Edward
Sorin

Edward Sorin, 1814–1893

Edward Sorin

MARVIN R. O'CONNELL

University of Notre Dame Press

Notre Dame, Indiana

Designed by Wendy McMillen
Typeset in 11.2/14.5 Minion by Em Studio, Inc.
Printed in the U.S.A. by Edward Brothers, Inc.

Manufactured in the United States of America

Title page art (Statue of Sorin), courtesy of Robert Ringel

*Unless otherwise noted, all photographs are courtesy of
the University of Notre Dame Archives*

Library of Congress Cataloging-in-Publication Data
O'Connell, Marvin Richard.
    Edward Sorin / by Marvin R. O'Connell.
      p.   cm.
    Includes bibliographical references and index.
    ISBN 0-268-02759-5 (cloth : alk. paper)
    1. Sorin, Edward.   2. University of Notre Dame.   I. Title.
LD4112.65.S65 O63   2001
378.772'89—dc21   2001002654

For

Theodore Martin Hesburgh

of the

Congregation of Holy Cross

Second Founder of

Notre Dame

Nisi Dominus aedificaverit domum, in vanum laborant qui aedificant eam.

Contents

Acknowledgments

THIS BOOK OWES ITS INCEPTION TO TIMOTHY O'Meara, Provost Emeritus of the University of Notre Dame, and to Harold W. Attridge, formerly Dean of Notre Dame's College of Arts and Letters and now Lillian Claus Professor of New Testament, Yale Divinity School. Their commission was accompanied by generous financial support. My friend and colleague, Wilson D. Miscamble, C.S.C., formerly Chairman of the Notre Dame Department of History and now Rector of Moreau Seminary, was tireless in his advocacy of this project. The text was reviewed in its entirety by Thomas E. Blantz, C.S.C., and Philip Gleason, both my esteemed and long-time associates at Notre Dame, and in part by James T. Connelly, C.S.C., Professor of History at the University of Portland; I profited immeasurably from their encouragement as well as from their criticisms and corrections. I owe special thanks as well to Professor Charles E. Parnell and to John E. Conley, C.S.C.

I was fortunate that my text was subjected to the keen eye and keener wit of E. Ann Rice of the University of Notre Dame Press; her editing skills are as formidable as her manner is gracious.

My work benefited very much from the monographic literature duly cited in the notes, particularly from papers prepared over the past twenty years or so for delivery at the annual conferences on the History of the Congregations of Holy Cross. Most important, however, was the material located in three archival collections and generously put at my disposal. I am grateful, therefore, to Wendy Clausen Schlereth and her staff at the Archives of the University of Notre Dame, especially to Kevin Cawley; and no less so to William B. Simmons, C.S.C., Archivist of the Indiana Province of Holy Cross, and his associates Thomas Balaz, C.S.C., and, especially, Jacqueline Dougherty. But my largest debt of all is to Robert C. Antonelli, C.S.C., formerly Archivist of the Holy Cross Generalate in Rome and now Archivist of the University of Portland, who guided me through the immense Sorin collection under his charge and provided me with copies of it. Without these several thousand pages of correspondence this book could not have been written. Due recognition must also be accorded, posthumously for the latter two, Father Antonelli's predecessors as general archivists: Jacques Grisé, Léandre Frechet, and, most particularly, Philéas Vanier, all members of the Congregation of Holy Cross.

Edward Sorin often approvingly quoted the first verse of Psalm 127 and consistently tried to abide by it. It seems to me that his distinguished successor has adhered to the same biblical dictum, and so, *ex intimo corde,* I have placed it next to his name in the dedication.

Marvin R. O'Connell
Notre Dame, Indiana 1996–2000

Edward
Sorin

Prologue

AHUILLÉ, IN THE DEPARTMENT OF MAYENNE, lies about seven miles southwest of Laval. The approach to the village from the east passes through open fields of rich brown soil, in the midst of which stand conventional farm buildings, most of them of weather-faded stone and many of them dating back to the nineteenth century. Herds of enormous black and white milk-cows, on this October day, contentedly munch the withered grass in their pastures and now and then look up vacantly at a swooping, chirping bird. The terrain has a gentle roll to it, and, at the very edge of Ahuillé, dips down, only to rise sharply into the center of the village. Here pervades that bright orderliness so characteristic of French towns, however small, and Ahuillé is small indeed, a cluster of neat old houses and shops built along a couple of twisting streets that issue into modern roads along which contemporary buildings meander out into the surrounding farmland. Here and there narrow evergreens provide splashes of color, as do the windowboxes of begonias, yellow daisies, and golden chrysanthemums. The gentle breeze is a reminder that the village rises modestly above the placid countryside.

Not quite at the top of the hill stands the church, by far the biggest and most impressive building in Ahuillé. Constructed of large blocks of beige stone, embellished by decorative rock held in place by mortar, it is well kept and attractive in its way, though hardly different from hundreds of other steepled, imitation gothic churches to be seen in western France. Nor is its interior in any way exceptional; the liturgical and devotional paraphernalia proper to Catholic worship and piety are much the same here as elsewhere, as are the dampness, the faintly musty smell, the peaceful gloom which the colored window-glass of indifferent quality does not disturb. Yet there is one remarkable feature in this otherwise pedestrian setting, a plaque dating from 1978, set into the wall just above the ornate baptismal font, which is older than the mid-nineteenth century church. "To the memory," it reads, "of Father Edward Sorin. Born at La Roche February 6, 1814. Baptized the same day in the parish church of Ahuillé. Ordained a priest in 1838. Admitted into the Congregation of Holy Cross in 1839. Sent to America in 1841. He founded the American province of Holy Cross and established the foundations of one of the greatest Catholic universities in the world, at Notre Dame du Lac, in the state of Indiana, in the United States of America. He became Superior General of Holy Cross in 1868. After a life devoted to apostolic endeavor he died in 1893 at the University of Notre Dame."

Outside, along the church's north wall, stands a memorial, also a commonplace in French villages, to the men of the parish who died during the wars of 1914 and 1939. This one is small and tasteful, with the statue of a young soldier in battle gear on the top. On its pedestal are carved the names of the twenty-two Ahuilléans killed during the first World War and the eight who suffered the same fate during the second. Attached to the base of the monument is an addition of very recent date, a tablet which bears this inscription: "To the memory of R. H. Krookshanks, American soldier, killed at Ahuillé at the time of the Liberation." Nudged against this plaque is a fresh bouquet of gold, red, and purple flowers.

Edward Sorin left Ahuillé a century before R. H. Krookshanks paid the ultimate price to help free the village from the grip of a brutal enemy. But it remains eerily appropriate that these two men—different as they surely were in almost every respect—should be memorialized within a few yards of each other. As the American soldier gave his life for France, the French priest gave his life and his heart and all his being to America.

chapter one

The Best of Times, the Worst of Times

DURING THE COURSE OF 1814, THE GUNS THAT for two decades had shattered the cities and countryside of Europe from Madrid to Moscow fell silent, if only for a little while. In April of that year, with his enemies pressing in on him from all sides, Napoleon, emperor of the French, abdicated and was bundled off to exile on the coastal island of Elba. He remained there, restless and scheming, until, eleven months later, he slipped past the careless watch kept over him and for a hundred days rallied his weary soldiers for one last campaign to recover their former glory. But the desperate gamble failed, amid massive carnage, at the little Belgian town of Waterloo.

Meanwhile, across the ocean, the young republic of the United States of America was embroiled in a war with Britain so ill-defined that it took its name from the year in which it began. Here 1814 witnessed organized violence similar to that which had so long tormented Europe, though less blood was spilt because fewer combatants were engaged. Nevertheless, the British, freed for several crucial months from their struggle with the French, sent reinforcements to America, and, in August, they captured Washington. They burned the capitol and other public buildings and left standing only the walls of the presidential mansion, which when painted a fresh white, after the war and the British withdrawal, still by its scorch marks testified—and does till this day—to that moment of national humiliation.

Such were the dramatic events that at the time preoccupied the élites on both sides of the Atlantic and that, since then, have absorbed the attention of historians. But, as is ever the case, ordinary people, far removed from the concerns of the powerful and the worldly-wise, continued their ordinary pursuits: coming to terms with an unpredictable nature, keeping the proverbial wolf from the door, alternating laughter with tears, pondering the eternal mysteries of love, of death, of birth. So the ageless rhythm of human experience was affirmed once more, even if the great world took no notice, when during that year of 1814, on February 6, the seventh of the nine children of Julien Sorin and Marie-Anne-Louise Gresland was born in the large house the local people called La Roche, only a few hundred yards outside the boundaries of the commune of Ahuillé, in the *département* of Mayenne. The baby boy was baptized later that very day and given the name Edouard-Frédéric.[1]

ONE WHO TRAVELS OUT of Paris west and a little south passes first through a golden panorama ripe and rich and so flat that the horizons appear to merge, at immeasurable distances, into the cloud-studded sky. So flat is it indeed, that the magnificent cathedral of Chartres, sixty miles or so from Paris, arises to the eye like a great ship floating on the air, even though the traveler can as yet see nothing of the town that encompasses it. But shortly thereafter, as one approaches the jurisdictional line between the Department of Eure et Loir and the Department of Sarthe, the terrain begins to change, subtly at first and then more dramatically. The almost treeless prairie gives place little by little to clusters of hills which grow higher and sharper the farther west one goes. Cultivated fields and pasture, divided from each other by hedgerows, flourish in the little valleys, or else compete for space on the hillsides with scrub oak and undergrowth. This irregular, rolling landscape is the consequence of the immemorial workings of a complex water-system, constituted of mere brooks as well as of streams broad and deep—the Loir and the Sarthe and the Mayenne—and all of them tributaries of the Loire, at five hundred miles from source to mouth the longest river in France and the arbiter, in its mute fashion, of a distinct style of life and of a history all its own.

By the time of Edouard Sorin's birth, the centralized departmental policy of administration had been successfully implemented across France by the various revolutionary governments after 1789, and indeed it had been if anything en-

---

1. Charles Lemarié, *De la Mayenne à l'Indiana: le Père Edouard Sorin* (Angers, 1978), 5. This is a special issue of *Impacts: revue de l'université de l'Ouest.*

hanced by the ruthless efficiency of the succeeding Napoleonic regime. These administrative units, each headed by a prefect appointed from Paris and each subdivided into *arrondissements*, cantons, and communes, were assigned names reflecting a prominent physical feature of the particular region, more often than not a river. Thus the River Sarthe intersected the department of that name and flowed through its captial, the ancient Roman city of Le Mans, while, in the district directly to the west, the River Mayenne similarly shared its name with the locality. This bureaucratic arrangement with its nomenclature was maintained by the restored Bourbon monarchy after the fall of Napoleon.

The Department of Mayenne had been carved out of the sprawling pre-Revolutionary provinces of Maine and Anjou. To have rationalized this old and largely inefficient political structure made perfect sense to the dominant Parisian intelligentsia, but, like much else characteristic of the Enlightenment, it had little impact upon the people who lived there. Like the Sorins, the vast majority of them were farmers, and their customs and values were rooted in the unchanging land itself. The only town of any size was the departmental capital, Laval, its medieval charm already in Edouard Sorin's childhood giving way to a drab modernity. And even there, as in the lesser communes like Chateau-Gontier and Craon, the cadence of economic and social life followed the beat of the countryside. To be sure, remnants of the primeval forests of chestnut, beech, birch, elm, and oak still stood atop the hills, *les mamelles boisées*—the wooded breasts—as one fanciful native had dubbed them. There were modest deposits of coal available, enough slate and marble to warrant quarrying, and some unpretentious enterprises in textiles and brick-making offered employment in the towns. Small arts and crafts served ordinary needs, as they always have. But none of this could alter the reality that untold generations of human work and ingenuity had created in Mayenne an overwhelmingly rural culture, one which depended upon the cycle of the seasons, upon the tempo imposed by planting and harvest, upon the brute strength of some domesticated animals and the sustenance provided by others. The department abounded, as had the old provinces, in pigs and cattle and especially horses, famed for their size and vigor. In a good year the cultivated fields, rich in limy soil and freshened by abundant moisture, produced a hardy yield of oats, barley, maize, buckwheat, maslin, all manner of vegetables, and forage for the animals. One momentous development that Julien Sorin witnessed during his lifetime was the gradual replacement of flax by wheat as the premier crop, a mark of the decline of the venerable linen industry. Orchards of pear trees were tended everywhere, and even more of apple trees: only in the extreme south of Mayenne were vineyards to be found, and elsewhere cider was the common table-beverage and Calvados the brandy of the rich.

Thus the physical environment which Edouard Sorin knew as a boy was similar in many respects to that in which he would distinguish himself as a man, the midwest of the United States. Yet there were differences, too. The generally benign climate he experienced growing up could not have prepared him for the extremes in temperature and especially for the often brutally cold and snowy winters of northwest Indiana, most of all when the winds swept across nearby Lake Michigan. More welcome possibly was the drier air Sorin was to find in a region where the average rainfall was twenty inches less than in his birthplace. Yet when he did settle in America he was to do so in a tract where two small lakes and the contiguous soggy ground must have reminded him uneasily of the profusion of ponds and marshes in Mayenne—including the *etang* of Goulia, near Ahuillé—which, according to local lore, occasioned many mysterious ailments.

But perhaps the greatest difference had to do with vision and brought with it, albeit unconsciously, a psychic effect. There were no wide vistas for the young Sorin to delight in; the terrain he saw every day was chopped up by hills and trees and the innumerable hedges which girdled the fields, so much so that it was easy to sense as intrinsic to it deep limitation and constraint. And, thanks to the frequent rains and the heavy morning dews, the landscape of Mayenne was an undeviating green, fetching enough to the eye at first, but then increasingly monotonous and melancholy, as it seemed to absorb every other color and to blur into a tedious uniformity all that it enveloped. It is not mere whimsy to suggest that the mature Father Sorin discovered in the immense sweep of the American plains and in the great variety of their flora and fauna a more appropriate setting in which to play out his remarkable assortment of gifts and his boundless ambitions.[2]

The ultimate fulfillment of those ambitions was not unrelated to the social class into which Edouard Sorin was born. Considerably more than half the rural population in the Department of Mayenne were day laborers or sharecropping peasants. Not so the Sorins. Julien Sorin was a *propriétaire-cultivateur* who owned the land that had originally belonged to his wife's grandparents. The plot he farmed was admittedly small by the American standards his son would become acquainted with later, but it was his, unencumbered by any feudal dues or memories, and the handsome house he and his family lived in was known respectfully among the locals as a *manoir*. A large, square, three-storied structure, with chimneys jutting upward at either end and flanking the slanted roof, it stood on a wooded knoll at the northeast edge of Ahuillé. Not quite grand enough to be clas-

2. See L. Gallouédec, *Le Maine* (Paris, 1925), 4–10, and A. Jardin and A.-J. Tudesq, *La France des notables. La vie de la nation, 1815–1848* (Paris, 1973), 28–36.

sified a chateau in the usual sense of that term, the manor-house of La Roche nevertheless bespoke a solid economic and social prominence, as much as it did a legendary past. Upon this elevated site, upon this "Rock," men of war long ago had built a sturdy bastion of defense for the surrounding countryside.[3] Approached by way of a long, tree-lined avenue and surrounded by numerous outbuildings, the house, no fortress now, seemed rather the peaceful center of a little hamlet all its own. The master of La Roche even sported a genteel prolongation of his name—Julien Sorin de la Gaulterie—though he seldom invoked it and Edouard never did. By status and income, therefore, the Sorins belonged to the lesser gentry and could presume to mingle on roughly equal terms with the rural bourgeoisie of notaries, physicians, and petty government officials.[4] French employs the noun *notables* to designate such persons.

It is hardly surprising that from childhood Edouard perceived himself to be a notable, a member of the local élite, at least with regard to most of his neighbors and playfellows. It may overstate the case to conclude that this farmer's son was early on imbued with a sense of *noblesse oblige*. But certainly the posture of command he so readily assumed during his career, his self-confidence, his willingness to take up any challenge and embark on any adventure, and, less attractively, his propensity to ride rough shod over opponents—all these characteristics of leadership reflect to some degree the position of relative privilege in which Edouard Sorin was reared.

Apparently such traits were in evidence from the beginning. The scraps of anecdotal evidence available suggest that Edouard was the leader of the other lads, in the village schoolroom and on the playing field. On one occasion he stormed out of the school and refused to return when he believed the teacher had unjustly punished him. This fracas was resolved, it seems, by the intervention of the pastor of Ahuillé, who had much time on his hands and so willingly took on himself the instruction of Edouard and a few other promising pupils. In his mid-teens, young Sorin was sent for his secondary education to a *collège* in nearby Laval, which was itself a sign of his family's privileged standing. He stayed there, however, only a year, because he had already decided that he wanted to become a priest. At that time—and until 1855 when the diocese of Laval was erected— Mayenne fell under the ecclesiastical jurisdiction of the bishop of Le Mans, who maintained a preparatory seminary at Précigné, a charming little town in the

---

3. The house still stands though much refurbished during the nineteenth century. My thanks for information about it and photographs of it to my colleague, Professor Charles Parnell.

4. See Maurice Agulhon et al., *Apogée et crise de la civilisation paysanne de 1789 à 1914*, vol. 3 of Georges Duby and Armand Wallon eds., *Histoire de la France rurale* (Paris, 1976), 83–87.

southern part of Sarthe. There Edouard went into residence in the turreted seminary building hard by the imposing church, and there he remained until 1834 when, his humanities and Latin courses completed, he entered the major seminary in Le Mans to do his theology.[5] His family took great pride in the hearty and yet pious young man who, when he returned home on scholastic vacations, "went hunting with the same eagerness as his professors observed he gave his studies when at college."[6]

No record survives to describe the circumstances under which he first met one of his new professors in the *grand séminaire,* the thirty-five-year-old Basile-Antoine Moreau. But it was a fateful meeting indeed.

A SORIN FAMILY TRADITION maintains that Edouard-Frédéric as a boy used to pretend he was a priest, dressing himself up in Mass-vestments made of stiff paper. If so, there was on the surface nothing particularly startling about it: Catholic boys of every generation, those at any rate brought up in pious households and taught from their earliest days to revere the priesthood, have often indulged in such playful fantasies. But during Edouard Sorin's childhood the game involved a seriousness and poignancy which only recent events could have warranted. His parents and perhaps his elder siblings recalled all too well the terrible days when priests were hunted down all over France and when some of them, at no small risk to the family, found secret refuge in the *manoir* of La Roche. As many as 3,000 clergy lost their lives during the persecution of the 1790s—guillotined, starved, drowned, bludgeoned to death—and more than ten times that many were driven into exile. The bloodbath ceased with Napoleon Bonaparte's seizure of power at the end of the decade, but the wounds continued to fester for more than a century afterward.

The great Revolution of 1789 had not in its beginnings involved a clash between church and state. Though no doubt the anticlerical and even antitheistic program of *philosophes* like Voltaire and Condorcet exerted much influence in many quarters, it had been the utopian if uneasy alliance between the first and third estates—the clergy and the bourgeoisie—that had first put the revolutionary

---

5. Lemarié, *De la Mayenne,* 5–6. Much of the same anecdotal material can be found in a short fragment prepared by P. Livenais, "Notes sur la vie du T. R. P. Sorin," Archives of the Generalate of the Congregation of Holy Cross, Rome (hereafter cited as AGEN), folder 232.1.

6. Lemonnier to "Father Superior," December 6, 1893, AGEN, folder 232.1. Auguste Lemonnier was Sorin's grandnephew. He should not be confused with the Auguste Lemonnier, Sorin's nephew, who during the 1870s served as president of Notre Dame. See chapter 23, below.

wheels in motion. And if the impetus to reform the financial structure of ecclesi-astical institutions had figured prominently in the purposes of those who gath-ered in Versailles for the meeting of the Estates General that spring, pulsing with idealism—"Bliss was it in that dawn to be alive," sang the ecstatic Wordsworth—the first estate, or at least its overwhelming majority composed of parish priests and lesser clergy, was not in basic disagreement. Indeed, such a reform would have been to the considerable material advantage of the *curés* and curates, how-ever much the bishops, aristocrats to the man, might have bridled at it.

Not much time passed, however, before the clergy came to recognize to their distress that events were moving swiftly far beyond their relatively modest intent. Succeeding revolutionary governments—the Constituent and Legislative assem-blies and the National Convention—shifted ever more radically to the left. In Au-gust 1789 the venerable tax called the tithe, the chief source of clerical income, was abolished without compensation. The following November the whole prop-erty of the church—somewhere between six and ten percent of the total real es-tate in France—was confiscated and placed "at the disposal of the nation." The government indeed assumed responsibility for "the expenses of religious wor-ship, the upkeep of its ministers, and the relief of the poor." But this largesse, such as it was, asserted a philosophical principle which troubled a large number of the otherwise sympathetic clergy. The issue now transcended the mere computation of francs and sous. The state had arrogated to itself the right to define the pa-rameters within which the church had traditionally performed its apostolate, es-pecially with regard to the care of the poor. This latter function, since beyond memory the responsibility of the local parish priest or of the local convent or monastery, and thus a source of immense popular prestige, now fell under the supervision of the state—a key affirmation of that complexus of policies that has since come to be included under the heading of "modernity."[7]

Yet even this assault upon their prerogatives as an independent corporation failed to ignite the clergy's active resistance. Nor did the decree (February 13, 1790) which suppressed all the religious orders and rendered invalid the swearing of the religious vows of poverty, chastity, and obedience. Monks, friars, and nuns—from the Cluniacs of the tenth century to the Dominicans of the thir-teenth to the Lazarists and Visitandines of the seventeenth—long the objects of

---

7. A point made with particular force in Ralph Gibson, *A Social History of French Catholicism 1789–1914* (London, 1989), 34–35. This is an enormously informative book, a compilation and distilla-tion, as it were, of the vast monographic literature on the subject. Its major flaw is too univocal a defi-nition of what the author calls "the Tridentine model of Catholicism," the important nuances of which he has completely failed to grasp.

the ribald contempt of the *philosophes* as society's useless parasites, thus became non-persons in the new legal order of things. The secular clergy for their part, neither to their credit nor, in the long run, to their advantage, watched impassively the overthrow of their historic ecclesiastical rivals, much as their English counterparts had done three centuries before, when Henry VIII launched his attack upon the monastic orders.

Despite the differences of time and place, there was more than a superficial similarity between these two series of events. King Henry had determined to destroy the independence of the clergy, and—acting under very different ideological criteria, to be sure—so did the French revolutionary regime. In this regard a point of no return was reached on July 12, 1790, when the Constituent Assembly passed the Civil Constitution of the Clergy. By its detailed provisions, this section of the larger constitution definitively established lay supremacy over the Catholic priesthood. *Curés* were to be chosen by electors in the parish, bishops by those in the newly constituted *départements*. Sacerdotal ordination and episcopal consecration could indeed occur as needed or desired, but these ritual acts were no longer to be discerned as themselves conferring authority, spiritual or otherwise, on any individual. All authority stemmed from the organs and procedures of the modern state.

The next year, 1791, the government attached an oath of allegiance to this *fait accompli*. Virtually all the bishops refused to swear acceptance of the Civil Constitution, and so did about half their priests. This meant that roughly 30,000 of the secular clergy—to say nothing of the majority of the 26,000 monks and friars and 55,000 nuns, already dispersed—explicitly repudiated a first principle of the revolutionary settlement and, as a consequence, were deprived of all civil standing. In this act of recusancy they were supported by the pope who, however, could do nothing to protect them from the wrath to come.

Indeed, the Revolution's attack upon clerical independence and privilege transformed itself, with dizzying speed, into an onslaught upon the Christian religion itself. The nonjuring priests had scarcely been driven from their parishes or, many of them, conveyed by the tumbrelful to the guillotine, when the government unleashed its rage against the constitutional church it had so recently founded. Those priests who had taken the oath suddenly found themselves hardly better off than their confreres who had refused it. "Marry if you want to be free," some of them were told, "marry or you will be sent before a revolutionary tribunal!" Others were forced to dunk their heads into a tub of water and so "debaptize themselves." A spectacular example involved no less a personage than the constitutional archbishop of Paris, who was compelled in a public ceremony to abjure the priesthood itself: "Today when liberty is advancing with great strides, today when there should be no national cult but that of liberty and equality, I renounce my functions as a minister of the Catholic cult." (Even so abject a surrender did not, in the end, save that prelate from the guillotine.) What had begun as schism evolved swiftly into massive national apostasy. By the mid-1790s churches had been closed down or converted into secular uses, and all sacramental activity forbidden under the harshest penalties. Ecclesiastical buildings were routinely looted and sacred vessels either stolen and sold or else subjected to the blasphemous ridicule of the mob. Typical of the mockery of traditional worship was a procession of donkeys organized in Nevers in 1794; the animals had crucifixes tied to their tails and were made to drink from the chalices out of which, so the Catholic faithful believed, the very Blood of Christ had once been consumed.[8]

This orgy of hatred and destruction was, no doubt, the work of a small if dominant minority and part of a larger mania: it could be argued that no movement ever devoured its own children with greater relish than did the French Revolution. By the end of the decade at any rate it had exhausted itself, and had paved the way for the *coup d'état* of Brumaire (November 9, 1799), and once Bonaparte had secured power he moved quickly to make peace with the church by means of the concordat he entered into with the papacy in 1801. This initiative had had nothing to do with the new dictator's own religiosity—he believed in nothing but in himself and in his destiny—but, shrewd politician that he was, he recognized that the oppression of a majority, as traditional Catholics continued to be in France, was a policy that could not be sustained over the long term. And moreover he concluded that the church, if handled properly, could contribute to his regime the same unique measure of social control it had supplied the pre-Revolutionary monarchy. So the persecution of the 1790s ended. Churches were reopened, and seminaries and other ecclesiastical institutions proscribed by the Revolution were granted civic recognition once more. As what was left of the constitutional clergy faded away, the nonjurors, like the *curé* of Ahuillé, Abbé Noyer, who had christened Edouard Sorin, were allowed to come home from exile and assume parochial duty once again.

T HEY WERE, as Charles Dickens would later observe, the best of times and the worst of times. High idealism mingled indiscriminately with

---

8. Adrien Dansette, *Histoire religieuse de la France contemporaine* (Paris, 1965), 82–89, 92–101. See also Simon Schama, *Citizens: A Chronicle of the French Revolution* (New York, 1989), 630–637, 776–779, 836–39.

blood-lust and brutality. Dedication to the Rights of Man and the Citizen gave birth to the Reign of Terror. Lofty aspirations summed up in the immortal motto of *liberté, égalité, fraternité* were honored by many, and courageously so, but they were also betrayed and manipulated by a succession of fanatics until, in the end, they were appropriated by that most cynical of opportunists, Napoleon Bonaparte. Young Edouard Sorin, as he grew toward manhood and reflected upon all these events that had shaped his world, could not have failed to learn some important lessons.

That world, it must be remembered, was narrower than France as a whole, and far removed from the nation's glamorous and sophisticated center in Paris. In the departments of Mayenne and Sarthe, and in the West of the country generally, the Revolution had encountered its stiffest internal resistance. As early as March 1793—in the wake of the execution of *citoyen* Louis Capet, once known as King Louis XVI—full-scale rebellion broke out in the Vendée, on the south banks of the Loire, and it required two ruthless campaigns by regular troops to put it down.[9] Even then disaffection continued to smolder just beneath the surface and to flare up in spasmodic waves of violence directed against those known to sympathize with the central regime—the "white terror" as the "red" terrorists in Paris designated it. North of the river, the reaction was never so organized as in the Vendée. In Mayenne and Sarthe resistance tended rather to coalesce into independent guerrilla bands which sprang up in villages or parishes and were usually led by some colorful local figure. Their hit-and-run tactics succeeded for a time in reducing the whole region to virtual chaos, and even the departmental capitals of Laval and Le Mans were not spared the rebels' violent attentions. The group of insurgents centered at Ahuillé was under the command of one Bézier, nicknamed "the Mustache."[10] The exploits of these so-called *chouans* became the stuff of legend in the manor house of La Roche and indeed across the western departments during those troubled years and for long after.[11]

THE MOST PUZZLING ASPECT of the demography of French Catholicism has been the wide divergence in adherence and practice within the various regions of the country. Signs of this anomaly appeared even before 1789:

---

9. See J. C. Martin, *La Vendée et la France* (Paris, 1987), 247–284.

10. Gallouédec, *Le Maine,* 212.

11. For background see Michel Denis, *Les Royalistes de la Mayenne et le monde moderne* (Paris, 1977), 49–59.

in Paris and its environs, for example, the common statistical measurements—attendance at Sunday Mass and reception of the Eucharist during Easter time—showed that a significant proportion of the populace of all classes had already been dechristianized. After the Revolution, however, this trend had been spectacularly intensified, but by no means everywhere. If, at the time Edouard Sorin entered the seminary, in the 1830s, only 35 percent of the Catholics living in the Ardennes made their Easter duty, and considerably less than that did so in the valley of the Marne, in Strasbourg, on the eastern frontier, the figure hovered around 90 percent and in the far west of Brittany around 95. There seemed to be neither rhyme nor reason nor a discernible regional pattern to explain the differences: in the diocese of Clermont, at the geographical center of the country, nearly all the men received Easter Communion, while in the contiguous diocese of Limoges hardly any of them did. Collateral indices relevant to the vigor of the church—vocations to the religious life, publication and purchase of religious books, wills drawn up to favor pious purposes—exhibited a drastic decline in some areas and an increase in others. A great religious revival was underway here, a powerful progression toward apostasy was underway there.

This strange discrepancy defies explanation, even to this day, as does the attitude frequently assumed by many French intellectuals during the early nineteenth century, summed up best perhaps by the aphorism of Alexis de Tocqueville: "*Je crois, mais je ne puis pratiquer* (I believe, but I cannot practice)."[12] Which is not to say that certain conclusions cannot be safely derived from the evidence at hand. It is clear, for instance, that after the tumults of the Revolution of '89 never again would there prevail in France that universal fidelity to ordinary Catholic practice that had characterized the mid-eighteenth century and indeed many centuries before. Nor could the political clash over the succeeding hundred years between French Catholics and their deistic and anticlerical adversaries have been avoided, given their diametrically opposed policies and beliefs and, more practically, the roughly equal constituencies that each side could count upon.

And, in a narrower ambit, it appears similarly decisive in understanding the career of Edouard Sorin to recall that he sprang from the western provinces of France where the Catholic faith not only survived the challenges of the Revolution but had even flourished amidst every conceivable vicissitude. Once again, the statistics tell at least something of the tale. In the diocese of Versailles, just to the west of Paris, no more than six percent of the total population made their Easter duty in 1834, the year Sorin entered the major seminary. At Chartres, the next

---

12. See George Pierson, *Tocqueville and Beaumont in America* (New York, 1938), 17.

ecclesiastical jurisdiction to the west of Versailles, the story of nonparticipation was much the same. Crossing over into the *département* of Sarthe the eastern parishes, practically bereft of worshippers like their neighbors in Chartres, gave way, as one moved westward, to a scene of lively parochial involvement. In Sarthe 54 percent of the populace, most of them in the west, received the Easter Eucharist, while in Mayenne the number was 76 percent.[13]

As THE BOY Edouard Sorin listened to accounts told around the family board of the feats of the Mustache and his men—much embellished, no doubt, in the telling—he came to realize that the rising in the Vendée and the similarly inspired if unsynchronized resistance movements elsewhere in the West, including his own village, had stemmed as much, if not more, from religious fervor as from royalist commitment. Or perhaps it would be better to say that in the minds of the people like the Sorins the king and the faith had been indissolubly wedded, a point of view apparently confirmed by the Revolution's assault upon both the church and the monarchy. The king who mounted the throne in 1815, however, proved to be a feeble shadow of his anointed brother who had been guillotined, and the king who came to power in 1830 was not even a legitimate successor but merely an upstart princeling who called himself "the citizen-king," affected bourgeois values and wielded an umbrella instead of a scepter.

The accession of Louis-Philippe wrote finis to the attempt to restore the monarchy of the *ancien régime,* but the old faith, far from sharing the same fortune, stood stronger and, in the West, more vital than ever. The lesson was not lost upon the seminarian Edouard Sorin, now twenty years old. He was as yet too raw and unsophisticated to appreciate the force of that mantra of nineteenth-century liberalism, "a free church in a free state." But seeds of doubt had been sown in his mind about the necessity or even the desirability of the union of throne and altar, seeds which at a later time and in a different place would blossom into full flower. Meanwhile he could observe at leisure the progress of the Catholic revival as it spread unevenly across France and revivified the church in his own *patrie,* those western districts which had withstood most firmly the excesses of the Revolution. And central to that revival was the enhanced position of the priesthood whose ranks he proposed to join, in order not only to offer sacramental ministry to his fellow-believers—that went without saying—but also to exercise those gifts of wider leadership which he sensed, even then, lay within him.

---

13. See Gibson, *Social History,* 8–9, 170–175.

chapter two

The Founder

PERHAPS THE LEAST DRAMATIC REFORM INTRODUCED during the early stages of the French Revolution was the establishment throughout France of registers of vital statistics under the aegis of government officials. Yet, prosaic and sensible as this policy may appear to have been, it was also a conscious step in the process of secularization. Ever since such records had been kept they had fallen within the responsibility of the local *curé* who, by implication, exercised control over the rites of passage of his parishioners. Birth, marriage, even death and its testamentary consequences: all these were bound up with the sacramental ministry over which the priest alone had enjoyed jurisdiction. Indeed, the status of a newborn's citizenship, to the extent that that term had meaning before 1789, had been determined by his baptism into the Catholic community, and not even members of the small Protestant minority had been able to contract valid nuptials without the agency of the *curé*. For a regime that had not hesitated to impose civil marriage and to legitimate divorce, such an arrangement was not only irrational but intolerable. With a wave of its legislative hand, therefore, it swept away the venerable method of record keeping and all that that system had implied.

Passage of an ordinance by anticlerical politicians in Paris, however, could not guarantee the automatic existence of a competent or even a literate civil service. So it happened that the oldest extant document relating to the man who was to become Edouard Sorin's mentor and later, under tragic circumstances, his sternest antagonist, was entered into the official books in scarcely grammatical French and contained at least one serious error of fact. The date, written at the head of the entry, equivalent to February 12, 1799, reflected the conceit of the revolutionary calendar, soon to pass away.

On this the twenty-fourth day of Pluvius in the year VII of the French Republic, one and indivisible, before me, René Gorget, municipal agent of the commune of Laigné-en-Belin, appointed to record births and deaths in this commune, has appeared citizen Louis Moreau, merchant, domiciled at Haut-Ecler, aged forty-three, in the company of citizen René le Baillieuil, wheelwright, thirty-two years old, and citizeness Marie Moreau, daughter of the above and domiciled with her father, aged twenty-one, who have attested to me that Louise Pioger, Moreau's lawful wife, has yesterday borne a son to whom has been given the name Basile-Antoine. After this declaration and the presentation of the infant, I have entered his name and signed it, as have the others, except the aforesaid Moreau.[1]

The baby's father, that is to say, could not sign his name. But then the registrar, citizen Roget, apparently could not distinguish a little girl from a grown woman: Marie Moreau was twelve years old when her brother was born, not twenty-one. The designation of the father as "merchant" was also somewhat misleading. Louis Moreau did indeed carry on a modest wine-distributing business and behind his house in Haut-Ecler—a huddle of low-slung dwellings on the eastern edge of Laigné—stood a small stone shack in which he stored various vintages until the time was ripe to peddle them across the district. But in essence Louis was a peasant, as had been his and his wife's forebears, and tilling the land and pasturing the animals near the village continued to provide the basic support for his enormous family. Louise Pioger bore fourteen children, of whom Basile-Antoine was the ninth. It was not without long-term significance that Moreau belonged to a family of lower social rank than that of Edouard Sorin.

Laigné-en-Belin lay some twelve miles south of Le Mans, in the *département* of Sarthe. In 1799 about a thousand people lived in the district, three hundred of them in the village itself, all served by a parish church whose oldest segment, the nave, dated back to the eleventh century and whose slender slate steeple was reassuringly visible some distance into the countryside.[2] The suffix to the town's name referred to the cult of a long forgotten regional deity, Belin, and was shared by several nearby communes, like Moncé-en-Belin and Saint-Gervais-en-Belin.

---

1. The ungrammatical entry and a corrected version printed in *Recueil documentaire. Le très révérend père Moreau, d'après ses écrits, ses correspondants et les documents de l'époque (1799–1835)* (n.p. [New York], 1945), 11–12.

2. The street that now runs beside the church toward what was Haut-Ecler is called Rue Basile Moreau (1799–1873).

The gently rolling land round about was fertile and productive, but the remains of the ancient forests out of which the fields had been carved were never far away.[3]

Basile-Antoine was not baptized until ten days after his birth, a remarkably long interval in that era of high infant mortality. One of his elder siblings, however, had had his christening delayed ten months. The reason in both instances was that the Moreaus, like most of their neighbors, wanted no truck with the constitutional priest who was given charge of the parish after their *curé* and his assistant, having refused the oath to the Civil Constitution of the Clergy, had been deprived of office, then arrested and imprisoned. The parishioners preferred to await the clandestine ministry of one they identified simply as "a Catholic priest," by which they meant a nonjuror. Though a half dozen of these men came and went during the decade of persecution, their arrival could never be predicted. One of them, however, an Abbé Guyon, did become available in the latter days of February, 1799, to perform the rite of Christian initiation for the latest Moreau baby.[4]

So the reaction to the religious policy of the Revolution in Laigné-en-Belin did not differ much from what had prevailed at the same time to the northwest, in Ahuillé, though the former place could not boast the likes of the Mustache and his intrepid partisans. But Basile Moreau, fifteen years older, retained a keener awareness of the travails of the 1790s than Edouard Sorin did. For Moreau the word "republic" possessed dour connotations that eluded the younger man. Later on this difference in perspective would complicate the relationship between the two of them.[5]

A few years after the Napoleonic concordat had been signed, and something of pre-Revolutionary normalcy restored, Basile Moreau, aged nine or ten, became a pupil in the little school presided over by the *curé* of Laigné-en-Belin,

---

3. Laigné's economic and social foundations are still symbolized by the town's coat-of-arms: three shocks of golden wheat on an azure field.

4. See Etienne Catta and Tony Catta, *Le T. R. P. Basile-Antoine Moreau (1799–1873) et les origines de la Congregation de Sainte-Croix,* 3 vols. (Paris, 1950–53). I have used the English translation by Edward L. Heston, *Basil Anthony Mary Moreau,* 2 vols. (Milwaukee, 1955), in this instance 1: 3–10 (cited hereafter as Catta, *Moreau*). This enormous study—more than 2100 pages in the English text—is marred by its deeply apologetic and hagiographical tone, by its undisguised hostility toward Sorin, and by its practically unusable index—a serious flaw in a work of this size. Some readers may also object to the authors' apparently obsessive concern for detail, but I would submit that this is the book's greatest merit, this and the quotation of a huge number of hard-to-find contemporary documents.

5. "Father Moreau never despaired of his country. At the end of 1871 [and the Franco-Prussian war] he was fearing a new revolution in France, while still hoping for the return of Henry V." Catta, *Moreau,* 2: 985. "Henry V," the comte de Chambord, was the grandson of Charles X and the legitimist pretender to the throne of his Bourbon ancestors.

Abbé Julien le Prevost. This brave priest, who had risked his life for the ministry in Le Mans and its environs during the Reign of Terror and after, took up his pastorate in 1802 and persevered in it for thirty years. He convened classes in the fours r's—the fourth of course was religion—in his own home, the presbytery itself. Such humble grammar schools, similarly sited, became commonplace across France during these years, when local communities attempted to revive some semblance of the of the educational system disrupted by the Revolution.[6] The young Moreau soon caught the priest's eye as one singularly gifted intellectually and spiritually. Basile, who at home played at saying Mass and at preaching to his mother and sisters—one wonders at their patience with the lad—was assigned by the *curé* the task of training and overseeing the parish's altar servers.

Before long Prevost became convinced that the boy had a calling to the priesthood. When, after some hesitation, he submitted this opinion to Basile's parents, he was confronted with some skepticism. Characteristic of a French peasant, Louis Moreau looked upon his large brood of children, and particularly upon his sons, as not only the beloved fruit of his loins but also the guarantors of the economic well-being of his own present and future—offspring considered, that is, in biblical terms, as "olive plants around the table," as a quiverful of arrows which armed aging parents against the uncertainties of capricious fortune. A compromise of sorts was in the end arrived at: Basile would continue to perform his usual chores and yet be allowed, even as he conducted the family's cows to and from the pasture, to pursue his study of Latin and other esoteric subjects—as such inquiries must have seemed to the members of his family. Finally, with whatever level of reluctance, Louis Moreau succumbed to the *curé's* exhortations and agreed to Basile-Antoine's matriculation at an ecclesiastical *collège* where he might try his vocation. In October 1814, father and the son made the fifty-mile trek on foot west to Chateau-Gontier, in the Department of Mayenne. Edouard Sorin was eight months old.

YOUNG MOREAU spent two years at Chateau-Gontier, a town on the River Mayenne quite unremarkable except for its cattle market. The establishment he attended there was not essentially different from the one at Precigné to which Sorin was to be sent some years later: a secondary school staffed by a handful of diocesan priests, which nudged its way modestly into collegiate sub-

---

6. For a contemporaneous example of another influential presbyteral school, this one in the Department of Ain, near Lyon, see my *John Ireland and the American Catholic Church* (St. Paul, 1988), 21–23.

jects and which catered both to lay and clerical students. This kind of Catholic preparatory seminary—*un petit séminaire*—flourished all over France during the nineteenth century[7] and also in other places where French missionary influence was strong, as in the United States. One contrast, however, between Moreau's *collège* and Sorin's clearly manifested itself: the wounds inflicted by the depredations of the Revolution and by the sternly statist monopoly over education created by Napoleon—the *université*—were fresher in the memory and more keenly felt in Chateau-Gontier than in Précigné.

Moreau witnessed much the same measure of very recent tribulation when, in the autumn of 1816, he entered the major seminary in Le Mans. The bishop had set up this institution in the old abbey of Saint-Vincent, founded near the city during the sixth century. From 1790, when the monks were expelled, till the year before Moreau arrived the government had utilized the monastic buildings as military barracks. There was no question of restoring the Benedictines to their ancient status—the Napoleonic concordat, which remained in force after 1815, did not mention, much less recognize, the existence of the religious orders—and so the bishop had secured possession of the property and, at no small expense, had repaired and converted it into a training center for those who aspired to join the secular priesthood. Here Basile Moreau spent five years under a regimen that emphasized the strict observance of moral norms much more than it encouraged intellectual inquiry. He survived this period of austere probation, and, on August 12, 1821, he was ordained priest for the diocese of Le Mans.

As was (and is) the Catholic custom, Basile returned to his home parish to celebrate, in the presence of family and friends, his first solemn Mass. Assisting him at the altar was his patron, the venerable and painfully gouty *curé* of Laigné-en-Belin, Julien le Prevost. A festive banquet followed the liturgical ceremony. Later that night Moreau, a guest in the presbytery, was awakened by a messenger from an outlying farmstead who brought news of a dying parishioner. The pastor, too crippled to answer the call himself, commissioned the stripling priest to take his place. As indeed he did, and there were those who remembered that a half-century later Basile Moreau found himself in a similar situation. Substituting for a country pastor, incapacitated by some undefined illness, the old man was again awakened in the night, this time by the abdominal pains that presaged his own final illness. So he ended his apostolate much as he had begun it.[8]

---

7. For examples see my *Ireland,* 43–45, and my *Critics on Trial: An Introduction to the Catholic Modernist Crisis* (Washington, 1994), 79–80.

8. Catta, *Moreau,* 1: 23–28 and 2: 996–97. See also chapter 27, below.

THE BISHOP OF LE MANS was clearly impressed, once he became aware of it, by the record Father Moreau had made during his student days. Instead of routinely assigning this newly ordained priest as curate to a parish in his enormous diocese—as his successor was to do with Edouard Sorin seventeen years later—he decided to send Abbé Moreau to Paris, specifically to the seminary of Saint-Sulpice and its retreat center in suburban Issy. The bishop's intent was that, once the young man had experienced this postgraduate training, he would be ready for appointment to the staff of the bishop's own seminary.

The time Moreau spent at an impressionable age—he was in his early twenties—under the auspices of Saint-Sulpice was no doubt the most formative of his life. This society of priests, which took its name from the Parisian parish where it had had its origins in the midseventeenth century, was devoted exclusively to seminary education, to the training, that is, of the men who would be the parochial curates and pastors of tomorrow. It was, in fact, this mission alone that gave cohesion and purpose to the Sulpicians: they did not form a religious order, they did not take vows like the Jesuits and Dominicans did. Their sole occupation was to mold the boys and young men the bishops sent to their institutions into parish priests who would serve their people virtuously and selflessly.

Such at any rate was the ideal, and it would be wrong to insinuate that it was an unworthy one. And, what is more, the reputation the French Catholic clergy earned during the nineteenth century for personal rectitude and dedication stands as an enduring tribute to the work of the Sulpicians. Indeed, so successful were their methods perceived to be that the Sulpician model was adopted virtually everywhere in the Latin church—including in the United States, where four French Sulpicians arrived, in flight from the Revolution, in 1791.[9] Even the seminaries they did not staff themselves, like the one in Le Mans, strove to follow the example they set, which is the reason his bishop put young Father Moreau under their direct tutelage.

Nevertheless, for all their merits, the Sulpicians inevitably carried with them some negative baggage. The strict regimen they imposed upon their students—with its careful and elaborate schedules, its often petty preoccupation with detail, its insistence that the candidates cultivate an exclusive priestly piety—tended to encourage a spirituality which was, it might reasonably be argued, too introspective, too self-indulgent, too individualistic. There also ran through their system a vein of Jansenism, that peculiarly French phenomenon which, despite repeated

---

9. See Christopher J. Kauffman, *Tradition and Transformation in Catholic Culture: The Priests of Saint-Sulpice in the United States from 1791 to the Present* (New York, 1988), 37–41.

condemnations, had injected into the fiber of the Gallican church its withering pessimism about the human condition. A kind of cosmic gloom and tension enshrouded a Sulpician seminary, testified to in the personal rules written down by a student who was in residence at Saint-Sulpice at the same time Basile Moreau was there.

> To remember that God is my beginning and my last end. To ask often of myself, when I pass from one exercise to another, what ought I to do? What am I doing? Why and to what intention? To perform the present act as if it were the last of my life. To act as if there were on earth only God and myself. To examine myself carefully after each act, and should I be obliged to acknowledge guilt, to humble myself before God, to crave pardon from him, and to impose on myself some penitential act of self-denial. To beg from God that he make me more humble, more void of myself, that he extirpate within me all love of myself.

The seminarian who recorded these sentiments was wearing a hair shirt.[10]

Certainly it could be maintained that aspirants who passed through such an indoctrination would find it difficult to relate to the ordinary men and women in the pew. And so in fact it was. But the priests produced by the Sulpician method never thought themselves intended to fit comfortably into the parochial milieu in which Providence situated them. Dispensing comfort was not their charge. Theirs, they had been taught, was a prophetic office, meant to build surely, but also to root up. They were to be in the world, but not of it. They were divinely commissioned to raise the spiritual consciousness of those of lesser status in the church than themselves. The vagaries of popular superstition, the empty vanities involved in so many parish-activities, the sexual promiscuity that seemed to the suspicious celibate living alone in the presbytery to disfigure much of village life: these were some of the evils that Sulpician-trained clergy aimed to rectify. The instruments at hand to accomplish this end, besides their own austere example, were the confessional and the pulpit, the administration and, no less, the withholding of the sacraments, and the constant warning that iniquity committed in this life had to be accounted for in the next.[11]

The two years (1821–1823) Moreau spent with *les messieurs de Saint-Sulpice* were divided about equally between the houses in Paris and in Issy. In both places

10. Quoted in O'Connell, *Ireland*, 23–24. The student was Joseph Cretin of the diocese of Belley, later missioner in Iowa and Minnesota and first bishop of St. Paul.

11. See the comments in Gibson, *Social History*, 56–61, and the sources cited, 281–282.

he was required to take advanced courses in philosophy and theology. These he found much more rigorous than the formal study he had experienced before: "I have never taken so many notes as I have at Saint-Sulpice," he remarked early in 1822.[12] This observation may be seen as a reflection on the caliber of education offered at Chateau-Gontier and Le Mans, but it also says much about the character of the intellectual training favored at the time by the Sulpicians. The 1820s marked the nadir of a long-decaying scholasticism shot through, at least in France, with Cartesian anomalies, Gallican arrogance, and sour bits of Jansenism. Even postgraduate students like young Father Moreau were put through a dull routine of rote-learning and memorization. They read the dreary manuals assigned to them, and carefully wrote down their professors' comments, professors who themselves had studied little else than other dreary manuals. With an emphasis almost exclusively apologetic, two hours of class a day were deemed sufficient.

The only philosophical breeze to roil the still waters of Saint-Sulpice while Moreau was in residence there issued from the novel theories of Félicité de Lamennais, who appeared to challenge the conventional scholastic epistemology and even to question the Gallican church's traditional independence from the pope. Moreau became mildly interested in these speculations or, perhaps more precisely, mildly troubled by them. The advice he received from his spiritual director was terse and unequivocal: "The best course to follow is to resolve to pay little attention to such things, never to discuss them, to remain neutral, and to suspend judgment for a half-century." "I hear no more talk about M. de Lamennais," he added, "and I shall wait ten years to see what will be thought of him then. Do the same yourself."[13] Moreau took these admonitions to heart. "What is given in class is quite enough," he decided, "and, besides, arguing is to no point, especially on this subject [raised by Lamennais], because even great minds do not understand the problem clearly."[14]

The director just quoted was a priest named Gabriel Mollevaut. He was descended from a family of the lesser nobility in Lorraine, where his father was a prominent politician. During the tumultuous decade of the 1790s young Mollevaut—he had been born in 1774—served at different times as a soldier, a teacher, and a minor diplomat. He also became something of a *bon vivant* and gave up all practice of religion. Largely self-educated in the classics and mathematics, he eventually joined the faculty of a *collège* in Metz and soon acquired the reputa-

---

12. Catta, *Moreau*, 1: 40.

13. Letters of January 15 and April 24, 1825, in *Recueil documentaire: le très révérend Père Paul Moreau, d'après ses ecrits, ses correspondants et les documents de l'époque (1799–1835)* (New York, 1945), 106–109.

14. Quoted in Catta, *Moreau*, 1: 75.

tion of a gifted teacher. About the time of his thirty-fifth birthday he underwent a profound conversion-experience, after which his previous indifference gave place to a religious fervor that startled as well as edified his academic colleagues. Indeed, the stark mode of life he now adopted seemed to them to signal a flight from the world whose joys he had so avidly sought before. They were not mistaken. Nor were they surprised, late in 1813, when Mollevaut risked his life to nurse the wounded and typhus-infested French troops retreating through Metz after Napoleon's defeat at Leipzig.[15]

Three years later, at the age of forty-one, this austere and driven man was ordained a Sulpician, and in 1819 he was appointed superior of the house in Issy. The Solitude of Issy, as it was called, served as a novitiate for the Sulpicians as well as a retreat center and a residence for young priests, like Moreau, destined for posts in various diocesan seminaries. Mollevaut's influence upon two generations of French priests was immense, not only because of the pivotal position he held for eighteen years but also because of his own strong, not to say domineering, personality. Nor did his ascendancy over his charges necessarily cease after they left Issy and no longer had direct contact with him. His counsel followed them by way of occasional visits and especially through the correspondence he exchanged with them, often over many years.

There is no question that Father Mollevaut had more to do than anyone else with the formation of Basile Moreau's ideas and ideals. It is instructive to compare the guidance the former proposed and the resolutions the latter made in response to them. "I note with pleasure . . . that you will be able to continue the life of the Solitude," Mollevaut wrote shortly after Moreau had returned from Issy to Le Mans, "which you find so attractive, and rightly so. A life of retirement, regularity, and obedience is the best thing in the world." "We should humiliate ourselves, especially when things are going well." "It is quite true that we must despise ourselves in all things and desire nothing but to be forgotten." "Try to make it your principal joy to have an ever more ardent desire to do something for the love of our good Master, remembering always that an act of humility and meekness is worth more than the conversion of many souls." And when in 1830—seven years after his departure from Issy—Moreau had been named professor of Scripture in the seminary, Mollevaut sent him this bleak warning: "The teaching of Holy Scripture . . . demands much humility and prayer. One's vanity is exposed to the danger of research out of mere curiosity, of subtle discussions, of superfluous treatises which are useless and dangerous. Thus it happens that a man

---

15. See the sketch in Catta, *Moreau*, 1: 44–49, and the biographical references there.

can become as vain in this field as in the study of Homer and Virgil."[16] Mollevaut in his youth had been an accomplished Greek and Latin scholar. Now, in the continued heat of his conversion, he disdained such studies or any other remotely like them. Probing too much within the sacred sciences was "useless and dangerous." "You are too much of a theologian," he once told a seminarian who persisted in asking questions. "Theology will kill you."[17]

Moreau, at Issy and afterward, tried to mold his own attitudes in accord with those of the master. Spiritual distinction, consistent with the dignity of the priesthood, was what he sought, not intellectual enlightenment. Aside from a smattering of Hebrew and the development of impressive verbal and compositional skills, the results of Moreau's education were mediocre at best. What he did learn from the Sulpicians was a method of conducting his daily life. A widely quoted dictum of the superior of Issy, addressed to all his disciples, Moreau wanted desperately to apply to himself: "Without a love of regularity, you will never be anything but street-peddlers. For such priests, their only interest eventually will be to collect the income from their parish. Be faithful to your little exercises, and they will bring you big results."[18]

So Father Moreau, seminary professor, drew up for himself a highly detailed rule of life. Arise at four o'clock in the morning (four-thirty in the darkling winter), recite the *Memorare* of the Virgin, read a chapter of the Old Testament, pray the so-called little hours of the breviary (prime, terce, sext, and none), spend some crucial time in mental prayer, offer the sacrifice of the Mass, make a thanksgiving not to exceed twenty minutes for this privilege, eat a simple breakfast, and then read a chapter of *The Imitation of Christ,* visit the Blessed Sacrament and, following that act of piety, lecture to the students until noon, at which time engage in a detailed examination of conscience, read a theological tract, eat dinner and afterward reverently visit the Blessed Sacrament once more. During the afternoon he would share in the period of community recreation, reflect upon any verbal faults he had committed during that talkative interval, and finally join in the community's recitation of vespers. After a meager supper, having already anticipated the next day's matins and lauds, he would pay a final visit to the chapel, retire to his room, where he would recite the *Memorare* again and kiss the floor while he made an act of contrition.[19]

---

16. Letters of October 10, November 22, December 30, 1823, January 28, 1827, and March 26, 1830, in *Recueil documentaire,* 97, 99, 100, 123, 136.

17. Quoted in Catta, *Moreau,* 1: 52.

18. Quoted in Catta, *Moreau,* 1: 51.

19. Catta, *Moreau,* 1: 62–64.

Such was the daily schedule of the man into whose orbit Edouard Sorin came in 1834, under whom he was to serve, and with whom, eventually, he was to do battle. Moreau's stern devotion to these ascetic principles—his endeavor to tame the baser human instincts through a rigid and undeviating set of religious exercises—was not without its admirable characteristics. Regularity in fulfilling his duty, as he saw it, and steadfast adherence to resolutions freely determined upon were no doubt virtues in him and in many of his priestly contemporaries as well. The voluntary denial of creature-comforts—Moreau resolved, for instance, not to have a fire in his room during the winter—conformed to Christian usage over the centuries.

Yet there remained in this brand of spirituality a chilling and forbidding aspect. It had no biblical roots, or liturgical ones either; the sacramental and communitarian elements in the Catholic tradition played as small a role in it as did the intellectual. So obsessively personal, so much dependent upon constant probing into the murky bog of motivation, so often demanding a faithfulness to the letter rather than a blossoming in the spirit, the standards Basile Moreau had adopted seemed bound to lead him into a kind of perilous if splendid loneliness—bound as well to make his relationships with other people prickly and mutually fault-finding. Sulpician ritual moreover, as mediated by Gabriel Mollevaut, required its votaries to indulge in repeated avowals of self-loathing, and so Moreau conformed: "How wonderful a lost soul I shall make"; "What a wretch I am"; "[I] desire to be among the despised."[20] How far removed were such pro forma protestations from the reality revealed in future years of an imperious personality, of an iron will, of a capacity and an inner strength extraordinary enough to found and direct a great religious order which would affect the lives of millions, from France to Bengal, from Algeria to every corner of the United States.

But the portrayal of the sources of Moreau's ministry—and their impact upon the likes of Edouard Sorin—remains incomplete without reference to two more youthful incidents. During his time in Paris and Issy it was Basile's custom to write regularly to Cécile Moreau back in Laigné, apparently because she alone among his siblings was literate enough to read his letters to the rest of the family. He had always addressed Cécile with the familiar *tu*, as would be normal between brother and sister. Always, that is, until shortly before he departed Issy when he wrote again, affectionately as ever, but now employing the formal *vous*.[21] One

---

20. Letters of July 9 and August 27, 1822, and retreat resolutions, December 29, 1822, in *Recueil documentaire*, 56, 58, 84.

21. Letter of April 13, 1823, in *Recueil documentaire*, 34–36.

more Sulpician lesson had been learned: the dignity of the priest was so exalted that even those most intimately related to him had to be kept at a ceremonial arm's length.

And then a few years later, in 1825, the fifty-nine-year-old Louise Pioger Moreau lay dying in Laigné, her son Basile-Antoine in dutiful attendance. The mother, he recorded thankfully, suffered little during her last illness. "Fortified by the Bread of the strong [the eucharistic Viaticum] some days before my arrival, she received extreme unction the day before she died with a lucidity of mind that evoked the admiration of all." Then in so laconic a manner that it might have seemed an afterthought he wrote: "I might add that in the middle of the night, while I was praying at her bedside, two angels appeared carrying a crown which they held over her bed."[22] One who had so easily taken in stride a direct revelation from God would appear to have had little to fear from the ordinary vicissitudes of life or the machinations of mere men.

---

22. Letter of February 3, 1825, in *Recueil documentaire*, 70.

chapter three

Sainte-Croix

WHEN BASILE-ANTOINE MOREAU RETURNED FROM
Issy to Le Mans in the summer of 1823, the bishop, as expected, assigned him to the staff of the *petit séminaire,*
located in the former *hotel* Tessé hard by St. Julien's Cathedral, a massive pile as
impressive in its own way as its more famous neighbor at Chartres. Here his
classroom duty was to teach philosophy to the young men in their late teens—
this preparatory seminary, like the one at Precigné that Edouard Sorin would
attend later, was in effect an ecclesiastical *collège* or secondary school—but for a
Sulpician-trained instructor in a Sulpician-inspired institution like Tessé the intellectual component of his work was of secondary importance. Moreau's knowledge of academic philosophy, beyond what he had picked up out of humdrum
scholastic manuals, was in any case restricted to a trifling acquaintance with the
controversial tenets of Lamennais. Nor did the fledgling professor consider this
circumstance a deficiency, because for him the real object of seminary education
was moral and spiritual. The advice of the assiduous Father Mollevaut, which
followed him in a steady stream of correspondence, confirmed him in this view:
"My dear friend, let it be our principal task now to set up the Solitude [of Issy] in
the depths of our heart."[1]

Such a goal was by no means out of harmony with the general tenor of the
clerical opinion that prevailed in the seminary and in the diocese at large. Perhaps
his confreres did not adopt ascetical and prayerful exercises as relentlessly as Father Moreau or recommend them as strongly as he did, but neither did they dis-
agree with his principles. And among the devotions that characterized the French

---

1. Letter of July 22, 1823, in *Recueil documentaire,* 97.

Catholic ethos as it emerged out of the dark shadows of the Revolution, the chief one was the cult of the Virgin Mary.[2] It was as though the devout enthusiasms of the Middle Ages had come alive again, the era of St. Bernard and St. Louis, when Marian hymns were joyously sung in innumerable cloisters and village churches, when the magnificent gothic cathedrals had been constructed in every corner of France and routinely placed under the patronage of Our Lady, *Notre Dame*. Moreau introduced at Tessé the relatively recent cycle of devotions to be performed during the month of May. "The sweet month of Mary," Mollevaut wrote approvingly to his disciple in Le Mans, "is the joy of the Solitude. . . . I share in the zeal of your dear children, and thank our Lord for inspiring you with this holy practice."[3]

Despite his youth Basile Moreau quickly won the esteem of his colleagues in the seminary and of his superiors, including that of the bishop, who, in 1825, named him an honorary canon of the cathedral. This title in itself brought with it no practical advantage, monetary or otherwise, but to have won it at so early an age was a sign of present regard and of promise for the future. The same year he was promoted to the faculty of the *grand séminaire* at St. Vincent's Abbey, the institution in which he had been a student a few years before. Here he taught dogmatic theology until 1830, when he was shifted to the chair of Sacred Scripture. Thus, during a five-year span, he presided over courses in philosophy, dogma, and Scripture, disciplines which differed radically in content and methodology. This feat may have been a tribute to Moreau's flexibility, but it was surely one more indication of how low intellectual attainment ranked among the seminary's priorities. Meanwhile, he was pleased to be almost "overwhelmed (*surchargé*)" by students clamoring to make their confessions to him.[4]

The person most responsible for the young priest's swift advancement was the rector of St. Vincent's, Jean-Baptiste Bouvier. Born in 1783, Bouvier had endured his share of tribulation during the revolutionary period. He emerged from those trials something of an old-fashioned Gallican, almost as suspicious of ultramontanes as he was of Jansenists.[5] He began his teaching career in 1811. He was a

---

2. See the comments in Thomas A. Kselman, *Miracles and Prophecies in Nineteenth-Century France* (New Brunswick, N.J., 1983), 16–18, 198–200.

3. Letter of May 11, 1824, in *Recueil documentaire*, 103.

4. See the comment of Mollevaut, letter of November 23, 1826, in *Recueil documentaire*, 121.

5. "Gallican" refers to the Catholic Church in France, with an emphasis upon its administrative independence of Rome. "Ultramontane," literally "the other side of the mountains," means in this context the promotion of papal prerogatives and centralization located on the other side of the Alps, in Rome.

prodigious worker and was never burdened by undue modesty: between 1818 and 1823 he published first his class-lectures in theology and then those in philosophy, which ultimately went into fifteen and fourteen editions respectively and which were widely used as manuals in French seminaries. Toward the end of his life the exuberant Gallicanism in these works got him into some trouble in Rome, but by that time he had been for years a distinguished bishop with whom even the powerful bureaucrats in the Vatican had to deal cautiously.[6]

Along with his position at St. Vincent's, Bouvier was also one of the vicars general of the diocese and therefore enjoyed the special confidence of the bishop, and, in 1833, he was himself appointed bishop of Le Mans. Any protégé of his might have been expected to enjoy official favor. But there was much more than mere patronage involved in this instance of upward mobility. Moreau was virtually the definition of clerical respectability. He was eminently dependable. He was industrious as well as intelligent. He demonstrated early on that he could discharge capably any assignment given him. He organized his own life down to the smallest detail, and he carried over that punctiliousness into his relationships with others. The demands placed upon him as a teacher may have been minimal, but he willingly assumed collateral duties within the seminary and without. He became a popular preacher and retreat-master in the parishes around the diocese. When a group of Good Shepherd sisters wanted to open a convent in Le Mans and minister to wayward young women, Moreau was put in charge of them. He showed himself indefatigable in the nuns' service; he not only acted as their spiritual director, but he also saw to their more mundane needs and—most crucial of all—drummed up the financial support necessary to sustain their activities.

Yet this happy turn of events exposed also a dark side which proved to be a harbinger of the future. Various houses of the Good Shepherd fell to squabbling among themselves, and Moreau, as superior of the new establishment in Le Mans, was inevitably drawn into their disputes. He was probably more sinned against than sinning in this incident—the tangled details of which need not be recounted here[7]—but the manner in which he dealt with his opponents, if it revealed a principled controversialist, displayed also a stiff refusal to appreciate the merits of a position other than his own, an assertiveness that merged almost into the self-righteous, a reserve that could be labeled at times disingenuous. Such a man,

---

6. The standard biography is P. Sebeaux, *Vie de Mgr. Jean-Baptiste Bouvier* (Paris, 1889). See also the article in the *Dictionnaire de théologie catholique*, 2 (1923): 1117–1119.

7. The story is told in enormous detail in Catta, *Moreau*, 1: 142–276, and more succinctly in Gary MacEoin, *Father Moreau, Founder of Holy Cross* (Milwaukee, 1962), 47–57, as well as in Gaetan Bernoville, *Basile Moreau et la Congrégation de Sainte-Croix* (n.p. [Paris], 1952), 40–50.

especially one fired with zealous ambition, might have been expected to lead a contentious life. So at any rate it turned out for Basile Moreau who, despite all his admirable qualities, regularly found not peace but a sword.

THE SET OF STERN CONVICTIONS that Father Moreau carried with him was rooted in a sublime self-confidence which was by no means misplaced. He was a man of rare ability who knew his own mind and who had so disciplined his energies that no task seemed too formidable to him. That this strength of character entailed a concomitant weakness—a propensity to quarrelsomeness—does not perhaps, upon reflection, arouse much surprise. However that may be, Moreau's battles with the nuns of the Good Shepherd were only the first. Soon he fell out with his sometime patron, Jean-Baptiste Bouvier, and particularly so after the latter became his bishop. Indeed, a kind of strange love-hate relationship developed between these two strong and stubborn men.[8] But at least during the first stages of what proved to be Moreau's great work he had been able to count on Bouvier's unstinting support.

One of the most serious problems confronting the Catholic Church in France in the wake of the tumults of the Revolution was the virtual absence of any catechetical structure. A whole generation had grown up religiously illiterate, and, in most rural districts, illiterate in the ordinary sense as well. Though Napoleon's concordat had brought an uneasy peace to church-state relations and restored something of the normal parish life of the old regime, it had done nothing to address this predicament. In the Department of Mayenne alone, for example, the 341 parochial schools that had flourished in 1789 were gone a decade later, with nothing to replace them. Bishops and pastors quickly recognized that if a solution were to be found the impetus must come from themselves. The acceptance of this reality had more to do than any other factor with the astonishing proliferation in early nineteenth-century France of new religious associations and congregations dedicated to primary and secondary education. This phenomenon manifested itself across the entire country, but in the West the model most imitated was probably the Institute of the Brothers of Christian Instruction, founded in Brittany in 1817 by Félicité de Lamennais's much less controversial older brother, Jean-Marie.[9]

In the far southeast corner of the diocese of Le Mans, in the village of Ruillé-sur-Loir, another effort of the same kind was simultaneously being undertaken.

---

8. See the comments in MacEoin, *Moreau,* 70–73.
9. See André Merluad, *Jean-Marie de La Mennais: la renaissance d'une chrétienté* (Paris, 1960).

The *curé* of the parish there, Jacques-François Dujarié,[10] had established two foundations pledged to provide a cadre of teachers who would instruct the children of the locality to read and write and to do simple arithmetic, and instruct them also in the rudiments of the Catholic religion. Dujarié, born into a relatively prosperous family in a commune just north of Laval, was nearing the completion of his theological course when the Revolution broke out and the seminary he was attending in Angers was closed down. As a consequence he, like so many others, went underground. For a while he was employed as an apprentice in a weaver's shop, and later—so at any rate the popular story had it—he worked as a shepherd and then, in Paris, he roamed the city streets as a lemonade vendor. Whether or not he had ever in fact been reduced to this last occupation, Paris was the site of his ordination, performed secretly in 1795 by a bishop who was himself in hiding from the revolutionary regime. A native of Mayenne, Father Dujarié, even in such unsettled times, therefore belonged to the diocese of Le Mans, to which he now made his way back, and in 1803 he became pastor of the parish in Ruillé-sur-Loir. He was in his thirty-sixth year.

Dujarié, a round-faced man given to corpulence and the physical ailments often attributed to a careless diet—gout especially—found in Ruillé the same difficulties that countless other pastors faced in countless other parishes at the same moment: the church-buildings in disrepair, the people of the district ambivalent toward the new priest who might not last any longer than the former one had, the children unschooled and indifferent, the ordinary religious cycle of fast and feast long neglected, and, overarching all else, widespread poverty. That Father Dujarié brought with him a modest income of his own was surely a mark in his favor. But his parishioners soon learned that their new *curé* had projects in mind that would far outstrip his resources and theirs. What he had endured during the 1790s had toughened him and left him impatient to right all the wrongs which, as he saw it, the Revolution had brought about. Long after he had left Ruillé old people there recalled his kindliness but, even more so, his inflexibility which, as he grew older and his health deteriorated, inclined to render him cantankerous and secretive.

---

10. See Moreau's hagiographic sketch of Dujarié in Basil Moreau, *Circular Letters,* 2 vols. (n.p. [Washington], 1943–1944), 1: i–xxvi. This is the translation by Edward L. Heston of *Lettres circulaires du Supérieur-général de la congrégation de Sainte-Croix,* 2 vols. (Montreal, 1941–1942), which in turn is a reprint of the original edition published at Le Mans. Fuller treatments, though hardly less laudatory, are Philéas Vanier ed., *Le chanoine Dujarié, 1767–1838* (Montreal, 1948), a collection of documents, and Tony Catta, *Le père* [sic] *Dujarié (1767–1838), curé de Ruillé-sur-Loir* (Montreal, 1960). I have used Heston's translation of this latter work, *Father Dujarié* (Milwaukee, 1960).

Yet without such rigid dedication he would not have accomplished what he did. For out of this little village, out of this rustic and backward corner of France, there emerged two religious congregations destined to distinguish themselves the world over. In 1806 Dujarié enlisted a handful of pious young women to nurse the sick and to teach the appallingly ignorant children in Ruillé and the surrounding countryside. After a few false steps—like the early directress of one school who proved to be a termagant nobody could get along with[11]—the enterprise modestly prospered. Fourteen years later, with the encouragement of the bishop of Le Mans and the rector of the *grand séminiare,* Abbé Bouvier, the curé repeated the formula, only this time with a few well-disposed young men. The first two aspirants the *curé* housed with himself in the presbytery, but within weeks they had departed. Others, however, soon came to replace them, almost all of them farm boys or the sons of artisans, more at home in the fields or the workshop than the schoolroom. Most notable among these early recruits, and a particular blessing to Dujarié and to the community, was André-Pierre Mottais— Brother André, as he was subsequently known—a young man of remarkable steadfastness and probity who early on displayed strong gifts of leadership as well.

Such were the humble beginnings of the Sisters of Providence and the Brothers of St. Joseph. However much theoretical support he received from the larger ecclesiastical establishment, both groups remained very much Dujarié's creations. He acted as their spiritual director, he wrote their rules, he provided food and shelter for them, he heartened them with things went badly, as they often did, and he chastised them when he judged it necessary. The two associations, which Dujarié considered as forming a single spiritual entity, expanded prodigiously in numbers over a brief time-span; the kinds of services they performed were clearly in demand across the whole region, and soon dozens of houses were opened.

Indeed, they grew too rapidly for their own good. If Dujarié had a predominant fault as an administrator, it was to allow his reach to exceed his grasp. When he sifted through the piles of requests for assignment of the sisters or brothers to parishes round about, he tended to let his zeal rather than his prudence guide him. Often enough the villages to which he dispatched them offered no support-facilities, not even a decent place to live. Nor could the rural parishes afford to maintain more than one or at most two teachers, which circumstance readily brought with it a dispiriting sense of isolation and loneliness. A further disadvantage stemmed from the cavalier manner in which Dujarié sent his subjects

---

11. See the charming account in "Zeal for the Gospel" (Paris, 1989), 14–16. This is a romanticized story of Dujarié's life in cartoon form, distributed in several languages by the Sisters of Providence.

out into their missions without ensuring that they had been adequately prepared. Frequently those meant to teach reading and writing were scarcely literate themselves, and, called upon to deport themselves as dedicated religious, they seldom received from their putative superior more than a cursory spiritual training. The result was that successes were accompanied by an ominously large number of failures and disappointments.

THE WOMEN COMMITTED to this great endeavor came to grips with the structural problems much more quickly than did the men. Thanks largely to the strong leadership of the first two mothers-superior, the Sisters of Providence gradually edged away from the governance of their revered but impulsive founder and set up for themselves conventional procedures for the spiritual and intellectual formation of their postulants. These steps were logically followed by the determination that their status had to be detached from that of the Brothers of St. Joseph. Legislation passed by the Chamber of Deputies and ratified by the king in 1825 confirmed the sisters in their intention: a congregation of women devoted to teaching, stated the new law, could be recognized as a corporate person capable of receiving benefactions and owning property. No such legal privilege was accorded to religious associations of men. Up till then Dujarié could declare, consistent with the law formerly in force, that the assets of both communities were legitimately held only in his own name. Clearly the new statute put his relations with the sisters into an entirely different posture. Even so, he resisted the separation with all his might and, though now chronically ill and often bedridden, managed to hold it off for some years. But then, in 1831, the bishop of Le Mans intervened and insisted that the sisters be allowed to go their own way. And so they have, and to this day they flourish in their imposing motherhouse in Ruillé-sur-Loir and in missions from Mozambique to Sri Lanka. To their credit they have never forgotten the unsophisticated *curé* who first called them into being.[12]

Left to themselves the Brothers of St. Joseph soldiered on, but misfortune continued to harry their efforts. Dujarié, his health continuing remorselessly to decline, eventually managed to erect in the village a separate novitiate for the

12. There was much bitterness on both sides at the time of the separation. See Catta, *Dujarié,* 164–166. Dujarié died and was buried in Le Mans in 1838 (see below), but thirty-five years later his remains were brought back by his spiritual daughters to Ruillé-sur-Loir. Today they lie buried fittingly in front of St. Joseph's altar in the beautiful chapel which stands in the center of the Sisters of Providence's compound. The street outside is called the Rue l'abbé Dujarié.

brothers, which, at least in theory, should have prepared the young men for the spiritual and pedagogical demands that would be put upon them once they had been sent on assignment. But this institution proved slapdash at best, as did the boarding school for boys that the curé had founded in 1824, and the number of the brothers who defected was hardly less than that of those who remained. The political unrest of 1830, which sent the Bourbons packing and replaced them with the bourgeois monarchy of Louis-Philippe, further undermined their confidence and sense of mission. A wave of anticlericalism accompanied the palace coup, and fears were rife that a new Reign of Terror might be just around the corner. No such calamity occurred, but many of the brothers, stuck off in their lonely village outposts, nevertheless seized the moment to give up what must have seemed to them a thankless task. The figures tell the story. In 1829 more than a hundred Brothers of St. Joseph were managing forty-seven schools in ten dioceses; two years later their numbers had been almost halved. By that time too Abbé Dujarié's physical condition was so wretched that he could not even walk without help.

But help in a broader sense was on the way. In 1831—the year the Sisters of Providence declared their independence—the brothers' annual retreat was preached by Abbé Basile Moreau. A year later he returned to Ruillé-sur-Loir to perform the same function. And a year after that, in 1833, the bishop of Le Mans died and was succeeded by Jean-Baptiste Bouvier. At that point, the situation growing more chaotic by the day, Brother André took the initiative and, in concert with Moreau and two of his own senior confreres, proposed to Bouvier that the administration of the Brothers of St. Joseph be turned over to a specially constituted association of diocesan priests. It was hardly a coincidence that at that very moment Moreau was setting up just such an association—a project, incidentally, the ever-creative Dujarié had suggested years before.

The Auxiliary Priests of the Diocese of Le Mans—as this, their formal title, implied—were intended to serve as helpers to the parochial clergy, to give retreats and missions in the far-flung parishes of the diocese, and to substitute for curés who were ill or otherwise unable to discharge their duties. In 1835 there were five of them living at St. Vincent's Seminary with Moreau, who was, it will be recalled, a professor there (and Edouard Sorin a student). So few pledged to this ministry may have seemed a trifling factor in a jurisdiction as vast as Le Mans—which included the two departments of Sarthe and Mayenne and counted as many as 1200 active clergy—but Bishop Bouvier judged that it might increase in numbers and become useful. He therefore endorsed the project and, perceiving an opportunity to solve simultaneously the conundrum at Ruillé-sur-Loir, he approved as well the jointure between the Auxiliary Priests and the Brothers of St. Joseph.

And so, at the end of August, 1835, as the brothers were concluding their annual retreat, the venerable Jacques-François Dujarié made his painful way into the sanctuary of the community chapel. Bishop Bouvier was in attendance, as was Father Moreau. The old man, one hand resting on the corner of the altar and the other leaning on a cane, addressed the prelate in tremulous tones. "Your Lordship, you see how my infirmities have made me incapable of governing any longer the Congregation of the Brothers of St. Joseph which divine Providence has raised up by my hands. Today I come to lay it in the hands of your Lordship, begging you to turn to Monsieur Moreau ... to make him my successor. . . . I have been associated with him for a long time in the best of relationships, and I have placed in him all my confidence." Bouvier replied with conventional, though no doubt heartfelt, tributes to the revered founder, and then added: "I can only approve your choice of Monsieur Moreau to direct the Institute of your Brothers, because he well deserves your entire confidence."

Ironic as it may appear, Bouvier shortly demonstrated that "entire confidence" was precisely what he was unwilling to grant Father Moreau in other respects. In 1836 Bouvier dismissed Moreau—who was not only a professor but also by that time vice-rector—from the seminary faculty, because, presumably, the latter had shown too little enthusiasm for the traditional Gallican positions which Bouvier called his own. Thus did the shadow of Félicité de Lamennais and his ultramontane theories (which by then Lamennais himself had repudiated, furthering the irony) darken the scene once again. Yet Bouvier gave Moreau free rein in his other enterprises and encouraged the amalgamation of the Brothers of St. Joseph and the Auxiliary Priests. Accordingly Moreau, who owned a house on seven acres of yard and garden in Sainte-Croix, a suburb of Le Mans, transferred the brothers' novitiate as well as their little boarding school to this property from Ruillé, and, after a time spent in rented lodgings nearby, the Auxiliary Priests went into residence there as well. Abbé Dujarié then resigned his parish and came to live out his last days in the company of his brothers at the foundation now predictably called Notre Dame de Sainte-Croix. He was treated with fastidious consideration until the day he died, February 17, 1838.

Moreau fell to the task of organization with his usual diligence and attention to detail. The aspiring brothers—the postulants and novices—now directly under his eye, received a relatively rigorous and orderly spiritual indoctrination, and they were also subjected to a more carefully planned academic experience. The ambitious curriculum, offered by "various professors," included "reading, writing, arithmetic, geography, linear drawing, surveying, architecture, singing, sacred and profane history, not to mention bookkeeping and the courses on Christian

Doctrine and the Religious life."[13] Not that more mundane affairs were neglected. Moreau had already proved himself adept at securing financial support—the house in Sainte-Croix, for example, had been a gift. Now he organized an Association of St. Joseph, a group of lay persons pledged to support the new society through regular donations. Unhappily, Moreau had to contend, as had Dujarié, with the French government's refusal to recognize associations of religious men as legal persons and the consequent necessity to assume financial responsibility for the larger body in his own name, like a corporation sole. Indeed, this problem was to dog his steps through much of his career, leaving him on one occasion liable for the enormous debts contracted because of the dereliction of one of the brothers.

Nevertheless, he tried to anticipate any fiscal confusion that might arise between the two branches of the new society. Eleven months before Dujarié's death, on March 1, 1837, Abbé Moreau, in his capacity as "Superior of the Association of Holy Cross," drew up a brief written instrument spelling out the terms of union between the Auxiliary Priests and the Brothers of St. Joseph. Nine of its ten articles dealt with income and disbursement of funds, with accounting procedures, or with the property rights of each group and each individual. It was specified in article four, for instance, that the brothers originally invested in the association capital to the value of 45,000 francs,[14] this sum "comprising, besides the money received from the actual or possible sale of their property at Ruillé, all the furniture already brought by them, or to be transported to Sainte-Croix, all contributions made up to the present day by their various Establishments, and finally all the work done or to be done by their working Brothers." Therefore, if the two groups were for some reason to separate in the future, the brothers could claim one-half of the association's total valuation, less 45,000 francs (article five). The document was signed by seven priests and fifty-four brothers, and so the first step had been taken toward the founding of *la Congrégation de Sainte-Croix*— the Congregation of Holy Cross.[15]

---

13. Moreau, *Circular Letters*, 1: 2.

14. In 1837 five francs were roughly equivalent to one U.S. dollar, as is the case one hundred sixty years later. To ascertain value in contemporary terms, however, is extremely difficult. What $9,000 could purchase in 1837 and in 1997 is a meaningless comparison. Only by comparing prices in terms of common commodities can some reasonable appreciation of relative standards of living be attained. Even then the result is more often than not unsatisfactory.

15. See Catta, *Dujarié*, 53–79, 105–120, 185–206 and Catta, *Moreau*, 1: 277–337. An excellent summary is James T. Connelly, "In the Beginning There Were Two" (Notre Dame, Ind., 1987), which also prints the text of the Act of Union (22–24).

This "Fundamental Act of Union" left no doubt as to who would be in charge of the new society. "Abbé Moreau declares," "Abbé Moreau in proposing this decision," "Abbé Moreau wishes": phrases like these peppered the two-page agreement. Only in article nine, however, were the basic assumptions about governance given explicit statement: "Abbé Moreau will present later the principles by which he desires to establish the government of the Brothers of St. Joseph, which direction is to be confided to the Auxiliary Priests." The prerogatives of the chief executive officer, so to speak, were clearly affirmed. Moreover, though equality was to be maintained in matters related to property, there was to be no quibbling about who were to be the moral seniors in this partnership. So "a book of [day-to-day] receipts and expenses" was entrusted to the care of a brother, who, however, had to submit it every week to "the examination and verification" of a supervising priest (article one). This directive function of the ordained over the unordained was to have a profound effect upon the life and career of Edouard Sorin. When the call came to Father Moreau to dispatch missioners to Indiana, it was teaching brothers who were wanted. But they could not have been sent without a priest put in charge of them.

CLEARLY BY THE TIME of the "Act of Union" Basile Moreau had determined to found a religious order, a "congregation." There was nothing unique in this intention: nineteenth-century France witnessed the establishment of hundreds of new orders, along with the revival of many of the old ones banned during the Revolution.[16] This creative outburst was astonishing, especially when the alternating suspicion and hostility of successive civil governments is taken into account. From one point of view at any rate the phenomenon merely restored the normal mix of the Catholic Church's specialized personnel: the secular clergy, ordained priests bound directly to their diocese and their bishop, balanced by the religious or regulars, men—some ordained, some not—and women as well, dedicated to a specific ministry, committed to a common rule (*regula*) and lifestyle, and owing their first allegiance to the society of which they were members. From another perspective, however, the resurgence of the orders also meant a renewal of the age-old tension within the church between secular and religious— overall a healthy tension perhaps but one that brought with it a distinct set of problems.

These lay particularly within the scope of governance. The great traditional orders, like the Jesuits and the Dominicans, were international organizations, each

---

16. See the figures in Gibson, *Social History,* 104–133.

with its own internal structure and rules of procedure different from any other and—the important point here—each relatively independent of the immediate jurisdiction of the bishop in whose diocese they happened to be working. They maintained headquarters in Rome and enjoyed direct access to the Vatican bureaucracy and even to the pope. A thousand years of canon law had endeavored to define the respective rights and duties of the local bishop on the one hand and the local religious superior on the other, and, on paper at least, had produced a workable system.

Yet a Gallican bishop like Jean-Baptiste Bouvier put as minimalist an interpretation as possible on the theory of the "exempt" status—to use the technical term—of the religious in his diocese, while in practice he strove to control their activities much as he did those of his own clergy. Clashes were inevitable, and the feisty Bouvier engaged in his share of them.[17] Not surprisingly, he watched the unfolding of Abbé Moreau's plans with mixed emotions. The bishop appreciated that the *congrégation* emerging in Sainte-Croix, composed of secular priests and unordained brothers who were also his subjects, could provide much needed services to the diocese of Le Mans and indeed was already doing so. But at the same time he was anxious that the society should not evolve into a full-fledged religious order of the traditional variety, with its commitments and energies diffused outside his diocese and its policies determined outside his authority.[18] So the struggle was joined between two stubborn and principled men; Moreau won in the end but only after Bouvier died.[19]

Meanwhile the contention manifested itself in a series of small confrontations. When Moreau, with the sturdy support of Brother André, proposed that a third group be added to the society—laymen-teachers who were tentatively called "Sons of Mary"—the bishop vetoed the idea. Similarly, a few years later, he declined to allow the women who did the domestic chores at Notre Dame de Sainte-Croix to be organized into a formal sisterhood. He and Moreau quarreled

---

17. The most notable of these disputes was that between Bouvier and Prosper Guéranger, who was largely responsible for restoring the Benedictines in France. In 1837, with direct papal sanction, he refounded the ancient abbey of Solesmes, in the south of the Department of Sarthe. Guéranger was also a strong promoter of standardized Roman liturgical practice, while Bouvier supported what remained of the local Gallican liturgies. For instances of tension see Paul Delatte, *Dom Guéranger, abbé de Solesmes,* 2 vols. (Paris, 1909), 1: 139, 221, 239–240.

18. The intent by a bishop to maintain religious societies as diocesan institutes was by no means unusual. The contemporaneous foundation of the Marists in the diocese Belley provides another example. See the summary in O'Connell, *Ireland,* 56–58.

19. Bouvier died at the end of 1854. The Constitutions of Holy Cross received formal approval of Pope Pius IX on May 13, 1857.

when the latter decided to open a secondary school—a *collège*—at Sainte-Croix. Yet when Bouvier heard rumors and rather more formal complaints as well that Father Moreau was exercising too imperious a control over his confreres, the no less imperious bishop dismissed them as idle gossip.

The crucial issue, however, was a larger one. Within the Catholic scheme of things, the fundamental distinction between the secular clergy and the religious, whether ordained priests or not, was that the latter swore the venerable vows of perpetual poverty, chastity, and obedience, and the former did not. The religious were meant to find their means of sanctification in the fulfillment of those vows, in explicit imitation, as they maintained, of Christ himself. The seculars, by contrast, sought to achieve their spiritual advancement by the service they gave to the Christian people, service sustained by their promises to obey their bishop and to remain celibate and thus free from the obligations and distractions of family life. So at least ran the theory.

Abbé Dujarié had timidly attempted to implement the distinction by asking his Brothers of St. Joseph to take an annual vow of obedience; in fact only a handful of them had done so. Basile Moreau was made of sterner stuff: though most of the Auxiliary Priests were reluctant to agree to such a step, and the brothers as well, he insisted upon it as a condition to the survival of the new and untested community. As always, he placed more stock in the opinion of Father Mollevaut than in the resistance of lesser mortals. "I am glad that you are making vows," wrote the sage of Issy. "The older I get, the more convinced I am that the youth of today cannot acquire stability by any other means."[20]

By "youth" it may be assumed that Mollevaut would not have ruled out young persons of the fair sex. If Moreau gave up the proposal for a confraternity of laymen, he was determined to complete his grand scheme by founding a congregation of women who would commit themselves by religious vows—this in the teeth of Bishop Bouvier's oft-stated objections. A first the domestics at Sainte-Croix had been local charwomen under the direction of Victoire Moreau, Basile's sister. By 1839 a more formal arrangement had emerged: five country women, dressed in an unpretentious uniform, did the chores each day and returned at night to a house in the town where they lived together under a simple rule devised by Father Moreau. When he asked the bishop for canonical endorsement of this group, however, Bouvier brushed the request aside: "These girls," he said, "are only an adjunct to the house." Undeterred, Moreau, in the spring of 1841, placed four of these young women with his friends at the Good Shepherd convent in Le Mans, where, he trusted, they would learn to be nuns. And indeed

___
20. Letter of July 10, 1840, in *Recueil documentaire*, 170.

they did. By the end of that year they were located in a house of their own, and by 1845 a total of twenty-five women had joined the community, eighteen of whom persevered. However much the bishop of Le Mans might grumble, these Marianites[21]—in their habit of black serge skirt, black cape and veil, with a fluted cap of white, a rosary round the waist and a small metallic heart, symbolic of the wounded heart of the sorrowful Virgin Mother, worn on the bosom—became a common sight along the streets of Sainte-Croix. Moreau gave them the kind of relentless spiritual direction now habitual with him, and even drew up a set of constitutions for their governance. These Bouvier, predictably, refused to approve, nor did he ever do so—a decision which was to have startling ramifications for the Holy Cross mission in America.[22]

Moreau remained in any event adamant that his institute would be composed of vow-takers. After the community Mass offered on August 15, 1840, the feast of the Assumption of the Virgin, in the presence of an unenthusiastic Bishop Bouvier, the superior formally swore the conventional vows and, as a sign of his altered status, took on an added name: henceforward he would be known as Basile-Antoine-Marie Moreau. At evening vespers the same day four of the Auxiliary Priests followed suit, each of them confirming the Marian piety so prominent at the time: they pledged their lifelong loyalty to the foundation that bore the title Notre Dame de Sainte-Croix. Among them was Edouard Sorin.

---

21. Moreau consistently planned for an integrated *Congrégation de Sainte-Croix*—in Latin, *Congregatio a Sancta Cruce*, abbreviated to C.S.C.—with separate branches for sisters, brothers, and priests of Holy Cross (*not* "the" Holy Cross). But the terminology that emerged along the way, not always consistently, often spoke specifically of the Marianites (sisters), the Josephites (brothers), or the Salvatorists (priests).

22. Catta, *Moreau*, 1: 431–441. Not until 1858, after Bouvier's death, did the Constitutions of the Marianite Sisters receive canonical sanction within the diocese of Le Mans. The papal approval given the Institute of priests and brothers granted the year before (see note 19, above) specifically excluded the sisters.

chapter four

"Here I Am. Send Me"

ÉDOUARD SORIN FIRST MET BASILE MOREAU IN THE autumn of 1834 when he matriculated at St. Vincent's Seminary in Le Mans. The student was twenty, the professor thirty-five. The immediate influence exerted by the elder upon the younger has not been documented, but their later association suggests that it was weighty. There is little doubt that Moreau towered above his rather lackluster colleagues—Bouvier, the forceful longtime rector, was gone from the seminary by then, having been enthroned as bishop the preceding March. The seminary-community was strictly closed, but it was not large, and the oversight exercised by the faculty directors, adhering to the Sulpician standard, was all-inclusive and minute. In such a setting the impression created by the professor of Sacred Scripture and his vibrant, self-assured personality can hardly be exaggerated. As teacher and confessor, perhaps most of all as priestly role-model, he stood out as one to be admired and imitated. Mature and accomplished enough to inspire reverence and yet young enough to relate credibly to the aspirations of the next generation, Moreau came across as some one up and doing, as someone prepared to tackle the really strenuous challenges of his time and place, and as implicitly disdainful of the timidity of his more conventional brethren. Witness, as young Sorin did in 1835, the founding of the Auxiliary Priests—who promptly went into residence at St. Vincent's—and, that same year, Moreau's assumption of responsibility for the Brothers of St. Joseph.

In one regard at least a seminarian was (and is) no different from any other idealistic young man of twenty: he was impatient with the status quo, with established conservatism, with old-fogeyism. Moreau offered an alternative ideal, a positive program realistically and even aggressively geared to address the problems of the day. He offered, in a word, leadership. Even his physical appearance— the slight figure garbed in a severe black soutane, with the distinctly clerical French double-tailed rabat at the throat, the thick hair sprinkled with gray and now receding from a high forehead, the lean ascetic face with its wide, thin-lipped mouth and, most striking, the piercing dark eyes—persuaded the seminarians who listened to his lectures, who confessed their sins to him, and who stood in awe of his austere mode of life, that he possessed a singular inner strength. Nor did his summary dismissal from the seminary faculty in 1836 diminish his reputation among his devotees at St. Vincent's. Quite to the contrary; to have quarreled on principle with an authoritarian bishop was to them another sign of Moreau's stature.

Seminarians, almost by definition, were (and are) an anonymous lot, and Edouard Sorin was no exception. However, one valuable if suspiciously conventional snippet of information has survived. "I knew Monsieur Sorin at the major seminary in Le Mans," wrote Guillaume Meignan, Cardinal-Archbishop of Tours shortly after he learned of his contemporary's death. "He was amiable and pious and a friend of all. He always edified us, his fellow-students."[1] Sorin was ordained two years before Meignan, on May 27, 1838, and went home to Ahuillé a fortnight later to offer his first solemn Mass. He was then assigned as curate to the parish of Parcé-sur-Sarthe, a commune some thirty miles southwest of the see-city.[2] This was the sort of normal appointment any young priest, the oils of ordination still moist on his hands, might have expected. His charge was to assist the ministry of the curé in whatever ways the latter determined. Routine the assignment no doubt was, but the setting was not: among all the charming villages in western France, Abbé Sorin could not have found himself in a lovelier one than Parcé. The commercial district was strung along a single street high above the west bank of the River Sarthe. But the real character of the place could best be perceived in the oldest quarter, with its tangle of little streets and alleys, lined by small shops

1. Meignan to "Father Superior," n.d. [after October 31, 1893, the date of Sorin's death], AGEN, folder 232.1. Meignan (1817–1896) after his ordination in 1840 became a noted Scripture scholar. As bishop of Chalons-sur-Marne (1864–1882) he was the first patron of the Modernist exegete, Alfred Loisy. See O'Connell, *Critics on Trial*, 12–13, 20–21.

2. Sorin's first sacramental ministrations in Parcé were dated July 22, 1838, in the parish register. See Hayes [the local priest] to "Father Superior," December 2, 1893, AGEN, folder 232.1

and bistros and ancient houses with flower-boxes decorating their windowsills, and brooded over by a stone tower built for defense during some long-forgotten war. At the center of this jumble of hopes and memories stood the big parish church, added to by one generation after another, and, by 1838, a hodgepodge of architectural ambition and style, the oldest section of which went back nearly three hundred years. The river meanwhile flowed placidly past the town, its waters taking on the rusty hue of the soil in the fields that abutted it.

Parcé provided, to be sure, a much more fetching and beauteous scene than did the Ahuillé where Sorin had grown up. Yet the two locales were in essence very similar, and, as far as the mission of the priests was concerned, both parishes shared the same goals: to carry on the traditional sacramental ministry, to create a viable catechetical structure, and to maintain the church's moral ascendancy over an often unruly peasant populace. Perhaps it was this very similarity that left Father Sorin bemused and depressed and even bored as he performed his various parochial duties. Or perhaps he sensed already that he was meant for a larger field of endeavor. The fourteen months he spent in Parcé-sur-Sarthe were at any rate too brief a time for him to have left much of a mark there beyond "an edifying recollection." One parishioner recalled that Sorin's ministry to the young had been very effective, "but it was also fruitful among the rich of the neighborhood"—most notably he had brought back to her religious duties a noblewoman who later became renowned for her good works.[3]

The young curate moreover had clearly made an impression elsewhere in the diocese. Sometime in the summer of 1839 he received a formal invitation from Basile Moreau to join the Auxiliary Priests in Le Mans. Bishop Bouvier was duly consulted, and by August 18 he had given his consent. "God be praised," Sorin wrote that day to Moreau, "the bishop leaves me free, and I hasten to tell you that I accept your invitation with the liveliest joy. So from now on I am at your service, since you are willing to receive me. I place myself in your hands." He remained uneasy, however, on one score at least. "I leave for my home tomorrow. . . . Be so kind, Father Superior, to give me all the advice you judge useful both for myself and my relatives. I am perplexed as to how to break this news to them; my resolution is completely firm, but I know it will pain them." Whatever counsel Moreau may have offered, and however difficult Sorin's family may have found it to accept his decision, the upshot was that Sorin, after a brief retreat with the Jesuits at Laval, returned to Parcé and remained on duty there "until the feast of the

---

3. Cited in Lemonnier to "Father Superior," December 6, 1893, AGEN, folder 232.1.

Nativity of the Holy Virgin [September 8] in order to hear confessions," and then departed for Le Mans to take up his new challenge.[4]

By that time Moreau had established a makeshift novitiate in Sainte-Croix for the priests associated with him as well as one for the brothers. Having passed through this spiritual regimen successfully, Sorin, like the founder and director, was permitted on August 15, 1840, to swear the conventional religious vows of poverty, chastity, and obedience in the name of the Congregation of Holy Cross.[5] The experience left him ecstatic. "I am happy," he wrote to a friend three days afterward, "as happy as a mortal can be here below. Under Our Lady's protection I had the happiness of binding myself to her service by the three ordinary perpetual vows." And, exhibiting a combination of youthful idealism and the brand of introspective spirituality Moreau had imbibed from Mollevaut, he added: "Imagine how happy I am to be obliged by vow to live now apart from the world, dead to the world, broken with the world forever."

These self-satisfied words were addressed to a young priest named Alexis Granger, whom Sorin had known in the seminary.[6] Granger was then serving as curate in a country parish near Chateau-Gontier, but Sorin was convinced that he, "whom I esteem and love with all my heart," had really "been called to come here," to Sainte-Croix. Granger, though attracted, was hesitating, mostly because of family considerations: for one thing his spinster sister planned to become his housekeeper once he was given a parish of his own. "Be not surprised," wrote Sorin, "that I fail to understand your intention of passing some time in the ministry as a way of testing your vocation to the community life such as we observe it at Holy Cross." Father Moreau, when informed of it, had dismissed such a notion out of hand: "It is an illusion of the devil."[7]

A few days later the Founder elaborated. "This good *abbé* [Granger]," he told Sorin, "does not understand our work at all. It is, however, very clear, that once we consider all the various kinds of good to be done, it ought to be clear to every-

---

4. Sorin to Moreau, August 18, 1839, AGEN. In the archives of the Holy Cross Generalate in Rome Sorin's correspondence is arranged chronologically without further designation and so will be cited hereafter in accord with that system. I owe an enormous debt to the former archivist, Robert C. Antonelli, C.S.C., who supplied me with copies of these letters.

5. Lemarié, *De la Mayenne*, 6–7. It is unclear what the novitiate for the priests may have entailed at this early date, since Moreau expressed the intention (January 1, 1840) to open it "next year." See Moreau, *Circular Letters*, 1: 21.

6. For a later but still contemporary appreciation of Granger, see Joseph A. Lyons, *Silver Jubilee of the University of Notre Dame* (Chicago, 1869), 80–82.

7. Sorin to Granger, August 18, 1840, AGEN. The concluding salutation to this letter was "*Totus tibi* (All things to you, *Tout à vous*)," a phrase Sorin used in his correspondence throughout his life.

body that one can do more good in our Society than anywhere else in the ministry." This breathtaking self-assuredness was fully shared by Moreau's young disciple, who brushed aside Granger's reservations as so many trivialities. Thus, Sorin wrote, "If your good sister be too put out over not being able to live with her brother, the curé, you might perhaps find a still more agreeable situation for her," though he provided no clue as to how this might be done. At any rate, "I should tell you that it is not at all Father Moreau's intention to despoil [members'] families." True enough—with Sorin, even this early in his career, the ideal was not allowed to obscure the practical—the Auxiliary Priests received no set salary, but then they did not have demands placed upon their resources like ordinary pastors, and they kept their Mass stipends for their own needs. So Sorin urged his friend to set aside his doubts and reflect upon the "precise goal" of the congregation, as expressed in the constitutions Moreau had drawn up: "The spirit of the Society is a great zeal for the glory of Jesus, Mary, and Joseph, a burning desire to save souls, especially through forming in young people the Christian and ecclesiastical virtues, and a continual commitment to imitate the Holy Family." Upon such grounds Edouard Sorin was prepared to offer his personal testament.

> I will tell you, my dear Father [Granger], since you ask me to reply with utmost frankness, that personally, if I did not believe that I could do more good in the Society than in the world, I would never have entered. If I did not believe that I would make my eternal salvation more secure, I would never have entered. If I did not believe that I would be more acceptable in the eyes of God in choosing a state of life evidently more perfect in itself than the life commonly lived in the priestly ministry, I would still never have entered.[8]

ONE SOURCE OF ANXIETY felt by Alexis Granger, also related to a concern for his family, had been the fear that if he joined Holy Cross he might be dragooned off to the foreign missions. "You can rest assured," Sorin told him, "that you will not be sent out of France during the lifetime of your relatives or indeed during the whole of your own life except at the will of the Superior coupled with your own request. Nobody is ever obliged to go."[9] No such apprehension apparently troubled Edouard Sorin Even so, it may be doubted that

---

8. Sorin to Granger, August 31, 1840, AGEN.
9. Sorin to Granger, August 31, 1840, AGEN. Granger joined Holy Cross in 1843 and was sent to Notre Dame a year later. His death there 1893 occurred only weeks before Sorin's.

before 1836 he had ever heard of Indiana. But that year, his third at St. Vincent's Seminary in Le Mans, he and the other students were addressed by the first bishop of Vincennes, Simon-Gabriel Bruté de Rémur, whose diocese included the whole of that state as well as a third of neighboring Illinois, more than 50,000 square miles in all. Bruté,[10] born in 1779 of an affluent family in Rennes, was a medical doctor who had become a priest and a Sulpician—Basile Moreau's mentor, Father Mollevaut, had exerted much influence on him—and had emigrated to Baltimore in 1810. There he had taught a variety of subjects in the several institutions established in Maryland by the French Sulpicians since the 1790s. He was more a bibliophile than a scholar; none of the many literary projects he initiated ever came to anything, but by the time he went to Vincennes in 1834 he had accumulated a private library of some five thousand volumes.[11]

In some respects a curious combination of prayerful ascetic and unpredictable eccentric, Bruté nevertheless touched the lives of innumerable people attracted by his simple, unselfish character. His capacity for inspiring intimacy and trust was boundless and extended far and wide. As a young physician he had caught the favorable notice of the Emperor Napoleon. Before he left France he had become a close friend of both the brothers Lamennais, Bretons like himself. Once in America, he counted among admiring colleagues or grateful students most of the prelates who guided the Catholic community during its difficult early days: Carroll and Maréchal of Baltimore, England of Charleston, Purcell of Cincinnati, Dubois and Hughes of New York, Rosati of St. Louis, and his particular confidant, Flaget of Bardstown. But the most significant relationship of his life, personal and spiritual, was the one he formed with the saintly Elizabeth Ann Seton till her death in 1821.

Few of his associates, however fond of him they may have been, thought the diffident and seemingly insecure professor would succeed as administrator of a diocese, much less a diocese located on the raw frontier of the old Northwest Territory. Bruté quickly proved the doubters mistaken. Armed only with a few of his precious books and $245 in the pocket of his threadbare coat—money given him by Mother Seton's Sisters of Charity—he assumed his new duties with verve and

---

10. Standard accounts are Mary Salesia Godecker, *Simon Bruté de Rémur, First Bishop of Vincennes* (St. Meinrad, IN, 1931), and Charles Lemarié, *Monseigneur Bruté de Rémur, premier évèque de Vincennes aux Etats-Unis* (Paris, n.d. [1974]). More readable is Theodore Maynard, *The Reed and the Rock* (New York, 1942). Brief notice of Bruté's visit to Le Mans is given in Godecker, 429, and Lemarié, 232–233. Bruté was an incessant letter-writer. Much of his correspondence is preserved in the Archives of the University of Notre Dame (hereafter AUND).

11. The library is preserved in its own building next to the Basilica of St. Francis Xavier (the original cathedral) in Vincennes.

determination. His single-minded devotion to his faith, tempered by a universal kindliness and courtesy, won the love of many and the respect of almost everyone. In the scant five years allotted him, he put together across his vast jurisdiction the basic elements of an institutional structure upon which others could build.

What brought Bruté back to Europe in 1836, with the stopover in Le Mans included, was his need to solicit support for his missionary diocese in terms of both money and personnel. What success he enjoyed—and it was considerable—did not stem from an impressive physical presence or from eloquence. Indeed, virtually toothless by this time, his speeches were very difficult to understand, whether delivered in the French he had half-forgotten or in the English which, even after a quarter of a century in America, he had never quite mastered. Yet in this little man, more aged than his fifty-seven years, a perpetual half-smile playing across his lips, was embodied a priestly dedication and a spirit of adventure that lit up the young heart of at least one of those who listened to him in Le Mans that day.

AMONG THE RECRUITS for his mission whom Bishop Bruté enlisted during his tour of France in 1836 was a thirty-eight-year-old priest named Célestin Guynemer de la Hailandière. Like the bishop of Vincennes, Hailandière came from prominent Breton lineage, and, also like Bruté, he had attained a certain professional status before he entered the priesthood. Trained in the law and destined, it was widely believed, for a brilliant legal career, he had suddenly given up such prospects and enrolled in the seminary of Saint-Sulpice. There he too had encountered the seemingly all-pervasive influence of Gabriel Mollevaut. After his ordination for the diocese of Rennes in 1825 many predicted that a miter would shortly be his, but five years later the fall of the Bourbon monarchy, to which he and his family were notoriously loyal, made ecclesiastical advancement unlikely, since under the concordat of 1801, still in force, the government nominated the candidates to all French bishoprics.[12]

Hailandière had scarcely arrived in Indiana when Bruté named him vicar general and then, in 1839, instructed him to return to Europe to seek more financial support and more volunteers for the mission.[13] By this time Bruté had entered upon his last illness; he died June 26 of that year, without knowing that Hailandière had already been appointed his coadjutor and successor. Given his

12. Charles Lemarié, *Les missionaires bretons de l'Indiana au xix siècle*, 3 vols. (n.p., n.d. [Montsurs, 1973]), 3: 9–14.
13. Hailandière's decennial faculties, AUND, CAVI, "Diocese of Vincennes," were signed in Rome March 29, 1840.

habitual self-deprecation, Bruté probably did not take sufficient account of his statistical achievements. They were nevertheless significant: instead of the virtual nonexistence of Catholic institutions and specialized personnel in the infant diocese when he arrived in Vincennes in 1834,[14] there were, five years later, twenty priests ministering to twenty-eight parishes, three schools for girls, one for boys, and a fledgling seminary. Hailandière accordingly made the case, as he traveled from Alsace to Brittany, that these firm beginnings deserved reinforcement from French Catholics who appreciated the importance of the missionary apostolate. At the end of July, 1839, while he was in Paris preparing for his episcopal consecration, he took up his pen and composed a letter to be delivered in Le Mans. "Monsieur Mollevaut told me of the Congregation of which you are the superior and counseled me to write to you."

> I have come to France [Hailandière continued] with the desire of finding some Brothers who would be willing to devote themselves to the instruction of the people in our country. It is so saddening for the heart of a priest to see our children deprived of Catholic schools and going to ask for instructions from the Protestants. I have looked for help, but in vain. . . . Here, Reverend Father Superior, is the problem we have to solve: to establish in the diocese of Vincennes a community of Brothers to spread religious instruction among the people, as also the instruction needed for business and the needs of daily life, first in this diocese and then, God willing, beyond its limits.[15]

This appeal, addressed to Basile Moreau, was not without its effect. The superior of Holy Cross had himself, at least in his imagination, hankered after a vocation to the foreign missions, and to hear such an eloquent entreaty, especially one endorsed by the revered Father Mollevaut, could not leave him unmoved. Yet prudence dictated that he not decide precipitously. He already had in hand requests to send brothers to Algeria—incorporated into the French Empire in 1830—and to Canada. At issue for him was not only the genuinely religious objective to spread and bolster the Catholic faith but also the opportunity to enhance the congregation's reputation and to ratify its status as an institute with

---

14. Thomas T. McAvoy, "Bishop Bruté's Report to Rome in 1836," *The Catholic Historical Review*, 29 (July 1943): 177–233. The Latin and French texts of the report are printed here, along with some additional notes Bruté made and an English translation of all the material.

15. Quoted in Catta, *Moreau*, 1: 496.

more than merely local relevance. On both these scores there was much enthusiasm for missionary ventures among the priests and brothers at Sainte-Croix.

A month later—about the time Edouard Sorin joined the Auxiliary Priests—
the new bishop of Vincennes arrived in Le Mans to plead his case in person.
Moreau, now committed to send two priests and three brothers to Algeria, listened to Hailandière sympathetically and promised to assign some men to his
diocese once they had completed their religious formation. Such formation, however, as he pointed out to the bishop, could not include training in a foreign
tongue. Hailandière brushed aside this reservation with the remark that English
was easy to learn—a quaint assertion seeing that he himself after three years in
the United States could scarcely make himself understood in that language.[16] But
the bishop was in fact animated by a different conviction altogether. True, he said,

> English is the language in which the Brothers will have to do their teaching,
> and it would seem for this reason that we ought not to come to France
> looking for recruits. But we cannot hope to find in America, at least in the
> beginning, young people who have the qualities necessary for founders.
> With time and God's help we shall come upon such people. Indeed, there
> are two young and pious boys in Vincennes who await a guide to direct and
> form them. But the religious spirit has to come from France which seems
> chosen by God to take the lead in doing good.[17]

Another obvious question Moreau raised had to do with the physical survival
of the mission. Sainte-Croix and Vincennes were both virtually penniless; how
then were the brothers to live? After inconclusive negotiations, continued by post
after Hailandière had returned to Indiana, the bishop agreed to provide the Holy
Cross contingent with a farm that could sustain them while they learned English;
once that was accomplished the brothers could open their schools and then—a
plum shrewdly calculated to appeal to Moreau—there would be sufficient funds
even to establish an American motherhouse, modeled on and subject to Sainte-
Croix.

---

16. Lemarié, *De la Mayenne*, 9.

17. Quoted in Anon, *Histoire du T. R. P. Basile-Antoine-Marie Moreau* (La Chapelle-Montli-
geon, 1923), 131 cited hereafter as Charles Moreau, *Moreau*). A sister of Holy Cross and the Seven Dolors (Canada) prepared this abridgment of the biography of Moreau written by his nephew Charles,
a two-volume work useful for the documents it prints but compromised by its bitter bias against almost all Basile Moreau's associates.

The ill-fated Holy Cross ministry in Algeria began in May, 1840, and, after a series of desperate travails, ended thirteen years later.[18] It cost Father Moreau immense pain and trouble, and it cost him as well his most trusted lieutenant: the redoubtable Brother André Mottais died in 1844 of a disease contracted in North Africa. But the Algerian project, in its early euphoric days, acted if anything as a spur to attempt a similar venture in America. Moreau, with the concurrence of his self-appointed administrative council, decided to send to Vincennes a larger group than Hailandière had hoped for. He picked out three brothers who would be teachers and who would find practical support in three others, a farmer, a tailor, and a carpenter. And, in accord with the principle within the *congrégation* that priests should always rule, he appointed one of the auxiliaries to lead the delegation. His choice was Edouard Sorin.

Sorin promptly addressed the bishop of Vincennes in a letter that breathed the spirit pervading post-revolutionary French Catholicism.

Monseigneur, Never has Divine Providence seemed to me more kind and merciful or lovable. Never before have I thanked God with a heart more deeply touched by his goodness, or with a heart happier than mine since I have been assured that it is upon me that his eyes have fallen, in order to give you one more priest to work in your immense diocese for the glory of God and the salvation of souls. . . . It seems to me that our good Master is leading me towards you by the hand, and it is this particularly which has filled me with unspeakable joy. . . . After all, I am not saddened at seeing myself so poor; this is only another reason for placing my whole hope in God. . . . How happy I am to be able to assure you that the road to America stands out clearly before me as the road to heaven. . . . Henceforth I live only for my dear brethren in America. America is my fatherland. It is the center of all my affections and the object of all my thoughts. . . . At the present time I see clearly that our Lord loves me in a very special manner as has been told me many times. I look forward to sufferings of every kind, and I know ahead of time that the good Master will maintain his protection over me, which is all I aspire to. I have a great need to suffer! Our Lord has done so much for me already, and I have done so much contrary to his will! The only thing I fear is to be ungrateful to him.[19]

---

18. See the announcement in Moreau, *Circular Letters*, 1: 22–24. The Algerian enterprise is described in detail in Catta, *Moreau*, 1: 457–489.

19. Sorin to Hailandière, n.d. [summer, 1841], AGEN.

Moreau recognized that in dispatching across the sea this most promising of its younger ordained members he was imposing a hardship on his infant congregation. He felt a personal loss as well: "What a sacrifice I have made!" he observed privately, nor did he neglect to urge the same conclusion upon Bishop Hailandière. For his part, Sorin displayed not the least hesitancy in accepting this charge. Neither his youth—he was twenty-seven—nor his ignorance of English, nor his inexperience of the world outside one little corner of France, nor even the prospect of working in nearly absolute poverty could dampen his spirits or undermine his aplomb. Even as he remembered the impact the sweetly unaffected Bishop Bruté had had upon him five years earlier, Sorin now built upon that recollection a larger vision: "The road to America is the road to heaven." The conviction that this was so, whatever the terrors and difficulties to be encountered along the way, had spiritual roots peculiarly French in that it combined noble dedication with a melancholy affirmation of the need for personal catharsis. "I hunger and thirst for suffering," Sorin had confided to a friend soon after his arrival at Sainte-Croix;[20] that aspiration, healthy or not, was to be amply fulfilled.

But to say this is not to say enough. Father Sorin's response to the call from the west must also be seen as in accord with an exalted tradition as old and universal as revelation itself. Obedient to God's summons, Abraham left Ur of the Chaldees for an unknown land, Moses defied Pharaoh and led his people into the wilderness, and Jonah, almost paralyzed with fear, went to Nineveh to preach penance along the city's endless pagan streets. Or perhaps an even better model to invoke is the Prophet Isaiah whose mystical experience at the beginning of *his* ministry might well have been, in the August of 1841, the subject of Edouard Sorin's meditations. "Then I heard the voice of the Lord saying, 'Whom shall I send? Who will be our messenger?' I answered, 'Here I am. Send me.'"[21]

ALL SIX BROTHERS chosen for the mission in Indiana were natives of Mayenne or Sarthe. The eldest was Brother Vincent, born Jean Pieau in 1797 (and thus Sorin's senior by seventeen years). He was the eldest too as a religious, having joined Father Dujarié's society in Ruillé-sur-Loir in 1821. A quiet, self-possessed man, he had proved his worth as a teacher and an administrator, and, along with André Mottais, he had provided Moreau with stout assistance during the crucial negotiations that resulted in the union of the Brothers of

20. Quoted in Catta, *Moreau*, 1: 501.
21. Isaiah 6:8–9.

St. Joseph with the Auxiliary Priests of Le Mans. Upon Brother Vincent rested Sainte-Croix's best hopes for the establishment of a solid and well-trained community in America.

Not that Basile Moreau had repeated Dujarié's signal fault as a superior, that of sending subjects upon a mission without attempting to school them adequately in the religious life. Four of Brother Vincent's colleagues, though they differed widely in age and experience, had spent at least a year in the community at Le Mans, and the fifth, Brother Joachim (Guillaume Michel André), was a mature thirty-two years old when he entered Holy Cross in March 1841; he took his vows a few days before the departure to Indiana. A tailor by trade and a cook by necessity, he worked hard and devotedly until he died of consumption in the spring of 1844. Brothers Laurent (Jean Ménage) and Marie (René Patois, who later changed his religious name to François Xavier) had been professed the same day as Joachim. Laurent, at twenty-six, had been a successful farmer, and he was to demonstrate in future years a keen business sense that would serve the American community well. Marie, twenty-one years old, was a carpenter whose skills were similarly put to long-term use; he was destined to outlive all his companions. Finally, Brothers Anselm (Pierre Caillot) and Gatien (Urbain Monsimer),[22] both in their midteens and unprofessed, were explicitly designated as teachers for the mission; presumably they had been selected on the basis of Bishop Hailandière's recommendation that younger persons could learn English more readily and so move quickly into the classroom. Anselm died tragically early (1845), while Gatien, though he did display uncommon intellectual gifts and a rare talent for teaching, also exhibited and even flaunted a turbulent personality much given to conspiracy and dubious emotional attachments; eventually he left the community (1850), and thus was the only member of the original colony not to have persevered in the religious life.[23]

Once the decision to send missionaries to Indiana had been determined, money had to be found to get them there. The bishop of Vincennes was no help;

---

22. Monsimer's religious name is alternately and frequently spelled with a second a, Gatian.

23. See Garnier Morin, *From France to Notre Dame* (Notre Dame, Ind., 1952), 32–35. A shorter treatment is Sabinus Herbert, "Vanguard of Our Lady," *The Associate of St. Joseph,* 24 (September-November, 1954): 3–4, 16. See especially George Klawitter, ed., *Adapted to the Lake* (New York, 1993), xvii–xxi. This is a collection of letters written by various of the brothers between 1841 and 1849. The book also possesses many helpful charts and tables, as well as a very useful "Introduction" by the editor and translator. A capsule description of each of the original six can be found in Kilian Beirne, *From Sea to Shining Sea: The Holy Cross Brothers in the United States* (Valatie, NY, 1966), 21–39.

all he was prepared to offer was an intimation that if funds became available travel-costs from New York to Vincennes might be reimbursed. Father Moreau therefore turned to the lay people of Le Mans who had aided him financially in the past. These Associates of St. Joseph sponsored a lottery which featured a particularly fine gold chain[24] donated for the purpose by a local lady. This transaction raised a total of 1,682.37 francs, to which was added a further 1,565.15 contributed by other donors.[25] So Father Sorin had the equivalent of about $600 in his wallet when the practical preparations for departure were completed.[26] The seven had followed Hailandière's advice and had collected "all the linen, all the clothing, too, you can procure; these things cost much here. I always regret not bringing enough." Besides such personal items the bishop hoped the missionaries would also bring liturgical supplies—"chasubles, chalices, candlesticks, church lamps"—and so they did, several crates full.[27]

"At last," as Edouard Sorin recalled the moment, "on August 5 [1841], the feast of Our Lady of the Snows, the first colony took its departure after a most impressive and touching ceremony."[28] That he and his six companions should have set out on their adventure on a feast of the Blessed Virgin surely struck them as an auspicious omen. Indeed, three of them—Sorin, Brother Marie, and young Brother Gatien—when fifteen months later they found themselves knee-deep in the snows of northern Indiana and routinely invoked the protection of Our Lady, recalled perhaps on this wintry occasion how she had long ago signaled her intentions by

---

24. Not "a golden chair," as in Edward Sorin, *Chronicles of Notre Dame du Lac* (Notre Dame, Ind., 1992), 2. This is a translation of *Chroniques de Notre Dame du Lac* prepared by Father John Toohey, C.S.C., during the 1890s. The rules of Sainte-Croix required that each house keep a running account of "all that is pertinent to the enlightenment of the general administration as to persons, things, and important events, and is of such a nature as to edify the community." Much of the manuscript was written in Sorin's hand, and all of it appears to have been inspired and approved by him. It covers the years 1841–1866, with a brief appendix dated 1880. The publication used here was edited and annotated by James T. Connelly. For "gold chain" versus "golden chair," however, see ms. *Chroniques*, 2, Archives of the Indiana Province of the Congregation of Holy Cross (hereafter cited as AIP).

25. See notation for August, 1841, in AUND, CSCM, "Miscellany, Indiana Province, Accounts between Motherhouse and Notre Dame." Sorin, *Chronicles*, 2, remembered slightly lower figures, but see note 35, below.

26. Catta, *Moreau*, 1: 500–503.

27. Quoted in Morin, *From France*, 30.

28. Sorin, *Chronicles*, 1. Sorin's memory of the feast-day remained fresh: see Sorin to Moreau, July 6, 1845, AGEN.

causing snow to fall on the Esquiline hill in Rome during the hottest time of the summer.[29]

Father Moreau, "more dignified and serious than usual," presided at the departure ceremony, which took place in the community chapel after the celebration of Mass. "We are, it is true," he said, "ever exposed to dangers of both soul and body; hence the attention of Christian souls never to lose sight of God's holy presence, for we always need protection, but especially when starting on a journey."[30] Sorin rather ruefully remembered that the "dangers" uppermost in his mind as he listened to his superior were those the missionaries were likely to encounter from savage Indians or bigoted Protestants. Such fears, happily unfulfilled, nevertheless "prepared and encouraged them to meet a thousand lesser crosses chosen for them by God and of which they had never thought."[31] And so, late in the afternoon, they boarded the stagecoach for the hundred-mile, twenty-hour trip northward over the rutted roads between Le Mans and the port of Le Havre on the Normandy coast, the blessing of Isaiah echoing in their ears: "How beautiful are the feet of them that preach the gospel of peace, of them that bring glad tidings of good things."[32]

They were accompanied on this first leg of their journey by a young nun, a member of Dujarié's Sisters of Providence, who had already heeded Bishop Hailandière's appeal and established a convent in Terre Haute, Indiana.[33] Also in attendance was a dedicated layman named Léon Papin-Dupont, a lawyer originally from Rennes, who had assumed the task of giving aid and succor to French religious volunteering to serve in the diocese of Hailandière, his fellow-townsman. "He was with me in the front part of the stage," Soeur Saint-François-Xavier reported later, "while [Sorin and the brothers] were [in the larger rear section]. We

---

29. During the pontificate of Pope Liberius (352–366) a church dedicated to the Virgin Mary was built on the Esquiline, replacing an ancient temple of the goddess Juno. A much later tradition asserted that Mary had indicated the exact location for the church by causing snow to fall there on August 5. On the same site a century later was erected Santa Maria Maggiore, still one of the four major Roman basilicas. This monument represented the great outburst of Marian devotion that followed the definition of the divine maternity (*theotokos*) at the councils of Ephesus (431) and Chalcedon (451). See Prosper Guéranger, *L'Année liturgique*, 15 vols. (Tours, 1922), 4: 328–37. This work appeared originally in 9 vols. (1841–1866). The commemoration of Our Lady of the Snows on August 5 was in accord with the calendar of the Roman liturgy, not formally recognized by the Gallican Bishop Bouvier. Sorin's invocation of it was a small sign of the continuing tension between Sainte-Croix and the local chancery in Le Mans.

30. Morin, *From France*, 36.

31. Sorin, *Chronicles*, 2–3.

32. Isaiah 52: 7. This text was incorporated into the departure ceremony.

33. See Lemarié, *Missionaires bretons*, 3: 134–141.

spent the night as if at the gate of heaven. We spoke continually of Jesus and Mary. [Dupont] is twenty-five times more devout than I am. After the beads he asked me to say a great many 'Aves' for the conversion of sinners. . . . Then from eleven o'clock till midnight we made the Way of the Cross on an indulgenced crucifix. We took turns meditating aloud."[34]

Fortunately for the travelers Dupont proved worldly-wise as well as pious. He arranged housing for the Holy Cross contingent over the three days they spent in Le Havre and helped correct some minor technical flaws in their passports. A more serious difficulty arose with the discovery that Moreau's agent had carelessly booked cabin passage for them on a ship called the *Victoria* at 500 francs apiece, almost as much as the all the money they had in hand.[35] But this obstacle too was quickly disposed of, thanks to the intervention of a group of five French nuns bound for New York. These Mesdames of the Sacred Heart,[36] ticketed aboard the *Iowa,* had been forbidden by their superior to sail without having a priest on board. The consequence was that the sisters loaned Father Sorin, the only priest available, 1,000 francs to free himself and the brothers from their commitment to the *Victoria,* and all of them were then accommodated on the *Iowa,* the nuns in cabin-class and the Holy Cross men in steerage. Soeur Saint-François-Xavier attributed this very practical solution to a higher power: "Monsieur Dupont began to pray, and I waited in peace." As for Edouard Sorin, he too was grateful for all the good prayers and good wishes—especially for those expressed by Basile Moreau, in a note delivered to him just after the ship slipped anchor—and grateful perhaps most of all that he still had 1,500 francs in his pocket.[37] At any rate he stood on the deck at three o'clock in the afternoon of Sunday, August 8, 1841, and watched fresh winds fill the *Iowa's* sails as she glided out of the harbor and into all the unknown challenges that lay ahead.

---

34. Quoted in Morin, *From France,* 42.

35. See notation in AUND, CSCM, "Miscellany, Indiana Province, Accounts between Motherhouse and Notre Dame:" "Aug. '41—versé à moi meme à mon départ, 3,500 francs."

36. A congregation founded by Madeleine-Sophie Barat (1779–1865) in 1800 and established in the United States in 1818.

37. Sorin, *Chronicles,* 3–5, and Morin, *From France,* 44–46. It is not altogether clear whether the 1,000 francs ($200) Sorin received from the Sacred Heart nuns was a loan or a contribution. Indeed, in recounting as early as 1844 his party's original financial situation Sorin made no mention at all of a benefaction from the nuns. "When we left Le Mans in the August of 1841 we had in hand a total of 3,620 francs, which would have left us less than 200 once we paid for our passage. . . .We managed to exchange cabin-accommodation for steerage, and in this manner, at the cost of some discomfort, we arrived in New York having preserved 1,500 francs." Sorin to "Messieurs" of the Propagation of the Faith (Paris), February 2, 1844, AGEN.

chapter five

The Way West

THE *IOWA*, CAPTAIN PELL COMMANDING, WAS AN
American packet-ship which sailed regularly between Le
Havre and New York. She was a good-sized vessel, a hundred
fifty feet long, and handsomely appointed with "cabin-doors of citron and ma-
hogany and locks of silver." And she was a good sailor: the voyage took only
thirty-five days. "We met several vessels on our route," recalled Sister St. Francis
Xavier, "but we outsailed them all."[1] This speedy passage was especially remarkable since the first eight days were virtually lost as the ship stood becalmed in the
English Channel. "Those were bad days for the whole crew. Although the sea was
not in one of its furious moods, the rolling was greater and all the passengers suffered much." Of the Holy Cross contingent, at first all were ill save Brother Vincent who valiantly nursed the others. And "hardly had the little colony regained
a little health and energy when Brother Vincent . . . needed to be waited on
himself."[2] "The feast of the Assumption [August 15], so beautiful ashore, so exquisitely observed this year at Sainte-Croix," Sorin reported to their recent benefactor, Léon Dupont, "was a very sad time for us here: it seemed that we, like the
Psalmist, had hung up our harps by the rivers of Babylon. We were then still en-
snared in the backwaters of the Channel. Nevertheless we have since learned
again that Mary has not deserted her poor pilgrims. That was the last day of our
illnesses, and three days afterward I was able to say Holy Mass." The brothers and

---

1. Quoted in Morin, *From France*, 46. It is appropriate from now on to employ English usage in
proper names. Soeur Saint-François-Xavier thus becomes Sister St. Francis Xavier, Edouard Frédéric
Sorin becomes Edward Frederick Sorin.

2. Sorin, *Chronicles*, 5.

nuns were all by then well enough to attend, and "only the good Sister St. Francis Xavier was unable to receive Communion: she had inadvertently taken three sips of water!"[3]

They were not troubled by sea-sickness during the balance of the voyage. There remained, however, much physical discomfort to contend with. Quartered among the two hundred emigrants packed into steerage, Sorin and the brothers resorted to using spare boards to block off a corner twenty feet by ten and thus secured a modicum of privacy. Even so, the only light and air accessible to them came from opening a hatch. Captain Pell, an easy-going Episcopalian who treated the Catholic religious with every courtesy and consideration, not only furnished a small cabin for use as an oratory—Sorin said Mass eleven times altogether during the voyage—but he also allowed the Holy Cross men deck privileges. This latter was a considerable boon, as Sorin remembered it, because in steerage "we had to suffer from the continuous confusion of this strange group of people, . . . persons of all sorts, dispersed indiscriminately with barely any distinctions," crowded, bored, noisy, "sometimes quarreling, sometimes in bursts of joy." Yet "the good God more than once furnished us with the occasion of making ourselves useful toward our neighbors who were distressed and even poorer than we were."[4] Whatever these ministrations may have been, they appear to have won for the religious the esteem of the ship's complement, including, rather surprisingly, that of a troop of traveling vaudeville performers. Though there were some predictable exceptions—"The Devil," Sorin observed darkly, "also has his apostles and always at least double the number of those of Jesus Christ"—

an unexpected event brought into strong light the general sentiments of the ship towards the little band [of religious]. A child of two years of age, daughter of a German Protestant, fell sick, and it soon became evident that there was no hope of recovery. After many fruitless pleadings, the Ladies of the Sacred Heart finally succeeded in obtaining the consent of the father to have her baptized. . . . The ceremony took place in the little [oratory] room on deck. The event caused a great sensation among all the ship's company. . . . Two days later the new Christian went to take possession of the heritage that had just fallen to her. . . . The captain . . . invited Father Sorin to perform the funeral ceremony. . . . At the appointed hour the body was borne by four sailors on a plank five or six feet long. It was made to rest on

---

3. Sorin to Dupont, August 20, 1841, AGEN. The letter was posted to Dupont at Tours from New York by way of Le Mans.

4. Sorin to Moreau, September 14, 1841, quoted in Morin, *From France,* 47.

the edge of the vessel until the priest had recited the usual prayers, and during all that time the crew and passengers stood uncovered and silent as if they had been in church. The prayers being finished and the signal given to the bearers, the plank . . . was raised at one end, the little corpse slid gently off, and the next instant was heard dropping into the sea. But the soul which had taken its departure was already in heaven.[5]

This poignant incident was doubtless a bonding moment for all those aboard the *Iowa* who experienced it, a fact the men of Holy Cross came to appreciate fully by the end of the voyage, when "every one bade them good-by with thanks and wishes of happiness in the New World." But for them the christening and death of "little Mary," as they called her, amounted to a good deal more, to a providential token which, sentimental as it may seem in retrospect, appeared to them further assurance that in undertaking this perilous mission they were fulfilling God's special designs. "The little Mary, they said to one another, owes us much; she will not forget those who have made her so happy. Many years afterwards they still loved to recall their little Mary, who on her side appears not to have forgotten them."[6]

"On September 13 [1841] the vessel entered New York bay, probably one of the most beautiful in the world. It would be hardly possible to describe the sentiments of the pious band at the sight of this strange land which they had come so far in search of, through so many dangers and fatigues."[7] Hardly possible or not, one reaction Edward Sorin did scribble on the margin of a letter he had written aboard the *Iowa:* "All hail to God and Mary, we have landed in New York. Oh my dear Monsieur Dupont, how beautiful is the sky of America!"[8] The sky had dark-

---

5. Sorin to Dupont, August 20, 1841, AGEN.

6. Sorin, *Chronicles*, 7–8.

7. Sorin, *Chronicles*, 9. Sorin and his companions were more fortunate than two celebrated travelers a decade earlier. It took thirty-eight days for the ship carrying Alexis de Tocqueville and Gustave de Beaumont to sail from Le Havre to New York. Due to poor provisioning there was virtually no food or drinkable water aboard during the last three days of the voyage. See Pierson, *Tocqueville*, 52–57.

8. Sorin to Dupont, August 20, 1841, AGEN. Sorin may have expressed the same exultant sentiment to Moreau: "We have arrived in New York full of life, health, and joy. . . .What a delicious day it is here—how beautiful is the American sky! Here is the portion of my inheritance; here will I dwell all the days of my life." Quoted in James J. Trahey, *The Brothers of Holy Cross* (Notre Dame, Ind., n.d. [1904?]), 47. But Trahey gives no source for this quotation, and, since his account of the trip from New York to Vincennes (48–49) is so filled with errors, his whole description of the arrival of Holy Cross should be treated with caution. For a fuller quotation see Timothy Edward Howard, *A History of St. Joseph County Indiana*, 2 vols. (Chicago, 1907), 2: 613–614.

ened into evening by the time Sorin disembarked, noting the happy omen that he and his companions had arrived on the eve of the feast of the Exaltation of the Holy Cross. Next morning he celebrated the feast itself by offering Mass for the first time on American soil.

The six brothers, however, did not experience that moving moment with him, because, due to routine quarantine regulations, they had to remain aboard the *Iowa* until September 15. That Sorin himself escaped this irritating delay was due perhaps to Captain Pell's intercession with the sanitary inspectors or, more likely, to the direct action of one of the customs officers. Samuel Byerley at any rate proved to be the good angel to Holy Cross in New York that Léon Dupont had been in Le Havre. Though English-born Byerley, a successful merchant as well as a port-official, had formally joined the Catholic Church only a week before, his involvement with French missionaries had begun a year earlier. Dujarié's Sisters of Providence of Ruillé, it may be recalled, had responded to Bishop Hailandière's pleas and had dispatched a group of nuns to Terre Haute, Indiana, in 1840. But the bishop's agent had failed to meet them in New York as promised, and Byerley, present at quayside in his official capacity, had offered to assist them; it was thanks largely to his kindly interest and material help that they had survived their early difficult days in the United States. Holy Cross's winsome companion on the journey from Le Mans, Sister St. Francis Xavier, belonged to the Providence order and was in fact on her way to Terre Haute. The superior there, however, the formidable Mother St. Theodore Guérin, worried lest the negligence of the year before be repeated and the young nun find herself alone in a big, brawling, foreign city. So Mother St. Theodore shrewdly sent her a letter in care of Samuel Byerley, which guaranteed that that gentleman would meet the *Iowa*.[9]

It was well that he did, because once again the bishop of Vincennes's representative failed to turn up. Byerley took charge of the situation, and even before the little launch they steamed ashore in together had reached the docks, he had won the heart of the wonderfully guileless Sister St. Francis Xavier and of Father Sorin as well. "He has already proved himself almost as perfect as my dear Monsieur Dupont," gushed the young nun.[10] And Sorin echoed her: "As I

---

9. Morin, *From France,* 55–59. See also Clémentine de la Courbinière, *Life and Letters of Sister St. Francis Xavier* (St. Mary-of-the-Woods, Ind., 1934), 146–163. I am indebted for this reference to my friend James T. Connelly, C.S.C. See the passenger manifest of the *Iowa,* September 1841, in the geneological library (microfilm), Allen County Library, FortWayne, Indiana. I owe this reference to my friend Joseph L. Walter, C.S.C.

10. Sister St. Francis Xavier to her mother, September 13, 1841, quoted in Lemarié, *Missionaires bretons,* 136.

boarded the steamboat, I heard my name called by a new Monsieur Dupont."[11] Once the formalities of the quarantine were satisfied, and the Madams of the Sacred Heart and their luggage moved from the *Iowa* to that order's convent on Houston Street, in lower Manhattan (and Sister St. Francis Xavier there also, as a temporary guest), Byerley turned his benevolent attentions to the men of Holy Cross. He opened his own home to them, escorted them round the city, introduced them to the venerable Bishop Dubois,[12] and helped with the necessary arrangements for the next leg of their journey to Indiana. Like the missionaries who had come before them, they were impressed by the size and bustle of New York, though disappointed in the rather shabby appearance of the Catholic churches there—even the cathedral—and slightly scandalized that the Protestant ones had no crosses atop their steeples ("*ces hauts clochers pointus*").[13] Edward Sorin had three days to form an opinion of his own, which included surprise "to find in a land not long since inhabited by savages a city whose streets and stores might compare, sometimes even favorably, with those of Paris and London"—an observation as gratuitous as it was condescending, seeing that Sorin's acquaintance with cities was restricted to the likes of Laval and Le Mans. Nevertheless he displayed his keen eye for the practical when he added: "New York cannot fail before long to rival both [Paris and London], since it surpasses them in the promises of the future on account of its maritime and commercial location."[14]

Bishop Hailandière's New York agent, however lackadaisical he may have been about meeting ships, did see to it that the Holy Cross men were furnished with 1,500 francs ($300) to pay their expenses from New York to Vincennes. By following the relatively cheaper water-route they spent only 940 francs ($188) of this sum.[15] On Thursday September 16, they departed the west side of Manhattan on board a paddleboat steaming up the lordly Hudson River. "The shores of the Loire are renowned in France," Sorin wrote, "but I do not believe they should be compared to those of the Hudson.... Here it is less the variety which pleases and charms than the prodigious grandeur which surprises.... All was new for us;

11. Sorin to Moreau, September 14, 1841, quoted in Morin, *From France*, 57.

12. John Dubois (1764–1842), born and educated in Paris (he had Robespierre for a schoolmate), fled the Revolution to America in 1791 and was named third bishop of New York in 1826.

13. Sister St. Theodore Guérin's remark (1840), quoted in Lemarié, *Missionaires bretons*, 49.

14. Sorin, *Chronicles*, 10.

15. See the accounting in Sorin to Hailandière, n.d. [January, 1842], AGEN: New York to Albany 60 francs; Albany to Buffalo 245; Buffalo to Logansport 435; Logansport to Vincennes 200.

none of us had ever seen nature on such a grand scale." Next morning, at five
o'clock, they landed in Albany, and within hours had boarded "one of the five or
six thousand boats that ply the famous canal from Albany to Buffalo."[16]

The Erie Canal was indeed famous by then, fifteen years since its completion
and thirty years since it was first proposed by DeWitt Clinton and his associates.
And American plans and aspirations to duplicate the venerable canal-systems
in England and France went back much further still. But the Erie was the great
breakthrough, and not only as a remarkable feat of engineering. Its commercial
and cultural success ushered in an era of feverish construction, so that by the
time Sorin and his companions rode westward on "Clinton's Ditch" a network of
interconnected waterways had been built or planned from New England through
the mid-Atlantic states as far south as Virginia and across the Alleghenies into
Ohio and Indiana and then circling north and east toward the Great Lakes.[17]

Whether in fact "five or six thousand boats" worked the Erie, as Sorin had
heard, there were at any rate enough of them to create a fierce competition that
kept prices down. In 1836 a ticket to travel the whole length of the canal, 350
miles, on a so-called packet boat, which catered exclusively to passengers, cost
fifteen dollars, while one on a line boat, which also carried freight, cost nine dollars. Five years later the Holy Cross men, who doubtless chose the cheaper alternative, paid only seven dollars apiece to go from Albany to Buffalo.[18] By then
various refinements had improved the service, but the boats, packet or line, remained essentially barges drawn along the forty-feet-wide channel by teams of
horses on the abutting towpath at an agonizingly slow pace of four miles per
hour. Passengers in 1841, especially those paying the lowest fares, enjoyed few
amenities. They had to bring their own food and water aboard, and complaints
were common—especially among Europeans, accustomed to the better developed
canal systems back home—about the primitive sleeping conditions available. How
much colorful distractions—canal-men singing or telling stories, for instance—
may have compensated for the boredom and overall discomfort over a journey that
lasted nearly eight days probably differed from passenger to passenger.[19]

16. Sorin to Moreau, September 26, 1841, AGEN.

17. See Madeline Sadler Waggoner, *The Long Haul West: The Great Canal Era, 1817–1850* (New
York, 1958), 29–63. A useful map of canals in 1850 forms the endpapers of this book.

18. That is, 245 francs for the seven of them. See note 15, above.

19. See Ronald E. Shaw, *Erie Water West: A History of the Erie Canal, 1792–1854* (Lexington, Ky.,
1966), 202–218.

Such diversions or indeed any sense of camaraderie with the bulk of the vessel's company were hard to come by for Sorin and his companions. Their ignorance of English and their unfamiliar garb set them off as not only foreign but peculiar. Nor did the rough fraternity of drummers, grain-factors, and assorted peddlers who frequented the Erie Canal rest easy with a group of papists in their midst—papists who huddled together on deck and regularly performed unintelligible devotions. On at least one occasion bafflement may well have mingled with an age-old Yankee hostility: when the boat's progress was halted for a while due to a low water-level in one of the locks, the Holy Cross men went ashore, and the priest was seen hearing the confessions of the brothers "at the foot of a fallen oak."[20] However distasteful such a sight was to Protestant sensibilities, for the seven Frenchmen—or rather the five men and two boys—the sacramental act was merely one more sign of a deepening interdependence, an increasingly vibrant sense of community rising out of an environment where everything, even the work-songs, was strange and new.

Meanwhile they stood on the deck of the *Archimedes* or the *Anti-Masonic Republican* or the *Assiduity*—many of the canal boats sported idiosyncratic names[21]—and marveled at the vastness of the land through which they were passing. The valley of the Mohawk not only moved them by its somber beauty; it also stirred up pious memories of earlier French missionaries who had had thrust upon them the palm of martyrdom.[22] Off to the south Brother Vincent discerned the hazy outline of the Catskills and wondered what lay behind them. Edward Sorin for his part remained astonished at "the great number of forests, the unbelievable abundance of wood which the settlers do not know what to do with." Nor was the son of that prosperous farmer, Julien Sorin of Ahuillé in the Department of Mayenne, favorably impressed by the husbandry he observed. "Agriculture does not seem to have made much progress in this part of the country. . . . Everything here exhibits a great negligence. . . . Some fields seem to have been plowed wretchedly before the seed was planted. . . . One sometimes sees in the middle of a planted field a great number of trunks of trees two or three feet in height, blackened by flames. . . . In this way they clear the land and burn over the fields. I do not know whether they have ever uprooted a tree in America."[23] The condescending mood was still on him, but it was destined not to last very long.

---

20. Morin, *From France*, 73.

21. For a list in 1839, see Shaw, *Erie Canal*, 204–205. There was even one boat called the *Clergyman*.

22. Notably the Jesuit Isaac Jogues (1607–1646), who was mutilated and later decapitated in an Iroquois village some forty miles west of Albany.

23. Sorin to Moreau, September 26, 1841, AGEN.

At Lockport, the last entrepôt on the Erie Canal before its terminus in Buffalo, Sorin and Brother Vincent disembarked in order to indulge a tourist's fancy. It was Friday, September 24, and, more significant to them, another Marian feast day, that of Our Lady of Mercy. Thanks to money given them in New York by Samuel Byerley,[24] they had the wherewithal to spend a day visiting Niagara Falls. The eighteen-mile train ride—surely the first for both of them—took but an hour, and then, having each paid the 25 cents admission charge, "we hurried to get up there and enjoy the beauty of the spectacle."

> As for myself [Sorin continued] I have never seen anything which could enter into comparison with the scene which spread out before our eyes. The huge forest which surrounded us on all sides seemed to act as a background to the scene. We were completely beside ourselves. In going around the gallery which topped the turret we saw to the right a second falls larger yet and deeper than the first. We stopped for some time as if rendered immobile by astonishment. Then we dropped to our knees, and there amid the noise of the surge of the torrent, amid marvels so new to us, we adored the infinite power of the Creator of all things.

At noon they said the Angelus too, and, instead of contributing to the graffiti by "mingling our names with those which one sees cut in the bark of all the trees, we made a small cross out of some oak branches and planted it in a prominent place. That was our name and surname." The trip by rail from Niagara to Buffalo took only two hours, after which they collected "our good Brothers" and all the luggage from the canal-depot, before enjoying the hospitality of a local pastor, an "excellent priest," a French-speaking German native to whom Sorin made his confession, the first time since Le Mans.[25]

The next day was Saturday, September 25. Father Sorin said Mass and several of the brothers received communion. By late morning, thus fortified, they had embarked upon the next stage of their relentless journey, down the entire length of Lake Erie from Buffalo to Toledo, Ohio, a distance of 250 miles. Steamboats had been plying the Great Lakes for the better part of twenty years. They were curious looking vessels, with side paddles and a smoke stack situated amidships between two conventional masts. Their engines tended to exert more propulsion than their fragile wooden construction could sustain, and many of them were

---

24. See the figures in Sorin to Hailandière, n.d. [January, 1842], AGEN.
25. Sorin to Moreau, September 26, 1841, AGEN.

damaged and even wrecked. Indeed, the men of Holy Cross were nervously aware that only six weeks before they boarded their vessel a similar one had burnt and sunk off the south shore of Lake Erie, hardly forty miles from Buffalo; 175 people had been killed.[26] No such mishap happened to Sorin and his confreres, but they did experience a miserable three days of apprehension, delay, and a roiling of the waters unpleasantly remindful of the English Channel aboard the *Iowa*. It was a great relief when the wharves of Toledo finally hove into sight.

But frustration awaited them there. They had assumed that by employing the canal system—the Miami and Erie linked with the Wabash and Erie—they could travel by water across northwestern Ohio into Indiana. Due to various financial and engineering difficulties, however, sections of these two canals remained unfinished in the early autumn of 1841, including the one leading out of Toledo.[27] Hampered now more than ever by their inability to obtain information—"None of them spoke any English, [and] it was harder for them to understand than to make themselves understood"[28]— they finally decided to follow the proposed canal route[29] by steamboat up the Maumee River as far as Maumee City, where they transferred to another, probably smaller vessel.[30] By seven in the evening, September 28, they arrived in Napoleon, Ohio, where the navigable waterway ended and where, Sorin noted ruefully, nobody spoke French, despite the name of the town. Next morning, after much haggling, most of it in sign language, they hired two carts and four horses and set out overland for the point of entry into

26. See Dana Thomas Bowen, *Lore of the Lakes* (Daytona Beach, Fla., 1958), 10, 60, 302.

27. Construction of the Wabash and Erie began at Fort Wayne, Indiana, in 1832, proceeding sectionally in both directions. It took ten years to complete the connection to Toledo, Ohio, in the east and Lafayette, Indiana, in the west.

28. Sorin, *Chronicles,* 11.

29. For a useful sketch see Thomas H. Smith, *The Mapping of Ohio* (Kent, Ohio, 1977), 220–221.

30. There is considerable difficulty in unraveling this portion of the journey because Sorin's later memory conflicted with his contemporary account. See the discrepancies between Sorin, *Chronicles,* xv, 11–12, written sometime after the event, and Sorin to Moreau, October 1, 1841, AIP. Also Sorin called Toledo "Miami," which compounds the confusion, because, although there is no "Miami" in Ohio, the Maumee River was familiarly known as the Miamis River or the Miami of the Lakes River (see Smith, *Mapping of Ohio,* 12, 58, 99–100) and the canal in question was called the Miami and Erie. Finally, Sorin refers in his accounts either to places that no longer exist, like Providence, Ohio ("three or four houses" between Maumee City and Napoleon: see Henry Howe et al., *Historical Collections of Ohio,* 3 vols. [Columbus, 1891], 2: 184–187), or to places that never existed, like "Miami" or a town called "Junction," by which he really meant the "junction" of the Miami and Erie and the Wabash and Erie canals. The continuing use of "Miami" by Sorin and his contemporaries testifies to the wide presence of the Miami Indians one hundred fifty years before. On the site of the present Fort Wayne there was earlier a Fort Miami. See also chapter 7, note 4, below.

the finished section of the canal that led into Indiana. There followed the worst two days of their heroic trek. Accompanied by two young brothers who acted as guides and three other backwoodsmen "of no religion" who amused themselves by continually firing their rifles—their presence remains a mystery—the men of Holy Cross "became involved in the most deplorable roads ever built."

> Think of a road rutted everywhere by rain, strewn with mud, where the wheels of our carts sank up to the hub. . . . We also had to cross streams, and such was their force that we often . . . went downstream . . . with the current until we were swept into a vast pond where our horses went in up to their breasts. . . . How can I tell you of the frightful precipices which we skirt, not by feet but by inches.

Nevertheless Sorin boasted that they covered twenty-five miles that day, September 29, arriving at ten o'clock at Defiance, Ohio, "a small village situated in the middle of the woods."[31] The travails on the second day were, if anything, worse than those of the first. "I forced myself to appear gay," Sorin remembered, "but in reality I was consumed with fear. I had to watch over our six Brothers and all our baggage. At each ravine, at each mud hole, I muttered an Ave with my gaze fixed on the danger."[32]

Finally, after hours of toiling directly westward from Defiance on the last day of September, they reached the eastern terminus of the completed section of the Wabash and Erie Canal, and the seven of them, "slightly tired, it is true, and covered with mud," found a small boat to take them into Fort Wayne, Indiana, on October 1, 1841, the fifty-eighth day since they had left Le Mans.

INDIANA HAD BEEN ADMITTED to the Union as the nineteenth state in 1816, when its population totaled about 65,000. By the time of the arrival there of Edward Sorin and the six Brothers of St. Joseph (as they still designated themselves) that number had increased more than tenfold. Those who

---

31. Actually Defiance was seventeen miles from Napoleon and roughly halfway between Toledo and Fort Wayne. It took its name from Fort Defiance, one of a string of forts built in the mid-1790s during the Indian wars of that decade. See Howe, *Historical Collections*, 1: 539–41 and the maps in Hilda Huen Kagan, ed., *The American Heritage Pictorial Atlas of United States History* (n.p. [New York], 1966), 124–25.

32. Sorin to Moreau, October 1, 1841, AIP, and Morin, *From France*, 81–84.

had flooded into the state were mostly farmers who found the land and climate suitable for the cultivation of corn, wheat, and beans, for the raising of hogs and dairy cattle, and, in the north especially, for poultry, vegetables, and even spearmint and peppermint. The forests which had astonished Sorin and his companions as they traveled along the Erie Canal were by no means diminished now that they had penetrated farther into the west. Seventeen species of oaks flourished in Indiana, along with hard and soft maples, hickories, yellow poplars, sycamores, beeches, elms, and even a few pine trees. Out of such materials the pioneers could, and did, build the houses they needed, as well as the barns and wagons and furniture that helped define their way of life. They could rejoice as well, according to the season, in the gorgeous blossoming of sumac, dogwood, ivy, and honeysuckle, and—understandably more crucial for them—they could supplement their diet by hunting the red deer, the plentiful small game, and the varieties of waterfowl.

The overwhelming majority of these 700,000 people lived in the southern half of the state, and it was here that the word "Hoosiers" was coined to denominate them. The origins of this word are obscure, though most likely it derived from a dialect spoken in northern England during the eighteenth century, which used "hoozer" to characterize a highlander, a rough-hewn, uncouth man. So the nickname at first was derisory—much like "Quaker" or "Shaker" or, perhaps more analogously, like "Cracker" to denote a poor white in Georgia. But early on residents of Indiana wore it defiantly like a badge of honor.

The state's official name acknowledged that long before whites from Virginia, the Carolinas, and Kentucky had thronged across the Ohio River, the land had been home to various tribes of native Americans. There were in fact Indian burial mounds that went back a thousand years and more. The people who had built them, however, had mysteriously disappeared, and only after many centuries did the "modern" tribes immigrate to take their place: the Miami, the Potawatomi, the Kickapoo in the north; the Shawnee and the Delaware in the south. But these too, by 1841, had been virtually swept away, victims first of the imperialist struggles over "this dark and bloody ground" between Britain and France, victims then of American "manifest destiny" and the crushing numbers of land-hungry white settlers who justified their depredations by invoking that dubious mandate, victims finally of an inability to cope with a culture more developed in skills and organization than their own. Indian resistance to the inevitable, brave but forlorn, had been eliminated long before Edward Sorin became a Hoosier, by dramatic set-piece battles, to be sure, like Fallen Timbers (1794) and Tippecanoe (1811), but even more by the systematic destruction of native American village life and the forced removal of the survivors to reservations west of the Mississippi.[33]

This dénouement occurred first in the southern part of Indiana, which helps to explain why so large a proportion of the early white settlement was concentrated there. In the north the tribes lingered somewhat longer, but finally they too, reduced by disease and drunkenness to a pathetic remnant, were remorselessly evicted from the lands of their ancestors. Thus it was that Father Sorin, the Holy Cross mission, and the future Notre Dame had practically nothing to do with an apostolate to the Indians, not because of racial or any other kind of prejudice but because there were no Indians at hand for them to serve. What Bishop Hailandière intended in inviting the men of Sainte-Croix to his diocese was the establishment of an institutional structure of parish and school of the kind flourishing just then in the west of France. Earlier missionaries, and indeed a few later ones, did keep "the poor savages," in the terminology of one French-born prelate, as the primary object of their solicitude.[34] But Moreau and Sorin, whatever differences they may have had with the bishop of Vincennes, understood Hailandière's injunction that the duty of Holy Cross in Indiana was to provide a conventional Catholic milieu for white immigrants, viewed as displaced Europeans. Sorin's later brief encounter with the Potawatomi notwithstanding, this episcopal directive was simply taken for granted.

The preponderance of southern Indiana in population and influence, so striking in 1841, was not destined to last. The state's 36,000 square miles were divided into roughly equal halves by the action of the primeval glacier, which antedated by many thousands of years even the earliest Indian presence. North of the line of latitude reached by the glacier—approximately where the great Cumberland Pike or National Road which began in Wheeling, Virginia, already bisected Indiana[35]—lay 400 lakes and bogs and, more importantly, land left relatively flat and blessed with much more fertile soil; this was particularly the case in the geographical center of the state, around Indianapolis, the site which had been selected for a state capital in 1821, twenty years before Sorin and his companions reached Fort Wayne. (These were comparatively simple days: the transfer of the state treasury and official records from Corydon, the former capital located in

---

33. See the maps in Kagan, ed., *Pictorial Atlas,* 118–119.

34. For observations on this shift of missionary emphasis, see O'Connell, *Ireland,* 29–34. The prelate quoted was Joseph Cretin, first bishop of St. Paul (1850–1857).

35. Now Wheeling, West Virginia. See Kagan, ed., *Pictorial Atlas,* 150–151.

the southernmost part of the state, cost $118.07, but furniture sold in Corydon brought in $52.50, so the total expenditure amounted to $65.55.)[36]

Nothing in the long run could gainsay the geological facts: the southern half of Indiana, left untouched by the glacier, remained an area of rugged, hilly terrain and thin soil. The narrow valleys and cluttered countryside determined that the railroads, harbingers of an industrial future, would arrive there later rather than sooner. Though neither cotton nor tobacco could be grown in southern Indiana, and though hardly any of the residents were slave-holders—in the census of 1850 11,200 "free Negroes" were recorded[37]—the culture developed there nevertheless reflected the pace and customs and, to a degree, even the values that prevailed on the other side of the Ohio River and eastward toward the Alleghenies. There remained there also a whiff of the utopianism that had led Robert Owen during the 1820s to locate one of his experimental communities in New Harmony.

Meanwhile the northern half of the state, much more suited to agricultural and industrial development, began to assert its economic ascendancy.

Fort wayne would prove to be a center of this commercial vibrancy once the Wabash and Erie Canal reached Toledo and regional railroad construction began, both achieved by 1847. But even six years earlier, when Sorin and the brothers, "covered with mud," arrived there, it was already a bustling community of eighteen hundred. The town stood at the point where the St. Joseph[38] and St. Mary rivers joined to form an arrowhead into which the Maumee fitted like a shaft. The famous revolutionary general and Indian-fighter, "Mad" Anthony Wayne, had built a fort on the site in 1794, but it had long since disappeared. Destined to last much longer was the testament of John Chapman, kept green in popular memory as the legendary "Johnny Appleseed," gentle and eccentric apostle of fruitful orchards and virtuous living, whose mission had reached its westernmost terminal in Fort Wayne. He died there a few years after the weary Holy Cross men passed through.[39]

---

36. Howard H. Peckham, *Indiana* (New York, 1978), 50–54.

37. Peckham, *Indiana,* 65.

38. Not to be confused with the other St. Joseph River which turned north at South Bend, Indiana, and flowed into Lake Michigan.

39. See Robert Price, *Johnny Appleseed, Man and Myth* (Bloomington, Ind., 1954), 187–188, 234–239.

The Catholic parish, which counted several hundred communicants, was in the charge of two French priests, the senior of whom was away visiting in France. His curate, a recently ordained young man named Joseph de Murtzig Hammion, received the muddy travelers kindly, but he was desperately ill—he died a few months later—and they did not trouble him for long. Two days of hard overland travel out of Fort Wayne brought them to Logansport, a town set in the valleys of the Eel and the Wabash, which, according to a visitor a year earlier, "presented a most picturesque aspect."[40] Here they were welcomed by another French priest, a hardier specimen named August Martin, destined for long life and a bishop's miter.[41] Martin "received them," Sorin recalled, "with all the amiability and cordiality of a genuine Frenchman, waiting on them at table with his own hands after himself doing the cooking. . . . He was too poor to pay a housekeeper."[42]

After a short rest, the Holy Cross men were on the road again, accompanied by Father Martin and an orphan girl named Mary Johnson, whom the pastor of Logansport had arranged to place under the care of the Sisters of Providence at their foundation, St. Mary of the Woods, at Terre Haute. Had they followed the same relatively benign route a few months earlier they would have been charmed by the sprinkling of "wild flowers of every rich and varied tint," by "the hawthorn, wild plum and crabapple bushes, . . . overspread with a tangle of vines, grape, wild hops, honeysuckle, and clambering sweet briar, fantastically wreathed together."[43] But now it was autumn, and the foliage had begun to display a tinge of gold, and the nights were chilly. On October 5, at Lafayette, Martin saw the little party safely aboard the boat that would take them down the Wabash River.

This last leg of their journey seemed tortuously slow to the seven men whose patience had worn thin, but at least they were spared the apprehension the young orphan must have been experiencing. By October 7 they had reached Terre Haute, where the boat paused long enough for them to bid adieu to little Mary and dispatch her off to the convent, no doubt remembering, as they did so, another little Mary. Sorin sent with her—"*le petit paquet*" he called her—letters for the sisters brought from New York as well as a note of his own. "My very honored Mother,"

40. Kate Milner Rabb, ed., *A Tour through Indiana in 1840: The Diary of John Parsons of Petersburg, Virginia* (New York, 1920), 203–204.

41. Martin (1803–1875), a native of Rennes, became vicar general of Vincennes in 1842 and bishop of Natchitoches, Louisiana, in 1853.

42. Sorin, *Chronicles*, 12–13.

43. Rabb, ed., *Tour through Indiana*, 222. Parsons rode the stage from Logansport to Lafayette in June, 1840.

he wrote the superior, "you will understand the sacrifice I have to endure at this moment," the sacrifice of not being able to offer salutations in person. "Oh, how painful it is for me not to able to converse with you about the good God and about France." Then, recalling his traveling companion from Le Mans to New York, he added: "If the dear Sister St. Francis Xavier has arrived among you, do me the favor of recommending me to her good prayers." And in case Mother St. Theodore had not heard the happy news, "Mr. Byerley is a Catholic now for four weeks!!! What a worthy man." Another worthy man, through Sorin, sent muted greetings of his own: "The good Brother Vincent, the only one of our little troop who has some acquaintances among the dear sisters of Terre Haute, asks me to recall him to the memory of those whom he knows."[44]

Finally, on the morning of Sunday, October 10, 1841—the sixty-sixth day since their departure from Le Mans—Edward Sorin and his six companions "beheld the tower of the new cathedral of Vincennes."[45] At 3:30 A.M., they disembarked some distance upriver—presumably at a wharf where merchandise was routinely unloaded—and, with their baggage, made what Sorin called "a forced march across the sands" until they reached the church several hours later.

> We should have been exhausted, [he wrote exultantly to Basile Moreau] but at the sight of Vincennes the feeling of fatigue gave way to a thousand other sentiments, our energies revived, and soon we were in the cathedral where we offered our first homages to God, to the holy Virgin, and to the angels of our new homeland. . . . My reverend and much beloved Father,[46] we have come at last to the end of our long pilgrimage. . . . Thanks, a thousand times thanks, to all the holy souls who have prayed to God for us, thanks particularly to you, good Father, who has given us the chance to

---

44. Sorin to Mère Saint-Théodore Guérin [Mother Theodore], October 7, 1841, AGEN. Sorin also wrote to reassure Martin at Logansport about Mary Johnson: "I am going to deliver your dear and precious packet by sure hands." Sorin to Martin, October 9 (?), 1841, AGEN. The "sure hands" belonged to one S. Buteux, who added a few lines to Sorin's letter: "I received from the hands of the priest the young female orphan whom I have taken today to St. Mary of the Woods and delivered to the sisters."

45. Sorin, *Chronicles,* 13. The cathedral was completed in 1826. Much refurbished, though no longer a cathedral (the seat of the diocese was translated to Indianapolis in 1898), the building is still in use, under the title of the Basilica of St. Francis Xavier.

46. In formally addressing a Catholic priest, French draws a distnction that English does not. The latter employs the catch-all term "Father." In French, however, *Père* refers to a priest who belongs to a religious order and takes vows; *Abbé* refers to a secular or diocesan priest. It is significant that here and consistently Sorin addresses Moreau as *Père.*

taste such lively consolations. . . . We have seen Vincennes, the Vincennes that we had so much desired to see, that we have talked about so much, . . . and our entry into this other Jerusalem makes us feel, I believe, something of what the elect of God must feel upon their entrance into heaven."[47]

The imagery Sorin chose in his enthusiasm was prophetic, though in a way he did not intend. The euphoria he felt lasted hardly longer than that occasioned by the entry of another Personage into the first Jerusalem eighteen centuries before.

---

47. Sorin to Moreau, October 14, 1841, AGEN.

chapter six

Black Oak Ridge

L IKE THE MEN OF HOLY CROSS A YEAR LATER, JOHN
Parsons fretted at the agonizingly slow passage down the Wabash from Terre Haute to Vincennes, but he, like them, exulted in what he found at the end of the trip.

> [Nothing could] in the least temper my amazement over the beauty, the antiquity, the interest of this town. Its situation is of great loveliness, being on what the early writers term a "savannah" of irregular size, some miles in extent, with the dense woods behind it, and the placid river at its feet. Along its streets small century-old houses alternate with more recently erected magnificent mansions. Its inhabitants, I have learned, are extraordinarily interesting, high-bred people among whom I have spent some of the most enjoyable days of all my enjoyable journey.

He ruefully admitted that, "although I endeavor to keep the knowledge from others," he was of "a most romantic temperament," which may indeed have colored his judgment that no "spot, it seems to me, [is] so full of charm as this town of Vincennes, a charm that I find it impossible to describe."

> From the beginning there has always been hospitality here; the place has been sought by visitors from the old world. . . . When I close my eyes I can see, against the background of forest, the picturesque figures: the painted Indian, the Jesuit father, the French coureur-du-bois, the English soldier,

the titled visitors, the backwoodsman with his rifle—ah, small wonder my pen fails me when I attempt to write of Vincennes![1]

Parsons's evocation of the storied past of Vincennes did smack of fashionable romanticism, which, however, was not altogether out of place. "The painted Indian," "the Jesuit father," "the English soldier," along with the other icons Parsons heard about when he disembarked had indeed all left their stamp upon the town. As for "the coureur-du-bois," there had been a French presence on the lower Wabash as early as 1702, and thirty years after that the settlement had received its name from its most prominent resident, the scion of an old Montreal family, the Bissot, sieurs de Vincennes, long active in the French penetration of the region between lakes Erie and Michigan. This young entrepreneur and adventurer, whose authority rested on the commission awarded him by the governor of Louisiana, also French, played his part in the century-long competition between the French and the English for access to the lucrative fur trade with the Indians who roamed the vast basin between the Great Lakes and the Ohio River. This sort of enterprise involved artfully maneuvering among the various tribes and sometimes fighting them. The Sieur de Vincennes proved unlucky in the latter endeavor and was ultimately captured and burned at the stake by the Chickasaw. A Jesuit father suffered the same fate with him.[2]

By 1763 French Canada was no more, and sovereignty over what had been French Louisiana remained ambiguous.[3] But the victorious British had scarcely begun to assert their dominion along the Wabash when the American Revolution broke out. The decisive battles in that conflict were fought, to be sure, along the Atlantic seaboard, but the war eventually spread into the west as well. Thanks to the exploits of George Rogers Clark and his handful of Virginia volunteers, much of what is now Illinois and Indiana was wrested from British control, such as it had been, and Vincennes became an American town.[4] From 1800 till 1813 it was the territorial capital and the headquarters of the young and ambitious governor

---

1. Rabb, ed., *Tour through Indiana,* 337–338.

2. There has been some controversy about the precise identity of the Sieur de Vincennes. See an analysis of the various theories in Edmond Mallet, "Le Sieur de Vincennes, fondateur de l'Indiana," *Bulletin des recherches historiques,* 3 (1897): 3–15.

3. See the maps in Kagan, ed., *Pictorial Atlas,* 76–77, 92–93. By the treaty of 1763 Spain ceded to Britain West Florida (i.e., the panhandle and a wide strip along the gulfcoast as far west as the Mississippi) and received Louisiana in recompense. In 1800 Napoleon forced the Spanish to recede Louisiana to France, and three years later he sold the vast region to the United States.

4. See Peckham, *Indiana,* 25–28 and Joseph Somes, *Old Vincennes* (New York, 1962), 61–64.

William Henry Harrison, victor at the battle of Tippecanoe and later ninth president of the United States.

Vincennes, however, perched atop a gentle rise on the east bank of the Wabash, did not lose its gallic character all at once. Honored locally almost as much as Rogers Clark was "the patriot priest," Pierre Gibault, who at a decisive moment had rallied the French population to resist the British.[5] Succeeding Gibault, other pastors came and went, all of them French, to serve the nominally Catholic majority in the town and hinterland or, in one celebrated instance, to act as the federally appointed tutor to the remnant of Indians still living nearby.[6] Then in 1834—it may be recalled—Vincennes welcomed its first bishop in the person of Simon Bruté de Rémur, followed five years later by Célestin Guynemer de la Hailandière.

THE SECOND BISHOP OF VINCENNES was by any accounting a difficult man to get on with. This was not due to a lack of talent or resolve. He displayed during his brief tenure admirable zeal and not a few administrative gifts. His willingness to labor without respite in fulfilling his charge was never in question. The crude circumstances of life he encountered on the Indiana frontier—notwithstanding the youthfully euphoric testimonies of John Parsons and Edward Sorin—must have been a constant trial for this cultivated French lawyer. He nevertheless confronted his duties and his problems bravely and straightforwardly.

Perhaps too straightforwardly. Hailandière was a man utterly without tact. He recognized no way to deal with opinions that differed from his own except to beat them down. As a result he appeared, even to those who wished him well, as arrogant, high-handed, and quarrelsome. And not everyone wished him well: as settlers from other states of the Union came in ever-increasing numbers into Indiana, many brought with them a nascent nativism disdainful of foreign popery and of its leading spokesman who could not—or would not—learn English.[7] A sweet-tempered Bruté might have turned aside small signs of bigotry; Hailandière, made of sterner stuff, tried rather to ride roughshod over them.

---

5. Somes, *Old Vincennes*, 57, 66 and James D. McQuaid et al., eds., *A Guide Book to Historic Vincennes* (Vincennes, Ind., 1965), 32–33.

6. Jean-François Rivet (d. 1804), "Indiana's first public school teacher," was paid $200 annually by the federal government. See McQuaid et al., eds., *Guide Book*, 39–40.

7. For instances of bigotry see Lemarié, *Missionaires bretons*, 291–296 and Morin, *From France*, 136–139.

The bishop often seemed just as implacable in dealing with members of his own flock. One of his first decisions upon taking office was the replacement of the popular Irish pastor of the sole parish in Chicago—eastern Illinois remained part of the diocese of Vincennes until 1843—an initiative that brought about a virtual schism, settled only by the intervention of the Irish-born bishop of Cincinnati.[8] In 1842 Hailandière appointed as his vicar general August Martin, the pastor of Logansport who had treated the Holy Cross men so kindly; after four years of wrangling with the bishop Martin relinquished his post and then withdrew from the diocese. Even members of Hailandière's own family, a layman and a cleric who had come out from Brittany at their uncle's behest, soon found the situation in Indiana intolerable.[9] Most melancholy of all, perhaps, was the bishop's quarrel with the Sisters of Providence at Terre Haute whom he treated with feline cruelty.[10] He persecuted with special ferocity their founder and superior, the saintly Mother Theodore Guérin, and he eventually excommunicated her. This ill-advised judicial decision, rendered on the eve of Hailandière's resignation of the see in 1847, was quickly quashed by his successor, but it left scars behind nonetheless.[11]

This is not to say that blame for these disputes should have been laid at Bishop Hailandière's door alone. If he possessed a strong, even an abrasive and domineering personality, so did many of the religious who came to Indiana from Europe, else they might not have had the courage to undertake so arduous a mission. And some of them proved to be—to put the kindest word on it—so eccentric that they inevitably elicited episcopal displeasure and even censure.

---

8. Lemarié, *Missionaires bretons,* 86, and Mary Carol Schroeder, *The Catholic Church in the Diocese of Vincennes, 1847–1877* (Washington, D.C., 1946), 3.

9. Lemarié, *Missionaires bretons,* 161–162.

10. See Georgia Costin, "Hailandière of Vincennes: His Views on Women Religious," a paper read at the Conference on the History of the Congregations of Holy Cross (1991). This paper summarizes material found in the first volume of Mary Borromeo Brown et al. *The History of the Sisters of Providence of Saint-Mary-of-the-Woods* (Chicago and Terre Haute, 1949–1991), 3 vols.

11. Anon. [Mary Theodosia Mug], *Life and Life-Work of Mother Theodore Guérin* (New York, 1904), 340–356. Sister Theodosia was cured of cancer through the intercession of Mother Theodore. For her testament see Penny Blaker Mitchell, *Mother Theodore Guerin: A Woman for Our Time* (Saint Mary-of-the-Woods, IN, 1998), 166–169. A popular treatment is Katherine Burton, *Faith Is the Substance* (St. Louis, 1959), and a brief, hagiographical notice is Eleanor Ryan, "With Courage and Faith," in Joseph N. Tylenda, ed., *Portraits in American Sanctity* (Chicago, 1982), 137–152. In American parlance, the "St." was dropped from Guérin's religious name, a curiosity in that she was beatified in 1998, the last step before formal canonization. For a detailed picture of her quarrel with Hailandière, see *Positio super virtutibus concinnata . . . servae Dei Theodorae Guérin* (Rome, 1987), 413–519. This book of more than 800 pages contains all the documents pertinent to Mother Theodore's canonization process.

The superior of the Eudists,[12] for example, who had arrived in Vincennes in 1839 to staff the little college Bruté had founded, was a peculiar guitar-playing priest named Jean-Pierre Bellier, who mismanaged the institution in every conceivable way and who left the diocese a debt of more than $10,000 when he drifted away to Alabama a few years later.[13]

But there was more to these contentions than simply the clash of aggressive or idiosyncratic personalities. At the root of almost every dispute, first of all, was a desperate and pervasive impoverishment—not a genteel lack of luxury or an abstract poverty of the spirit but real destitution which affected the amount of food on the table and of coals in the stove. The missionaries who came out to Indiana were by no means a pampered lot—among the Holy Cross contingent only Edward Sorin could be said to have sprung from comfortable circumstances—but, physically tough as they may have been, the vows of poverty they swore as religious took on a radically new meaning when lived out on the American frontier. For his part, the bishop could count on hardly any resources, aside from what he could beg in Europe. Indeed, he had to acknowledge that he was not financial master even in his own see-city: just prior to the arrival of Bruté in 1834 the lay-trustees of the parish in Vincennes had denied funds to the hapless resident-priest and, in the end, had sent him packing.[14]

Compounding these seemingly endless fiscal difficulties was the ancient tension between a bishop and the religious orders serving in his diocese, a tension which had surfaced in Vincennes as surely as it had simultaneously—between Moreau and Bouvier—back in Le Mans. And when a bishop was as jealous of his authority and as prone to micromanagement as Hailandière, arguments and misunderstandings were unavoidable. The bishop had only a handful of specialized personnel directly subject to himself; he had therefore to depend upon the cooperation of the nuns, priests, and brothers who belonged to religious congregations if the church's work were to be done in his diocese. Even so, Hailandière

---

12. The popular name for the Society of Jesus and Mary, founded in France in the seventeenth century by St. John Eudes (1601–1680).

13. Schroeder, *Diocese of Vincennes*, 29–30 and Lemarié, *Missionaires bretons*, 205–208. The ever-enthusiastic John Parsons (Rabb, ed., *Tour through Indiana*, 350–351) called the college "a most interesting Catholic institution," which offered courses in nine languages as well as in anatomy, botany, philosophy, mathematics, painting, vocal and instrumental music, including lessons on the guitar. He was apparently quoting Bellier's outrageous prospectus. For a later insight into Bellier see Portier [bishop of Mobile] to Hailandière, February 24 and March 10, 1846, AUND, CAVI, "Diocese of Vincennes."

14. Lemarié, *Missionaires bretons*, 278–281 and McAvoy, *Catholic Church in Indiana, 1789–1834* (New York, 1940), 181–182.

remained deeply suspicious if any of them showed the slightest trace of independence or a hankering to maintain a connection with their motherhouses back in France. Mindful of the old saw that he who pays the piper calls the tune, he displayed an almost hysterical anxiety whenever he discovered that the congregations were seeking funds without reference to himself. The irony was that Bishop Hailandière had recruited a good many of these people; the tragedy was that he proved temperamentally incapable of meeting halfway not only the outlandish Père Bellier but also the genuinely staunch likes of Mother Theodore and Edward Sorin.

THE CATHEDRAL OF ST. FRANCIS XAVIER at which Sorin and his six companions arrived on the morning of Sunday, October 10, 1841, was not a prepossessing place. Hardly more than a hundred feet long and sixty wide, the small, squat building with its modest appointments—the unadorned high altar was made of wood—was a far cry from the glorious gothic pile of St. Julien's cathedral in Le Mans. The men from Sainte-Croix, however, hardly noticed the difference, so relieved were they after their long and fatiguing journey. They attended the pontifical Mass at 10:00 A.M., and afterwards Father Sorin, in a little side chapel, offered a private Mass, at which the brothers received Communion and after which they all sang a Te Deum in thanksgiving. They walked then toward the bishop's homely residence along the path carpeted with pine needles that abutted the French and Indian cemetery, whose mostly unmarked graves were gently sheltered by chestnuts, sweet gums, and white pines. Hailandière received them "like well-beloved children," as Sorin put it, and they dined with him along with several seminarians and one or two priests.

After the meal Sorin and the bishop repaired to the latter's private room and conversed tete-à-tete until time for vespers in the late afternoon. It soon became clear that, contrary to their expectations, Hailandière had not yet determined a specific locale in which he wanted the Holy Cross men to exercise their ministry, or, if he had so decided (which Sorin later concluded was the case), he kept that fact for the moment smoothly to himself. Instead, Sorin diplomatically recorded, "the good bishop [said he] had several places in view [and] did not wish to decide by himself without giving [Holy Cross] a chance [to choose]."[15] In other

---

15. Sorin, *Chronicles*, 14. In his letter to Moreau of October 14 (AGEN) Sorin wrote: "Since the bishop had not yet picked out a place for our establishment, it was determined that the brothers should remain in Vincennes while he and I would visit various farms that might serve the purpose." It is significant that the negative in the first clause of this sentence was expressed, not by the ordinary *ne . . . pas* but by the much more emphatic *ne . . . point,* suggesting perhaps irritation as well as surprise on the writer's part.

words, there was as yet no house or center prepared to receive the missionaries from Le Mans.[16]

Next morning the two of them on horseback cantered over the bridge spanning the Wabash, turned south, and rode four or five miles until they reached a little settlement called Francisville. (Neither of these Frenchmen—nor any one else for that matter—took notice that eleven years earlier an ever-restless journeyman-carpenter and farmer named Thomas Lincoln, his second wife Sally Johnston, and his son Abraham, aged twenty-one, had crossed this same bridge into Illinois, one more American family willing to go west in search of a new life and new opportunities).[17] Sorin looked round at the gaggle of cottages that composed Francisville, and, as he reported to Basile Moreau, "I decided that this first proposed location was not a suitable place for us, though I cannot exactly tell you why." So bishop and priest returned to Vincennes in midafternoon, Monday, October 11, and Sorin, accustomed to the lordly habits of prelates in the old world—likely he had Bouvier of Le Mans in mind—admiringly described the plebeian style of the hardy bishop of Vincennes, "who himself took the saddle off his horse and carried it 200 paces to his rooms, without giving me the pleasure of acting as his esquire."[18]

Within a few hours Sorin was to demonstrate a robust physique of his own. During the critical discussion of that evening, Hailandière described in the most positive terms another mission about twenty-seven miles east of the Wabash. He called in to confirm the glowing portrayal of this site the testimony of the priest, Parisian-born Julien Delaune, who had served there for some months and who was now briefly in Vincennes before reporting to another pastoral assignment. Or so at least it seemed on the surface: Sorin came to suspect later that the bishop had intended all along to send him and the brothers to this eastward station and that Delaune's presence just then at Hailandière's house was perhaps more than a coincidence. However that may have been, Delaune showed himself in the long run a good friend to Holy Cross.

The conversation among these three continued until 11:00 P.M., when it was decided that the two priests should set out right then to examine the proposed location. So Sorin, with little or no sleep, mounted a horse again and, with Delaune beside him, rode out of the silent town. They followed a route made famous years

16. The same thing had happened to the Sisters of Providence the previous year. See Morin, *From France*, 96–98.

17. Peckham, *Indiana*, 47–48. A handsome monument commemorating Lincoln's crossing now stands on the Illinois side of the Wabash.

18. Sorin to Moreau, October 14, 1841 (AGEN).

before as the Buffalo Trace, along which great herds of bison had passed regularly on their way to and from the salt licks in Kentucky. By nine o'clock the next morning, Tuesday, the two weary men arrived at St. Peter's Mission, Black Oak Ridge, between the villages of Washington and Mount Pleasant.[19]

> There is a farm here [Sorin reported to Moreau] of about 160 acres, of which only sixty are under cultivation. Its location seems to me sufficiently agreeable. The air, I am told, is very healthy. The buildings are large enough, but they are a little old. There is even a small but quite pretty chapel built of wood, but I can see already that repairs will be necessary in many places. All in all, I am pleased with the place. The compound was built originally for the Sisters of Nazareth who, however, only stayed here for one year.[20] I do not doubt now that this is the place in which the bishop intended all along to establish us. Nor do I know what internal attraction told me that Providence wished us to settle here.

Perhaps it was the same inner voice that had induced him the day before to reject the site at Francisville. Sorin at any rate, when faced with an important decision, never hesitated to trust his own instincts, then or ever. But on this occasion he was not prepared to make a final commitment. "We shall not engage in a great deal of repair-work," he told Moreau, "because it is not yet certain that with the spring we might not choose to go somewhere else."[21]

Just at sunset the next evening, Wednesday, October 13, the six brothers, in response to Sorin's summons, reached St. Peter's from Vincennes, and the whole company gathered in the crude log chapel to sing a second Te Deum. Along with their scanty luggage, the brothers also brought with them five boys—most likely orphans—selected by Bishop Hailandière to be boarding-pupils in the school which, in succession to the Sisters of Nazareth, had begun to function again somewhat awkwardly under the direction of a thirty-three-year-old German immigrant named Charles Rother. Rother, whose later career showed him to be a

---

19. The site was about five miles east of Washington. Mount Pleasant is now Montgomery.

20. The Sisters of Charity of Nazareth, a congregation founded in Kentucky in 1812 and composed in its early days of the daughters of Catholic pioneers. The first log house used by the nuns as a convent was piously called "Nazareth," hence the society's popular name. Four of these sisters were in residence at St. Peter's 1832–1833 but then withdrew for lack of financial support. This was the second venture the order had undertaken in the diocese of Vincennes. See Morin, *From France,* 107; McAvoy, *Catholic Church in Indiana, 191–192,* and J. Herman Schauinger, *Cathedrals in the Wilderness* (Milwaukee, 1952), 285–286.

21. Sorin to Moreau, October 14, 1841, AGEN.

well-intentioned eccentric, had confided to Hailandière his wish to join a religious community, and the bishop had sent him to St. Peter's to await the brothers' arrival—a convincing indication that Sorin was correct in concluding that this was indeed the mission intended all along for him and his companions. Rother's religious aspirations were quickly fulfilled: he entered the community as Holy Cross's first postulant in America and was duly professed as Brother Joseph two years later.[22]

"Black Oak Ridge" was a rather whimsical name which suggested more than the gentle rise upon which stood St. Peter's mission. True enough, woods grew prodigiously over the land roundabout, and, though sycamore and elm aplenty could be found, most of the trees were oak. The Frenchmen were astonished at their size and at the suffocating thickness of the forests in which they grew. "We've measured oaks twenty feet around," reported one of the brothers, "straight as candles and as high in proportion. These poor oaks die standing. You can't take a step without encountering a rotten tree."[23] Yet in other respects the rolling countryside around St. Peter's reminded these natives of Sarthe and Mayenne more of home than had the Indiana prairie they had recently traveled over from Fort Wayne to Vincennes.

The first few days on mission were spent at humdrum tasks necessary to complete before the winter set it. "We have yet many supplies to secure," Sorin wrote to Moreau. "We have already begun to put in a well and to build a bake house. These should be finished shortly." There may not have been as many mouths to feed at St. Peter's as at Sainte-Croix; nevertheless "there are already twelve of us, counting the five pupils the bishop has entrusted to our care at least through the winter, and not counting the old and pious housekeeper we have inherited for the time being, who will be very useful for initiating Brother Joachim into the secrets of American cuisine."

But Sorin realized fully that Basile Moreau's priorities did not include the digging of wells or the construction of bakehouses and assuredly not "*les secrets de*

---

22. See Klawitter, ed., *Adapted to the Lake*, 370. A postulant (*postulare*, to request) was a person formally admitted to candidacy in a religious order. After a certain period of trial, if candidate and superiors agreed, the person became a novice (*novare*, to make new) and had the right to wear the order's habit (distinctive garb). After passing successfully through the novitiate—lasting normally a year—the candidate could become a professed religious—that is, a full-fledged member of the order—by taking vows, whether temporary or permanent.

23. Brother Francis Xavier to Moreau, n.d. [autumn/winter, 1841–42], quoted in Klawitter, ed., *Adapted to the Lake*, 1. The date given here, October 1, 1841, is clearly incorrect. René Patoy originally took the religious name Mary, changing it to Francis Xavier in 1848. See Klawitter, ed., xviii.

la cuisine américaine." So he carefully chronicled other early activities at St. Peter's which would have appealed much more directly to his superior's predilections.

> We have been here two days, and already our house is in order. . . . We have made a day's retreat. A council has been formed. Obediences[24] have been distributed so that the community is properly organized and the rule is in full vigor. Everyone appears content with his assignment, everyone appears forearmed with the best will possible to accomplish good. How would I not be happy about all this! Oh yes, we are happy. We have our good Lord close by us. This very evening we have hung up in our little chapel our beautiful [sanctuary] lamp, only the second to be found in this vast diocese.[25] It burns now before our modest altar, and I cannot speak of it without shedding tears of happiness. . . . If you could experience as we do, good Father, our little chapel. We gather there as though lost in the middle of an immense forest; when across the woods we see the lamp that lights up the mean dwelling where our good Master resides, we know full well that we are not alone. Jesus Christ dwells in our midst, and so we take courage. We come to visit Him, and in the night as in the day our eyes are fixed upon the tabernacle. But now it is well into the night, and the rest of the world here at St. Peter's is asleep in the Lord; only I now, along with you, well-beloved Father, am on watch. If you would permit it, I should now offer a prayer at this moment for you and for my little family.[26]

This declaration, penned by Edward Sorin at the very beginning of his apostolate in America, is rife with intimations of his character and his intentions. In the primitive circumstances in which he found himself, the practical necessities of life for him and his fledgling community at St. Peter's—the need for bread and water and whatever else contributed to communal survival—possessed an immediacy that could not be denied. He and his six colleagues had come to live within a vast wilderness which only now, in recent years, had begun to assume a certain conventional civic form. Only months after his arrival at Black Oak Ridge,

---

24. An "obedience" in this context meant a specific assignment or office given by a superior to a particular religious.

25. The Eucharist was reserved relatively rarely, not so much because of a lack of oil or wax for the required light as because so few churches had permanently residing pastors. At St. Peter's the lamp burned olive oil. See Morin, *From France*, 105–106.

26. Sorin to Moreau, October 14, 1841, AGEN.

Sorin was pressing to have a United States postal office located there. Accommodation with the political and social realities of the Indiana of the 1840s seemed to him to be a condition of success that hardly needed saying.

But what about his assertion of pietistic values, his almost rhapsodic description of nights of prayer before the Blessed Sacrament in the log chapel at St. Peter's? "I have but a single step to take," he assured Moreau, "in order to stand at the foot of the altar where yesterday I said Mass here for the first time on the feast of my patron."[27] It does not suffice to say that he expressed these warm sentiments because he knew they would please his superior, though no doubt they did. The fact is, however, that Sorin was as much a product of postrevolutionary French religiosity as were the brothers Lamennais or, certainly more to the point, as Basile Moreau himself. Yet a tension always exists between a believer's spiritual aspirations and his adaptation to the demands this world imposes upon him. And perhaps the more ambition, the more vigor, a person brings to bear upon these often conflicting compartments of his life, the keener that tension becomes. One conclusion at any rate emerges from the decision to accept the mission at St. Peter's and from the events of the first days spent there: Edward Sorin was determined to take charge over, as he put it, "my little family—*ma petite famille*"—and all its doings, spiritual or otherwise.

A START HAD BEEN MADE. St. Peter's primary school, though hardly a citadel of scholarship, was in operation. Three of the brothers—Vincent, Gatien, and Anselm—had commenced a serious study of English. The meager crops sown before Holy Cross's arrival were duly harvested. The well and the bakehouse had been finished, and putting together a modest mill assured the colony a supply of flour. Though Sorin had determined that no major repair work should be undertaken, enough was done to secure the flimsy buildings against the coming cold winds. With the same thought in mind a store of cut timber was laid in to provide firewood for the winter. In November the Sisters of Providence at Terre Haute dispatched a most welcome and practical gift to St. Peter's, a team of oxen. "A thousand thanks for your generosity," Sorin wrote their superior; "God will take note and recompense you a hundred times over."[28] By December Brother Francis Xavier, the carpenter, had seen to it that each man, instead of sleeping on the floor, now had a bed of his own hewn out of logs.

---

27. Before the recent changes in the liturgical calendar, Catholics commemorated King St. Edward the Confessor on October 13.

28. Sorin to Mother Theodore, November 12, 1841, AGEN.

At the end of that month Charles Rother was admitted to the novitiate.[29] By then three more postulants had been received at St. Peter's; a year later the number of recruits to the community had risen to twelve, two of them sent from Logansport by Father August Martin.[30] This apparent surge of prosperity proved, in the end, a mixed blessing; barely half of these candidates persevered. The sheer physical hardships involved was surely one cause of such a high percentage of withdrawal. Another factor, more crucial in the long run, was the failure to provide the postulants and novices with an appropriate introduction to the religious life, and this, in large measure, was Bishop Hailandière's fault. In mid-November the bishop ordered Brother Vincent to go into residence in Vincennes and teach in a school there for French-speaking children. His departure left at Black Oak Ridge five brothers, two of them teenagers, who taken together had had scant experience as religious. Vincent—it may be recalled—had joined Father Dujarié's Brothers of St. Joseph as early as 1821; indeed Moreau had assigned him to the mission in America with the intent that he should act as mentor to any young men attracted to the brotherhood and direct their formation. Now he was gone, and no one was spiritually or temperamentally equipped to replace him. Even Sorin, for all his talents and self-confidence, was not a mature religious, and, even if he had been, the training required for the brothers was different from what he had undergone as seminarian and young priest. Vincent's removal, moreover, later preyed on Sorin's mind as an early indication of Hailandière's chronic lack of candor. "It appears that from the time of our arrival [the bishop] intended to locate one of our brothers in Vincennes." When Sorin pointed out that to do so—especially if the candidate were Brother Vincent—would "render very difficult if not well-nigh impossible the success of the novitiate, he seemed to abandon the idea," only to renew it "in so explicit a manner that I judged it necessary to acquiesce."[31]

Still, it would have been totally out of character for Sorin not to have had a strong opinion about this vocations crisis. The young men who had applied for

29. Klawitter, ed., *Adapted to the Lake*, 370 gives the date as December 28. Sorin in a letter of December 2 speaks of "*un prise d'habit*" on "*dimanche dernier.*" Sorin to Bouvier, December 2, 1841, AGEN.

30. Sorin to Martin, March 8, 1842, AGEN. The elder of Martin's two recruits, Sorin said, "will be particularly useful to us, because we have here no English-master." See also Sorin to Martin, July 14, 1842, AGEN, inviting Martin to preach the annual retreat to the community, after which exercise, Sorin wrote, "I will present five candidates for the habit, if the good God confirms them in their vocation. Ah, this will be a celebration for you and for us!"

31. Sorin to Martin, n.d. [January 3, 1842], AGEN.

admission to postulancy at St. Peter's had been mostly Irish and German immigrants. "The former," Sorin mused a year or two later, "are by nature full of faith, respect, religious inclinations," but they "lack stability." The Germans "are ordinarily less obedient, prouder, more singular in their tastes and less endowed with the qualities of the heart; but they are more persevering." Then, echoing Bishop Hailandière's earlier appraisal, Sorin offered a sour commentary on the religious capacities of his new fellow-countrymen.

> As to genuine Americans, there is no hope of finding subjects amongst them for a religious house of this kind. We might look upon it as a miracle of grace for a young American to persevere in the humble and difficult employment of a Brother of St. Joseph. The spirit of liberty as it is understood in the United States is too directly opposed to the spirit of obedience and submission of a community to leave any hopes for a long time to come of any addition of subjects in a country in which the nature of the men appears to offer so few dispositions towards the religious life. Hence it comes to pass that the young men who spend some time amongst Americans soon imbibe their spirit and manners and become in reality all the more unfitted for the religious life the more years they have passed in the new world.[32]

This, as time would prove, was not a judgment inscribed in stone.

EVEN IF EDWARD SORIN had had, like Brother Vincent, the aptitude or the formal mandate to train the postulants and novices, his other preoccupations would have made such a commission highly problematic. From October 1841 till November 1842, he was for all practical purposes parish priest of St. Peter's, Black Oak Ridge, though over the first two months of this span the kindly and helpful Father Delaune, still awaiting his new assignment in Illinois, lingered nearby. Perhaps forty Catholic families lived in the vicinity of St. Peter's, most of them dirt-poor immigrants.[33] Sorin also had responsibility for two dependent stations, one five and the other nine miles away. This meant that he, like most ministers on the frontier, Protestant and Catholic alike, was in effect a cir-

32. Sorin, *Chronicles*, 16–17. For Hailandière's similar views, see chapter 4, above.
33. Sorin, *Chronicles*, 15, says thirty-five families; Sorin to Bouvier, December 2, 1841, AGEN says fifty. Perhaps the larger number was meant to include those belonging to the other two missions, St. Patrick's near Glendale and St. Mary's at Bogg's Creek.

cuit rider, traveling regularly with his Mass-kit and gospel book from one place to another.[34] This work was not without its consolations. "Yesterday," he reported to the bishop of Le Mans, "I performed my first baptism in America. The sacraments are the same here as in France, but you will permit me to say, Monseigneur, there is some difference in the heart of a priest between baptizing a little American and baptizing a Frenchman."[35] Nevertheless, these frequent absences from St. Peter's inhibited Sorin's influence on the motley crowd of aspiring brothers, as did his inability to converse in their languages, whether English or German: free-and-easy communication would have necessitated, he ruefully confessed to Basile Moreau, "that the Holy Spirit repeat the miracle of Pentecost."[36]

Learning to speak and particularly to preach in English was, predictably, a hard struggle for Sorin. "Some weeks after their arrival [he] set to work as well as he knew how to prepare and preach sermons in English every Sunday. Sometimes he was told on the following day that half of what he said was not understood, but nothing discouraged him, and towards the end of the year [1841] nearly all understood him."[37] This account, though in the third person, was Father Sorin's own, and it may have been more sanguine than factual. Well into 1842, so one Holy Cross tradition has it, his practice was to speak a few words in French to the congregation and then give way to one of the postulants who would then expound the doctrinal message in English.[38] However that may have been, Sorin, although of course he eventually became fluent in English, nevertheless maintained throughout his life an affinity to the French language and to French patterns of thought, a fact attested to by his massive correspondence.

By all surviving accounts Edward Sorin was from the outset an extremely forceful pastor of souls. Brother Vincent reported to Basile Moreau a typical illustration.

---

34. See Morin, *From France,* 102–103.

35. Sorin to Bouvier, December 2, 1841, AGEN.

36. Sorin to Moreau, December 10, 1841, quoted in Morin *From France,* 118.

37. Sorin, *Chronicles,* 20.

38. See Klawitter, ed., *Adapted to the Lake,* 368–369. The postulant became Brother John, an enigmatic figure who may have been Frederick Steber, born in Trieste in 1815, or born in Dover, England, in 1820. Given his proficiency in English, the latter scenario seems the more likely. Sorin, who put great store in his abilities, claimed to have first met him at Samuel Byerley's house in New York, shortly after which meeting Steber (?) became a Catholic and then a postulant at St. Peter's. Sorin, *Chronicles,* 38, described him as "an Englishman by birth," and a later letter (Sorin to Moreau, March 20, 1843, AGEN) speaks of "an excellent postulant from New York [taking] the habit" at Notre Dame on March 19, 1843. It is doubtful, however, that he was the "Jeremiah Cronin" mentioned in an editor's note, also 38. See chapter 8, note 38, below.

On Easter Monday [1842] after Benediction of the Blessed Sacrament [Sorin] made an excursion. Here's an abridged version. First he went to an old fox who hadn't made his [Easter] duty for a long time. "Come with me," said [Sorin], "to such and such a place." Not suspecting any mystery [the man] mounted his horse and led the Father [to the homestead indicated]. After the ordinary greeting, . . . the missionary says to the master of the house, "I come to hear your confession. Let's get going, get out of here the rest of you!" The poor man, seeing himself grabbed by fate, falls to his knees, makes his confession, and admires the priest's charity.

"We haven't finished yet," says [Sorin] to his guide, "let's go to a certain man's house." When they got there everyone was sleeping. . . . Nevertheless, the head of the house gets up, seemed surprised to receive a visit at that hour. "But I'm going to hear your confession," said the priest. "Wait. Let's go into the little bedroom so as not to disturb your family." Without more explanation he goes with the priest, made his confession, and admired, like the first man, the charity of the priest-missionary.

But let's come now to the guide who found himself in the same case [of not having received the sacraments of penance and the Eucharist during Eastertide]. He saw he was going to have his turn, but coming in front of [Sorin], he asks him for three or four days to prepare himself.[39]

Sorin's forthright assertion of the canons of the Catholic faith did not apparently alienate the Protestant majority in the area. Members of the various denominations, he reported—except the Presbyterians who, he had been told, were notorious for their antipathy toward popery—had been more than cordial.[40] The primary reason for their guarded friendliness was the hope they had that a successful school, even one operated under Catholic auspices, would benefit the whole community. But there were other factors too. Sorin's very bearing and appearance—this square-shouldered young French *gentilhomme*, clean-shaven at this time in his career, striding along purposefully in his black soutane and cloak, his big, muscular hands swinging at his sides, his upright posture making him look taller than he really was—cut an impressive figure.[41] And to a degree unfamiliarity with Catholics and their ways seemed to exert an attraction of its

39. Brother Vincent to Moreau, April 10, 1842, quoted in Klawitter, ed., *Adapted to the Lake*, 6. Vincent had come out to St. Peter's from Vincennes to spend Holy Week and the Easter holiday with his confreres.

40. Sorin to Bouvier, December 2, 1841, AGEN.

41. See the description in Morin, *From France*, 141.

own: there were more Protestants than Catholics in attendance when Charles Rother received the habit, and crowds of them, manifesting a kind of reverent curiosity, were present for the elaborate Corpus Christi procession held outdoors in the late spring of 1842. Some of them found contact with Holy Cross compelling: by the time he left St. Peter's Sorin had received about twenty converts into the Church.[42]

WITH THE WISDOM OF HINDSIGHT it is easy to conclude that the Holy Cross mission on Black Oak Ridge was doomed from the start. Clashing personalities, mutual suspicions, the high-handedness of Bishop Hailandière, the apathy of Basile Moreau, the mood-swings of Edward Sorin: all these factors combined to set the stage for trouble. But the root problem was the failure to resolve two fundamental questions: how were the men of Holy Cross to be supported; and under whose jurisdiction were they to exercise their ministry. These questions, moreover, were intertwined; to answer one was, in effect, to answer the other. If the bishop took it upon himself to maintain the mission until it was self-sustaining, it was not unreasonable for him to suppose that he should enjoy authority over the personnel involved; the Holy Cross community would be, in other words, a diocesan institute. If, on the other hand, such support came from the motherhouse in Le Mans, then Holy Cross in Indiana would be what Moreau intended, a part of an independent religious order in the service of the universal Church. This was an uneasy scenario, one that could readily evolve into deadlock, particularly since neither Le Mans nor Vincennes had any significant financial resources. The 1,500 francs Sorin had with him when he arrived at Black Oak Ridge sustained the community for barely three months,[43] after which the stalemate inevitably came into effect. It was ultimately broken only when the bishop appeared to have blocked Sorin's plan to enable St. Peter's to support itself, which resulted—as will be seen below—in the fateful decision to move the mission northward.

From the beginning of their association, in 1839, there had been a lack of frankness between Hailandière and Moreau. This is not to say that either man meant to deceive the other; rather, each of them entertained certain preconceptions which, unhappily, remained unspoken. Nor is it irrelevant that both of

42. Sorin, *Chronicles*, 15, 20; Morin, *From France*, 103, 114; Brother Vincent to Moreau, June 6, 1842, quoted in Klawitter, ed., *Adapted to the Lake*, 11–13.

43. See Sorin to "Messieurs" of the Propagation of the Faith (Paris), February 2, 1844, AGEN, and note 32, chapter 4, above.

them lacked experience in dealing with the age-old tension between a local bishop and a religious order: Hailandière had scarcely donned his miter when he visited Le Mans, and Moreau was in the very earliest stages of fashioning his congregation, in the teeth of the obstruction, coincidentally, by his own bishop. Perhaps, finally, an excess of zeal, praiseworthy if naive, helps explain why no formal agreement was put in writing.

Edward Sorin at any rate, amid the euphoria occasioned by arrival at his destination, found himself squarely in the middle of a discord not of his making. "Scarcely had we set foot in Vincennes," he recalled a few months later, " when I discovered with the greatest surprise that our status in the diocese was not understood by Monseigneur in the same way as it was by our Father [Moreau]."[44] This predicament became painfully clear during that first private conversation he held with Hailandière on the Sunday afternoon, October 10. After handing over $112 of the money the bishop's agent had advanced him in New York—the journey for the seven missionaries had cost 940 francs or $188[45]—Sorin requested the sum of "three thousand and several hundred francs," which, as he understood it, the bishop had pledged to support the colony. "His Lordship looked surprised and even offended at the amount, and after telling Father Sorin he would not pay it, he added that he would write to Father Rector [Moreau] to decide the important question: shall the Brothers be subject to Le Mans or to the diocese?"[46]

Sorin would hardly have presented the bishop this *mémoire* had he not been instructed by Moreau to do so. Underlying Hailandière's settled argument—to the degree that the vacillating prelate ever did settle it in his own mind—was the understandable anxiety that if he did not control the brothers they might be withdrawn at the whim of Le Mans. But, he said, in 1839 he had some money; now he had none. If Sainte-Croix had dispatched the missioners at the time he petitioned for them—and, he intimated, at the time they were offered to him—he could have given them some support; now he could not. He would, to be sure, let them utilize one of the farms the diocese owned, though without giving them title to the land.[47] More he could not and would not do, at least not until the question of ultimate authority had been cleared up.

On this latter point Father Sorin quickly learned that his very presence was a bone of contention. The bishop of Vincennes had asked Le Mans for brothers to

44. Sorin to Martin, n.d. [January 3, 1842], AGEN.
45. See the figures in Sorin to Hailandière, n.d. [January, 1842], AGEN.
46. Sorin, *Chronicles*, 17.
47. See Morin, *From France*, 142.

staff the schools he aimed to organize across his sprawling jurisdiction; he had not asked for a priest. Not that he did not need men ordained to carry out the sacramental ministry; far from it. But Sorin had come out to Indiana primarily as superior of the brothers, as a link therefore to the motherhouse, as an agent of Basile Moreau. This circumstance did not sit well with Hailandière, who, however good his intentions, could never quash his autocratic instincts. Since Sorin displayed a similar temper, altercation between the two was probably inevitable. "I would like in the priest . . . youth, piety, and above all humility," Hailandière observed later. As for Sorin, who was young and, for all the bishop knew, pious enough, "I have been vexed with him more than once. He seems to me to want to accomplish too swiftly what no establishment in America could obtain without years of labor. . . . Could I be oblivious to his shortcomings?"[48] But in the long run personal differences proved to weigh less in this series of misunderstandings than did institutional ones.

In the course of their first conversations Hailandière had indicated to Father Sorin his intention to seek clarification from Le Mans about the jurisdictional situation. Now, on October 17, ensconced for some days at St. Peter's, Sorin wrote anxiously to Moreau that he wanted "to take measures to see to it that my communiqué reaches you before his," which *cannot possibly be pleasing to you*." The bishop appeared ready to throw upon Sainte-Croix the financial responsibility for the mission. "He would probably prefer," Sorin continued, "that I say nothing to you prior to your response to him," but there are "some insights that I have been able to acquire on the spot that I think I should acquaint you with." First, "you cannot prudently assume to satisfy the expenses for the Brothers for less than a fixed subsidy of 300 francs [$60] per head," a sum that would need to be furnished also for "every postulant who might come to us in the future. The reason is that the revenues neither from the school nor from the farm will amount to anything for some years."

Secondly, "you must lay down very clear and positive conditions with this bishop, because (I have to tell you) he has the reputation here of being a consummate politician [*politique achevé*] who never finds himself cornered and who possesses a thousand resources to extricate himself from any embarrassment." This information about Hailandière's "reputation," for what it may have been worth, could have come from nobody but Julien Delaune, who was the only local source with whom Sorin, at this early date, was acquainted. It would seem devotions during the long evenings at St. Peter's were interspersed with gossipy conversation.

So, in any event, money had to be sought elsewhere

---

48. Hailandière to Moreau, quoted in Morin, *From France*, 126.

You had assured me, my Father [Moreau], that the Council of Lyon[49] had allocated us 4,000 francs. The bishop, with whom I shared this intelligence, did not appear to believe me. If it were possible, I would love to have these monies sent here directly, because I fear that if they pass through the hands of the bishop he will deduct the 1,500 francs he claims to have paid for our passage here from New York. The greater part of such a benefaction ought to be spent on the indispensable repairs to the buildings here [at St. Peter's]. I have reread today a letter Bishop Hailandière sent you in 1840 in which he spoke of the house where he promised to receive us. In fact we are located in a place where we are authorized only to take on repairs without knowing who will pay for them.

The ever-informative Father Delaune pointed out to Sorin that he, during his brief pastorate at Black Oak Ridge, had had to assume payment himself "for his own food and clothing." "In a month or two," said Sorin, once Delaune had gone, "the same will be the case with me." Yet, notwithstanding Delaune's admonitions, Sorin judged that the three congregations served by the parish priest at St. Peter's would not let him starve or go naked. The problem was the brothers. "If you can, my Father [Moreau], impress upon the governors of the Propagation of the Faith at Lyon or at Paris that we must have 500 or 400 or at the very least 300 francs a year for each brother. It is very clear to me that the permanence of our apostolate here would then be assured. We cannot depend upon the resources of the diocese, which will be very poor for a long time to come."[50]

ON OCTOBER 20, three days after Sorin set down this bill of particulars, Bishop Hailandière visited St. Peter's. He came, in part at least, in response to a message sent him by Sorin: "I had asked his Excellency in a letter for a frank and precise explanation of his intentions toward us, and, so far as I could understand him from a single interview, I think he has given it." Hailandière was distressed, so he said, by two recent communications from Le Mans which he took to mean that Moreau expected the bishop to assume support of the Brothers of St. Joseph but reserved to himself the right to withdraw them from the diocese of Vincennes at his pleasure. Three words (in French), which Sorin underscored,

---

49. This is a reference to the Society for the Propagation of the Faith, an international organization for the support of Catholic missionaries, founded in Lyons in 1822. During the course of the nineteenth century the society disbursed about $80,000,000, nearly $11,000,000 of it in America.

50. Sorin to Moreau, October 17, 1841, AGEN.

stuck in the bishop's craw, "and he based his whole argument on them:" Father Moreau had written that the present commitment would be maintained "*jusqu'à nouvel ordre—until a new arrangement was called for.*"[51] Hailandière protested further that Moreau "had changed both the timing of the foundation and the manner in which it was carried it out, since he had sent a priest to represent him and to take charge." As far as expenses were concerned, Moreau "had reneged on his original promise to pay them," and anyway he, the bishop, had already advanced the mission the equivalent of 1,800 francs.[52] Finally, he professed himself "unable to understand how [Moreau] could demand from him more than 3,000 francs when what was at issue was a work of charity and devotion. . . . He said all this in a very grave tone."

Sorin, as he reported it to Moreau, replied with no less gravity, but even as he did so the charged atmosphere began to lighten a little. It was as though the bishop's blustery outburst had left him too spent to press the matter to a crisispoint. "At heart he is very happy we are here, as he said over and over." The simple fact is "that he has no money, and so he thrashes about looking for scapegoats." But Sorin also felt that one of Hailandière's apprehensions was genuinely felt,

> that, once he had paid the expenses to establish them here, the brothers might still be withdrawn without replacements. I do not know whether Monseigneur wished me to leave unspoken the crux of his concern—I rather think he did—but when he voiced this conclusion I could not refrain from responding to him, smilingly, that if this was all he wanted I could assure him, in writing or viva voce, that he would obtain the assurances he desired immediately upon [*de suite*] his agreement to pay the founding expenses. To which he said again that it was physically impossible even to dream of such a thing, that he had nothing, and that he had learned recently that he was to get nothing over the next year from the Propagation in Lyon.[53]

51. This passage is mistranslated in Morin, *From France,* 109.

52. See the quotation and commentary in Morin, *From France,* 113. This assertion is difficult to accept, given Hailandière's pleas of utter penury. Perhaps he meant to include the $300 (1,500 francs) advanced to Sorin in New York. But this sum was for travel-expenses, and a substantial portion of it was returned (see note 36, above). Perhaps the bishop also was thinking of the value of farm-implements and of the horse he had put at Sorin's disposal.

53. Sorin to Moreau, October 21, 1841, AGEN. A charming and accurate paraphrase of Hailandière's position is in Arthur J. Hope, *Notre Dame. One Hundred Years,* revised ed., introduction by Thomas J. Schlereth (South Bend, Ind., 1978), 29–30.

This tense conversation between Hailandière and Sorin did not end here, and there were to be other conversations, and letters exchanged, and recriminations tossed back and forth over the next twelve months. But the impasse of October 20, 1841, remained in place, unsolved and perhaps insoluble. Nor was Basile Moreau of much help. He did indeed express confidence in Sorin's behavior in a general way: "Maintain your independence, and be sure I will approve whatever you decide."[54] But his communications to Hailandière continued to be vague and infrequent and to Sorin even more so.[55] Indeed, the lack of direction from Le Mans was a sore trial to the young priest who had been sent into the wilderness of Daviess County, Indiana. Moreau, to be sure, had many demands placed upon his time and energy, and the mails were excruciatingly slow.[56] Nevertheless, his failure to respond to his subordinate's long and detailed reports may well have nurtured the seeds of independence in one who was anyway, by temperament and breeding, disposed to self-direction.

The bishop of Vincennes meanwhile often felt personal vexation, while Sorin at one moment, after he had received two harsh letters from Hailandière, was moved to reply with an anguished *cri de coeur*.

My God, have I come all this way to seek you out just to make you sad? I, who desire only to do everything to console you; I, who had brought with me from France such lively and sincere sentiments of veneration and devotion. And have you believed that these very painful months, *which I desire to see an end to,* have perverted my spirit, so that now all you see in me are dispositions contrary to yours. Well, Monseigneur, you may believe what you like about it. I have the same respect for your Excellency as I did when I arrived here. I hope that time will convince you of this better than my words have done.[57]

But it would be wrong to assume that this squabbling had wrung all the idealism out of these two men who had sacrificed home and comfort and worldly prospects to come as missionaries to America. During the testy discussion of October 20 Hailandière had suddenly turned to Sorin, looked him full in the face, and said: "*I will share my last scrap of bread with you, and when I have nothing left,*

---

54. Moreau to Sorin, November 20, 1841, quoted in Catta, *Moreau,* 1: 511.

55. Sorin, *Chronicles,* 20.

56. An example of the slowness of the mails: a letter Sorin wrote to Bishop Bouvier of Le Mans on December 2, 1841, reached that prelate on March 31, 1842.

57. Sorin to Hailandière, n.d. [January, 1842], AGEN.

I shall go begging for you from door to door." And then the two of them, wrangling only a moment before, went outside and stood in the clearing and looked beyond the log huts that now stood there. "*Monseigneur and I,*" wrote Sorin, again with emphasis, "[began to] form some magnificent plans. We marked out the place where the church should be built, and where the missionaries' residence should stand. We laid out in our minds the design of the garden and of the orchard." A little farther on they spied "a superb location for the convent of the Sisters of Sainte-Croix," a real necessity in the near future, Sorin observed parenthetically, "because the local populace will quickly grow irritated with us if we do not provide a school for girls. But [the bishop and I] will look forward to this."[58] It was a golden moment and much to be cherished, since so often the relationship between the two men was spoiled by haughtiness and "obstinacy."[59]

EDWARD SORIN MAINTAINED for most of his time at St. Peter's a hopeful optimism. Sometimes that optimism merged into fantasy, as when during the harsh winter he declared: "In the spring we will count our oxen, cows, pigs, and calves as one counts chickens in France, [not to] mention the three or four winter mares that we will have, our sheep and ducks."[60] Or as when in later years he claimed to have accumulated at St. Peter's during that same spring of 1842 the materials—"one hundred thousand bricks, ten thousand feet of lumber, and some thousands of feet of cut stone"[61]—necessary to construct the buildings he and the bishop had dreamed about. He consistently mingled sober analyses of the dire straits the community was in with extravagant predictions of future success. "In two or three years," he assured Moreau, "our farm will support ten or fifteen people, and shortly our school, with forty or fifty pupils, will turn a profit of 500 or 800 francs."[62] He was even more expansive in a report to the bishop of Le Mans: "Our future in this country is full of the most beautiful hopes for the advancement of Catholicism. If heaven continues to bless us, as it has so far, I believe I can guarantee that in seven or eight years we shall have placed our Brothers

---

58. Sorin to Moreau, October 21, 1841, AGEN.

59. Sorin to Moreau, February 21, 1842, AGEN: "[Hailandière calls] me obstinate [*enteté*] and says I get too many of my ideas from France, in other words, your ideas, dear Father, though he refrained from saying this explicitly."

60. Quoted in Morin, *From France,* 115.

61. Sorin, *Chronicles,* 19. See the comment in Morin, *From France,* 149.

62. Sorin to Moreau, October 21, 1841, AGEN.

in every parish in this diocese where there is a resident priest."[63] In the midst of these euphoric speculations there did occur one stroke of real good fortune. Early in the winter, during an evening's somber conversation with Sorin, Julien Delaune volunteered to go on a begging tour of the northeast United States and French Canada in behalf of the mission. To the astonishment of both priests, Bishop Hailandière agreed, provided that a percentage of the collection be applied to diocesan needs. Delaune's year-long undertaking proved gratifyingly successful, bringing in a total of 15,000 francs ($3,000), three-quarters of which were allocated to St. Peter's.[64] This generous intervention kept the community afloat for many months, but, as a once-only event, it could not meet the long-term financial problems. By the time Delaune returned triumphantly to the diocese of Vincennes, Sorin had already given up on St. Peter's and had departed for northern Indiana.

Other disappointments followed. Brother Joachim fell ill, with the result that cooking for the community became problematic. In the late summer of 1842 the precocious young Brother Gatien, who had learned English very quickly, was dispatched four miles or so away from St. Peter's to open a little school, but there was only a pathetic shack to house this venture, and in a few months it had to be given up. Meanwhile Brother Anselm had joined Brother Vincent at the French-speaking school in Vincennes and was miserable there. Vincent, for his part, though he protested that he was "very happy in America," felt frustrated by his inability to learn English and by his removal from the community. "My talent isn't to teach, very reverend Father," he told Moreau, "but to obey."[65] Sorin meanwhile grew increasingly impatient with his confreres. The mission needed another priest and some sisters, he contended, as well as a shoemaker and an "intelligent Brother who can construct brick and wood walls." "I have no complaint," he wrote testily to Le Mans, "about the Brothers you have already put here. They are quite full of good will, but I am forced to observe and report that poor Brother Vincent supports me only slightly, has almost no foresight, no memory."[66] This

63. Sorin to Bouvier, December 2, 1841, AGEN.

64. Sorin, *Chronicles*, 18. But in Sorin to Moreau, February 21, 1842, AGEN, Sorin says Holy Cross was to receive two-thirds of the collection, not three-quarters. Hailandière maintained possession of the money collected and parceled out a total of $1,832.50 to Holy Cross as needs arose. See John Wack, "The University of Notre Dame du Lac: Foundation, 1842–1857," unpublished doctoral dissertation, University of Notre Dame, 1967, 24 and 32, and the authorities cited there.

65. Klawitter, ed., *Adapted to the Lake*, xx–xxi and 8 (Brother Vincent to Moreau, April 10, 1842). Vincent and Anselm were paid $37.50 a year, with the promise from Hailandière that this salary would increase to $50.00 after two years service. See Morin, *From France*, 144.

66. Quoted in Morin, *From France*, 115.

criticism of Brother Vincent, who was languishing in Vincennes against his will, presents a sad contrast to the dogged loyalty and devotion he consistently afforded his superior.[67] Another priest at any rate did become available, though not from France. At the end of the summer of 1842, Etienne Chartier, a thirty-two-year-old native of Montreal and recent arrival in Indiana, preached the brothers' retreat at St. Peter's, and then requested to be admitted to the community. Such impulsiveness, as the coming months would show, was characteristic of Father Chartier.[68]

During the previous spring, expending some of the money Delaune had raised, eighty more acres had been cleared at St. Peter's for cultivation, but by the autumn the results at harvest belied the community's sanguine expectations. "Unfortunately," commented Sorin some time later, "the Brothers, who had very little knowledge of agriculture in this country simply wore themselves out without much benefit. . . . A plan excellent for a country like France, might be very imperfectly adapted to the requirements of a strange soil, and the precautions called for in France were a mere waste of time in the United States." Whatever exactly he meant to imply, he had apparently changed his mind about the American agricultural methods which he had derided when he had first observed them from the deck of a boat on the Erie Canal. Nevertheless, as he described it on a later occasion, the failure stemmed more from the caprices of nature than from the brothers' ignorance: "At St. Peter's we had cleared seventy acres at great expense; three weeks before harvest a hail-storm destroyed all our hopes."[69] The poor harvest of 1842 was at any rate a severe setback for the struggling community. "Here in America," Sorin added somewhat obscurely, "time is everything, land nothing. In Europe it is just the contrary. . . . Thus it appears that devotedness is not always the sole requisite, but that an experienced guide is needed, otherwise devotedness will wear itself out to little purpose."[70]

He might well have applied this sentiment to the whole adventure at Black Oak Ridge. In the interval between planting and harvesting, relations between Holy Cross and the bishop of Vincennes continued to deteriorate, and Father Sorin, without "an experienced guide," did not, and probably could not, avoid a final confrontation. "Devotedness had worn itself out to little purpose." The paranoid Hailandière, who saw enemies everywhere, at one point accused Sorin

67. For examples see Klawitter, ed., *Adapted to the Lake*, 4, 6, 8, 10, 13.

68. Sorin, *Chronicles*, 20–21.

69. Sorin to Moreau, July 6, 1845, AGEN.

70. Sorin, *Chronicles*, 19–20.

of intriguing with the disgruntled priests of the diocese. "My great crime in his eyes," Sorin retorted, "is that I lived here for nearly two months with a priest of spirit—Monsieur Delaune—who like most of his colleagues does not love the bishop. I did not ask to have [Delaune] here, but of course I do not deny that this priest made me au courant with the secular clergy's unhappiness with the bishop, which is perfectly true." When Hailandière upbraided Sorin in a face-to-face meeting "for giving advice to the malcontents, I answered first by asserting my astonishment to him. He insisted, saying that I did not deny the charge he was making. So I told him frankly it was not true."

Then the bishop shifted ground in order to press the cause that remained most important to him. If, he said, a diocesan priest, Delaune, had gone abroad to seek funds for Holy Cross, it followed that Holy Cross must be considered a diocesan institute, directly under his own control. This assertion "made me very angry," Sorin recalled, "but I did not say a word."[71] Hailandière, outlandishly in this instance, apparently chose to interpret silence as implying consent. He informed Moreau that Sorin had finally agreed that Holy Cross in Indiana should sever its relationship with Le Mans and become a foundation of the diocese. Moreau scribbled in the margin of Hailandière's letter: "Father Sorin wrote me just the contrary of what His Lordship says here."[72] The likelihood that Sorin was playing some sort of double game seems extremely remote. Citing the experience of the Sisters of Providence at Terre Haute as well as that of Holy Cross, he wrote tersely to Moreau in June, 1842: "It is clear that [Hailandière] is the enemy of every independent society."[73] And a few months later he added: "I saw clearly that your intention has been to see us here as dependent on Sainte-Croix, and I bless the good God for this; for my inclinations and my manner of understanding our work have always made me desire what you have decided on this subject."[74] Nevertheless, there may have been an implicit rebuke to his superior in the tense of the verb in this last clause—"*vous avez résolu à ce subjet.*" Why should this tortured and endlessly debated subject have been settled only now?

After all the quarrels and misunderstandings—some principled, some petty— the end came quite suddenly. As he and the brothers sadly regarded the meager results of their harvest, Father Sorin announced a renewed determination to open a boarding school at St. Peter's. What he intended was a French *collège*—a

71. Sorin to Moreau, February 21, 1842, AGEN.

72. Quoted in Catta, *Moreau*, 1: 513.

73. Sorin to Moreau, June 25, 1842, AGEN.

74. Sorin to Moreau, August 11, 1842, AGEN.

secondary or high school for boys—though he used the word *pensionnat* in the vain hope of warding off the bishop's opposition. He was aware that Hailandière had given a commitment to the Eudists that their *collège* in Vincennes should operate without competition. Though that institution was in a miserable state, the bishop considered himself committed to it by the prior agreement. Nor was he taken in by the clever semantic distinction between *collège* and *pensionnat;* he would not permit such a school, whatever it was called, to function only twenty-five miles from Vincennes. Sorin insisted in rebuttal that secondary education was precisely what the Brothers of St. Joseph were trained to offer and what the bishop had wanted them to offer in the first place. This line of argument may have strained even Sorin's own credulity, but another did not: given all its financial problems, the Holy Cross mission at Black Oak Ridge could not survive unless it were allowed undertake a profitable venture of this kind.

There followed one last exchange of rancorous correspondence. Then "Father Sorin made a journey to Vincennes about the end of October [1842] to treat of the matter. The Bishop repeated to him what he had already expressed in writing and ended by saying that if he wished to build a college, he would give him the lake property near South Bend, in the northern part of the diocese," and would expect that a college and a novitiate for the brothers to be in place there within two years time. Whether Hailandière's unexpected offer was to be considered a gesture of reconciliation or merely an admission on his part of weariness after a year's bickering, the prospect of separating themselves by a distance of more than two hundred miles was more than welcome to both men. The bishop, however, insisted that Holy Cross continue to staff St. Peter's as well as the school in Vincennes.

This condition presented Sorin with a canonical problem: the Constitutions of Notre Dame de Sainte-Croix required that any house of brothers had to have a priest as superior.[75] But so anxious was Sorin to shake the dust of Vincennes and Black Oak Ridge from his feet that he brushed aside this difficulty in the most high-handed and imprudent fashion: he named Father Etienne Chartier, a postulant of only a few weeks standing and a man he scarcely knew, to act as director of those brothers to be left behind.[76] Then with some impatience he went through the formality of submitting the matter to "the council of administration"—two or three of the brothers whom he had appointed—and finally, after "several

---

75. See chapter 3, above.
76. The best treatment is that in Morin, *From France,* 151–152.

days . . . spent in ineffectual deliberations, . . . the offer was accepted." On November 16, 1842, "seven of the most industrious Brothers set out with their superior for South Bend."[77] Obviously—and significantly—Basile Moreau had been neither consulted nor informed about any of these decisions.

The end had indeed come quite suddenly. But in the end was a beginning.

---

77. Sorin, *Chronicles,* 21. Why the deliberations were "ineffectual" remains unclear. Morin, *From France,* 193, assumes that most of the brothers were opposed to the move.

chapter seven

Sainte-Marie-des-Lacs

WHEN EDWARD SORIN AND THE SEVEN BROTHERS of St. Joseph set out with their ox-cart from the mission at Black Oak Ridge, Daviess County, it was as though in anticipation of lines to be written many years later by one of the great poets of the twentieth century.

> "A cold coming we had of it,
> Just the worst time of the year
> For a journey, and such a long journey:
> The ways deep and the weather sharp,
> The very dead of winter."[1]

Not "the dead of winter" according to the calendar, to be sure, but this was the winter of 1842–43, one of the longest and most severe that ever befell Indiana, "a true cold of Siberia," as Sorin later described it.[2] "Our first day out," he reported to Basile Moreau at the time, "the cold became so biting that we could not go more than two and a half leagues"—less than eight miles, that is, of the more than 250 that lay before them.[3] Their route took them first through Washington and west to Vincennes, where Bishop Hailandière provided them with horses

---

1. T. S. Eliot, "The Journey of the Magi."

2. Sorin to Moreau, April 10, 1843, AGEN. See Timothy Edward Howard, *St. Joseph County* 2: 619. "Snow was fifteen inches deep as far south as Georgia."

3. Sorin to Moreau, December 5, 1842, quoted in Moreau, *Circular Letters,* 1: 59.

and a wagon. Then, under the direction of a guide named Colliche, they proceeded northward up the Wabash valley. (Whether the wagon had been loaned or given—it broke down four times during the trip—later became one more source of contention between Sorin and the bishop. After some delay, Colliche returned the horses to Vincennes.[4]) Most of the time the men walked, guiding the draught-animals over the frozen ground.[5] Little wonder that Sorin praised his companions to Moreau not only as "industrious" but "courageous." Two of their number—Brothers Gatien and Francis Xavier—had been members of the original colony, while the other five—four Irish immigrants and an Alsatian—had joined the community at St. Peter's.[6]

A short distance out of Vincennes an impatient Sorin, with the horses, the wagon, and four of the brothers, decided to push ahead, leaving the other three brothers and the ox-drawn cart to follow at a necessarily slower pace. He reached Terre Haute on November 20 and paused there long enough to scribble a note to Mother Theodore. "I am passing through here today. It may be that you already know of our shift of location to South Bend. I am here with four of the brothers, and three others are traveling more slowly behind us. The rest of the community will winter at St. Peter's and rejoin us in the spring." He regretted—as he had thirteen months before[7]—that shortness of time did not permit a visit. "Perhaps you should be surprised at such a change, but I cannot tell you any more about it at the moment," he added rather cryptically. If the two of them had had "the pleasure of passing some hours together," it is not unlikely that they might have exchanged anecdotes about the difficulties involved in getting along with Bishop Hailandière.[8]

The Holy Cross men continued to follow the track along the Wabash northeast to Lafayette and then to Logansport, where they left the valley and turned straight north for the last leg of the frigid journey. On Thursday, November 26, 1842,[9] at three o'clock in the afternoon, eleven days out of St. Peter's, Edward Sorin reached South Bend, the village that had taken its name from the unique

---

4. Sorin to Martin, January 5, 1843, AGEN.

5. Lemarié, *De La Mayenne,* 26.

6. Klawitter, ed., *Adapted to the Lake,* 347, 362, 366, 373, 374, 377. By 1850 all but one of these five—Brother Patrick, né Michael Connelly—had left the community.

7. See chapter 5, above.

8. Sorin to Mother Theodore, November 20, 1842, AGEN.

9. November 26, 1842, remains the traditionally sanctified date (Sorin, *Chronicles,* 23), though there has been some dispute about its precision (see Hope, *Notre Dame,* 35, Morin, *From France,* 159, 194–195, and Wack, "Notre Dame Foundation," 350–351).

configuration of the St. Joseph River.[10] He and his companions repaired to the impressive home of Alexis Coquillard, a businessman and civic leader who had begun his career as a fur-trader in the area nearly twenty years before.[11] Coquillard welcomed Sorin cordially, not least because the missioner brought with him a letter of credit from Bishop Hailandière to the value of $231.12 and ½.[12] Anxious to see the site where this latest decree of Providence had brought him, Father Sorin, after a brief rest, asked to be directed there forthwith. His host accordingly assigned his seventeen-year-old nephew, also named Alexis Coquillard, to guide the weary but excited travelers to that tract of land two miles away known locally as Sainte-Marie-des-Lacs. The sweep of snow obscured from their eyes the fact that, as its name attested, more than one body of water lay on the property. "Everything was frozen over," wrote an enchanted Sorin. "Yet it all seemed so beautiful. The lake [sic] especially, with its broad carpet of dazzling white snow, quite naturally reminded us of the spotless beauty of our august Lady whose name it bears. . . . We went to the very end of the lake, and, like children, came back fascinated with the marvelous beauties of our new home."[13]

Even on this first, emotional visitation the Holy Cross men could see that their holding was heavily forested; later examination revealed that stands of timber and a tangle of undergrowth covered all their 524 acres, except for ninety or so taken up by the lakes and another ten tilled in a desultory fashion by a mixed-race trapper named Nicolas Charron, whose clapboard shack stood up a gentle rise from the edge of what appeared on that November day to be one large lake.[14] Aside from a storage shed, the only other extant building, located close to Charron's little house, was a structure in bad repair, forty feet by twenty-four, which had been put up ten or eleven years before to serve as a chapel and a residence for a priest. Charron owed his undefined tenure on the land to his service as interpreter for the itinerant missioners who had not spoken the Indians' language.[15]

---

10. Actually there were two villages, South Bend on the river's west bank and the much smaller Lowell on its east. The latter, never incorporated, was eventually absorbed into the former. See Howard, *St. Joseph County*, 1: 135, 366.

11. See Howard, *St. Joseph County*, 1: 131–135.

12. Mary Clarke Coquillard, "Alexis Coquillard—His Time: A Story of the Founding of South Bend, Indiana" (South Bend, Ind., 1931), 15–20, 41.

13. Sorin to Moreau, December 5, 1842, quoted in Moreau, *Circular Letters*, 1: 60. Sorin always associated the snowy arrival at Sainte-Marie with the departure from Le Mans on the feast of Our Lady of the Snows. See, for example, Sorin to Moreau, July 6, 1845, AGEN.

14. Klawitter, ed., *Adapted to the Lake*, xviii.

15. Sorin, *Chronicles*, 23–24. See also the commentary and pictorial material in Thomas J. Schlereth, *The University of Notre Dame. A Portrait of Its History and Campus* (Notre Dame, Ind., 1976), 8–13.

Their euphoria checked somewhat by the bitterly cold temperature, Sorin and the brothers, as evening fell, returned to South Bend where the elder Coquillard had prepared temporary accommodations for them. During the days that followed they began to lay their plans for their future work, even as they learned something of the lore associated with the place to which the hand of God—as they firmly believed—had led them.

SIMON BRUTÉ DE REMUR, first bishop of Vincennes, never quite lost the professorial mindset he had acquired in Maryland during the decades preceding his assignment to the Indiana frontier. The detail with which he embellished the report on the state of his new diocese, sent to the Roman Curia in 1836, filled as it was with graphs and elaborate lists and historical precedents, suggested the habits of the classroom lecturer he had long been.[16] But, pedantic as his disposition may have appeared, Bruté combined with it an understandable pride that he, as a Frenchman and a Catholic priest, had assumed a position by no means out of harmony with a long and honored tradition. He could justifiably point to Pierre Gibault, the patriot-priest of Vincennes and ally of George Rogers Clark, but also, long years before that, to Fathers Marquette, Hennepin, and Allouez, Frenchmen all, his precursors as missionaries in what was now, since 1816, the state of Indiana.[17] "The St. Joseph portage," Bruté observed, "was used by Father Marquette long before La Salle."[18]

These two proper names, Marquette and La Salle, recalled the glory days of the French exploration of the region between the Great Lakes and the Mississippi valley during the last quarter of the seventeenth century.[19] And the term "St. Joseph portage" was pregnant with historical significance. The St. Joseph River[20] rises in central Michigan, flows southwestward until it reaches a point six or seven miles below the Indiana-Michigan border, then bends toward the northwest, re-

16. McAvoy, ed., "Bishop Bruté's Report," French, Latin, and English texts.

17. Claude Allouez (1620–1689) and Jacques Marquette (1636–1675) were Jesuits, Louis Hennepin (c.1640–c.1701), a Franciscan. For Gibault, see chapter 5, above.

18. Quoted in Howard, *St. Joseph County* 1: 22.

19. For a recent summary see Anka Muhlstein, *La Salle, Explorer of the North American Frontier* (New York, 1994).

20. Sometimes called the "Big St. Joseph," to distinguish it from the St. Joseph River near Fort Wayne. See chapter 5, note 30, above. La Salle called it "the River of the Miamis," who were the dominant native American tribe in the area in his time. At the mouth of the Big St. Joseph, on the site of the present cities of St. Joseph and Benton Harbor, Michigan, the French established a post originally called Fort Miamis.

crosses that border, and empties ultimately into Lake Michigan, forty-five miles or so away. But only four miles from the south bend of the St. Joseph,[21] amidst a tangle of underbrush and crooked trees and bogland in Marquette's and La Salle's time, lies the source of the Kankakee River, which twists its way west until it joins the Illinois and then the Mississippi just above St. Louis. The vagaries of the prehistoric ice age had dictated the westward flow of the Kankakee and the northward flow of the St. Joseph, a circumstance which lent incalculable importance to the St. Joseph portage for a man like La Salle, who dreamed imperialist dreams. The physically daunting task of dragging vessels and supplies four miles over treacherous terrain was a triviality compared to the prize at the end of it, because this passage provided a link between two vast basins of the North American continent, that of the Great Lakes and that of the Mississippi. In other words, a French explorer or missionary, were he intrepid, tough, and lucky enough, could depart Quebec on the St. Lawrence, proceed along the chain of lakes, sail down the eastern shore of Lake Michigan until he reached the mouth of the St. Joseph, paddle his canoes up that river to its south bend, then haul them in a southwesterly direction across the swampy grounds of the St. Joseph portage, launch them again on the Kankakee and float down that river to the Illinois and then to the Mississippi until, finally, he reached the Gulf of Mexico. This is the sort of adventure Marquette and La Salle, each for his own purposes, engaged in, at a time when the place names just mentioned had yet to be determined.

Bishop Bruté therefore had justice on his side when he asserted the longevity of the French Catholic presence in Indiana and specifically in the state's northwest corner. This latter portion of his immense jurisdiction he visited only once during his brief episcopate.[22] But in 1835, the year after he took up his charge in Vincennes, Bruté became—or rather his infant diocese became—the beneficiary of the enterprise of another remarkable Frenchman. On July 31, 1835, the ownership of 524 acres of land, which enclosed two small lakes located near the south bend of the St. Joseph River was formally transferred to the bishop of Vincennes. This parcel had been acquired from the federal government, which, in accord with its routine policy, had seized it from the local Indians by way of an exploitative treaty. The original purchaser had imposed two conditions for his benefaction to the diocese: that he be reimbursed a total of $750 to cover his original

---

21. The portage began on the south bank of the St. Joseph where the Riverview and Highland cemeteries—intersected, appropriately, by Portage Avenue—are now located. See the maps and photographs in Otto M. Knoblock et al., "Historic Background of South Bend and St. Joseph County in Northern Indiana" (South Bend, 1927), 7–13.

22. McAvoy, ed., "Bishop Bruté's Report," 190.

investment as well as the "improvements" he had added to the estate, and, secondly, that "an orphan asylum or some other religious or charitable project" be set up on the property, to which he had given the euphonic name Sainte-Marie-des-Lacs.[23] By the time Bruté died, this latter stipulation had not yet been fulfilled, and so his successor, Bishop Hailandière, after failing, in 1840, to interest one order of French missionaries in the project,[24] turned three years later to another, judging that he could thus satisfy both the letter and the spirit of the donor's intentions—and rid himself at the same time of an irritating source of controversy—by offering the tract to Edward Sorin and the Congregation of Holy Cross.

NOT TILL 1845 did Sorin meet that original donor,[25] by then a short, paunchy old man of seventy-six, bald except for a fringe of white hair that fell over his ears. His jowls were heavy, his nose sharp and pinched, the corners of his mouth turned down as though in chronic disapproval of the world around him. He walked with a shambling gait, and, because of a partial paralysis in his right hand and forearm, "he generally appeared with his left hand and arm caressingly thrown around the diseased member."[26] But despite the disabilities with which years of relentless work and harsh living conditions had burdened him, Stephen Theodore Badin's gray eyes snapped and sparkled with undiminished vigor.

In his last will and testament he described himself simply as "Roman Catholic Missionary," surely an appropriate designation for this tireless priest who spent six decades ministering to his co-religionists all across the near Middle West. But as the terms of that will indicate,[27] he was also a dogged real estate speculator; his procurement of the parcel of land destined to become the site of the University of Notre Dame was only one among many such transactions. Not that he or any of his colleagues saw any conflict between their ministry and the accumulation of property. Their objective was to forge in America an institutional Catholicism on the European model—the only kind of Catholicism they knew—

---

23. Hope, *Notre Dame*, 50–51.

24. The Fathers of Mercy, founded in France in 1808, and introduced into the United States in 1839. They were active especially in New York, Mobile, and New Orleans. The member of the order who negotiated fruitlessly with Hailandière was Ferdinand Bach, who later became president of Spring Hill College in Mobile. See Hope, *Notre Dame*, 51, and Wack, "Notre Dame Foundation," 39.

25. Sorin, *Chronicles*, 54.

26. Quoted in J. Herman Schauinger, *Stephen T. Badin, Priest in the Wilderness* (Milwaukee, 1956), 272.

27. Text (1840) printed In Schauinger, *Badin*, 295–298.

and to accomplish this goal required the provision of sacred space for the cele-bration of the sacraments, to be sure, but, hardly less crucial, permanent locations also for schools and colleges, orphanages and hospitals, convents and presbyter-ies. America between the Alleghenies and the Mississippi offered abundant op-portunities in this regard to the missionaries of Badin's generation; much of the land there was scarcely inhabited, once the Indians had been expelled, or else it was tantalizingly cheap, though, as Badin perceived, it would not much longer re-main so. He was by no means unique in recognizing these realities, but the zest with which he entered into buying, selling, and transferring real estate, and his failure to distinguish carefully enough between what belonged to him and what belonged to the Catholic community—as a secular priest he had every right to purchase and own property himself—to some extent set him apart. His activities at any rate brought about almost as much confusion and contention as they did long-term benefit.

Born in Orléans in 1768 and educated in the classics at the venerable Collège Montagu in Paris, the short and wiry young Badin matriculated in the seminary of his home diocese the year the Revolution broke out. Two years later, in 1791, the institution was closed down by the hostile government, and the following Janu-ary, Badin, in the company of another seminarian and three Sulpician priests—among them Benedict Flaget with whom, in later years, Badin would have a poignant love-hate relationship—set sail for America. Arrived in Baltimore and greeted warmly by Bishop John Carroll, Badin found himself once again in a Sulpician seminary identical in spirit, if not in material resources, to what he had experienced at Orléans. Since he had received a goodly portion of his theological training as well as the minor orders[28] in France, his progress toward his ultimate goal was relatively swift. Raised to the subdiaconate in September, 1792, and to the diaconate five months later, he received priest's orders at Carroll's hands in May 1793. So it was that Stephen Theodore Badin bore the distinction of having been the first Catholic priest to be ordained in the United States of America.[29]

And he bore the distinction well for more than sixty years, but not without controversy. He was indefatigable in his work on the frontier missions, first in Kentucky where Carroll appointed him fresh from his ordination, and then in

---

28. Prior to revisions introduced by Pope Paul VI (d. 1978) candidates for the Roman Catholic priesthood passed through several ritual stages before ordination, beginning with formal admittance to the clerical state (tonsure), followed by the minor orders (acolyte, exorcist, porter, lector), the sub-diaconate, and the (transitional) diaconate. Only the last of these is considered an integral part of the sacrament of Holy Orders, and so it continues while the others have been suppressed.

29. Schauinger, *Badin*, 6–8.

Ohio, Michigan, and Indiana. He was a circuit-rider *par excellence* at a time when Catholic settlers were scattered across trackless prairies and woodlands. The labors he took upon himself—as emotionally draining as they were physically—were almost Homeric in their scope and diversity. Afoot and on horseback, he traveled in all kinds of weather from settlement to settlement and presided, as he reported to Bishop Carroll, at 300 baptisms, 40 weddings, and 30 funerals a year, not to mention hearing 2,100 confessions. Alone for the most part during his first decade in Kentucky—over one stretch of nearly two years he never encountered another priest and so could not enjoy the solace of the confessional he offered to others— he put together nonetheless a viable institutional structure upon which his successors could and did successfully build.

But he quarreled with almost everybody, including, in due time, with Edward Sorin. His unrelenting rigidity on moral matters smacked of that Jansenism so characteristic of the French Catholicism from which he had sprung. Thus, for example, festive dancing, so cheering an amusement among those on the frontier who had few diversions from the harshness of their lives, was for Badin a particular *bête noire,* because he fancied this recreation to be the occasion of unspeakable sexual sins among his flock. Next to harping on the evils flesh was heir to, litigation seemed to be his favorite pastime. He was constantly at loggerheads with prominent Catholic laymen who, he thought, perversely withheld support from him and who denied him the kind of financial control over parish and school he considered his clerical status entitled him to. The lash of his sarcasm was felt even by those guilty of trivial transgressions, like coming to church late for Mass or being there improperly dressed. He once began his sermon at the funeral of a distinguished parishioner: "[The deceased] had not much sense, to be sure, but we are not to forget that he had all the sense God gave him." Hurt feelings were immaterial to him; "A priest is God's surgeon, and he must cut to cure," he liked to say.[30]

Nor were his relations with fellow clerics any more pacific. When the Dominicans began work in the Kentucky missions and expressed a more relaxed attitude toward dancing, Badin reacted toward them in such a hostile manner that their American-born superior complained to officials in Rome: "[Badin] is generally more zealous than prudent—in fine more of a Frenchman, . . . [with] his overbearing, hasty temper and his harsh, strict, and rigid practice."[31] In 1811

---

30. See Schauinger, *Badin,* 268 and 107.

31. Quoted in Schauinger, *Badin,* 114. Needless to say, Badin took a different view of the characteristics proper to his countrymen (Schauinger, 68): "I preserve the serenity of mind natural to Frenchmen," he wrote to Bishop Carroll, "tho' I meet with a thousand crosses daily in my way."

Benedict Flaget—a rather more temperate Frenchman and one of Badin's companions on the voyage to America—assumed his duties as first bishop of Kentucky, with his see-city in Bardstown. Within a year the two had fallen out, and the usually gentle Flaget had denounced Badin from the pulpit. Their unedifying dispute over property rights dragged on for years, until, Badin, in 1818, left Kentucky in disgust and returned to France.

He stayed abroad for a decade, but his restless heart continued to roam the missions he had left behind. Indeed, during that time of self-imposed exile he displayed his charmingly contradictory nature by crisscrossing Europe seeking support for the people he had quarreled with in America. Then, in 1828, he came back, not to Kentucky, inhospitable to him now, but to the rawer pioneer settlements in the old Northwest Territory, to Illinois and Michigan and northern Indiana, a priestly wandering minstrel, an anointed *chevalier errant* jousting once more with the world, the flesh, and the Devil. Badin's canonical credentials may have been uncertain—was he subject to the bishop of Bardstown, to the bishop of Cincinnati or, later, to Vincennes or Detroit?—but the niceties of the canon law did not much matter on the edge of a wilderness and certainly did not hamper the ministry of one who had begun to enjoy almost legendary status among Catholics as America's proto-priest. Though the fracas with the Dominicans had long been forgotten,[32] and a kind of wary truce had been patched together between him and Bishop Flaget, Badin showed himself on this second foray into the missions no less cantankerous than before, no less prepared to wield the painful scalpel as "God's surgeon," no less anxious to summon into a courtroom all his enemies, real and imagined, and no less zealous either, it is only fair to say, to preach Christ's gospel to the poor.

His unparalleled experience at any rate gave him the right to fix the qualifications a French missionary needed to bring to the American frontier.

Much as priests are wanted in your Diocese [Badin wrote the newly-appointed bishop of Vincennes in 1835], it seems to me that it is a lesser evil to have none than to have bad ones. There must be a very particular grace, especially for such as are young or novices in the holy ministry, to live so remote from both the Diocesan Bishop and a confessor. The air breathed in our Backwoods is far from being pure. Profound humility, diffidence of one['s] self, the fear of God and Divine charity, the love of mortification and disinterestedness, a competent learning, and a spirit of piety are all

---

32. While in Rome in 1826–27, Badin even became briefly a Dominican novice. See Schauinger, *Badin*, 209–211.

equally necessary. Some knowledge of the world and prudence in the world (not of the world) are also desirable ingredients in the character of a missionary, who must deal with all sorts of people of different nations, of all ages, sexes, conditions, various dispositions, etc.[33]

Recommending "diffidence" may not have rung altogether true given the old man's contentious career, but the ideal he described was not less worthy because of that.

D URING THE YEARS between 1828 and 1833 Badin's preachment was largely addressed to the poorest of the poor, the pathetic remnant of native Americans not yet ruthlessly transported from the old Northwest Territory to reservations beyond the Mississippi. Despite his age and wide experience, this ministry was new to Badin; in his time there there had been no Indians in Kentucky to minister to. But along the great loop of the St. Joseph River there perdured among the scattering of French Canadian and *métis* families still living in northwest Indiana and the southwest corner of Michigan Territory (as it was until statehood in 1837) a hazy memory of the "blackrobes," the French Jesuits, who had come into the region with the explorers, soldiers, and *coureurs des bois* during the seventeenth and eighteenth centuries.[34] This tradition of Catholicism, muted as it may have been, was kept alive by occasional visits to the area by itinerant priests, most recently by a French-speaking German named Frederic Résé,[35] who expanded his apostolate to embrace the local Indians. These were the Potawatomi, who in their various clans had for more than a century inhabited the lands adjacent to the shores—east, south, and west—of Lake Michigan. In 1830 a notable Potawatomi chieftain, the fifty-six year-old Pokagon, whose village lay four or five miles downstream from the south bend of the St. Joseph, received baptism at the hands of Résé, who at the same time christened one of the chief's wives and some scores of his dependents.[36]

---

33. Badin to Bruté, January 28, 1835, AUND, CAVI, "Diocese of Vincennes."

34. Classic treatments are John Gilmary Shea, *Discovery and Exploration of the Mississippi Valley* (New York, 1852) and many works by Francis Parkman, including *The Jesuits in North America in the Seventeenth Century* (Boston, 1867). For a recent and succinct summary see Richard White, *The Middle Ground. Indians, Empires, and Republics in the Great Lakes Region, 1650–1815* (Cambridge, 1991), 7–10, 25–28, 53–56.

35. Born in Hanover, Résé or Reese (1791–1871) was named first bishop of Detroit in 1833. Ill health later forced transfer of his jurisdiction to a coadjutor and ultimately his resignation.

36. McAvoy, *Catholic Church in Indiana*, 174–175.

Legends abounded about Pokagon, during his lifetime and afterward. It was said, for instance that his name—meaning something like "Mr. Rib"—was given him because, as a ferocious young warrior, he habitually wore a human rib in his top-knot. But later in life he conformed to standards more acceptable to the white man, became a decorous *chef de parti,* and stoutly resisted that most destructive scourge to his people, the whisky trade. It was also said that Pokagon himself cherished a vague tradition honoring the religion taught by the Jesuit blackrobes in the St. Joseph valley so long ago, which allegedly explained why he asked for and received the ministrations of Father Rese.

The truth appears to have been both simpler and more complicated. The chief's Potawatomi name—Sakekwinik, "Man of the River's Mouth"—characterized his position within the tribe much better than did the blood-curdling *sobriquet* the white men favored—favored perhaps because it implied how successfully they had tamed him. Certainly the mature Pokagon practiced sobriety and urged his followers to do likewise. But, though his conversion to Catholicism was no doubt genuine and heartfelt—he kept the faith according to his lights with considerable devotion till he died—it did not involve abandoning the polygamy he had practiced all his life. Nor does evidence exist to support the notion that his decision to become a Catholic stemmed from faint memories of the blackrobes. Indeed, there was a measure of practical calculation in that decision.[37]

For the overriding motive that determined Pokagon's behavior was his determination that he and his little band not be removed with the other Indians to the reservations west of the Mississippi. To become a Christian was one way to accommodate to the intruding white world. To become a Catholic Christian was to accommodate to a familiar white world, that of the French, which was composed of traders whose interest was to preserve the Potawatomi way of life, in contrast to Anglo-Protestant farmers who would surely destroy it. By way of confirmation, the well-intentioned American Baptist missionaries, with whom Pokagon had long maintained friendly relations, urged him to accept the inevitable and lead his people to the open lands reserved for them in the west. Conversely, even as he listened to this earnest appeal, the chief observed that the Catholics, far from recommending removal, were opening new mission-stations along the valley, most conspicuously Father Badin's 524-acre acquisition near the St. Joseph's south bend, Sainte-Marie-des-Lacs, where the priest had had constructed a log

---

37. See the illuminating account in James A. Clifton, *The Pokagons, 1683–1983: Catholic Potawatomi Indians of the St. Joseph River Valley* (Lanham, Md., 1984), 56–68. See also Everett Claspy, *The Potawatomi Indians of Southwestern Michigan* (Dowagiac Mich., 1966), 7–11.

building to serve as a chapel and a residence and where he intended to establish a school for "young squaws" as well as an orphanage for children of both races and all denominations.[38]

Meanwhile, Stephen Badin for his part cordially embraced the Potawatomi convert and even lived for a time in the same hut with Pokagon and his number-one wife—now since their submission to the Catholic faith known by the respectable European names Leopold and Elizabeth. Soon the indefatigable missionary could count twenty-four other Potawatomi adults under his instruction as catechumens. He was edified, he said, by the Indians' "attentive and intelligent attitude, [by] the meekness, simplicity, and innocence" of their lives.[39] But, ever pragmatic and by now somewhat Americanized, he also urged that Pokagon and his braves should concentrate their energies on farming rather than on hunting and trapping, should, in other words, by cultivating corn and wheat adapt themselves to the agrarian realities of a culture which, if they failed to do so, would overwhelm them. Pokagon accepted this advice, and, though it was the women of the clan who did most of the work, the productive fields the Potawatomi could boast of demonstrated how well, if left to themselves, they might have coped with the demands of a set of economic values not their own.

How much this modest accomplishment contributed to Pokagon's ultimate success is debatable. Similarly, it remains difficult to estimate how effective Badin's mediation may have been. To his eternal credit, in any case, the priest traveled across the Midwest, from Louisville to Detroit to Fort Wayne and back again to the Potawatomi villages along the border between Indiana and Michigan Territory, always seeking support and sustenance for his Indian converts, always arguing in their behalf with federal commissioners and other officers of local and state government. Concrete events, however, as they always seem to do, intervened. In 1832 the rising of the Fox and Sauks in Illinois known as Black Hawk's War—young Abraham Lincoln was a volunteer, though he saw no action—by arousing white fear and animosity sealed the fate of other Indian tribes entirely uninvolved in the insurgency, including the widespread Potawatomi. Over the next several years northwest Indiana was practically cleared of natives, who were transported to what are now Oklahoma and Kansas under the most appalling conditions. Only the handful of Catholic Potawatomi led by Leopold Pokagon, who proved himself a supple and inventive bargainer through a series of treaty-negotiations, was spared removal. The handsome, silver-haired chief died July 8, 1841, a little less than a month before Edward Sorin and his companions departed

38. Schauinger, *Badin*, 219, 241.
39. Schauinger, *Badin*, 227.

Le Mans. But the memory of his leadership endures even to this day among those pockets of native Americans who still survive in southern Michigan and who are referred to routinely as Pokagons.[40]

At the moment of the great chief's death, the ever-restless Stephen Badin had long since moved on to other apostolates. He left in charge of the mission at Sainte-Marie-des-Lacs a Belgian priest named Louis DeSeille, who, besides fulfilling his strictly sacerdotal duties, tried his best to mitigate the sufferings of his Indian congregations shortly to be transported to the west. He lived in Badin's log chapel, and there in 1837, stricken by a fatal disease, he administered to himself the Viaticum at the altar and then died in a bed a few feet away; his Indian disciples buried him in the floor.[41] Bishop Bruté sent north as DeSeille's successor a young Frenchman he had just ordained, Benjamin-Marie Petit, a native of Rennes, for whom dedication to his Indian flock was the touchstone of his ministry. In the late summer of 1838, the militia rounded up some 800 Potawatomi out of the St. Joseph valley, Pokagon's clan excepted, and herded them westward. Benjamin Petit went with them over this cruel "Trail of Death," along which every day five or six children perished. By the time they crossed the Mississippi, after two months of excruciating deprivations, their number had been reduced by one-fifth. The twenty-nine year-old Father Petit, worn out by fever and depression, died in St. Louis on February 10, 1839, a martyr surely to that dubious American dogma called, later, "manifest destiny."[42]

SOME MONTHS after he had settled in northwest Indiana, Edward Sorin was made aware—by way of a rare occurrence, a cordial communication from Bishop Hailandière—of the more remote historical significance of the place to which he had come. This information—broadly correct if flawed in detail—Sorin passed on in a letter to the man who had acted as friendly patron

40. Clifton, *Pokagons,* 74, 91–135.

41. Viaticum is the Eucharist administered to a dying person to strengthen him on the way (*via*) to judgment. For the burial see Hope, *Notre Dame,* 43–44. DeSeille, already ordained, had come to the United States in 1832 (i.e., before the erection of the diocese of Vincennes), had joined the diocese of Cincinnati, whose bishop, Edward Fenwick, had sent him to assist Badin.

42. Howard, *St. Joseph County,* 2: 608–611. See also R. David Edmunds, *The Potawatomis, Keepers of the Fire* (Norman, Okla., 1978), 264–266. An excellent summary of the pre-Sorin apostolate at Sainte-Marie-des-Lacs is Joseph M. White, *Sacred Heart Parish at Notre Dame: A Heritage and History* (n.p. [Notre Dame, Ind.], 1992), 15–26. For Sorin's considered appreciation of DeSeille and Petit, written in 1880, see *Chronicles,* 316–318.

and companion at the time of Holy Cross's departure from Le Mans and Le Havre, Léon Dupont

> The site of Notre Dame du Lac is perhaps the first locality in the West that was visited by missionaries and moreover had missionaries in residence. It is at least certain, the bishop tells me, that Père Marquette was here in 1669 and that he resided here until his death in 1675, when he was replaced by Père Allouez. The latter had himself already since 1669 worked among the Potawatomi and the Miami (the local savages). It is astonishing how many memories crowd around this parcel of land.[43]

Less removed from the endeavors of the blackrobes of two centuries before was the all too poignant and futilely heroic ministry of Fathers DeSeille and Petit. Sorin's romantic soul was powerfully, if temporarily, moved by the example of these two selfless missionaries. Indeed, the first prayer he had offered in the crude and bitterly cold log chapel hard by St. Mary's Lakes had been over the grave of Louis DeSeille.[44] And the first communication he sent back to Le Mans—in the first days of December, 1842, about the time the other three brothers and the ox-cart had finally arrived at Sainte-Marie—testifies to the effect this recollection had upon his usually pragmatic nature. The institution Holy Cross proposed to establish on this site, he told Basile Moreau, "cannot fail to succeed, even if it receives only a little help from our friends in France, because, in the whole United States, it is evidently the one college whose location offers it most chances of success." Presumptuous as such a prophecy may have seemed at the time, it proved over the long term essentially correct. And yet the shrewd prophet, who confidently uttered it, was also a warm-hearted young man, not yet thirty years old, who, at least for the moment, thought he discerned another calling altogether.

> But the deeper my gratitude for all these many heavenly blessings on our work, the more keenly do I realize my inability to direct it any longer. It is all well and good that you should give me five or six brothers to be brought to America. But you must understand the situation is different now. Now we need an able leader, possessed . . . of all the qualities called for by our

---

43. Sorin to Dupont, May (?) 1843, AGEN. Léon Dupont by this time had begun to be known as "the holy man of Tours." See Pierre Janvier, *M. Dupont and the Work of the Holy Face* (New York, 1886).

44. In 1857 Sorin arranged to have Benjamin Petit's remains brought back to Notre Dame and interred next to DeSeille's.

Constitutions. It is for you, Reverend Father, to make your choice in keeping with the requirements of such a position. For my part, in all honesty, I recognize my inability as well as my reluctance to have any further part in this undertaking, unless it be to live in it under obedience. This alone can make me happy. This does not mean I am tired of the work of the Brothers and that I want to be recalled to France. No, neither is true, dear Father. I love the work of the Brothers, . . . and less than ever do I think of returning to France. But to be entirely frank with you, I also love the savages of Father DeSeille and Father Petit. I thank heaven that I am now among them. . . . Over many years [God] inspired me with such a great desire to labor for them. . . . I see nothing in the world comparable to the life of a missionary among the savages. . . . I am still young; I shall learn their language quickly. In a year I hope to understand them. I shall write to you frequently about my dear Indians, and, no doubt, everything about them will interest you. . . . Please write as soon as possible, so that I may see your permission with my own eyes. Tomorrow . . . I shall begin to study their language, and when your letter arrives, I hope to be able to express my thanks in Indian.[45]

An aura of make-believe hangs over this extraordinary effusion, and a series of legends emerged from it, some of which persist to this day. Perhaps the closest one can come to the truth of the matter is that this petition reveals Edward Sorin to have been an intriguingly integrated blend of the romantic idealist and the practical man of affairs. Much evidence from across the full spectrum of his career tends to support that broad conclusion. But with regard to the case at hand, little if any evidence confirms that such a hankering to repudiate his leadership position—at which he had already demonstrated considerable proficiency and which he manifestly enjoyed—in order to lose himself, as it were, in the service of the tiny remnant of the Potawatomi, was anything more than a passing fancy. Significantly, he never repeated the proposal,[46] and a more jaded generation than his own can be forgiven for wondering whether he might have been indulging in histrionics calculated to please his austere superior in Le Mans. This surmise, however, hardly fits the person or the times. Sorin was a man whose emotions ran very deep, whose fancies sometimes burned with a white heat. The accounts he

---

45. Sorin to Moreau, December 5, 1842, AGEN, and also quoted in Moreau, *Circular Letters,* 1: 61–62.

46. See Catta, *Moreau,* 1: 523.

had heard about the brutal expulsion of the Indians in 1838–1839 and of DeSeille's and Petit's noble self-sacrifice had no doubt moved him keenly.

But reality soon pressed itself upon him. When he wrote this letter to Father Moreau late into the night of December 5, Sorin had been settled scarcely ten days at Sainte-Marie-des-Lacs. He knew little about Indians in general—there had been none in southern Indiana—and even less about the peculiarities of the local Potawatomi—for instance, he was probably unaware at this early date that their numbers had been reduced to a mere handful. And despite his claim that the "great desire to labor for them" had been divinely inspired, the fact is that in coming to America he had clearly understood, and had accepted, as his mandate, from both Moreau and Hailandière, the establishment of European-style institutional Catholicism among the white immigrants to the diocese of Vincennes. It would seem in any event that within a week his original ardor had begun to cool. "I have not yet seen the savages," he remarked somewhat laconically on December 13. "They are off hunting."[47] Shortly after the hunters returned to their villages, early in the new year of 1843, a delegation came to Sainte-Marie to greet the new blackrobe, and Sorin, at their request, baptized fourteen of them.[48]

The Indians, however, were seeking more than spiritual solace, and Sorin had already had intimations of the person causing some of their difficulties. "It appears certain," he informed August Martin, "that Monsieur Bernier has taken away with him all the possessions of Messers. DeSeille and Petit that had been left behind here. We are all much pained about this, and for myself I sincerely regret not having these precious reminders of two men whom I venerate to a high degree. Ah, Monsieur Martin, this wretched priest has done much harm here. May God efface as soon as possible his memory from this whole country!"[49] In the formal record he composed later, Sorin made only oblique reference to this "Canadian missionary from Detroit, who spent nearly three years in the country, which he did not edify as his predecessors had done."[50] At the time he was more explicit.

I have just come from visiting the village of Pokagon [he reported again to Martin], which is in greater trouble than ever because of the report of the land-transfer. For some months a Presbyterian schoolmaster has been per-

---

47. Sorin to Martin, December 13, 1842, AGEN.

48. Schlereth, *Notre Dame,* 10–11. On the latter page is reproduced a romanticized version of this meeting, painted in 1883.

49. Sorin to Martin, December 13, 1842, AGEN. By this date Martin had become Hailandière's vicar general and had moved to Vincennes. Sorin addressed him as "Monsieur le Grand Vicaire." See chapter 5, note 4, above.

50. Sorin *Chronicles,* 27.

suading the Potawatomi that Monsieur Bernier has sold their land, and that it no longer belongs to them, no more than to the bishop. Everything appears in a pitiable state. Have the goodness to persuade the bishop to renounce purely and simply all his rights to this land. I for one could never recognize this as property legitimately acquired. The good of religion urgently demands such action at this moment.[51]

The shadowy career of Stanislaus Bernier, "this wretched priest" in Sorin's estimation, demonstrated that, while the Catholic missions gave scope to figures of heroic stature, like DeSeille and Petit, they could also offer opportunity for mischief to less admirable individuals, a few of whom—misusing the relative freedom from direction they enjoyed and giving vent to eccentricity or self-interest—actually did damage to the cause they purported to serve. The situation to which Sorin referred had its origins in the summer of 1840 when Father Bernier, who had been in and out of the South Bend area since the year before, on some unknown but certainly specious pretext, persuaded Leopold Pokagon to accept $800 in exchange for deeds to 674 out of the 874 acres the chief actually owned. The following January control over the tracts in question was formally transferred to the bishop of Vincennes. The details involved in these transactions are by no means clear—particularly Hailandière's part in them—but Bernier's motivation appears to have been a desire to curry favor with certain government officials who were once again contemplating ways to expel the remnant of the Potawatomi from the St. Joseph valley. After Pokagon died (July 1841) the confusion and consternation Father Sorin witnessed dragged on for some years, but in the end the chief's reliance on the treaty system he had so skillfully exploited when alive, was vindicated once more. In 1848 a Michigan circuit court voided the deeds to the 674 acres and cited Bernier and Hailandière for employing "fraud and undue influence."[52]

In light of the judicial decision ultimately rendered in the case, it seems unlikely that Hailandière adopted Sorin's forthright recommendation, that he renounce "purely and simply" any property acquired through Bernier's intrigues. On the other hand, it is equally unlikely that the bishop in fact shared the court costs with Bernier, as the judge directed, since he, Hailandière, had resigned his see and returned to France a year before the verdict came down. Sorin at any rate, noting that unease at the diocese's perceived land policy had spread to another nearby Michigan settlement, remained dubious about the line the bishop

51. Sorin to Martin, January 31, 1843, AGEN.
52. Clifton, *Pokagons*, 73–76.

had apparently chosen to take at the outset of the scandal. "I went recently to Pokagon," he wrote him sometime in the early spring of 1843, "where I tried to make them understand the reasons you have given me. I hope things will go better, despite the fact that the business might well cause more commotion than ever in Niles."[53]

This visitation to the Potawatomi was the most extended Sorin ever paid to the local Indians. His proposal to establish a school for them was vetoed by Bishop Hailandière, a decision Sorin accepted almost too readily; he assumed, he said (not without a touch of sarcasm) that the bishop had "grave reasons" for denying this "satisfaction" to "the interests of these dear Indians."[54] Though he spoke no more of a desire to devote himself exclusively to their service, he did describe to Father Moreau the time spent with them in the pietistic terms that would have been most appreciated in Le Mans. And he did not refer to *l'affaire Bernier*.

> I stayed three weeks at Pokagon with our dear Indians. It is there that I celebrated this year the Forty Hours devotion.[55] I have seen their primitive dwellings; I have eaten and slept with them. I have said Holy Mass twice in the midst of these good savages. I have listened to their chants, a thousand times more touching to me than all the concerts of the world. They had learned the songs from Monsieur Petit. If time permitted I would report to you the principal peculiarities of this visit to the dear family of Monsieur Petit. All I can say today is that for four years these dear savages have been almost entirely abandoned. For the last six months they have had as schoolmaster and catechist a Presbyterian, the most implacable enemy of our holy religion. I have happily succeeded in driving this ravenous wolf from the midst of this innocent sheepfold.

Yet Sorin's practicality never let him stray for long from considering possible future problems and solutions, this time perhaps with the hint of a smile.

> I propose to send Brother Joseph to Pokagon Easter week. Afterwards, if the expenses of his mission prove too burdensome for our poverty, and if you approve, Reverend Father, we will dispatch to you a pretty little savage

---

53. Sorin to Hailandière, April (?), 1843, AGEN.

54. Sorin to Martin, April 3, 1843, AGEN.

55. A devotion originating in the sixteenth century as an acknowledgment of the Real Presence of Christ in the Eucharist. Continuous prayer is offered for forty hours before the Blessed Sacrament exposed, that is, outside the tabernacle.

who, I hope, will not return from Le Mans with empty hands. I realize that there are many who come to France soliciting funds for good causes, but few may be of this type.[56]

Sorin did indeed persuade the Indians to send the objectionable Presbyterian packing and to accept Brother Joseph—né Charles Rother, the young immigrant who had joined Holy Cross immediately upon its arrival at Black Oak Ridge[57]— in his stead. This initiative had a twofold result. The talented if erratic Brother Joseph, relying on the agricultural practices he remembered from his boyhood and youth in Germany, was able during his brief stay among them to help the Potawatomi—as Stephen Badin had done fifteen years earlier—to improve their farming methods and thereby to increase the productivity of their fields, an important consideration for a people whose resources were so limited. But this very success tended to solidify, secondly, the political and social control exercised over the two hundred or so Catholic Potawatomi from Sainte-Marie-des-Lacs, a control which, as so often the case during the nineteenth century, manifested much insensitivity to hallowed customs and values.[58]

AN INDIAN MINISTRY was an ephemeral preoccupation for Edward Sorin, and soon it became a readily delegated one. Meanwhile, the primary obligation and commitment of Holy Cross was to provide a *collège* in the far northern reaches of the diocese of Vincennes. Plans for such a venture had already been drawn up, to no avail, at St. Peter's; now the bishop who had thwarted them indicated his desire that the institution, safely far away, be established by the summer of 1844. Even as the $400 Father Moreau had sent the community just prior to its northward trek was fast running out,[59] the larger project was never far from Sorin's mind. "If we had $4,000 assured to us," he reflected during those bitterly cold days of early December, "I think we would be able reach the bishop's goal. But you," he told August Martin, "know our resources as well as our expectations. I wonder what Monseigneur will give us to compensate for our expenses at St. Peter's." Clearly there would be a genuine advantage in building soon:

56. Sorin to Moreau, March 20, 1843, AGEN.
57. See chapter 6, above.
58. See the severe strictures in Clifton, *Pokagons*, 75–83.
59. Sorin to Moreau, March 20, 1843, AGEN. This money came through Moreau from one Sorin identifies only as a "*bien cher confrère*" in Le Mans, perhaps from Father Narcisse Hupier, an early member of the Auxiliary Priests. See Wack, "Notre Dame Foundation," 48, and Catta, *Moreau*, 2: 73–75.

"Several [local] families have already expressed a strong desire to send us their children. But by ourselves we simply do not have the capacity. Do you think, Monsieur Vicar General, the bishop would be able to help us a little this coming summer? . . . I believe that even $3,000 would cover most of the expenses we would incur in implementing that part of the plan I shall soon submit to the bishop."[60] Over succeeding weeks Sorin carefully priced the materials necessary for the proposed building and concluded the total would amount to about $3,080. Add to this figure "$200 for the architect and at least $600 to pay workers needed, besides our brothers, to construct ledges, doorways, stairways, and a little bell-tower, and, *voila*, you have already spent $3,880, and I have not mentioned painting, etc."[61]

So for the moment construction of the *collège* had to be held in suspension. Sorin nevertheless moved smartly on another initiative. The only accommodation available at Sainte-Marie-des-Lacs for the community, and the only place in the immediate area where Catholic services were conducted, was Badin's run-down log chapel, hardly more commodious or more secure from inclement weather than a large hut would have been. Once the eight Holy Cross men had settled into their new home—Father Sorin had said Mass there for the first time on the feast of St. Andrew, November 30[62]—they made the ground floor of the chapel their residence while the attic continued to function, as it had during the tenure of DeSeille and Petit, as a little parish church, "although it was open to all the winds."[63] This situation was clearly intolerable on several fronts, and Sorin determined to alleviate it at least temporarily by constructing another facility a little farther east up the bank from the lake, "a suitable place in which the Christians of the area might assemble." Once a new church was completed, the space made available in the Badin chapel could be converted to some other use, like a carpenter shop.[64] At the beginning of that harsh December, therefore, "an appeal was made to all the Catholics [of the area]. But what could be expected of people so poor?" Over the three weeks before Christmas "trees enough were cut down and hauled to the place to put up a building forty-six feet by twenty. On the day appointed, the [local] men assembled and raised the walls of the new temple."

60. Sorin to Martin, December 13, 1842, AGEN.

61. Sorin to Martin, January 31, 1843, AGEN. Breakdown of the cost of material: $1,000 for the foundation, $1,250 for bricks, $200 for glass, $250 for wood, $200 for limestone and iron-work; and $180 for finished steel, equal $3,080.

62. Sorin to Moreau, December 5, 1842, quoted in Moreau, *Circular Letters*, 1: 60.

63. Sorin, *Chronicles*, 24.

64. See Schlereth, *Notre Dame*, 10–12. Fire destroyed the original Badin chapel. A replica was put up on the site in 1906, wherein the remains of Petit, Deseille, and Badin himself are interred.

However, "the efforts of their liberality," Sorin observed with some sarcasm, "did not go beyond that."[65]

Thus it was that the new year of 1843 began with the shell of the half-finished log church standing forlorn amidst the snows of Sainte-Marie-des-Lacs. But this disappointment was not enough to leave Edward Sorin disconsolate. He had plenty to do and plenty of reason to feel satisfied that even at its inception his ministry was needed and appreciated. Aside from overseeing the construction of the new church, planning the *collège,* and peremptorily taking charge of the Pokagons, he was also the busy missionary tending to the spiritual wants of the Catholics settled in and around South Bend—a circuit rider as he had been at St. Peter's, but now on a much more extended scale.[66] None of these occupations, however, distracted him from his determination to reunite the Holy Cross community as soon as possible.

Brothers Vincent and Anselm were still teaching school in Vincennes, and their colleagues from the original colony, Joachim and Lawrence, together with seven or eight novices and a postulant, still lingered at Black Oak Ridge—all of them under the titular authority of Father Chartier, himself technically a novice.[67] Bishop Hailandière for his part wanted the brothers to remain in their original assignments indefinitely, wanted indeed to have their novitiate established at St. Peter's or in any event at a place close to Vincennes, so that he could more easily exert his control over them. But Father Sorin was having none of it. "Please be our mediator with the bishop," he appealed to Vicar General Martin, who, Sorin reminded him, had always understood how important it was to maintain the unity of "our little family" and how "deeply inconvenient is a separation of this kind. . . . Can you not make the bishop understand that I cannot under any circumstances consent to his wishes and that it pains me to witness his Excellency *bickering* and *quibbling* in a situation in which he would do honor to himself by an act of generosity."[68]

---

65. Sorin, *Chronicles,* 30–31.

66. See Sorin, *Chronicles,* 28–29 for a list of missions located in northwest Indiana and southern Michigan. "For five or six years the priest of St. Mary of the Lake was accustomed to visit several places in the neighborhood at stated times and to say Mass for the people." This pastoral activity was carried on as far away as Kalamazoo, Michigan, in the diocese of Detroit, to whose bishop, Pierre Lefèvre, Sorin wrote on March 16, 1843 (AGEN): "By the authorization of Monseigneur, the bishop of Vincennes, I have already visited several congregations in your diocese; if your Excellency cannot give them a priest of their own diocese, I shall do for them all that I do for those places directly dependent on me."

67. See chapter 6, above. Klawitter, *Adapted to the Lake,* 348, lists Chartier as a novice, though this designation was perhaps too generous.

68. Sorin to Martin, January 31, 1843, AGEN.

Distance, it seems, had not made hearts grow fonder, nor had the passage of time resolved the disagreement over the brothers' allegiance that had soured the relationship between Hailandière and Sorin from the first. The two men differed on an important matter of principle, though they often gave expression to it over relatively mundane concerns. When Sorin asked to be compensated for ill-defined "expenses" incurred at St. Peter's, Hailandière (or his agent) countered by demanding detailed statements of monies received and spent by Holy Cross.[69] And sometimes the disputes became simply petty, as to whether, for instance, the bishop had given or only loaned the wagon the Holy Cross men had used on their journey north. But on the issue of reuniting the community at Sainte-Marie-des-Lacs, Sorin would brook no compromise, and he probably took a certain perverse satisfaction in reporting to Vincennes that "Brother Anselm complains about the unwholesomeness of his [and Brother Vincent's] rooms. I am very anxious about their health."[70]

Luck was with him. Father Chartier—postulant one day and local superior the next—soon enraged the bishop by asserting his own prerogatives with regard to the governance of the brothers. At the end of January, Sorin wrote blandly to the vicar general that he was "pained to learn that Monsieur Chartier had so forgotten himself as to claim a commission he did not have. Nevertheless I want to believe that he acted so out of an excess of zeal rather than out of bad will. I still hope that he may prove useful to us."[71] Indeed he did, and, given the fluidity of the situation, in a manner not altogether exceptional. Restive and unconventional like so many missionaries who served on the American frontier, he simply drifted away from Hailandière's jurisdiction and, in so doing, gave Sorin the perfect excuse to summon northward the now priestless community in southern Indiana.[72]

This second exodus of Holy Cross began in mid-February, 1843, and lasted two weeks. There were eleven of them—Brothers Vincent, Lawrence, and Joachim together with six novices and two postulants. As a sop to Hailandière, Brother Anselm, to his immense sorrow, was left behind to continue teaching school in Vincennes, and so left as well to the not-so-tender mercies of the often mean-

---

69. Sorin to Martin, January 5, 1843, and Sorin to Hailandière, April (?), 1843, AGEN.

70. Sorin to Martin, January 31, 1843, AGEN.

71. Sorin to Martin, January 31, 1843, AGEN. Sorin observed later (*Chronicles,* 21) that Chartier "was a man of talent but too hot-headed."

72. Sorin's explanation to Father Moreau was somewhat ambiguous: "Consequent to events completely unrelated to the community, Monsieur Chartier retired from the diocese. His residence for four months at St. Peter's at least allowed me to come here and pass the winter, which I could not have done without him." Sorin to Moreau, March 20, 1843, AGEN.

spirited bishop.[73] Preparations for the journey showed that the community had prospered modestly during the sixteen months spent at St. Peter's. "Our mode of conveyance," one of the novices reported, "was a large wagon made under the direction of Brother Lawrence [which] contained our beds, provisions, and four trunks well filled with kitchen apparatus, our load in all amounting to near three thousand pounds weight. The wagon was drawn by four large horses. Besides that we drove on foot eight head of large working [sic] cattle," while a frisky dog named Azore loped along ahead of them.[74] They arrived at Sainte-Marie on February 27—it was Mardi Gras—hale and hearty enough, except for a couple of cases of frostbite. The joy of reunion was expressed in many ways, not least in the work resumed on the church in order to complete it in time for the brothers' patronal feast, March 19. "Our dear Brothers," Sorin wrote Moreau next day, "have arrived from St. Peter's, full of health and joy and devotion.... I had told them of my desire to see them [here] for the feast of St. Joseph, and indeed they are here. Yesterday we all together celebrated the feast of our glorious patron in our new church of *logs,* where we said Holy Mass for the first time."[75]

THE SPRING MELT, once the high waters receded, revealed that the lakes on the property were indeed separate, divided only by a stretch of marshland, but by then plural had already given way to singular.[76] From the beginning Father Sorin called the mission Notre-Dame-du-Lac rather than Sainte-Marie-des-Lacs. The distinction between the titles accorded the Virgin meant nothing, except no doubt as a way of underscoring a connection with Notre-Dame-de-Sainte-Croix in Le Mans. But to disregard cavalierly topographical reality may have said something about the masterful temperament of him who quite consciously did so. "The more I reflect upon it," Sorin wrote six weeks after his arrival, "the more convinced I become that Heaven, out of love and mercy, has designs for this apostolate of ours, which from now on will be called the apostolate of Notre Dame du Lac."[77] By 1855, when the marshes had finally been drained, the two little lakes had already received the names they have borne ever since, St. Mary and St. Joseph.

---

73. For poignant examples of Brother Anselm's distress, see his letters to Sorin of July 26 and October 26, 1843, quoted in Klawitter, ed., *Adapted to the Lake,* 30–35.

74. Brother John (Frederick Steber?) to Moreau, February 28 (?), 1843, quoted in Klawitter, ed., *Adapted to the Lake,* 21–24, and in Morin, *From France,* 173–176.

75. Sorin to Moreau, March 20, 1843, AGEN, and Sorin, *Chronicles,* 31.

76. See the discussion in Morin, *From France,* 195.

77. Sorin to Martin, January 5, 1843, AGEN. It seems appropriate from this point to omit the hyphens required in the French spelling.

chapter eight

The American Way

T HE HOUSE AT WHICH EDWARD SORIN AND HIS FOUR
companions had arrived on that late November day in 1842
was the third built in South Bend by Alexis Coquillard. The
first, put up in 1824 when he was twenty-nine years old, had been a rude if relatively large log cabin. Here he had brought his bride, Françoise Comparet, and
from here he watched over the trading post he had opened only a short distance
away. Seven years later he and Françoise moved to a new frame house nearby, and
here their only child, a son named Theodore, was born. They moved again in 1839,
this time a city block or so north to a handsome, commodious brick dwelling located on the thoroughfare by then (and still) called Michigan Street.[1]

These domestic changes told a typically American tale of upward mobility.
Coquillard's first enterprise, as agent for John Jacob Aster's American Fur Company, had depended upon the trade with Indian hunters and trappers practically
monopolized for generations by men of French or French-Canadian stock, most
of whom had Indian blood as well. When Coquillard established his trading post
in 1824, virtually the only other whites in the vicinity were in fact *métis* who
bore gallic names like his own: Pierre Navarre, François Comparet—his wife's
brother—and Joseph Bertrand, who had a small settlement named for him five
or six miles down the St. Joseph from the river's south bend. Not that Coquillard

---

1. Coquillard, "Alexis Coquillard," 30–31. See also 28, where a photograph of the third house is
reproduced. Wack, "Notre Dame Foundation," 35, inappropriately calls this house a "cabin" and Coquillard himself "a French-American trapper."

for his part could have been labeled an interloper, seeing that he had been born in Detroit and belonged to a family that had worked the fur trade across the Great Lakes region since the seventeenth century.

By the end of the 1820s, however, that business was waning fast. As the local native Americans were gradually and then more swiftly dispossessed of their hunting grounds and white farmers began to press in ever-swelling numbers into the St. Joseph valley, bartering for furs became an increasingly problematic way to make a living. True enough, the earliest Anglo of note to settle in South Bend, Lathrop Taylor, also came originally, in 1827, as an Indian trader, but he, like Coquillard, soon had to face up to the demands of rapidly changing times. They did so with genuine éclat.

Alexis Coquillard continued to maintain a cordial if somewhat sternly paternal relationship with the dwindling Indian population; it was said that Potowatomis who came to seek his counsel or financial help often spent the night sleeping in the big porch that stretched across the rear of Coquillard's brick house. But simultaneously he shifted his priorities with an eye to the future, which rendered his former enterprise marginal at most. His trading post—as did Taylor's—evolved into a general store. Both of them began methodically to buy up federal lands, ceded by the Indians, on either side of the river, at the standard price of $1.25 an acre. When in 1830 the ingress of immigrants warranted the organization of a new civil entity, St. Joseph County, the relevant negotiations were carried out in Coquillard's house; indeed, for some years his residence was for all practical purposes the hub of civic activity. The next year, 1831, Coquillard and Taylor, as proprietors, had the village platted, donating numerous lots for county use as well as for space for schools, for a courthouse, jail, and cemetery, and for Methodist, Presbyterian, United Brethren, and Catholic churches. House lots sold for as high as $40 and as low as $4. The final step in setting up a conventional polity was to locate the county seat at South Bend—called Southold at first—and to secure this concession a bond valued at $3,000 was offered by the town's residents, $600 of it pledged by Alexis Coquillard and $500 by Lathorp Taylor. These arrangements were in due course endorsed by the Indiana legislature.[2] In 1833, 200 people lived in South Bend in twenty brick and frame houses; they were served by two physicians, two lawyers, one newspaper, and three "mercantile stores."[3]

---

2. Coquillard, "Alexis Coquillard," 26–30, and Howard, *St. Joseph County*, 1: 155–176.

3. See Dean R. Esslinger, "The Urbanization of South Bend's Immigrants, 1850–1880" (unpublished doctoral dissertation, University of Notre Dame, 1972), 21.

By 1840 the population of the town had grown nearly fivefold and that of the county as a whole stood at 6,500.[4] Coquillard was active in almost every phase of the area's development. He and Taylor, for instance, were instrumental in securing for South Bend a branch of the state bank of Indiana.[5] In accord with the economic realities of the era, Coquillard was particularly anxious to take advantage of the South Bend's location on a navigable river like the St. Joseph. The projects he initiated, however, bore at best mixed results. His plan to institute regular shipments of commodities—flour especially—by flatboat down the river to Lake Michigan was eventually implemented and expanded by others,[6] while his scheme to forge a canal between the St. Joseph and the headwaters of the Kankakee, the venerable portage route to the west, came to nothing. Yet he seldom overlooked a chance to turn an honest dollar. Early on he controlled the ferries across the St. Joseph, and in 1837, when the first bridge was built over the river, it belonged to him and to Lathrop Taylor. And, frustrated as Coquillard may have been in some of his endeavors, he was always ready to seize upon other opportunities. He inspired and helped to finance construction of a dam on the St. Joseph and the digging of a race on the west bank, designed to exploit the potential of waterpower. Indeed, Coquillard's own three mills (two flour, one saw), thus made productive, may well have defined the economy of this midwestern community until, later in the century, steam-driven machinery dictated a shift away from the river and the advent of industrial giants with memorable names like Studebaker, Oliver, and Singer.

Edward Sorin was never intimate with Alexis Coquillard.[7] The two of them maintained a warily mutual respect until Coquillard's sudden and untimely death in 1855.[8] It may have been that they were too much alike, both strong-willed and

---

4. See J. D. B. DeBow, ed., *Statistical View of the United States, . . . being a Compendium of the Seventh Census* (Washington, D.C., 1854), 230. For Coquillard's later relations with the local Indians, see Edmunds, *The Potawatomis*, 266–274.

5. Howard, *St. Joseph County*, 1: 409–410.

6. See Esslinger, "Urbanization," 20–21, and John Joseph Lyon, "The Pioneer Farmer and the Settlement of St. Joseph County, Indiana, 1830–1851" (unpublished master's dissertation, University of Notre Dame, 1955), 61–64.

7. There is only one passing reference to Coquillard in Sorin, *Chronicles*, 175–176, a rather grudging acknowledgment of his civic importance.

8. See Coquillard, "Alexis Coquillard," 42, quoting the local newspaper, *The St. Joseph Register* for January 9, 1855: "The sad disaster [the destruction by fire of one of Coquillard's mills] had an unexpectedly tragic termination. . . . Mr. Coquillard was examining the ruins of his mill . . . and accidentally fell from a beam on which he was walking, striking with his whole weight on the front part of his skull, crushing it in, so that he lived but an hour." He was sixty years old at the time of his death.

self-directed, to have become close friends. Coquillard was moderately helpful to the fledgling Notre Dame du Lac—for example, in the spring of 1843 he offered to supply laborers to help bring down the excessively high waters of the lakes[9]—but he had many irons in the fire and, though a Catholic, he had a position to maintain among an élite which was increasingly Anglo and Protestant. It would seem that Françoise Coquillard—"Aunt Fannie" to many of the townspeople—took a more direct interest in the doings at Notre Dame than did her husband.[10]

Sorin for his part may well have harbored some qualms about the Coquillards. Benjamin Coquillard, who at his brother's urging had settled in South Bend in 1829, operated a tavern which, on the hard-drinking frontier, was an establishment routinely viewed with suspicion by any missionary priest. But in this instance there was an added and most peculiar feature: Benjamin struck up a friendship with an itinerant Methodist preacher who organized his first Sunday school in, of all places, the Coquillard taproom. This bizarre ecumenical event occurred long before Sorin arrived in the area, but, as his abhorrence of the Protestant clergy ran like a refrain through his early correspondence—"ministers who are nothing more than ignorant impostors" in agreement only in "their common hatred of the slaves of superstition at N. D. du Lac," ministers who proclaimed from the pulpit "that the Pope of Rome had already sent Father Sorin ninety thousand dollars and that he would send another ten to make the even number"[11]—it might, even if only heard as an anecdote, have raised questions in his mind about the Coquillards' firmness in the faith. More troubling still, especially to a priest fresh from France, was the fact that a lodge of Freemasons had been founded in 1842 in Alexis Coquillard's very house, with Alexis himself a charter member.[12]

Yet despite whatever reservations he may have entertained about them, the Coquillards provided Edward Sorin with a useful model. Tall, burly, fair-haired Alexis and his small, dark, vivacious wife, both of whom spoke English fluently, had risen to the top of a largely Anglo-Protestant community. They had done so by adjusting to rapidly evolving economic circumstances and, no less, by a willingness to take risks and to make compromises. They combined a zest for making money with a stern commitment to civic and political duty and a lively social

---

9. Sorin to Martin, May 19, 1843, AGEN.

10. See Sorin, *Chronicles*, 88–89.

11. Sorin to Dupont, May 10, 1843, and Sorin to Bouvier, November 17, 1843, AGEN. See also Sorin, *Chronicles*, 25.

12. Coquillard, "Alexis Coquillard," 24, 41. The membership dues for the lodge were set at 12 and ½ cents a month.

conscience. Theirs in microcosm was the story of America expanding ever westward, when it seemed that no target was beyond reach, no secular dream impossible to fulfill. During the eighteen years between the Coquillards' arrival in South Bend and that of Father Sorin, the backwoods had given way to a bustling community, strongly agricultural, to be sure,[13] but with an increasingly robust industrial element as well. Indeed, the men of Holy Cross had come into northwest Indiana at a momentous cusp of time: the Indians and their primitive culture were gone, and a rambunctious, individualistic, capitalist civilization had just passed through its birth pangs. More than 200,000 bushels of corn and more than 150,000 bushels of wheat and barley grown in the county annually, along with the nurturing of 10,000 swine and a similar number of sheep and cattle, undergirded the new market economy, but flourishing also were the flour mills and the two distilleries which produced 10,000 gallons of whisky and the blast-furnaces up the river a few miles from South Bend—at the settlement soon to be called Mishawaka—which forged each year upwards of 700 tons of locally mined iron-ore. Though many jobs were seasonal, a sixty-five-hour work week was the norm. A farm-laborer could earn $10.50 a month, with board, a female domestic $.90 a week, and a carpenter $1.30 a day. A yard of seersucker cost $.28, a pound of bacon $.15, and eggs a penny apiece. During 1837, a year of severe economic depression nationwide, St. Joseph County had spent $210.50 on poor relief.[14]

Alexis Coquillard, French-Catholic-*métis* trapper turned American entrepreneur, had witnessed all this development, had helped mightily to shape it even as he had shared in its ups and downs. Honors and tribute were paid to his achievements during his lifetime, and when he died the funeral cortège was composed of two hundred carriages stretched out over a mile.[15] Edward Sorin could hardly have failed to ponder how this new land had opened seemingly boundless opportunity to a man much like himself, a forceful, ambitious, risk-taking man. He may well have recalled from his school days the scraps of a couple of Latin maxims: *Carpe diem!* and *Si alii, cur non ego?* If others, like Coquillard, had seized the chance America had given them to succeed, why should not he? And especially so since his optimism and aspirations were rooted in an ardor the worldly

---

13. A few years later (1850) there were 847 farms in St. Joseph County, valued at more than $1,500,000. See DeBow, ed., *Compendium of the Seventh Census*, 232.

14. See Robert A. Margo, "The Labor Force in the Nineteenth Century," Historical Paper no. 40, National Bureau of Economic Research (Cambridge, Mass., 1992), 23–24, 62, and compare the figures in Lyon, "Pioneer Farmer," 36, 48, 58–59, with those in DeBow, *Compendium of the Seventh Census*, 164, 232–235.

15. Coquillard, "Alexis Coquillard," 42–43.

could never match and were sustained, as he firmly believed, by the special favor of the Virgin Mary. "The road to America," he had written in the first flush of enthusiasm over his assignment to the Indiana missions, "seems clearly to be for me the road to heaven. . . . I long now only for my dear brothers in America. There is my fatherland, there the center of all my affections and the object of all my godly thoughts."[16]

And yet the parallel must not be pushed too far. At the time he settled in South Bend Alexis Coquillard represented the sixth generation of his family to have made a living in the rough and tumble of the North American fur trade. It was not so great an adjustment for him to accommodate to hard-driving, individualist Yankee standards as it would have been for a young priest only two years removed from Basile Moreau's cloister in Le Mans. Edward Sorin had sprung from a social structure which superficially appeared similar to the one he now had to adapt to, a structure overwhelmingly rural, yet possessing a vital urban component. But the differences between the two amounted almost to a clash of cultures. The agricultural rhythms governing life in Mayenne and Sarthe were rooted in ancient and immutable tradition, a strong commitment to communal enterprise, and a hierarchical system of land-tenure that emphasized familial continuity over generations and even centuries. In booming northwest Indiana it was far otherwise. "The Americans have arrived but as yesterday on the territory which they inhabit," Alexis de Toqueville had observed only a decade before Sorin and his companions made their way into the St. Joseph valley, "and they have already changed the whole order of nature to their own advantage. . . . In America . . . every man owns the ground he tills. . . . America . . . stands alone in this respect." Even so, that uniquely independent American farmer remained ever alert to other economic prospects: "The cultivation of the ground promises an almost certain result to his exertions, but a slow one." As likely as not, the "active, enlightened, and free man . . . sells his plot, leaves his dwelling, and embarks on some hazardous but lucrative calling." The reason for such impatience, and for the social volatility that followed upon it, lay beyond the reach of an economic rationale; it could only be understood "in democratic times," Toqueville had concluded, by "what is most unstable, in the midst of the instability of everything, . . . the heart of man," to which the American experiment had offered unprecedented scope and latitude.[17]

---

16. Sorin to Hailandière, n.d. [summer 1841], AGEN.

17. Alexis de Tocqueville, *Democracy in America*, 2 vols., ed. by Phillips Bradley (New York, 1945), 2: 154–157, 186–188.

Edward Sorin was not a deep thinker like Toqueville, not given, as was his compatriot and contemporary, to cosmic musings. But as a priest he also had to seek out the hidden places in "the heart of man," in whatever context he might find it. Salvation of souls was his business, gospel and grace, as he defined these terms, were the wares he had on offer. For him they were endowed with an eternal worth that overrode any distinction of space or time. But they came garbed in the vestments peculiar to the spirituality—regimented, austere, sentimental, centered in devotion to the Virgin Mary—that characterized the revival of Catholicism in post-Napoleonic France. Sorin, after all, was a disciple of Moreau, as Moreau had been of Mollevaut.[18] Catholic though he was, Alexis Coquillard, who signaled his Americanization by cheerfully joining the Freemasons, carried no such psychic baggage.

Yet that same French spirituality, born out of travail and persecution, was undergirded by a sublime confidence in its capacity to overcome any challenge, and, thus armed, even an émigré priest, struggling to master a foreign tongue and to accommodate to unfamiliar customs and values, might feel at home in America, might share the buoyant vision of a nation on the march. Father Sorin, like his new countrymen, did not doubt for a moment that he had been offered an opportunity to accomplish great things in a future which held nothing but promise. His "manifest destiny," however, did not rest upon the secular ground of an ever-expanding frontier for entrepreneurs to exploit, but upon an unshakable confidence that he was doing God's work, that he was in the hands of the Providence he never ceased to invoke. "Ah," Sorin wrote in the depths of the grim winter of 1842–43, "if heaven grants our prayers a great work will be done here under the auspices of our august Mother. . . . My only fear is to spoil the work of God by trying to advance it by means that are too human. To God, therefore, and to Mary, I confide all my desires and all my needs. *In Domino confido, non confundar.*"[19] A few months and several setbacks later he added, more prosaically: "Happily, our hopes do not rest upon men."[20] Such uncomplicated trust in divine beneficence could well lead to absurd exaggeration: hardly had the springtime come when Sorin was proclaiming that "as a *collège* [Notre dame du Lac] has attracted the attention of the whole country,"[21] when in fact there was no college, not yet. But that same confidence carried him through all sorts of adversity and

---

18. See chapter 2, above.

19. "I trust in the Lord, lest I should fall into confusion." Sorin to Martin, January 31, 1843, AGEN.

20. Sorin to Moreau, March 20, 1843, AGEN.

21. Sorin to Dupont, May 10, 1843, AGEN.

disappointment, so that his splendid optimism never wavered, and as the years passed he framed his own version of the American dream.

An early indication of this ever-sanguine approach to his new surroundings was the manner in which he dealt with a religious milieu far removed from the one he had grown up in. Though Sorin had encountered instances of tepidity and even of unbelief and anti-clericalism in Parcé-sur-Sarthe and Le Mans, he had been acquainted with few if any Protestants there, and certainly the multiplicity of organized sects that flourished even in a village as small as South Bend astonished him. At first their bitterness toward him and his apostolate he returned in kind. "The Protestant spirit," he wrote toward the end of 1843, "is very far from diminished in our midst. On the contrary, the very fact of our arrival seems to have reanimated the fervor of the sectarians, namely the Methodists, Presbyterians, Baptists, Episcopalians, Universalists, etc., etc. About the only thing upon which they can agree is their common hatred for the poor idolaters at N. D. du Lac."[22] But within a few months he recorded an event which showed, if nothing else, unbending high spirits in confrontation with "the sectarians."

> Last Sunday I preached before a very large crowd which did not include a single Catholic. When we arrived here, fifteen months ago, we were greeted by most people as great enemies. We had come in effect into the heart of Protestantism. Catholics were described as a sect of the superstitious and absurd, even more vicious than gullible. Now the veil has lifted, the truth has forced its way through! Not only have the locals grown accustomed to seeing priests and religious in their midst; now they want to listen to us. God grant that soon they will love us! Oh, how admirable is the future of N. D. du Lac in this country heretofore populated by savages, infidels, and Protestants.[23]

It may be that this account contained a measure of exaggeration, but, if so, it was that of an unflappable American optimist.

THE MEMBER OF THE COQUILLARD FAMILY probably best known to Edward Sorin was Alexis the younger, Benjamin's teenage son, who had acted as guide to the Holy Cross men on the day of their arrival in South Bend and who may well have been one of the first students enrolled at Notre

---

22. Sorin to Bouvier, November 17, 1843, AGEN.
23. Sorin to "Messieurs" of the Propagation of the Faith, February 2, 1844, AGEN.

Dame.[24] In order for him to achieve that status, however, the *collège* first had to be established. In handing over the property at Sainte-Marie-des-Lacs, Bishop Hailandière had imposed upon Sorin a two-year deadline for the school's opening—the end, that is, of 1844—though he hoped for its accomplishment even sooner. So did the elder Alexis Coquillard and other civic boosters who were urging Holy Cross to establish the *collège* in South Bend itself and promising ample financial support if this were done. "I concede," Sorin observed, "that this proposal would bring a considerable advantage to the town and a genuine saving for the mission; for in place of two churches"—South Bend had as yet no Catholic church—"one would suffice, a simple wooden chapel which would serve also the original needs of our novitiate. Yet I would agree to this plan only if we find it absolutely impossible to build at the Lake."[25]

It seems unlikely that Sorin gave more than a passing nod to this overture.[26] His determination to locate the center of the Holy Cross mission on the grounds that had so enthralled him at his first sight of them remained unwavering from the beginning. And, from a practical point of view, the 524 acres at the lakes were already in his hands, if not yet the formal title to them.[27] Straitened as he was financially, his sanguine temperament nevertheless pressed him forward. "Obviously," he wrote at the beginning of 1843, "this is the time to build, and I am reluctant to believe that we cannot begin something with the $1,500 we possess."[28] That sum, however, was soon diminished. Once the transfer of the community from southern Indiana had been completed, and furnishings, animals, and "indispensable tools" had been purchased for the new site, "there remained in hand," Sorin noted ruefully, "scarcely 5,000 francs ($1,000)." To construct the log church had cost $240.[29] So, as the long harsh winter drew finally to a close, "our

---

24. The evidence is ambiguous. The student-records speak of "Theodore Alexis Coquillard," and Wack ("Notre Dame Foundation," 62) concludes they refer to the elder Alexis's son, Theodore, who, however, was only seven years old in 1843. See also Hope, *Notre Dame*, 54.

25. Sorin to Martin, January 5, 1843, AGEN.

26. In fact South Bend did not have a Catholic church of its own until 1853. See Thomas T. McAvoy, "The History of the Catholic Church in the South Bend Area" (South Bend, 1953), no pagination [18–19].

27. See Sorin to Hailandière, April 28, 1843, AGEN: "As to the deed your Excellency intends to put in our name, I desire it to be made out in a form of a pure and simple donation in favor of the societies we compose (although both groups hold all in common), that is to say, the Auxiliary Priests of Sainte-Croix and the Brothers of St. Joseph, represented here respectively by Edward Frederick Sorin and Jean Pieau [Brother Vincent], without privilege of one of these groups over the other."

28. Sorin to Martin, January 5, 1843, AGEN.

29. Sorin to "Messieurs" of the Propagation of the Faith, February 2, 1844, AGEN.

resources," Sorin told Bishop Hailandière, "amount to the $500 you have passed along to us [from the funds collected by Father Delaune], the $117 the brothers brought from St. Peter's, and the 4,000 francs ($800) Father Rector [Moreau] sent us three weeks ago," plus perhaps several hundred dollars still left over from the winter's exertions, which Sorin discreetly decided not to mention to the bishop. Against this total sum of between $1,500 and $2,000 stood debts of $500, $300 of which had to be paid by the August of 1843.[30]

Such slender means made the construction of a college building problematic at best, when so shrewd an observer as Alexis Coquillard estimated the cost could run as high as $10,000. Bricks and lumber were nevertheless purchased, and, with the coming of spring, architectural plans were submitted both at Notre Dame and at Vincennes. The bishop determined that the latter set, drawn up by an émigré named Marcile, should be accepted, a decision Sorin, after a predictably edgy exchange over the costs involved, finally agreed to.[31] To some extent he was moved to do so by the bishop's commitment that the architect would come to Notre Dame in person to supervise the project and would bring with him some skilled workmen. "We accept with great pleasure," Sorin wrote at the end of April, "the masons your Excellency proposes to send us at such advantageous terms."[32] Yet no one should fail to realize that "the situation is very serious. We will need freed up fifteen to twenty thousand francs [$3,000–4,000] over some months in order to build our [*collège*]. . . . We are going to begin in any case; we will pay what we can up to the month of August with whatever comes to us from France."[33]

But, as spring changed to summer with the brothers busy putting in a crop and clearing more woodland, Marcile, "unfaithful to his promises," failed to appear, and Sorin faced the prospect that "the season for building" would pass by with nothing accomplished. So, partly out of exasperation and partly out a desperate need for space, he directed that the matériel already on hand should be used to put up quickly on the shore of St. Mary's Lake a more modest, multipurpose brick building of two stories which could (and eventually did) serve as a dormitory, a bakery, a kitchen and dining hall, and even as a place to hold classes.[34] At the same time a couple of crude additions were tacked on to the rear of the

---

30. Sorin to Hailandière, n.d. [April 1843], AGEN. For Delaune's collection see chapter 6, above.

31. Sorin to Hailandière, n.d. [April 1843], AGEN.

32. Sorin to Hailandière, April 28, 1843, AGEN.

33. Sorin to Moreau, April 10, 1843, AGEN.

34. See Sorin, *Chronicles,* 34, and Schlereth, *Notre Dame,* 14–16 (with photographs on the latter page). This is the building, with two more stories added shortly afterward, that came to be called Old College. It still stands on the Notre Dame campus and is still in use.

new church, which gave it, at ninety feet by twenty, the peculiar appearance of a log tower set on its side.

Such unpretentious expansion was by no means a luxury. There were already eighteen men in permanent residence at Notre Dame du Lac, and room had to be provided as well for the hoped-for boarding students. Moreover, the community was shortly to be expanded by a second infusion of personnel from France. Since the summer of 1842, at St. Peter's, Father Sorin had been petitioning Le Mans for reinforcements. The following May 16 he received "a letter from Sainte-Croix [saying that] two priests, two brothers, and three sisters are being sent to us."[35] Aware some weeks earlier of Moreau's intentions—though in the end the Founder altered the composition of the colony somewhat, assigning to it two priests, a seminarian, a brother, and four Marianite sisters—Sorin decided to dispatch an emissary to accompany the party to Indiana.

"This dear Deputy of our forests," as he called him,[36] was the same Brother John who, at Black Oak Ridge, had served as interpreter of Sorin's early sermons. There was by this time less need for the young Englishman to furnish that particular service, but Sorin continued to hold a high opinion of his gifts and of his potential usefulness to the community. "Our dear Brother John," Sorin rhapsodically described him, "my catechist and my companion on the [parochial] missions, our English master, indeed I can say our *everything*." Since he joined the community at St. Peter's "he has not ceased to render us the greatest services." He has been "for the whole house the object of our most beautiful aspirations. And for me, if I may say so, he is the object of my hopes. . . . I have no one here so close to me and who understands me better." Who more appropriate than this confidant to serve as guide for those about to depart Notre-Dame-de-Sainte-Croix for Notre Dame du Lac? "In a few weeks," Sorin assured Moreau, "[Brother John] will be in your arms; and the joy you will have in pressing him to your heart will amply compensate for the sacrifice we must make in allowing him to depart."[37]

This well-laid plan went awry, without, however, serious mishap, except perhaps to the enigmatic Brother John. Unaccountably he did not arrive at Le Mans in time to join the departing company, which sailed from Le Havre on June 3 and, after a voyage marked by the usual bouts of boredom and seasickness, landed in New York on July 11. Samuel Byerley and his wife, still the good angels for weary missionaries in transit, welcomed them to their spacious home and, after they

35. Sorin to Martin, May 19, 1843, AGEN.

36. Sorin to Sister Francis Xavier, May 11, 1843, AGEN.

37. Sorin to Moreau, April 10, 1843, AGEN. See also chapter 6, note 26, above.

had rested for some days (and had been suitably impressed by the magnificence of the city), saw them off along the water route to Detroit, where they were kindly received by the local bishop, the Belgian-born Pierre-Paul Lefèvre.[38] On the eve of their scheduled departure overland for South Bend, however, one of the priests, François Cointet, accidentally fell and suffered a painful injury to his back. The upshot was that five of the party set out, leaving Cointet behind to recuperate, along with the brother and one of the sisters to look after him. These three eventually followed, so that by the middle of August the newly enlarged community, its numbers swelled to twenty-six, was intact.[39] A sad participant in this otherwise happy reunion was young Brother Anselm, who had come to Notre Dame to make his retreat but who then had to return sorrowfully to Vincennes, to the teaching position he hated, and to the petty persecution of Bishop Hailandière.[40] Anselm grew increasingly lonely and unhappy, and Sorin, his spiritual mentor and superior, did little to lighten his disciple's inner burden. Aware of the bishop's antipathy, Sorin did repeatedly recommend Anselm to the "paternal solicitude" of Vicar General Martin: "I wish him to eat something at four o'clock after his last class. And I don't want him in a room that is too humid."[41] But this sort of pragmatism was small consolation to Anselm, who wanted, and needed, the community life to which he had committed himself at Sainte-Croix.

Brother John, meanwhile, duly made an appearance in Le Mans, but his confrères at Notre Dame remained in the dark about his movements there and elsewhere over the succeeding months. By early November Sorin was clearly alarmed: "Brother John has not yet come," he informed Moreau. "I very much fear that he is ill. Please God that he returns home safe and sound." John did indeed return a week or so later, bringing with him a fifth sister and a handsome bronze bell, a gift to the mission from Father Moreau.[42] His health seemed satisfactory, but, for whatever reasons, his alienation from the Holy Cross community had plainly

---

38. For a detailed account of the journey see M. Eleanore Brosnahan, *On the King's Highway* (New York, 1931), 16–26.

39. M. Georgia Costin, *Priceless Spirit: A History of the Sisters of the Holy Cross, 1841–1893* (Notre Dame, Ind., 1994), 11–14. Sorin wrote formally to the bishop of Detroit, thanking him for the care he gave the colony. Sorin to Lefèvre, August 20, 1843, AGEN.

40. Brother Anselm to Sorin, July 26 and October 26, 1843, in Klawitter, ed., *Adapted to the Lake*, 31–35. Hailandère commented to Sorin: "[Brother Anselm] is far from being above reproach. He appears proud to me." See Sorin to Martin, June 2, 1843, AGEN.

41. Sorin to Martin, October 9, 1843, AGEN.

42. Sorin to Moreau, November 8, 1843, AGEN. An addition, dated November 14, in another hand: "Father Superior [Sorin] met Brother John, safe and sound, at Goshen, eight leagues from here. We expect them at Notre Dame tomorrow."

begun. Perhaps in him, as in so many other missionaries, the original fires of enthusiastic devotion burned brightly for a while, too brightly to be sustained, and
then quickly withered away. Maybe the trip to Europe released within him heretofore unacknowledged ambitions and aspirations. Around this undoubtedly talented young man in any event rumors swirled for some years to come: he had
failed dismally as a teacher in Fort Wayne and Vincennes, he had gone to France
to study for the priesthood, he had left the Catholic Church and married a Protestant woman.[43] Whatever the truth may have been, before long Brother John was
gone, and his commitment to Notre Dame du Lac was all too soon only a memory. How severe a blow his withdrawal was to Edward Sorin—for whom John
had been "the object of my hopes," for whom indeed he had been *"everything"*—
can only be guessed at.

THE ELONGATED LOG CHAPEL had two stories; religious ser-
vices were conducted on the lower level, and the sisters went into residence in the
loft.[44] Here the Convent of Notre Dame du Lac remained for a heroic two years.
"Except for the fact that there was only one window and that in consequence of
the close atmosphere there was a large stock of fleas and bedbugs, they were, as
they say in America, pretty comfortable."[45] As Father Moreau had insisted—in
accord with the common Catholic practice—all the nuns bore the name Mary,
with some biblical or devotional reference added to distinguish them; thus the
first stalwart four were called Mary of the Heart of Jesus, of Calvary, of Nazareth,
and of Bethlehem, while the fifth, who had arrived later with Brother John, was
known as Sister Mary of Providence. They took charge immediately of the domestic needs of the community, including tending the cows and the poultry, and
no doubt performed such tasks much better than had been the case before, while
at the same time releasing the brothers to work in the fields and clear the woodland and to prepare for the building projects that always seemed to be in the

---

43. See Klawitter, ed., *Adapted to the Lake*, 368–369. But the "Brother John" complained of for
his "frivolity" in Brother Anselm to Sorin, December 13, 1843 (Klawitter, 38), can hardly have been the
"Brother John" who returned from France only in mid-November. Perhaps Anselm's "Brother John"
was Jeremiah Cronin (see chapter 6, note 36, above). Confusion in identification is compounded by
the suggestion (see Costin, *Priceless Spirit*, 13) that it was a "Brother James" whom Sorin sent to Le
Mans. But there is no "Brother James" to be found among the early American rosters.

44. This arrangement was later reversed, with the sisters moving to the rather more limited first
level. See Wack, "Notre Dame Foundation," 46.

45. Sorin, *Chronicles*, 33.

offing. Behind this division of labor, and indeed basic to all the community's activity, was the prospect that soon there would be a flourishing *collège* in operation at Notre Dame.

Nursing and cooking, sewing and laundering were understandably the first order of business for the sisters, who were, after all, country women, but from the moment he first asked for them to be sent to Indiana, Father Sorin had intended the nuns eventually to be teachers as well.[46] Meanwhile, as their superior, he saw to it that all the canonical formalities were observed—the sisters had a distinct ruling council of their own—and that they were given the spiritual direction called for in Moreau's constitutions.[47] On a more pragmatic level, he personally tried to help them learn English, even as he was striving to improve his own proficiency in that language.[48]

Besides the bruised Father Cointet, the male contingent of the new French colony included another priest, Théophile de Lascoux-Marivault, a seminarian in minor orders named François Gouesse, and Brother Eloi, né Jean-Marie Leray. The latter, a twenty-five-year-old farmer and locksmith, showed little aptitude for the religious life and soon left the community, leaving behind only the memory of his "ungovernable temper."[49] Father Marivault, aged thirty-four and so five years Sorin's senior, was welcome not only for the priestly service he could offer the mission but also for the likelihood, as it seemed at the time, that he could bring with him 6,000 francs ($1,200) due him out of a family trust. This benefaction, however, was challenged in the French courts and ultimately came to much less than was planned for.[50] Marivault himself soon indicated a particular interest in the apostolate to the Indians, but from the beginning Sorin found him a trouble-making and ineffective associate: "Even the savages have no better opinion of him than do the whites."[51] François Gouesse, once professed and ordained priest (1847), served the Notre Dame mission fitfully but not without effect until, by 1850, he had fallen victim to drink, the all too common curse that

---

46. Sorin to Moreau, October 21, 1841, AGEN. Sorin reiterated his position to Moreau, December 5, 1842, AGEN. Once in northern Indiana, Sorin expressed, almost guiltily, his hope to have sisters available to serve the Indians at Pokagon. See Sorin to Moreau, March 20, 1843, AGEN.

47. See Catta, *Moreau*, 1: 437–441.

48. See Costin, *Priceless Spirit,* 9–16.

49. Sorin, *Chronicles,* 33.

50. The amount eventually realized was $500. See AUND, CSCM, "Miscellany, Indiana Province, Accounts between Motherhouse and Notre Dame."

51. Sorin to Moreau, December 4–12, 1844, AGEN. Marivault eventually became a missionary to Indians in Arkansas. See Wack, "Notre Dame Foundation," 50.

afflicted the Catholic clergy in America during the nineteenth century. Afterward he was a painful thorn in Edward Sorin's side.[52]

François Cointet, by contrast, came to be a most valued aide and confidant. Only two years younger than Sorin, whom he had known well at the seminary in Le Mans, Cointet had been a country curate when one day by chance he met Basile Moreau, who shared with him a letter from Sorin filled with characteristic enthusiasm. Cointet then, after some reflection, petitioned to join the Auxiliary Priests and asked further to be assigned to the mission at Notre Dame du Lac. This request Moreau granted, and after his rough introduction to America, the young priest's gifts of mind and temperament immediately made themselves felt. Of a scholarly bent, he was a highly competent teacher, once the *collège* had begun to operate, but he was also a benign and effective parochial minister, relieving much of Sorin's burden in furnishing pastoral care to the scattered communities of Catholics in northern Indiana and southwestern Michigan.

> It was [with] the sons of the forest, the remnant of the red race passing from the plains of Indiana, and to the advanced guard of civilization, the poor Irish laborers of the railroad that [Cointet] delighted to break the bread of life. . . . Now riding at nightfall over a wide extent of country to reach some Indian wigwam, or seated in a shanty by the side of an unfinished railroad, hearing the confessions of poor Irish women, explaining the catechism to a crowd of wild ragged little children who formed a circle around him; or collecting the men at the close of the day as they returned from their hard toil, he taught them their duty as citizens and Christians. How often have their shanties by the railroads of Michigan and Indiana been converted by his presence into holy temples where the poor laborers, strengthened by the Blessed Sacrament and the consoling voice of the priest, become new beings.[53]

The interlocking system of railroads, with all its revolutionary consequences, and whose Irish workers Father Cointet so diligently ministered to, did not reach South Bend until 1851, a momentous event for the area and hardly less for Notre Dame. In the interval, the mild, self-effacing Cointet mingled solicitude for the

52. For the probability of Gouesse's drinking problem, see James T. Connelly, "Charism: Origins and History," in *Fruits of the Tree,* 3 vols. (Notre Dame, Ind., 1988–1991), 1: 111, and the authorities cited there. For Sorin's later difficulties with Gouesse, see below, chapters 14 and 15.

53. [Mary Angela Gillespie], *Life of the Rev. F. Cointet, Priest and Missionary of the Congregation of Holy Cross* (Cincinnati, 1855), 38–47. For a shorter appreciation, see Lyons, *Silver Jubliee,* 83–85.

Catholic gandy dancers with steady support, until he suddenly died in 1855, for his sometimes impetuous superior. Little wonder that Sorin, his hopes for Brother John sorely disappointed, should have been sharply struck with grief at the death of François Cointet, aged only thirty-eight years: "I was in no way prepared for it. The day I saw that Father Cointet was going to die my mind almost failed me. I still cannot get it into my head that he is really gone. Ah! would that I had gone in his place and he remained in mine! The void he has left behind grows more frightening every day."[54]

THE ORIGINAL HOLY CROSS COMMUNITY had hardly welcomed the men and women of the new colony when, out of the blue, the elusive architect from Vincennes, Monsieur Marcile, dropped into their midst, along with the two workmen Bishop Hailandière had promised. It was August 24, 1843, a date too far advanced in the year, it would have seemed, to undertake major construction. The chronic shortage of available funds was another reason to delay. Indeed, every consideration of prudence dictated that the best course was to put the project off until the spring. But Edward Sorin refused to listen. Perhaps he feared that Marcile, who was to supervise the work, might disappear again. Perhaps he felt in his bones that the time was too precious to waste, or in his heart that the Virgin wanted him to proceed forthwith. Or perhaps he was beginning to imbibe something of the American entrepreneurial spirit that had lifted Alexis Coquillard above his fellows: nothing ventured, nothing gained. "No one," Sorin mused once his decision had been made, "no one knows how to live and to manage things like the Americans." The cornerstone for the college building was laid on August 28, at which ceremony a collection netting about $200 was taken up.[55]

The risk, if that is what it was, paid handsome dividends. Monies came from Le Mans and from the Propagation of the Faith in Paris—not nearly enough, to be sure, to cover all expenditures but enough to secure credit for the remainder. What must have struck Sorin as a special intervention of Providence was the decision just at this moment of that peerless friend of Holy Cross, the prosperous Samuel Byerley, to leave New York and to settle in South Bend; he promptly loaned Notre Dame $500 and provided a line of credit for another $2,000 in the general store he opened.[56] As for matériel, there was still on hand an accumulation of lumber and bricks left over from the small building put up in the spring, and "the

---

54. Sorin to Mother Theodore, October 16, 1854, AIP.
55. Sorin, *Chronicles*, 37, 35.
56. Howard, *St. Joseph County*, 2: 623–624.

inexhaustible supply of white marl" along the banks of the lakes assured a ready stock of lime.[57]

Even the weather cooperated. A mild autumn continued deep into December, and the winter as a whole was as benign as the previous one had been severe. "The construction of our new house is going well," Sorin reported in early October. "In three weeks the roof will go on, I hope."[58] That aspiration was not quite met, occasioning a moment of anxiety. "Our house is half-covered," he wrote a month later. "It will be magnificent if we can finish it."[59] A rubbish fire on the building site caused more consternation than damage and very little delay, and the roof was duly in place before the snows came. Interior finishing, plastering, and painting were carried out at a more leisurely pace through the spring so that in time for the academic year of 1844 the first Notre Dame Main Building was completed. Due to continuing financial strictures it was somewhat smaller than Marcile's original blueprints—and Sorin's hopes—had called for: four and one half stories high, one hundred forty feet by sixty, with the central section flanked by two wings in the form of a double hammer. Attaching the two annexes to the center had to await a later day. Nevertheless the multifunctional structure was adequate in size to house the whole collegiate enterprise, from study halls, classrooms, music salon, refectory, and kitchens to dormitories, a recreation area, private rooms for faculty members, a president's office, and even an art gallery. And atop the roof perched a modest cupola which sheltered Father Moreau's bronze bell. The total cost was $6,000, "not counting our own labor. In order to finish the interior it will be necessary to spend another $800."[60]

Fortune, it is said, favors the brave. Edward Sorin's determination to build his *collège,* despite the unfavorable circumstances, had seemed foolhardy to many, but once the gamble in brick and mortar was well on its way to success, it yielded an unforeseen and remarkable consequence. "The edifice is of Brick," reported the *South Bend Free Press,* "four and a half stories high, and not inferior in point of style of structure to any colleges in the United States, and is situated upon a commanding eminence of the two picturesque and commodious Lakes, which with the River St. Joseph and the surrounding country present a most magnificent prospect."[61] Local pride then played its part, even among the non-Catholic

57. Sorin, *Chronicles,* 34, 24.

58. Sorin to Martin, October 9, 1843, AGEN.

59. Sorin to Moreau, November 8, 1843, AGEN.

60. Sorin to "Messieurs" of the Propagation of the Faith, February 2, 1844, AGEN. See also Wack, "Notre Dame Foundation," 47, and Schlereth, *Notre Dame,* 26–28.

61. *South Bend Free Press,* December 2, 1843. I owe this reference to my friend, John Conley, C.S.C.

élite. "We have found a patron," Sorin told Basile Moreau even before the Main Building was fully roofed, "a man without faith or religious principles but full of good will, who has become very devoted to us." The Honorable John Dougherty Defrees, a South Bend lawyer who sat in the Indiana state senate, was perhaps less devoted to Holy Cross than to the prospect that an institution of higher learning might indeed be about to become a reality in his constituency. However that may have been, "he has proposed," Sorin continued, "to obtain articles of incorporation for our brothers and, linked to similar recognition for our priests, all the powers of a college, that is, the right to confer all scientific degrees, like all the great colleges in the United States. . . . [We shall] enjoy the title and all the rights of a university. I would be only half-surprised if he sends us soon from the capital confirmation that this is so." Defrees was as good as his word: on January 15, 1844, the Indiana legislature granted that title and those rights to the University of Notre Dame du Lac. "We shall not fail to find a blessing here," Sorin commented. "It will be for our work a major development." But not even Edward Sorin, for all his optimism, could deny that such a lofty designation was anomalous at best. "Of course we shall not at first be prepared to justify this title thus given us. But later it cannot fail to have the most profound results for the good."[62]

Whatever may have been Senator Defrees's sentiments—or indeed whatever may have been his understanding of the word "university"—it seems unlikely that he would have put forward his bill had Father Sorin not gone ahead with his building project in the late summer of 1843. If the nay-sayers had had their way, and the *collège* had not been built, civic endorsement might have been deferred or perhaps have taken a different tack altogether. Upon such imponderables do the histories of institutions depend. The result in this case at any rate was that in the woodland of northwest Indiana a university was born, even though it was hardly more than a random collection of modest brick structures and log shacks, attended by no more than a half-dozen students, and staffed by a faculty only a few of whom spoke English with any facility. It remained to be seen whether such an institution would "have the most profound results for the good."

---

62. Sorin to Moreau, November 8, 1843, AGEN.

chapter nine

The Battle of Bertrand

WHILE EDWARD SORIN WATCHED WITH SATISFACTION the swift rise of the much-desired collegiate building, his fertile mind, during that autumn of 1843, was already plotting further expansion of the mission of Notre Dame du Lac. He knew full well that Bishop Hailandière had imposed a double condition when he gave over to Holy Cross the land at the northern extremity of his diocese: a *collège* was to be opened there and a brothers' novitiate was to be established, both within a two-year timespan. As to the need for this latter foundation, Sorin was, for once, in perfect agreement with the bishop of Vincennes, who had reasonably pointed out that, if the brothers were to fulfill their vocation in the new world, their formal training had to be seen to.[1]

In late November, just as the final section of the roof was being attached to the main building, Father Sorin withdrew from the community for some days to make a spiritual retreat. He chose to perform this religious exercise on the higher reaches of the marshy land between the lakes, which, since he insisted on considering the two bodies of water one, he habitually referred to as "the island." This was not an implausible conceit on his part, because much of the land at the entry to this elevation lay at such a low level that, during the spring melt or after heavy rains, it was often cut off by standing water and was then accessible only by boat.[2] Prayer and reflection no doubt provided the strong spiritual meat for Sorin during his retreat, but he also had energy left over to put the ax to many a tree with

1. See Sorin to Martin, June 2, 1843, AGEN.
2. See Schlereth, *Notre Dame*, 19–20.

the thought that here, once the ground was cleared, would be a perfect site for the brothers' novitiate. Indeed, he had already decided that this should be so.[3]

"The island" had in fact attracted Sorin's romantic attention many months before.

> Do you know, good Father [he had written Basile Moreau the preceding April], how we shall observe this year the month of Mary? You may recall that I told you of an island in the middle of the lake. It is there that we shall erect a modest altar which we shall adorn each day with the most beautiful [wild] flowers from the island and from along the shores of the lake, since we do not yet have a garden. On the last day of April, when all has been prepared, toward sunset we shall embark our whole family in our little canoes and paddle silently toward the object of our pious pilgrimage. Arrived at the island we shall bless it and dedicate it to our Lady under the title *the Isle of Mary of the Lake.*

Devotions, he promised, would continue through the month of May, and eventually "in honor of the Immaculate Conception and of the Seven Dolors" a shrine to the Virgin would be set up on the island and then the fourteen stations of the cross, "each of which will be enclosed in a grotto surrounded by oak trees." He concluded in the pietistic mode he so often adopted in his communications to Le Mans: "Allow me, good Father, to offer you excellent advice. When you have something close to your heart that you want for God's glory, vow a pilgrimage to St. Mary of the Lake. You will not regret it."[4]

But seven months later he had enlarged the pious possibilities offered by the island into a definite plan, and he believed his decision had secured divine endorsement. "Since I last wrote you," he told Moreau just before he retired to the island for his retreat, "the holy Virgin has given a striking sign of her protection over our little family." One of the sisters who had arrived from France in August—he did not name her[5]—had been stricken by a grievous illness. For two days the community despaired of her recovery. "Humanly speaking there was no hope for her," and Sorin spent a sorrowful night reciting the prayers for the dying over her. "Then we promised to build as soon as possible a chapel to the holy Virgin on the island which bears her name. Some moments later we had the strong hope that

---

3. Sorin, *Chronicles*, 40, and Hope, *Notre Dame*, 57.

4. Sorin to Moreau, April 10, 1843, AGEN.

5. Costin, *Priceless Spirit*, 17, says the sick nun was Sister Mary of Calvary. See also the editor's note in Sorin, *Chronicles*, 39.

[the nun] would become better, as indeed she did." Moreover, Sorin continued, we were about to lose one of the brothers to a sickness similarly severe: "During one half-hour period he thought he was dead (*il se crut mort*). Then we promised to dedicate the future chapel [on the island] to the most holy Heart of Mary. [The brother] is still bedridden, but out of danger."[6]

For Sorin these promises amounted to a solemn commitment—"a vow," he called it later.[7] Nor was there in thus swearing to honor the Virgin the slightest trace of hypocrisy or inconsistency. Marian devotion had been the core of Sorin's spirituality from his childhood, and it did not diminish as he approached old age. He liked to recall that "my first sermon, written at home in 1837, when I was a subdeacon, was on our Blessed Mother. . . . I read it all to my dear Parents before I preached it, and they seemed to be more than pleased. . . . My first love [increased] year after year." He never doubted for an instant "that the Blessed Virgin has taken this mission of the Holy Cross in America under her special protection, from its very incipiency throughout."[8]

But even as he moved to fulfill this vow made over a nun's sickbed, it was characteristic of his pragmatic temper to judge that two purposes might be achieved as well as one. The chapel on the island dedicated to our Lady could serve as the place of worship for the novices. With the main building still unfinished, however, these projects had to wait their turn; not until the beginning of June, 1844, was the cornerstone of the chapel put in place. Though immediately thereafter other distractions were such that little could be done on the island, Father Sorin's confidence in the undertaking did not flag. In mid-September he told Mother Theodore at Terre Haute that "we are building a pretty little octagonal chapel to the Blessed Virgin on the isle of Mary, and next to it a novitiate for the brothers."[9] This assertion reflected aspiration rather than fact, as did his request, a few days later, for Bishop Hailandière's authorization to bless the chapel, at that moment hardly more than a hole in the ground. But it was important that the bishop be informed also that "a very simple two-story novitiate" was going up on the same site, thus fulfilling one of the conditions Hailandière had imposed prior to the move from St. Peter's to Notre Dame. Father Sorin—such was his self-assurance—even offered to put off the dedication of these nonexistent buildings if Hailandière would deign to visit Notre Dame du Lac "before winter" and per-

---

6. Sorin to Moreau, November 8, 1843, AGEN.

7. Sorin to Moreau, June 7, 1844, AGEN. See also the ambiguous reference to it and to the "miracle" of the nun's recovery in Sorin to Moreau, December 4–12, 1844, AGEN.

8. Sorin, *Chronicles*, 308–309.

9. Sorin to Mother Theodore, September 13, 1844, AGEN.

form the ritual himself.[10] The bishop declined this invitation, which was just as well, because not till two months later did serious construction on the island get under way, and then the speed with which it was done suggests that structural quality was not a primary consideration: "In seven and a half days the walls [of the chapel] were up and eight days more sufficed to build those of the novitiate."[11] On December 8, 1844, a year and a month after Sorin's "vow," the chapel and novitiate were dedicated to "the most Holy and Immaculate Heart of Mary."[12]

THE NEW BUILDINGS on the island, once finished, may have been jerry-built structures, neither durable nor destined for long retention, but their construction, along with the successful completion of the collegiate building, would meet Bishop Hailandière's original two-year requirement. That cantankerous and unpredictable prelate, however, soon found occasion to object to the location of the novitiate, and even earlier he detected other reasons to quarrel with Notre Dame du Lac and its superior.

The most serious of these broils originated far from Indiana. Basile Moreau had consistently seen his calling as that of a founder of a religious order with three distinct and yet integrated branches: the Auxiliary Priests of Le Mans (in the early days often referred to as Salvatorists), the Brothers of St. Joseph (whom he had inherited from Abbé Dujarié), and the Marianite Sisters, all under the aegis of Sainte-Croix. If Moreau was a man of iron will, so was Jean-Baptiste Bouvier, bishop of Le Mans, who, while granting the priests and brothers canonical status in his diocese, adamantly refused to do the same for the sisters.[13] But Moreau, just as stubborn, was not to be gainsaid, and, during the late summer and the autumn of 1843, he pondered a plan to circumvent his bishop's *non placet*. Why not establish the nuns and their motherhouse in the diocese of Vincennes, with Father Sorin as their superior. He accordingly instructed Sorin to

---

10. Sorin to Hailandière, September 17, 1844, AGEN.

11. Sorin, *Chronicles*, 39–40. Here it is stated that the cornerstone of the chapel was blessed in May, 1844, but Sorin's letter to Moreau of June 7 specifies that the ceremony took place six days earlier, that is, on June 1.

12. The chapel also served as the center for the newly founded "Archconfraternity" (Sorin, *Chronicles*, 40), a voluntary association of the Catholic faithful established by ecclesiastical authority and pledged to the performance of certain good and pious works. It should be borne in mind that Notre Dame continued till 1853 to be the sole Catholic parish in the South Bend area.

13. There was irony in the fact that one reason for Bouvier's refusal to recognize the Marianites was the approval already granted in his diocese to the Sisters of Providence of Ruillé, also founded by Dujarié. See chapter 3, above.

draw up a summary of the Marianite rule for submission to Bishop Hailandière. If the latter gave his approval, the sisters, whether working in France, America, or indeed anywhere, would do so with formal ecclesiastical sanction.[14]

Sorin received this communication sometime in November, 1843, on the eve perhaps of his withdrawal to "the island" to make his retreat. He took his time at any rate mulling the matter over in his mind. Then, on New Year's day following, he broached the subject to Hailandière's vicar general.

> It appears that at the meeting of the general council at Sainte-Croix, held in August last, I have been named Superior of the Sisters, who make up the third and completing part of Father Moreau's magnificent plan. But instead of recalling me to France, Father Rector has written me . . . that he is ready to transfer the motherhouse of the Sisters from Le Mans to Notre Dame du Lac. He also pledges to send us next spring three more sisters, two of whom are very accomplished, as well as a sum of money sufficient to establish them in a condition I think the bishop would approve. He adds, furthermore, that in order to give me more latitude, he is leaving me free to make a selection [*extrait*] from the nuns' constitutions, if these cannot be fully approved as they now stand. Do you think Monseigneur would turn a favorable eye upon the foundation of a new community of women in his diocese? As for the fittingness of them living with us here at Notre Dame, that poses no problem; I can locate them as far enough away as would be judged necessary.

The "fittingness" to which Sorin referred had to do with the consideration—in public perception as well as in fact—that men and women religious, especially the presumably more susceptible young, should not reside in too close proximity to each other. But in raising this problem, even as he dismissed it, he was revealing a hidden agenda.

> Or perhaps [Sorin's letter to August Martin continued] I should pause on a second thought that has come to me, one that would probably be welcomed with pleasure, that is, to offer the sisters to the bishop of Detroit. I have in mind for their establishment a magnificent place in Bertrand, four miles from here in Michigan. The nature of the questions I pose to you is

---

14. Catta, *Moreau,* 566, who adds, after the fact, that Moreau had acted "perhaps somewhat imprudently."

enough proof, Father, of the degree of confidence I have in you as well as the reasons why I ask you to keep all this a secret.[15]

It strains credulity almost to the breaking point to imagine that the proposal of Bertrand, Michigan, as a site for the sisters' motherhouse had occurred to Sorin only as "a second thought—*une seconde pensée qui m'est venue.*" He could not but have seen the analogy between his own tense and quarrelsome relations with Bishop Hailandière and those that had put Moreau and Bishop Bouvier at loggerheads. The happy circumstance was that the border separating Indiana and Michigan, only a few miles from Notre Dame, also marked the divisions between the jurisdictions of Vincennes and Detroit. Canonical establishment required the consent of a diocesan bishop; why should it not be the bishop of Detroit, who had offered kind hospitality to the new Holy Cross colony the previous summer?[16] And, since the men and women had to be physically segregated in any case, location of the sisters four miles north of Notre Dame made as much sense as one four miles away in any other direction. Nor does Sorin's statement to Father Martin, that he had already found "a magnificent place" for the sisters in Bertrand, support the claim that this solution had come to him as "a second thought."

The inquiry to Martin was posted on January 4. Less than a week later— much too brief a time for him to have received a reply from Vincennes—Sorin took up his pen again. "Monseigneur," he addressed the bishop of Detroit, "some two months ago Father Moreau, our founder, informed me that at the last general council of the Society of Notre Dame de Sainte-Croix I had been named superior for a five-year term of the sisters founded at Le Mans." Then, after he had stated the essentials of the arrangement as he had done for August Martin, he raised the crucial issue.

Up till now I have not written about this matter to the bishop of Vincennes, and my reasons are two. First, because he already has in his diocese a house of religious women,[17] and so perhaps he would not like to make the great sacrifice of having another group almost identical in its purpose and means. Second, because if the sisters were to be established here, the malicious Protestants could find reason to raise salacious questions about their too

---

15. Sorin to Martin, January 1, 1844, AGEN. The letter was mailed on January 4.

16. See chapter 8, above. Strictly speaking Pierre-Paul Lefèvre (1804–1869) was at this time a titular bishop and coadjutor and administrator of the diocese of Detroit, acting for Frederick Rese (see chapter 7, above), whose ill-health had forced his return to Europe.

17. The Sisters of Providence at Terre Haute.

close proximity to the brothers and to the college. My thought is that in fixing their house some miles from us we would avoid many implications of this kind, and we would reap at the same time many advantages. I do not know whether your Excellency wants an establishment of this kind in your diocese and for your diocese; but if you believe it could contribute to the glory of God and to the salvation of the souls confided to your care, I believe I can say that I am ready to do anything in my power to support your benevolence, to do anything possible in this regard. If such is agreeable, it would be at Bertrand, four miles from here, that I think the sisters might take up their abode.

In the very nature of the case, he added, "I must ask your Excellency to consider what I have said confidential, . . . at least for the present."[18]

This communication, when compared to that sent a few days earlier to Vicar General Martin, displays Edward Sorin at his most disingenuous. The assumption that the bishop of Vincennes would not have welcomed to his enormous diocese an order of dedicated French nuns because there was already one such group in place there was, to say the least, presumptuous. Nor did it, as Sorin maintained, explain why the bishop should not be informed of the possibility, why, indeed, as he said to Martin, the whole matter be regarded "a secret." As for the second reason advanced—Hailandière would object to the sisters' "too close proximity to the brothers and to the college"—Sorin had already, in his letter to Martin, dismissed this as "not a problem," since appropriate living arrangements away from the Notre Dame campus could be readily secured, and by no means necessarily in Michigan. The conclusion is difficult to avoid: Edward Sorin saw Moreau's commission with regard to the nuns—Moreau's difficulty in France, one might reasonably say—as an opportunity to deliver at least a portion of Holy Cross from the often witless and petty interference of Célestin Hailandière.

The response from Detroit was enthusiastically positive. You are to be congratulated upon your appointment as superior of the sisters of Sainte-Croix, Bishop Lefèvre wrote Sorin on February 5: "I believe your worthy founder could have suggested nothing wiser to promote the glory of God and the advancement of our holy religion, and the spiritual well-being of these sisters as well." Sorin's "arguments (*raisons*)" the bishop found "very plausible and even urgent," though, significantly, he did not refer to the first of them, the surmise that his colleague of Vincennes would "perhaps" suppose it "a great sacrifice" to welcome a second congregation of religious women into his diocese. Instead Lefèvre simply en-

18. Sorin to Lefèvre, January 10, 1844, AGEN.

dorsed the maxim that the sisters needed to be located a discreet distance from Notre Dame: "For we must always avoid as much as possible anything which could give our erring brethren the pleasure of accusing us or even of suspecting us. . . . Far from having any objection to locating them at Bertrand, it would give me great pleasure to see them established there and occupied, I assume, more or less in teaching. I have always hoped, and now I do so with more confidence, that you would honor us with a visit to Detroit, where we can discuss this matter more amply." The bishop concluded this cordial communiqué with a canonical gesture, granting Sorin the right to delegate to any Holy Cross priest faculties to perform sacramental ministry in his diocese "to the same degree as I have accorded them to you."[19]

Sorin wasted no time in taking the next step in his campaign, an appeal to Moreau to endorse "this latest avenue offered us by Providence." Within the week he forwarded Lefèvre's letter to Le Mans, covering it with an explanation of his own. "In what I wrote to the bishop of Detroit I suggested that my appointment as superior of the sisters had probably been a reason for you to fix the motherhouse here, . . . and that I did not despair of obtaining your agreement for its foundation in his diocese, if he were in favor of it. What I intended," he added somewhat lamely, "was just a preliminary and succinct inquiry in order to find out his feelings on the matter. I thought it likely his reaction would be more favorable if he were given some solid hope that the thing would come to pass. . . . The only remaining question is whether you will agree."[20]

Meanwhile, Sorin and his two recently-arrived priestly colleagues, Fathers Cointet and Marivault, diligently cultivated the Michigan connection. During February retreats were held at the parishes in Bertrand and St. Joseph and at the Indian mission at Pokagon. "In the space of fifteen days the good God has given us the consolation of baptizing eighteen adults and twenty-six infants, almost all resident in the diocese of Detroit." Sorin himself planned to visit the Catholics in Kalamazoo "before the end of Lent."

As to Bishop Lefèvre's agreeable response with regard to the sisters, "please," Sorin assured him, "accept my gratitude for it." Anxiety about a final decision continued to mount, however, because

we have presently offered us some good postulants whom I dare not receive until I know where we can put them. If I had sufficient means, I would place them either at Bertrand or at St. Joseph. Indeed, the latter

---

19. Lefèvre to Sorin, February 5, 1844, AGEN.
20. Sorin to Moreau, n.d. [posted February 13, 1844], AGEN.

place might be preferable, since it provides easier access to your diocese and is scarcely more inconvenient for us. There is the further advantage that in St. Joseph a large and beautiful house is available at a good price, which would be perfectly suitable for a novitiate and a boarding-school.[21]

Though St. Joseph, on Lake Michigan, was a larger and livelier community than Bertrand—the latter had become a backwater, "a dead town," in Sorin's own words,[22] destined to disappear as a recognizable entity within a few years—nothing came of this particular "second thought."

B UT EVEN AS EDWARD SORIN was maneuvering his way around the flank of Bishop Hailandière with regard to the sisters of Sainte-Croix and their status, he was also opening an offensive against that prelate on another front. In doing so he enlisted the support of his new ally, Bishop Lefèvre. At this juncture he would have preferred "the sacrifice of ten or twelve days" for a visit to Detroit so that he could air his "very important concerns" to the bishop in person. Since such a trip was just now not possible, Sorin had to content himself with consultation in writing.

Aside from the topic of the sisters, the most urgent subject I am obliged to raise with you . . . is to learn whether [you think] we must consent that our brothers are to be employed exclusively in the diocese of Vincennes, when that diocese has done almost nothing for us except to give us the land where we now reside. Or rather whether it would not be better for the promotion of religion to listen sympathetically to the aspirations of the various [American] bishops and to afford them the hope that our good brothers might serve in their dioceses as soon as a place was made available to them. It is true that we came from France in order to serve the diocese of Vincennes. But since the original agreement, everything has changed. We are free of this diocese, and we have decidedly returned to the charge and dependence upon our motherhouse in Le Mans. The numerous requests for teaching brothers I have recently received from other dioceses has almost persuaded me that the good God does not intend that the destinies of our work be limited to the diocese of Vincennes.[23]

21. Sorin to Lefèvre, March 13, 1844, AGEN.

22. Sorin, *Chronicles*, 49.

23. Sorin to Lefèvre, March 13, 1844, AGEN.

This declaration of independence was but the first salvo. Ten days later Sorin addressed the archbishop of Baltimore and the bishop of New Orleans[24] identical letters, which began with a rather bold assertion: "Doubtless your Reverence is aware of the existence of a religious community formed here under the name of 'Brothers of St. Joseph;' it has been established a little more than two years, and under the special blessings of a wise and beneficent God has realized for its projectors [sic] infinitely more than the most sanguine of them could have wished." This institution has for its object "to form young men for teachers and, when duly qualified in attainments and piety, to send them out to originate schools where none had existed, or to take charge of those which had been previously established." What Sorin professed he needed from "your Reverence" was "advice and, if possible, cooperation upon certain points."

These points he summed up under three headings. First, "would it be advisable to admit little girls with the boys in schools of this description?" Second, should tuition be charged or should the teaching be "gratuitous?" But these questions, hardly meant to be taken seriously,[25] were clearly intended to give occasion for raising the third: "Should the labors of the brothers be confined to one diocese?"

> With regard to the latter, I beg to add that, although our Mother House in France had this principle at the origin of its institution, it abandoned it at the solicitation of the [French] Bishops, and is now engaged in sending teachers to all parts of the kingdom; at present I am not under any *exclusive* obligation, nor has anything occurred since my residence in this country that could induce me to wish it; on the contrary, the demands I have lately had urge me to reserve the privilege of supplying as many dioceses as shall cooperate with the institution.[26]

It would seem that Edward Sorin was at this moment playing, if not a devious game, then one of serpentine subtlety. About a month before he sent out the broadside just quoted, he had received from Bishop Hailandière a communication "which expressed astonishment at the question whether we depend upon

---

24. American-born Samuel Eccleston (1801–1851), fifth archbishop of Baltimore (1834–1851), and French-born Anthony Blanc (1792–1860), fifth bishop and first archbishop of New Orleans (1835–1860).

25. The question about coeducation hardly seems relevant given Sorin's settled views on the matter: "As to having little girls admitted to the brothers' schools, I will never consent to this." Sorin to Martin, June 21, 1844, AGEN.

26. Sorin to Eccleston and Blanc, March 5, 1844, AGEN. These letters were written in English.

him or upon Notre Dame de Sainte-Croix." The bishop's surprise had been based, apparently, upon word that had come to him from Moreau, which he interpreted "as a desire that we should be changed from what we have been from the beginning, so that we belong now to the diocese, a conclusion he subscribes to with his whole heart."[27] Sorin, sensing perhaps that here was one more example of the failure of communication between Le Mans and Vincennes, forwarded this statement of the bishop's perception to Father Moreau without comment, but obviously he, Sorin, had no intention to abide by it. Certainly it was equally obvious that the contentious definition of where the fundamental loyalty of Holy Cross in America belonged remained unresolved, at least in Hailandière's mind.

No doubt Father Sorin was encouraged in his determination to spread wide the apostolate of Holy Cross when he reviewed the requests for the services of the Brothers of St. Joseph that reached him from various dioceses, or—if imitation is the highest form of flattery—when some bishops proposed to establish similar institutes of their own. For instance, Mathias Loras, the French-born bishop of Dubuque, Iowa—who presided over a missionary territory even more primitive than Vincennes—sent his vicar general to Notre Dame "this past winter" to consult with Sorin and to observe the functioning of the brothers in northern Indiana. "[Bishop Loras] wants to found such a society; he will fail," Sorin laconically observed. But there was, he said to Basile Moreau, a larger lesson to be learned.

> Yet at the very least [Dubuque] will for some years monopolize vocations in that region. If two or three other bishops imitate [Loras], *voila,* we will be deprived of a large share of potential postulants. The only thing to do in order to save these good bishops from expense and useless embarrassment (they simply do not have the resources needed for success), and for us to obtain the vocations available in their dioceses much more than in Vincennes, is to establish branches which will not prove onerous to the motherhouse (quite to the contrary) and will secure for the [Holy Cross] institute [in the United States] very rapid development.[28]

Sorin was seconded in this appeal to Le Mans by the gentler tones of Brother Vincent. "The bishop of Philadelphia wrote recently to Father Superior that he wanted at least eight brothers immediately. He would entrust the schools of the city to them, then some principal places in his diocese. . . . [There have also been]

27. Sorin to Moreau, February 13, 1844, AGEN.
28. Sorin to Moreau, June 26, 1844, AGEN.

numerous requests made to us by other dioceses. . . . We groan at not being able to satisfy these venerable bishops."[29]

B̲UT TO SATISFY THEM inevitably involved further alienating their colleague of Vincennes. Indeed, Bishop Hailandière now deemed himself, as well as the lofty view he held of his office and authority, under assault on two fronts. His resistance to the first of these—the brouhaha over the location of the Marianite Sisters—took the form of a proposal, made first in the late winter of 1844 and repeated some weeks afterward, that the novitiate and motherhouse be set up in Madison, Indiana. It is difficult to believe that the bishop thought this absurd idea would invite serious attention; Madison, a town on the Ohio River, in the extreme southeast corner of the state, lay hundreds of miles from Notre Dame and, therefore, was practically inaccessible to the ministrations of the priest whom Moreau had appointed the nuns' superior and spiritual director. But absurd or not, this move prompted Sorin to press Detroit "for a final decision, so that I can put an end to all my doubts and hesitations relative to [the sisters'] establishment." Madison is clearly too far away, and, if, as Hailandière maintained, "Bertrand like South Bend is too close," perhaps St. Joseph would serve better. In any event, he wrote Bishop Lefèvre on April 12, "I can assure your Excellency that in this particular matter I have in view only the greatest possible good; as soon as I know what to do on this subject to please God, no merely human consideration will I take into account. And understanding Father Rector [Moreau] as I do, I know that in whatever place it is finally established, he will not neglect to develop it and to render it useful to diocese to which it belongs." On these grounds "I pray that you have the goodness to grant your episcopal approbation. . . . I do not actually have the funds in hand for a foundation of this kind, but it appears to me less urgent to know where we shall find financial support than to know what God asks of us."

Money he may, as usual, have lacked, but now at least he had a confidant, an associate he could trust. Since he could not just then travel himself to Detroit, "I am sending to you dear Father Cointet whom you already know. I have as much as possible communicated to him all my thoughts on this subject. You can learn from him all the information you need, and share with him any advice you would want transmitted to me." He concluded with what was almost an ultimatum. In this affair

29. Brother Vincent to Moreau, April 11, 1844, in Klawitter, ed., *Adapted to the Lake*, 48.

I seek no personal satisfaction nor any earthly advantage, but only the good of souls and thereby the glory of God. After all, I cannot prove that our sisters should have an establishment of this kind in America. Our Father Rector desires it, I myself believe it possible; but if your Excellency sees some obstacle which ought to make us stay where we are, I have not, as far as my personal preference is concerned, the least objection. I do not know that a venture of this kind can be taken on without a great deal of difficulty. And we already have more to do than we can ever do.[30]

So now it was the bishop of Detroit's turn to be caught between two fires. Sorin insisted that he render "a final decision," while Hailandière bombarded him with vehement protests. It was not a comfortable position. Whatever may have been the fruits of the conversations between Lefèvre and Cointet, Sorin decided in early June that his own presence in Detroit was necessary. "[I have come here] to see his Excellency and to finalize, without possibility of reversal, the question of the establishment of our sisters, and to dissipate the fear that the influence of Vincennes should be felt too much as far away from there as Detroit. Providence decreed that I should consult the bishop yesterday and this morning [June 7], and everything has ended in accord with my wishes, that is to say, I must now do whatever is possible to attain the house offered to us near Niles [i.e., at Bertrand] and to move all our sisters there a few at a time [*de suite*]."[31] It would seem, however, that Lefèvre's backbone had been stiffened less by Sorin's powers of persuasion than by the intervention of the very forceful bishop of Cincinnati, John Baptist Purcell. On a visit to Detroit, he was asked to comment on Hailandière's opinion that settling the young nuns at Bertrand and brothers and priests at Notre Dame du Lac would be dangerously compromising. Such an assumption, said Purcell—who, like almost every one else, had already quarreled with the bishop of Vincennes—was preposterous.[32] This was not the last time that Purcell's consideration for Holy Cross was to make itself felt.

Meantime Lefèvre's positive decision, whatever its source, left Sorin free to formulate final plans for the establishment of the sisters' motherhouse and novitiate. Whatever precisely his fall-back position may have been, the prospect of locating the nuns at St. Joseph—most likely no more than a gambit to head off

30. Sorin to Lefèvre, April 12, 1844, AGEN.

31. Sorin to Moreau, June 7, 1844 (fragments), AGEN.

32. Sorin, *Chronicles*, 47, and Costin, *Priceless Spirit*, 17. For an instance of disagreement between Purcell and Hailandière, see Anthony H. Deye, "Archbishop John Baptist Purcell of Cincinnati. Pre-Civil War Years" (unpublished doctoral dissertation, University of Notre Dame, 1959), 274–275.

Bishop Hailandière's gloomy misgivings—swiftly faded in favor of the original site, Bertrand. Scarcely returned from Detroit, "I found at my door this morning [June 19] a deputation from the nearby village of Bertrand, composed of Catholics and Protestants. They presented me with a list of subscriptions that the whole village had recently made, urging me to establish the sisters in their village." They were ready to offer 3,000 francs ($600) in support of their petition. "When I asked them whether the sisters would be burned alive at Bertrand, the spokesman for the Protestants replied, 'Be not afraid of it, Father. There is no danger for them among us.'" Does not, Sorin asked rhetorically, such a reaction from "a town of black Presbyterians, Methodists, Episcopalians, Baptists, etc." demonstrate how "the work of Notre Dame du Lac has advanced through tribulations and sufferings?"[33]

So Bertrand it was to be, though grumbling from Vincennes continued as did puzzlement in Le Mans, so that Sorin was impelled to offer a final, not altogether convincing, *apologia*. Serious negotiations with Detroit, he claimed, had been initiated only after an especially mean and unwarranted provocation from Bishop Hailandière. Soon after their arrival from France, the sisters had attracted three candidates for admission to the order, all local girls of Irish extraction. When the bishop learned of this, he reacted "with a severe accusation that I wished to set up a novitiate of sisters without speaking to him first." This was not true: "My intention had been to secure a number of female domestics [*ouvrières*], perhaps a total of eight or ten, sufficient to serve the immense needs of the [Notre Dame] community." So informed, Hailandière held his peace, until "five months later when I asked his permission to clothe these young women in the religious habit, and he refused in a most shocking manner. It was then that I entered into positive arrangements with the bishop of Detroit."[34]

The substance of this explanation, dispatched to Basile Moreau, helps to account for Edward Sorin's "second thought," that the sisters might be best situated in a nearby Michigan village. The details, however, leave some uncertainty. Nobody acquainted with Célestin Hailandière would have doubted him capable of "shocking" rudeness. Nevertheless, postulancy within a religious congregation is by definition a temporary state; postulants, after a relatively brief trial, become novices, and the bishop could hardly be blamed for making this point. Also Sorin's chronology remains murky. Exactly "five months" passed between the sisters' arrival at Notre Dame from France—early August, 1843—and Sorin's original revelation of his "second thought"—January 1, 1844.[35] Therefore Sorin's

33. Sorin to Dupont, June 19, 1844, AGEN.

34. Sorin to Moreau, July 2–20, 1844, AGEN.

35. See note 14, above.

sequence of events assumes that the three recruits joined the sisters immediately; but even if that were the case, it seems unlikely that Hailandière's reprimands could have been received and replied to within so short a time-frame.[36]

Perhaps this was why Sorin did not include the "five months" version when he later recorded what happened in his *Chronicles*. Nor did he mention it or indeed even describe the occurrences precisely the same way when, contemporaneously, he shared his anger with August Martin.

> I asked Monseigneur [Hailandière] for permission to give the habit to some postulants of whom we have need, not to form a novitiate but to complete the number of necessary domestics. The manner in which my request was received disgusted me completely [and turned me away] from trying any more to have a foundation in Indiana. Afterward I entertained the thoughts of sending the sisters away or even sending half of them back to France in order to have the number his Excellency wanted. Then Providence sent me a considerable gift, $3,000 at least to be used to establish the sisters in Michigan.[37] Negotiations were then easily and definitively entered into with the bishop of Detroit. The residents of Bertrand have themselves subscribed nearly $600.[38]

But once again Sorin's chronology appears skewed: surely negotiations with Bishop Lefèvre began many months *before* the providential benefaction "to be used to establish the sisters in Michigan."

So Bertrand in any case it was to be. "If I wish to proceed here in a manner somewhat artful [*rusée*]," Sorin informed Moreau, "I am authorized by the bishop of Detroit to establish a foundation anywhere in his diocese. I shall do it this very week at Bertrand."[39] The day chosen was July 16: "Our sisters have been at Bertrand since the feast of Our Lady of Mount Carmel. They have a house leased for fifteen months. It has an ample cloister . . . and a parlor for visitors. A good old brother of some sixty years is their gardener and wood-cutter. . . . The sisters appear happy."[40] One of them remembered, when she was an old lady, that

---

36. Costin, *Priceless Spirit*, 16, says that the three postulants had been clothed by Christmas, 1843.

37. This money came from the sale of real estate in Detroit donated by a Mr. and Mrs. Beaubien of that city, who wanted it used for support of the Marianite Sisters but who left the details of its disposal to Sorin. See Sorin to Moreau, June 7, 1844, AGEN, and Sorin, *Chronicles*, 36.

38. Sorin to Martin, June 21, 1844, AGEN.

39. Sorin to Moreau, July 2–20, 1844, AGEN.

40. Sorin to Moreau, December 4–12, 1844, AGEN.

wild roses and sweetbriar had grown near the convent's front door, and on the second floor, where the dormitory and community room were located, a sign on the wall had read, "God sees me."[41]

Edward Sorin had been "artful" indeed. The establishment of the sisters in accord with his desires was now a *fait accompli*, and his main political objective, if one may label it so, had been achieved: "The bishop [of Detroit] appears very content; and if he has not in his power the resources to help us very much, at least he does not seem disposed to meddle at all in the governance of this foundation."[42] However, the contest with Célestin Hailandière, for whom meddling was second nature, was far from over: "The sisters remained at Bertrand," Sorin observed dryly, "but the bishop of Vincennes did not forget."[43]

41. Costin, *Priceless Spirit,* 19.
42. Sorin to Moreau, June 7, 1844, AGEN.
43. Sorin, *Chronicles,* 47.

chapter ten

"Ad Vesperum Fletus, ad Matutinum Laetitia"

WITH THE ARRIVAL OF THE SPRING OF 1844, Edward Sorin had reason to feel satisfied, or perhaps even a bit euphoric, at the progress of his little mission. The collegiate main building was practically finished (though its furnace was to prove an expensive failure);[1] Notre Dame du Lac had been granted a state charter as a "university"; construction of the novitiate for the Brothers of St. Joseph had begun; and the Marianite Sisters had been settled at Bertrand. And he would have been less than human had he not seen these accomplishments as having check-mated, for the moment at least and to a degree, the ever-critical Bishop Hailandière. Much more land had been cleared as well—150 acres during the course of 1843–44—and wheat, corn, and potatoes became the staple crops of a farm which, if at first it barely broke even, gave promise of a stable source of sustenance and perhaps, in time, of profit. The men and women of Holy Cross, mostly country folk from Mayenne and Sarthe, could find consolation in this rustic setting, which happily committed them too to the care of numerous hogs and sheep, cows and horses. Indeed, they may have had wistful thoughts of the orchards back home when, a little later, they planted three hundred peach trees along the shores of the lakes.[2]

---

1. Sorin, *Chronicles*, 37.
2. Sorin, *Chronicles*, 49–50.

But all these activities involved expense—about $10, for example, to clear an acre of woodland—and a lack of sufficient funds continued to dog Sorin's every step. He was not always clear or candid in stating the financial straits of the mission, but neither did he leave any doubt that mounting debt and borrowing defined its condition—this despite relatively generous grants from France and rather niggardly ones from Vincennes,[3] not to mention the unpaid labor of the nuns and brothers. Thus on the credit line offered by Samuel Byerley in his new store in South Bend, Notre Dame promptly ran up a liability of $1,600.[4]

Sorin faced this precarious situation with his convictions unaltered: it could be reversed, he continued to insist, only by setting up a boarding school catering to fee-paying students. Thwarted in such a venture at St. Peter's, he was all the more determined to succeed at Notre Dame. But this was more easily intended than done. The completion of the collegiate building did not in itself guarantee a pool of male youngsters capable of following something akin to a French secondary education. Despite the heady implications of the word "university"—a term used very loosely at the time all over the United States—Bishop Hailandière, when he had invited the Brothers of St. Joseph to Indiana, had not had in mind even so exalted an institution as a *collège*. What he wanted, not an ignoble purpose, were religious men to staff a system of *primary* education across his vast diocese, wherein would be taught the basic verbal and numerical skills, along with a dollop of Catholic doctrine. Or, to express his intention negatively, he wanted to deliver Catholic children from the dominant Protestant culture.

But Father Sorin discerned early on that, since the bishop had no financial resources to speak of and support from France could not over a long span of years be more than marginal, Holy Cross in America would have to become self-sufficient. And it would never attain that happy status simply by dispatching teaching brothers to serve in the far-flung parishes of the diocese of Vincennes. "I understand," Sorin observed sarcastically, "that his Excellency intends to offer $50 for each brother, out of which sum we are to support him and to pay his traveling expenses. I have so little inclination to make our brothers objects of monetary speculation that I shall grant in advance everything his Excellency will propose, trusting that divine Providence will not let them die of want."[5] But in fact he proved also to have "little inclination" to assign any brothers to Hailandière's jurisdiction, with the exception of the unfortunate Brother Anselm, while,

---

3. For an example see Sorin to Martin, January 1, 1844, AGEN, in which Sorin complains about the non-payment of a $500 pledge made in the name of Bishop Hailandière.

4. Sorin, *Chronicles*, 36, which speaks vaguely of an overall debt of between $4000 and $4400.

5. Sorin to Martin, June 21, 1844, AGEN.

to that choleric prelate's fury, he sought to place them in locales as far away as Pennsylvania and Louisiana.

Meanwhile Sorin soldiered on in his attempts to found a respectable and profit-making *collège*. In the autumn of 1843 five new students were in residence, taking their classes in the small structure put up the preceding spring.[6] A year later, with the multipurpose main building a reality, the total number had risen to twenty-five, though, as the recorder, Brother Gatien, noted, several of them stayed only a few weeks and others drifted away without settling their accounts. Tuition, board, room, laundry, and medical attention (which meant the use of the community infirmary) cost $100 per year, and partial payment in kind was not unusual. The curriculum as it was described in various advertisements sounded impressive enough: courses available at the University of Notre Dame du Lac included Latin and Greek, composition, mathematics, oratory, grammar, geography, ancient and modern history, French, botany, and zoology. The trouble was that, with the possible exceptions of Father Cointet (the classical languages) and the precocious Brother Gatien, aged seventeen (history and French), the proposed faculty had little acquaintance with the disciplines listed.[7] What in the short term was most disheartening, however, was that the brags of local boosters had proved illusory: the South Bend area was simply too limited in population to provide enough candidates to make such a scholastic project viable. Even the modest day school the brothers operated briefly—"a Free School opened at South Bend, by the Brothers of St. Joseph, for the reception of boys, . . . [meeting] from 8:00 A.M. till 4:00 P.M., with instruction . . . in Spelling, Reading, Writing, and Arithmetic [and without] religious qualifications"[8]—did not prosper.

When he visited Detroit in early June 1844, Sorin contacted two or three young men who expressed some interest in the collegiate program offered at Notre Dame. But when he returned home he was accompanied, not by prospective students, but by two orphans, entrusted to his care by the same pious couple who had donated property to Holy Cross for the support of the sisters at Bertrand.[9] These unfortunate children, soon joined by others similarly deprived and then by boys not orphaned, came to form the nucleus of a labor-school at Notre Dame, which was eventually sanctioned by state charter. "The Apprentices," as Sorin called them, at least twelve years of age, "spen[t] all their time at work in . . . [the] shops" managed by the brothers, and some of them made "remarkable

6. The building known today as "Old College." See note 34, chapter 8, above.

7. See Council of Professors, minutes, August 3. 1844, AUND, UFMM.

8. *South Bend Free Press,* February 3, 1844. I owe this reference to my friend, John Conley, C.S.C.

9. See note 36, chapter 9, above.

progress. . . . It [was] understood as a matter of course that at the end of their time [at the maximum age of twenty-one] they should have received a good common education," not in letters, to be sure—they were carefully segregated from the collegiate students—but in trades and crafts that would help them find jobs in the larger economy. This work of charity, appropriate and indeed admirable as it may have been, did not, however, do much to alleviate the community's financial uncertainties. If the apprentices did supply some free labor to the campus, they were not a significant source of cash: "When it was possible," Sorin noted, "the relatives or guardians should, at the entrance of the child, pay the sum of two hundred francs [$40]"—which, even if it were paid, was in a sense already committed, because "the house . . . furnished [the apprentices] at their departure with two complete suits of clothes."[10]

Though the Manual Labor School—its formal title—could itself yield little ready money for the struggling mission, the Providence which Sorin so often and so confidently invoked had reserved a special reward for its founder. Or so at least it seemed in July 1844, when Stephen Badin quite unexpectedly turned up at Notre Dame. The venerable proto-priest, now seventy-seven years old, was delighted by what he saw on the campus, and particularly by the provision made for the boys in the trade school; his original intent in purchasing the 524 acres upon which the Holy Cross mission now stood, it may be recalled, had been the establishment of an orphanage. So pleased was he that he offered Sorin what looked like a heaven-sent benefaction: he would turn over to Holy Cross several city lots he owned in Louisville, Kentucky, valued, he claimed, at between $12,000 and $15,000, and, besides that, would purchase and donate to Notre Dame a 200-acre tract that lay between the campus and the St. Joseph River. In return for such munificence the old missioner and real estate speculator requested only that he be paid an annuity of $400. Sorin agreed with appropriate enthusiasm and gratitude. He urged Father Badin to stay on at Notre Dame, and so he did through the following spring, intending, it appears likely, to end his days there.[11] Meanwhile he taught catechism twice a week to the collegiate students and did Sunday duty in neighboring parishes, preaching the abusive sermons for which over the years he had become notorious across the Midwest. Perhaps the by-now habitual truculence displayed in these pulpit performances should have forewarned Edward Sorin that any negotiation with Badin risked the sowing of dragon's seeds; a bitter harvest at any rate was not far off.[12]

10. Sorin to Moreau, June 7, 1844, AGEN, and Sorin, *Chronicles,* 43–45.
11. See Wack, "Notre Dame Foundation," 104–105.
12. See chapter 11, below.

But for the moment the likelihood of financial deliverance by way of the sale of the Louisville property buoyed up Sorin's spirits amidst the rumbles he was beginning to hear from Le Mans—softly, so far, in accord with Basile Moreau's characteristic diffidence, and yet insistent. Holy Cross in America must follow proper accounting procedures and, above all, must cease soliciting loans on the credit of Sainte-Croix du Mans without first securing permission from the motherhouse. These were by no means outlandish requirements. "I demand," Moreau decreed as early as August 1843, "that Brother Vincent send me every July, over the signature of Father Sorin, a financial statement of . . . receipts and disbursements." The following March, Moreau wrote again, in a gentle and yet firm tone: "As for your note of five thousand francs [$1,000], you should, my dear friend, at least have warned me ahead of time, for by not doing so, you left me open to the risk of losing my credit here and making you lose yours in America, if I had refused to honor the note, as my council wanted me to do."[13]

DEBT OR NO DEBT, with or without warnings of too rapid expansion, Edward Sorin's plans and ambitions continued to soar. He was beginning to dream of Notre Dame as the center of a vast Catholic enterprise, embracing schools at every level to serve toddlers and collegians, rich and poor, men and women (once the sisters were properly mobilized), an occasional Indian, and even Protestants of good will who, he guaranteed, would never feel any undue papist pressure.[14] The educational enterprise established on the campus by the lakes would serve as a dynamic hub from which would radiate other apostolic activities, including the parochial work already well begun and the teaching the brothers and later the nuns might do in far-flung venues. Yet the dismal truth remained that neither the number of available personnel nor their religious or scholastic training could immediately warrant even a modest fulfillment of these schemes. Little wonder, then, that Father Sorin—and Bishop Hailandière too, for reasons of his own—put such emphasis on launching a proper brothers' novitiate. In terms simply of numbers, the situation was somewhat unsettled. From the arrival of the original six Brothers of St. Joseph from France in the autumn of 1841 to the end of 1844, twenty-five men had applied and had been accepted as postulants for admission to the order. Only about half of these, however, persevered, and,

---

13. Catta, *Moreau*, 1: 530.

14. See Wack, "Notre dame Foundation," 86. Non-Catholic students were excused from catechism classes, though they did attend Mass (but only as observers) and "were expected to participate in the prayers before classes." This policy was frowned upon by several bishops.

indeed, in succeeding years the number of applicants declined while that of the departures remained statistically constant. This state of affairs tended to confirm Edward Sorin's earlier negative view that the success of the mission could not depend, at least in its early years, on native vocations.[15]

> Not only are vocations rare, but one-third of the time they do not present the qualities necessary to put the men to study. One-half are too old, and the others too ignorant to begin the necessary studies. And then they have less desire than they seem to have in France to become teaching Brothers. . . . Here, even more than in Europe, those that succeed in making money in the world do not think of giving it up. It would be better for some years to bring young postulants from beyond the sea, who are unacquainted with the spirit and morals of the Americans. These would be easily formed and would offer a better assurance of perseverance.[16]

For this reason, among others, Edward Sorin welcomed the colony that arrived at Notre Dame from Le Mans in the autumn of 1844, after enduring a particularly tumultuous and dangerous voyage.[17] In this group were three sisters, two brothers, and—a particularly happy omen for him—his confrère from seminary days, Father Alexis Granger, whom he had tried to persuade to join the Auxiliary Priests of Sainte-Croix four years before, and whom he had assured that service in the foreign missions was not a requirement for entry.[18] Granger had finally presented himself to Basile Moreau, and, his inhibitions about overseas duty apparently stilled, had petitioned the founder to serve in Indiana. Granger proved a lifelong support for Sorin—they died within months of each other—though his diffidence and shyness sometimes hindered his effectiveness. Yet over the years Edward Sorin had reason to feel blessed by the presence of a man who was his friend and who, like François Cointet, would stand as a stalwart and reliable co-worker.

But, Sorin might have reflected, as the Lord giveth, so he taketh away.

---

15. See chapter 6, above.

16. Sorin, *Chronicles,* 42–43.

17. "The ship, riding now on one side, now on the other, seemed at every moment on the point of being swallowed up by the waves." Granger to Moreau, October 3, 1844, in Moreau, *Circular Letters,* 1: 94–97.

18. See the correspondence quoted in chapter 4, above. For a brief sketch of Granger see Wack, "Notre Dame Foundation," 79–80.

I recommend to your prayers [he wrote Mother Theodore in the early spring], and to those of your whole pious community, our dear Brother Joachim who came here with us from France, whom the good God has called unto himself . . . after an illness of fifteen months. The courage and love (*sentiments*) with which he suffered to the very end lead us to believe that soon he will be in possession of his reward. If we can hasten the day of his deliverance [by prayer] and so assure ourselves of one more Protector in heaven, we shall assuredly be sufficiently recompensed.[19]

So the sturdy sometime tailor, a victim of tuberculosis, was the first of the original missionaries of Sainte-Croix to die in America. Some weeks later death, also from tuberculosis, took Brother Paul, a clever Irishman born John de la Hoyde, who had joined Holy Cross at St. Peter's and who had been a valuable asset to the community both as an instructor in English literature and as a bookkeeper.[20] These two pioneers were followed the next year by the young and frail Brother Anselm, who, cruelly isolated from his confreres, had known so few happy days since he had departed his home in Mayenne at the tender age of sixteen.[21]

Anselm was fated to drown while swimming in the Ohio River, near the town of Madison, Indiana. His assignment there as the lone teacher for sixty pupils in November 1844, after an illness in inhospitable Vincennes, meant that he had been at last delivered from Hailandière's petty bullying and into a more congenial environment—the parish priest in Madison was Holy Cross's old friend from the days at Black Oak Ridge, Julien Delaune. But it also stands as a black mark against Edward Sorin as a religious superior; he appears to have been almost callously insensitive and indifferent to Anselm's desperate need for community support.[22] Since Brother Mary Joseph had been sent to Vincennes as a replacement for Anselm,[23] it seemed in any event that Sorin was abiding by the letter if not

---

19. Sorin to Mother Theodore, April 25, 1844, AGEN.

20. Wack, "Notre Dame Foundation," 61, says Brother Paul died May 8, 1844, Klawitter, ed., *Adapted to the Lake*, 374, says May 27.

21. See chapter 4, above.

22. See Anselm to Sorin, August 4, 1844, quoted in Klawitter, ed., *Adapted to the Lake*, 68–69, as well as Klawitter's own apt comments, xx–xxi. Moreau's reaction (*Circular Letters*, 1: 103) was characteristic: "I must take advantage of this terrible warning to forbid forever, in virtue of holy obedience, any and all members of our association to go swimming in rivers or in the sea without the express order of a doctor or a formal permission from me."

23. Sorin to Mother Theodore, September 13, and Sorin to Hailandière, September 17, 1844, AGEN. Mary Joseph, né Samuel O'Connell, a native of Ireland, was the first postulant to become a novice at Notre Dame. He also succeeded Brother Anselm in Madison. See Klawitter, ed., *Adapted to the Lake*, 372.

by the spirit of the original agreement with the diocese. But this minimal conformity did not appease Bishop Hailandière, especially in the light of what he perceived to be Sorin's desire to dispatch the brothers hither and yon. The bishop was of course not mistaken in this perception, but his dark suspicions led him to register some rather dubious reproaches. He protested, for example, that Brother Joseph had been sent to the Potowatomi at Pokagon, to which criticism Sorin replied with some heat: "I had not other means of *reconciling him* [the bishop] to the savages," after the scandalous land deal associated with Father Bernier.[24] Hailandière also thought it "strange" and suspicious that Brothers Vincent and Augustine should have traveled to France "immediately after the return of Brother John."

In fact several months had elapsed between these two journeys abroad. As for Brother Augustine, Father Sorin explained, "he would probably have been lost to the community if I had not taken this measure to conserve him." In France "he can regain his health, continue his medical studies, give some English-lessons at Sainte-Croix, and then return in a couple of years formed and capable, I hope, of rendering great services here."[25] Brother Vincent, on the other hand, had gone to Le Mans, not so much as Augustine's companion as Sorin's emissary, to report to Father Moreau and to persuade him, if possible, to visit Notre Dame du Lac. "I have many reasons to desire that our Father-founder should come and pass some time with us and stay probably through the winter. His presence here would do more good than anything else; he will then see the situation with his own eyes" and so be able to make the proper administrative decisions.[26]

Sorin's hopes in this regard, however, did not materialize; many years were to pass before Basile Moreau paid his single visit to Indiana. Had he decided otherwise at this moment, perhaps later painful events might have been avoided. But that is mere speculation. At the time rumor gave Sorin reason to worry rather that Moreau would not only decline to come to Notre Dame himself but might also keep Brother Vincent in Le Mans. Sorin's conviction was the same as before: solicitations for teaching brothers from various dioceses, notably New Orleans and Philadelphia, both potentially sources for abundant vocations, promised a rich future for Holy Cross in America. The pertinent fact that there were no brothers presently trained and available—some would be ready within a year, he

---

24. Sorin to Moreau, July 2, 1844, AGEN. For Bernier and Brother Joseph at Pokagon, see chapter 7, above.

25. Brother Augustine (Jeremy O'Leary) did return to Notre Dame in 1845, but soon afterward he left the community. See Klawitter, ed., *Adapted to the Lake*, 361.

26. Sorin to Martin, June 21, 1844, AGEN.

asserted with characteristic bravura—he brushed aside, as he did the objections of Monseigneur of Vincennes: "I know that [Hailandière] would prefer that we establish our first foundations in Indiana; but having received from various American bishops responses so contrary to the idea of circumscribing our Brothers to the limits of a single diocese, I have told him I could not agree with his position"—a stance he was confident the Founder would support.[27] But what if Moreau were to resolve not to send Brother Vincent back to Notre Dame to take charge of the brothers' preparation? "I pray you, my reverend Father, to consider these reflections of mine which I think are of the highest importance for the success of our work. But if contrary to my very strong opinions on this matter you were to retain Brother Vincent at Sainte-Croix, it would be necessary to give up all these plans until I do not know when." Obviously three years in America had worked a sea-change in Sorin's estimate of the value of his "dear" senior colleague, to whom he pledged his "special love and respect."[28]

BROTHER VINCENT did indeed return to Notre Dame du Lac and brought with him, not Father Moreau, but the colony of 1844, headed by the young Father Granger. That event, agreeable as it was, found Edward Sorin in a bruised and discontented mood. Eighteen forty-four, despite its early victories, was a year which brought him its share of gloom. He felt, perhaps for the first time, intellectually isolated and homesick. "It has been more than two years since I received any news from our dear France. Not a newspaper, not a contemporary pamphlet, not a treatise even, nothing. When you find something in the journals you are reading," he appealed to Léon Dupont, "that you think might interest us, please have the goodness to send it to me; and when you have read some new worthwhile book, could you not offer it to our good fathers of Notre Dame? We are almost as poor in books as we are in money."[29]

Nor was he without temptation to exchange his difficult mission in Indiana for a softer life elsewhere. *"Shall I tell you,"* he informed Moreau, underscoring the words, *"that I have been offered the title of sole heir to a very good family* (worth perhaps two hundred thousand francs) *if I want to settle in Detroit?* To be sure, he brushed this inducement aside: "I love my dear family at N. D. better than two hundred thousand, better than four hundred thousand francs."[30] But the many

27. See Moreau to Hailandière, August 28, 1844, quoted in Catta, *Moreau,* 1: 532.

28. Sorin to Moreau, June 26, 1844, AGEN. For Sorin's earlier and negative judgment of Brother Vincent, see chapter 6, above.

29. Sorin to Dupont, June 19, 1844, AGEN.

30. Sorin to Moreau, June 7, 1844, AGEN.

"tribulations and sufferings" he was enduring led him to assert his dedication in terms stark indeed for a young man of thirty: "I ask of the good God only one thing: to see the work at Notre Dame firmly established before I die."[31]

Although the men and women at Notre Dame remained his "dear family," Sorin, in his present humor, was not above finding fault with many of them— obliquely at first, and then more directly. "Even if," he lectured Basile Moreau, "it becomes impossible for you to come and visit us this autumn and bring yourself the new colony, it will be indispensable to take new precautions in light of the dangers involved in the voyage." The dangers he had in mind were spiritual, not physical.

> I now know from experience that if I were charged with a similar commission, I would wish that, once the first indispositions of seasickness had passed, all religious exercises should be regularly carried out without exception at their appointed hours, that in case of necessity something more be done to conserve fervor *which runs such great risks during these two months.* For example, there could be a half-hour meditation at three in the afternoon on the need to die to self in order to be afterwards in a proper state to fulfill the grand mission that is approaching. Another half-hour, at, say, ten in the morning, of silence, of mortification of the eyes, and so forth, to maintain a great desire to do well. . . . I would wish the world to serve as a novitiate upon the sea, and whoever does not pass the test by the time the ship docks at New York *should not come any farther.* Five weeks at sea can tell more about a religious man or woman than a five months' novitiate anywhere else.[32]

Whichever members of his "dear family" he was thinking of when he wrote this stern admonition—Father Marivault, Brother Eloi, and perhaps others of the second colony seem likely targets—certainly its hectoring tone no less than its substance marked a new departure in his relations with Moreau.

More, much more, was to come in succeeding months. Meanwhile the barrage of grievances shot off by Bishop Hailandière continued unabated. He was still smarting from Sorin's *coup* at Bertrand, still angry that more brothers were not being assigned to his parishes, still annoyed that the novitiate, now going up on St. Mary's Isle, was to be located in a place remote from his own control—

---

31. Sorin to Dupont, June 19, 1844, AGEN.
32. Sorin to Moreau, June 7, 1844, AGEN.

though he had originally agreed that it should be so—still convinced that Holy Cross would somehow take financial advantage of him. As any one can see, Sorin observed bitterly, "he knows how to give to his complaints a ring of truth which can be persuasive. But hardly so for me. Ah! if I wished to accuse in the same manner all the chiefs I have had to deal with these three years—but no, at least until I am formally instructed otherwise, I prefer to keep such things to myself." The bishop even accused Brother Lawrence of having been rude to him and of having spread the rumor that he, Hailandière, was about to resign his bishopric.[33] "Brother Lawrence has assured me," Sorin retorted, "that he had not spoken to or about Monseigneur in that manner, and I believe him." But such petty allegations stood far from the heart of the matter. "[Hailandière] sees all too clearly that we are withdrawing from his administration and governance. . . . What he cannot abide is that we have received some assistance from the Propagation of the Faith [in Paris], that we eluded him in this regard despite his efforts. He is too intelligent not to feel the weakness of such accusations. That he should leave us in peace is all that I want from him. For my own part, I do not want to deal with him."[34]

The intimacy between Sorin and August Martin that had begun at Logansport in 1841[35] was, for the time being, a sad and unintended casualty of this unseemly wrangling. Sorin's ceaseless quarrels with Hailandière put Martin, the bishop's right-hand man as vicar general, in an impossible position. In mid-September 1844, Sorin mourned the confidant he had lost and penned a sad little note: "It appears that you have entirely given up corresponding with me. At least your silence allows me to suppose so. I regret to be deprived of the pleasure and advantages I have derived from our association. . . . Oh! pray sometimes for me and my family."[36]

Internal troubles surfaced as well. As the autumn term proceeded, the difficulties in providing an education of even minimal quality to the collegiate students appeared ever more daunting. What few books were available were written in English, which few of the faculty could read. The students themselves proved a

---

33. Brother Lawrence (Laurent, Jean Menage) was one of the original six—see chapter 4, above. The rumor, whether Lawrence propagated it or not, was not far-fetched. Hailandière did resign his see in 1846 and return to France where he lived another thirty-two years. See Lemarié, *Missionaires bretons*, 251–269.

34. Sorin to Moreau, July 2, 1844 ("*pour vous seul*"), AGEN.

35. See chapter 5, above.

36. Sorin to Martin, September 15, 1844, AGEN. But Martin himself departed Vincennes to serve as a priest in Louisiana early in 1846 "for reasons of health," he said, but in fact to escape the tyranny of Hailandière. He became first bishop of Natchitoches in 1853. See Lemarié, *Missionaires bretons*, 336–337, 341, and chapter 11, below.

rough and unruly lot; hardly any of them, children of the frontier, had had the slightest preparation for formal schooling, and many of them resented the strictures of a regime that got them out of bed at 5:30 A.M., put them into classes taught by foreigners they could scarcely understand, and made them say more prayers in a day than their pious mothers did in a week. Discipline was theoretically strict, but in fact it was tempered almost into laxity. Troublesome students seldom felt more than the softest slap on the wrist.

This circumstance was a bone of contention from the start and the source of serious annoyance for Father Sorin. As Superior of the community, he presided *ex officio* over the so-called Council of Professors, which served as the college's governing board. At this body's frequent meetings—one more drain on his time and energy—Sorin often found himself pitted against the brash Brother Gatien, who spoke for those faculty members who wanted stern punishment meted out to delinquent students. To Gatien's mounting irritation, Sorin consistently overruled him. A kind of unhappy climax was reached with the case of one Louis Fontaine, a mixed-race boy who from the day he arrived at Notre Dame was the source of constant disturbance. Gatien wanted him expelled, but Sorin pointed out that Louis was paying full tuition and that his father—once a chief of the Miami—had loaned the institution $2,000, payable on demand. If the chief were moved to issue that demand, Notre Dame simply could not meet it. The wretched boy, therefore, had to be put up with, however odious his conduct might be. This "decision of the Rev. mild-measure-taking Superior," as Gatien sarcastically called it, may have marked the beginning of the disenchantment of that talented young man who, not untypically of one his age, tended to see events in starkly moral tones of black and white. Edward Sorin for his part was famous later in his career for being a firm disciplinarian, but this he saw as a luxury, so to speak, to be indulged in only after Notre Dame was a going concern. As the grim autumn of 1844 gave way to winter, survival had to enjoy pride of place, even if it meant alienating one of the most gifted of his "dear family."[37]

On DECEMBER 8, 1844, the feast of the Immaculate Conception of the Virgin, all the members of that family gathered on St. Mary's Isle for the dedication of the just-completed chapel and novitiate.[38] Two sisters, including Mother Mary of the Five Wounds, the superior, made their profession and took

---

37. See Wack, "Notre Dame Foundation," 87–92. Brother Gatien left the community in 1850. See Klawitter, ed., *Adapted to the Lake*, 367.

38. The interior of the novitiate was still unfinished. See Sorin, *Chronicles*, 56–57.

vows, and a third received the habit as a postulant. The heart of bronze that Father Moreau had sent as a gift rested upon the chapel's altar, and on its rough floor lay the "magnificent carpet" donated by Mrs. Samuel Byerley and specially decorated for the occasion. Over the next several years this modest sanctuary was to be the focal point of the community's devotional life.[39]

But even as this celebration was going on, with all its pious overtones, Edward Sorin was giving vent to a catalogue of grievances and passing judgment, with remarkable candor, on his religious brothers and sisters. He did so, first, by drawing up between December 4 and December 12 a brief report on each of the persons under his charge: three priests, one seminarian, twenty-two brothers (including one novice), six brothers-postulant, and, among the women, eight nuns, two novices, and two postulants, divided between the convents at Bertrand and Notre Dame. Missing from the list—much, no doubt, to Sorin's sadness—was the name of Brother John, who apparently by this date had gone his own way.[40]

Much of the material contained in the roster of personnel, sent on to the motherhouse in Le Mans with a covering letter, was predictable. Father Cointet, for example, was described as achieving "astonishing progress" in the study of theology and Scripture and, moreover, had shown himself "a lively, happy man . . . [who] will do great work both within and outside the community." Father Granger, similarly, "will accomplish, I hope, much good. *He is very much loved*," even though he had arrived at Notre Dame only a few months before. Father Marivault, on the other hand, was a miserable student and, though physically sturdy enough, demonstrated "frailty of spirit, hypercriticism, and poor judgment. At thirty-two years of age, he appears fitted for nothing."[41]

Among the Brothers of St. Joseph, Sorin reserved his highest praise for those who had accompanied him from France. Brother Joachim was dead, but Vincent, Lawrence, and Francis Xavier received plaudits as charitable, hardworking, regular in performing their religious exercises, devoted to the well-being of the house. Lawrence was especially valuable as overseer of the farm, and Francis Xavier was "the most beloved of all the brothers." And, to his credit, Sorin testified to the sterling contribution of Brother Gatien, with whom he had been recently so much at odds: Gatien had made "extraordinary progress" in the study of English and German, he was a first-rate teacher, and, if his capacity for cool judgment

---

39. Sorin to Moreau, December 4–12, 1844, AGEN, and Sorin, *Chronicles,* 39–41.

40. See chapter 8, above.

41. Though ordained priests, Cointet and Marivault were still novices in the congregation and so technically still "students." Granger had made his profession in France. He was listed in the roster as "master of novices," as was Brother Vincent.

was somewhat "ill-directed," he remained "extremely precious here, and well-regarded by his pupils." Of those who had composed the original Holy Cross colony to Indiana, only poor Brother Anselm, now within months of his tragic death, received adverse grades because, Sorin said, of his "weak personality, fragile health, contrary spirit, and bad judgment."

As for those brothers who had either come from France since 1841 or who had joined the community after its arrival in America, Sorin's assessment was, with some exceptions, on the whole positive. Brother Joseph—né Charles Rother, the young German who had been the earliest recruit at St. Peter's—may have been "somewhat brusque in manner," but he also possessed "sound judgment," an opinion, however, Sorin eventually came to regret.[42] The thirty-four-year-old Brother Eloi, who had come to Notre Dame with Cointet in August, 1843, reputed to be a good farmer and skilled locksmith, was a dead loss; indeed eighteen months had been long enough to prove to Sorin's satisfaction that Eloi was "a foul-mouthed man [*jureur*]," full of inane criticism and "without piety."[43] Yet among the others, so many in their thirties and forties and so many of the Irish-born, Sorin discerned more good than bad. Brother Anthony, for example, a forty-nine-year-old Irishman, exhibited "limited" powers of discernment, but he was "a good brother."[44] Brother Joachim—the second to bear that revered name—displayed "a pious spirit" and consistently made himself "useful." Brother Thomas, a very young man, a mason by trade, may have on occasion given offense by his "habitually curt manner," but he possessed "an excellent heart."

When he addressed the status of the Marianite Sisters for whom he was ultimately responsible, Father Sorin appeared to be, perhaps not surprisingly, less confident in his critique. Their immediate superior he was content to specify simply as one whom he "hoped would do well." Several of the other nuns he designated as "excellent daughters," while still others he judged to be "good sisters." By contrast, the thirty-year-old Sister Mary of Calvary—whose sudden recovery from illness had supposedly prompted Sorin to build the chapel on the island[45]—he held in deep suspicion; whatever her considerable strengths, he maintained, she had "a mischief-making spirit and an extravagant [*folle*] imagination. Up till now," he declared, Mary of Calvary "has been my cross." Sister Mary of Providence, a Frenchwoman aged forty-two, he found harder to categorize; if she was

---

42. See chapter 6, above, and Klawiter, ed., *Adapted to the Lake*, 370.

43. A slightly less harsh judgment but also negative is in Sorin, *Chronicles*, 33.

44. Sorin's roster in this instance differs from that in Klawitter, ed., *Adapted to the Lake*, where none of the three brothers called "Anthony" matches Sorin's description.

45. See note 5, chapter 9, above.

in many respects a vulgar woman [*grossière*] and given to "scandalous" behavior (about which he did not elaborate), she was nevertheless an excellent cook and therefore "very useful" to the community.

But it was in the letter to Moreau which accompanied these analyses that Sorin registered his own flagging spirits as his second year at Notre Dame du Lac came to a close. "I join [to the roster]," he began, "some reflections which I pray that you receive, my reverend Father, less as an act of censure on my part than as a proof of the interest I take in the development of our work." Despite this disavowal, what he wrote surely sounded like a rebuke when read in far-off Le Mans.

> You have sent here Father Marivault along with two confrères [the seminarian François Gouesse and Brother Eloi], none of whom has the true spirit of Sainte-Croix. I have often [since the summer of 1843] had reason to deplore that your choice could not have been more appropriate. I want to believe that you have done your best, but I cannot regard as a benefit what, humanly speaking, is bound to injure our mission rather than strengthen and extend it. Father Marivault has done us great damage among the diocesan clergy; he may well have cost us our entire reputation. And he has done as much damage inside the community as outside, with his fickle and emotional outbursts (*épanchements journaliers*) against priests, brothers, sisters, and so forth. What a poor head he has. If he does well with his money somewhere else,[46] he will do great evil among us. What am I to do with him? Even the savages [among whom Marivault said he wanted to work] have no better opinion of him than the whites.

About the other two malcontents Sorin was less precise and less strident, but his indictment of Moreau's judgment was not less clear. "You have sent here Mr. Gouesse, a person whom some one told you I had known since childhood." Gouesse, three years Sorin's junior, came from Courbeveille, a village only a few miles from Ahuillé. "Could you not, before sending him so far, have consulted with me ahead of time? It is absolutely necessary that the work be sustained by the highest authority, my Father." As for Brother Eloi "who came with them, he remains in a constant state of indecision about his future. . . . If he does not change his ways, he will soon be gone."[47]

---

46. The reference was to the benefaction Marivault was supposedly bringing with him from France. See chapter 8, above.

47. Eloi left the community the next year, 1845.

"And the sisters. You know that Mary of Nazareth has left us, though," he added mysteriously, "she is less culpable in our eyes than the woman who caused her departure."[48]

> I have nothing more to say on this subject, except for what I have said before. I marvel at the readiness at Sainte-Croix and at the Good Shepherd[49] to accept on faith inconceivable things and to receive them at Le Mans as though they were well authenticated. God knows I am very little troubled by the mischief . . . personally, . . . convinced as I am that they are simply lies. But [I cannot be silent] when I see arrive here certain persons predisposed against me, uncertain of the obedience they owe to a Superior who has been guilty of such wickedness, although by a certain delicacy they do not yet dare to say so to him openly; and when some one allows me to infer that we are suspected at Sainte-Croix of marching toward independence and *separation from Sainte-Croix.* If you, my reverend Father, were to inform me of similar opinions of your own, I would bless heaven for them and hope they would be meritorious to the same degree that they would be painful; but at the same time I feel the need to repeat to you my astonishment at the prospect of similar behavior motivated by complaints of the kind I have described. I have too much repugnance to think about this any longer or to write about it. If you think me so culpable have the goodness to command me to recount these matters to you myself. I will do so under obedience, and you can then be the judge.

Wounded pride on Sorin's part was one source of this outburst, and frustration at tale-bearing and gossip—so often the bane of religious and clerical establishments—was another. But the roots of the problem went deeper. If a hurt and angry Sorin did indeed grant Moreau the right to be final arbiter, he did not thereby relinquish his position as the man *en scène,* as the person directly responsible for the work at hand. Clashes between the operator-in-the-field and the administrator at headquarters, even though they share the same ultimate objective, have gone on since the invention of government. Sorin had urged Moreau to come to Indiana and see the situation there for himself, but the Founder declined. What then, it was not impertinent to ask, did Moreau know about America

---

48. Costin, *Priceless Spirit,* 21–22, sheds no light on the identity of Sorin's villainess, saying only that Sister Mary of Nazareth decided she could not live in such "straightened [sic] circumstances."

49. For the connection between Moreau and the Marianites with the Good Shepherd convent in Le Mans, see chapters 2 and 3, above.

and, more specifically, about Holy Cross in America? Only what members of the congregation there chose to tell him, including some whom Sorin believed to be his own chattering and disloyal subordinates. "Have the goodness to command me to recount these matters to you myself."

This was not an unreasonable request. But, on the other hand, Sorin, weighed down by all sorts of problems, had become a prickly subordinate himself. Never one to doubt his own competence, the experience of three years in Indiana had given him warrant, he thought, to determine what was best for the mission there. And he had reached a stage at which his requests often sounded like demands. So it was, for example, when he urged that the novitiate for the priests Cointet and Marivault, which in theory, at least, curtailed their parochial activity, be drastically shortened: "For two whole years our Catholics have been completely neglected by priests living in their midst." Protestant ministers had not been slow to take advantage of "our apparent idleness. . . . In my opinion it would be much more worthwhile to redo part of the novitiate a few years from now."

But more than any single factor it was the status of the Marianite Sisters in America that troubled, and would continue to trouble, the relations between Notre Dame du Lac and Le Mans.

> Even though you might have a still poorer opinion about my ability to govern your sisters, and might want to pay even less attention to our observations about them, I nevertheless hold my ground not less than before as to what I have said . . . about what they ought to have as their objective here: the establishment of orphanages, hospitals, care for invalids, education of the poor, and domestic service for the houses of the community. And they are going to have to change their garb.[50]

Before he sent this letter to Moreau, Sorin prudently showed it to Father Cointet, who endorsed its contents and observed that he too thought some in the community sent complaints to Le Mans without due reflection. And it may have been the gentle Cointet who urged Sorin to mitigate the letter's otherwise harsh contents by writing an affectionate conclusion. Or it may very well have been the

---

50. Sorin's point here remains unclear. Reception of the habit, says Costin, *Priceless Spirit*, 20, "does not mean that any two of [the sisters] were dressed alike. There was an attempt at uniformity in the headdress, which was still undergoing various changes; otherwise 'habits' were made out of whatever material happened to be available." Moreau replied mildly (Catta, *Moreau*, 1: 535): "Before changing the habit of the sisters . . . give me time for study and reflection." See the description of the habit in chapter 3, above.

La Roche, near Ahuillé, Department of Mayenne,
birthplace of Edward Sorin
Photo courtesy of Indiana Province Archives Center

Garden gate at La Roche
Photo courtesy of Indiana Province Archives Center

Basile Moreau (1799–1873), founder of the
Congregation of Holy Cross

Edward Sorin at Black Oak Ridge
Photo courtesy of Indiana Province Archives Center

Célestin Guynemer de la Hailandière (1798–1882),
second bishop of Vincennes

Stephen Badin (1768–1853), proto-priest of
the United States, founder of Sainte-Marie-des-Lacs

Brother Vincent
(Jean Pieau, 1797–1890),
the patriarch

Photo courtesy of
Indiana Province Archives Center

Brother Francis Xavier
(René Patois, 1820–1896),
last survivor of the
founding seven

Brother Lawrence (Jean Ménage, 1815–1873),
sturdy farmer and gold prospector
Photo courtesy of Indiana Province Archives Center

Mother Ascension (1826–1901), among the most steadfast of Sorin's allies

St. Mary's Academy, Bertrand, c. 1850

Photo courtesy of St. Mary's Archives

The Main Building at Notre Dame, c. 1847

Old College

Photo courtesy of Robert Ringel

Manual Labor School

Photo courtesy of Indiana Province Archives Center

Notre Dame Post Office, c. 1856

John Baptist Purcell (1800–1883),
archbishop of Cincinnati, Sorin's favorite prelate

Michael Shawe (d. 1854), peripatetic English priest,
pioneer crafter of the Notre Dame curriculum

Notre Dame du Lac, c. 1865

mercurial Sorin's own deep feelings of regard for the Founder. "Do not believe, my very dear Father, that all these comments mean that my attachment for you has diminished in the least degree, nor my devotion to the work you have entrusted to me. By tomorrow morning, all will have passed away." And then, after paraphrasing in Latin the thought contained in Psalm 90—"Tears in the evening, joy in the morning (*ad vesperum fletus, ad matutinum laetitia*), I have hoped in the Lord, and I shall never be put to shame"—he wrote: "Pardon me, very beloved Father, if I have caused you pain. I love you as I always have. . . . *Adieu, bon Père, adieu.*"[51]

"You write me things which astonish and pain me," Basile Moreau replied, "and which have no foundation in fact. . . . No one has written me the least word of complaint about you or anyone else. That is all a lie." However unpersuasive this blanket assertion may sound in retrospect, there appears no reason to question the sincerity of Moreau's essential pledge: "My friend, . . . more than ever before, I am all yours."[52] And so this small crisis passed, without, however, the root tension being relieved. Perhaps no relief was possible, since the tension is rooted so deep in the ethos of Catholicism and often manifests itself with particular force within religious orders. Here was being played out again the old story of Mary and Martha, of the contemplative and the activist, each respecting the other and even loving the other, and yet never quite understanding the other. In the face of this dilemma the tears of evening were not always followed by the joy of morning.

---

51. Sorin to Moreau, December 4–12, 1844, AGEN.
52. Moreau to Sorin, January 20, 1845, quoted in Catta, *Moreau*, 1: 534–535.

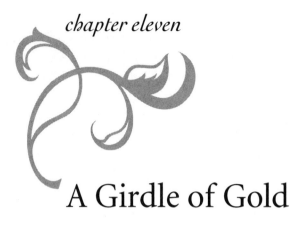

chapter eleven

A Girdle of Gold

W HEN EDWARD SORIN CELEBRATED HIS THIRTY-first birthday, in the February of 1845, there was a promise of spring in the Indiana air. There was promise also that the prodigious labors of the preceding two years would in due course bear abundant fruit for the mission of Notre Dame du Lac. Nor was physical affirmation of such hopes lacking. Where before a vast forest had been broken only by a couple of ramshackle huts huddled on the shore of St. Mary Lake now stood a complex of structures of brick, frame, and log. Dominating the scene, like a great ship surrounded by a flotilla of smaller vessels, was the new collegiate building, plain indeed in its appointments but impressive nonetheless, soaring up four storeys and surmounted by a clock-tower and a fine iron cross, which faced southward and seemed to stand watch over the dirt road that passed through heavy woods toward the village of South Bend, two miles or so away. In front of the college was a fenced-in lawn, and behind it, stretching east to west, were the modest shops of the Manual Labor School and, on the "island," the chapel of Our Lady and the brothers' novitiate. Just east of Father Badin's original chapel stood the log church, whose loft also served for the time being as the sisters' residence, and, a little closer to the lake, the small stand-by collegiate building, "Old College," which had already housed bakery, dormitory, and classrooms and which soon would be converted into a more livable convent.[1] And all around were the newly planted fruit trees and the cleared fields ready for spring sowing.

---

1. Wack, "Notre Dame Foundation," 110–111, and Costin, *Priceless Spirit,* 24.

Eighteen forty-five was to witness further expansion of the Holy Cross compound, but it brought with it some disappointments as well. An infirmary, begun the preceding autumn just to the northeast of the main building, was completed; its second-storey rooms were to be utilized often for temporary residents. Of permanent value was the commodious barn constructed at a cost of $750. Unsuccessful, however, was the print-shop which Sorin, with his habitual optimism, expected to promote religious and pedagogical projects, and at the same time turn a profit.[2] He purchased a printing press for $700 with the intent of publishing pious tracts and schooltexts, and put the mercurial Brother Joseph in charge; but aside from a few trifling jobs, the venture proved "impossible to continue.... The expenses were not sufficiently justified, and the attempt was given up." A similar fate befell an ambitious plan—formulated, Sorin maintained, not by himself but by the brothers—to exploit "the rich banks of [the] lakes to make lime out of the marl" and thus produce commercially plaster, mortar, and even bricks. A limeyard was accordingly set up, but "the first years did not pay expenses, either on account of [the brothers'] ignorance or through mistakes." Nor did persistence pay any dividends: "Not until 1847 and 1848 ... was it recognized that the making of lime here was the most sterile of enterprises." Only the hope remained that with the increase of population in the area, and a consequent growth in the construction industry, some monetary advantage could be gained from what was in itself a valuable natural resource.[3]

In due time the kilns did indeed pay dividends,[4] but even when such projects did not at first prosper, undertaking them was not without benefit. They demonstrated the stubborn intention of these French and Irish men and women, under Father Sorin's leadership, to persevere whatever the difficulties, and to do so in a peculiarly American fashion. Every initiative, moreover, and particularly the work done to enlarge and improve the farm, enhanced the intrinsic value of property which had been a few years before a patch of wilderness. Edward Sorin, his mind ever attuned to expansion, understood that this reality opened for him opportunities to raise cash either through mortgages or, in an extremity, through sale, and local bankers and real-estate brokers understood it too. It may well have been that this circumstance led him to a financial recklessness that his bishop and his superior in France disapproved of—a dissatisfaction heightened by Sorin's careless and sometimes deceitful keeping of accounts. But in the little world of

---

2. Sorin to Moreau, October 13, 1845, AGEN.
3. Sorin, *Chronicles*, 53, 52.
4. See Schlereth, *Notre Dame*, 18.

northwest Indiana the almost incredible transformation in so short a time of Ste.-Marie-des-Lacs into a thriving community exercised an impact of it own. Whatever ideological unease Protestant merchants in South Bend and its environs may have felt at this abrupt appearance of aggressive popery in their midst, they recognized the dozens of religious already at Notre Dame and Bertrand as potential customers over the long term; and day-laborers had already found in those places a source of employment. If the college were to thrive, Notre Dame, with a full complement of students who would also be consumers, might well become an economic dynamo stimulating the whole region. That condition, however, remained throughout 1845 glumly unresolved: during the spring a depressingly small number of thirty-one students were in residence, and in the fall only nineteen of them returned, joined by eight others.[5]

But, as that new year began, Father Sorin painted a much rosier picture of his fellow-workers in the mission than he had in the confidential report he had sent to Le Mans a few weeks before.[6] He may have done so, because he was aware that Father Moreau frequently gave publicity to news from America, when that news was sufficiently edifying.[7] Sorin in any case heaped praise upon the colony that had arrived from France the previous October "after having suffered through such great dangers."[8]

> The more I see of the truly limitless devotion that this new colony exhibits each day, the less surprised I am that the demon . . . tried so hard to prevent them from surviving their voyage. Happily, since they have set foot on the soil of Notre Dame, the enemy appears to have lost all power to harm or molest them any more. Though they have been working exceedingly hard and have shared the sufferings and privations inseparable from a new mission of this kind, they appear full of health and joy. I have scarcely had the time, dear Superior, to thank you adequately for this new gift; we had never before so well understood how deeply indebted we are to you. . . . All of them have filled glaring needs: only since their arrival have we had the satis-

---

5. Wack, "Notre Dame Foundation," 112. Sorin characteristically predicted that the number would reach sixty by the spring of 1846. See Sorin to Moreau, October 13, 1845, AGEN.

6. Sorin to Moreau, December 4–12, 1844, AGEN. See chapter 10, above.

7. What follows is taken from Sorin to Moreau, January 22, 1845, AGEN. Excerpts from this letter were published in Moreau's *Etrennes spirituelles* (1846) and, before that, in *La Province du Maine*, April 26, 1845.

8. The reference was to the rough trans-Atlantic voyage the colony experienced. See chapter 10, above.

faction of seeing . . . reproduced at Notre Dame du Lac the propriety and decency of the motherhouse [in Le Mans], which we original toilers had not had the capacity to secure by ourselves.

As to the presence of "dear Father Granger, he is more precious than silver and gold." Not that silver and gold were ever far from Sorin's mind: each brother, he said, "can save us 100 francs a month and each sister at least as much."

Important as expansion of the mission was to Sorin, scarcely less so was the necessity to put down roots. That too would cost money. In mid-February, so he told Bishop Lefèvre, he received a handsome offer of support if he would transfer the sisters' establishment from Bertrand to Fort Wayne. "I merely thanked those who suggested this," he wrote, "because my set purpose is to leave the nuns where they are, since God himself appears to wish them to stay there." He did not add that Fort Wayne fell under the jurisdiction of the unfriendly bishop of Vincennes, while Bertrand was subject to the benign bishop of Detroit to whom he was writing.

Besides, as ever with Sorin, he saw more in the divine will than may have struck even an episcopal eye, and he did not hesitate to exert some gentle pressure. "Soon it will be necessary for us to build a house of some kind in Bertrand, but the means to do this are now entirely lacking to us." Renting a residence for use as a convent depleted the Holy Cross coffers that were anyway always nearly empty. "I realize that a contribution from your Excellency is not now possible, given your present necessities." But if the bishop would apply to the Propagation of the Faith for aid, "I have confidence that, besides the establishment of the sisters at Bertrand and the opening of an orphanage [for girls] attached to the novitiate, we will be able to staff a permanent school at Pokagon as well as parishes in St. Joseph, Kalamazoo, and Pokagon. Put simply, I believe that with this aid we are going to do more for Michigan than we have done up to now for Indiana." He had thought at first of writing himself directly to Paris and Lyon "and so spare your Excellency any embarrassment," but the latest information he had received was that the Propagation "will in the future accept petitions only from the bishops themselves for religious communities serving in their dioceses."[9] What might have been thought at Le Mans or Vincennes of a direct appeal from Notre Dame to

9. It appears that the Propagation disbursed funds to Notre Dame du Lac through local bishops and through Holy Cross's superior. A separate sheet, enclosed in "Ledger A, August 1841–June[?] 1847, Cash Book," in AUND, ULDG, "Early Records," indicates that between 1842 and the end of 1846 the Holy Cross mission in America received 63,320 francs ($12,664) from the Propagation, all of it through Hailandière, Lefèvre, or Moreau.

the Propagation in France did not appear to trouble Sorin overly much. He contented himself with the observation that "Providence is pleased to give our little family growth week by week," but he also reminded Bishop Lefèvre that the Propagation allocated its disbursements toward the end of April, two months away: "I pray that your Excellency consider this request of mine as soon as possible."[10]

The end of April was also the eve of May, the Virgin Mary's month, the prospect of which brought forward that other, non-monetary, side of Sorin's complex psyche. "As we come to begin the observances of this beautiful month," he wrote Mother Theodore at Terre Haute, "I want to assure you of my intention to profit spiritually for myself and to reap advantage for all those whom I love. And let me tell you that your dear house ranks as much in my affections as my own. . . . Pray God that these thirty-one days of grace and happiness will unite me and my whole family with your dear family of St. Mary of the Woods."[11]

The month of Mary came and went, during which most of the pious exercises were carried out, to Sorin's satisfaction, in the "decent chapel" now available on the "island." But lively devotions to the Virgin did not rule out exhibiting some weeks later another form of piety, the crucial importance of which Sorin shrewdly grasped. "You know," he explained to Basile Moreau,

> that the fourth of July is a day of universal celebration across America. It would be highly impolitic for a public institution to ignore the joy felt throughout the country. So we took part in a way that could not be misconstrued by anyone. On the morning [of July 3] we sent invitations to all the families of note in South Bend, Mishawaka, and Bertrand. About sunset the road leading to the collegiate-building was thronged with visitors. For an hour the guests were conducted on tours of the college facilities. At eight o'clock all repaired to the music hall in which every seat was promptly filled. . . . The performance (*séance*) began with the reading of the Declaration of American Independence.

There followed a speech in praise of that sacred document, delivered by "the professor of mathematics, an Englishman by birth,"[12] and then a short play, the student-performers "fully-costumed," on a patriotic theme. "The applause—

---

10. Sorin to Lefèvre, February 24, 1845, AGEN.

11. Sorin to Mother Theodore, April 30, 1845, AGEN.

12. Most likely the orator was Michael E. Shawe, an English-born priest who had arrived in the Inidana missions in 1839 and served on the Notre Dame faculty for a brief time. See Wack, "Notre Dame Foundation," 129–130, and chapter 12, below.

clapping of hands and pounding of feet on the floor—went on with such vigor that the room seemed to tremble."

So the first formal contact between town and gown came off successfully. Entertainment of any sort on the frontier was rare enough, and the pleasure experienced on this occasion by the local "families of note," Protestant and Catholic alike, could not but foster amiable feelings. Nor were these diminished by the fact that Father Sorin had brought to the *"grand fete,"* as he called it, a measure of calculation.

> This was a spectacle as surprising as it was agreeable to our American neighbors, to witness the anniversary of their independence celebrated in this way in a house peopled by foreigners from the corners of the world. Later they will understand why we rejoice with them on this same day. The [United States] constitution (*charte*) guarantees to us also certain privileges which we have not yet been allowed to enjoy fully; but the day when we do cannot be far off.[13]

He may have overstated the case by identifying France and Ireland as "the corners of the world," but his civic instincts were sound.

At the conclusion of the July fourth festivities Sorin issued a blanket invitation to the audience to return to Notre Dame du Lac for another celebration in less than a month's time. On August 1 the local worthies duly appeared, once again in considerable numbers, to observe the *distribution des prix* which marked the end of the summer collegiate term. The ceremony was properly academic, to be sure, though not a commencement or graduation: the awarding of formal degrees or certificates was still some years off. But most of the thirty or so students in attendance received some kind of prize: thus "at least three of the four" youths from Detroit, Sorin assured Bishop Lefèvre, "would probably be mentioned very honorably."[14] Father Sorin confidently expected Lefèvre and Governor Whitcomb to grace the event by their presence,[15] but, though these distinguished personages failed to appear, the enthusiasm of the other guests was not thereby diminished. As in July they toured the campus, and most of them were particularly enthralled by the "museum" Sorin had recently purchased and assembled on an upper floor of the collegiate building—"a splendid collection of beasts, birds, fishes, reptiles, antiquities, etc., from the various parts of the globe," as one observer described

13. Sorin to Moreau, July 6, 1845, AGEN.
14. Sorin to Lefèvre, June 30, 1845, AGEN.
15. Sorin to Moreau, July 6, 1845, AGEN.

it.[16] Edward Sorin, poor as a churchmouse, nevertheless gloried in *grands gestes* of this kind.

And in the midst of these public comings and goings there emerged during this high summer of 1845 another sign that Notre Dame had perhaps turned a crucial corner. The fields of grain, Sorin cried exultantly, "form a rich girdle of gold" around the compound and give promise of a yield of as many as 1,800 bushels. "The sky seems to invite us to gather up its abundant blessings. . . . What a pleasure it is to see with what eagerness this little army of religious pluck the first fruits of their fatiguing labors." In 1844 an infestation of "worms" had reduced the crop by two thirds, a disaster reminiscent of the driving hail that had leveled the fields at St. Peter's two years before that. "Thanks be to God, this year is going to make up for those past losses," with abundant harvests, besides the wheat, of potatoes, oats, buckwheat, turnips, carrots, onions, and melons. "In short, we should have sufficient produce to support the house and to sell the rest at a profit of at least 10,000 francs [$2,000]."

> It is true that in order to achieve such remarkable results in so short a time has cost our good brothers plenty of sweat: 200 acres of land cleared in less than two years by a handful of religious who have been employed half the time in constructing the chapel, the college, and the novitiate. . . . I assure you [Moreau] that the opinion of this area regarding *the indolence of lazy monks* . . . our brothers have worked [to transform completely]. Even today, in the broiling heat, they show their courage in not allowing themselves to flinch at the sight of so painful a task. And when I see them forgetful of their fatigue in order to give their attention only to the ultimate happy objective, I believe I see the fulfillment of the words of the prophet, "Going forth weeping . . . but they return exultant carrying their sheaves."[17]

WHAT MATTERS IN ASSESSING the person and career of Edward Sorin is not whether his euphoric predictions came true—very often they did not, as was the case with the harvest of 1845—but whether they were consistent with the ideals and ambitions he had set for himself. To say that he constantly looked on the bright side, that he was a kind of clerical Pollyanna, is to underestimate profoundly the force of his character and, moreover, to miss the vein of melancholy that lay deep within him. Whether sad or happy, however, he

---

16. Quoted in Wack, "Notre Dame Foundation," 101.
17. Sorin to Moreau, July 6, 1845, AGEN.

simply refused to entertain the possibility of failure. So confident was he in his own powers, so sure of the ultimate righteousness of his goals, and so deep his faith that God and the Virgin Mary had summoned him to America to accomplish a great work, that no obstacle could confound him. He was no saint. He was capable of duplicity and pettiness and even ruthlessness. But for sheer courage, and for the serene determination that courage gives birth to, he was hard to match. He never doubted for a moment that he was destiny's child and that all would turn out to the good.

It was well that in 1845 Father Sorin could count upon this aplomb, for, in the midst of his triumphs in local public relations, the pressures upon him were beginning to mount. "I think you will soon see the bishop of Vincennes," he wrote Moreau at the end of 1844. "Please give him a good reception—but that may be more easily said than done."[18] Célestin de la Hailandière had indeed with the new year departed for France, and at the beginning of February—a few weeks before Sorin's birthday—had arrived at Le Mans. On the third day of that month, a written agreement was signed between the bishop and Basile Moreau.[19] It has not been recorded whether either of them acknowledged on this occasion that had such a formal instrument been entered into three or four years earlier much misunderstanding might have been avoided, but, given the unyielding personalities involved, it seems unlikely. However that may have been, the terms of the agreement were clear enough. The priests, brothers, and sisters of Holy Cross serving in Hailandière's diocese were free to observe their own rules and were to remain subject to and dependent upon the motherhouse in Le Mans. At the same time they were to regard "their worthy bishop as their local superior, to whom they owe the greatest respect and obedience required by religion. . . . They were to regard themselves as fortunate to enjoy the privilege of his regular [canonical] visit." More directly pertinent to Edward Sorin's aspirations and initiatives, it was agreed that no school under Holy Cross auspices could be founded outside the diocese of Vincennes without the bishop's written consent. Also serious consideration was to be given to transferring the brothers' novitiate from the hallowed confines of St. Mary's Isle to Indianapolis, for some years now the state capitol and the largest town in Indiana and, more to the point, much closer to Vincennes and hence to the bishop's oversight. In return for these substantive concessions Hailandière granted final approval—the deed to this date was still in his possession—of the transfer of the property at Notre Dame du Lac to the Congregation

---

18. Sorin to Moreau, December 4–12, 1844, AGEN.

19. See a copy of the agreement of February 3, 1845, signed by Moreau, AUND, CSCM, "Miscellany, Indiana Province."

of Holy Cross, together with a commitment to add 375 acres more to the original allotment and to contribute to the mission $500 in cash were his desires about the location of the brothers' novitiate complied with.[20]

The apparent advantage Bishop Hailandière won through these negotiations proved to be a pyrrhic victory. Edward Sorin either ignored the agreement's provisions or interpreted them as it suited him, on the grounds that to act otherwise was to imperil the Holy Cross mission in America. He was particularly adamant that the removal of the novitiate to Indianapolis was a bad idea. "It appears to be decided," he wrote glumly to Mother Theodore. "What can be the designs of Heaven in this matter is quite beyond me."[21] However, if such a step were to be taken "in accord with your desires," as he put it sourly to Moreau,[22] let it be linked, as it was at Notre Dame, to a commitment to provide collegiate education to the American Catholic middle class, such as it was. The bishop entertained a much more modest objective: let the novitiate, he said, serve at the same time as a center of instruction for prospective converts to Catholicism. For example, a brother might be assigned to sell cheap religious books door-to-door. As for the general lines of the agreement, Hailandière, in his frustration, wrote later to Sorin: "I ask you, tell me frankly, is your past conduct and your plans for the future exactly what I went to Sainte-Croix to ask for?"[23]

But Sorin had nothing to say to this appeal, convinced though he was that a novitiate located in Indianapolis would fail, as ultimately it did. At the moment, however, this intuition was conditioned by possible alternatives suggested and encouraged by Sorin's old friend and benefactor, Julien Delaune. Delaune—who had gone on a begging tour in behalf of Holy Cross during the desperate days at Black Oak Ridge[24]—was now pastor of the parish in Madison, Indiana, on the banks of the Ohio River. Sorin had kept in touch with him and had sent him several brothers to serve as teachers in his school; indeed, it had been Delaune who had had to report the sad news of Brother Anselm's drowning.[25] From the beginning of their association Delaune had shown himself an enthusiastic

20. Resumé in Catta, *Moreau*, 1: 536–537. The additional acreage had been in the bishop's hands since the failed mission of the Fathers of Mercy in 1840. See chapter 7, note 24, above, and chapter 12, note 64, below.

21. Sorin to Mother Theodore, April 30, 1845, AGEN.

22. Sorin to Moreau, July 6, 1845, AGEN.

23. Hailandière to Sorin, August 31, 1845, AGEN.

24. See chapter 6, above.

25. See Klawitter, ed., *Adapted to the Lake*, introduction.

supporter of Sorin and of the latter's various projects, so much so that it was thought in some quarters that he might well join Holy Cross.[26] In the meantime he remained a lively source of ideas and proposals much in tune with Sorin's own predilections.

Chief among these was the desire to convert the Brothers of St. Joseph from a diocesan institute to a teaching organization which could serve any bishop in any corner of the United States. In this ambition he had been confronted by adamant resistance from Bishop Hailandière, a resistance which appeared to have received final and formal sanction in the agreement of February 1845, signed by the bishop and Father Moreau in Le Mans. But Julien Delaune knew full well that that scrap of paper had not changed Father Sorin's mind, and, in the late summer of that year, he intimated that a powerful ally might be put in play. "It appears, my dear friend," Delaune wrote, "that Monseigneur Purcell shares your views about the establishment of brothers in different dioceses." Delaune cited an article recently published in which the bishop of Cincinnati indicated that he would "solicit support for this enterprise among the prelates attending the forthcoming council."[27] What Purcell apparently had in mind conformed precisely with Sorin's aspirations for his brothers: a single congregation whose members could be dispatched to any diocese requesting them. Approval of this scheme by the council seemed to Delaune a foregone conclusion. Of course, he added, the choice of the specific congregation and its director had to be left to the bishops themselves, but "I would think it a very happy result if Providence . . . would have them cast their eyes upon the man most capable of conducting this work in accord with their intentions. Not for me to give that man counsel, but I think it is by no means too soon for you to open a correspondence with Monseigneur Purcell." Delaune further offered to go to Cincinnati himself and argue the case with Purcell, if Sorin desired it.

Nor was this the only proposition the energetic pastor of Madison had to share with this friend at Notre Dame du Lac. He was ready to found a college of his own. "I have just received a letter from the bishop of Vincennes, and here is an extract from it which concerns you."

Education has to be always our principal business [wrote Hailandière]. I am delighted to see you full of zeal for this cause. Madison requires that this take priority. The town's locale is very advantageous, and a *collège* could

---

26. See Catta, *Moreau*, 1: 553.
27. The sixth Provincial Council of Baltimore was convened in May, 1846.

succeed there.[28] I believe this just as much as you do, but I have less means even than you. I think the only way our hopes can be fulfilled over the long term is through employment of some [teaching] brothers. Two or three capable brothers to begin with, under the direction of a priest, would perhaps be enough, and Father Sorin could perhaps furnish them to you.

"What do you think of this new idea?" Delaune asked Sorin. "His Excellency would leave you free to do it, and it would release you from any obligation with regard to Indianapolis, because obviously you could not staff both places."[29] Most likely Sorin's response, if any, to these ideas would have leaned toward endorsing any initiative that would deliver him from the dead hand of Célestin de la Hailandière.

MEANWHILE FINANCIAL TROUBLES continued apace. In mid-April of 1845, Sorin, desperate for ready money in support of the new infirmary, the printshop, and the limeyard, issued a note, without prior notification to Le Mans, for 3,000 francs ($600) on collateral to be guaranteed by the mother-house at Sainte-Croix. The reaction was swift and predictable.

Father General [Moreau] was quite surprised and deeply pained to learn that you had made, or had promised, new foundations . . . without consulting him and despite the prohibitions which Father Granger and Brother Vincent[30] must have made known to you. . . . From all this he can draw only one conclusion, and it is that he forbids you, in virtue of holy obedience, to undertake anything extraordinary, either in foundations or new buildings, without previously submitting your plans and your reasons, and securing permission.[31]

It does not appear likely that Father Sorin felt unduly constrained by this admonition. Indeed, without bothering to receive permission from Le Mans, he had already dispatched the superior of the sisters resident at Notre Dame to France

---

28. The Eudist *collège* in Vincennes—the existence of which had led Hailandière to forbid the founding of such an institution at Black Oak Ridge (see chapter 6, above)—was by now on the verge of dissolution. See Lemarié, *Missionaires bretons*, 206–208.

29. Delaune to Sorin, August 2, 1845, AIP.

30. Granger and Vincent had arrived from France the previous autumn.

31. Catta, *Moreau*, 1: 540 (letter to Sorin of May 15, 1845, signed by six members of Moreau's council).

on a begging tour. Apparently he did so quite unaware of giving offense, since after the fact he informed Basile Moreau about her mission quite openly.[32] But the latter was so annoyed by this initiative that, once he became aware of it, he forbade the nun—named appropriately, in light of her painful position, Sister Mary of the Five Wounds—to solicit any funds and kept her in penitential seclusion at Sainte-Croix for fifteen months. Her endeavors, even before this authoritative intervention, had in any case produced only negligible results.[33]

The excursion of two other sisters, however, in itself entirely innocent, became a source of annoyance to Sorin himself. The culprit in this instance was Stephen Badin, who, pleading age and fragile health, persuaded two Marianite nuns to accompany him on an ill-defined junket from Indiana to eastern Wisconsin.[34] This happened in the spring of 1846, but the trouble with the ever-cantankerous Badin, "who," Sorin maintained with justice, "never agrees with anybody," had begun the preceding August, when Sorin had traveled to Louisville in order to dispose of the city lots Badin had so generously donated to Notre Dame.[35] Upon arrival in the Kentucky town he discovered to his dismay that the property Badin had cheerfully estimated as worth upwards of $15,000 had in fact a market value of only a fraction of that sum. Sorin duly sold the lots for something less than $7,000,[36] arousing the wrath of Father Badin, who, insisting on his original appraisal, promptly accused the younger priest of haste, carelessness, and naiveté. Sorin countered by pointing out that in the transaction he had employed the local real-estate agent recommended by Badin himself, a gentleman presumably well-informed about the economic realities of the region. The cash from Louisville in any case, though much less than had been hoped for, gave a welcome if temporary reprieve to the by-now habitually strapped Holy Cross community, but the earlier cordial relationship between Sorin and Badin was gone beyond recall.

32. Sorin to Moreau, July 6 and October 20, 1845, AGEN.

33. Costin, *Priceless Spirit*, 22, and Brother Augustine to Sorin, August 4, 1845, in Klawitter, ed., *Adapted to the Lake*, 92. Moreau's treatment of Sister Five Wounds shows clearly that appointing Sorin superior of *all* the Marianite nuns (see chapter 9, above) had been done merely to elude the strictures of the bishop of Le Mans. The Founder had no intention of ceding to Sorin a jot of his ultimate authority.

34. Sorin, *Chronicles*, 55. Costin, *Priceless Spirit*, 24–25, says the trip was not to Milwaukee but to Detroit where one of the sisters sought medical attention.

35. See chapter 10, above.

36. The amount recorded, AUND, ULDG, "Early Records, August 1841–June [?] 1847, Cash Book," was $6,948, but after the agent's fees and miscellaneous expenses were paid the final figure was probably closer to $6,000, as Sorin himself maintained (*Chronicles*, 54).

Indeed, the old proto-priest, never one to suffer opposition gladly or to hesitate to turn a disagreement into a grudge, took up his pen and addressed his complaints directly to Basile Moreau. "While we recognize [Sorin's] good intentions," he wrote, "we cannot but resent his blunders, his hastiness, and his impetuosity in trying to accomplish all the good that comes into his imagination."[37] What Badin was denouncing were capricious projects, like the print-shop and the lime-yard, and, as he judged them, other improvident plans and initiatives for expansion. More sardonically, he reserved particular scorn for the "museum," for which Sorin had set aside space on an upper floor of the new collegiate building. This assortment of curiosities and artifacts had been purchased for nearly $1,000 from a dealer in Detroit,[38] and already had become a source of wonderment and interest to the local community. This reaction was sufficient to justify the museum in Father Sorin's eyes: if Notre Dame du Lac were to succeed—indeed, if it were to survive—it would have to mark itself as an institution culturally worthy of the attention of a wide public.

To Badin, however, to buy a "collection of beasts, birds, and reptiles" represented the kind of extravagance which, aside from its inherent foolishness, could jeopardize the annuity which Sorin had guaranteed him in exchange for the property in Louisville. Negotiations on this matter, Notre Dame laboring under the disadvantage of its empty treasury, dragged on into 1846 and 1847, by which time the peripatetic Badin had moved back to Bardstown, where his apostolate had begun nearly a half-century before, and then to Cincinnati. Sorin finally worked out a settlement with Badin's lawyers,[39] but so bitter was the mutual hostility that payment of the annuity had to be done through an intermediary.[40] Soon the Louisville money was gone and Badin's animosity—"he continues to say all the evil he can [about Sorin]"—rendered his promise of buying and donating to Notre Dame the 200-acre tract between the campus and the St. Joseph River a dead letter. Sorin's bitter ambivalence toward Badin, despite the latter's "venerable white hairs," revealed itself in a few lines he sent the old man in the midst of

---

37. Badin to Moreau, n.d., AGEN (copy).

38. Hope, *Notre Dame,* 71. The collection, assembled by Dr. Louis Cavalli, is described more fully in Peter Leo Johnson, *Stuffed Saddlebags: The Life of Martin Kundig, Priest, 1805–1879* (Milwaukee, 1942), 146. The museum "cost 4 or 5,000 francs and . . . now doesn't pay its rent." Brother Gatien to Moreau, November 21, 1846, in Klawitter, ed., *Adapted to the Lake,* 117.

39. The tortuous negotiations described partially in Sorin to Badin, September 3, 1846, AGEN.

40. See Quinn to Sorin, May 16, 1848, AIP. John Quinn was a pastor in Louisville. His relationship with Sorin over succeeding years remained cordial. Upon reception of a check for $100 he wrote Sorin: "I certainly must praise you for your promptness. You will by such a course give no handle whatever to our very Reverend friend to complain." Quinn to Sorin, May 22, 1851, AIP.

the controversy: "No one has done more good for our institution than you, Monsieur, and no one has done it more harm."[41] He was even more cryptic in summing up the dispute: "From the end of 1845," he wrote in the third person, "Father Badin was evidently angry with Father Sorin. The latter was well aware of the cause, which was not a matter of Dollars, but one that must be kept to himself, leaving it to God to settle accounts whenever it is his good pleasure to do so."[42]

THE DEITY might indeed be supposed capable of maintaining a creditable set of celestial account books; analogous credit, however, could never have been accorded his earthly servant, Edward Sorin. The ledgers meant to keep track of Notre Dame's financial condition had become by 1845 a chaos of paper. All the records were jumbled together indiscriminately, so much so that occasional efforts to reduce them to some intelligible pattern were fruitless. Receipts were entered without distinction, so that charges for tuition, priestly stipends of one kind or another, the small sums now and then earned by the brothers and sisters, and loans from various sources all jostled each other in a single register. Such an arrangement, or lack of it, reflected the practice of dumping all monies into a single fund out of which expenditures, often undefined, were drawn and debts paid, if and when they were paid. Francs mingled with dollars on a series of blotched pages filled with apparently random excisions and additions. Records from the manual-labor shops lay cheek-by-jowl with lists of contributors and with student accounts, many of which were paid partially in cash and partially in kind.[43] It may have been that Sorin's remarkable gifts of courage and decisiveness, his sweeping vision, his sublime confidence that God and the Virgin Mary would provide, left no room in him for the humdrum and pedantic precision required of an accountant. There is no question that in the long run his dreams and ambitions were amply fulfilled, that his willingness to run risks for the sake of the high ideal that had brought him to America yielded rich dividends. But for those who had to deal with him at the time his inability or, troublingly often, his nonchalant refusal to explain how Notre Dame's rapid institutional development was

---

41. Sorin to Badin, August?, 1846, AGEN, which lists in detail the "falsehoods" Badin had been telling about Sorin "here [South Bend], at Chicago, Milwaukee, etc., and even Le Mans."

42. See Sorin, *Chronicles*, 56. Stephen Theodore Badin—who had done "more good and more harm" to Notre Dame than anyone else—died in 1853, in his eighty-fifth year. He was buried in the crypt of St. Peter's Cathedral in Cincinnati. In 1904, eleven years after Edward Sorin's death, Badin's remains were transferred to Notre Dame and now rest in the replica of Badin's log chapel (which was destroyed by fire in 1858), located near the original site. See Schauinger, *Badin*, 284–288.

43. See "Ledger A, August 1841–June [?] 1847, Cash Book," AUND, ULDG, "Early Records."

to be sustained gave understandable cause for alarm. Add to this consideration Sorin's penchant for borrowing money or throwing up a building or committing personnel without consulting his legitimate superiors—to one of whom, Moreau, he had sworn a vow of obedience—and it is hardly surprising that strained relations were the result.

The contrast between Sorin's slapdash management style and Moreau's rigidity should not be underestimated in any analysis of the growing disaffection between the two priests. Basile Moreau was a man for whom attention to detail was a matter of the gravest import; his own schedule was inflexibly organized and compartmentalized, so that not an hour, not a minute should be wasted—all to the honor of God, to be sure, but hardly less to the self-satisfaction of that driven soul.[44] At the feet of Gabriel Mollevaut he had learned and then whole-heartedly adopted the Sulpician model that defined religious maturity in terms of a strict adherence to a regular routine. In Moreau's scheme of things there was no room for intuition or instinct; instinct indeed could well be a snare and a delusion inspired by the devil, while commitment to a carefully spelled-out behavioral system was the key to genuine spiritual progress. Virtue, after all, was simply the supernatural expression of habit. So it was that he delighted in drawing up extremely elaborate sets of rules and constitutions, that he insisted upon the fulfillment of all due formalities, that in his circular letters and in his *Etrennes spirituelles*—short, pious essays composed for the guidance of lay supporters of Sainte-Croix[45]—he consistently placed emphasis upon the need for uniformity of conduct.

It was a short step from this conviction born of religion—almost, one might say, this obsession—to a demand that in secular concerns the Congrégation de Sainte-Croix conform to the highest standards of bourgeois probity. The insistence upon responsible bookkeeping, perhaps not in itself high in the heavenly hierarchy, was nevertheless attuned to Moreau's religious ideals. Orderliness in keeping accounts, if not next to godliness, was not far removed from it. Nor could he as a practical matter—he, the head of an organization already operating on three continents—ignore the obligation to maintain intelligible records of monies received and expended.

But Edward Sorin, spun off into a world Moreau knew nothing of and captivated by what seemed unlimited possibilities offered to the apostolate both of them were committed to, simply could not confine himself to such pedantic preoccupations. He was dreamer of dreams, a designer of vast if sometimes

---

44. See chapter 2, above.
45. See Catta, *Moreau*, 1: 740–758. The *Etrennes* were discontinued in 1851.

chimerical projects, a romantic *chevalier*, a troubadour, a Pied Piper—he could never be a clerk with ink stains on his fingers. His instinct, that untrustworthy faculty in Moreau's judgment, told him that a singular moment had arrived in the history of the Catholic Church: the new, raw, bustling American republic opened vistas heretofore unimagined to those religious alert enough to take advantage of them. What seemed ordinary prudence to others smacked to Sorin of pusillanimity. His own piety ran deep, but it ran in a different current from Moreau's; it was more expansive, more pragmatic, more elastic. And it appeared to some, and not only to Basile Moreau, to be increasingly compromised by American mores. Sorin, complained one of those who had accompanied him from France, "is not much on his guard against subtle flattery and the assurances of Americans, whom he believes in preference to his [confrères] and with whom he often shares plans before saying a word to those in his own house."[46]

Murmurs of discontent from within his community, and, as he rightly suspected, eventually heard through the post at Le Mans,[47] were troubling enough for Edward Sorin; much more so was the order he received late in 1845 to repair to the Holy Cross motherhouse in France and give an account of his stewardship. This unwelcome news came after a late summer and early autumn turned sour by uncertainties and internal disputes. The portion of Father Marivault's inheritance that had survived litigation in the French courts, originally earmarked for Notre Dame, was now, by Moreau's order, to be diverted to Sainte-Croix.[48] This decision, Sorin complained, together with a less than anticipated grant from the Propagation of the Faith, amounted to shortfall of 13,000 francs ($2,600).[49] Less weighty a problem, but even more unpleasant, was a series of clashes with Francis Gouesse, the seminarian Sorin had disliked from the start. So truculent and abusive did the young man become that an angry Sorin banished him to Pokagon.[50] Ten days spent among the poor Potawatomi was apparently a chastening experience for Gouesse, who, Sorin reported, returned to Notre Dame "wiser, more tractable, and a consolation to us all."[51] The consolation was not destined to last.

46. Brother Gatien to Moreau, November 21, 1846, in Klawitter, ed., *Adapted to the Lake*, 121.

47. See his complaints on this score, Sorin to Moreau, December 12, 1844, AGEN.

48. See chapter 8, above.

49. Sorin to Moreau, August?, 1845, AGEN.

50. Sorin to Moreau, August 27, 1845, AGEN.

51. Sorin to Moreau, October 13, 1845, AGEN.

The formal directive to Sorin to appear at Le Mans was not couched in combative terms; it merely stated that the annual chapter of Holy Cross priests, from
attendance at which Sorin had been dispensed in previous years, would in 1846
require his presence.[52]

But, sanguine as he habitually showed himself, he knew that at such a conference he would be confronted with complaints and even reproaches, and that he
would be expected to justify his future plans as well as his past actions. Such an
eventuality was, to say the least, distasteful to him. On the other hand, he never
lacked confidence in his powers of persuasion: an appearance at the chapter would
give him an opportunity to contest the repugnant provisions of the Le Mans agreement of February 1845. Moreover, if he were indeed to undertake a journey to
France, he might well use it as an occasion to try to secure new funding and to recruit additional personnel. It seems likely also that he found attractive the prospect of seeing friends and family at Ahuillé after so long an absence.

Upon balancing the options Sorin decided to resist the summons. His avoid-
ance-strategy, however, a curious combination of bluster and disingenuousness,
proved to be in the end self-defeating. "My absence over four months"—which
such a junket would inevitably involve—"I am convinced," he wrote Moreau,
"would wreak real harm on the community here as well as on [relations with] the
larger public. . . . At the moment there is no one, neither an outsider nor somebody in-house, who could conveniently replace me." At the same time—and here
his attempt at artfulness came into play—"there are extremely strong reasons for
me to desire to make this trip," so that he could describe for the chapter the invitations recently received at Notre Dame du Lac, invitations highly advantageous
to the congregation, to establish houses of the Brothers of St. Joseph in Canada
and in the diocese of Cincinnati: "Canada, more pious and more Catholic even
than France," and so a rich source of vocations, and Cincinnati, presided over by
a bishop who "is one of the most respected prelates in the United States." Other
bishops will follow John Baptist Purcell's lead, Sorin argued, and, though "Vincennes will probably refuse to agree," we must not fail to seize this advantage of
an opportunity "to establish ourselves across America." What we need at this moment, he maintained, is more personnel.

> Please take account, my dear Father, that this set of circumstances may
> never come again. It will be a boon for our brothers; but if the bishops do
> not in the immediate future find assignment to their dioceses of our people,
> they will in six months time go to Ireland to satisfy their needs. If that hap-

---

52. Catta, *Moreau*, 1: 544.

pens, five-sixths of the vocations we might have expected in the eastern United States and [French] Canada will have been lost to us. I make bold to say that a proposal so advantageous to our brothers has never been on offer, at least not that I know of. The consequence of your agreement to this request would be to guarantee over the next twenty years the prosperity and usefulness of our brothers throughout the country. If you refuse to agree, not only would you renounce doing an incalculable good but also, strictly speaking, you would compromise what we have been able to accomplish here. This is a vital decision which is demanded of you now.

What Sorin was arguing in this rather hectoring tone was the need for immediate agreement to these possibilities of expansion, after which it would be imperative for him to stay at home and see them through; a trip to Europe to plead his case would involve *ipso facto* unacceptable delay. But whatever its intrinsic merits, such a contention had little chance of finding concurrence in Le Mans. Indeed, it was Father Sorin singing the same old song—expand the operations of Holy Cross now and worry about resources later; here was an instance of his weakness, so it was judged, for sweeping proposals that warranted calling him before the bar of his colleagues at Sainte-Croix in the first place. Nor could they or their superior have been much reassured by a sunny prediction that all Notre Dame's debts would be paid, once the lots in Louisville were sold, nor by a recital of plans for new construction on the campus, including a grand church—to replace "the poor log-cabin, . . . this poor shed in which we now suffer"—and, "in accord with the original blueprint," an addition for the collegiate building which would cost a mere 9,000 francs.

But Edward Sorin remained blissfully unaware that explanations of this sort simply confirmed the anxiety felt by Moreau. "If, despite the arguments adduced here, you still think it my duty to come to France," Sorin concluded, "let the summons be considered a conditional one, dependent *upon when the state of our house shall permit complying with it*. . . . Simple prudence urges me to beg you not to expose our community to the dangers my absence would now entail. . . . If one of our dear fathers would be acceptable [as emissary to the chapter], the house here will suffer less. Whom would you like to have?" To substantiate that this appeal represented the views of senior members of the Notre Dame community, the letter was signed by Fathers Cointet and Granger and Brothers Vincent and Gatien, as well as by Sorin himself.[53]

---

53. Sorin et al. to Moreau, October 20, 1845, AGEN.

Whatever hopes he may have had about the reception of his request, Father Sorin was in a despondent mood as this checkered year of 1845 neared its close. In mid-November "we had the honor of a visit from the worthy bishop of Milwaukee, Dr. Henni,[54] who was seeking brothers to serve in his diocese. You understand, dear Father [Moreau], the pain I feel on these occasions when I have to reply that our hands are tied." He was pained also now that he had learned that Moreau had expressed his displeasure at the attempt of Sister Mary of the Five Wounds to raise money in France by detaining her at the motherhouse. And pervasive was a growing sense of isolation. "I must tell you, my reverend Father, despite all my efforts to prove our affection for Sainte-Croix, Sainte-Croix seems to have completely forgotten us. Not a word from a single priest or brother or sister or student, not the least bit of news, not the least account of goings-on for a whole year, and very little the year before. Yes, a few lines written in haste to me, but nothing for the others here." Though he had been named superior of the Marianite sisters,[55] he was "left in total ignorance as to the growth, the successes, and even the trials of these good daughters of Le Mans." Perhaps these "reproaches" sounded harsh, "but my constant desire to see all the members of our dear family united by genuine bonds of charity makes me fear exceedingly that this charity is not being very carefully nurtured."[56]

The splendid fourth of July celebration was but a memory now. The golden girdle was gone. The fields around the little lakes stood empty and starkly brown. And soon the icy winds from the north would begin to blow once more.

54. Swiss-born John Martin Henni (1805–1881), first bishop of Milwaukee (1843–1875), first archbishop (1875–1881).

55. This nominal appointment had been Moreau's maneuver to evade the authority of the bishop of Le Mans in securing canonical status for the sisters. See note 33, above.

56. Sorin to Moreau, November 17, 1845, AGEN.

chapter twelve

Threats and Alarums

"MY DEAR SUPERIOR," EDWARD SORIN WROTE ON February 12, 1846, "only yesterday evening did I learn positively that I have to make the journey to France this year." His attempt to avoid what he predicted would be a time-wasting appearance at the chapter of Holy Cross priests in Le Mans had come to naught. "If I can be of any service to you while there," he continued in his note to Mother Theodore Guérin in Terre Haute, "I hope you will afford me this opportunity to prove of benefit to you—at any rate, you must keep me in your prayers during this long voyage to come." He was scheduled to sail from New York between March 5 and March 10 and to return sometime after July 15. "I assure you that my thoughts will be often of our dear America. I shall do all that I can to put to good use the approaching fatigue and distress which I would dread were it not that I believe God wants me to go."[1]

But even on the eve of his departure, with the likelihood that he would receive upon his arrival at the motherhouse some kind of reprimand, he continued to dabble in the type of negotiations that had been explicitly forbidden him. "I would like very much," he assured the archbishop of New Orleans, "to send you three or four brothers in accord with the wish you have expressed several times. If you had some new proposal or some greater advantages or resources to offer us, it would be very good for me to know about them during my sojourn at the motherhouse in Le Mans, where I shall pass the whole month of May."[2] Associa-

---

1. Sorin to Mother Theodore, February 12, 1846, AGEN.
2. Sorin to Blanc, February 16, 1846, AGEN.

tion between Notre Dame and New Orleans, a highly contentious one, did indeed come to pass a few years later, but it did not figure, except in a general way, in the discussions at Sainte-Croix in the spring of 1846.

Not so another initiative that reached Father Sorin at about the same time. It arrived at Notre Dame in the form of a letter from Bishop Guy Chabrat, coadjutor to the venerable Benedict Flaget of Bardstown / Louisville, Kentucky.[3] Chabrat explained that the Society of Jesus, which for some years had operated St. Mary's College located near Lebanon, about forty-five miles south of Louisville, was departing that institution for greener pastures. St. Mary's had been founded by an energetic Irish-born missionary named William Byrne ,who conducted it almost single-handedly for twelve years: he was "president, prefect of discipline, procurator, and [sole] professor." Despite the typically straitened circumstances involved in such a venture, the college from its beginning attracted a considerable number of students and not only from Kentucky. In 1832, the year before he died, Byrne, with the bishop of Bardstown's approval, turned the college over to the Jesuits. During their tenure St. Mary's—situated on "four hundred acres of excellent land on which the Jesuits, according to [Chabrat], had just spent fifty thousand dollars and whose buildings could lodge three hundred persons"[4]—had held its own and indeed had continued to serve up to a hundred students a year; it could also boast, among other things, a library of 5,000 volumes.[5] But now, at the end of 1845, the Jesuits, invited to staff what would become Xavier University in Cincinnati and Fordham University in New York City, determined to shift their personnel to these more favorable sites, much to the annoyance of the diocesan authorities at Louisville. And thus it was that Bishop Chabrat offered St. Mary's to the men of Holy Cross.

Edward Sorin was more than intrigued by this proposal, which clearly was more attractive than invitations he had received from other bishops. Here on tender was an institution that had demonstrated its viability over a twenty-five-year period. To bring it under the aegis of Holy Cross could open a host of possibilities and, perhaps, might even deliver Sorin himself from some of his troubles.

---

3. The diocese of Bardstown, with Flaget (1763–1850) as first bishop, was founded in 1808. Chabrat (1787–1868) was named his coadjutor in 1834. Seven years later the diocesan seat was transferred to Louisville.

4. Sorin, *Chronicles*, 66.

5. See Francis Cassidy, "Catholic College Foundations and Development in the United States (1677–1850)" (doctoral dissertation, The Catholic University of America, 1924), 28–30; Ben. J. Webb, *The Centenary of Catholicism in Kentucky* (Louisville, 1884); and M. J. Spalding, *Miscellanea*, 4th ed. (Baltimore, n.d. [1866]), 729–735. This last was a eulogy preached in 1843, the tenth anniversary of William Byrne's death.

He replied immediately to Chabrat, tentatively accepting the offer, provided that the St. Mary's property pass to Holy Cross intact, that the bishop apply for a 20,000 francs-grant from the Propagation of the Faith in order to pay initial expenses, and, finally, "that his Lordship would do his best to organize at St. Mary's a central [teaching brothers'] novitiate for the United States, sanctioned by all the Bishops of the Union."[6]

This last condition reflected an idea that had been forming in Sorin's mind for a goodly time, an idea he had been exploring since at least the previous summer with Julien Delaune and Bishop Purcell.[7] Nothing had frustrated Father Sorin so much as Bishop Hailandière's insistence that the Brothers of St. Joseph serve exclusively within the diocese of Vincennes. But in a parallel situation Sorin had adroitly eluded that prelate's intransigence by establishing the Marianite Sisters in the diocese of Detroit. That precedent could not have been lost upon him as he pondered Chabrat's offer. Yet, if there were similarity between the two cases, there was a major difference as well: Bertrand, although in Michigan, lay only a few miles from Notre Dame du Lac, which remained the center and headquarters of Holy Cross in America. Lebanon, Kentucky, on the other hand, was hundreds of miles from northwest Indiana. To set up at St. Mary's a kind of national novitiate, and to assume direction of a college markedly more successful than the one at that moment barely surviving at Notre Dame, could not but leave the original foundation in limbo at best. Though Sorin did not say so explicitly, the possibility that the focus of Holy Cross's missionary endeavors should shift to Kentucky, even to the extremity of abandoning Notre Dame, undoubtedly occurred to him.[8] So baneful was the unending quarrel with Hailandière.

The timing of Chabrat's overtures was inopportune for Sorin, since they came on the eve of his departure for France. But he made the best of it and, with his habitual, not to say presumptuous, optimism, he assured Louisville that he would formally submit the proposal at Le Mans, confident that it would be favorably entertained there. Chabrat responded cordially, accepting the conditions Sorin had laid down and "saying that he regarded the matter as settled." With Chabrat's letter in his pocket, Sorin, just before boarding ship in New York, wrote Julien Delaune, "informing him of what was happening and requesting him to go in person to St. Mary's and to send him without delay at Sainte-Croix an account of the property and buildings with as close an estimate as possible of the

---

6. Sorin, *Chronicles,* 66.
7. See chapter 11, above.
8. See the comments of Wack, "Notre Dame Foundation," 139–140.

expenses required in order to establish a community there."[9] No proposition could have sounded more sweetly in Father Delaune's ears than one that would directly associate him with the work of the man he admired more than any other. Cheerfully shaking the dust of Madison, Indiana, from his feet—and so exchanging humdrum parochial duties for a share in what promised to be a much more rewarding and exciting project—he sped off to Kentucky, Father Sorin's faithful agent, to be sure, but also anxious to carve out a significant niche for himself.

BEFORE HE LEFT FOR NEW YORK, Sorin held a conference with the Marianite Sisters under his charge and warned them, not altogether playfully, to bear in mind the venerable pietistic saw that when a spiritual director was absent the devil sought to take his place.[10] It did not please him, when he learned of it later, that a few weeks afterward two of the nuns, as though substantiating his admonition, had gone off on a frivolous expedition, as he viewed it, with the ineffable Stephen Badin.[11]

The old proto-priest was discerning enough to perceive that the administration during Sorin's absence was not likely to obstruct his activities, frivolous or otherwise. To serve as acting superior at Notre Dame and Bertrand, Sorin had appointed Alexis Granger. The choice proved to be a not altogether happy one; Father Granger was loyal and conscientious, but he was also diffident to a fault, a priest who placed spiritual premium upon passive virtues like humility and forbearance rather than upon the forcefulness required of a leader. In fact Sorin had set aside the advice of some of his senior colleagues, who had formally pronounced that "Granger could not do it" and that he, Sorin, should instead designate Francis Cointet as his vicar.[12] But Cointet—the only other possible candidate given Sorin's antipathy toward Father Marivault—refused to give up the pastoral commitments he had made to the far-flung parishes he was serving. This imbroglio was merely the first step in what proved to be a wholly unsatisfactory venture for Father Sorin.

And indeed during Granger's brief tenure the institution, collegiate and religious, did drift under a feeble administrative hand. The good and pious priest shunned any hard decisions, like reining in Stephen Badin. The morale among the seminarians plummeted over these months—three of the five in residence

---

9. Sorin, *Chronicles*, 67.
10. Costin, *Priceless Spirit*, 24.
11. See chapter 11, above, especially note 32.
12. Wack, "Notre Dame Foundation," 126.

had left before Sorin's return. These defections had in turn a negative effect in the college, where several of the seminarians had acted as instructors.[13] The nuns, deprived of their mother superior for more than a year, were restless and peevish. But Granger, incapable of dealing with serious problems, confined himself to trivialities, such as determining how many table napkins should be allotted to each sister.[14] "There's no one here who can replace [Sorin], and human prudence," Brother Gatien predicted, "expects only disorder and ill-fortune." Not that the hypercritical Gatien did not detect plenty of "disorder" already in place. "Father Superior's great kindness (or timidity or lack of vigilance)," he informed Moreau about the time Sorin left for New York, "lets him be easily fooled in his moves and in his dealings with hypocrites and flatterers, who get from him everything they want." He went on to recount how Sorin had overlooked the "scandalous behavior" of several postulants "who merited expulsion; . . . he preferred to imagine that those who complained [about them] were mistaken." One of these miscreants had since "married without a priest at the door of the university."[15]

Such peccadilloes were hardly uppermost in Edward Sorin's mind when he confronted his revered founder and his peers at the chapter at Sainte-Croix. The statistics he presented, testifying to the growth of the mission in America, duly impressed his hearers in the course of the meetings held in late April and May. There were committed to the mission of Notre Dame du Lac, its superior reported, four priests, five seminarians, thirty-two brothers, eight postulants, and nineteen sisters. Fifty apprentices and other workmen were associated with the Manual Labor School on campus, as were numerous orphans. Two sisters had gone into residence in Pokagon and were instructing the Potawatomi children there in religion and in reading and writing. But, significantly, the numbers of fee-paying students in the college, disappointing as they were, remained unstated.[16]

But sharp questions were raised by the capitulants about the prudence of some of Sorin's initiatives, about the trustworthiness of his accounting procedures, and, more specifically, about the overall financial condition of Notre Dame du Lac. In answer to this last query, Sorin admitted an accumulation of debt, but he maintained that the liabilities the mission had accrued were scarcely more than the assets in hand in real property, domestic animals, and capital goods, like

---

13. Wack, "Notre Dame Foundation," 113.

14. Costin, *Priceless Spirit*, 25. For broader indications of the faltering leadership, see Minutes of the Council of Administration, AUND, CSCM, "Miscellany, Indiana Province," March 9–August 17, 1846.

15. Gatien to Moreau, February 18, 1846, in Klawitter, ed., *Adapted to the Lake*, 103–104.

16. "Report," dated May 27, 1846, AGEN. See Catta, *Moreau*, 1: 544–545.

farm machinery.[17] On other issues, convinced that "more than one calumny had preceded him" to Le Mans, "he, perhaps too readily, looked upon it as beneath him to justify himself against charges whereof he had never been guilty; his silence was taken as a tacit confession of the things laid to his charge."[18]

This assessment was Sorin's own, written in the third person sometime after the fact. On the chapter's side, in all probability, lay an unspoken current of suspicion, that the waywardness of the mission in Indiana betokened an inclination of its chief to separate it and himself from Sainte-Croix.[19] It would no doubt have been better in the long run for all concerned to have had the air cleared on this matter, but neither Sorin nor his inquisitors were prepared to do so. Then, just as the waters were at their muddiest, Stephen Badin's letter of complaint arrived in Le Mans.[20] Moreau promptly showed it to Sorin, who seized his pen in fury.

> You have believed it right, after mature consideration, to accuse me to my Superior of the gravest derelictions possible for one in my position to commit. Your white hairs have so far prevented any reply. . . . If this accusation launched by a very old priest affected only me personally, so that the consequences would concern me uniquely, I would not level at you the least reproach. But when I see that in doing this you compromise the future of a work which not long ago excited your lively sympathy, of which you spontaneously made yourself the first benefactor, and about which you still protest loudly that you have always desired its success—when I see all this I have to inform you that, whether you are sincere or not, you have *in effect* already advanced the ruin of that very work.

However seriously Father Moreau and the members of the chapter took Badin's specific grievances, there existed a disquieting similarity between the old man's grumbling and the qualms they already harbored about the situation in Indiana. Sorin for his part had no doubts: "You are the cause," he told Badin, "that my journey to France . . . has had no success, . . . that some at Sainte-Croix think it right to take action against a man they now consider, in all probability, an un-

17. See report of the General Chapter, April 17, 1856, AUND, CSCM, "Miscellany, Indiana Province."
18. Sorin, *Chronicles*, 60.
19. So at least opines Catta, *Moreau*, 1: 546, without attribution.
20. See chapter 11, above.

worthy priest, without faith or honor, whom they leave for the moment at his post only because here and now they have no one to replace him."[21]

It was hardly uncharacteristic of Sorin to overstate his case, but neither his outrage nor the list of Badin's allegations that had so provoked him seemed to sway the capitulants. They forgave a considerable debt allegedly owed the motherhouse by Notre Dame,[22] and then put together a set of bland recommendations which, rather timidly, asserted the precedence of the motherhouse and which imposed upon Sorin an obligation to abide by financial strictures consistent with the overall commitments of Holy Cross.[23] On one issue, however, they were precise and adamant. When Sorin exultantly described the advantages of an annexation by Holy Cross of St. Mary's College, the chapter instructed him to leave all future inquiries on the matter to the motherhouse. This decision was prompted by the news that the enthusiastic Julien Delaune, once arrived in Kentucky, had immediately spent 9,500 francs ($1,900) of borrowed money for furnishings left behind by the departing Jesuits. Sorin protested to the chapter that such expenditure went beyond any directives he had given Delaune and that in any case the 20,000 franc subsidy the diocese of Louisville would presently receive from the Propagation of the Faith would easily liquidate this momentary if imprudent indebtedness. Moreau and the other capitulants, however, already deeply suspicious of Sorin's financial dealings, remained unpersuaded: the superior of Notre Dame du Lac was to restrict his attentions to that mission and was not to meddle in the Kentucky affair. The door was left open to a possible agreement between Le Mans and Louisville, but only after mature deliberation and, particularly, only after the Propagation's grant was in hand.

This ruling put Edward Sorin in an awkward and humiliating position. It was to him and to Notre Dame, after all, that Bishop Chabrat had offered St. Mary's, and it was he who had dispatched his friend Father Delaune to inquire into the feasibility of the transaction. The latter had indeed, albeit in perfectly good faith, exceeded his instructions, but it was Sorin upon whom the chapter's rebuke had

---

21. Sorin to Badin [summer, 1846], AGEN. The context of this undated letter suggests it was written at Notre Dame in late August or early September. But its origin was certainly what Sorin had read at Le Mans, where Badin's letter to Moreau arrived in early June (Catta, *Moreau*, 1: 543), weeks before Sorin's departure.

22. The records are not altogether clear, but it would appear by a statement dated June 15, 1845, and confirmed by another document dated April 21, 1846, that Notre Dame was in arrears to Sainte-Croix by 13,943.37 francs. By June 20, 1846, that indebtedness had been reduced to 95.88 francs. See AUND, CSCM, Miscellany, Indiana Province, "Accounts between Motherhouse and Notre Dame." Negotiations were in any case extensive, and one entry indicates that Sorin bought "une paire de souliers" for six francs.

23. A summary in Catta, *Moreau*, 1: 546–547.

fallen. And as Delaune labored at his behest in Kentucky, he himself had been reduced, under religious obedience, to an embarrassing silence. Here was one more reason for Sorin, in retrospect, to dismiss the prolonged conversations at Le Mans as irrelevant—they "did not remove . . . dispositions on one side or the other"—and even to resent them as having caused havoc at home.

> Of all the endeavors of Father Sorin since his arrival in the United States, none perhaps was more injurious to him than his voyage to Europe at a time when his presence was far more necessary to his house than he could have imagined. During his absence, which lasted for about six months, . . . the evil spirit made ravages in his flock which even two years later he had not been able to repair. Not that Father Granger, who took his place, was negligent or spared himself in any way, but being overburdened with duties and having daily to fight against bad will, which took advantage of the superior's absence to heap difficulties in the way, he could not oppose a sufficiently strong resistance to the passions of others which had become more exacting, nor maintain everywhere the spirit of submission and of peace.[24]

Nor had Sorin's hopes that while overseas he might secure fresh funding come to fruition. He made a side trip to Paris in early May and filed a formal application for aid from the Propagation of the Faith, but this charitable organization was already granting as much support as it considered feasible. In the end he had to admit that "financially this journey was hardly more successful; [I] made expenses and very little over." His only consolation—a considerable one—was the large number of new personnel who accompanied him back to America: nine sisters, three brothers, a priest, a seminarian, and a brother-postulant. After a tedious voyage of forty days, they landed in New York on August 15, and a week later they arrived safely at Notre Dame.[25] However trying the journey, it was child's play compared to what the seven men of Holy Cross had endured five years before.

ONCE BACK HOME IN INDIANA, Edward Sorin offered a melancholy report to his confrères.

---

24. Sorin, *Chronicles*, 59.

25. Sorin to Moreau, September 3, 1846, AGEN, says the date of arrival was August 22, while Sorin, *Chronicles*, 61, says August 24. See following note.

The Reverend Father Superior assembled the Council of Administration in order to give an account of his journey and to acquaint us with the unfavorable dispositions of the Mother House towards us, occasioned by the misrepresentations of individuals belonging to our American branch of the institution, and especially those of the late Superior of the Sisters in Bertrand.[26]

But Sorin shortly afterward acknowledged that, at least in one area and at least for the time being, the criticisms leveled at him during the chapter in Le Mans had more substantive roots than merely the complaints of a disgruntled nun. "I am alarmed about the payment of our debts," he wrote Moreau on September 3. "Although our assets do exceed them by a little"—not quite what he had maintained at Le Mans—"nevertheless there is no assurance that monies owed us will arrive in time to pay what we owe. . . . Without cash I do not know what will become of our mission." He was particularly concerned about a note for 10,000 francs ($2,000) plus interest which was to fall due by the following February. "I had counted upon using the same sum pledged to us by the Propagation of the Faith, but when I returned I discovered that Father Granger had already spent part of it, and most of the rest had to go to settle a multitude of small debts amassed during my absence.[27] . . . Please believe me this time, my reverend Father, I am going to do all I can to free us from these embarrassments. Help me with all your might."[28]

"Please believe me this time. . . ." Chastened into good resolutions about the handling of finances Edward Sorin may have been by the confrontation at Le Mans, but, even so, he remained convinced that the whole undertaking had been a mistake. "If I were not persuaded that God had some designs for my trip to France, designs which I do not yet see, I would say that it was the greatest error in administration that I have committed in my five years here." The vexation he felt, however, he carefully ascribed to what had happened at Notre Dame during his absence, not to any disappointments he may have experienced in the bosom of

26. Minutes of the Council of Administration, AUND, CSCM, "Miscellany, Indiana Province," August 23, 1846. The nun in question was Sister Mary of the Five Wounds, who had gone to France on a begging tour and whom Moreau had detained in Le Mans. See chapter 11, above, and Costin, *Priceless Spirit*, 21–22.

27. At the moment of Sorin's departure for France the cash on hand amounted to $538. A week later it stood at $273. See the minutes of the Council of Administration, March 2 and 9, 1846, in AUND, CSCM, "Miscellany, Indiana Province."

28. Sorin to Moreau, September 3, 1846, AGEN.

the motherhouse at Sainte-Croix. Nor did he care to "blame many of my confrères here who deserve sincerest praise for the unlimited devotion they have shown since my departure." But there had been internal "crisis" enough, and, "to tell you [Moreau] my whole thought, . . . seeing that the establishment did not succumb during the past six months, demonstrates clearly that God watches over us and takes care of us."

The unspecified troubles had arisen out of a lack of discipline, and Sorin moved quickly to cure them by prescribing a stiff dose of spirituality. Within days of his return the brothers went on retreat, followed by the sisters, and then by the priests, the latter joined by Francis Gouesse, who was shortly to be ordained. The results were gratifying: "The more trouble there had been this year, the more each one seemed to take to heart the making of this retreat well, and at the same time it seemed to pleasure them."[29] New assignments and obediences were distributed within the community, the most significant of which were Father Granger to be master of novices for both priests and brothers and Sorin himself "to remain financial officer (seul économe)"—this last inevitable but hardly calculated to inspire elation at Sainte-Croix.

After their retreat, four brothers, to whom Father Moreau had given prior approval, made their profession, as did, on what must have been a poignant occasion, "two other good brothers, John Baptist and Anthony, who are dying; I did not ask permission for them when I was in Le Mans, and yet I believed I could admit them to the happiness of the vows, for fear that their deaths would occur before your response could reach us."[30] Final profession for Cointet, Marivault, and Gouesse was put off till the Christmas season. Sorin could not muster even faint praise for Marivault: "[He] is much the same as he was at Sainte-Croix," he told Moreau. Gouesse, by contrast, had for the moment won back his superior's approbation: "[He] has astonished the whole community by the way in which, over the last year, he has reversed his earlier reputation. He certainly merits to be encouraged, and I hope, reverend Father, you will permit him to be ordained priest during Christmastide at the latest."[31]

And despite Sorin's repeated use of the alarming word "crise" to describe the state of affairs at Notre Dame during his absence, only one member of the community was formally censured upon his return. "The conduct of Sister Mary of

29. Sorin, Chronicles, 52.

30. John Baptist (William Rodgers), born in Ireland in 1815, died October 13, 1846; Anthony (Thomas Dowling), born in Ireland in 1780, died January 10, 1847. See Klawitter, ed., Adapted to the Lake, 369, 360.

31. Gouesse was ordained in the spring of 1847. See Bazin to Sorin, December 1, 1846, AIP.

the Heart of Jesus," he reported, again without giving specifics, "has been as hurtful to us in America as it was in Le Mans. God pardon the poor girl." By unanimous vote the nuns' council, over which Sorin presided,

> decreed that she must put off the religious habit. Only then did she seem to
> appreciate the seriousness of her fault. The next day her physical and moral
> despondency was so great that I feared for her life. . . . I took pity on her
> and offered her pardon, on condition that she should go and do penance at
> Pokagon, under the eye of one of the senior novices until such time as I
> judged it proper to recall her to Bertrand. She received this favor with every
> sign of lively gratitude. For ten days she has been living with the [Pota-
> watomi] savages, and she appears to have abided by her promises. God
> grant that she always be faithful to them. . . . All the other sisters are doing
> well, and Bertrand is as quiet and peaceful as possible. I was there yesterday
> and found everything very satisfactory.[32]

THERE WAS A CERTAIN AMOUNT of hubris in Sorin's ac-
count, as though his simple presence were enough to restore tranquillity to a
mission which had fallen into disarray over his six months' absence. Or perhaps
he was merely whistling in the dark, as he contemplated the sea of troubles that
threatened to engulf him. Even the powers of nature appeared hostile. During
the autumn and winter of 1846–47 nearly everyone at Notre Dame fell ill at one
time or another. Besides Brothers John Baptist and Anthony, one of the seminarians died and, a year later, so did the prize-recruit just brought back from France.
In Le Mans, before his original departure for America, young Father Sorin had
acted as spiritual director to Louise Naveau—Sister Mary of the Cenacle, once
she took the veil—"a woman," he said, "of tried virtue, of more than ordinary
merit for her knowledge of the world, of tact, zeal, devotedness," in whom he had
placed high hopes as the best person to lead and invigorate the motherhouse at
Bertrand and the convent of domestic nuns stationed at Notre Dame itself. Her
premature death he considered one of the harshest blows endured by the mission
in its early days.[33]

---

32. Sorin to Moreau, September 3, 1846, AGEN.
33. Sorin, *Chronicles*, 60, 76–77. Once professed, Sister Mary of the Cenacle became superior of
the sisters stationed at Notre Dame. In February 1847 she moved to Bertrand and assumed the same
position there. See Costin, *Priceless Spirit*, 26–29; Brosnahan, *King's Highway*, 149, and Catta, *Moreau*,
1: 588.

The college continued to struggle. The number of students remained dispiritingly low, not least because some parents, understandably in an era when cholera, typhus, and other infectious diseases were mass killers, hesitated to send their sons to, or to keep them at, a locale they suspected to be inherently unhealthy. Father Sorin viewed the predicament gravely. "It appears clear," he observed, "that the location of Notre Dame du Lac actually is noxious and particularly so since our arrival here. The sicknesses we have experienced we attributed as long as possible to ordinary causes, but instead of ceasing or diminishing they have increased every year. . . . A reputation for unhealthiness cannot fail to jeopardize the fortunes of the college." Yet, as always, Sorin could find a bright side or at any rate a credible embellishment to a pressing problem. "Many people say that the health-prospects for this place will soon change totally, because the illnesses have really been caused by the immense quantity of earth that has been excavated here [for farming and construction], in proximity to our living-quarters." Even if worse came to worst, Sorin mused—at the back of his mind was the slim hope that the venture in Kentucky might still prove fruitful—"thirty persons could easily live here, . . . a seminary for our Society and a novitiate for our priests, along with two other priests to serve the [parochial] mission and a sufficient number of brothers to tend the farm."[34]

But, besides the fears and suspicions about the incidence of disease, contributing also to the college's precarious condition were the deplorable state of the faculty and the attempt to impose a French regimen, academic and disciplinary and, for secular students, unduly ecclesiastical, upon rough-hewn and individualistic American youths.[35] Advertisements trumpeting Notre Dame's virtues did not help, and so Father Sorin, shortly after his return from France, moved to reform the scholastic program, reorganizing the collegiate and preparatory departments, dropping some courses and adding others, and significantly lessening the time and energy to be spent by students on religious observances.

In this endeavor he was aided by Father Michael Shawe, who joined the faculty in the autumn of 1846. Shawe—who had delivered the July 4 oration a year earlier[36]—was an Englishman in his mid-fifties who brought with him to Notre Dame the panache of a veteran of the battle of Waterloo and of a world traveler. After many and varied adventures he had entered the seminary of Saint-Sulpice

---

34. Sorin to Moreau, September 7, 1847, AGEN.

35. For example, the number of times a week older students were allowed to shave was determined by rule. See Wack, "Notre Dame Foundation," 114.

36. See chapter 11, above.

in Paris, from which Bishop Bruté had recruited him for the Indiana missions. From 1839 he had achieved a modest reputation in Vincennes and its environs for pulpit eloquence, and he was certainly a man of relatively wide cultivation and *savoir-faire.* Sorin was originally much impressed by him: "If you should ever change your relations with Vincennes," he told the Englishman, "I shall receive you with welcome here."[37] Shawe remained at Notre Dame for only two years— he was peripatetic by nature and, besides, his unabashed English tastes and mannerisms eventually grated upon his French colleagues, Sorin included: "Father Shawe whom we have had here for two years has finally departed. He has gone to Detroit.[38] What a burden has been lifted from my shoulders! May God bless him, but I think his true vocation would be with La Trappe! I have nothing precise against him, but I would prefer to have him there rather than in the active ministry."[39] Even so, Shawe's effectiveness as a classroom teacher and his realistic appraisal of the college's curricular needs have left him a memorable place in the roster of Notre Dame faculty.[40]

Michael Shawe exerted his noteworthy influence on academics through his membership on the Council of Professors. Sorin chaired this body, as he did two other committees charged with overall supervision of the community's affairs. The first of these was the Council of Administration and the second the so-called Minor Chapter—the latter term applied to a smaller group of advisers who, in accord with the Constitutions of Sainte-Croix, would presumably function until the mission in America attained the maturity of provincial status and would then merit a full-fledged chapter of its own.[41] Membership on both these boards was restricted to Holy Cross priests and brothers, who served at the pleasure of the local superior. In late 1846 the Council of Administration was made up of Brothers Vincent, Francis Xavier, Lawrence, and Gatien—all of whom had accompanied Sorin from France in 1841—Brother Joseph (né Charles Rother, who at St. Peter's had been the first to join the community in America), Fathers Cointet and Granger, and Francis Gouesse, both before and after his ordination in the spring

---

37. Sorin to Shawe, March 4, 1846, AUND, COSR, "Sorin, Edward."

38. See Shawe to Sorin, July 6, 1848, AIP.

39. Sorin to Martin, January 31, 1848, AGEN. The reference to the Trappists is obscure, but the inference can be drawn from Shawe's verbose correspondence that Sorin judged a dose of Trappist silence would be good for him. Among many examples in AIP, see Shawe to Sorin, March 20, 1849.

40. Wack, "Notre Dame Foundation," 129–132, 166. Some records, followed by Hope, *Notre Dame,* 57, render the name as "St. Michael E. E. Shawe." Shawe died (1853) as rector of the cathedral in Detroit.

41. See Sorin, *Chronicles,* 62.

of 1847. The Minor Chapter included all of these, with the significant exceptions of Gouesse and Brother Gatien.[42]

Significant because these two, Gatien in the lead and Gouesse a somewhat unpredictable follower, spearheaded resistance to Father Sorin within the community. It is by no means clear why Notre Dame du Lac required two almost identical panels,[43] but Gatien was in no doubt: the arrangement allowed Sorin to manipulate events to suit himself. If the larger Council of Administration proved reluctant to endorse a particular policy, he brought it to the subservient Minor Chapter which supinely did his bidding. So at least contended Brother Gatien, who did not hide his contempt for the capacity of several of his colleagues on the Council: "Brother Francis Xavier is almost a zero. Brother Lawrence and Brother Joseph have good ideas, but they express them in an odd and ridiculous way which Father Superior [Sorin] uses adroitly to diminish the influence their observations could have. . . . Brother Vincent . . . has never expressed himself clearly." Father Granger, Sorin's close friend who, along with his membership on the council and the chapter, was Sorin's "monitor"—a moral counselor called for by the Holy Cross Constitutions[44]—was too frail a reed for the superior to lean upon; Sorin's monitor should be a strong person, Gatien maintained, "a priest whom Father Superior could consider his equal or even more able than he in the handling of affairs and for whom he had a certain deference."

Young Gatien demonstrated a degree of courage in that he made no secret of his objections to Edward Sorin's policies. It may be recalled that from the beginning of the collegiate enterprise at Notre Dame he had taken a strong and public line against what he conceived to be his superior's disciplinary laxity.[45] And since he acted as secretary for all three deliberative bodies at Notre Dame, his strictures often found their way into the minutes of meetings and hence into the permanent record. Indeed, Sorin was intensely suspicious of Gatien's note-taking, which, though it "did not falsify the acts of the chapter, did underscore certain

---

42. See the list in Moreau's hand and with his signature, dated June 20, 1846, AUND, CSCM, "Miscellany, Indiana Province." In the same file a printed document, undated but bearing Moreau's signature, provides the expanded membership list.

43. Wack, "Notre Dame Foundation," 148, says that the Minor Chapter replaced the Administrative Council. But it is clear from Gatien to Moreau, November 21, 1846, in Klawitter, ed., *Adapted to the Lake*, 114–126, that the two bodies coexisted until early 1847. See below.

44. "In order to work with greater ease and assurance of success at the correction of his faults, each religious is encouraged to choose a monitor and to see him at least once a month. This provision applies also to Superiors." See *Constitutions of the Congregation of Holy Cross* (n.p., 1951), 113. This article is no longer in force.

45. See chapter 10, above.

words and add some [provocative] points after certain phrases."[46] Certainly less laudable on Gatien's part was his litany of private complaints against Sorin, which he sent directly to Moreau. Nor was Moreau's willingness to receive such communications much to *his* credit.

Gatien was a clever youth, and he displayed the cock-sureness not seldom associated with clever youths. But he also had a hard heart and a core of juvenile self-righteousness readily given to rash judgment. "Now," he wrote Moreau toward the end of 1846—at a moment when Edward Sorin was struggling through perhaps the darkest days of his life—"now I'm going to give you some information on our administrative acts . . . with all the frankness I'm capable of, because your last letter and recent ones led me to believe you'd be happy to know everything of possible consequence to our America." Sorin, he reported first, had returned from France resentful because "he had been received coldly at Sainte-Croix" due to insinuations made "to you that we wanted to separate from the motherhouse." Gatien had heard no one at Notre Dame actually assert this, but "I nevertheless have to tell you that in my opinion Father Superior has . . . believed he had the same powers as you and that Notre Dame du Lac would govern its subjects and establishments . . . in the same way as [you do at] Sainte-Croix."

It is difficult to imagine a more damaging "opinion" to have unveiled itself in Le Mans at that moment. But Gatien had scarcely begun his bill of indictment, which included items both substantive and trivial. Thus Sorin had tried to convince the Administrative Council that "the accounts he had given to Sainte-Croix were proper. But the account was done from memory, . . . and I assure you that if a bad memory exists it is Father Superior's. . . . We have no books here except the foul copies of Father Superior, which he didn't even want to use himself." Gatien had since discovered "considerable errors" amounting to additional debt of 8,000 francs ($1,600), and he was certain there were many more.

The accusatory drum beat relentlessly on. "Father Superior, for the least complaint and the most frivolous reason, caves in to employees." "He sometimes misleads his councilors in making them see only the bright side." "He proposes certain money matters to the Minor Chapter alone, from which, seeing the members who constitute it, he can expect no opposition." "Father Superior holds to his opinion too much . . . and acts without consulting when he foresees that the majority will be against him." "Father Superior is *too* good. He always seems fearful of offending. . . . He prefers disorder to correction." "Father Superior [is] good (*too* good), forgetful, neglectful, and variable, forgives everything, and lets himself be led by those who know how to say kind words to him." "Father Superior . . .

---

46. Sorin to Moreau, June 22, 1847, AGEN.

always believes American rogues in preference to his councilors, . . . because they know how to flatter him."

Perhaps it was the relatively free-and-easy mores of "roguish" frontier Indiana that Brother Gatien found most offensive. He was "shocked" at any rate at the undisciplined comings-and-goings of the nuns whom

> you can . . . meet . . . every time you turn around, even after nightfall and after supper, sometimes in the stairways where there is hardly any light. . . . But what seems more scandalous is to see the new Sister Superior [Sister Mary of the Cenacle[47]] spend hours with Father Superior, often in his bedroom, although he ordinarily receives nobody except in his office. I'm making you aware of this disorder, because I have in mind you wouldn't tolerate it if you knew about it.

Gatien's willingness to retail squalid gossip about one of his confrères in Christ does not invalidate the legitimacy of some of his complaints. Even so, the malice revealed in this secret dispatch seems to rise to a pathological level. As Othello had his Iago, so Moreau, all too willingly, listened to his Brother Gatien, who, predictably, contrasted his own heroic candor to Edward Sorin's villainy and duplicity. "I'm very young, it's true," Gatien wrote (he was barely twenty). "But fearing no one has the courage or imprudence to speak frankly to you about these affairs, . . . I'm going to tell you what I, as well as the majority of the Council [of Administration], think about them." Almost as an afterthought he invoked for Moreau's favorable notice his, Gatien's, single ally within the community. Sorin, he maintained, did not get along with Francis Gouesse, because the latter was "our better administrator." And as Sorin played fast and loose with the rules of Holy Cross, Gouesse, "on the contrary, firm and regular, wants to follow the Constitutions in everything and submit everybody to them."[48]

IN DECEMBER 1846, Edward Sorin, harried in his own house and under a cloud of suspicion at the motherhouse in France, traveled to Vincennes,

---

47. See note 33, above.

48. Gatien to Moreau, November 21, 1846, in Klawitter, ed., *Adapted to the Lake*, 114–126. There are many problems in the printed version of this long and important letter. Even the date given is suspect, since internal evidence indicates, though far from conclusively, that it was written some months later. Both its length and, toward its conclusion, its fragmentary character suggest that it might be the melding of several communications. Nevertheless the critical tone and substance remain consistent throughout.

another place where he could expect to endure tension and unpleasantness, especially since his intention was to justify to Bishop Hailandière the necessity to "delay the Indianapolis foundation, since we had neither funds nor personnel." Instead Sorin "found his Lordship in good spirits."[49] But the bishop's cordiality vanished when the discussion turned to Notre Dame's dalliance with St. Mary's of Kentucky; he even threatened that if any sort of union occurred, he would banish the Holy Cross community from his diocese.[50] He remained moreover adamant that, despite Sorin's explanations, the transfer of the brothers' novitiate to Indianapolis was a sacred commitment made by Moreau nearly two years before.[51] After such a mixed reception, Father Sorin may have been heartened when he heard the clerical rumors around town that the bishop was planning to resign his see.

Back home at the beginning of the new year Sorin gave no sign that he had heard such gossip which, even were it in the end to prove true—as he hoped it would—had not done so yet. In the meantime the bishop had to be dealt with, and in doing so Sorin as usual found himself on the defensive. Hailandière, for example, had complained that requests for teaching brothers submitted by several parishes in the diocese had been ignored at Notre Dame. "I truly do not know," Sorin wrote in rebuttal. "what priests could have possibly accused me of not responding to them, nor am I aware of the so-called conditions you yourself reprimand me for imposing on them before any brothers are assigned." On another issue, the bishop's impatience at the delay of the transfer of the novitiate was understandable, but "I regret that you have not chosen to believe that lack of means alone has prevented us from proceeding immediately to setting up the foundation in Indianapolis. I can however reiterate to you that once our debts are paid it is my intention, as it has been all along, that our first expenditure will go to fulfill this promise." In this and all other regards, Father Sorin claimed, the bishop had failed to recognize that Holy Cross had remained "most attached" to the diocese of Vincennes. And then, sliding rather too readily into the disingenuous, he added: "I have been consistent in believing that I have dealt . . . with your Excellency so candidly and simply, so that you could easily understand me and know that I have not even a thought of dissimulation. . . . In order to give you a small proof of my good intentions I am going to send Father Saint-Palais a third

---

49. Gatien to Moreau, April 20, 1847, in Klawitter, ed., *Adapted to the Lake,* 151.

50. Sorin, *Chronicles,* 63.

51. The transfer had not been finalized, but Hailandière had every reason to assume Moreau's agreement to it. See Catta, *Moreau,* 1: 536.

brother a month or six weeks after he caused me to lose two others by conduct which he tried vainly to justify."[52]

Jacques Maurice de Saint-Palais, another of Bruté's recruits for the Indiana missions,[53] had succeeded Julien Delaune as parish priest in Madison. The incident to which Sorin referred had occurred the previous October when Brothers Mary Joseph and Francis reported for duty there, only to have the pastor receive them coldly and rudely. Mary Joseph, who had served in Madison before, recounted their opening interview with Saint-Palais: "He asked me who had told Father Sorin he wanted Brothers. I said that I had, that the people were asking me . . . when I passed through when they could have two Brothers." Afterwards, when Mary Joseph and Francis attended Sunday Mass, "everyone welcomed us to Madison. They asked us when the school would commence, as their children were running wild for want of a school." The welcome, however, was not quite universal; a small but influential group of parishioners "circulated through the town that Reverend J. Delaune had taken the people's money from Madison to buy the college and farm in Kentucky." This charge against Sorin's friend and agent was not true, but it was enough to explain Saint-Palais's antagonism. "He . . . said . . . he would rather we would return to South Bend. He would pay the expenses back and would send for us when he wanted us. He wished us to leave Madison."[54]

They did indeed leave that Ohio River town, and as Sorin protested bitterly to Hailandière, they had formally left the Holy Cross community as well. Mary Joseph went off to Kentucky to join the embattled project at St. Mary's—Delaune specifically requested him[55]—while Francis, one of those who had made the trek with Sorin from St. Peter's to Sainte-Marie-des-Lacs in 1842, simply drifted away.[56] Their departure may well have been occasioned by Saint-Palais's bad manners, but surely the root causes went deeper than that. The harsh frontier life, made harsher by the demands of religion, could relentlessly erode even the best intentions. Nor could the withdrawal of these two young men be ascribed to that inconstancy of spirit which Father Sorin believed rendered Americans unsuitable for the religious life: Mary Joseph had been born in Ireland, Francis in Alsace. Sorin was nominally the superior of a large community, but his control over personnel was limited at best.

---

52. Sorin to Hailandière, January 1, 1847, AIP.

53. See Lemarié, *Missionaires bretons*, 86, 361–364.

54. Mary Joseph to Sorin, October 26, 1846, in Klawitter, ed., *Adapted to the Lake*, 111–112.

55. Delaune to Sorin, June 28, 1847, AIP.

56. Brother Francis should not be confused with Brother Francis Xavier (originally called Marie), one of the original seven who had come to Indiana in 1841.

Another stern and depressing reminder of this fact came early in 1847. In order to pacify Bishop Hailandière at least to a degree, Sorin proposed to the Minor Chapter that a brother be dispatched to Indianapolis "to travel around like a peddlar to sell Catholic books. . . . Father Superior," Brother Gatien reported to Moreau, "had a mind to test this new and odd enterprise, laying out all the advantages. Everyone concurred with his opinion . . . except me who, taking everything as a joke, kept silent."[57] Brother Joseph—no longer required to preside over the failed print shop—was chosen for this "new mission," as Sorin put it, "which his Lordship was desirous of establishing, namely, to sell Catholic books cheap and thus to fill every house of the country with them. He made hardly any sales; he was more concerned, it seems to me, in buying than in selling."[58] This bit of sarcasm notwithstanding, Sorin had also instructed Joseph "to look around and see whether there was any property for sale in Indianapolis which might be suitable for a Novitiate." But as Delaune had done in Kentucky, Brother Joseph expanded his limited mandate into an authorization to commit a serious amount of money when the community had literally no money. He bought twenty-seven acres of property, "most excellent land, . . . a good little orchard with all kinds of fruit and many grape-vines, . . . a nice well, [a] a good-sized new brick house just finished, a good cellar under it," along with sheds and barns and "an excellent stable. In a word, it is the most complete thing that can be desired."[59] The total cost was 22,500 francs ($4,500), half to be paid by May 1, when Holy Cross was to take possession, and the rest in a year's time.

This act of "stupidity," as Sorin called it, caused consternation at Notre Dame du Lac and brought down a storm of abuse on Joseph's head, to which the impetuous brother reacted with alternating petulance and penitence. "I easily can perceive that you must be sorry for my having concluded the bargain. . . . I cannot be sorry; my only wish is to see you, to communicate to you my views, and to show you all the advantages we have in our hands." But another critical missive from Notre Dame some weeks later left him forlorn: "I was for several hours nearly out of my senses, not with anger or rage, but with grief bordering on despair."[60] Nevertheless, "to refuse to sanction what [had been] done would compromise the house in the eyes of the public and especially in those of the bishop." And so the purchase was approved by Sorin and his Minor Chapter as "the lesser

---

57. Gatien to Moreau, April 20, 1847, in Klawitter, ed., *Adapted to the Lake,* 151.
58. Sorin, *Chronicles,* 63.
59. Joseph to Sorin, January 25 and February 2, 1847, AIP.
60. Joseph to Sorin, February 8 and March 31, 1847, AIP.

evil." But such approval did not magically generate the funds to cover the transaction, and Sorin, however reluctantly, had to appeal once more to the motherhouse. He consoled himself with the thought that "Father Rector [Moreau] himself
seemed to be of the opinion that some sacrifices might be made in order to preserve the last remnants of the favorable dispositions of the bishop," who so much
wanted the novitiate transferred to Indianapolis.[61] So with in hand only the argument that the "favorable dispositions" of Hailandière might be in the end "preserved" by this initiative, Sorin addressed himself to Father Moreau. It was a faint
hope indeed, but Sorin, even so, put on as bold a face as he could.

> In accord with your letter of November 5 last, received here on February 4,
> in which you order us *to observe scrupulously the terms of the agreement
> reached between yourself and the bishop of Vincennes in order to avoid all
> grounds for discontent on his part or even dismissal* [from his diocese], we
> find ourselves forced to accept and to ratify, contrary to our personal wishes,
> a contract to purchase twenty-seven acres of land, situated on the outskirts
> of the city [of Indianapolis], with a new house built of brick, stables, mews,
> various outbuildings for carriages and farm implements, and so forth, all
> for 22,500 francs, half payable in six months and the remainder in a year.
> The Minor Chapter here has believed itself obliged to consent to this trans-
> action, though we have no money. Hoping that cognizant as you are of the
> state of our finances, you would manage to help us recover this debt, which
> we would not have dared to incur without your orders.[62]

"Orders" was a word Sorin may well have come soon to regret. The agreement of February 1845 between Moreau and Hailandière had called for a reasonable and conditional accommodation to the bishop's desire for the transferal of
the novitiate, without, however, any formal or final commitment to do so. Certainly Le Mans had not "ordered" Brother Joseph without any consultation to
spend almost $5,000, not a single cent of which Holy Cross in America could
possibly pay. Sorin, who himself acknowledged Joseph's "stupidity," could hardly
have been surprised by the reaction at Sainte-Croix: the motherhouse adamantly
refused to honor the debt.[63]

Before he learned of this decision, however, Father Sorin appeared to take the
problem in stride. "We are going to buy property at Indianapolis for $4,500 to

---

61. Sorin, *Chronicles*, 64.

62. Sorin to Moreau, February 6–8, 1847, AGEN.

63. Catta, *Moreau*, 1: 552.

serve as our brothers' novitiate," he remarked in May, and then added rather laconically: "We shall have to borrow almost the entire amount."[64] Perhaps he sensed that rescue from this acute embarrassment was close at hand, whatever Sainte-Croix decided. If so, he was right. Even though help for the project from the Propagation of the Faith was not forthcoming, Bishop Hailandière remained delighted that at last his aspirations vis-à-vis the brothers' novitiate were within sight of fulfillment. After much hemming and hawing over the spring and summer of 1847, Brother Joseph was able to report exultantly to Sorin: "I must inform you that I received from the bishop a draft of $3,000."[65] The rest of the debt was negotiated successfully, and in September Father Granger as novice master and six aspirants took up residence in Indianapolis. "The location was agreeable" for the formation of the novices, Sorin conceded, but "the expenses for the support of this house were three times as great" as they would have been at Notre Dame. This was a burden that clearly could not be sustained over a long period, and Sorin, who had resisted as long as he could—who indeed was at that moment anxious to set up a national novitiate outside Hailandière's jurisdiction—did not have to wait long for its termination.

BUT, FOR THE MOMENT AT LEAST, Célestin de la Hailandière had gotten his way; despite Sorin's reluctance and delaying-tactics, the brothers' novitiate had moved from hallowed St. Mary's Isle to Indianapolis. Nor, to his credit, had the bishop been niggardly in providing financial support for that establishment as well as in fulfilling related commitments.[66] The final terms of the transaction, however, were still pending when Notre Dame received an unexpected and unwelcome guest from abroad.

Augustin Saunier was only a few months younger than Edward Sorin, and, like Sorin, he had been ordained for the diocese of Le Mans before joining Moreau's Auxiliary Priests; indeed, all three of them had taken religious vows the same day in 1840. Saunier's assignment to the United States had grown out of the

---

64. Sorin to Martin, May 2, 1847, AGEN.

65. Joseph to Sorin, September 5, 1847, AIP.

66. Hailandière promptly discharged his pledge to grant Notre Dame $500 in cash and 375 more acres of land near Bertrand, in accord with the agreement of February 1845. See chapter 11, above, and Sorin, *Chronicles,* 73. In return for his $3,000 he was granted by Holy Cross a pension of $330 per annum. Sorin's hopes to amortize this obligation shortly were fulfilled when the novitiate returned to Notre Dame in 1848. See Sorin to Moreau, September 11, 1847, and Sorin to Martin, January 31, 1848, AGEN, and chapter 13, below.

still ambivalent position Sainte-Croix had adopted toward association with St. Mary's College. But before proceeding to Kentucky, in June, 1847, Saunier had been instructed by Moreau to go to Indiana and to deliver what amounted to an ultimatum. "He was the bearer of a document," Sorin recalled, "which he had orders to read in [the minor] chapter on the very day of his arrival." He did so "scrupulously" and with so "little tact" that his performance left "the most painful and regrettable impressions on nearly all the members of the chapter. For his part, Father Sorin never entirely forgot the annoyance that it gave him."[67]

Later developments suggest that Father Saunier, who had known Sorin since their days together in the seminary at Le Mans, might well have considered himself a rival to the superior of Holy Cross in America. At any rate he apparently promulgated the memorandum from the motherhouse with a brutal relish which only exacerbated the festering resentment between Notre Dame and Sainte-Croix. Along with rebukes for Sorin, explicit and implied, the document went over wearisome old ground, only now with more specificity: along with regular and precise accounts of money received and expended, the motherhouse also required it be sent a full inventory of assets, copies of all administrative acts, and prior submission of any building plans. Such reports were to be signed by all members of the Minor Chapter. As for the property in Indianapolis, Saunier merely recited Moreau's formal refusal to honor its purchase, with the clear implication that while Sorin's continued imprudence might well threaten the dissolution of Notre Dame du Lac, Sainte-Croix could not and would not be involved in its ruin. These directives were gall and wormwood to Sorin, who had had already to accept ominous challenges to his authority. "The Council of Administration, pursuant to an order from France, was abolished the 22nd day of March, 1847, by the Minor Chapter, which henceforth shall do everything."[68] And then, as though to drive home his point, Moreau had reconstituted the chapter simply by adding to its membership Sorin's harsh critics, Brother Gatien and Francis Gouesse.[69]

Later in June, when Saunier departed for Kentucky, he left much indignation behind him. Sorin later confessed to "annoyance" at this turn of events, but at the time his feelings were much sharper than that. Amid the scurry to put together at least some of the paperwork the motherhouse now demanded, he told the mem-

---

67. Sorin, *Chronicles,* 65.

68. The last entry in book of Minutes of the Council of Administration, signed by Fathers Sorin, Granger, and Cointet and Brothers Lawrence, Vincent, and Gatien, AUND, CSCM, "Miscellany, Indiana Province."

69. See the list signed by Moreau, n.d., AUND, CSCM, "Miscellany, Indiana Province."

bers of the chapter that, if Moreau and his council "were not pleased and contented by the reception of these documents, he was quite determined to abdicate his charge" for the sake of unity.[70] On June 22 the reports were sent to Le Mans, along with Sorin's somber covering letter. "My Reverend Father," he began abruptly,

the actual situation here seems to me too serious to conceal anything from you that could be useful to you in remedying what is, in my strongest opinion, an evil, but one different from what you think. If you allow Notre Dame du Lac to go under, you will undo much good. This would be a mortal blow to all your hopes in the United States for a long time to come, and hardly less so at Rome with regard to Sainte-Croix's various projects, to say nothing of the shock that would be felt in France. We should do everything possible to support Notre Dame du Lac, but I fear understanding this fact will come too late.

I have been accused, he continued, of maladministration so pronounced that "it has threatened the future of the whole Society of Holy Cross. Let me assert the contrary: there is certainly, at this moment, no danger of insolvency here," since our assets are five times the worth of our debts—a remarkable ratio to have claimed "at this moment." "But what I fear is that the ruin you yourself appear so frightened of will come, my reverend Father, from the very policies you seem to have adopted in our regard." And then the bitterness spilled out.

Some men and even some women without a true religious spirit and usually without much judgment write to you without reflection or else under the influence of some discontent or of envy or of some other passion, and you believe them. And so you are brought to suspect the probity and decency [*délicatesse*], even the veracity, of a [local] superior whose devotion has never once been compromised since he entered the Society, who has never told you nor written you a single lie, whose blood boils when confronted with duplicity. Him you no longer believe.

Sorin had prepared "a detailed response to your memorandum of April 23"— the date on the document Saunier had read out so zestfully to the Minor Chapter—but, "since it seems to me more urgent to secure peace than to justify myself,"

70. See the "Statement," n.d., AUND, CSCM, "Miscellany, Indiana Province."

he refrained from forwarding it to Le Mans. Nevertheless, "let me say this, my Father: as you will recognize some day I am innocent of at least two-thirds of the accusations laid at my door in that memorandum." But he had a threat of his own to impart.

> I have thought seriously of leaving the Society, and it is only since this morning that I have promised the good God to take up my cross again. But you know even better than I, my reverend Father, that, if circumstances do not change, my position here will no longer be tenable. There must be a full and complete reconciliation between the motherhouse and Notre Dame du Lac; perhaps it should begin by providing a successor to me. Only you can predict the results, but I repeat: it is impossible for me to keep the post I occupy in the present state of things. To have been expelled from the Society would have distressed me less than your memorandum did. . . . You did not even deign to send me a personal word through Father Saunier. Your memorandum is the only manifestation of your sentiments in my regard. . . . I mourn at the effect this change of yours has upon our work.[71]

Within days, however, sorrow had evolved into anger. On a visit to Bertrand during the first week of July, Sorin found his friend and specially-loved spiritual daughter, Mother Mary of the Cenacle, distraught "and in a state of suffering and dejection such as, so she tells me, she has never experienced before." The immediate cause of her unhappiness was a letter just received from the superior of the newly founded Holy Cross mission in French Canada, Father Louis Vérité.[72] It was "a tactless and pointless" communication in which Vérité presumed to "order" the nuns at Bertrand "to observe strictly and *scrupulously* not only the rules of the congregation but also the prescriptions related to the habit." The propriety of the sisters' garb had long been a sore point with Sorin,[73] but his deeper irritation arose from the fact that both he and Vérité had known Louise Naveau, and her worth, before she entered religion. "As far as I am concerned, my reverend Father [Moreau], I have been acquainted with Father Vérité for sixteen years, and I certainly deplore it that the Society of sisters should be represented by such a superior in Canada. Wait for a few months," he added sarcastically, "and

---

71. Sorin to Moreau, June 22, 1847, AGEN.
72. Early in 1847 two priests, five brothers, and four nuns departed Le Mans to establish a mission at Saint-Laurent, near Montreal. See Catta, *Moreau,* 1: 579–582. At one time Verité had hoped to be assigned to Notre Dame du Lac.
73. See chapter 10, above.

you will have ample proof of his knowledge and prudence. I beg you to make him understand that he should write here or to Bertrand as rarely as possible."

At the same time that one of Sorin's intimates was being subjected to outside interference, another was being victimized by internal dissension. "This very morning I have had to communicate to Father Granger as delicately as I could the gossip within the house to the effect that he has written to Sainte-Croix in order to repudiate policies which he had formally approved of in council and chapter." Granger denied the allegation, as Sorin had been confident he would, but the sensitive young priest also said that "he was going to write you [Moreau] and ask for a change of assignment, because he could not hope to do any good in a place where he was accused of such hatefulness." Sorin wondered rhetorically what he himself should do "in accord with this principle? What unpleasantness has not been said to me face-to-face? What has not been written [to Le Mans] about me? If I have not yet heard that I have been called unchaste or a drunkard, at least not till now, I have been called just about everything else."[74]

N EWS FROM VINCENNES, however, received at the end of this summer of discontent, gave Edward Sorin some much needed relief from a dreary period marked by threats and alarums. When Célestin de la Hailandière returned from his European tour in October 1845, fears that he would promptly initiate "a reign of terror," as one of his priests put it, were mitigated by rumors that, while in Rome, he had submitted his resignation to the pope. He had indeed done so, but the pontiff had refused to accept it, had refused as well to appoint a coadjutor for Vincennes,[75] and had urged Hailandière to return to his diocese and to keep his hand to the plow. The thought of fleeing his burdens, however, remained strong within him, even as the incessant quarrels, including the scandalous one with Mother Theodore,[76] were renewed, the alienation of all elements of the little Catholic community continued as before, the unraveling of the diocesan administration was, if anything, accelerated. In late March 1846, Edward Sorin's once and future friend and patron, the vicar general August Martin, who, seven years before, had so ardently heeded Bishop Hailandière's challenge to come and serve Christ in the missions of Indiana, fled Vincennes for Louisiana, "not out of distaste for the work, for he loves it," a confidant explained, "but weary at numberless

---

74. Sorin to Moreau, July 7, 1847, AGEN.
75. See Eccleston to Hailandière, February 24, 1846, AUND, CAVI, "Diocese of Vincennes."
76. See chapter 6, above.

miseries, continual vexations, incivility, and I may say even the insults he has had to endure since the bishop's return."[77]

Shortly after Martin's departure for the diocese of New Orleans, Hailandière, depressed by the report of complaints lodged against him in Rome,[78] renewed the petition to resign his see. The Roman authorities, as was (and is) their wont, moved slowly, especially since the current pontificate was drawing to a close.[79] In the interval the bishop did not moderate his conduct a whit: his haughtiness, his savage sarcasm, his unreasonable demands upon and almost hysterical suspicion of those who dealt with him daily, persisted in all their vigor. Finally, in the late spring of 1847, it was announced in the public press that a new bishop of Vincennes had been appointed, Jean Bazin, vicar general of the diocese of Mobile, who duly addressed Hailandière a courteous inquiry about routine matters of transition.[80] But the latter, despite the praise heaped on Bazin by the bishop of Mobile,[81] coldly took the line that he recognized no bishop of Vincennes but himself until he had received official notification from Rome. And to the worthies of the Roman curia he sent off a blistering protest, because they had at first held in abeyance his petition to resign, and then, when it suited them, had precipitously published its acceptance.[82] Nor was he entirely without local support. Michael, the Holy Cross brother then in residence in Vincennes, who served the bishop's Mass each morning at 5:30, told Sorin that "the bishop and all his house continue their kindness to me. The more I know him, the better I like him."[83] And Simon Lalumière, the pastor at Terre Haute—who had the distinction of being the first native-born Indianan ordained to the priesthood—attributed Bazin's appointment to "intrigue among priests and bishops. There is not simplicity and honesty enough. . . . I am sad and afflicted almost to be sick when I look into the future."[84]

77. Lemarié, *Missionaires bretons*, 337.

78. See the comments in [Peter Richard] Kenrick to Hailandière, September 2, 1847, AUND, CAVI, "Diocese of Vincennes."

79. Pope Gregory XVI died June 9, 1846.

80. See Bazin to Hailandière, June 25 and July 17, 1847, AUND, CAVI, "Diocese of Vincennes."

81. Portier to Hainlandière, June 25, 1847, AUND, CAVI, "Diocese of Vincennes."

82. Lemarié, *Missionaires bretons*, 264. Bazin's faculties were signed at Rome on July 4, 1847, but the official notification to his predecessor was dated September 2, 1847, Franzoni to Hailandière, AUND, CAVI, "Diocese of Vincennes." Cardinal Franzoni was the prefect of the Congregation of Propaganda, the Vatican bureau in charge of the missions.

83. Michael to Sorin, April 24, 1847, AIP. Brother Michael (né James Flynn), after teaching in Vincennes, served in a variety of capacities at Notre Dame—including fire chief—until his death in 1884.

84. Lalumière to Sorin, September 28, 1847, AIP.

Nevertheless, the inevitable day came, in November, 1847, and Hailandière participated in the episcopal ordination of his successor, looking, commented one in attendance, "as though he were presiding at his own funeral."[85] Even then he tarried in the Vincennes area—as Lalumière, for one, hoped he would—pondered whether to build a permanent home there, and badgered his successor over the $400 per annum pension he claimed due him from the penniless diocese.[86]

Both the ancient Greeks and Romans had a proverb which seemed to apply to Célestin de la Hailandière: "Those whom the gods have determined to destroy, first they drive mad." He was a man of considerable gifts and of undoubted, if conventional, piety and good intentions, and yet on more occasions than could be counted he appeared genuinely unhinged. He had generously exchanged the comforts and prerogatives a cleric of his social standing could have expected in nineteenth-century Brittany for the lonely and physically rigorous, indeed the primitive, existence on the American frontier. But once arrived there he utterly failed to adjust to the realities of the situation, in contrast to so many of his contemporaries among the French missionaries. Thus Stephen Badin was a quarrelsome man too, but he also possessed charm and wit and a single-minded dedication to the tasks at hand. Whether Hailandière was deluded by a false understanding of a Catholic bishop's function in the raw New World, or whether he succumbed to weaknesses inherent in his own personality, his in any case was a tragedy of classic proportions.

When his successor, Bishop Bazin—whom Hailandière grudgingly decided was good-hearted, though ill-educated[87]—died after only a few months in office, rumors immediately sprang up to the effect that Hailandière was willing to take up the mantle in Vincennes again. If indeed he were so inclined, he was dissuaded from this potentially disastrous scheme by the archbishop of Baltimore.[88]

---

85. This comment was made by Sister Francis Xavier, Holy Cross's traveling companion from Le Mans to New York in 1841.

86. See Schroeder, *Vincennes, 1847–1877*, 2–5, 19–20, 40–41.

87. Audran to Hailandiere, December 14, 1847, AUND, CAVI, "Diocese of Vincennes." Ernest Audran was Hailandière's nephew; he served as a priest in the diocese of Vincennes until his death in 1902.

88. Eccleston to Hailandière, May 3, 1848, AUND, CAVI, "Diocese of Vincennes": "My respect for your views and feelings would not permit me even to suggest your return to the See of Vincennes, after having read the objections in which you [expressed] your repugnance to such a measure." Based on this remark, Schroeder, *Vincennes, 1847–1877*, 46–47, doubts that Hailandière seriously entertained this course of action. But see Lemarié, *Missionaires bretons*, 270–272. A recent precedent no doubt precipitated these rumors: Benedict Flaget had resigned the see of Bardstown/Louisville in 1833 and had been reappointed in 1841.

So in 1848 he returned to his hometown, near Rennes, and lived on another thirty-four years. He was received in retirement by his Breton confrères with respect and with even a measure of affection. Some years before he died he began to ponder whether it would be appropriate for him to be buried next to Simon Bruté, his predecessor, and his two successors who predeceased him. Inquiries to this effect, made by his clerical nephew still resident in Indiana, did not receive a sympathetic response: "If Bishop Hailandière is interred in France, he will find himself on the last day among friends, not among those who have forgotten him, as is the case in America." The nephew persisted nevertheless, and shortly after he died on May 1, 1882—the eve of his eighty-fourth birthday—the remains of Célestin René Laurent Guynemer de la Hailandière were transported from France and lodged in the crypt of the old cathedral in Vincennes. Few remained in Indiana who remembered him, and fewer honored him. Perhaps Jean Bazin composed a seemly epitaph that underscored, in a kindly way, the tragic futility of Hailandière's brief episcopate: "Like Don Quixote, he was a man who tilted at windmills."[89]

---

89. Lemarié, *Missionaires bretons,* 407–410, 231.

chapter thirteen

New Beginnings

EDWARD SORIN GREETED THE NEWS OF BISHOP Hailandière's impending departure from Vincennes with a frank statement of purpose. "The new bishop, Monseigneur Bazin, will arrive any day now," he wrote jauntily to Basile Moreau. "Our first business with him will be to have abolished the treaty which bound our brothers to service in this diocese only."[1] There may well have been an implicit rebuke in this assertion, since the other signatory to the objectionable "treaty" had been Moreau himself. Yet at this moment Sorin was basking in a "great joy that peace between us has been reborn, and that my original affection for Sainte-Croix has little by little replaced the sad thoughts that have filled my soul these past eighteen months."[2] And in any case the agreement of February 1845 was indeed abrogated, though the formalities did not occur for some months.

Meanwhile there remained one last joust with the unhappy Hailandière, who lingered in Vincennes after the enthronement of his successor, a ceremony, incidentally, that Sorin did not attend. Even out of office the former bishop found cause to accuse the superior of Notre Dame du Lac of "duplicity" and "insincerity." Almost exactly a year earlier—in December 1846, when Sorin had visited him in Vincennes[3]—Hailandière had requested that four Marianite Sisters be assigned to St. Peter's, Daviess County, the site of Holy Cross's first mission in America, and had offered $500 as initial support for them. Sorin, whose memories of Black Oak Ridge were by no means entirely happy, had expressed grave

---

1. Sorin to Moreau, September 15, 1847, AGEN.
2. Sorin to Moreau, October 22, 1847, AGEN.
3. See chapter 12, above.

reservations about the proposal but had agreed to consult the relevant persons at Notre Dame and Bertrand. "On my return here," he explained, "the mother-superior and the members of the Minor Chapter appeared to share my . . . fears. Five hundred dollars was not in their judgment a sum sufficient to guarantee the sisters establishment nor to gain the approval of Sainte-Croix." The matter had therefore been deferred. Then, a few months later, Sorin learned that a certain Father Delisle was to be sent from Le Mans to Notre Dame, and, once he knew that gentleman had landed safely in New York, Sorin had made Hailandière a counteroffer. "I wrote you from South Bend that if you wished to raise the amount of your contribution to $1,000, I could send you the sisters as well as a priest and a brother. You replied you could not do this." On the heels of this exchange came intelligence that Delisle—"a *flawed* priest who has clearly made sport of Father Moreau"—had run off to Alabama. "If you had agreed to the $1,000 you would have had the four sisters immediately, even after the defection of a priest I had counted on.[4] I will be extremely pained if this explanation does not satisfy you, for it is all the justification I can offer."

It may be doubted that Hailandière was satisfied. The Providence whom Father Sorin so often invoked seems to have decreed that these two men should always have been at odds. The stormy saga was at any rate at an end now, and Sorin managed to summon up a courteous if conventional farewell: "Monseigneur, please pardon all that in my conduct has caused you pain, bless me and mine, and believe me to be, along with my associates, cordially and sincerely, your humble and respectful servant."[5]

BUT THE WITHDRAWAL of one major combatant from the field did not by itself bring about a cessation to all hostilities. From late 1847 and into 1848 Sorin stood at cross purposes with two of his confrères, neither of whom he much liked, Augustin Saunier and Louis Vérité.[6] The immediate issue in each case was the same as that which had triggered the last dispute with Bishop Hailandière: the provision of Marianite Sisters. Sorin had reluctantly, and only when directed formally by Sainte-Croix to do so, dispatched four nuns to Saunier at St. Mary's in Kentucky. At the same time that negotiations over this transfer were

---

4. Sorin alerted the bishop of New Orleans in case Delisle, who was rumored to be in Mobile, "should offer his services to your Excellency or has already done so." Sorin to Blanc, December 6, 1847, AGEN.

5. Sorin to Hailandière, December 3, 1847, AIP.

6. See chapter 12, above.

dragging out, Notre Dame and Bertrand were being bombarded by appeals from Vérité at the mission of Saint-Laurent, in Canada, where the group of sisters recently arrived from Sainte-Croix had been, for reasons unclear, separated and dispersed by the local ecclesiastical authorities.[7] This development ran contrary to one of Moreau's spiritual imperatives—communal life was an absolute necessity for religious in his scheme of things—and so, suggesting several possible nominees presently at Bertrand, he directed that reinforcements, so to speak, be sent to Montreal. After consultation with the mother superior, Sorin chose Sisters Mary Heart of Jesus and Mary of Providence, and to accompany them a priest, Francis Refour, who had come to Indiana from Le Mans in 1846 and who appeared to be experiencing some difficulty in adjusting to his new environment.[8]

They had been gone only a few weeks when—on the eve of the departure of the four religious women destined for Kentucky—a weary and disheveled Sister Mary of Providence, "having traveled 500 leagues," appeared on Sorin's doorstep. She brought with her $75, "the amount advanced by us to pay expenses for the three travelers" to Canada. She also carried "a pathetic communication" from Vérité "in which he said, among other things, . . . that . . . he could send no more money and that he felt no concern about this, because this was all that Notre Dame had spent" sending Refour and the two nuns to the north. Vérité wrote further that he had no need for the questionable skills of Mary of Providence— she had been infirmarian at Notre Dame[9]—and indeed he was annoyed that Moreau should have designated any individual sister without consulting him first. "As for other matters," Sorin reported scathingly, "the Theologian of Saint-Laurent coolly declares *that we shall talk them over later.* . . . What delicacy, what tact!" The real costs to Notre Dame, Sorin contended, which had paid for transportation of the three persons in question from France to Indiana in the first place, amounted to $400. Reimbursement is manifestly a matter of simple justice, Sorin insisted to Moreau: "I ask you to be the judge, and we shall await your decision, my reverend Father."[10]

The machinations of "the Theologian of Saint-Laurent," however, proved to be a pin-prick compared to the relentless deterioration of the situation in Kentucky, largely the fault of Augustin Saunier. The negative impression created at Notre Dame by his rendition of the scolding memorandum from Le Mans in

---

7. Catta, *Moreau*, 1: 587.

8. Sorin to Moreau, September 11, 1847, AGEN. Refour remained in Canada, and from there he withdrew from Holy Cross in 1851. See Klawitter, ed., *Adapted to the Lake*, 374.

9. Costin, *Priceless Spirit*, 16.

10. Sorin to Moreau, October 22, 1847, AGEN.

June 1847 had not dissipated when a couple of months later he returned to Indiana for a conference with Edward Sorin. The chilly discussions, which took place within the framework of the Minor Chapter, touched largely on jurisdictional issues. Saunier predictably argued that the center of the Holy Cross mission in America should be shifted from Notre Dame to St. Mary's. Sorin at one time had mused over this possibility, but that had been before Saunier had intruded into the scene and before he, Sorin, knew of the imminent change of bishops in Vincennes.[11] Indeed, that good news had prompted him a few weeks earlier to bless the cornerstone of a new church building at Notre Dame. Saunier may well have pointed out that "it was in reality somewhat bold for a man who had nothing collected, nothing even promised for the new enterprise." But "it seemed to [Sorin] a matter of necessity. He left to God the care of finding the resources. Who has ever hoped in the Lord and has been confounded?"[12]

Another, bolder idea advanced during the discussions was to operate both Notre Dame and St. Mary's under a single administration, which led in turn to a proposal both Sorin and Saunier liked: the establishment of a full-fledged province in North America or at least in the United States, so that most decisions could be made without the inevitable delays imposed by the slow mails to and from Le Mans. Of course a proposition of such magnitude would have had to secure the approval of Sainte-Croix, and in the end all parties to the deliberations, fearful of Moreau taking offense, shrank from submitting any petition in this regard. But Moreau soon learned what was afoot, because Brother Gatien, who recorded the minutes of the meetings and drew up the various drafts and working-papers, kept him informed. "In the document I had prepared," he wrote, "I had been ordered not to put in the word 'provincial,' but when they want the thing I don't know why they wouldn't want the name. The word 'provincial,' they told me, would scare you." Not that Gatien opposed the notion of an American province which, he predicted, would eventuate sooner or later. What concerned him was the choice of provincial: "He should be a thinking man who loves discipline, rather young so he can learn the language to perfection, a very good administrator, and very wise." The gossipy brother did not quite say that this description was a self-portrait, but he left no doubt that the potential candidates *en scène* were unsatisfactory: "In the discussion there was a kind of jealousy between the Rev-

11. Still, the possibility of shifting the center of Holy Cross operations lingered in Sorin's mind. "I feel . . . certain that I will do my best to make [a mission in the diocese of Cincinnati] beneficial to the class of Society to which I have devoted my life. May the Almighty bless our humble efforts! I do not mean that I could abandon N. D. du Lac entirely; but I must admit that the same exertions might be far more useful in Cincinnati." Sorin to Purcell, July 23, 1848, AGEN.

12. Sorin, *Chronicles*, 74.

erend President [Sorin], . . . who always more or less dissimulates, . . . and Father
Saunier; . . . each seemed to want to pull the provincial [administration] to his
place," to Notre Dame or St. Mary's respectively.[13]

Augustin Saunier then returned to Kentucky and immediately began to quarrel with Julien Delaune and to insist that he, not Delaune, was to be in charge
of the operation at St. Mary's. Despite all the uncertainties, that operation had
begun propitiously enough; a few professors had been hired and classes opened
in 1846[14]—the fifty or more students enrolled each semester easily exceeded the
number at Notre Dame—but by the time the ambitious Saunier had settled in,
Delaune found himself confronted by a situation at once tragic and farcical. The
Kentucky enterprise had depended from its inception on Bishop Chabrat's assurances that the Propagation of the Faith would underwrite it with a subsidy of
20,000 francs. Sainte-Croix, while forbidding Sorin to involve himself further in
the matter,[15] showed enough interest in St. Mary's to send Father Saunier there
and to promise more personnel, but this had been done on the understanding
that the money from Paris would be forthcoming. Due to a clerical error, however, only 2,000 francs had been requested, $400 instead of $4,000, and the Propagation duly granted them, but when apprised of the *faux pas* declined to make
good on the omitted zero.

Father Sorin all this time was, under obedience, reduced to silence, or rather
to plaintive remarks like this one offered to Moreau early on: "Think of Monsieur Delaune, if possible."[16] The sensitive Delaune was suffering keen sorrow
and annoyance at what seemed to him desertion by the man who first sent him to
Kentucky. "My dear friend," he appealed to Sorin, "I have waited for some lines
from you for several months. Let us no longer speak of the past. I absolve you
from all excuse or apology. Let us concentrate on doing good. Time is short, and
we love one another in the bowels of Christ."[17] Father Moreau, for his part, was
not without sympathy for Delaune, nor without hopes of salvaging the undertaking at St. Mary's, but, though he quashed Saunier's more egregious pretensions
as soon as he learned of them,[18] he appeared unable to act decisively in other

---

13. Gatien to Moreau, September 14, 1847, in Klawitter, ed., *Adapted to the Lake,* 173.

14. See the prospectus, printed over Delaune's name, AIP. "Board, tuition, washing, bed, and
bedding" cost a student $75 per annum. There was a separate charge for mending.

15. See chapter 12, above.

16. Sorin to Moreau, September 3, 1846, AGEN.

17. Delaune to Sorin, June 28, 1847, AIP. The last clause quoted was written in a combination of
French and Latin.

18. Brother Theodolus to Sorin, March 1 [?], 1848, AIP. Theodolus was at this time stationed at
St. Mary's.

respects. Indeed, he sent conflicting signals to Kentucky, first declaring Delaune to be in charge at St. Mary's and then giving priority to Saunier.[19] The lack of firm direction and a shortage of funds combined to check whoever held the reins. "I cannot believe that you understand how critical is my position," Delaune wrote desperately.[20] Meanwhile, Bishop Chabrat, hearing not a word from Notre Dame du Lac, not unreasonably assumed he had been duped by Sorin, to whom he assigned blame for what was swiftly becoming a debacle.

Edward Sorin had no doubt as to where the fault lay.

> A man of talent, prudence, and tact [he concluded in retrospect] could even then have succeeded in arranging things satisfactorily. The prospects [for St. Mary's] were encouraging. Monsieur Delaune was willing to remain there for at least another year for the sake of the Society [of Holy Cross], on condition that he received a modest compensation, and before the end of that time all the debts of the college could have been easily cleared off. We may as well say it: the prospect of such a fair future turned the head of the poor newcomer [Saunier]. It appears indubitable that at his arrival at St. Mary's he conceived of having himself made president, independent of [Notre Dame], whence, however, he expected to draw all the necessary help, but treating directly with Sainte-Croix in everything.[21]

Yet not every witness to the events in Kentucky agreed with this judgment. Sister Mary of the Five Wounds, back in America from house-arrest in Le Mans, believed that Julien Delaune was more anxious to make a name for himself in some other foundation than to build up St. Mary's; this was why, she said, he was so "in a hurry to place on the shoulders of another the burden which ought to be his own here."[22]

At any rate, before 1847 was out, Sorin determined, despite the formal prohibition still on him, to intervene personally in the Kentucky affair, though it was not till the following April that he actually got there.[23] The situation was as chaotic as he feared. A disillusioned Julien Delaune had already decided to give up the struggle, not without considerable forbearance. "Father Saunier will never be able to deal with the problems here," he told Sorin, "and things will never get

---

19. At least so claimed Saunier to Sorin, March 30, 1848, AIP.
20. Delaune to Sorin, September 10, 1847, AIP.
21. Sorin, *Chronicles*, 69.
22. Mary of the Five Wounds to Sorin, April 10, 1848, AIP.
23. Wack, "Notre Dame Foundation," 173.

better. He is a good and holy man, but here he is out of his depth. . . . The impossibility of me sharing administration with him has obliged me to fix my departure for July 19 [1848] at the latest."[24] He accordingly returned to France, where he died a year later. Chabrat was gone too, having retired as old Bishop Flaget's coadjutor and having been replaced by Martin John Spalding.[25] The young and feisty Spalding was not a man to suffer gladly or for long the confusion which had fallen upon the institution he himself had attended as a boy,[26] and, as Sister Five Wounds had warned Sorin,[27] it was the decisive bishop with whom negotiations had to be entered into. A tentative agreement was patched together whereby, presuming Moreau's endorsement, Notre Dame guaranteed sufficient personnel for the college to reopen in September. But Saunier, enraged at the prospect that another priest might be named president of St. Mary's in preference to himself, "positively refused to act with anyone whatsoever from Notre Dame du Lac."[28] Spalding, by now weary of the interminable wrangling and impatient at the apparent ambivalence in Le Mans, decided to terminate the diocese's connection with Holy Cross. "We have been for two years left in a state of uncertainty," he wrote Sorin in June, "as to whether your order would take the College, and we can be left in suspense no longer."[29]

Sorin hurried to Louisville again in July, but his efforts to persuade the bishop to reverse his decision were fruitless. Spalding had had his fill of dealing with a two-headed monster: "Father Saunier, . . . it seems, together with Father Delaune, caused most of the *disagreement* in this curious transaction."[30] On his way home Sorin experienced a bizarre confrontation.

Last week [he reported to Moreau] I met Father Saunier by chance on the street in Cincinnati. Without forewarning me, he had left us and had come to offer himself to the Jesuits, who have to send him to their novitiate in New York, along with Father Marivault. His two principal reasons for leaving the Congregation are, first, that Father Moreau has treated him with

---

24. Delaune to Sorin, April 30, 1848, AIP.

25. Chabrat's retirement, at the end of 1847, was necessitated by his approaching blindness. Spalding (1810–1872) succeeded Flaget as bishop of Louisville in 1850 and became archbishop of Baltimore in 1864.

26. Spalding had taught mathematics at St. Mary's when he was fourteen years old. See Thomas Spalding, *Martin John Spalding, American Churchman* (Washington, D.C.: 1974), 6–7.

27. Mary of the Five Wounds to Sorin, April 10, 1848, AIP.

28. Sorin, *Chronicles*, 71.

29. Spalding to Sorin, June 17, 1848, AIP.

30. Spalding to Sorin, July 25, 1848, AIP.

disdain, particularly by annulling his acts [at St. Mary's] after having authorized and approved them; and, second, that our Congregation will not survive in France and has scarcely a better chance to do so in America. This he plans to say *publicly* to anyone who wants to listen to him. He treats you with scant respect and often honors me with the same treatment; of course the disciple is no greater than the master. It is astonishing that you sent here to represent the Congregation *a child who does not even have common sense.* I think he is diseased in the brain. In Kentucky, in the diocese of Louisville, in the college—in all these he has left the sorriest perception of Holy Cross.

Here was a missed opportunity. "I have seen St. Mary's, and *I regret losing the place.* It is a great loss for our Society. Nevertheless, I cannot take it upon myself; I have only done what I was told to do." Cincinnati too seemed closed to Holy Cross as the Jesuits entrenched themselves there.[31] Then, in a softer tone, he added: "As you see, my reverend Father, heaven does not leave us very long without a cross."[32]

Yet, however critical Sorin may have been of Augustin Saunier, he could not easily forget a man with whom he had been an idealistic seminarian and in whose company he had sworn religious vows on that fateful day in 1840. Disquieting news came shortly from the Jesuits in New York. "Father Saunier came here, it is true with the intention of joining our Society," wrote the novice-master, despite the latter's attempts to dissuade him. Saunier made a retreat and then simply departed. Rumor had it that the bishop of New York had refused to incardinate him and that he was seeking acceptance in the dioceses of Philadelphia or Providence.[33] These applications also proved unsuccessful, and Saunier then went first to Canada and not long afterward, for some unspecified reason, to Missouri. There Sorin tracked him down and sent him a letter that gave him "the greatest pleasure." He recalled, in his reply, their friendship that went back to seminary days and lamented "the painful travail" he had endured in Kentucky. "My good

---

31. "Oh! How happy I would feel to see my dear N. D. du Lac somewhere about Cincinnati.... May I candidly declare [my] desire [that] you procure me as soon as possible an introduction into your diocese; of its being a blessing for our Society I remain perfectly confident." Sorin to Purcell, July 23, 1848 AGEN.

32. Sorin to Moreau, July 22, 1848, AGEN.

33. Thebaud to Sorin, November 17, 1848, AIP. Thebaud did not mention Marivault, who appears to have returned for a while to Notre Dame. It would seem that his last service as a priest of Holy Cross was to substitute for Father Baroux at Pokagon, 1849–1850. See the congregation's roster, *La Matricule générale de la Congrégation de Sainte-Croix,* 476, AIP.

friend, I believed that I acted prudently before God who will judge me, and I believe the same today about leaving the Congregation to which you devote yourself entirely. I shall explain my reasons to you in Paradise."[34] The word "*entièrement*" may have caused Father Sorin a moment of uneasy self-examination, given his growing alienation from the authorities in Le Mans.

HOWEVER THAT MAY HAVE BEEN, a heavy cross had by that time been lifted from his shoulders. On his first journey to Kentucky, in April 1848 he had traveled by way of Vincennes, where he met Bishop Jean Bazin for the first and, as it turned out, for the last time. Before setting out he sought the advice of August Martin, now the parish priest in Baton Rouge, with whom he had resumed cordial correspondence.[35] "Do you not now agree, my dear Confrère," Sorin wrote, "that it would be better for us not to be bound by any contract with this diocese? Is it not really prejudicial to the development of our work to link ourselves thus exclusively to any diocese, and this especially when our brothers in the schools are still paid only $50 a head? You know the total repugnance I have for the restrictions of such a treaty."[36]

The agreement of the former vicar general of Vincennes was welcome but that of the new bishop would be decisive, and this Sorin obtained with astonishing ease.

> Once at Vincennes [Sorin recorded in the third person] his first concern was to have canceled the former agreement which bound the Brothers in such a manner to the diocese that they had no liberty to make any foundations elsewhere, no matter what advantages might be presented. The first point being secured, Father Sorin himself drew up a new agreement which the good bishop consented to sign.[37]

Once the key issue of exclusivity had been settled, the agreement consisted of five articles, which Sorin carefully recorded.

> Monseigneur Bazin consents, first, to grant us full title to the property at Notre Dame du Lac, reserving to himself a mortgage (*hypothèque*) of $3,000

---

34. Saunier to Sorin, August 9, 1849, AIP.
35. See Sorin to Martin, May 2, 1847, AGEN.
36. Sorin to Martin, January 31, 1848, AGEN.
37. Sorin, *Chronicles*, 75.

should we ever come to sell it. Second, that we should be allowed to sell the property in Indianapolis presently serving as the brothers' novitiate and restore to him the $3,000 [Hailandière had contributed to that establishment in 1847], in return for which he holds us free of the pension granted [Hailandière]. He further allows us in compensation the $500 and the [375 acres of] land given us by Monseigneur Hailandière and permits us as well to use for the construction of the new church at Notre Dame du Lac the $600 advanced by his predecessor for churches in South Bend and Mishawaka. Third, [Bazin consents] to ordain to sacred orders candidates presented to him by the Congregation [of Holy Cross] under the jurisdiction of said Congregation and to leave any decision about releasing them from their duty to the judgment of the Superior at Notre Dame or to the Rector [Moreau] of said Congregation. Fourth, Monseigneur Bazin also approves that the Brothers of St. Joseph should be assigned in pairs to each [parochial] establishment and that they should teach boys only; further that they should take the schools they teach in into their own control when the pastors who have asked for their services fail to fix a sum sufficient to support them, which must be in every case in excess of $50 [annually]. Fifth, his Lordship promises to recommend to the Clergy of the Diocese from time to time the need to promote vocations for the novitiate of the Brothers of St. Joseph.

Sorin could not help expressing a small *cri de triomphe:* "The treaty concluded at the motherhouse," he scribbled at the bottom of this document, "has been, thanks be to God, buried in oblivion—I mean to say the agreement [of February 1845] between Monseigneur Hailandière and the motherhouse."[38]

On Easter Sunday 1848, less than two weeks after affixing his signature to this "contract," Jean Bazin died. This native of Lyons—not, like so many missionaries in Indiana, from the west of France—had never enjoyed robust health, and the burdens and anxieties imposed upon him by his promotion to Vincennes had helped to undermine his frail constitution.[39] Edward Sorin, when he heard the news, reacted with characteristic pragmatism, softened by characteristic eloquence: "However great was the pain of everyone on learning of the sudden death of this pious prelate, . . . all admired so much the more the Providential ac-

---

38. "Copy of a contract between Monseigneur Bazin and Father Sorin," April 10, 1848, AGEN. Sorin, *Chronicles,* 75–76, summarizes the five articles but very inadequately, one of many instances in which the *Chronicles,* composed after the fact, requires clarification and, sometimes, even correction from contemporary documents.

39. Schroeder, *Vincennes, 1847–1877,* 38–39.

tion on the house [at Notre Dame], whose important interests had been secured by this worthy bishop almost immediately before he took his departure from this world of misery and strife."[40]

On HIS DEATHBED Jean Bazin designated Father Saint-Palais, the pastor at Madison, to be administrator of the diocese pending the appointment of a new bishop—the same Saint-Palais, incidentally, who had so annoyed Edward Sorin the year before by rudely refusing to accept the two brothers assigned to him. In the rough-and-ready manner in which the canon law was applied in the missions, Saint-Palais immediately assumed his new duties.[41] With a few bizarre exceptions—one unhinged priest accused him of being the agent of Satan—the secular clergy agreed to the arrangement, and indeed most of them indicated a willingness to accept the administrator as their bishop. So in the end it worked out, though the American prelates who were consulted, and who sent their recommendations to Rome, were less keen, placing Saint-Palais fourth out of four possible candidates. Hailandière, who had not yet departed for France, dismissed Saint-Palais as a feeble nominee, and—surely a tribute to his basic evenhandedness—asserted that the only priest in Indiana who could effectively govern a diocese was Edward Sorin. Jacques-Marie-Maurice Landes d'Aussac de Saint-Palais—his full name testified to his noble ancestry in the southeast of France—aged thirty-seven, was nevertheless consecrated fourth bishop of Vincennes in January 1849, a post he held for nearly thirty years.[42] A mild-mannered man, with deeply pastoral instincts, "a second Bruté" his admirers called him, he proved to be the antithesis of the confrontational Hailandière. Sorin's relations with him were cordial but distant, and, after 1857, when the diocese of Fort Wayne was instituted, there were no official relations between them at all.[43]

Even had he been so inclined, Saint-Palais could have scarcely found the time or energy to interfere at Notre Dame du Lac, so crushed was he by the financial and related problems he had inherited. For his part, Sorin was willing to forget

40. Sorin, *Chronicles*, 76.

41. See the circular letter, Saint-Palais to the clergy, May 1, 1848, AUND, CAVI, "Diocese of Vincennes": "The Bishop, before his decease, had appointed me administrator of the diocese. You will, I sincerely trust, do all that will be in your power to render lighter the burden that has been imposed upon me."

42. See Fransoni to Saint-Palais, October 1, 1848, AUND, CAVI, "Diocese of Vincennes." A copy of Saint-Palais's faculties, dated at Rome October 1, 1848, can be seen in the Sorin papers, AIP.

43. See Schroeder, *Vincennes, 1847–1877*, 43–51, and Lemarié, *Missionaires bretons*, 361–364.

his earlier irritation so long as the new bishop honored the compact reached between his predecessor and Holy Cross, as indeed he did. And though his own financial distress remained as acute as before—except for the $600 Bishop Bazin had agreed to contribute to the construction of the new campus church—for Father Sorin the beginning of the Saint-Palais-regime in Vincennes proved to be coincidental to a period, welcome albeit brief, of relative calm and harmony. The return, on June 25, 1848, of Alexis Granger and the novices from the ill-fated experiment in Indianapolis—"the little family returned to their own with sentiments of reciprocal affection which the temporary separation had only made stronger and more perceptible"[44]—seemed an omen of more tranquil times to come.

Back in France, however, and indeed across the whole of Europe, signs of tranquillity were hard to come by just then. In February the barricades had gone up in Paris, and the July Monarchy, after eighteen pallid years, had collapsed with barely a whimper. As King Louis-Philippe fled into exile across the English Channel, the fires of revolution were ignited in a score of European cities, and the old order trembled at the prospect of a renewal of the anguish of 1789 and 1830. But the promulgation of the French Second Republic at least was marked more by euphoria than by the violence of those earlier upheavals, and the old jacobin hostility to the clergy and to religion was strikingly absent. Indeed, after the elections in April, Father Lacordaire took his seat in the National Assembly, resplendent in his white Dominican habit, the rosary beads at his waist rattling against the benches. This era of good feeling did not last, to be sure: in June the street-fighting that broke out in Paris signaled an initial wave of reaction, and by the end of the year the republican experiment began to give way to a revived napoleonic tyranny.[45]

The February Days inevitably had their impact in Le Mans, where Basile Moreau, a convinced monarchist but no admirer of Louis-Philippe, at first viewed the situation with alarm. Aside from the threats of a few hooligans, however, and some absurd rumors about goings-on within the religious compound in Sainte-Croix—it was whispered, for example, that the brothers were secretly manufacturing and selling cloth and thus threatening textile-workers' jobs—it soon became clear that the public at large bore Holy Cross no ill-will. Indeed, Moreau's reputation as a benefactor of the poor as well as his own humble origins—"Everything that I have undertaken and founded has been in the interest of the people, to which I myself belong"—gave the lie to the preposterous charge "that I have or

44. Sorin, *Chronicles*, 77.
45. See Maurice Agulhon, *1848, ou l'apprentissage de la République* (Paris, 1992), 36–42, 67, 78–84, and 239–244. Louis-Napoleon was elected president by a huge margin in December, 1848.

want to have in our house any machines or trades shops which may harm the laboring classes."[46] But he was prudent enough also to instruct his religious not to meddle in what was an essentially political affair: "In view of the grave events which are taking place in Paris, I exhort you to remain calm. . . . I also urge you not to mix in matters not connected with your vocation, for you should be persuaded that to 'those who love God all things work together unto good.' . . . I advise you not to show any opposition to the new government, but to give it your generous support and to cooperate to the fullest extent with the authorities who have taken over the maintenance of public order."[47] During the heady weeks that followed, cooperation in Le Mans included allowing the band made up of students boarding at Sainte-Croix to lead the frequently held patriotic parades and participating in the ceremonial planting of "Freedom Trees." "Let the ministers of religion have faith in the Republic," proclaimed crusty old Bishop Bouvier, no more a republican than Moreau.. "What is our duty? To continue to carry on peacefully our ministry of charity and union, going about, like our Lord, doing good and, as far as possible, offending no one."

Within Holy Cross itself, however, the democratic enthusiasm produced moments of distress. In early April, the boarders, lustily singing the *Marseillaise,* threw up barricades of their own in the study hall, until faced down by Father Moreau himself. "He did not scold the students," a witness recalled, "but rather put all the blame on the spirit of evil, which is the source of all bad inspirations." Nevertheless, the boys' restlessness necessitated sending them home for a time, and when they returned one of the more disgruntled among them actually started a fire in the dormitory. "He felt quite sure that if his plan worked, we would be obliged to send him home." A more permanent misfortune, traceable in Moreau's view to the revolutionary turmoil loose in the land, was the decision of four priests to leave the community and return to the diocesan ministry, and the departure also of five brothers, two of whom "abandoned their post of duty to learn by experience in the world whether there is greater calm on the high seas than in port."[48]

THESE EVENTS had little direct relevance to the backwoods of northern Indiana, though the Frenchmen resident there undoubtedly took a keen

---

46. Catta, *Moreau,* 1:690, quoting a statement Moreau inserted in the local newspaper, *Le Courrier de la Sarthe,* March 6, 1848.

47. Moreau, *Circular Letters,* 1: 136–137, dated February 24 and March 2, 1848.

48. Moreau *Circular Letters,* 1: 144, dated January 5, 1849.

interest in them. The unrest in France, and particularly in Le Mans, did, however, produce one result important to Edward Sorin. "For several years Father Rector [Moreau] gave it to be hoped that he would be seen in person at Notre Dame du Lac. Perhaps he would have actually carried out his intention this year had not the troubles in France made it a duty for him to remain at Sainte-Croix."[49] The ever-confident Sorin believed that such a visit, during which the Founder could see and then judge for himself what his congregation in the United States was accomplishing, would easily put to rest the doubts that had been raised at Sainte-Croix by what Sorin considered unwarranted and gossipy criticism of his objectives and methods.

Whether or not Moreau had in fact intended to travel to Notre Dame in 1848, his presence there would not have been a casual "visit" but rather a formal "Visitation," a canonical inquiry into the spiritual and material state of a daughter-house of Sainte-Croix. Since for obvious reasons he deemed such an investigation a necessity, the Founder decided to commission a trusted lieutenant to act as official "Visitor" to the Holy Cross mission in America. Victor Drouelle was thirty-six years old and so two years senior to Edward Sorin, whom he knew well. Ordained for the diocese of Le Mans in 1837, Drouelle had been one of the first to join Moreau's association of Auxiliary Priests. He had served for a time in the ill-starred mission in Algeria. He did not enjoy robust health, but his intellectual gifts were considerable. He had a flair for diplomacy—what Sorin characterized as his "tact and fairness"—and a fondness for poetic expression. In many respects stylish and sophisticated, Drouelle was not notable for constancy, nor did he over his career ever disdain the uses of flattery and intrigue.

In the late spring of 1848 Father Drouelle set out from Le Mans bound for the New World. He spent a month at the Holy Cross mission near Montreal. He arrived at Notre Dame du Lac at the end of August and remained there as accredited Visitor for nearly three months, to the complete satisfaction of Edward Sorin.

> Father Drouelle acquitted himself . . . with tact and fairness and restored peace and union wherever they were found wanting. The material state of the house appeared to him very encouraging, and in spiritual matters, if he did not find all the religious spirit desirable, he had at least the satisfaction, before [his departure], of finding the dispositions in general very consoling. His stay at Notre Dame du Lac, more than anything else, succeeded in restoring a perfect understanding between the Mother House and this foundation.[50]

49. Sorin, *Chronicles,* 78.
50. Sorin, *Chronicles,* 79.

Such an encomium was hardly surprising given the laudatory report about Notre Dame Drouelle sent back to Le Mans. Indeed, the Visitor and the local superior clearly shared a bond of mutual admiration. In the new collegiate building, wrote Drouelle,

> we find a sort of little workroom, where Father Sorin maps out his pious projects, writes his heart-stirring appeals to the charity of his numerous friends, and draws up plans with his fellow-workers, as with people who form only one heart and soul with him. . . . There he listens to the respectful suggestions of some and the disrespectful outbursts of others; there he is obliged to pass out to others consolations which he does not himself have and to give them the encouragement which is refused him. There he congratulates those whose work is satisfactory and pardons those who pain him. There he goes even to extremes in order to be pleasant to all, and there also he receives blame for a thousand and one things.

The other priests at Notre Dame received similar if less lengthy and intense plaudits. The learned Father Cointet "speaks the language of St. Teresa. . . . [N]othing holds back his zeal, neither the effort he puts into his preaching, nor that which he manifests toward the priest-novices, meditating on the practices of religious obedience in order to teach it to them.[51] Francis Gouesse has "succeeded in uniting in himself a genius for music, the rod of scholastic discipline, the task of steward, and the secret of regularity." As for "good little Father Granger,"

> do not form an idea of his sacrifices or of his mortification by the expression on his face. To look at him you would think he were living in the midst of all the pleasures and satisfactions of life. But you would be very much mistaken. His bed nothing but a poor cot, and his furniture consists of a small table, one chair, and three boards with a few books on them.

Drouelle was especially affected by a journey he took in Sorin's company to Pokagon, where Father Louis Baroux and two nuns were laboring among "the proud children of the forest, obedient like Carthusians. . . . I had never before me any more perfect picture or more heart-touching representation of the apostolic life of the early missions." He was less impressed by the four sisters stationed at

---

51. At this time Cointet had been named master of the priests and seminarians who aspired to take vows in Holy Cross. Gouesse took his place caring for the parochial missions, and Granger remained master of the brother-novices. See Sorin, *Chronicles,* 79.

Notre Dame, who, he commented sarcastically—an echo of Brother Gatien's strictures—observed the rule of silence "as ordinary women observe it" and were besides, several of them, incompetent and uncharitable. By contrast the eighteen nuns at Bertrand—three professed, fifteen novices almost all Irish—were "edifying as Carthusians," who were, apparently, the Visitor's *beau idéal* among religious orders. The sisters were very poor but cheerful, and if their habit did not meet the norm established for the Marianites in France—only the cord and the rosary at the waist and the heart worn on the bosom had been preserved—Drouelle sided with Sorin in maintaining that this alteration was a legitimate adaptation to local circumstances.[52] The twelve brother-novices, they too mostly Irish immigrants, appeared pious and devoted. Not so most of the Americans Drouelle encountered: "Converting them to the religious life would require a miracle similar to that which hurled St. Paul to the ground." Not surprisingly, neither did he much like the forty or so lay students he found enrolled in the college, whom he judged "of an extremely independent character, proud to the point of haughtiness, and so cold as to make one forget they are children."

The Visitor, finally, painted an idyllic picture of the material well-being of Notre Dame du Lac, calculated to reassure the authorities in Le Mans. In less than seven years, he pointed out, a forested wilderness had been transformed into one of the finest farms in Indiana. More than 300 acres were under cultivation. Grazing in the pastures were a dozen thoroughbred horses and fifty cattle, and 200 swine grunted happily in the pens nearby. Add to this agricultural achievement the flourishing shops where eighteen orphans and apprentices worked under the supervision of the brothers, and the limeyard which, though not yet a commercial success, could potentially reduce substantially the costs of internal construction by providing needed building materials.

And so Drouelle concluded that the institution he had been designated to examine was fundamentally sound in its personnel, in its financial base, and in its apostolic strategy. In issuing this verdict he amplified his findings with an admonition which, though somewhat oblique, must nevertheless have sounded like music to Edward Sorin's ears.

> One of the main causes of suffering for the religious at [Notre Dame], but at the same time something which reflects much honor on them, is their false impression that Sainte-Croix, and especially Father Rector [Moreau], are forgetting the exiles. If they understood that any such forgetfulness

---

52. See chapter 10, above.

would be black ingratitude, they would certainly never dare to give expression to any such accusation. Nevertheless, if there be accusation, let observations be made to the proper persons.[53]

EDWARD SORIN took advantage of the presence of the congenial Father Drouelle to grasp at the first fruit of the willingness of the post-Hailandière administration in Vincennes to waive the exclusivity arrangement with regard to the assignment of the brothers. Among the prelates who had in the recent past petitioned Notre Dame for teachers to serve in their schools was John Hughes of New York.[54] The usual questions had immediately arisen as to the sources of financial support for the project, and with Hailandière still in office—the inquiry from Hughes had come in September 1847—the solicitation had been set aside, at least for the time being. But when Drouelle had passed through New York on his way to Montreal he had conferred with Hughes, who had urged him to renew the request once he, Drouelle, had arrived in Indiana. He had done so, and Sorin, seconded by the Minor Chapter, had agreed to explore the matter.

Accordingly, the two priests traveled to New York in mid-September, 1848. The bishop explained that his need was especially acute in the borough of Brooklyn,[55] and, though he was more strapped for money than he had been at the time of his original entreaty, he promised to do his best to channel funds for the brothers from a "considerable legacy" controlled by a committee over which he presided. Once on the scene in Brooklyn, Sorin and Drouelle found several pastors more than eager to employ brothers from Notre Dame to teach "letters and trades." The hitch was that the use of the legacy's funds was restricted to instruction in "letters and trades . . . in favor of the orphans of Brooklyn." Such a task was certainly not foreign to the brothers' experience at home, "but the members of the committee [were] not able to come to an understanding" over what appeared to be a possible conflict of endeavor, with the result that Sorin decided to adopt Bishop Hughes's first proposal and assign brothers to the two parishes most anxious to receive them. On November 1

five brothers arrived in Brooklyn. Unfortunately, the Jesuits had learned of these arrangements. One of their Fathers had been employed for some

---

53. Summary of Drouelle's report in Catta, *Moreau*, 1: 927–932.

54. Irish-born Hughes (1797–1864) was fourth bishop (1842) and first archbishop (1850) of New York.

55. The separate diocese of Brooklyn, embracing all of Long Island, was not erected until 1852.

time in the principal parish; they had probably formed their plans for these same schools. In a word, it was impossible then to find employment for more than two Brothers, and the other three returned [to Notre Dame] at once.

Sorin was neither the first nor the last Catholic leader to resent the aggressiveness of the Society of Jesus. Indeed, he had already encountered it: "The history of Kentucky and of Cincinnati," he noted wryly, "serve as keys to explain this little phenomenon." Nevertheless, he described himself as "satisfied" at having secured a "foothold in Brooklyn, one of the first posts in the United States."[56] But there was more to the story than simple Jesuit malevolence. For the two brothers assigned to serve in Assumption parish—thirty-eight-year-old Basil and eighteen-year-old Aloysius, both Irish-born—the foothold seemed to be, as they put it, not in Brooklyn but in Purgatory. It did not take them long to realize that they were not competent to control, much less to teach, the hundred unruly boys placed under their charge. No formal agreement had been drawn up between Notre Dame and the parish, and so the pastor felt no obligation to offer any support to the brothers beyond what they could collect from their pupils' parents. Ill-paid and ill-housed, cut off from the larger religious community, and sick a good share of the time, they grew increasingly desperate. "The predicament in which we are placed," Basil complained bitterly to Sorin early in the new year, "[stems from your] sending us here; you could not treat us worse if we were really slaves, and you may be sure we shall never forget this."[57]

Father Sorin, anxious to maintain Holy Cross's "foothold," sent Brother Vincent to Brooklyn to try to calm the waters, but his gentle persuasion bore no results. So Sorin determined to dispatch to the scene the cleverest and most obstreperous member of the community and let him try his hand.[58] Brother Gatien found the situation deplorable in the extreme, and, quite in character, he did not hesitate to point the finger of blame. "No one," he informed Sorin,

is as responsible for the ill-success of your establishment [in Brooklyn] as Brother Vincent and yourself. Permit me to speak frankly: you generally do things only by halves, and you require real miracles from your subjects and then blame them when these miracles are not really wrought. . . . You

---

56. Sorin, *Chronicles*, 80–81.

57. Basil to Sorin, January 30, 1849, AIP. Both brothers left the Holy Cross community soon after their experience in Brooklyn, though Basil spent a brief time in New Orleans. See chapter 15, below.

58. See Minor Chapter Book, minutes, April 2, 1849, AIP, instructing Gatien to remain in New York.

should not have sent [Basil and Aloysius] to New York; they were not and are not able to teach. . . . If I retrieve your affairs, as I have some hopes of doing, it will be the result of my innate capacity and energy. . . . I don't see, Reverend Father Superior, how you manage to be continually getting yourself and others into scrapes, while if you would profit by experience and get a man to do business for you with the necessary business-like nicety, you would avoid these petty difficulties which greatly endanger the reputation of [Notre Dame].[59]

Sorin did not reply to this caustic, not to say impudent, missive which was followed by several more, some written in French, some in English, some in a combination of both, each one longer and more scathing than the last, each one brimming over with underscorings, exclamation points and other signs of passion.[60] And despite Gatien's "innate capacity and energy," he did not manage to "retrieve" the situation for Holy Cross in Brooklyn. The brothers were withdrawn, but not before Gatien had reported to Moreau the disastrous plight of the mission and, predictably, denounced the man he held responsible.

Father Superior and [Drouelle] went to New York where they made their arrangements so well and examined things so well that, having sent five Brothers in November, three had to go home immediately, and the two that Mr. Bacon [pastor of the Assumption] wanted to keep preferred Purgatory to being at his place. . . . The result of this inconceivable imprudence, or rather this illegal enterprise to work miracles, which is pretty common with Father Superior, was the cause of useless expense, trips, etc., and a loss at the time of 3,000 francs, and he'll no doubt have to spend more than a thousand francs before the thing goes ahead or folds. . . . I've been here five weeks trying to mend everything, because my sole duty is to unravel what superiors tangle here. . . . Father Superior bought five or six thousand francs worth of experience by this affair. I don't see how Father Superior takes on a heap of impossibilities with such calm indifference. He must think he's capable of doing miracles. I'm really afraid his faith is presumptuous! But it doesn't matter much—if he gets himself in a mess, I'll help

---

59. Gatien to Sorin, February 23, 1849, AIP.

60. This series of letters, AIP, can be seen in Klawitter, ed., *Adapted to the Lake*, 244–300. On April 11, 1849, Gatien wrote: "You reproach me with my numerous letters. You should have praised me. For I obeyed you with a vengeance. . . . *Truly a Brother must have an iron vocation to stand the trials you make him undergo* [emphasis Gatien's]."

him with all my heart to pull himself out of it even at the risk of my life. It's possible that God blesses his presumptuous faith [with] my rash courage.[61]

In this instance, as often in the past, Brother Gatien's criticisms were not without merit. But quick-witted as he may have been, he failed to understand that every visionary displays a measure of presumption, "or what's a heaven for?"[62] At any rate, of all the crosses Edward Sorin had to bear, none was heavier than the "rash courage" of Brother Gatien.

Even as the situation in Brooklyn was fast deteriorating, Sorin was working what might have been a minor miracle back home. On November 12, 1848, a week before his departure, Father Drouelle performed a final duty as canonical Visitor to Notre Dame du Lac, a pleasant one, by singing the solemn high Mass which inaugurated use of the new church, whose cornerstone Sorin had laid fifteen months before without any money in hand and "nothing even promised."[63] Father Cointet conducted the formal blessing of the structure, and a recent addition to the novitiate was the festive preacher; he gave "an excellent sermon," Sorin thought, "but a little long."[64] Dedicated to the Sacred Heart of Jesus, the church stood ninety feet long, thirty-eight feet wide, and twenty-four feet high. "The style is Greek (*et à plein centre*). There are three arches and six fluted columns, which make a very pretty effect. It is already enriched by an organ, . . . which, though somewhat weak for the church, is all the same a principal and very precious ornament thereof."[65]

And the "miracle" was compounded a year later when the church was consecrated by the bishop of Vincennes—this was Saint-Palais's first visit to Notre Dame—with the bishop of Chicago in attendance. The celebration of this rite meant that Sorin, surrounded by creditors, had somehow devised a way to accumulate $1,500 to cover the costs of construction, because by canon law no church could be solemnly consecrated until it was debt-free. It was a day of splendid ceremony, beginning with a procession from the brothers' novitiate led by banners representing the three branches of Holy Cross—the Salvatorist priests, the Josephite brothers, the Marianite sisters—and featuring caskets containing relics

61. Gatien to Moreau, March 30, 1849, in Klawitter, ed., *Adapted to the Lake*, 289–290.

62. "Ah, but a man's reach should exceed his grasp, / Or what's a heaven for?" Robert Browning, *Andrea del Sarto* (1855).

63. See chapter 12, above.

64. Sorin, *Chronicles*, 82. The preacher was William Ivers, a forty-eight-year-old Irishman, who joined the community in 1848 and left it the next year due to ill-health. See Sorin to Blanc, August 29, 1849, AGEN.

65. Sorin, *Chronicles*, 81–82.

of the saints carried reverently beneath an ornamented canopy. "It was a moment capable of creating a profound impression, . . . when the main door was opened and the relics entered beneath their canopy to the sound of bells and music and the boom of a cannon, into the midst of the large crowd made up of various classes and religious persuasions, who had squeezed their way into the church."[66] "The solemnity," Sorin observed later, "had as much pomp as could be had. It lasted seven hours, including confirmation, which was administered to ninety persons."[67] The sermon was not entrusted this time to an untried neophyte; the preacher was that celebrated orator, Father Michael Shawe, who traveled down from Detroit for the occasion.

IT MAY BE RECALLED that this same Michael Shawe, during his brief tenure at Notre Dame, had inspired a modest adjustment of the curriculum in the college along with something of a relaxation of the disciplinary and religious regimen originally imposed upon the students in imitation of the Catholic *collèges* in France.[68] Sorin had adopted Shawe's recommendations, not out of any pedagogical principle, but simply in hopes of that such measures would help to increase enrollment. The result, however, had been disappointing; as Victor Drouelle noted in his report to Le Mans, only about forty pupils were in residence during the autumn-term of 1848. Something more drastic had to be tried, for Sorin remained as convinced as he had been at St. Peter's, Black Oak Ridge, that the success of Holy Cross's mission in America depended upon a flourishing residential college supported by fee-paying students. It was all very well that the state of Indiana had formally designated Notre Dame du Lac a university; now some steps had to be taken to convert that heady title into a reality.

Happily Sorin and those who labored with him could not have foreseen that this was to be the task not of years but of decades, else they might have given it up. Even so, they had plenty of company. West of the Alleghenies, and away from the staid eastern seaboard, institutions allegedly dedicated to higher education

---

66. Sorin to Moreau, November 14, 1849, AGEN.

67. Sorin, *Chronicles*, 86–87. The bishop of Chicago was Belgian-born (1795) James van de Velde, who in the evening presided at vespers and Benediction of the Blessed Sacrament. Of the ninety persons confirmed, thirteen were Potawatomi from Pokagon. For a full description of the festivities, see Joseph M. White, *Sacred Heart Parish at Notre Dame.*, 30–32, and the authorities cited there. Sacred Heart Church was much embellished over succeeding years, and it served the community until replaced by the present Basilica in 1875.

68. See chapter 12, above.

sprang up like weeds. Newly-formed states signaled their coming of age by chartering their own universities, however scanty were the resources at hand; Indiana did so in 1838, elevating a college already in existence at Bloomington. The government in Washington contributed mightily to this development through the instrumentation of grants of federal land, upon which fledgling institutions could enjoy an unfettered start. But besides these public initiatives, highly successful indeed but only over the very long haul, seemingly every religious denomination and sub-denomination had to have a college of its own. As for the Catholics, even within the relatively narrow ambit of Edward Sorin's direct experience, there were, besides his own Notre Dame, colleges in Vincennes, in Lebanon and Bardstown, Kentucky, and in Cincinnati, and soon to be another in Chicago.[69] It seemed as though at every country crossroads a *soi-disant* pedagogue, usually a clergyman or sometimes simply a displaced Englishman, was ready to nail a shingle to the façade of the general store announcing the availability of advanced courses in every science from algebra to zoology.

Such proliferation with so little sustenance guaranteed that with the passage of a brief time most of these fly-by-night academies would disappear with hardly a trace, as indeed they did. But what of those that survived? Not least among their problems was that of self-definition. The model before them was the one rooted deep in an aristocratic European tradition, replicated, *mutatis mutandis,* by the institutions founded in America before the Revolution. A university was intended to equip a young gentleman with the skills and knowledge adequate for him to assume his foreordained station in the world and to instill in him—as Newman would argue in his Dublin-lectures a few years after this—an "imperial intellect," a profoundly philosophical habit of mind which would render him serene in the face of all vicissitudes, confident in his own capacities, and prepared to contribute to the well-being of society.[70] The best way to achieve this noble and liberalizing objective was to immerse the student in the best of the Western intellectual tra-

---

69. Sixty-five Catholic colleges were founded in the United States between 1841 and 1860, of which 22 were in existence a century later. See Philip Gleason, "From an Indefinite Homogeneity: the Beginnings of Catholic Higher Education in the United States." I cite this unpublished paper, originally delivered to the Catholic History Seminar, University of Notre Dame (1975), with the kind permission of the author. Like everything Professor Gleason has written, this text is supported by a most formidable list of sources. Helpful also, for comparative purposes, is the same writer's "The Curriculum of the Old-Time Catholic College: a Student's View," *Records of the American Catholic Historical Society,* 88 (1977): 101–122.

70. Newman delivered the "Discourses," which later formed the core of *The Idea of a University,* in May and June, 1852. See A. Dwight Culler, *The Imperial Intellect: A Study of Newman's Educational Ideal* (New Haven, 1955), 144–152.

dition. He must be exposed to the rigor involved in learning the classical languages, so that he could plumb the wisdom of the ancients. He had to accept the unique mental discipline imposed by a study of Euclidean mathematics and the elaborations drawn from it. And if some acquaintance with a modern language—French being the obvious choice in Enlgish-speaking lands—along with a smattering of history and geography be added to the curriculum, all well and good. Such a "circle of sciences," another Newmanesque phrase,[71] would not so much enclose or confine the student as bring him into contact with the points along its circumference relevant to him: thus, for example, economics was merely a branch of moral philosophy and physics of natural philosophy.

This ideal, or some amplification of it, had proved its worth well enough at Oxford and Cambridge, and, refined by the ingenious French Jesuits, it had produced the likes of Descartes and Voltaire. It was not destined to achieve much in the desperately poor Ireland of Newman's day, though in America it had taken on a vigorous life at Harvard, Yale, and elsewhere. But Harvard (1636) and Yale (1718) seemed to those living on the Indiana frontier during the late 1840s as ancient and remote as any European institution. And in the rough democracy and commercial competitiveness that prevailed there, the conventional definition of "gentleman" had little pertinence. To be able to parse the Greek of a passage of Homer's *Iliad* or the Latin of Horace's *Eclogues,* or to examine the consequences of a demonstration in calculus, was hardly the criterion invoked in Fort Wayne or South Bend to evaluate the successful man. A "gentleman" in those towns was one who had struggled his way to economic and political prominence.

In Notre Dame's case, the difficulty of self-definition was complicated by verbal usage and by the experience of those who established the institution. The word "college" was highly ambivalent. For Frenchmen of Sorin's generation a *collège* was a private secondary school; when in his teens he himself had briefly attended such a place, operated by the Jesuits in Laval.[72] But in English too college was a word applied indifferently to secondary and postsecondary education: Eton claimed (and still does) the title "college" as much as did, say, Trinity College, Oxford, where Newman studied the classics and mathematics necessary to attain the status of a bachelor of arts.

Sorin received the bulk of his education in French seminaries, preparatory and theological, as did his priestly colleagues; the brothers and sisters, to the degree that they were educated at all—many of the Irish-American recruits joined

---

71. Culler, *Imperial Intellect,* 173–188.

72. See chapter 1, above. Even today the distinction between *collège* and *lycée* rests upon the fact that the latter is state-supported.

the community barely able to read and write—were products of a minimal training at best. Thanks to Senator Defrees, Notre Dame from 1844 could "enjoy the
title and all the rights of a university, . . . [including] the right to confer all scientific degrees, like all the great colleges in the United States."[73] But this token of
educational respectability formed only one part of a multifaceted enterprise.

It cannot be repeated too often that Edward Sorin saw himself as, first of all,
a Catholic missioner in a land full of savages, heathens, and heretics. The original
invitation to Holy Cross from Bishop Hailandière had been prompted by the need
for teachers for Indiana parochial schools, teachers who would deliver their teenage
charges from Protestant machinations. Indeed Sorin, as those teachers' religious
superior, had been only grudgingly welcome in the diocese of Vincennes, whose
bishop would have much preferred to have been himself the superior of the brothers. As Sorin warmed to his task, he brought to it no familiarity with "higher education" as that term would come to be consecrated in the late nineteenth century.
If the realities he encountered invited blurring the distinction that later times
would draw between "high school" and "college," Sorin did not hesitate to do so.
Nor was he alone in taking such a policy for granted; most of his contemporaries
who founded "colleges" or "universities," whether religious or secular, adopted
the same approach.[74]

Notre Dame from its beginnings was a polyglot affair. Its ministry to a dozen
parishes in Indiana and southern Michigan,[75] its benign care of and vocational
instruction for deprived orphans, its similar service offered to bereft girls by the
sisters in Bertrand, its much-debated endeavor to assure its long-term durability
through the institution of appropriate novitiates for priests, brothers, and sisters,
its heart-breakingly difficult struggle to secure economic viability based upon a
prosperous farm—these were the paramount concerns, none of them far removed
from Father Sorin's attention. As an alumnus of the seminaries at Precigné and Le
Mans, he had little interest in—indeed, he was entirely indifferent to—promoting
learning for learning's sake. "Imperial intellect" and "circle of sciences" would
have been empty phrases for him, had he ever heard them. But a college or *un
collège,* however defined, was the central piece in the puzzle, the one thing necessary, in the American context, to ensure that the work ordained by God and Our
Lady would triumph.

73. See chapter 8, above.
74. See Gleason, "Indefinite Homogeneity," 20.
75. During his visit to Notre Dame on the occasion of the consecration of Sacred Heart Church,
Bishop Saint-Palais appointed Sorin vicar general for the northern district of the diocese, as well as
granting him other canonical privileges. See Sorin to Haudebourg, December 15, 1849, AGEN. Father
Haudebourg was secretary of Moreau's council in Le Mans.

One of Edward Sorin's greatest strengths, one perhaps he hardly realized he possessed, was an ability to seize upon an idea and then adjust it to suit his needs. If the price of survival was a reform of the college's curriculum, so be it. If lip-service had to be paid to the ideal of a classical education, let that be done too. And if the most convenient model was that provided by the American Jesuits, or rather by mostly French and Belgian Jesuits translated to America, then make use of it. Sorin and his brethren still smarted from their recent confrontations with the assertive Society of Jesus. Nevertheless, the fact remained that the Jesuits and their famed *ratio studiorum* had succeeded in establishing viable institutions, and not only in the effete east with Georgetown (1791), their flagship college, but even farther west than Indiana, with St. Louis University (1819).[76] Fledgling colleges in Cincinnati and New York pointed Sorin toward the same conclusion, as did the recent painful fiasco at St. Mary's, Kentucky.

Through much of 1848 the community pondered the possibilities of adopting a Jesuit organization of studies for the college. Meanwhile, the drift continued, one sign of which was that Sorin, besides holding the presidency, was also officially listed as "Professor of the French and Spanish Department," as elaborate a title as it was meaningless. Brother Gatien voiced his usual complaint: "The discipline is exceedingly mild. This year [1848] pupils may do almost anything with impunity. There is indeed almost no other law than [that] of nature."[77] New faculty members came and went seemingly with the seasons, and in so haphazard a manner that institutional continuity was unthinkable. Father William Quinn, for example, drifted into northern Indiana and taught English literature at Notre Dame for a few months and, during this interval, indicated his desire to join Holy Cross. But after a while, like so many of his ilk, he simply disappeared.[78] As before a few of the brighter seminarians were used as teachers in the college, a makeshift solution at best, for they too were students and, as yet, unsettled about their future status.

All the more courage it demanded, therefore, to unveil, in the summer of 1849, an ambitious new curriculum. Modeled on the plan originally adopted at St. Louis University, the program called for six years of study, divided between a junior or preparatory and a senior "department." In the former, basic courses were to be offered over two years in Greek, Latin, and English grammar, penmanship and reading, history, arithmetic, and bookkeeping. The senior department's responsibility was more carefully delineated. Each year's sequence had a

---

76. The Jesuits actually took over the administration of a failed pre-existing institution in 1829.

77. Brother Gatien's "Journal" March 24, 1848, AIP.

78. Wack, "Notre Dame Foundation," 165.

specific title—"Humanities, Poetry, Rhetoric, Philosophy"—and each was divided into two sessions. From Lucian's *Dialogues* and geometry to Vergil's *Aeneid* and trigonometry; from "analysis of approved specimens in prose and poetry" to "analysis of the most famous specimens of eloquence;" from Tacitus, Demosthenes, and Quintillian to metaphysics, astronomy and chemistry—as complete a classical education, in short, as could be found anywhere. For an extra charge a student could also be tutored in French, German, Spanish, and Italian, as well as in music and drawing. The bachelor of arts degree was to be awarded to those who finished the whole six-year program, while the master's was reserved only to graduates who in some vague fashion "pursued" further philosophical studies or were admitted into one of the learned professions.[79]

It needs hardly be said that this curriculum was never anything more than an ideal or, to put a less kind construction upon it, never more than a façade. There were neither faculty to teach it nor students to follow it. "One cannot be serious . . . thinking of a half a score of brawny youths with huge bare feet and one suspender each, crooning over Greek paradigms, while all the people of [Indiana did] . . . battle with primitive forest, swamps, and wild varmints."[80] No doubt the most important notice contained in the college's descriptive materials was that proposing a practical alternative. Instead of the classical course, a student

> may take if preferred a partial course, which [for one] who already possesses a good knowledge of the common English branches and Latin grammar, may be completed in two years. This course, however, does not pretend to make of him a Classical scholar, but to give him a thorough English and Mathematical education, with that complete knowledge of Book-keeping and that fund of general information indispensable to young merchants.[81]

Even this, with its assumption of "a good knowledge of Latin grammar," was something of an overstatement as to the level of preparation "brawny Indiana youths" might bring to the college, but at least it had a ring of reality to it.

Sorin was too much the entrepreneur himself not to have been keenly sensitive to the demands of the educational market. During the autumn of 1848, as he

---

79. *Catalogue of the University of Notre Dame,* 1855. This is the oldest printed catalogue extant and available in AUND.

80. Logan Esarey, *History of Indiana, from its Exploration to 1923,* 3 vols. (Dayton, 1918–1923), 2: 995–996.

81. *Catalogue,* 1855.

was thinking through the possibilities of curricular reform, he received an instructive communication from the pastor in Fort Wayne, who passed along the views of one of his parishioners.

> The children of Mr. Wolke have written to their father to know what he wanted them to study. Mr. Wolke does not intend his children to follow any of the learned professions, but wants for them a business instruction, English language, its grammar, composition, etc., Arithmetic, elements of Algebra and Geometry, Modern Geography, and as extensive religious instruction as practicable. [This] is all he expects from them. Next year he may allow them to take an instrument of music, but for the present he thinks they have enough to learn.[82]

Though he was anxious that his sons be provided with "extensive religious instruction," Mr. Wolke apparently was not troubled by the absence from the Notre Dame curriculum of courses in theology. His boys could no doubt be adequately formed through the required daily spiritual exercises, Sunday sermons, and the ministrations of Father Sorin himself, who now exchanged the ludicrous title of Professor of the French and Spanish Department for the more appropriate Professor of Moral and Religious Instruction. Sorin and Mr. Wolke probably agreed, despite Newman to the contrary, that religion was a virtue to be practiced rather than a discipline to be examined by young Catholics uninterested in an ecclesiastical vocation.

Indeed, Edward Sorin assumed a predictably pragmatic attitude toward the new program. Results were what mattered, and the result that mattered the most was the number of students enrolled.

> This year [1849] the number of pupils was one-third greater than the previous year. . . . As to the intrinsic merit of the new plan, it consists chiefly in this, that in all the branches of English the same studies may be allowed without prejudice to their respective classes. . . . This new plan presents a great advantage in the United States, where everybody wants to be free to study what he likes. It pleases everybody. . . . While giving the pupils more liberty, [they] became more contented and their gratitude was shown by a greater assiduity than they had hitherto displayed.[83]

---

82. Benoit to Sorin, November 4, 1848, UNDA, COSR, "Edward Sorin."
83. Sorin, *Chronicles*, 83–84.

Over his career Father Sorin proved a friend and supporter of scholars without caring much about scholarship itself. The more demonstrative arts—music, oratory, painting—interested him, but the classics and philosophy and literature, to say nothing of the esoteric physical sciences, remained mostly blank pages to him. He cheerfully accepted the reformed organization of collegiate studies, and he presided benignly over it as it slowly evolved into a curriculum befitting a modern university. But he could not situate the "intrinsic merit" of academic life much beyond its practical consequences. It is true that without Edward Sorin, Notre Dame would never have endured, would never have been more than a footnote in the history of Catholicism in the United States. But it is also true that without collaborators of a different stripe, persons dedicated to the cultivation of learning and to the artful training of young men, Notre Dame's destiny would have been far different than it has proved to be.[84]

IT APPEARED THAT NOTRE DAME DU LAC had turned a corner in 1849. The reformed curriculum was in place, the number of students in the college had increased, a semblance of harmony had been restored with Le Mans, a new and, so far, friendly bishop had been installed in Vincennes. In May, Sorin had attended the provincial council in Baltimore and mingled cordially with the twenty-five prelates in attendance. Three months later he made another journey, this time to Canada, where he mended fences with Louis Vérité and consulted with Vérité's recently appointed successor as superior at Saint-Laurent, Joseph-Pierre Rézé—"they spent about a week pleasantly together." Sorin brought back with him to Bertrand a new mother-superior, Sister Mary of the Savior,[85] along with two other French sisters. "Soon afterward [the convent] was finished, . . . so that it presented a pretty front of ninety-two feet with two wings, less high, of forty feet each. . . . The Society of the Sisters appeared once more to become filled with life, order, peace, and happiness."[86]

But only a week after Saint-Palais had consecrated the new church amidst much jubilation, disaster struck. "On the night between Saturday and Sunday, 18

84. Both in description and analysis, Wack, "Notre Dame Foundation," 193–204, is particularly illuminating on the reformed curriculum and its consequences.

85. Sorin, in the wake of the death of his friend, Sister Mary of the Cenacle (see chapter 12, above), had failed in his attempt to "borrow" a sister from Mother Theodore's convent in Terre Haute to act as superior in Bertrand. See Sorin to Sister St. Vincent, June 1, 1848, AGEN. Mother Savior was described by one of her Marianite contemporaries as "a noble woman in every sense of the word, an educated lady, just and straightforward in her dealings." See Costin, *Priceless Spirit*, 48–51.

86. Sorin, *Chronicles*, 86.

November, fire started in the [apprentices'] workshops, it is not known how, and, in spite of the efforts of the Brothers, Seminarians, and of everybody, a line of buildings one hundred and thirty feet long and two stories high was wiped away by the flames in two hours." There had been fires in the compound before, but none of them, as he reported sorrowfully to Moreau on the morning after the tragedy, had approached this ferocity.

> It reduced to ashes the entire orphanage-complex (dormitory, study hall, carpenter's shop, as well as that of the shoe-maker, the tailor, and the baker) and also the kitchen that serves the whole institution and the work-room of the sister-sacristan where we have kept the linen and vestments for liturgical services. It is impossible at the moment to estimate the loss. . . . Such has been the fury of the flames. . . . that we have not been able to save any of the food in the kitchen, . . . or the good clothing of the orphans or even their beds. All the bread and flour kept in the bakery have been destroyed.[87]

Even the bishop's "beautiful alb" had been a casualty, Sorin told Mother Theodore; "Sister-sacristan is desolated."[88]

As he paced the charred ruins over succeeding days, Sorin calculated that the loss amounted to "at least sixteen thousand francs [$3,200]." So, as the cold of winter loomed immediately ahead, the rebuilding began with the kitchen and bakery, without which the community would simply perish.[89] All told, however, the process was painfully slow and indeed dragged out over the next eighteen months. Local benefactors, headed by Mrs. Alexis Coquillard, contributed food and clothing and a modicum of cash. Other well-wishers, from as far away as Detroit and Cincinnati, did the same. But not until Louis Baroux, the missioner at Pokagon, was persuaded, despite his reluctance, to leave his Potawatomi and go on a begging tour to France, were any substantial sums raised. "Father Baroux," Sorin reported approvingly, "devoted himself with zeal and earnestness to the work, and on his return in May 1851, he had the consolation of seeing all the shops springing up again."[90]

---

87. Sorin to Moreau, November 18, 1849, AGEN.

88. Sorin to Mother Theodore, December 12, 1849, AGEN.

89. Minor Chapter Book, minutes, November 19 and 22, 1849, AIP.

90. Sorin, *Chronicles*, 88–89, which says that Baroux collected $2,400 and that the Propagation of the Faith contributed another $1,150. The latter figure is confirmed in a Propagation statement, dated at Paris, January 19, 1850, located in the Sorin papers, AIP.

In the meantime, Edward Sorin demonstrated, once again, that no calamity, however severe, could for long weaken a self-assurance rooted in a child-like faith. Four months after the fire, the Minor Chapter, Sorin presiding, passed this resolution: "No lightning rod shall be placed over the college at least for the present, by a reason of confidence in God's Providence."[91]

---

91. Minor Chap Book, minutes, April 22, 1850, AIP.

chapter fourteen

Fool's Gold and Creole Conflict

T HE MANUAL LABOR SCHOOL, AS IT WAS EVENTUALLY rebuilt in the wake of the fire of November 1849, altered the configuration of the compound at Notre Dame. The new apprentices' shops and orphans' lodgings were situated, not behind the college-building as before, but in the area in front of it, abutting the road leading to South Bend.[1] Whatever the reason for this shift in locale, agreement soon became almost universal among those who worked and lived there that construction had been too hurried and too carelessly done. Before long disquieting suspicions arose that the shoddy work may have been the result of the diversion of money intended for the facility to other purposes. Cold winds at any rate blew through cracks in the walls during the winter, and, even more disagreeable, the oppressive heat in the summer was accompanied by an infestation of insects, especially of bedbugs, which made sleep virtually impossible.[2]

Some considerable time before the loss had been rectified, however inadequately—indeed, months before the disastrous fire itself—a quite different initiative had been discussed at Notre Dame and ultimately approved.

Whereas our debts and, of course, their interests [sic] are constantly increasing [and] we do not see any ordinary means to be able for a long while to pay so many debts, we have unanimously resolved to make use of a means

---

1. See Schlereth, *Notre Dame,* 134–135.
2. Brother Edward, "The Record of Notre Dame" (1849?), UNDA and AIP.

which, though it will appear extraordinary and strange to some, is in no ways [sic] unjust and unlawful; that is, three Brothers will be sent to California to dig gold. . . . None of them will go but of his own accord.[3]

The vote may have been unanimous, but the inspiration undoubtedly came from Edward Sorin. Even so, there was no immediate follow-up to the Minor Chapter's resolution. Then, in mid-November, the Holy Cross community awoke to discover the sorry devastation wrought upon one of its most promising enterprises. It did not take long to realize that the local élites were either unable or unwilling to offer substantial monetary aid to meet the crisis. As for Louis Baroux's assignment to seek funds abroad, there was no assurance in December 1849— when the chapter prevailed over the priest's reluctance to leave his Indians at Pokagon[4]—that his efforts would succeed, nor that a simultaneous appeal to the ever-generous but always-unpredictable Propagation of the Faith would bear fruit. So, as 1850 began, Notre Dame's perpetual, grinding need for money had been compounded by a fiery act of God. The search for a solution led Father Sorin to embark upon perhaps the most bizarre endeavor ever undertaken during his long and tumultuous career.

That he did so marked a major development in the Americanization of this young Frenchman who, like most of his fellow-missionaries, had at first looked askance at the moral and intellectual quality of the New World to which he had pledged to bring the blessings of the gospel. Nearly a decade of experience in Indiana had ripened Sorin into a more nuanced point of view, and repeated quarrels and misunderstandings with the authorities at Sainte-Croix had steered him toward the conviction that conditions in the United States dictated a different apostolic strategy from that which was appropriate for France. Moreover, perhaps because he came to listen sympathetically to "roguish" Americans rather than to his French confrères, as Brother Gatien cold-bloodedly put it, Sorin went further still and began, even if unconsciously, to subscribe to the tenets of Manifest Destiny. Nothing confirms this conclusion more forcefully than does the formation under his aegis of the St. Joseph Company, whose objective was to prospect for gold in California.

Neither geo-political nor military events figured explicitly in Edward Sorin's plans or deliberations. These were matters beyond his ken; indeed, he remained at this juncture of his career a relatively young immigrant, still uneasy trying to express himself in English and entirely innocent of the stratagems of American

3. "Minor Chapter Book," minutes, September 28, 1849, AIP.
4. See the chapter's resolution, dated December, 1849, AGEN.

politics. But in fact, during the very time he spent worrying over matters like the enrollment figures in his college or the morale of his community or the frowns of his superiors in Le Mans, the land of his adoption had entered a period of robust and even jingoistic expansion.

The election to the presidency in 1844 of Democrat James K. Polk of Tennessee over the perpetual Whig pretender to the highest executive office, Henry Clay, signaled a newly aggressive United States foreign policy that aimed to establish as its first priority to extend the sway of the American flag to the lands west of the Louisiana Purchase.[5] Polk may indeed have been, as his opponents maintained, a party hack, a narrow-minded, obstinate man of less than conspicuous intellectual gifts. Yet, for all that, he proved to be a strong leader, one capable of making a decision swiftly and without ambiguity, so much so that his presidency is remembered as the most impressive between those of Andrew Jackson and Abraham Lincoln.[6] The aims of Polk's administration, however, were not accomplished without war or the threat of war. Amidst a chorus of bombastic assertions and counterassertions, conflict with Great Britain over the borders of Oregon was averted in the end by hard diplomacy (1846), but not so with Mexico, too weak to maintain control over the rickety remains of the old Spanish Empire. The war of 1846–48 was an unvarnished war of conquest, and it netted the United States, besides an immense tract of picturesque deserts and mountains, an area called Upper California, a place about which most Americans knew nothing, except that it touched upon the Pacific Ocean and was populated by a handful of listless *vaqueros,* brown-robed friars, and docile Indians.

On January 24, 1848, quite by accident, gold was discovered by a workman employed in building a sawmill for one John August Sutter, a Swiss-born entrepreneur who controlled a huge piece of land in the Sacramento Valley, granted to him by the last Mexican governor. Sutter tried to keep the strike secret, but to no avail. By April word had reached the villages of San Francisco and San José, leaving them virtually deserted in favor of a hodgepodge of shantytowns that sprang up around the new mining camps. By mid-August official notification—along with a tea caddy containing $3,000 worth of gold nuggets panned from the vicinity of Sutter's mill—had been dispatched by the military governor of California to the secretary of war in Washington. As the news spread ever more

---

5. A personal note. In 1939, when I was a fourth-grader in Immaculate Conception School in Charles City, Iowa, Sister Benedicta, in a history lesson dealing with the accession of Texas to the union, taught me and my classmates this jingle from the campaign of 1844: "Hurrah for Polk and the Annexation,/ Down with Clay and high taxation!"

6. The judgment of Bernard DeVoto in his minor classic, *The Year of Decision: 1846* (Boston, 1943), 7–8.

widely, gold fever gripped the nation. Tens of thousands Americans, beguiled by the prospect of laying hands upon the unlimited natural riches sought in the far-off days of Cortez and Pizzaro, rushed toward California by land and, around Cape Horn or with an intervening trek across the Isthmus of Panama, by sea. In twelve months the population of the formerly sleepy province had quintupled, and over another year it more than doubled again. James Polk, who left office after a single term and died shortly afterward, in June 1849, did not himself witness this spectacular if unintended result of his expansionist policies. Nor did the former president live long enough to appreciate the chilling reality that for every millionaire who emerged from the California goldfields, a thousand others left them with much less or, in most instances, with nothing at all.

But whatever the odds against securing an instant fortune in the sandy river-beds that crisscrossed the Sacramento Valley, enthusiasm even for an outside chance of doing so was hard to restrain. And so it was that Edward Sorin and his colleagues at Notre Dame du Lac determined that they too should seek to find a solution to their unending financial troubles by an appeal, as it were, to the golden legends of El Dorado. Nearby examples were plentiful: During 1849, 112 hopeful prospectors set out from the South Bend area for the goldfields, and by the next spring another 170 had followed—these from a county where the total number of families stood at scarcely a thousand.[7] Among the 170 were seven who comprised the St. Joseph Company. They departed for California on the last day of February, 1850.

The Minor Chapter's rather vague resolution of the previous September had directed that three brothers should undertake an expedition "to dig gold," with Brother Lawrence in charge. But when, after the fire, the mission's financial straits were even more dire than before, and Sorin decided to put the project into motion,[8] he saw the necessity to buttress it with precise resources and with careful planning. He first contacted George B. Woodworth, a 45-year-old local farmer of some means whose two sons were enrolled in the college. Woodworth had been recommended to Sorin by their mutual friend, Samuel Byerley, as one ready and eager to try his luck in the goldfields. He was prepared moreover to contribute a wagon, a team of horses, and collateral equipment to the venture. For his part, Sorin pledged $1,450 as working capital for the St. Joseph Company. This was an enormous sum given the circumstances then prevailing at Notre Dame, and

7. For this statistic and for much of what follows, see Franklin Cullen, "Holy Cross on the Gold Dust Trail" (Notre Dame, Ind., 1989).
8. The expedition "will start by land for California as soon as possible." Minor Chapter Book, minutes, January 28, 1850, AIP.

its availability at that moment suggests it might have come from Baroux's fund-raising efforts in France.[9] In any event, such an expenditure at such a time on such an undertaking speaks eloquently of the gambler who dwelt deep in Edward Sorin's soul.

Woodworth was designated as "captain" of the company, and the burly, not always tactful Brother Lawrence—one of Sorin's original companions, now the 35 year-old director of the Notre Dame farm—as "lieutenant." Three other brothers were also recruited: Justin, aged 49, a gentle, simple man who had plied his shoe-maker's trade in the community; Placid, 38, noted for his sharp tongue, who had served as baker at Notre Dame; and, surprisingly, the irrepressible young Gatien, who was appointed the company's "secretary." Sorin later accounted in an ob-scure fashion for the addition to the roster of his most relentless critic: "Brother Gatien was going to leave the Society to marry and to settle down near the col-lege. He consented to depart for those distant regions,"[10] presumably on Sorin's plea that a brother's marriage would create scandal in the locality. If there had in-deed been a romantic attachment, it could not have gone very deep, since Gatien never returned to Indiana, nor did he ever marry.[11] A more mundane explanation at any rate is just as plausible: for some time this highly talented teacher had grown despondent about the increasing deafness which, in his own mind at least, rendered him unable to perform adequately any longer in the classroom.[12] Finally, the party bound for California was rounded off by two young laymen, Gregory Campau, a student in the college, and Michael Dowling, who had worked at Notre Dame, either in the now burned-out apprentice shops or on the farm under Brother Lawrence's supervision.

Formalities were scrupulously attended to. An elaborate contract comprising twenty-three articles was drawn up, signed by the seven participants, and duly witnessed. It mandated that whatever proceeds the St. Joseph Company acquired would be divided equally. Seventy percent of the total realized—all the shares of the four brothers and half those of Campau and Dowling—would go into the

---

9. See chapter 13, above, and Catta, *Moreau*, 1: 937–938, 942–943, a not altogether consistent treatment.

10. Sorin, *Chronicles*, 90–91.

11. Sorin may have had in mind a later romantic initiative. D. Bruneau, in "L'Odyssée d'un Mayennais aux Etats-unis de 1841 à 1860, Urbain Monsimer (Frère Gatien, C.S.C.)," published pri-vately in Angers in 1991, prints a letter from Monsimer/Gatien to Sarah Kennedy, dated March 2, 1856, in which marriage is proposed. Miss Kennedy had been a pupil of the Marianite Sisters and later joined the community. Her father, originally a South Bend–area resident, had gone to Califor-nia and by 1856 had renewed acquaintance with Monsimer.

12. See Gatien to Sorin, April 10 and April 14, 1849, in Klawitter, *Adapted to the Lake*, 297, 299.

coffers of Notre Dame, while Captain Woodworth would keep his share for himself. Besides putting up the original capital, Father Sorin also assumed the commitment that "in case of necessity, any check or draft signed by the captain, lieutenant, and secretary of said Company shall be honored by the President of the University of Notre Dame du Lac." Nor did the contract fail to insist on maintaining the norms of Catholic piety; several of the articles stipulated that the participants were obliged to pray regularly and, whenever a priest was available, to attend Mass and go to confession; in short, "they shall always endeavor to behave themselves individually and as a family fearing God and seeking for their success in their dangerous mission [by] showing themselves [in] every way good, religious men." For the four brothers such a covenant was a commonplace; with their lay colleagues it may have been less well-received, though Campau at least was known as the pious sort.[13]

Conventional wisdom had it that the overland journey from Indiana to northern California would take about four and a half months, and, in the case of the St. Joseph Company, so it did. The stalwart seven were relatively well-equipped. Their caravan included, besides Woodworth's team and wagon, nine more horses and two more wagons, paid for out of Sorin's $1,450, as were food-stocks like 100 pounds of ham and 50 of sausage, 75 pounds of sugar, and 100 pounds of salted codfish. Three gallons of brandy and of whiskey were brought along to ward off the chill of the night. Tools, kitchen utensils, blankets, and a few books, a dictionary among them, were also packed into the wagons which began their long and arduous trip on February 28, 1850. After passage through Illinois, where Woodworth's weakness for petty thievery disturbed Brother Lawrence,[14] they crossed the Mississippi at Burlington, Iowa, and by April 15 they had arrived at Independence, Missouri. They were in high spirits, having heard about "a piece of gold in California six inches long, two inches wide, and three inches thick."[15] From Independence, the jumping-off place for most of the wagon-trains ready to embark into Indian country, their exact route is less certain, although it most likely followed the track blazed a few years earlier by John Charles Frémont, over what seemed a never-ending, treeless prairie to Fort Laramie—10,000 wagons, heading west, passed this settlement in the course of 1850—and into the mountains, to Fort Bridger, and then across the immensity of Utah Territory, coming down

---

13. The contract is printed in Cullen, "Gold Dust Trail," 5–7.

14. Lawrence to Sorin, March 15, 1850, AIP.

15. Campau to John Woodworth, April 17, 1850, AIP. John was Captain Woodworth's son, a student at Notre Dame.

finally, in the middle of a hot July, through the Donner Pass into Placerville, only a few miles from Sutter's first strike.

The prospectors from Notre Dame soon learned that Placerville was also called Hangtown, due to the fact that shortly before their arrival vigilantes had hanged three miscreants, as Brother Gatien reported to Father Sorin, "on a tree still standing in [the] town." Indeed, it was that indefatigable writer of letters and keeper of diaries, Gatien, who maintained verbal contact with the anxious patron back in Indiana. Brother Lawrence wrote only with great difficulty, and Brother Placid was virtually illiterate. Gatien, by contrast, was a gifted observer who described with panache not only the hardships of the long trail—the grimly fatiguing physical exertion combined with a profound boredom—but also the curiosities animal, vegetable, and mineral that the St. Joseph Company encountered along the way.[16] Yet during that journey, however harsh it may have been, they had all been buoyed up by the hopes of a happy ending once they reached the goldfields, hopes dashed by a brief spell in Hangtown. They found no gold. "Gold is plenty," Brother Gatien wrote laconically on September 15, "but not uniformly distributed. It is hid in the ground and must be dug out only by dint of hard work and untiring perseverance. . . . The cream is gone. . . . There is scarcely an inch of ground not already dug."[17] They found no gold, but they found sickness and petty disputes among themselves and growing emotional depression and prices for ordinary commodities that beggared their midwestern imaginations. And by mid-November they found death.

> "I'm sick." "I am unable to work." "One of my acquaintances just died." [Remarks like these make up] the talk of nearly every group in town or out of it. The St. Joseph Company has not been spared. . . . Brother Lawrence has been in danger of death, and Brother Placid is gone, I hope to a better world. Doctor's bill is not far from $600. I have also been very sick for four weeks and have run a $60 debt. The majority of miners are as in the same case of the St. Joseph Company, unable to work and in debt. . . . The diggings in this vicinity scarcely pay board to the majority of new miners, and a great many are merely trying to make enough to take them home. . . . Fleas and lice are in the greatest prosperity in this country, and very few miners can get ahead of them.[18]

---

16. For a striking example, see Gatien to Sorin, May 19, 1850, AIP.
17. Gatien to Sorin, September 15, 1850, AIP.
18. Gatien to Sorin, November 29, 1850, AIP.

So Edward Sorin's roll of the dice had failed. The mission of Notre Dame du Lac was to receive no sustenance from the golden streams of California. The loss, however, was even more severe in human terms. Woodworth, Campau, and Dowling had simply drifted away from the dismal gold-camps, and Brothers Lawrence and Justin eventually made their way back to Indiana; by mid-1851 they had resumed again their honorable positions within the Holy Cross community. But Brother Placid lay in a pauper's grave on the outskirts of Hangtown. "You will be able to understand," Lawrence had written Sorin in his crabbed hand, "how painful it was for us to see him die without a priest, but it was useless to think of it, for one was not closer than San Francisco."[19]

And Gatien—that brilliant, ill-starred young missioner, that stormy petrel, that hard, Jansenist conscience of early Notre Dame—Gatien had discovered in California, not gold, but the courage to admit that the call to religion he had hearkened to as a boy had somehow gone silent. Whatever his inner turmoil, withdrawal from the Congregation of Holy Cross had become for him a moral imperative. Edward Sorin, with whom he had crossed the sea when only a lad of fifteen and with whom he had so often quarreled, treated the parting benignly, almost affectionately. In June 1851 he sent Gatien by post a set of "amiabilities and gratefully received grants and dispensations," to which Urban Monsimer—he had reverted to his given name—replied, not without his wonted exaggeration:

> I must say with a deep regret and a heartfelt sorrow for the disappointments which my frankness may have caused you, and, in spite of the inconceivable and ineffaceable attachment which I have for your Institution and my inexplicable love of the apprentices, you shall never see me again. . . . I am not impious, thanks to Mary, and as far as I can [be], I am a practical Catholic, abstaining from whoring, gambling, and drinking, from swearing, from meat on Fridays and mining [i.e., performing servile labor] on Sundays.[20]

A certain charming simplicity clings to this protestation, and even more so to the words addressed to Sorin nine years later.

> I have lost all hope of recovery [Monsimer wrote from San Francisco in April, 1860]. Doctors have given me up, and I am becoming daily weaker. I weigh but 105 pounds. My father wishes to see me before I die, and it is for

---

19. Lawrence to Sorin, November 10, 1850, AIP. Placid had died on November 6.
20. Monsimer to Sorin, August 15, 1851, quoted in Cullen, "Gold Dust Trail," 26.

this reason that I undertake a long voyage at the eleventh hour of my life. . . . Pray for me that I may not die during the voyage and that I may carry my cross patiently.

He had lost none of his assertiveness. "I die, I think, the victim of the wretched system followed in your Institution and so many others. No attention is paid to health. Your subjects have not enough exercise in the open air and the dress alike summer and winter, buttoning tightly across the breast as if the intention were to choke them as soon as possible." But there was sorrow too, for what had proved to be a wasted life. "My greatest sins were committed at Notre Dame du Lac. There I blasphemed God in my heart and publicly insulted the Blessed Virgin. There I was guilty of unnatural impurities. I repent chiefly of *one thing, namely that I ever was a Brother.*[21] Monsimer did survive the journey back to France, but once he had returned to the farm where he had been born he lasted only a few weeks. He died there, aged thirty-four, July 29, 1860, a bachelor still.

Aside from a very brief and self-serving account,[22] Edward Sorin said little about the disastrous enterprise he had sponsored. Others were not so reticent. Once he learned the details of the venture, Basile Moreau was vexed that his permission had not been sought, a permission, he said, he would have refused to give.[23] Sorin claimed that he had informed Le Mans of the expedition in a letter written in March 1850; such a communication, however, never reached its destination, and, even if in fact it had been sent,[24] it could not have contained a request for permission, since the St. Joseph Company had been by that date some weeks on the road. Moreau in any case remained unappeased, particularly after he learned of Brother Placid's death, and he circulated a public rebuke to Sorin throughout the Congrégation de Sainte-Croix.[25]

Louis Baroux was still on his begging tour in France when he got wind of the disaster in California. Suspecting as he did that to equip the prospectors Sorin had used funds he, Baroux, had raised and forwarded to Notre Dame, his harsh reaction was not surprising.

---

21. Monsimer to Sorin, April 23, 1860, AIP.

22. Sorin, *Chronicles*, 90–91.

23. See Moreau to Sorin, March 30, 1851, AGEN.

24. In the light of Sorin to Moreau, May 11 and June 10, 1850, AGEN, it seems extremely unlikely that Sorin ever informed Moreau of the expedition. In neither of these letters does he mention the brothers on "the gold dust trail," which he surely would have done were Moreau aware of their departure.

25. See Moreau, *Circular Letters*, 1: 258, dated December 8, 1851.

Our fears [he scolded Sorin] that all the money went to pay for the trip of
the California colony—this saddens everybody and makes us blush. One
blushes to see Religious placed in the ranks of all the greedy who run after
gold; one is humiliated by these proceedings. . . . One finds neither charity
nor humanity to sacrifice these subjects whom you have exposed to dying
without the sacraments to find gold with the adventurers and dregs of society who people this California.[26]

But perhaps Sorin felt the sharpest sting from the reproach leveled at him by
the young woman who had sailed to America with him nearly ten years before.
Aboard the *Iowa,* wrote Sister Francis Xavier from Terre Haute. "the Brothers were
so happy to be near you."

I remember you saying: "I would like the ship to have an accident which
would cause us to throw all our trunks and supplies into the sea, and we
would have only the cross of Jesus left." Oh, you said that with a sincere
heart; you were far from thinking that one day you would send those dear
children who, like you, gloried in poverty to look for gold. Their trip from
New York to Vincennes was indeed dangerous, but they had their Father
with them. . . . But today they do not have a priest to console them, nor a
priest to absolve them. This week twenty-two men from our area are leaving for that wretched country. When we told them about the dangers to
which their souls would be exposed, they answered: "The Brothers from
South Bend are going there, why shouldn't we?"[27]

Alas, *l'affaire Californie,* far from Edward Sorin's finest hour, was only prelude to
a renewed drama of struggle and disillusionment.

W‌HEN HE DEPARTED Notre Dame du Lac in November 1848
the genial "Visitor" from Sainte-Croix, Sorin's good friend Victor Drouelle, was
bound for Guadeloupe, the French possession in the Caribbean where a member
of the Congrégation de Sainte-Croix had been appointed by Rome vicar-apostolic.
This prelate, a champion of the indigenous colored population of the island, had
for that reason fallen into disfavor with the colonial office in Paris; he therefore

---

26. Baroux to Sorin, September 30, 1850, and April 9, 1851, quoted in Cullen, "Gold Dust Trail,"
29–30. See also Baroux to Sorin, August 28, 1851, AIP.

27. Sister Francis Xavier to Sorin, November, 1850, AUND, COSR, "Edward Sorin."

had need of the smooth diplomatic gifts of which Drouelle was an undoubted master and in which Father Moreau had every confidence. Drouelle's itinerary called for him to take ship in New Orleans, and to get there he followed the river route disembarking in mid-December from the Mississippi paddle-steamer *Champion* at what was already nicknamed the Crescent City. While there he held several conversations with the French-born Catholic bishop, Antoine Blanc, conversations that went far beyond mere courtesy.[28]

Indeed, it is difficult not to assume that, before he left Indiana, Father Drouelle had heard a great deal about the possibilities of the expansion of Holy Cross to New Orleans and its environs. For nearly three years Sorin had been in touch with Bishop Blanc, who was anxious to acquire religious to staff various institutions in his rapidly expanding diocese.[29] August Martin, former vicar general in Vincennes who had fled the cantankerous Célestin de la Hailandière, was now parish priest in Baton Rouge, and Sorin had renewed correspondence with him. Moreover, in the spring of 1847, "the Patriarch of our good Brothers," Brother Vincent, had been dispatched from Notre Dame to reconnoiter in person the situation in Louisiana.[30] The ground had been prepared, and the consultation between Drouelle and Blanc could hardly have been a spur-of-the-moment matter, especially in light of the speed with which an agreement was concluded.[31] In short, Sorin commissioned Drouelle to inform the bishop that, with the collapse of the initiative in Kentucky, Holy Cross personnel were now available to him. Accordingly, at the beginning of May, 1849, five brothers and three sisters—all of them, it is important to stress, subjects of Notre Dame du Lac—went into residence in New Orleans.[32]

It was then a brawling, boisterous town of some fifty thousand. During the years immediately preceding the arrival of Holy Cross, it had enjoyed prodigious if unruly growth. Hardly a trace survived of the Spaniards who had briefly governed it, but the French presence remained strong: native Normans and Bretons, to be sure, and also Cajuns, descendants of the fabled Acadian refugees who had fled eastern Canada during the previous century. But the Irish had also begun to immigrate, and even more the Germans, and not a few free Negroes from the

---

28. Sorin sent with Drouelle a formal letter of introduction: Sorin to Blanc, November 20, 1848, AGEN. See also a statement confirming Drouelle's negotiations, Sorin to Blanc, January 9, 1849, AGEN.

29. See, for example, Sorin to Blanc, February 16, 1846, AGEN.

30. See Sorin to Martin, May 2, 1847, and January 31, 1848, AGEN.

31. Catta, *Moreau*, 1: 932, 934, is mistaken to assert that Drouelle's was "a passing visit" to New Orleans and that he only "happened to be in the city."

32. See Costin, *Priceless Spirit*, 91.

West Indies, all of them jostling together in the unkempt streets. Out of this racial and national diversity had developed a creole culture, warm, spontaneous, and artful, its love of life signaled by its already celebrated carnival, the Mardi Gras, not thwarted even by a physical environment notoriously prone to epidemics of yellow fever and cholera.[33]

Yet another factor played, if anything, an even more significant role than the hi-jinks of Shrove Tuesday and the seductive charm of the French Quarter. New Orleans was an American city now, and had been for nearly fifty years, and, despite its old-world flavor, it shared the characteristics of other outposts of western expansion. Anglo commercial assertiveness had by 1840 to a large degree tamed its frontier exuberances and had brought the city gaslight, a viable railway spur, and steam-driven machinery to process cotton. The harbor was thronged by river steamers and ocean-clippers, and produce of all kinds crowded its docks. Great fortunes were amassed, and grand houses were built; still, amidst the opulence and the mercantile audacity that produced it, poverty, neglect, and hopelessness haunted its alleyways, and the huts of black slaves were sober reminders of the foundations on which the bustling economy was based. But overall there clung to New Orleans a romantic aura, a kind of brash flamboyance, memorialized best perhaps by the moment when the redoubtable General Jackson had repelled a British incursion only with the help of the swashbuckling pirate, Jean Lafitte.

The brothers and sisters of Holy Cross, however, experienced nothing of the romance of the place during the early months of their new duty. Indeed, this was a time, brief but harrowing, of illness and deprivation. Bishop Blanc had put in their charge St. Mary's Orphan Asylum, a shelter for about a hundred indigent boys, founded fifteen years before. The nuns assigned to the mission, along with one of the brothers, had come to New Orleans directly from Kentucky, while the other brothers, including Basil, so recently involved in the unhappy undertaking in Brooklyn, had traveled there from Notre Dame by coach and paddleboat, their expenses of $150 paid for by Bishop Blanc. Father Granger had accompanied these latter, but, once they were settled, he returned to Indiana.[34] A certain ambivalence resulted: according to the constitutions of the Congregation of Holy Cross each community had to have a priest at its head. In this instance, however, as Father

---

33. See Sorin to Rousselon, April 12, 1849, AIP, announcing the imminent departure of the colony for New Orleans. Father Rousselon was Blanc's vicar general. Sorin also expressed concern about the dangers from disease, especially cholera, to which the community would be subjected.

34. Sorin had hoped to accompany the brothers from Indiana himself. See Sorin to Blanc, January 9 and April 4, 1849, AGEN, and, for details of the agreement, February 9, 1849, AIP.

Sorin maintained, no priest was immediately available. He therefore dispatched Brother Vincent to take charge.[35]

This assignment testified to the change of mind Edward Sorin had undergone about Vincent's worth since their early days together on the apostolate in America. Almost a generation Sorin's senior, both in years and in religious service, Vincent's very presence had at first suggested that the younger man owed him deference, a circumstance Sorin had resented and even protested against.[36] And Vincent had, on occasion, exercised a mild paternalism and had admonished his impulsive young chief.[37] Time, however, and above all experience, had brought their association into harmony. If Brother Vincent was a gentle and accommodating man, he was also a loyal and sturdy support, one whose spiritual testament threatened nobody and yet who never forgot the commitment he had made when Canon Dujarié had enrolled him among the original Brothers of St. Joseph so many years before. It was he whom Sorin had sent to Brooklyn in hopes of saving an ill-fated enterprise there, and now, at the age of fifty-three, he assumed the role of acting superior in New Orleans.

It was not a burden he carried easily or with marked success. The orphans were served diligently enough—so much so, Vincent lamented, that the brothers had no time for communal prayer[38]—but, though St. Mary's Asylum received a modest subsidy from the state of Louisiana, it was nevertheless necessary that each morning a brother, usually Vincent himself, go out "with a cart to beg from the hotels the leftovers of the day before," which solicitation routinely reaped debris like cigar-butts and apple-peelings as well as the remnants of the meat, bread, and vegetables "so badly needed."[39] Brother Vincent, in accord with his vow of poverty, did not consider begging a trial, but wrangling within the community rendered life sore for him. "Brother Louis is always fickle and changing, [and] he beats the children too much," Vincent reported sadly to Notre Dame. "Brother

---

35. Sorin assured Blanc that he would send a priest as soon as possible. "I hope the good God will bless our sacrifice." Sorin to Blanc, January 22, 1850, AGEN.

36. See chapter 6, above.

37. For example, see Vincent to Sorin, February 23, 1847, AIP. "I find you rather often too reserved with your assistant. . . . I do not think you follow through on the plans you form. . . . People complain that you do not observe college rules."

38. This complaint troubled Sorin enough for him to ask Blanc to make proper arrangements for common religious exercises. "The spiritual interests of these good Brothers cannot be neglected without threatening the work confided to them." Sorin to Blanc, July 17, 1849, AGEN. A month later he thanked the bishop for "ameliorating" the situation. Sorin to Blanc, August 19, 1849, AGEN.

39. See the first-hand account quoted in Costin, *Priceless Spirit*, 91, and Vincent to Moreau, August 1, 1849, in Klawitter, ed., *Adapted to the Lake*, 321.

Francis de Sales . . . criticizes everything done." "Sister Mary of the Five Wounds . . . is, in my opinion, a little busy-body or at least too moody."[40] That formidable lady, however, was not without complaints of her own. "The Brother Director of an establishment where there are some Sisters," she irritably informed Sorin, "should not believe that he has the right to keep the same Sisters in ignorance of what concerns them."[41] The solution to the squabbling was, for Brother Vincent, simple as well as consistent with the constitutions of Holy Cross: Sorin had to send a priest to shoulder direction of the mission in New Orleans.

His conviction on this score was to a degree based on an uneasiness stemming from the absence of regular sacramental ministry. "I am troubled," he told Moreau in September, 1849, "that there is no priest to hear [the orphans'] confessions and administer communion to them. For the three months I have been here I have got only twenty of them to confession." But Vincent was no less disturbed that the Holy Cross religious themselves would languish spiritually until a priest from Notre Dame reached them: "The Brothers and Sisters long for this moment."[42] Combined, however, with this reverential regard for the ministerial priesthood was his characteristic diffidence. "You say in your last letter," he remarked to Sorin somewhat peevishly, "that 'old Brother Vincent ought to know how to give orders.' I have never been able to, not even to our blacks. You knew it before sending me here." "Do you think you'll be able to replace me soon?" he asked a couple of months later. "The thing is perhaps more urgent than you could believe." He worried that without proper leadership antagonism might spring up between the brothers and the sisters; if so, "everybody will see, and they will grieve. . . . You must consider, my good Father, that you have to replace me as soon as possible, or else you'll see this beautiful establishment decay little by little."[43]

After its early tenuous months the Holy Cross mission in New Orleans did indeed give promise of becoming, relatively speaking, a "beautiful establishment." The speedy success the religious enjoyed in their supervision of the orphanage was soon translated into substantial support from the local elites. The sisters were moved into a new house, and a community chapel was being constructed. By the end of the summer of 1849 the project appeared as though it might compensate for the failures in Kentucky and New York. "If the New Orleans establishment is well-directed," Brother Vincent opined, "it will encourage

---

40. Vincent to Sorin, May 17, June 22, and September 19, 1849, AIP.
41. Mary of the Five Wounds to Sorin, n.d. [December, 1849], AIP.
42. Vincent to Sorin, August 8, 1849, AIP.
43. Vincent to Sorin, June 11, August 27, and August 6, 1849, AIP.

others."[44] Far away, in Indiana, Father Sorin granted the principle even as he pondered the possible nominees to take on that direction. That a priest be sent to Louisiana—especially that Sorin might come to the bayous and see the potential for himself—was a constant theme in Vincent's correspondence. In the early autumn he received a strong and yet not quite decisive hint as to Sorin's intentions: "You haven't told me if it's Father Gouesse whom you are going to send or not."[45]

Francis Gouesse was indeed Sorin's choice to go to New Orleans.[46] But the antipathy between the two, which stretched back to the day Gouesse arrived at Notre Dame and had been exacerbated since by disputes trivial and substantial,[47] inevitably affected this transaction. Gouesse was a gifted young man, fluent in German and English as well as in his native French. He was moreover a talented if amateur musician, and the performances over which he had presided had enthralled audiences from the South Bend area no less than they had Father Victor Drouelle when the latter paid his formal visitation to Notre Dame in 1848.[48] But Gouesse had also been Brother Gatien's ally during the sometimes heated debates within the Council of Administration and the Minor Chapter. Not so demonstrative or voluble as Gatien, Father Gouesse nonetheless never bothered to disguise his hostility toward many of Sorin's plans and ambitions nor his dislike of Sorin himself.

It is tempting to conclude that on the eve of Gatien's departure for California Sorin grasped the opportunity to rid himself of both of his most severe internal critics. In any event, at the end of January, 1850, he noted formally that "Father Gouesse was sent as Visitor to the orphans' establishment of New Orleans." Not, it should be noted, as superior but as "Visitor." Sorin, it appears, could not bring himself to assign a man hostile to himself and his ideals to more than what was, by definition, a temporary position. Nor did he doubt, since all the personnel in New Orleans were subjects of Notre Dame, that in making the decision he stood on firm canonical ground. "The truth is," he claimed afterward, when all the bitterness had bubbled to the surface, "that [Gouesse] had been sent to New Orleans merely to rid [Notre Dame] of his presence, without any intention of leaving him there for long, still less of ever giving him any other title but that of Spiritual Director of the [Orphans'] Asylum."[49]

44. Vincent to Sorin, September 18, 1849, AIP.

45. Vincent to Sorin, October 2, 1849, AIP.

46. See a copy of the formal appointment, signed by Sorin and dated January 21, 1850, AGEN. Sorin refers to Gouesse as "*notre cher confrère.*"

47. See chapters 10 and 12, above.

48. See Catta, *Moreau,* 1: 929.

49. Sorin, *Chronicles,* 91, 95.

Gouesse arrived at the delta at the end of February, and, whatever his title, he acted for all practical purposes as local superior. From the outset his administration received mixed reviews. Archbishop Blanc—his see had been elevated that same year, 1850, to metropolitan status—thought Gouesse performed adequately.[50] The Holy Cross sisters, however, to whom he ministered were less convinced; there was a good measure of acceptance among them but also not a little skepticism: "He showed a coldness, an air of contempt with a certain distrust," one of the nuns recalled.[51]

Francis Gouesse's behavior in New Orleans during the ensuing months gave rise to questions about his personal habits. Some thought his inconsistent and sometimes contradictory deportment indicated that he might have been drinking heavily. No one explicitly charged him with insobriety, however, and the archbishop was not alone in commending his overall effectiveness. Sorin, meanwhile, though he had not moderated his antipathy, and though revelations sent to him by various members of Holy Cross in New Orleans did nothing to lessen his rancor, nevertheless extended Gouesse's term as Visitor. Then, in July—just as the prospectors of the St. Joseph Company were coming down out of the mountains into northern California—Sorin traveled himself to Louisiana, because he believed "that the existence of our members was seriously threatened unless instant means were taken to check the evils that [that] turbulent and ambitious individual was causing to grow . . . day by day." Over the eight days of his stay he conducted distinct retreats for the brothers and the sisters, "arranged everything in a satisfactory manner for those two branches," but failed "to make any impression on the haughty dispositions of the man who ought to have given all the others the example of submission." A week of bitter quarrels might have augured Gouesse's removal, but, "having no one to put in this man's place just then," Sorin chose to leave him in New Orleans for the time being and appeal the matter to Sainte-Croix.[52]

Father Moreau was at this time in Rome, overseeing a new foundation in the city and lobbying the papal curia for approval of Holy Cross's constitutions. From there he wrote his council on December 4: "I have decided that Father Gouesse will govern his house [in New Orleans] with a minor chapter, but will present his accounts to Father Sorin, who will then submit them to me. Father Gouesse will also depend on Father Sorin for visitation and admission [of candi-

---

50. See Blanc to Sorin, May 26, 1850, AIP.
51. Mary of the Angels to Sorin, April 21, 1850, AIP.
52. Sorin, *Chronicles*, 93–94.

dates] to profession."[53] Much preoccupied with other matters, Moreau apparently assumed that since Gouesse had been given a temporary assignment to New Orleans, a permanent one would be acceptable, so long as financial transactions and personnel decisions there remained subject to Notre Dame in the first instance. This arrangement also suggested that Moreau was edging toward granting Sorin the latter's strong desire, dating back at least to the initiative at St. Mary's, Kentucky, that a separate province of Holy Cross be created embracing the whole United States. No final decision on this point had as yet been made, but the Founder demonstrated a certain liberality in even considering it, particularly since the recent commitments, first to Brooklyn and then to New Orleans, had been entered into without consulting him.

But Edward Sorin saw the situation far otherwise. "What was his surprise to learn . . . that [Gouesse] had at last received from France the document naming him Local Superior of New Orleans." A protest was duly sent from Notre Dame to Le Mans, but "not a line came for six months to check an evil that was growing in a frightening manner." Sorin soon came to appreciate that Moreau's sojourn in Rome explained the silence and that Gouesse's appointment had been judged as "the one means of bringing about a general reconciliation," but Sorin dismissed this attempt at peace-making as misguided and worse. "Very Reverend Father," he wrote in a fury, "your sad [announcement] has arrived. You choose to support Father Gouesse and to take no account of our representations. *You want to reconcile everything,* even that which cannot be reconciled. What a page in the history of your life!"[54] Indeed, he observed later in a calmer tone, "it is still a mystery at Notre Dame du Lac how the Mother House could be so mistaken in a matter that had been so often set before the eyes of the people there." Sorin also, backed by his Minor Chapter, advised Archbishop Blanc that Gouesse's appointment "should not hold," that it was probably the result of a misunderstanding at Sainte-Croix about the real status of the case. "It appears," he wrote the archbishop directly, "that Father Gouesse, whose ambition is not unknown here, has managed to entrap the Mother House into naming him Local Superior, despite all the efforts of the Chapter at Notre Dame du Lac. We shall refrain from saying what means he has employed and simply register with you our surprise and pain in learning of a nomination so irreligious and, in our opinion, so damaging to the common good."[55] And to Brother Vincent he insisted that the community in New Orleans should not acknowledge Gouesse's authority. If these were bold steps,

53. Catta, *Moreau,* 1: 938.
54. Sorin to Moreau, March 30, 1851, AGEN.
55. Sorin to Blanc, January 7, 1851, AGEN.

even bolder was the announcement, sent to the archbishop some months later (June 1851), "of the positive dismissal of the same Father [Gouesse] from the Association [of Holy Cross] in the United States."[56]

Francis Gouesse, whatever his vices and shortcomings, was not one to suffer such treatment gladly. He complained, specifically to the well-disposed Archbishop Blanc, of Sorin's "crooked and tortuous conduct." Blanc assumed a cautious line, though he confessed himself "not a little astonished" that Gouesse should have been declared "irregular." "I can say nothing," he observed some weeks later, "about the measure taken by the Chapter at Notre Dame du Lac with regard to Father Gouesse; this is a family matter. We shall have to see what the motherhouse decides."[57] But Gouesse enjoyed less than enthusiastic or unanimous support from his brothers and sisters in religion, whether in Louisiana or Indiana.[58] And Sorin's accusation that he was "very unworthy (*très indigne*)" of the post Le Mans had formally given him, and not merely incompetent, raised the question as to Gouesse's drinking habits. Indeed, the Minor Chapter at Notre Dame denounced him as a man "who would probably never exhibit the spirit of submission and obedience appropriate for a religious," who appeared "to allow vanity to be the guide of most of his actions," and who "shows by his demeanor even at the Holy Altar that he thinks nothing is amiss with him, prompting the confrères who live with him to tremble for his soul."[59] Sorin at any rate was so convinced of the rightness of his cause that he did not hesitate to employ hyperbole in its defense: "Whilst heaven was blessing [Moreau's] work at Rome, the devil was sifting it here. If human ambition had no other examples to bring forward in proof of the unfortunate effects that result from it, ours would suffice to inspire every sensible man with disgust. . . . Of all the trials of the Association [of Holy Cross] in this country, there was none that brought it nearer to its fall [than this one]."[60]

---

56. Sorin, *Chronicles*, 94–95, claiming that he had received from Moreau "authorization to dismiss" several months before. But it appears in the documents cited in number 59, below, that such authorization was valid only if Gouesse "did not mend his ways." Whether he had or not remained in dispute.

57. Blanc to Sorin, February 1 and March 10, 1851, AIP.

58. See Blanc to Sorin, April 12, 1851, AIP, and Costin, *Priceless Spirit*, 97–98.

59. See copies of the resolutions debated and passed by the Minor Chapter, dated January 7, 1851, and signed by Sorin, Granger, and Cointet, AGEN. Documentation as to Gouesse's problem with alcohol is oblique but persuasive. See the authorities cited by Connelly, "Charism: Origins and History," 114. However, "unworthy" was also the word used later by Granger to describe Louis Baroux, a stern critic of Sorin but hardly a drunkard. Granger to Moreau, November 9, 1852, quoted in Catta, *Moreau*, 1: 963.

60. Sorin, *Chronicles*, 95.

Gouesse could, and of course did, point to the undeniable fact that the mission in New Orleans was prospering, thanks, he argued, at least in part to his own enlightened leadership. Since its foundation in 1835, St. Mary's Orphan Asylum had been subsidized by the state of Louisiana, which allotted $125 annually to each member of its staff, along with an additional $25 to whoever acted as its director.[61] This support, considerable for the times, had been augmented by the generosity of New Orleans Catholics, to the extent that Gouesse and others of Sorin's enemies charged that Notre Dame's sole interest in the mission stemmed from a desire to derive profit from it, a contention that fails to honor the complexities of the matter.[62]

As the old year gave way to the new of 1851, Father Gouesse, thanks to the *diktat* of Sainte-Croix, still enjoyed his status as local superior in New Orleans.[63] But thanks to Sorin, and his implacable animosity, Gouesse's tenure was still under threat. Nor was Sorin's hostility mitigated by Moreau's assurance that, regardless of Gouesse's position there, surplus funds garnered in New Orleans, if any, could be employed at Notre Dame's discretion, so long as two separate sets of books were kept and submitted annually to Le Mans.[64] This concession clearly did not satisfy Sorin, for whom two distinct accounts meant that the Holy Cross staff in New Orleans was directly dependent on the motherhouse, not on Notre Dame du Lac from which they had come, which indeed was Moreau's intent.

Serious financial concerns and high principles of administration were, to be sure, at stake in this dispute. But Edward Sorin's distaste for Gouesse was also intensely personal, and at the end of March he unleashed his sharpest broadside yet. "A thousand pardons, Monseigneur," he wrote Archbishop Blanc, "for addressing you now as I do. Yet I have believed it to be my duty, and especially since you have taught me to think of you as a father."

Allow me to ask you to maintain what is written here as a secret for yourself alone. Nothing pains me more than to reveal certain things I would sooner forget. Father Gouesse has deceived Father-Rector [Moreau], who however knows as surely as I do that Gouesse was expelled from the seminary in 1842, banished from here in 1845,[65] and dismissed from Sainte-

---

61. Sorin, *Chronicles,* 84–85.

62. See Catta, *Moreau,* 1: 938–941. The harshly anti-Sorin bias of this book is evident throughout, but its treatment of *l'affaire Gouesse* seems particularly mean-spirited.

63. Moreau to Sorin, March 30, 1851, AGEN.

64. Moreau to Sorin, January 13, 1851, quoted in Wack, "Notre Dame Foundation," 249.

65. Sorin punished Gouesse for insubordination by sending him for a brief time to Pokagon. See Sorin to Moreau, October 13, 1845, AGEN, and chapter 11, above.

Croix itself in 1850. (I kept here the document [*acte*] of expulsion for six months, and I returned it to France only when I learned of his nomination to a dignity [in New Orleans] which he has attained as a way of gratifying his vanity.) This document had been sent me originally as a just chastisement for his insubordination over many years and in particular *for his refusal, despite his promise, to report to New Orleans in the autumn of 1849, a refusal because I would not share with him my powers as a Local Superior, etc.* [Moreau] knows all this, but Father Gouesse has no doubt beguiled him with stories of the riches available in New Orleans, in order to make him dream about a magnificent affair, a plenteous future, etc. At least I believe myself justified in this conjecture, based on my knowledge of [Gouesse] and of his eagerness to meddle with the temporal affairs of the [Orphans'] Asylum, over which he desires to have sole responsibility. [Gouesse] speaks against me to [Moreau] as much as he can, against me, *to whom he owes everything,* after God. No one has taxed my patience and my credulity more than he. I tremble at the thought that I alone am responsible for his profession and his ordination.

Here was a sweeping indictment indeed. But there was more. "I beg you anew, Monseigneur, to keep vigilance lest further trouble should occur, beg you to watch over my dear brothers and sisters [in New Orleans] whom I love with all the affection of a father. [Gouesse] inhibits them from reading my letters and from sending me theirs. His intention is to treat them like slaves. He is going to do them even more evil. I hope the good God will soon put an end to all this violence."[66] Oddly enough, at this very moment Gouesse was boasting that the superior at Notre Dame had finally "recognized his [Gouesse's] rights."[67] Instead, two months later Sorin followed up his denunciation with the announcement to Blanc of Gouesse's "dismissal" from Holy Cross in the United States.[68]

These appeals to the archbishop of New Orleans, even as they shed new, if albeit diffused, light on the controversy, also raised new questions. How gullible, for example, was Basile Moreau? If he knew as much about Gouesse's bad conduct as Sorin did, how could he have promoted such an objectionable person? How easily might he have been seduced by the prospect of the "riches available in New Orleans?" The now chronic scuffling between Notre Dame and Sainte-Croix had clearly taken its toll; Sorin was almost as inclined to suspect his

66. Sorin to Blanc, March 30, 1851, AIP.
67. Mary of the Five Wounds to Sorin, April 17, 1851, AIP.
68. See notes 55 and 58, above.

revered Founder's judgment as to chide a truculent subordinate. More to the precise point, what was the "document" that expelled Gouesse from Sainte-Croix to which Sorin referred? He claimed to Blanc, and reiterated the contention later,[69] that it had been in his possession for "six months" before he sent it back to France when he learned of Gouesse's appointment as local superior in New Orleans. But no one in France appears to have seen it, and the support Gouesse enjoyed in Le Mans afterward strongly argues that no such *acte* had been issued. Sorin's "six months," moreover, given the timing of his letter to Blanc, would have meant that the document of expulsion had been dated about the end of September, 1849. Yet Sorin himself maintained that the major reason for the alleged censure of Gouesse had been the latter's refusal "in the autumn of 1849" to accept an appointment to New Orleans as Visitor, that is, his refusal to go there without the full powers of a local superior. Autumn began, then as now, on September 21. Even putting the most favorable construction on the chronology, it strains credibility to the utmost to suppose that news of Gouesse's defiance in late September could have reached France, been acted upon, and then transmitted back to Indiana, all within Sorin's "six months."

Archbishop Blanc in any event came once more to the embattled priest's defense, not least because he prized Gouesse's ability to minister to the numerous German immigrants in his diocese in their own language. Sorin, aware of this circumstance, assured the archbishop that he would send as a replacement "my assistant, Father Cointet, [who] speaks the three languages" and would guarantee his residence in New Orleans for a year.[70] Cointet arrived in early July in time to see Gouesse off for France; he "accepted your decision," Cointet reported to Sorin, "without any show of great emotion."[71] There was to be, however, no pause in the contest. Gouesse, once back in Le Mans, pleaded his case in person before the general chapter held at Sainte-Croix in August. His explanations, however biased, were well-received, and the chapter determined to censure Edward Sorin, not only for exceeding his authority in New Orleans but also for mounting the foolhardy expedition to the goldfields.[72] Moreau, hoping to soften the blow, commissioned one known to have maintained cordial relations with Sorin to impart the bad news. "Here you have sincere and devoted friends," wrote Father Louis-Dominique Champeau, "even though they do not always approve your own

---

69. See Sorin, *Chronicles*, 94.

70. Sorin to Blanc, June 2, 1851, AIP.

71. Cointet to Sorin, July 2, 1851, AIP. A week later Blanc wrote Sorin to the effect that Gouesse's reaction had been properly submissive and that he, Blanc, believed Sorin had "exaggerated the danger."

72. Catta, *Moreau*, 1: 945–946.

ideas. Consequently, receive these communications with religious docility and humility. . . . The mother house is simply following the Rules and, in order to be a tender mother, is waiting for submission and obedience."[73]

Father Sorin pondered this advice for several weeks. Then, at the beginning of December he took ship for France. This battle of New Orleans was far from over, and, with a strange twist, it was to have ramifications that extended as far away as the Asian subcontinent.

---

73. Champeau to Sorin, August 28, 1851, quoted in Catta, *Moreau*, 1: 946.

chapter fifteen

War over Bengal

THERE CAN BE NO QUESTION THAT THE CONTROVERSIES Edward Sorin was embroiled in as 1852 began had profound consequences in the unfolding of his career. But the incidence of these quarrels and misunderstandings, however distracting they may have been, could not disguise the fact that he and his colleagues of Holy Cross in America continued to press forward with their apostolate. If storm clouds hovered overhead, signs of progress nonetheless abounded. With regard to the college at Notre Dame, probably the single most crucial concern in everybody's judgment, the new curriculum appeared to have caught on, at least as reflected in the statistic most important to Sorin: in 1850 the number of matriculated students reached fifty-eight, and, though it dipped a little the following year, three semesters later it had risen to seventy or more—satisfying if not spectacular growth.[1] A few miles away, the Marianite sisters had also taken a significant step forward. "I have the pleasure of informing you," Sorin wrote Moreau in the spring of 1850, "that the legislature of the state of Michigan is about to incorporate the boarding school at Bertrand under the title of St. Mary's Academy." The details of this legal approbation remained unclear for the time being, and the actual enrollment of female *pensionnaires* amounted only to eighteen.[2] Nevertheless, Sorin's long-held ambition, that the sisters should conduct schools just as the brothers did, was on its way to fulfillment.

An agreement moreover had been entered into with the diocese of Chicago, whereby Bishop Van de Velde's "favor and protection of our three societies,"

1. Sorin, *Chronicles*, 92, and Wack, "Notre Dame Foundation," 231.
2. Sorin to Moreau, May 11, 1850, AGEN.

sisters, brothers, and priests, would eventually be implemented institutionally in that booming Illinois city. In return for forty acres of property—*"une concession pure et simple"*—Sorin offered the bishop as soon as practicable brothers to teach either "liberal or industrial" courses and to oversee orphanages as well, so long as the financial obligations of both parties were clearly defined.[3] "The good Bishop and priests of Chicago received me very kindly," Sorin's agent reported. "They have no money. But what none other ever got, I have permission to collect when and where I spoke."[4] It took some years for these plans to mature, but the seeds had been planted. Yet, as much as he rejoiced over this promising arrangement, Sorin could not banish the soreness from his mind. When he sent the good news about Chicago to Le Mans, he added this chilling stipulation: "If the question about New Orleans is not settled in accord with our desires, please consider all this null and void (*comme non avenu*)."[5] Even on that contested southern ground, however, admirable initiatives continued to be undertaken. The sisters there, despite the conflict swirling around them, gave further witness to their calling by opening, with Sorin's blessing, a modest hostel for foundlings.[6]

The parochial missions both in Indiana and Michigan went on unabated and indeed expanded; new parish churches served by Holy Cross were blessed in Michigan City and Niles, the cornerstone for another was laid in Kalamazoo,[7] and still another parish was established in Lake County, eighty miles west of South Bend. Sorin meanwhile had overseen the reorganization of the three novitiates at Notre Dame and Bertrand, and, though "defections" from the community still occurred—among them Brother Basil "who departed incognito" from New Orleans—they were far outbalanced by fresh aspirants.[8]

The departure of the enigmatic Brother Joseph, however, was a special case. Sorin bitterly called it "a scandal rather than a loss" and claimed that Joseph had become "unbearable" by reason of his "haughty temperament." Yet the secession from Holy Cross of the first man to have joined it in America—as Charles Rother had done at Black Oak Ridge in October, 1841[9]—had to have been hurtful for all concerned. Perhaps the failure that seemed to dog Joseph's every step had as much

3. See the copy of the agreement, dated December, 1850, AGEN.
4. Brother Stephen to Sorin, November 21, 1849, AIP.
5. Sorin to Moreau, December 29, 1850, AGEN.
6. Costin, *Priceless Spirit*, 104.
7. "The church progresses rapidly but the collection slowly." Shortis to Sorin, July 22, 1851, AIP. Father Richard Shortis, in charge of the Kalamazoo parish, had been professed and ordained a year earlier.
8. Sorin, *Chronicles*, 92–93, 97.
9. See chapter 6, above.

to do with his decision as his alleged "haughty temperament." He had failed as a teacher, failed as director of the printshop, failed spectacularly in the imprudent real estate venture in Indianapolis. He continued to live there after the novitiate returned to Notre Dame, supervising an orphanage and hovering at the margins of his religious community. "I am almost tempted to run away," Joseph cried in June of 1849, and eight months later he did so. Entry into the Trappists had for a moment crossed the mind of this rootless man, but when Bishop Saint-Palais asked him to direct the Catholic orphanage in Vincennes, he accepted the post. "Please charge nobody," he entreated Sorin. "If there is any guilt, I am the only one that is guilty. I have been influenced by no one."[10]

Sorin's harsh judgment of Joseph may have been sparked by the memory that, in the midst of the wrangle in 1847 over the purchase of property in Indianapolis, the much-maligned brother had had Francis Gouesse as his sole ally.[11] But even with the defection of his first disciple and even while the distracting and distasteful *affaire Gouesse* dragged on, Father Sorin never wavered in his confidence that his mission in America would prosper, nor did he stop lobbying in its behalf. When Bishop Bouvier of Le Mans sent Notre Dame some books, including copies of his own celebrated theology manual,[12] Sorin replied with "a thousand thanks" and, predictably, with a request for more of the same. Then he drew a tableau calculated to appeal to the sympathies of the prelate who had ordained him to the priesthood thirteen years before. "It will be a consolation for your Excellency to learn," he wrote in the late summer of 1851, "that over the last two years twelve priests have gone out from our dear little seminary on St. Mary's Island—four for us and the rest for neighboring dioceses." The number of brothers at various stages of religious profession had risen to forty-five. But the very success of the apostolate so far justified, in Sorin's mind, a petition for still more support, a direct petition that sounded, it should be noted, as though issuing from one autonomous operator to another.

> If among your good seminarians and young priests, zealous to convert Savages, Infidels, or Protestants of every imaginable sect (and who in Le Mans is without such zeal?) you were to throw out a word of approbation, of encouragement toward Notre Dame du Lac, our gratitude would be without

---

10. Joseph to Sorin, June 17, 1849, and February 9, 1850, AIP. See also Saint-Palais to Sorin, January 6, 1850, AIP. It would seem Brother Joseph—he kept his religious name—was no more successful in Vincennes than before. See Klawitter, ed., *Adapted to the Lake*, 370.

11. See Gouesse to Sorin, January 20, 1847, AIP.

12. See chapter 3, above.

limit. Shall I tell you about one of our professors who has brought nine Protestants into the Church in five months time, even though he can devote himself to such work only once a week? Our mission-area is almost as large as your diocese. Two rail-lines now cross it from east to west. It will be necessary to provide ever more churches and especially schools. . . . Without a Catholic school, conducted by brothers or sisters, nothing can be done in this country. But with such a school, a priest can reasonably hope to accomplish everything necessary. We now have eight parishes; in ten years, with God's help, we shall have ten more. But where shall we find pastors for them?[13]

Though he listed the "Savages" among those to be converted by putative recruits from Le Mans, Sorin had by this time long ceased to include the native Americans in his planning. Indeed, the shrunken number of Potawatomi at Pokagon received now only irregular service from Holy Cross, and even that was shortly to be discontinued. Sorin's passionate desire to devote himself exclusively to the Indians he first met had faded as quickly as it had arisen,[14] and after ten years in America he assumed toward them roughly the same attitude of subconscious guilt mixed with racial prejudice as did white society as a whole. "Poor Indians!" he wrote in 1851. "They are fast disappearing from the land which not long ago was covered by numbers of their warriors." In two centuries, he predicted, "they will be spoken of . . . as a nation completely destroyed. . . . It is as hard to keep them from drinking as it is to make them work. This tells plainly that religion alone can oppose a sufficiently strong check to their violent passions." But, alas, though "the Catholic Church alone is able to preserve them from . . . inevitable ruin, . . . there is a lack of personnel as well as of the funds to take such care of them as their weakness requires."[15]

IF THE TONE and substance of Sorin's communication to Bishop Bouvier smacked of his sense of his essential independence, just then under worried scrutiny at Sainte-Croix, so did another series of events, unrelated but roughly contemporaneous. At the beginning of 1850, Edward Sorin became a naturalized American citizen.[16] Shortly afterward he applied through Indiana Congressman

---

13. Sorin to Bouvier, August 6, 1851, AGEN.
14. See chapter 7, above.
15. Sorin, *Chronicles*, 102.
16. See the visa in AUND, COSR, "Edward Sorin."

Fitch for the establishment of a post office within the Notre Dame compound and the appointment of himself as postmaster. This solicitation was denied on the grounds that the proximity of South Bend rendered such an installation unnecessary. Sorin, however, was not deterred. Early in March he wrote Bishop Hughes of New York and enclosed a "petition with request to do us the favor of directing it afterwards to some influential gentleman in Washington." Already, he explained, arrangements had been made, "with considerable expenses, to bring the [Logansport to Niles] stage through the premises of the Institution," which meant that mail could be deposited at Notre Dame three times a week with no inconvenience to the postal service. To do so "would secure . . . peculiar and local advantages," as it would eliminate "the daily trouble for sending to South Bend for letters" and the danger imposed by the "continually increasing . . . mail robbery." Perhaps Sorin exaggerated on this last point—the distance between the campus and the post office in South Bend was, after all, less than two miles—but he was candid enough to tell the bishop that he was acting contrary to the wishes of his congressman: "Not long ago I sent to our Congress Member a similar petition, accompanied with all requisite informations; but it would appear that Dr. Fitch, our Deputé [sic], is not the right kind of Advocate we might desire."[17]

Hughes, however, refused to cooperate: "I can hardly see the propriety of a Catholic priest being appointed as Postmaster." The bishop hesitated to call such an aspiration "wrong," but "in this country at least it would appear very novel and somewhat extraordinary." Moreover, he added, he could claim no influence with the federal government.[18] Nevertheless, an "influential gentleman in Washington" did ride to the rescue. No less a personage than Senator Henry Clay, "one of the men," Father Sorin observed, "most likely to mark an epoch in the United States, obtained this favor for Notre Dame du Lac to the great satisfaction of [all]." This startling development appears to have been due to the intervention of one Gardner Jones, who was in residence at Notre Dame in 1850. This somewhat shadowy figure, who at the moment was teaching in the college subjects as various as metaphysics, Hebrew, and rhetoric, had brought with him a checkered religious past. Originally an Episcopal priest, he had converted to Catholicism and had taught for a while at Mount St. Mary's Seminary in Emmitsburg, Maryland. Then he had a change of heart, became a Calvinist minister, and wrote several

---

17. Sorin to Hughes, March 3, 1850. AGEN (written in English). This letter's syntax and word choice—particularly the anglicized *deputé* for congressman—suggest that the writer was a Frenchman progressing, if not yet accomplished, in English usage.

18. Hughes to Sorin, March 26, 1850, AIP.

pamphlets attacking Mount St. Mary's "with bold impiety and willful and deliberate mendacity." So at any rate charged the president of that institution, who added: "Some time ago we read in the secular newspapers a letter from the students of [Notre Dame] to Henry Clay, signed in their behalf by Gardner Jones." If Jones had returned to his Catholic allegiance, as indeed he had,[19] the president insisted that he be treated as a "penitent" and "not be allowed to appear before the public."[20]

But Edward Sorin had decided to give Jones a very public commission. On March 14, 1850—that is, weeks before receiving Hughes's refusal to intercede for him in Washington—Jones, under Sorin's direction, wrote a letter to Clay, congratulating the senator on the "just, wise, and moderate views" expressed in "your great compromise speech" delivered on the senate floor on February 5 and 6. This had been indeed one of Clay's most remarkable oratorical performances, especially considering how ill and frail he was at the time, and it played a significant role in bringing about the celebrated Compromise of 1850 between the free- and slave-states. Jones, in highly florid rhetoric, told Clay that "the President and Faculty of the Catholic Institution" of Notre Dame believes "the integrity, stability and unchecked progress of this land of religious liberty" is identified with "the highest interests of the Church of Jesus Christ and the highest hopes of humanity." Though the community at Notre Dame "profess[es] a creed widely different from your own," nevertheless,

> while you are assailed by the violent and insane of both sections of the Union, we thought it might be agreeable to you to know that in a secluded religious house, whose inmates have their citizenship and conversation in Heaven, who commune more with the mighty past than the present, and whose invisible companions are the noble army of saints, your kindling oratory has warmed and cheered many a heart inflexibly and altogether American.[21]

---

19. O'Donnell to Sorin, January 18 and February 15, 1850, AIP. Thomas O'Donnell was parish priest in Ottawa, Illinois. Though he recommended Jones to Sorin, he also cautioned him: "Men of [Jones's] kind of character require watching and training."

20. McCaffrey to Saint-Palais, June 10, 1850, AIP (Sorin papers). John J. McCaffrey was president of Mount St. Mary's from 1838 to 1872. He was vice-president in 1837 when Jones was a "tutor" there. See Mary. M. Meline et al., *Story of the Mountain*, 2 vols. (Emmitsburg, Md., 1911), 1: 365.

21. The letter is quoted and summarized in Melba Porter Hay et al., eds., *The Papers of Henry Clay*, 10 vols. (Lexington, Ky., 1959–1991), 10: 688.

Henry Clay clearly found this piece of adulation more than agreeable: he had it published in a Washington newspaper.[22] And Edward Sorin received his reward. However, when called upon to record this victory, which took effect early in 1851, Father Sorin offered a simple and characteristic explanation for it: "Recourse was . . . had to prayer. The Blessed Virgin and St. Joseph were alternately importuned by all the house," until the great Kentucky statesman intervened in the case under their mysterious impulse. Gardner Jones, meanwhile, metaphysician and Hebrew scholar, went off to Chicago, with testimonials from Father Sorin, to edit a Catholic weekly there; but before leaving the "secluded religious house" he promised to make his peace with Mount St. Mary's.[23] The position of postmaster did not prove burdensome for Sorin, nor did that of district road inspector which he assumed at about the same time; whatever small tasks were involved he left to brother-assistants to perform.[24] Yet securing these offices did enhance the status of Notre Dame, putting it literally, if modestly, on the map and rooting it as well as its leader ever more deeply into the American milieu.

Indeed, despite debts and quarrels and the comings and goings of oddities like Gardner Jones, Edward Sorin had secured for Holy Cross and himself a remarkable visibility. This achievement was testified to by Sorin's enormous correspondence. Appeals for services came to Notre Dame from all corners of the young United States. The urgent and repeated requests for brothers, which had issued in the past from New York, Philadelphia, and Louisville, continued and even accelerated: Florida and Mississippi were heard from as well as Cleveland and Nashville.[25] The bishop of Milwaukee sent his seminarians to be trained at Notre Dame.[26] The bishop of Chicago inquired whether Sorin would house for a time an alcoholic priest sentenced to do penance for his scandalous behavior.[27] Pastors from Baltimore and Detroit recommended virtuous young ladies in their parishes anxious to join the Marianite Sisters, and persons of good will, clerical and lay, brought to his attention the plight of orphans for whom they hoped to

---

22. It was printed in the *Daily National Intelligencer,* April 2, 1850, where no doubt McCaffrey saw it.

23. Jones to Sorin, September 16, 1851, AIP.

24. Sorin, *Chronicles,* 100.

25. See, for example, Madéore (vicar general of St. Augustine) to Sorin, November 12, 1848; Buteux (vicar general of Natchez), May 8, 1848; Rappe (bishop of Cleveland), October 28, 1847; Miles (bishop of Nashville), July 2, 1847, AIP.

26. See Henni to Sorin, June 27, 1849, AIP.

27. Van de Velde to Sorin, September 6, 1849, AIP.

find a home.[28] Even Martin John Spalding, now bishop of Louisville in his own right and one, on past experience, unlikely to entertain friendly feelings toward Notre Dame, did not hesitate to ask admittance to the Brothers of St. Joseph for one of his subjects.[29] Through all this flurry of activity, Father Sorin had manifestly demonstrated that he was the indispensable man.

ABOUT THE TIME he received the appeal from Bishop Spalding, Sorin had determined to travel to Le Mans, because, he observed later, he was "tired of representing in vain by letter [various] subjects of complaint."[30] Perhaps rumors had reached his ears that the motherhouse was proposing to send Francis Gouesse back to Louisiana.[31] This indeed was the case, though official notification of the fact, in the form of a letter from Pierre Chappé, one of his old friends at Sainte-Croix, probably did not reach Sorin before his departure for New York on December 2[32] and surely not by November 19, by which date he had made up his mind to undertake the journey.[33] At any rate, Gouesse's renewed tenure, Father Chappé explained, would put him under the direct authority of the archbishop of New Orleans, and he would have strict instructions not to interfere in the Holy Cross mission or the orphanage. Chappé invited Sorin to consider Gouesse's linguistic skills and his "active zeal." "I have the lively hope, as do all our Fathers, that an enduring peace might be arrived at between you and Father Gouesse. . . . With a sincere pardon on your part the rest will be easy, and all the miseries and your heavy cross will, I believe, be relieved."[34] In fact, however, when Sorin unexpectedly arrived at Sainte-Croix at the end of December, he discovered that, though "all our Fathers" did hope for peace, not everybody was in sympathy with Francis Gouesse; the resolution in council to send him back to New

28. See, for example, Lalumière to Sorin, September 28, 1847, and Young to Sorin, April 10, 1850, AIP.

29. Spalding to Sorin, November 3, 1851, AIP.

30. Sorin, *Chronicles*, 104.

31. Such rumors had reached New Orleans by mid-November. See Sister Mary of the Five Wounds to Sorin, November 15, 1851, AIP.

32. Catta, *Moreau*, 1: 949, says that Sorin's journey was a result of his learning of Gouesse's return to New Orleans. But Costin, *Priceless Spirit*, 100–101, demonstrates convincingly that the chronology renders this conclusion implausible. A letter dated at Le Mans on November 12 could not have reached Notre Dame by November 19. See note 34, below.

33. As testified to in Cointet to Sorin, December 7, 1851, AIP.

34. Chappé to Sorin, November 12, 1851, AIP.

Orleans only as the archbishop's factotum had passed by a single vote and had even been opposed by Basile Moreau.[35]

This circumstance may have heartened Edward Sorin when, on New Year's eve, the Founder's "Chapter was convened and the grievances of [Notre Dame du Lac] were discussed for four hours." Nothing substantive changed as a result, except for a renewed sense of personal regard: "Affection did not seem to be lacking," as Sorin rather obliquely put it. Other meetings followed without altering the situation in New Orleans nor, as time would quickly tell, without alleviating what Sorin considered "the serious and pernicious differences which the inattention of the Mother House had unfortunately allowed to grow out of all proportion." Nevertheless, he did not come away without a couple of victories which permitted him to boast that he had "settled matters satisfactorily at Sainte-Croix:"[36] first, he learned that Moreau had appointed him Provincial of the Congregation in the United States, a position he had long aspired to;[37] and, second, Moreau agreed to "invite" Francis Gouesse to take up residence at the Holy Cross house in Montreal, which the controversial young priest did in early March, 1852.[38]

Sorin meanwhile, once the deliberations at Sainte-Croix were finished, spent some pleasant weeks in the friendly haunts around Ahuillé and Laval, visiting relatives and old friends and at the same time searching out possible new patrons willing to support the mission at Notre Dame du Lac. He paid a call on the family home of Father Cointet at La Roe, much to the latter's gratification.[39] Then, "having received the sanction of the Very Reverend Father Rector," Sorin set out for Rome. This was his first visit to the eternal city, and no doubt like any pious tourist he took pains to see the sites made famous by eighteen centuries of Christian and papal history. Afterward he described his stay as "delightful (*mon délicieux séjour*),"[40] though curiously he said virtually nothing about any particular shrine or monument. Moreau's "sanction" in any event intended Sorin

---

35. Catta, *Moreau*, 1: 947.

36. Sorin, *Chronicles*, 104–105.

37. Actually the appointment was "provisional." It had been announced on December 8, 1851, when Sorin, unbeknownst to Moreau, was on his way to Le Mans. By the same decree Victor Drouelle was named Provincial of the new houses in Italy and Joseph-Pierre Rézé of those in Canada. See Moreau, *Circular Letters*, 1: 259. For Sorin's aspirations, see chapter 13, above.

38. Catta, *Moreau*, 1: 950.

39. Cointet to Sorin, February 29, 1852, AIP.

40. Sorin to Torlonia, May 8, 1852, AGEN. Marino di Torlonia, a papal duke, was a noted philanthropist and a patron of the orphanage conducted by Holy Cross at Vigna Pia. See below.

to help deal with a problem of ecclesiastical policy, not to afford him a Roman holiday.[41]

The interminable disputes between Sainte-Croix and the diocese of Le Mans were creeping toward a climax. Moreau had recently spent five months in Rome (November 1850–March 1851), lobbying the curia for the approval of Holy Cross's Constitutions, which would establish his congregation as a full-fledged religious order and thus deliver it from the control of the local bishop. The results of the Founder's efforts, however, had been disappointing. His petition had predictably become entangled in the notoriously sluggish Vatican bureaucracy. Moreover, though Bishop Bouvier, a crusty old Gallican, was not popular among Roman officialdom, he was a forceful individual, not a man to be trifled with in his own domain, especially since he had reached an age when his demise could not be far off.[42]

But impeding Father Moreau's purposes was still another sticking point. His ambition for the Congrégation de Sainte-Croix, its "general plan" as he called it,[43] was to assemble a religious society of three constituent parts—priests, brothers, sisters—all of them integrated and directed by a single authority. Indeed, he had already done so, albeit in an informal and, despite his own obsession with good order, an almost slapdash fashion, which remained under constant threat from the aggressive Bishop Bouvier. The timing, however, of his appeal for papal endorsement and regularization could not have been less fortuitous. A few years before turmoil had broken out in a congregation similar in structure to what Moreau proposed. To this society—spoken of familiarly as Picpus, from its headquarters located on the rue de Picpus in Paris[44]—Rome had given canonical approval in 1817. The order had come to grief, because its women members had protested, with good reason, that their male brethren had bullied and intimidated them. The Roman authorities, including Pius IX himself, were determined not to repeat the error of their predecessors by according formal status to a mixed congregation.

---

41. See Catta, *Moreau*, 1: 950, where the implication is that Sorin's trip to Rome was intended merely as a vacation. But, as the correspondence cited below makes clear, Moreau did not merely give Sorin "permission" to go to Rome, as Catta says; rather, he commissioned him to negotiate with the curia on the matter closest to his, Moreau's, heart. It hardly needs saying that this is only one among the countless instances of Catta's anti-Sorin bias. To enumerate all of them would necessitate a separate chapter or small book.

42. For the contention between Bouvier and Moreau, see chapter 3, above.

43. See Catta, *Moreau*, 1: 430–453.

44. The society's formal name was The Congregation of the Sacred Hearts of Jesus and Mary and of the Perpetual Adoration of the Blessed Sacrament of the Altar. It addition to its activities in France, it established houses in North and South America and as far away as the Sandwich Islands.

Such was the state of affairs when Edward Sorin arrived in Rome in the late winter of 1852, more eager, it seems safe to assume, to be a negotiator than a pilgrim. He resided first on the outskirts of the city, at Vigna Pia, an orphanage and agricultural school opened two years earlier on twelve acres of a former vineyard donated to Moreau by Pius IX—hence the foundation's name. Here presided his old friend Victor Drouelle, now a Holy Cross provincial like himself.[45] Drouelle, however, was ill through much of Sorin's stay, and by late March, as the latter wrote laconically to Moreau, "I am lodging now with Monsignore de Mérode."[46] This change of residence was a significant triumph in itself: Frédéric de Mérode, a thirty-two-year-old Belgian aristocrat and soldier turned priest and curial functionary, was a particular favorite of Pius IX. Contact with him guaranteed a measure of entré to the pope himself, and Edward Sorin was indeed granted two papal audiences during his seven weeks in Rome. Clearly the charm that warded off Protestant creditors in northern Indiana could also work its magic in the *gallerie* of sophisticated Vatican ecclesiastics.

The charm, however, did not necessarily guarantee success for the task at hand.

> It appears [Sorin reported to Le Mans] that Heaven intends to keep us upon the cross for some time yet. . . . The Approbation so ardently desired for the three societies cannot be attained now. The Pope himself has pronounced against it, while offering to endorse union between our priests and brothers. It is Picpus that has overwhelmed the pope with difficulties and has indisposed him toward us, as it has the Sacred Congregation. This very evening I shall have an audience with the pope, but that will change nothing, as he has declared positively both to Monsignore Barnabò and Monsignore Mérode.

The invocation of Archbishop Barnabò's name bore its own significance; he was secretary and spokesman for the Sacred Congregation de Propaganda Fide, that department of the Vatican bureaucracy, usually referred to simply as Propaganda, which supervised Catholic missions all over the world and which was, therefore, of more than ordinary consequence to Edward Sorin.[47]

---

45. See Léandre Fréchet, "Holy Cross in Rome and Italy," a paper delivered at the Annual Conference on the History of the Congregations of Holy Cross (1989), 2–4.

46. Sorin to Moreau, March 16, 1852, AGEN.

47. This Roman Propagation of the Faith (in English) should not be confused with the Propagation of the Faith, located in Paris and Lyons, which subsidized Catholic missions around the world.

At this time and place, however, he was directly concerned with another issue, that of the canonical approval of Holy Cross, and this he met with his wonted pragmatism. "I would counsel you," he wrote Father Moreau,

> to adopt one of two courses: either withdraw your request entirely, or else limit your petition to secure a license for our priests. I am very much inclined to the second alternative. If our priests were accorded formal approbation, this itself would be a giant step within the Church and also in the eyes of the world. The brothers and sisters would be encouraged thereby and beneficially (*salutairement*) kept within their original sense of their dependence, and such will suffice till it is possible and desirable to do more. No doubt Rome would prefer to approve the brothers with the priests, but then what would become of the general plan? I would therefore boldly ask for canonical status for the priests only, without imposing a decision upon the Church in regard to responsibility for the other two of our groups.[48]

A week later, while Moreau was digesting this advice in Le Mans (presuming the post had by then delivered it to him), Sorin wrote again.

> I have just come from seeing Monsignore Barnabò who had a conversation with His Holiness last evening about our affairs. He displayed a certain air of optimism; the Pope told him that he was not demanding that the sisters be kept completely separate. Perhaps they could remain under the direction of the *Pères de Sainte-Croix*. Perhaps there could be a way of preserving the general plan by adding to it some guarantee that the sisters would not be under the absolute control of the priests, as at Picpus where they were *tyrannized,* it is said here. They could in any case be approved separately, as indeed could a union of priests and brothers; so the Pope repeated again last evening.

The time had come for another strong personal intervention, Sorin argued with a mixture of flattery and reproach.

> If it is in any way possible, I urge you, my Reverend Father, to come to Rome without delay. Your presence alone can bring everything to a happy conclusion. The Pope loves you, talks about you, obviously thinks about you often. Come, and perhaps the whole project can be started anew. You

---

48. Sorin to Moreau, March 18, 1852, AGEN.

were greatly at fault in leaving Rome too soon [in March, 1851]. You would have had your [papal] Brief [of approval] had you stayed. Now Picpus, along with the bishop of Le Mans, has spoiled everything.[49]

There were more conversations during ensuing days with the influential likes of Barnabò and Mérode, and Sorin came to feel that his "position was marvelously favorable for our affair." Yet he recognized that he was "restricted to the office of a singular informant" for Moreau rather than an executor. If you are "adequately to judge the essence of what I have learned," he told the Founder—that "Picpus is considered in the curia akin to *Carthago delenda est,* and stands in the way of your hopes"—you must come to Rome yourself: "Monsignore Mérode wants to see you here, and so do I, more than ever." A visit to Cardinal Franzoni, Prefect of Propaganda,[50] "who was very gracious," confirmed Sorin's judgment.

[The cardinal] is always anxious to serve us. He does not love the holy bishop of Le mans. He exhorts you to come to Rome and advises me to wait for you here. Here are his words. "Your *Père* will be happy to have you here with him. You can consult with each other, and I offer you my house and my advice as needed; in a word, I will do all that I can to help you." In order to avoid the infamy of Picpus, the cardinal thinks that the sisters will have to be left free to choose a superior and even a confessor, the upshot being that the Superior General [Moreau] would not necessarily be a formal member of their society.

To this legalistic analysis, which in substance merely restated the original Roman position, Franzoni added matter-of-factly that under whatever canonical solution eventually emerged, the sisters' accounts would have to be maintained separate from those of the priests and brothers.[51] Here was a caveat Edward Sorin was all too familiar with.

Father Moreau chose not to follow the course thus pressed upon him; he remained in Le Mans. Sorin meanwhile, besides his diplomatic overtures, busied himself preparing a long and detailed report on Holy Cross in the United States for the cardinals of Propaganda. There was no missing his basic intent: "In order

49. Sorin to Moreau, March 26, 1852, AGEN. Over the months following he did not change his mind. See Sorin to Moreau, August 18, 1852, AGEN.

50. Each Roman Congregation was governed by a board of cardinals, presided over by a cardinal-prefect (in this case Franzoni) and administered by an archbishop-secretary (in this case Barnabò, who in due course would succeed as prefect).

51. Sorin to Moreau, March 28–29, 1852, AGEN.

to encourage the self-sacrifice of my worthy Confreres and Associates," he wrote in a covering letter to Franzoni, "I respectfully pray that your Eminence would deign to recommend Notre Dame du Lac favorably to the Propagation of the Faith in France." The report itself for the most part covered predictable ground, recounting the good works achieved by priests, brothers, and sisters, the chartering of the "university," the girls' academy at Bertrand, the care given to orphans and apprentices, the rich spiritual life of the congregation sustained by the three carefully supervised novitiates. More surprising was the large space allotted in the memorandum to Sorin's plan for "*une maison de retraite ecclésiastique*."

> It is scarcely fifty years since the Catholic Church was established in the United States, and already through her inexhaustible charity she has been able to offer specific remedies for the various ills of humanity. From the infant in the cradle to the old person on the edge of the grave, all have received her maternal tenderness, the efficacious assistance that answers their needs. This spectacle of limitless charity, even in the eyes of unbelievers, is sufficient proof of the superiority of Catholicism over the cold speculations of the Protestants. . . . Divine Providence has willed now to make known to Father Sorin the importance of adding another good work.

Divine Providence, aided and abetted by a decade of apostolic labor. "From his ten years of experience in America, Father Sorin has reached the profound conviction that he wishes to submit, respectfully and with a lively sense of his own unworthiness, to the attention of the Sacred Congregation: . . . a bad priest is a great evil, especially in a country of neophytes, infidels and Protestants."

> One cannot hide from this truth, that scandal given by a bad priest, especially within a young and immature Christian community, can unsettle the faith and paralyze the zeal even of the most fervent. One need not say more than that in a mission-country, like America, where the demand for missionaries has been and continues to be so great, ordinations often have to be hasty, and the need is such that it is necessary to accept and maintain in the exercise of the sacred ministry some men who, under other circumstances, would not have been called to the altar. Moreover, if one considers that a large number of poor priests already interdicted in Europe come to the United States, one will appreciate the magnitude of the wound that makes the Church in this New World cry out in pain.

This candid assessment of an unpleasant reality too often left in the shadows could not have failed to impress the eminent governors of Propaganda. Sorin then capped his plea for support by claiming that what he proposed now would merely formalize and solidify efforts to rehabilitate wayward priests undertaken at Notre Dame "for six years past." This may have been a somewhat extravagant claim, but at any rate he added to it an assurance that the house would be more than a *refugium peccatorum;* it could serve also as a place where diocesan priests, who had no other facility at their disposal, could make their annual retreats, "at which they can renew their zeal and the spirit of their vocation."[52] Approbation of this project by the Propagation in Rome would result, he fervently hoped, in money from the Propagation in Paris.

By early May, Father Sorin had returned to France. On the second of that month he presided at a family wedding at La Brulatte, a few miles west of Laval.[53] By the eighth he was in Le Mans, and a week or so later he set sail from Le Havre for home, "for our dear mission of Notre Dame du Lac. O! how great a need have I to see it once again!"[54]

E DWARD SORIN did indeed rejoice to be back again among the familiar, among the labors and the people and indeed the land that he had come to think of as peculiarly his own. But this is not to say that he had failed to enjoy his time in Rome. What is most intriguing about those seven weeks is the ease and confidence with which the farm boy from the Department of Mayenne, grown into the missionary in rough-hewn Indiana, moved among the dukes and cardinals and other sophisticates of the papal court. It had been indeed for him *un séjour délicieux,* an opportunity to learn that he could hold his own among the greatest movers and shakers in his clerical world, and he had every reason to feel satisfied with his performance. But whether or not pride goeth before a fall, just ahead of him lay a stern test to his mettle and indeed to the *raison-d'etre* of his life.

The remote cause of this new crisis was a communication, dated November 15, 1851, to Basile Moreau from Cardinal Franzoni, prefect of the Sacred Congregation of Propaganda—the same Franzoni whom Sorin was to confer with some months later in Rome. In his letter the cardinal inquired whether Holy Cross would be willing and able to send missionaries to Eastern Bengal. To assign

---

52. "Memoire sur la mission de Notre-Dame du Lac, Amérique du nord," Rome, April 6, 1852, AGEN (copy).

53. Sorin to Moreau, March 28–29, 1852, AGEN.

54. Sorin to Torlonia, May 8, 1852, AGEN.

responsibility for conducting missions in certain geographical locations to European-based religious orders was Propaganda's routine policy; for example, the Marists, another recently founded French congregation, had been commissioned to serve New Zealand and the islands of the western Pacific. The wily Franzoni, who knew how desperately Moreau wanted Roman approval for his Constitutions and the independent status such approval would ratify, was not above offering a subtle inducement: if the burden of the Bengali mission were accepted, "you will then have a claim to our kindest consideration." This was a diplomatic insinuation, not a commitment, but it had the desired effect upon Moreau. "All the priests and brothers of our Association," he replied, "as well as the sisters, have felt themselves impelled by the charity of our Lord Jesus Christ to undertake some apostolate to help the countless numbers of men who are still in the darkness of infidelity and the shadows of death."[55] That this pious assertion was no doubt quite literally true was not inconsistent with Moreau's further assumption that to accept Franzoni's invitation would redound to Sainte-Croix's advantage in the corridors of power at the Vatican.

A general pledge therefore had been made, though the details remained to be worked out. Over succeeding months Father Moreau examined what resources he could garner for this new enterprise, while fending off the predictable opposition of the bishop of Le Mans; Bouvier scoffed at the idea that Holy Cross, short of men and money, could undertake such a venture. Planning and discussion continued nevertheless, and in mid-June, 1852, Moreau was formally notified that Propaganda had entrusted the mission in Bengal to the Congrégation de Sainte-Croix.[56]

The original correspondence between Franzoni and Moreau had occurred at about the time Edward Sorin had decided to undertake his unscheduled journey to France. He was told nothing of the Bengali proposal while at Le Mans nor, later, in Rome, even though his host and friend, Victor Drouelle, was directly involved in the negotiations with Propaganda. Sorin first learned of the project from three letters written him by Moreau between June 18 and 22, in which the Founder stated his decision to transfer personnel from the American mission to Bengal, where, under the administration of the British Raj, fluency in English was a practical necessity. Specifically he required that either François Cointet or Alexis Granger be named superior of the venture in India. Sorin's reaction was swift and unequivocal.

---

55. Catta, *Moreau*, 1: 886–887. For the background see Raymond J. Clancy, *The Congregation of Holy Cross in East Bengal, 1853–1953*, 2 vols. (Washington, D.C., 1953).

56. Catta, *Moreau*, 1: 888–889.

First and foremost [he wrote], you only do us justice when you say that you count in every circumstance upon our obedience each time you invoke it. But since you wish to have my advice, let me give it to you very candidly: neither the one nor the other of the priests you mention can actually be removed without ruining the establishment in New Orleans, which in turn would involve a dangerous crisis for Notre Dame du Lac. Indeed, I would prefer to leave here if either of them left. . . . Neither of them can be expected to manifest the forcefulness or zeal of somebody departing for the foreign missions for the first time; but we can still work fruitfully for some years here in the place where we have invested our original zeal. . . . Let me say in summary: I believe that transferring either Father Granger or Father Cointet would bring about the ruin of our work here; neither of them will have my consent to leave, unless you should order them most formally, and, if you do, I then shall leave to you alone the consequences.

Perhaps, he added, "we could more easily find you a brother or even some sisters if need be." But in any case "I would have much preferred that your Reverence had spoken to me about this plan when I was staying with you at Sainte-Croix; I'm sure I would have been able to make you see what a difficulty (*embarras*) your proposal would involve for us."[57]

A month later Sorin reiterated his position. "I have already made known to you the impossibility of removing from our midst either Father Cointet or Father Granger, neither of whom, aside from everything else, is really fit for Bengal, particularly as superiors. Father Cointet is indispensable here; without him our [parochial] missions will collapse." Sorin thus conveniently brushed aside the fact that Cointet was at that moment languishing, ill most of the time, in New Orleans, some hundreds of miles from his beloved parishes in Indiana and Michigan. But that was a trivial consideration when compared with this fateful declaration: "In short, if you absolutely must take a priest from here, take me first. Otherwise *you will destroy our work.*"[58]

Or perhaps it should be said "possibly fateful," because it is uncertain whether Moreau had read this provocative statement of August 18 when he wrote Sorin the following on September 13.

After prayer and long consultation with my council, I come to make known to you the will of God, insofar as it is possible to know it. Notwithstanding

---

57. Sorin to Moreau, July 14, 1852, AGEN.
58. Sorin to Moreau, August 18, 1852, AGEN.

the serious difficulties which will be entailed by your departure, you will, in virtue of holy obedience as promptly as possible, and after advising your chapter and whomever you will appoint as your temporary successor, leave for Eastern Bengal, Dacca, near Calcutta, as superior of the Mission, to be later presented to the Holy See for the vicariate apostolic and a bishopric *in partibus* [*infidelium*]. In this same mail, I am sending your appointment to Propaganda.[59]

Moreau further directed that Cointet should be recalled to Notre Dame to assist in the transition, and that Francis Gouesse should resume the position of Holy Cross superior in New Orleans.

In all the disputatious exchanges that darkened the next twelve months, Moreau never claimed that he had simply made his own Sorin's suggestion of August 18; he maintained rather that he acted as a legitimate superior who had reached an informed and prayerful decision and who therefore expected his subject to adhere to it. Nor did Sorin ever refer to his remark, which was probably an offhand rhetorical gesture he forgot as soon as he offered it. As for the minor chapters at Notre Dame and Bertrand, Moreau, fastidiously proper as ever, informed them only to the extent of inviting them to submit the names of candidates to succeed Sorin. The consternation felt locally at the prospect of any change was keen, and, insofar as it was known, universal.

Sorin, for his part, assumed a hard line from the beginning. "Very Reverend Father," he wrote on October 6,

leaving it to our chapters to acquaint you with the grave difficulties and serious dangers my removal would involve at this time, I need to declare to you in my own person that after mature reflection before God, I believe it my duty to refuse unequivocally the charge you wish to impose on me, unless the pope himself should order me to accept it. I have absolutely neither the knowledge nor the virtues required to make a good bishop. I nonetheless remain, very Reverend Father, your very humble and devoted son in Jesus, Mary, and Joseph.[60]

---

59. Quoted in Catta, *Moreau*, 1: 954.

60. Sorin to Moreau, October 6, 1852, AGEN. A vicar apostolic is an ordained bishop, but, since a vicariate is by definition a missionary area without a settled ecclesiastical center, he takes his formal title from a city once Catholic but no longer so (*in partibus infidelium*); such places abound in North Africa and modern Turkey.

So the issue was joined. Basile Moreau was a punctilious man, and, though genuinely pious and dedicated to the highest good, he was never unaware of his status and dignity and the deference that was due him. Certainly his unstinting labors had earned him the esteem that any leader of a great movement has reason to expect. And within the religious system Moreau had put together, based as it was upon the vows, respect for his office included compliance with his directives; obedience to lawful authority was not negotiable. Neither officially, therefore, nor, it must be added, temperamentally was Father Moreau prepared to explain his motives in suddenly assigning Sorin to the subcontinent; nor did he ever do so. It remains tempting, however, to speculate that in arriving at this decision he intended to kill two birds with one stone. He fully appreciated Sorin's remarkable gifts, his drive, his courage, his charismatic personality, his ability to inspire loyalty. Despite incredible hardships and against all odds, his young confrère in a short ten-year span had created a successful and multifaceted mission in the middle of a wilderness. All signs pointed to Notre Dame du Lac developing as time passed into one of the most important Catholic centers in the United States. Surely such demonstrated talent, Moreau must have reasoned, was precisely of the sort needed in Bengal, which, if anything, posed a more formidable challenge than did northern Indiana.

But he also might well have thought—the second bird—that Sorin's transfer would assuage the long-standing discord between Notre Dame and the motherhouse. Moreau would hardly have been human had he not longed for a more docile local superior in Indiana, a superior who would keep an intelligible set of accounts, who would not assume powers beyond his mandate,[61] who would refrain from threats of separation and from offering unsolicited advice. He who had so scrupulously drawn up the Constitutions of the religious order he had founded did not listen gladly when told from three thousand miles away: "I would hope our rules will not impose anything strictly local, as for example the observance of the vow of poverty as it is carried out in France."[62] But what, Moreau might reasonably have asked, was amiss with evangelical poverty as it was practiced in France? If he did so ask, he left no record of it, and indeed Moreau seems to have treated his volatile subordinate's various initiatives with almost seraphic patience. Not so, however, everyone in his entourage. Joseph-Pierre Rézé, for instance, the

---

61. "I believe that it is extremely important that the Superior here himself visit at least once every two years all the establishments *dependent* on Notre Dame du Lac" (emphasis added). Sorin to Moreau, May 11, 1850, AGEN.

62. Sorin to Moreau, June 10, 1850, AGEN.

Holy Cross superior in Canada and no friend to Sorin,[63] confided to the Founder his conviction that "Father Sorin's position was becoming false for himself and dangerous for us. An ordinary subject, one without ambition and devoted to the Rule, can, it seems to me, govern the houses at [Notre Dame].... With the disappearance of Father Sorin the reform can be undertaken.... A superior with even only a little bit of experience will bring back order, piety, and devotion to the Rule, along with union between the motherhouse and [Notre Dame]." To bundle Sorin off to India was, in Rézé's view, "a stroke of genius."[64]

As Sorin had indicated they would, the chapters at Notre Dame and Bertrand quickly sent protests of their own off to Le Mans. The priests and brothers drew up a document which stated in rather legalistic terms that the removal of their superior "would cause the ruin of the work of Holy Cross in the United States, that this ruin would do an immense harm to religion in this country and, incidentally, to the Association of Holy Cross, . . . [and] that in the present circumstances [Sorin] is alone able to uphold [our work], because he alone has the confidence of his own subjects and of the public in general."[65] The nuns' response made substantively the same argument, though in the form of a personal letter to Moreau which, in parts, verged on the hysterical and which contained a veiled threat: if Sorin, out of "a spirit of obedience pushed too far," were to agree to leave them, "how could we believe that the motherhouse wished us well from [then] on?"[66]

Sorin himself, by contrast, appeared to maintain, at least outwardly, a measure of close-mouthed equanimity. He did not, however, fail to look around for allies. He turned first to the most notable Catholic ecclesiastic in the middle west. "A strange occurrence!" he wrote Archbishop Purcell[67] as early as October 16.

> I received recently a command from the motherhouse to go, in the name of obedience, as soon as possible to Calcutta in Bengal, as superior of the mission there which the pope has just assigned to our congregation and shortly afterward to become vicar apostolic and bishop of Dacca. I have quite simply refused, but in all likelihood the command will be repeated, and then how

---

63. See chapter 13, above.

64. Rézé to Moreau, October 2, 1852, quoted in Catta, *Moreau*, 1: 954.

65. Minor Chapter Resolution (copy), October 7, 1852, AGEN.

66. See Costin, *Priceless Spirit*, 60–61, and the authorities cited there.

67. Cincinnati had been created a metropolitan see or province in 1850, with Vincennes as one of its suffragans. The archbishop had no direct jurisdiction in the dioceses in his province, though he might rarely act in a judicial capacity if a canonical case were appealed. This circumstance had some relevance for Sorin in 1853; see chapter 16, below.

shall I extricate myself from this embarrassment? Happily I have no ambition of this kind, but rather a genuine dread of so heavy a burden so far beyond my weakness. On the other hand, it would be impossible for me to leave this Institution without serious fears for its future. It is, to be sure, in a prosperous state: we have here 80 boarding students, and our novitiates are in a good condition, and our possessions exceed our debts.

Here was an argument that cut two ways. If the mission at Notre Dame du Lac were indeed thriving, then the replacement of its superior should not put it in jeopardy. But Sorin, not without resentment toward unnamed and ungrateful mandarins in Le Mans, interpreted the progress over which he had presided otherwise.

I foresee prosperity and development here, despite the inconceivable opposition of those for whom we spent ourselves gratuitously over these past ten years. In the case in which, contrary to all my tastes and affections for this land of my adoption, I were obliged to depart, I would not be without apprehension for those very people from whom, before God, I sincerely believe that I have deserved better treatment. I cannot foresee what will happen when I am gone. . . . I expect to receive new orders from France, . . . [and] I would then need your wise counsels.[68]

Purcell was basically sympathetic to this appeal—born in Ireland, his own Americanization was far advanced[69]—but he was an exceedingly busy man, and, in any case, he had no direct canonical jurisdiction in Indiana, nor was he inclined, at least at first, to meddle in a matter already decided by Propaganda. He advised caution, as did the few other prelates Sorin consulted. His own bishop, Saint-Palais of Vincennes, was kept in the dark until much later. Nor was the growing crisis revealed to the rank and file at Notre Dame and Bertrand; only the members of the two chapters, Sorin supporters all, knew what was afoot. Meanwhile the routine occupations of the mission continued apace. Classes were taught in the college and the academy, the sacraments were duly administered in

---

68. Sorin to Purcell, October 16, 1852, AGEN. Sorin also teased the archbishop about a possible promotion. While in Rome, he wrote, "I heard conversations, mixed with some laughter, about our American pretensions to the Red Hat. There was much more admiration expressed for the Queen City of the West [Cincinnati] than for the premature enthusiasms of New York." Twenty-three years were to pass before the first American was elevated to the College of Cardinals, in the person of John McCloskey, archbishop of New York.

69. See, for example, Dye, "Purcell," 289–291.

the parishes, the apprentice shops functioned normally, the harvest was gathered into the barns, and, in late October, a grisly tragedy dampened the spirits of the whole community: two students, absent without leave from the campus and afraid to return, died when the stable in South Bend where they had taken refuge for the night was destroyed by fire.[70]

A day or two after this distressing episode, another missive arrived from Le Mans, confirming the appointment to Bengal. "Very Reverend Father," Sorin immediately replied, "I see that you persevere in your first decision, to make me go to Bengal. Had you not specified the *burden* that you wish to impose on me, I would not have had the same repugnance in obeying you." The "burden specified" was the episcopal rank to which the head of the Bengali mission was to be automatically promoted. This proviso, as he had indicated to Purcell, was the ground upon which he was to base his resistance. Holy Cross's Constitutions, he maintained, "perfectly express the sentiments of my heart," and those Constitutions oblige members not to seek ecclesiastical honors, except at the express command of the pope. "I therefore adhere to my original resolution which has left me with neither doubt nor remorse nor regret. . . . I do not see any way you can force me to submit to a charge for which I have absolutely no ambition, my ignorance and lack of virtue having long since suppressed in me any such fanciful pretensions." The very idea is "ridiculous" and "affected." "Dream no longer of coming to find bishops in our forests and amidst our snows. Neither I nor any of my confrères will accept responsibilities of this kind." For the honor implied and "for your testimony of confidence, we thank you with all that is in us," but a simple refusal appears "the unique way of meriting something of that confidence." Surely the motherhouse can provide better candidates; why not the worthy Father Champeau?

But Edward Sorin was too straightforward a person to try to hide his real feelings entirely behind a flimsy legalistic façade.

> Besides all this, you cannot deceive yourself, though you seem to be so engaged, that my presence here is any more dispensable than yours at Sainte-Croix, and that the existence of our Association in the United States will become problematic from the moment that I depart for any length of time. I am sorry that I have not done better than I have; but up till now, I have been like a small child whom one must take by the hand lest he fall. Nor would I want your Reverence to imagine that my attachment to Notre Dame

---

70. Wack, "Notre Dame Foundation," 261–262.

du Lac has made me close my eyes without adequate reason to any prospect of change. Surely it would break my heart to say adieu to those who have given me proof of their devotion and affection over these eleven years. But with the aid of Heaven, I hope I would find the courage. Yet what touches me most deeply is the warranted fear that drawing me away from their midst would expose them to probable ruin and . . . to an unhappiness which would quickly make me die of grief (*chagrin*). Where then would be your gain?[71]

Basile Moreau's reaction to Sorin's *gran rifuto* was kindly but firm. "Humility should induce you not to regard yourself as indispensable at [Notre Dame], although I understand, like everybody else, how necessary your presence may be. . . . Above all, it is important for you to remain in the spirit of obedience which . . . neither asks nor refuses anything." Most important, he cut the ground from beneath Sorin's contention that he could accept a bishop's miter only at the command of the pope; Holy Cross's rules were clear that papal intervention was called for only for promotion to offices unrelated to the congregation's own apostolate, which was not the case in Bengal. Finally, he ordered that Sorin be prepared to depart in six months time, not later, that is, than May 1853. "How I should like to be on hand," he concluded, "to tell you in person what I have just written, and to press you to my heart!"[72]

But Edward Sorin was in no mood for an *embrassement*. He brooded over the Founder's rather too artful distinction between "necessary" and "indispensable," and his anger welled up at the thought of Francis Gouesse returning to New Orleans as Holy Cross superior. Indeed, as the drama unfolded, Sorin's long-standing aversion toward Gouesse played an ever growing role. "The sole fact of [Gouesse's] unexpected recall to the same post, which he had been compelled to vacate in spite of himself six months before, appeared inexplicable to the Chapters of [Notre Dame] and of Bertrand. It was thought that there was reason to fear everything from this turbulent spirit who was the declared enemy of Notre Dame." Sorin therefore, countermanding Moreau's direct order, "thought it is his duty to telegraph Fathers Cointet and Gouesse to remain at their respective posts," New Orleans and Montreal.[73] There followed an inconclusive correspondence with Archbishop Blanc—increasingly weary of the quarrels going on in his

71. Sorin to Moreau, October 21, 1852, AGEN.

72. Moreau to Sorin, October 31, 1852, in Catta, *Moreau*, 1: 961–962.

73. Sorin, *Chronicles*, 108–109.

jurisdiction—until early December, when, in response to a telegram from an alarmed Father Cointet, Sorin decided to go to New Orleans himself.[74]

The journey began pleasantly enough. He spent three days in Cincinnati, which allowed conversations with a putative ally, Archbishop Purcell, and a reconciliation of sorts with an old antagonist. "I took dinner with Father Badin and spent a few hours with him very pleasantly. He desires me to remember him to the sisters at Bertrand and wishes to send them his likeness. On my return I shall call upon him for it."[75] Sorin then boarded a river steamer that took him down the Ohio and Mississippi in about a week's time. When he disembarked at New Orleans, he found that Francis Gouesse had arrived there some weeks earlier, armed with his reinstatement from Le Mans. Antoine Blanc, however, insisted that the mild-mannered Cointet remain in charge of the mission until Provincial Sorin could come and sort out "this deplorable state of things. [The archbishop] told me," Sorin chided Moreau, "how surprised and pained he had been at Father Gouesse's return. He could not understand how his superiors could have sent him back to New Orleans. He said he did not blame the priest who had simply been obedient in this regard."

There followed a tumultuous fifteen days. Supported now by the archbishop, Sorin confronted Gouesse and "demanded to see his documents of appointment."

He brusquely refused and left the room. I heard at the same time that he was telling the [Holy Cross] sisters that I had no authority with respect to this mission, that I had never been named Provincial, *that Notre Dame du Lac was no longer a provincial house, that St. Lawrence [in Canada] will be the governing house in America from now on.* . . . [One of Blanc's closest aides] told [Cointet and me], "Your Founder must be a very weak man. This return here of Father Gouesse makes no sense. It is a great calamity (*malheur*) that he should be a priest; but it is ridiculous that he should be a religious. He no more has a vocation to religion than I have to be pope". . . . I then asked Father Gouesse to come to my room again. He told me right away that he wanted nothing to do with me, that he recognized in me no authority whatever. A half-hour later I sent him an order, in writing, that

74. Sorin to Moreau, December 22, 1852, AGEN. Sorin had originally planned the trip to New Orleans in October, but, for some reason, changed his mind. See Sorin to Purcell, October 16, 1852, AGEN, upon which Catta, *Moreau,* 1: 964–967, bases an erroneous chronology, asserting that Sorin spent two months in New Orleans stirring up trouble.

75. Sorin to Mother Ascension, December 5, 1852, AIP. Stephen Badin died the following April. Mother Ascension was the superior at Bertrand.

he leave as soon as possible the mission and the archdiocese without hope
of ever returning. This decision had been agreed to by the archbishop who
promised to support me.

The tragi-comedy, however was far from over. On the morning of December
16 Gouesse, after a meeting with Blanc, agreed to set sail for France without delay.
"But in the evening of that day [Gouesse] came to see me, made his excuses, and
asked that the past be forgotten." Sorin replied warily that he would have an answer ready on the morrow. When they met again, "[Gouesse] promised to observe everything; I embraced him, and I was happy thus to maintain appearances
at least." The archdiocesan officials were not impressed. "They seem to dread the
prospect of Father Gouesse obtaining authority from abroad. They say they know
of a score of people, attached to him, who, when he departed before, would not
even make their Easter confession. According to them, this priest is totally without judgment." Archbishop Blanc, for his part, simply hopes that "his Superior
[Moreau] will find a way of removing him without scandal."

During the days leading to Christmas Sorin conducted a retreat for the New
Orleans community. "Father Gouesse remained amiable," even "very amiable." But
then on Christmas day he presented Sorin with a letter from Moreau "commanding that we recognize him, Gouesse, as *sole superior*. This time, Father Cointet told
me, you need not feel accountable for the conscience of this subject of yours;
Father Founder has very clearly taken that burden upon himself." True enough,
Sorin agreed, "but if things turn out badly"—he left the sentence unfinished,
merely adding: "I depart shortly for the north with dear Father Cointet, leaving
the situation here at peace. God grant that it may endure!"[76]

BACK AT NOTRE DAME shortly after the beginning of the new
year, 1853, Edward Sorin did not in his heart of hearts think peace would long
prevail in New Orleans or indeed in his relations with Le Mans. By this time he
had informed his two chapters that his proposed removal was related to the mission in Bengal and that he had based his refusal upon his unwillingness to accept
promotion to the episcopate. "Here therefore," he had written Mother Ascension
from Louisiana, " the debate has ended. . . . So I beg of you, my dear Daughter, to
explain this plainly to whomever it might concern and to remain well assured
that I have not the remotest idea or apprehension of leaving my dear children of

---

76. Sorin to Moreau, December 22–28, 1852, AGEN.

St. Mary's or of Notre Dame du Lac."[77] But, whatever his hopes, the debate had
not ended, a fact that became increasingly plain as the winter progressed. "I am
as we must all be at the disposal of Divine Providence," he told the same nun on
January 20. "You may remain assured, however, of my sincere desire to stay and
of my intention to leave nothing untried (save unlawful means) in order to avoid
my removal and promotion."[78]

To find, within the context of the religious vows he had sworn, a lawful way
of declining to obey a direct order from his legitimate superior was for Sorin the
sticking point, especially once Moreau had demolished his first argument related
to the bishopric. Not a canon lawyer himself, Sorin nevertheless turned over in
his mind various legal expedients. One idea that occurred to him was to take advantage of the canonical limbo in which the Congrégation de Sainte-Croix was at
that moment confined. Since Rome had not yet approved Moreau's Constitutions,
Holy Cross remained technically bound to the diocese of Le Mans. Could those
religious who lived and labored outside that diocese be constrained to abide by
unreasonable demands from the motherhouse, to be afflicted by "an almost un-
broken series of explanations, altercations, prohibitions under pain of disobedience, reproaches full of threats, . . . so that there was no more love for the duties
of the community nor of the ministry, [and] life itself was at times a burden"?[79]

In the midst of these ruminations, during the first week of February, an ominous communication from Le Mans arrived at Notre Dame. It comprised only a
few lines and began with a somber paraphrase of a verse from the gospel: "Every
house divided against itself shall fall." Moreau went on to berate Sorin for having
dared to countermand his directives to Cointet and Gouesse in New Orleans and
Montreal respectively—"a most grave violation of the vow of obedience and of
our Constitutions, an act of open revolt against the motherhouse. It is time for
this scandal to cease. . . . Father Gouesse will remain at the orphanage [in New
Orleans], or I shall immediately recall all those still faithful to their vows." He
signed himself, "Your distressed but resolved Superior, Moreau."[80]

The die, it seemed, had been cast. On February 10, Edward Sorin took pen in
hand. In a tone of pained courtesy, he first thanked Moreau for the "sign of
honor" inherent in the proposal to send him to Bengal. "I regret, however, that
my refusal of such a dignity has not sheltered me from suspicions aroused

77. Sorin to Mother Ascension, December 20, 1852, AIP.
78. Sorin to Mother Ascension, January 20, 1853, AIP.
79. Sorin, *Chronicles,* 111, 112.
80. Moreau to Granger, January 13, 1853, AGEN. The letter was addressed to Granger, because
Moreau assumed Sorin was still in New Orleans or in transit.

among your entourage, suspicions unworthy of both of us, so that, when I modestly stated my position in terms of our Constitutions, you had someone write under your dictation that 'Father Sorin's insubordination can be clearly discerned in this explanation.' . . . God is my witness that I persist in my refusal, not out of self-love or human ambition, but solely at the call of duty." Then he rehashed, in very general terms, "our sufferings over the last seven or eight years."

But Sorin also expressed in a couple of sentences a specific and weighty complaint which may well have summed up his determination and indeed his rage. "In a letter of June 22 last, you said to me: 'You understand, my dear friend (speaking of the foundation in Bengal), we must sacrifice everything at the behest of the Holy See.' This is to say very openly that if need be we shall have to sacrifice Notre Dame du Lac." Here was the crux of the contention, at least as far as Sorin was concerned. Moreau's eagerness to secure Roman approbation for his order—and thus to free it and himself from the malevolent Bishop Bouvier— moved him to accept responsibility for the Bengali mission, even though the human and material resources at his disposal were extremely limited. Edward Sorin had succeeded in establishing a viable, indeed a flourishing, foundation in America, and, despite his careless accounting procedures and his tendency to extend his mandate beyond that proper to a conventional French religious, Moreau must have concluded that he might well achieve the same happy result in India. He further judged that Sorin's dire predictions about "sacrificing" Notre Dame for Bengal were vastly exaggerated.

These conclusions, however sensible they may have appeared in Le Mans, failed to give sufficient consideration to Sorin's own frame of mind and to his estimation of priorities. Fundamental to his declaration of independence—for such is what the letter of February 10, 1853, amounted to—was Sorin's conviction that his presence to and direction of Holy Cross in the United States was essential to its survival. He may have been guilty of hubris in thinking so—this certainly was the view at Sainte-Croix—but, if so, it was an opinion shared by his religious colleagues *en scène* as well as by the allies he enlisted among the American hierarchy. "Knowing well the Father of the Congregation of Holy Cross, residing at the house of Our Lady of the Lake," the bishop of Chicago assured Moreau, "I am firmly convinced that there is not one of the Fathers who could replace the Reverend Father Sorin as Superior of this Mission, and that the departure of said Father would bring about the ruin of all the Institutions founded by him, which are now in a state of prosperity."[81] The archbishop of Cincinnati was more restrained

---

81. Van de Velde to Moreau, February 1, 1853, AGEN.

in his assessment, but the drift of his sentiment left little room for doubt: "I believe I know enough about [Holy Cross] to put my name to the request of all the worthy priests of this excellent community and of the bishop of Chicago, who knows the circumstances . . . better than I. May I ask you, Very Reverend Father, to withdraw your intention of transferring [Sorin] to Bengal." And Purcell's endorsement ended with a judgment much in tune with Sorin's own thinking: "It is in America that he will carry off great victories for the Faith."[82]

But such hearty testimonials had become irrelevant in the light of Sorin's present stance.

> During my recent visit to France, I was authorized by our chapters to break with the motherhouse, if I could discern no other means of assuring peace for our mission. A glimmer of hope closed my mouth [on that occasion]. I wrote and repeated here that everything had been arranged satisfactorily. . . . Our recent disagreements, however, have naturally resurrected the earlier intention, along with our conviction that we must do all we can to gain internal peace. The chapters here have unanimously, myself abstaining, indicated their intentions. Believe me, my Reverend Father, my dedication to the Congregation has been up to now sincere and without limitation; at this moment I have a horror of the very word 'treason.' I have always thought that separation [from Sainte-Croix] a species of crime. But when separation presents itself as the only avenue (*planche*) of survival for a work so visibly that of Divine Providence, I would hold myself culpable, as would my confrères here, for resisting the obvious for too long. However painful may be this proceeding to which you have forced us, we accept it as imposed by the same Providence that we must recognize at work in a set of circumstances to which we contributed not at all.

Convoluted as this explanation may have been, it was designed to justify the grave step Sorin and his associates had determined to take.

> I must say from the start that I believe my appointment [to Bengal] is the occasion rather than the real cause of the present declaration. We have suffered too much over too many years and entertained too little hope to allow us any prospect of amelioration; suffered too much to consent to have another yoke fixed upon our shoulders, *irrevocably this time, by imposition of Rome itself*. . . . In asking today for our emancipation we are acting consci-

---

82. Purcell to Moreau, February 7, 1853, AGEN.

entiously and fulfilling our duty. . . . Consequently, and in order to demonstrate that we wish to do nothing that would injure the work of our mission, instead of appealing to Rome, . . . we would be content if your Reverence would agree to our majority [i.e., independence] for a period of five years, at the end of which time we would without anxiety place the question of final separation or reunion in the hands of Canon Heuterbize, in consultation with yourself."

In all his correspondence with Basile Moreau, Sorin had always signed himself "your devoted son." In this letter the conclusion was significantly different: "I am not less respectfully and sincerely the very humble servant of your Reverence, E. Sorin, Missionary Apostolic."[83]

---

83. Sorin to Moreau, February 10, 1853, AGEN.

chapter sixteen

"I Lay Down My Arms"

T O DECLARE INDEPENDENCE WAS ONE THING; TO
secure it was something else, something that required a
thought-out campaign which in turn involved risk and the
likelihood of casualties. But Edward Sorin and his colleagues in the minor chapters at Notre Dame du Lac and Bertrand showed themselves stalwart as that campaign began. And they were consistent too in, so to speak, the disposition of their theoretical armament: Basile Moreau and Sainte-Croix had over many years, they charged, assumed an aggressive and unreasonable posture toward the mission in the United States, the unacceptable climax of which was the proposal to send the indispensable Sorin to the exotic lands of East Asia. The tactics they adopted were clear enough from the beginning, even if their strategy may have seemed muddled and uneasy. One sign of this disquiet may well have been their reluctance to share their intentions with the other persons most concerned, their fellows in the Indiana community. Indeed, the confidentiality they successfully maintained over many months was remarkable, given that hint and rumor have been from time immemorial the ordinary coin of daily discourse within large houses of religious.

In analyzing the ensuing struggle, several interrelated factors have to be taken into account. Obviously the most prosaic, and yet highly important, was the sheer difficulty in maintaining contact between France and Indiana. In an era when the trans-Atlantic mail depended upon the unreliable schedules of sailing ships, it took at least a month for a communication to pass from one place to the other and another month for a reply to be received. In the course of this considerable length of time, as letters inadvertently crossed each other, initiatives in the New World could be held hostage merely to its distance from the Old.

Combine this reasonable assumption with the sense of the needs of mission that twelve years in the United States had taught Edward Sorin. Those who resided in faraway Le Mans could not fully understand, he argued, the ethos that prevailed in the culture that was emerging with astonishing speed from its primitive beginnings. Norms taken for gospel in the departments of Sarthe and Mayenne could not be automatically applied to the necessities at hand in Indiana and Louisiana. Gone was the green young priest who had doubted that his adopted country could of itself ever produce the kind of apostolate appropriate to the Catholic tradition. In his place stood a mature man who had adapted to American ways and, more than that, had come to believe that the future of the universal Church was bound up inextricably with the progress it could achieve in the United States. He had, in a sense, gone native, had embraced the rough-and-tumble mores of a youthful and bustling America, had looked upon the individualism and the proto-capitalist culture around him and had found them good, good at least in their potential. The get-up-and-go mentality that was all the rage in America had beguiled Edward Sorin, because he discerned within its vital fiber a genuineness, a basic honesty and directness that distinguished it from a weary and outdated European conformity. The methodology with which Americans dealt with one another and with the vast opportunities that lay before them had become his own *modus operandi;* the choice was either to expand and therefore to hazard, or to be left behind.

This *nouveau* conviction of Sorin's caused consternation in Le Mans, to the extent that it was comprehended. In the unhappy controversy that now unfolded, Basile Moreau quite understandably took the unequivocal view that those who had sworn allegiance to the Constitutions of Holy Cross—the society he had brought into being in the teeth of formidable resistance—owed it by reason of their original commitment to abide by directives issued from the legitimate authority of the motherhouse. And such spiritually rooted considerations were not the only ones. After all, the mission to Indiana had been undertaken in the first place because of a basic agreement between Moreau and the bishop of Vincennes. Money and personnel had been regularly dispatched to Notre Dame from Le Mans, and Moreau more than once had offered Sorin strong support in the latter's disputes with Bishop Hailandière.

Sorin was surely not wrong when he differentiated the American and French milieus. But his distinction was not appreciated in Le Mans, precisely because of that difference, and it is puzzling that Sorin should have thought it would be. One of Moreau's advisers, appointed to examine the vagaries of the Indiana mission, stated the motherhouse's view this way: "Father Sorin is not a businessman; he is a religious."[1] This assertion was true as far as it went, but it was not the whole truth. A dozen years of exposure to American ways had taught Sorin that if he and his mission were to succeed in this competitive environment he had to become a kind of spiritual entrepreneur. The swashbuckling manner in which he dealt with the administrative challenges he faced first in Bertrand and then in Kentucky and Louisiana was testimony to his zeal as well as his enterprise, if not always to his prudence. There had developed within him at any rate some of the traits of a salesman, a characteristic reminiscent of the quintessential American activist who, as a playwright would express it much later, made his way with a smile and a shoe-shine.[2] Even so, not even his most adamant opponent ever suggested that Sorin was not a man of prayer and genuine piety; whether he was a "religious" in a sense acceptable to the conventions of nineteenth-century French Catholicism remained to be seen.

If the appointment to Bengal occasioned the quarrel, Francis Gouesse and New Orleans created the catalyst that brought these disparate ideals and methods bubbling to the surface. At first the issue was fundamentally financial: it was imperative that new sources of regular income be unearthed if Notre Dame were not to founder. "Since our house is very heavily in debt, and since the mother-house does not feel an obligation to assist us, and since [Notre Dame] cannot pay its debts without bringing under its jurisdiction other houses, . . . we have therefore set up a foundation in New Orleans." So read the formal document drawn up in the name of the Minor Chapter and sent off to Le Mans. But almost immediately the fiscal problem evolved into a constitutional one. Basile Moreau declared that the new house in New Orleans was to be directly subject to Sainte-Croix, and while he granted Notre Dame some consideration with regard to income, he sealed his decision by appointing Gouesse superior there. Sorin and his colleagues vehemently objected and even formally "requested humbly from the Reverend Father Rector abrogation of the decree which renders foundations independent of local superiors"—that is, in this instance independent of Sorin who had instituted and staffed the mission to Louisiana.[3]

The next turn of the wheel brought the personal factor into play. Sorin's dislike and mistrust of Francis Gouesse was of long-standing.[4] The younger man in

---

1. Quoted in Catta, *Moreau*, 2: 9.

2. Arthur Miller, *Death of a Salesman*, "Requiem" (1949).

3. Sorin, Granger, and Cointet to Moreau, January 7, 1851, AIP.

4. Gouesse had arrived at Notre Dame, still a novice, in 1843. Within a year Sorin protested to Moreau that the young man lacked "the true spirit of Holy Cross." See chapter 10, above. As Brother Gatien's ally in opposition to the policies adopted at Notre Dame, Gouesse further alienated Sorin. See chapter 12, above.

the estimate of the older was a troublemaker and an unworthy priest. This harsh judgment was substantiated in the end: in 1855 Gouesse was expelled from Holy Cross for unspecified bad behavior.[5] But in the meanwhile, accomplished a person as he was in many respects, he held his ground in the battle of New Orleans, and not without support from some in the community and from an admittedly vacillating archbishop. Sorin certainly made a tactical error when he assigned Gouesse to Louisiana as temporary "Visitor,"[6] thus lending him a status which invited Moreau to grant him many a benefit of the doubt. As time passed Sorin grew ever more resentful that Le Mans would not take his word that Gouesse was undeserving of confidence. Cointet and Granger robustly seconded their superior in separate communications to Le Mans.[7] This discrepancy of opinion, however, merely underscored a more complex administrative problem, one commonly experienced within the Catholic system and indeed within any large, centralized polity. Who is better equipped to adjudicate a particular situation: subjects who are on the scene and actually involved; or authorities who, farther away and uncommitted emotionally, might be less swayed by immediate circumstances and might therefore offer a more judicious analysis?

LOUIS HEURTEBIZE was, like Basile Moreau, an honorary canon of the cathedral of Saint-Julien in Le Mans. During his term as a professor in the diocesan seminary, he had taught Moreau as well as Granger,[8] Cointet, and Sorin, who remembered him as "an excellent theologian."[9] A man of ripe years now, he was widely respected within clerical circles for his even temper and for his knowledge of ecclesiastical lore. Sorin described him as "the most worthy and venerable clergyman in Le Mans, the peculiar friend of Father Moreau; he knows us all and our institution perfectly."[10] Before this distinguished secular priest the resolute if reluctant rebels at Notre Dame du Lac determined to bring their suit: at the end of five years, Sorin informed Moreau, "we would without anxiety place the question of final separation or reunion in the hands of Canon Heurtebize, in

---

5. "Renvoyé April 23, 1855," *Matricule générale*, 480, AIP. If not "unspecified," at least "vague": he had allegedly "disgraced himself" in the presence of the sisters at the motherhouse in Le Mans. See Connelly, "Charism: Origins and History," 114, and the authorities cited there.

6. See chapter 14, above.

7. See Connelly, "Holy Cross in New Orleans," 9.

8. Heurtebize was especially close to Granger. See his letters of 1842–1843, AUND, CAGR, "Granger, Alexis."

9. Sorin to Purcell, n.d. [summer, 1853], AIP.

10. Sorin to Purcell, March 24, 1853, AIP.

consultation with yourself."[11] This resolution was formally confirmed by the minor chapters: "We believe ourselves forced to emancipate ourselves for five years, after which time we leave it to Father Heurtebize to examine with the Reverend Father Rector what would be the best to do for the good of Religion."[12]

It is hard to fathom how Sorin could have expected this strategy to succeed. Heurtebize, for all his merits, was, after all, "a peculiar friend of Father Moreau." He was also an elderly Frenchman and therefore presumably no more attuned to appreciate Notre Dame du Lac's contention of its unique importance than Sorin's critics at Sainte-Croix. He could be counted upon no doubt to deal with the petition objectively, but, since Notre Dame's case appeared on its face to be a weak one, the canon's personal integrity might have been expected to prove a hindrance rather than a help. Similarly problematic was the condition that Heurtebize should reach a final decision only after "consultation" with Moreau; did Sorin, Cointet, and the others seriously anticipate that the Founder of Holy Cross would accede to a separation in five years time, or in fifty for that matter? Perhaps Sorin imagined that a former beloved teacher might still recall happy seminary days and harbor a residual sympathy for the aspirations of the missionary priests in Indiana whom he had helped to train; or perhaps, in an ironic reversal, an Americanized Sorin could no longer divine the normal dispositions of a man who had never left the west of France. Nor is it impossible that the appeal to Heurtebize was designed to leave slightly ajar a door to reconciliation.

However debatable its motivation, the memorandum sent to the canon—signed by the members of the two chapters, it should be noted, and not by Sorin—took a very hard line. It began, for Heurtebize's benefit, with a snippet of history about Notre Dame's foundation and a statement of its present prosperity, "composed now of sixty professed religious and three novitiates, . . . a flourishing college with a hundred students, a manual-labor school providing religious instruction and vocational training for upwards of twenty orphans," orphanages also in Cincinnati and New Orleans, a foundling hospital in the latter place "under the direction of our sisters, and, at Bertrand, a boarding school for young women conducted by these same sisters," while "seven parishes and five stations receive regular ministry from the priests of our Association over a circuit of fifty miles." But then the tone of the document turned melancholy. "However, in the midst of these successes, our hearts have very often been wounded by a profound sadness. More than once we have witnessed our very existence compromised, and if Provi-

11. Sorin to Moreau, February 10, 1853, AIP.
12. Sorin et al. to Moreau, February 12, 1853, AIP.

dence does not come promptly to our assistance, our ruin seems inevitable." The canon should know the reasons why.

> The experience of twelve years has taught us that, despite our great desire for peace and our endless efforts and sacrifices to secure it, it has been most of the time impossible to enjoy it, and now, far from being able to entertain any real hope of an amelioration, we have reason to fear the most painful experience yet. Deceived without doubt by lying reports, the motherhouse appears to have had from the beginning only mistrust and anxiety about Notre Dame du Lac. Desiring to administer everything by itself, [Sainte-Croix] has almost always taken too little account of the distance between France and America, too little account of the differing cultures (*usages*) involved. The motherhouse has almost always censured as insubordination, resistance, and disobedience any undertaking not absolutely in accord with its own opinions. . . . Many complaints have been registered, many explanations offered in rebuttal but nearly always without success. The accusations have been believed, the justifications almost never.

The memorandum displayed throughout a desire to demonstrate to Father Heurtebize that Notre Dame's present admittedly audacious proposal was by no means new or frivolous. "More than once the thought has come into our minds that separation is the only remedy for such great evils. Always we have rejected the idea with a kind of horror, preferring instead to suffer patiently rather than risk losing the merit and the splendor of our accomplishments by a secession of which God might not approve." But as recently as a year before, "pushed to an extremity by new vexations and accusations, we decided to send our worthy superior, Father Sorin, to negotiate for peace with the motherhouse, determined this time, however, that if he did not succeed we would consummate the fatal separation." Sorin's mission—the reference was to the journey at the end of 1851[13]—had "happily appeared to reconcile the disagreements, and . . . a new era of peace was proclaimed. But alas! joy soon vanished under another wave of recriminations and accusations, . . . and today our condition is worse than ever"— worse because of the wrong-headed decision of the motherhouse to send "our worthy superior" to Bengal.

> This choice which under other circumstances would have honored and delighted us has pressed into our hearts desolation and sadness, because it is

---

13. See chapter 15, above.

obvious to us that the removal of Father Sorin would cause the ruin of Notre Dame du Lac. In reality his name is so linked to the existence and to the activities of our house, his authority seems so necessary to its life and permanence, the confidence in his experience is so affirmed within our [religious] community and within the public at large, that there is not the slightest doubt among those who live here that his transfer would infallibly cause the devastation of Notre Dame, which is still too feeble to pass from the personal direction of him who founded it, a reality which is all the more relevant since there is no one here who could possibly replace him, and, even supposing some one could be found to do so, the works and endeavors in our mission have become so numerous and the priests among us are so few, that it is inconceivable that any individual could be displaced from his post without leaving a void which could not be compensated for.

This last rather convoluted sentence was characteristic of the passion with which the document was composed. It was not strong, however, in specificity; the complaints raised were of the imprecise sort unlikely to impress an objective observer. On the tangled matter of finances, for example, "the motherhouse has always taken care to be repaid down to the last franc; yet at the same time our dependence upon an authority so far away has been the cause of continual expenditures for us both in time and money, for the journeys undertaken, the correspondence, the rendering of accounts, all of it paid for by us." And while Sorin did not inscribe his name to the memorandum, he certainly inspired it and probably composed most of it, which explains why it gave off a breath of personal bitterness. "The steadfastness of the motherhouse in insisting upon [the appointment to Bengal] seems inspired not only by a consideration of the incontestable qualities of Father Sorin, but also by spirit of distrust in his administration. For it appears doubtless that the motherhouse has made inquiries about the said Father . . . and blames him for his activities, always on the basis of false accusations made against him."

Not till the end of the document was the sticky canonical problem addressed, and then only obliquely.

One difficulty remains. It lies in the set (*formule*) of vows that most of us have taken. We have sworn to consecrate ourselves to the foreign missions at the will of the Very Reverend Rector [Moreau].[14] Does this vow give Fa-

---

14. Here the Latin was cited: "pro beneplacito mei Rectoris."

ther Rector the right to recall us? Moreover, in the same formula we made the solemn promise to prevent so far as we can a separation of the house in which we serve from the motherhouse.[15] But have not our long patience and our strong expectation of an endangered future not sufficiently fulfilled these promises in God's eyes? We dare to hope so.

There was a final question Canon Heurtebize was bound to pose: why should not this appeal be directed to Rome? The memorandum's rationale smacked of the disingenuous: Since the Constitutions of Holy Cross had not yet received curial approval,

> our complaints would probably not be considered before this supreme tribunal, and in any case they would perhaps bring down upon the motherhouse discredit which, under present circumstances, might prove very damaging, without doing us any real good. The motherhouse now enjoys a favorable regard in the court of Rome and hopes for a speedy endorsement of its Constitutions. We have therefore preferred to let the odium involved in separation weigh upon us, satisfied for now by the testimony of our consciences and leaving to Providence and the passage of time care for our reputations.[16]

W̲HATEVER CONFIDENCE Edward Sorin may have had that his reputation would be safe at the hands of Canon Heurtebize, he nevertheless believed it prudent to enlist the support of a powerful ally closer to the scene: he immediately sent a copy of the chapters' memorandum to the archbishop of Cincinnati. "My Lord," he wrote in a covering letter, not quite candidly, "[this] is a step of too great moment for us all to consummate it without feeling perfectly assured that it is right. Therefore, instead of forwarding it at once, I deem it proper to place it under your Lordship's eyes with a plea to say whether you approve of it or not." Though it was true that the memorandum had not been sent to Sainte-Croix—a step Sorin hoped the archbishop would take, along with his own endorsement—Sorin neglected to tell Purcell that it had been "forwarded" to Huertebize in Le Mans, a fact he did not share with the archbishop until many

---

15. The Latin again: "Promitto me impetiturum que, quanto potero, ne domus in qua versabor a subjectione Domus Generalis se eximat."

16. Memorandum of the Chapters, February 13, 1853 (copy), AGEN.

weeks later.[17] Perhaps this mental reservation was irrelevant, since Sorin at this juncture had in mind not only Moreau's reaction but also that of his missionary colleagues who, except for the members of the chapters, were unaware of his fateful initiative. "As for me, I have no trouble of conscience about it, but in case of scruples arising hereafter in some consciences I would by far prefer having your authority than mine to bring forward to calm them and make them peaceful." He remained at any rate sanguine, even jaunty, about the prospects of success. "I have no doubt . . . that, situated as the motherhouse is, they will prefer saying at once *amen* before exposing the Society to the great inconvenience of any noise or publicity." This conviction, that Moreau would accede to a separation rather than risk adverse notoriety, illusory in the end, was central to Sorin's tactics.[18] It was important moreover for Purcell to understand that "a simple petition [to Sainte-Croix] would have been worse than useless, and our declaration, which leaves them the choice between a temporary and final separation, is more than sufficiently justified, I think, by their past conduct toward us."[19]

Whatever Purcell's "personal sentiments," his response to Sorin's overture was not particularly encouraging. Though the archbishop granted the difficulty "of religious Societies here suffering from their dependence on Superiors in Europe," he nevertheless thought a proposal for separation, permanent or temporary, was rash. "It would be temerity in me to advise you to separate, for a time or forever, from your motherhouse. . . . It would be impossible for me to decide, in my present ignorance of a thousand things that might combine, were I familiar with them, to enlighten and direct my judgment, whether you could *tuta conscientia* take the proposed step or not." It would be far better, the archbishop said, to work matters out privately with Saint Croix; if such a procedure failed to give satisfaction, the only recourse was an appeal to the pope. As for forwarding the memorandum to Moreau, Purcell declined, "leaving this to your better knowledge and prudence."[20]

Heurtebize's reaction was even less heartening. "It is perfectly correct to remind you," he addressed the chapters, "that superiors cannot always give commands agreeable to their subordinates and that if there are local disadvantages to the execution of their orders there may be still greater disadvantages, which you do not see, in allowing you to act according to your own desires. You always have

17. See Sorin to Purcell, March 24, 1853, AIP. Huertebize dated his reply to the memorandum March 5, which meant that it must have been dispatched on the date it bore. See previous note.
18. See Sorin, *Chronicles*, 116.
19. Sorin to Purcell, February 13, 1853, AIP.
20. Purcell to Sorin and Granger, February 18, 1853, AIP.

the right to make your observations, but, in the last analysis, you must either submit to authority or appeal to a higher authority, without ever setting yourselves up as a final court of appeal." As for the Bengali appointment, how, he asked rhetorically, can your successful foundation survive without Father Sorin? Well, "if your superior were taken away from you by death, the foundation would certainly not thereby be ruined. Why would it run the risk of any greater ruin if he were taken away from you by obedience?" Then, invoking a legal principle well known to a former seminary professor, the good canon concluded that the argument advanced by the chapters was at best doubtful. "Now in case of doubt, we must refrain from acting, because the superior retains his authority. In such situations, none but a higher authority can dispense you from your obligations."[21]

Here was a dash of cold water indeed. Even more chilling, however, and more directly crucial to the matter at hand was this observation, sent to Sorin himself a few weeks later: "If you separate, I do not see by what right you could continue to remain in a house which, as I see it, would cease to belong to you by the very fact that you should no longer belong to the Congregation of Le Mans." But the honest Heurtebize, though he thought "a separation would be deplorable," was not one to disdain the ordinary channels of ecclesiastical law. He refused Sorin's request, as Purcell had done, to present the contentious memorandum now in his possession to Sainte-Croix—not his business, he asserted—but he did suggest, albeit reluctantly, a course the disaffected religious of Notre Dame might legitimately follow. Since the Indiana mission was, strictly speaking, still a diocesan institute, why not register an appeal to the bishop of Vincennes for a dispensation from the vow of obedience?[22]

This was an approach which up till now had either not occurred to Sorin or, if it had, had seemed to him to involve dangers of its own. The compact thrashed out years before between Moreau and Bishop Hailandière had defined Notre Dame's ultimate dependence upon Sainte-Croix, a status which at this moment Sorin was anxious to disparage. Moreover, he may have feared that the present bishop, Saint-Palais[23]—with whom his relations had been minimal—was, in contrast to Archbishop Purcell, too much a Frenchman to accept with composure the essentially Americanist argument Notre Dame was propounding. Whatever his reservations, he decided now to follow Heurtebize's counsel at least in part, and in early April he dispatched a petition for a dispensation to Vincennes, "without [however] stating in detail the reasons that led to this step."

---

21. See Catta, *Moreau*, 1: 978–980.
22. Heurtebize to Sorin, March 21, 1853, AIP.
23. Catta, *Moreau*, 1: 981, confuses Saint-Palais with his predecessor, Bazin.

Sorin chose to interpret Saint-Palais's reply as positive when in fact it was predictably ambivalent. Although the mandarins in Le Mans had so far remained ominously silent, the bishop was aware of the rumors that Moreau himself or some official commissioned by him might be coming to America to deal with the crisis. "His Lordship," Sorin recalled, "granted the dispensation but expressed the desire that the coming of the Visitor, who was to be sent from Sainte-Croix to settle everything, should be awaited." However, "by the end of April, as there was no more talk of a Visitor and the time fixed for the departure of Father Sorin [for Bengal] had arrived, the bishop of Vincennes was informed of the embarrassment in which the latter was placed," and so a second dispensation was asked for.[24] Over the next six weeks an ominous silence emanated from Vincennes.

May, the month of Mary so central to Holy Cross devotion, began with nothing settled. Meanwhile, the situation of the community in Louisiana, caught between two competing authorities, was fast deteriorating. Father Moreau reiterated his threat to recall all Holy Cross personnel to France if his orders were not obeyed. Father Sorin continued to maintain that all such personnel were subjects of Notre Dame du Lac. The perplexed Archbishop Blanc tried to play the role of peacemaker, urging Moreau for the sake of harmony to transfer Francis Gouesse—to whom, however, Blanc still did not attribute personal fault—and urging Sorin on the same grounds to refrain from any imprudence.[25] But these efforts were in vain; both Moreau and Sorin refused to budge from their positions, and Gouesse, as stormy a petrel as ever, remained in place as local superior, while the nuns and brothers nominally subject to him fretted and quarreled among themselves. Sorin at first was not so frank about his ultimate purposes with Blanc—another Frenchman—as he had been with the Irish-born Purcell, but in mid-March he promised that "within a month I hope to have the honor to address your Excellency at length."[26] In early May he renewed this pledge, complaining at the same time: "Father Gouesse has not written me a line since my return [from New Orleans in January]." However annoyed at this impertinent secrecy, he nevertheless was full of assurances that "everything at Notre Dame du Lac has been arranged nearly satisfactorily, and we hope finally that more tranquil days lie ahead of us. God knows the troubles I have endured in recent years." Blanc should rest easy about Notre Dame's aspirations: "Believe me, my dear and

---

24. Sorin, *Chronicles*, 116. If he forgave it, Moreau never forgot Sorin's alleged insubordination in seeking the dispensation. See chapter 26, below.

25. See especially Blanc to Sorin, June 30, 1853, AIP.

26. Sorin to Blanc, March 18, 1853, AIP.

holy archbishop, we have sought and shall continue to seek for that amity with-out which religious houses are not worthy of the name."[27]

Such peaceful ambitions, however, did not mean that Sorin was willing to give way in the contest over the New Orleans mission. When one of the lay trustees of the orphanage admonished him about the continuing quarrel, Sorin replied vigorously. "You have no doubt perceived that Father Gouesse is not working much in our favor; I have every reason to believe that he aims at separating our establishment in your city from us here. I therefore think it my duty . . . to inform you that I am determined to hold you to your contract. I *shall stay* there and give up *none* of my rights."[28] To the archbishop he reiterated his intention to re-sist anyone who "would interfere or try to interfere with our contract" and violate its terms by diverting any funds. The obvious villain in this regard was Gouesse, though he was only an agent of a larger offense.

> His conduct does not surprise me in the least, but it opens our eyes and demonstrates what danger we shall be constantly exposed to with a mother-house which can over and over repeat appointments of this kind, among us and against us. We do not intend to make public our miseries. But if Sainte-Croix or Father Gouesse choose to inform the world we have not the slightest apprehension about the judgment that will result. Then people will know that one of the principal causes of our decision has been the aggressive appointment of this ambitious man who, since his arrival from France, has not let a year pass without justifying the measures we have taken in his regard, as was with the case with the superiors of the seminary, who originally dismissed him.

The "decision" to which Sorin referred was the five-year separation from Le Mans, about which the archbishop was finally informed through a copy of the memorandum of February 13 now sent to him. Sorin was apparently willing to risk Blanc's distress because he had in hand by this time Saint-Palais's first dis-pensation. Indeed, he even gave the archbishop a veiled warning: "The dispensa-tion from the vow of obedience to the motherhouse granted us by the bishop of Vincennes affects [the Holy Cross staff in New Orleans], since they all belong

---

27. Sorin to Blanc, May 6, 1853, AIP. Sorin's assertion was not literally true; Gouesse had written twice during calendar year 1853 (AIP), most recently on April 6, but both notes were brief and incon-sequential.

28. Sorin to Layton, May 11, 1853, AIP. For the contract drawn up by Drouelle and Blanc, see chapter 14, above.

here and can be called back as appropriate." Whether therefore Holy Cross continued to serve in his archdiocese was up to Blanc: "We shall in all deference, Monseigneur, follow your advice and leave the matter in your hands." But in fact staying in New Orleans "has become for us no more than a secondary consideration." The "documents" (*pièces*) formally declaring a unilateral separation have now been presented to Father Moreau, "and nothing will make us retract it before the five years have expired."[29]

The same determination was evident in Sorin's personal manifesto to Moreau. "I deferred making known to you the definitive resolution circumstances have finally forced us to adopt, because I hoped all along that you would spare us this common pain." The "secondary" importance New Orleans had assumed was still at the top of his mind as he searched for the way to put forward his best case.

> The question of New Orleans has doubtless been to a large degree the occasion but not the genuine cause of our determination. Our great object is not only to save [Notre Dame] from a crisis which could have destroyed it, but even more to assure it a boon of which it can no longer be deprived, the blessing of peace. It would be futile to repeat to you all the evils we have suffered . . . in the midst of these endless disputes. For many years we have picked nothing more than these sour fruits because of our dependence on Sainte-Croix and gained nothing else. We believe that the extremity to which you have reduced us gives us the right to declare this weighty separation from you as the only way of salvation. . . . Our dispensation obtained, we implore you today to pardon the pain we regretfully cause you, without, however, allowing you the slightest hope of our retracting this grave act until the expiration of the allotted time.

The argument for independence had subtly shifted from Bengal to New Orleans to, finally, a simple desire to be left alone. Canon Heurtebize and his future mediation were ritually invoked; in the meantime there was to be no compromise. "We are aware that you have it in your power to cause us some temporary embarrassment. But at heart we believe ourselves justified and secure. My very Reverend Father, I conclude by imploring you again to believe I am as pained as I am firmly resolved."[30]

As summer drew near the impasse dragged on with no sign of alleviation. In mid-June Sorin protested to the archbishop of New Orleans that Sainte-Croix

---

29. Sorin to Blanc, n.d. [May, 1853], AIP.

30. Sorin to Moreau, May 9, 1853, AGEN.

"as usual has told me nothing about the secret orders it has issued to *our* subjects at the orphanage." These directives involved the holding back of funds due the personnel from Notre Dame, money "of which I have an urgent need."[31] A few days later he elaborated more bitterly on this complaint to Moreau himself: "The steps you have believed it right to take recently in New Orleans without telling me—though obviously I had a right to know about them at the time—make me understand finally that there is nothing more to wait for from Sainte-Croix." Moreau's refusal to communicate with him directly had itself become an affront to Sorin, who increasingly moved into a mode of stubborn if ineffectual repetition. "I can no longer put off making known to you the arrangements the mother-house has led us to make, in spite of ourselves." Father Heurtebize will adjudicate the matter after five years. In the meantime, "if ever it becomes necessary to place this sad affair before the public, we are fully prepared to render an account of our conduct. . . . I have personally no ambition to be head of one day of a religious congregation in this country any more than I had for the honors of Bengal. I desire only the well-being of our work; any scandal would sadden me, but it would not be imputable to me."[32]

Basile Moreau may have judged it *infra dignitatem* to parley directly with his insurgent sons and daughters in the United States, but he was not behindhand in addressing the crisis in his own way. Nor did he make a secret of his anger and distress.[33] He considered for a while registering a formal complaint against Notre Dame du Lac in Rome, but in the end he refrained from taking such a drastic step.[34] Instead he set up an *ad hoc* committee in Sainte-Croix to examine the situation, and, on June 16, he appointed the long-rumored Visitor for the Holy Cross missions in North America. The findings of the committee contained no surprises. While granting Father Sorin credit "up to a point" for his undeniable achievements, and granting too the difficulties involved in communication between distant places as well as in attaining a mutual appreciation of two differing cultures, the report nevertheless concluded that obedience to the vows remained the decisive issue. Notre Dame's successes were all well and good, but if they represented "a prosperity belonging to the temporal order, and not to the supernatural order," they amounted to an illusion. By no means incidentally, the same could be said, as Heurtebize had already done, about Sorin's claim to property in America ceded, not to him, but to the Congrégation de Sainte-Croix.

---

31. Sorin to Blanc, June 15, 1853, AIP.
32. Sorin to Moreau, June 20, 1853, AGEN.
33. See the summation in Moreau, *Circular Letters,* 1: 307–308, dated June 15, 1854.
34. Moreau sent a draft of this document to Archbishop Purcell. See Purcell to Sorin, April 3, 1854, AIP.

The Visitor no doubt kept these conclusions clearly in view as he pondered the prospects of his delicate assignment. Pierre Chappé was a pious, genial man of forty-four and so five years Sorin's senior. He had been with Sorin among the first priests to make their profession as members of Holy Cross. He had become closely associated with the administration of the motherhouse, and Moreau, recommending him to the archbishop of New Orleans, described him as "a man who is serious-minded, prudent, worthy of confidence, and a great lover of peace." The Founder in later years would have reason to disavow this recital of virtues, but in early July 1853, when Chappé took ship for the New World, it was not unreasonable to expect that such qualities could indeed lend his delegate some effectiveness.[35]

W HILE CHAPPÉ was still at sea—it proved to be a long and diffi-cult voyage—tensions remained high. And in that pit of unhappiness for Holy Cross, New Orleans, they were intensified by the hand of death. From the end of June through August three brothers and one nun, as well as several children in the orphanage, were carried off by yellow fever.[36] The first to die was Brother Theo-dolus,[37] news of whose demise was recounted to Sorin from Archbishop Blanc. "Who would believe it?" Sorin cried in frustration. "Father Gouesse had not the heart to write a word about it to Notre Dame du Lac."[38] "Ah, had I foreseen the disappointments (*chagrins*) of every kind which were to plague our foundation in New Orleans, never would we have undertaken it. . . . My only consolation is the rightness and honesty of my proceedings since the beginning of our difficul-ties." His sense of resentment and isolation was only heightened by a severe per-sonal loss: "I see myself obliged to stifle in my heart the desire to recommend to the prayers of those who regard themselves as members of our family the soul of my own father whose death I learned about three weeks ago." And, thanks to the wrong-headedness of Sainte-Croix, the living symbol of all this unhappiness still strutted across the stage in New Orleans. "Father Gouesse is not a man of God, and he will succeed only in creating trouble and discord instead of peace. Sainte-Croix has committed an unpardonable fault in identifying itself with such a man. . . . Sainte-Croix is mischief-making (*tracassière*) inconsiderate, ambitious,

---

35. Catta, *Moreau*, 2: 5–10.

36. See Connelly, "Holy Cross in New Orleans," 5. There had also been a large number of fatali-ties among the orphans the year before.

37. Theodolus, né François Barbé, died June 25, 1853, aged thirty-five, *Matricule générale*, 347, AIP.

38. Sorin, *Chronicles*, 117.

and frivolous. It has well deserved the lesson it is now learning, a lesson that will be good for it."[39]

At the beginning of July the second dispensation from Vincennes finally arrived at Notre Dame. Pleading illness as an excuse for the delay, Saint-Palais displayed in this document—hedged about as it was with reservations—as much reluctance as before to grant Sorin the canonical relief he sought. And though he addressed Sorin as "My dear Friend," the bishop, sharply mindful that Holy Cross in his diocese had virtually ignored him as much as it had the motherhouse, wrote in a waspish mood and showed himself prepared to exact a high price for his cooperation: "Before approving your community, I wish to make arrangements which will assure me some voice in its government." Another unwelcome bird had come home to roost, casting the shadow of Bishop Hailandière: "If everything at Sainte-Croix had not been done and were not being done independently of the authority of the bishop," Saint-Palais said, "you would perhaps not find yourself now in such an embarrassing situation."[40]

Another disappointment came shortly afterward from Detroit. Once informed by Moreau of what was afoot at Notre Dame, the once friendly Bishop Lefèvre declared that past transactions of Holy Cross within his diocese were now subject to review. Specifically, he rescinded Sorin's faculties to act as confessor to the nuns in Bertrand. Furthermore "I strictly forbid any Sister of the Holy Cross, novice, or postulant, to go to the sisters established on the premises of [the] College of Notre Dame du Lac, or to receive within their community any sister coming from that college."[41] Since the nuns' novitiate had been shifted to Notre Dame a few years earlier, the bishop's decree in effect ruled out any formal connection across the diocesan and state line. "We shall have to adopt the course of abandoning Bertrand," Sorin wrote mournfully "and locating elsewhere everything which we have had there."[42] So much for past victories.

But he was not yet ready to give up the canonical battle. "We . . . wrote the Right Reverend Bishop of Vincennes who granted a dispensation," he told John Baptist Purcell in mid-summer. "I am now informed indirectly that they are extremely vexed at the motherhouse at our bold step, which, however, in our humble and unanimous opinion here, was nothing more than to place ourselves on the only plank of temporal salvation left to us. They speak of referring the matter to the Metropolitan to annul the dispensation of our Right Reverend Bishop."

39. Sorin to Blanc, July 16, 1853, AIP.
40. Saint-Palais to Sorin, June 19, 1853, AIP.
41. Lefèvre to Sorin, August 26, 1853, AIP.
42. Sorin to Moreau, August 30, 1853, AGEN. See Costin, *Priceless Spirit*, 83.

The "metropolitan" was Purcell himself who, in his capacity as archbishop of Cincinnati, did enjoy some ill-defined appellate jurisdiction over suffragan dioceses.[43] "In point of fact," Sorin continued, "they appear to me outrageous, and I have no doubt that their object is to frighten us and that they will very soon give up if they are once shown that we shall be supported."[44] But even had an appeal been directed to him from Sainte-Croix—it was not—Purcell, sympathetic as he may have been, had no intention of meddling in Vincennes's business.

Nor was an even more eminent prelate. To avert a possible crisis of conscience among that majority of his colleagues, who still did not know about the proposed break with Sainte-Croix, Father Sorin sought advice and implicitly support from Francis Kenrick.[45] In late July, Saint-Palais's vague dispensation in hand, Sorin described for the archbishop of Baltimore the planned separation, "which after the expiration of five years the two parties will examine anew and decide what course to adopt definitively. The dispensation has been accorded us. We have informed the motherhouse of this fact, but no reply has come from there. So I ask your Excellency, can we in conscience use this dispensation whether Reverend Father Rector approves or not? What means should we take to secure our objective, which in our opinion is to be preferred for a community like ours in this country?" Kenrick's lofty ecclesiastical opinion, however, was not helpful. Though the law, he said, was not altogether clear on a matter of this kind, it appeared to him most doubtful that a legitimate separation could be effected without Moreau's consent. "It would be a good thing for you and your superior to remain united," he added.[46]

Not even the friends of his youth rallied to him. "Your last letter, Father Sorin," wrote Victor Drouelle, the friendly Visitor of a few years before,[47]

has stupefied me. How deluded I have been about you, and how humiliated I feel to have been duped for so long a time by my devotion and my foolish (*niaeses*) assumptions about the uprightness and the sincerity of your conduct. I neither can nor want to tell you my true feelings. . . . In the

43. See chapter 15, above.

44. Sorin to Purcell, n.d. [July-August, 1853], AIP.

45. Francis Kenrick (1797–1863), coadjutor bishop of Philadelphia (1830), was promoted to Baltimore in 1851. His brother Peter (1806–1895) was bishop, then archbishop of St. Louis, a post he held for more than half a century.

46. Sorin to Kenrick, July 27, 1853, AGEN, and Catta, *Moreau*, 2: 7. When he became aware of it, the bishop of Vincennes was none too pleased at Sorin's initiative to Kenrick. See Saint-Palais to Sorin, October 4, 1853, AIP.

47. See chapter 13, above.

presence of a treason so clearly acknowledged, my heart fails me. Ah! my dear friend, I hope nevertheless that the mission of Father Chappé will open your eyes and scatter the seeds of trouble and division the devil . . . has sown among us.[48]

So IT WAS that at the moment Pierre Chappé landed at Quebec, on August 13, his embattled confrère in Indiana found himself increasingly isolated. Over the course of the next three weeks the Visitor toured the Canadian houses and reported to Le Mans that all was well with them. While in Montreal he received a note from Sorin advising him that he was not welcome at Notre Dame. He ignored this rebuff—given his mandate from Moreau he could scarcely have done otherwise—and arrived on September 7. In his first conversation with Sorin "he declared that he was not a man to be discouraged until he had tried everything in his power. However, it was clearly intimated to him that he was received as a friend, . . . but by no means in the capacity of Visitor."[49] For the moment he accepted this status and bided his time.

Nothing demonstrates better the volatility of the situation and of the personages involved than the treatment accorded the non-Visitor during his two-week stay at Notre Dame. Father Michael Shawe, the former faculty member who had come from Detroit to make his retreat, was bundled out of the best quarters in the collegiate building to make room for Chappé.[50] Everyone treated him with the utmost friendliness. Edward Sorin acted as his guide over the thirteen hundred acres that now comprised the foundations in Michigan and Indiana. He was enormously impressed by the signs of vitality all round the gleaming lakes: the bustling compound with the new church and the college and the apprentice shops, the novitiates bursting at their seams with aspirants, the great barn and the swine pens and the cattle herd, the orchards of fruit trees and the vegetable gardens and the fields of grain ripening under the late summer sunshine. The short journey to Bertrand revealed, among the sisters and the young ladies of St. Mary's Academy, a distinct and yet similar scene of productive activity. Chappé probably knew of the bishop of Detroit's displeasure with Sorin, which left the future of the foundation at Bertrand in doubt, and he certainly knew that the Potawatomi mission in Pokagon had been abandoned and an embittered Father Baroux sent off to

48. Drouelle to Sorin, July 24, 1853, AGEN.
49. Sorin, *Chronicles*, 118.
50. For Shawe see chapter 12, above.

Bengal.[51] "This news grieved me very much, for I had thought to spend the remainder of my life in my Indian mission, but now all was changed."[52] But such misadventures could not negate for a priest like Chappé the plentiful evidence he saw of the religious community's genuine piety and regularity; the requests for his blessing with which he was constantly greeted hardly seemed the stuff of truculent rebellion.

More sobering were his private conversations with the members of the chapters and particularly with Sorin and Granger. Among them he discerned no disposition for compromise. "He saw in all the members perfect unity of views, conviction, and determination. The administration, which he had never suspected to be any other than Father Sorin's, presented to him . . . evidence of a council of administration acting according to rule by the majority of votes. It was no longer, consequently, a single man that had to be taken into consideration."[53] He was shown the property deeds, all of them in Sorin's name, and told that, aside from a trifling 15,000 francs, nothing more was owed to Sainte-Croix.[54] The familiar charges against the motherhouse, in all their vagueness, were brought forward for Chappé's benefit. He parried them as best he could, without, however, changing any minds. However frustrated he may have felt as a result, it was nothing compared to his astonishment when he discovered that, aside from Sorin and the ten signatories of the notorious memorandum of February 13, nobody at Notre Dame or Bertrand was aware of the impending separation. This did not mean that Sorin lacked personal or institutional support among the larger body of sisters, brothers, and priests—quite to the contrary. Chappé swiftly came to appreciate the spirit that Alexis Granger recalled almost passionately many years later: "The enthusiasm of youth, the unknown future, and above all the visible assistance of God, with deep conviction spread around the young community an atmosphere of peace, of joy and holy alacrity, which made everyone forget his wants, his poverty, his suffering."[55]

So the emissary from Le Mans confronted a very delicate situation. Would it be prudent to reveal his commission as Visitor to a rebellious community, when doing so would render the scandal public and perhaps hasten the very catastro-

---

51. See Catta, *Moreau*, 1: 895–902, 979. Much to the distress of the bishop of Detroit (see Lefèvre to Sorin, September 14, 1852, AIP), the mission at Pokagon had to be placed in charge of the diocesan clergy. For the temperamental Baroux's earlier displeasure with Sorin, see chapter 14, above.

52. Louis Baroux, *Correspondence* (Ann Arbor, 1913), 76–77.

53. Sorin, *Chronicles*, 118–119.

54. For a detailed list of the properties, see Sorin's will, dated December 3, 1851, AUND, COSR, "Sorin, Edward."

55. "Memoir" by Granger, dated November 11, 1884, AUND, CGRA, "Granger, Alexis."

phe he had been sent to prevent? He decided not. All along Edward Sorin had counted upon Sainte-Croix's reluctance to risk adverse publicity,[56] and now the Visitor—who was not accepted as Visitor—experienced the effectiveness of that tactic.

Not surprisingly the discussions dragged on inconclusively. At one point, however, Sorin suddenly appeared to alter course. He offered to accompany Chappé back to Le Mans and lay the whole dispute before Basile Moreau one last time. The day of their leave-taking was set, September 16, and then, at the behest of the chapters, Sorin changed his mind again, and Chappé's joy withered into a renewed distress. This apparently erratic behavior, however, heralded a momentous and totally unpredictable turn of events. At nine o'clock in the evening of Tuesday, September 20, a despondent Chappé, packing his carpetbag in preparation for his scheduled departure for New Orleans, answered a rap on the door from a messenger who asked him to come to Father Sorin's room immediately. Once there, an agitated Sorin held up two sheets of paper and asked Chappé's consent to read aloud a letter he had just composed to Basile Moreau.

My Reverend Father, Never has it been clearer to me that the work of Holy Cross is from heaven and that will triumph over every obstacle. Confronted by the sad commotion we are about to present to the world, I feel that I am not the man to initiate such an enterprise, and however impregnable I see the fortress in which I am entrenched, my courage fails me at the thought of defending myself against those who attack us. I asked only for peace, and you forced me to a struggle whose consequences and limits you did not foresee. I have suffered too much for the Congregation not to recoil from the irreparable damage, which would result from an open rupture. I love my confrères too much to refuse a further sacrifice, even though it will be more painful than any other. Yet it appears to me unavoidable in order to ward off a storm such as has never yet broken out over our work. However justified I believed myself to be, and however right my intentions may have been, I lay down my arms and renounce any hope of victory, the fruits of which would have been so bitter. I surrender personally without reserve or condition. As to the mistakes in this matter our chapters [here] have been guilty of in your eyes, I assume full responsibility for them. To deprive any of these colleagues of your regard or your affection because of their cooperation [with me] would be an injustice, as you would readily understand were you to speak to them in person. If I can register here a

---

56. See, for example, Sorin to Purcell, February 13, 1853, AIP.

complaint, I would say in their behalf that their devotion to our work, so well known to me, has been badly appreciated elsewhere, at least in appearance. It would be useless to enter here into details about the motives that led us to the declaration we made to you. May the memory of it disappear entirely for you and for us. I prefer rather to tell you in this letter that I retract and regret everything that has offended you and the Congregation, from which I seek only peace in the blindest submission to your will. My Reverend Father, please bless your very humble and devoted son in Jesus, Mary, and Joseph.[57]

Five months afterward Sorin recalled the "truly fraternal embraces" he then shared with Chappé. He recalled too the thoughts and feelings that had prompted this almost incredible recantation. Up to that moment, he wrote in the third person,

Father Sorin had been sincere and honest in his opposition. He had wished to save the Association in the United States. But when he saw the direction that things were going to take, he yielded, and sooner than publicly raise the standard of revolt against the motherhouse, he asked himself, whilst reciting his [rosary] beads, if now that Sainte-Croix knew everything, it would not be more religious to surrender at discretion and to leave to God the consequences of a step that he could no longer defer without involving the whole Work in an atmosphere of scandal that would not be easily dissipated. He that changes the hearts of men of His own accord disposed that of the Father in question to give a favorable reception to this participation.[58]

"There is nothing more deceptive," he added, "than the human heart." And nothing more mysterious. Sudden conversions, like that of Saul of Tarsus on the road to Damascus, defy facile explanation. Such surely is the case in this instance. There is no reason to doubt Edward Sorin's word that his radical turnaround occurred while he was at prayer, specifically while praying the *Aves* of the rosary. He was a man of deep faith, who really believed that God "changes the hearts of men of His own accord" and for whom devotion to the Blessed Virgin was the wellspring of his life. He may have adopted many American manners and mores, but he remained as well a priest reared in the west of France where the kind of scan-

57. Sorin to Moreau, September 20, 1853, AGEN.
58. Sorin, *Chronicles*, 120.

dal Notre Dame's breach with Sainte-Croix would have occasioned was viewed with special abhorrence. Yet Sorin was a pragmatic man too, and, considering how tangled and complex human motivation often is, it does not seem amiss to wonder whether, even as the beads slipped between his fingers, he may have come to the realization that he had engaged in a battle he could not win. Canon Heurtebize had in effect rebuked him for the imprecision of his arguments; the American bishops he appealed to had failed to rally to him; the majority of his associates still had no notion of his intentions and might well repudiate them. Brooding over such realities on that fateful autumn eve would have been far from incompatible with a sincerely submissive prayer.

This war of Father Sorin with Sainte-Croix had been largely a war of harsh words, and now, at this dark and humiliating moment, he did not shirk the obligation to try to remove their sting. "I fear you are tired of the trouble we have given you," he wrote Archbishop Purcell on October 1, "and for that very reason I am glad to inform you at once that, contrary to all my previsions, a reconciliation has been effected by the parties at variance. Peace again reigns among all the members of the little family of Holy Cross. As to my staying or going, it is now left entirely to the Rector in France."[59] And to Archbishop Blanc, a few weeks later, he admitted the disconcerting uncertainty in which the events had placed him: "Doubtless by this time you have been informed by Father Chappé, before he left New York,[60] of the gratifying fact of his bringing home in haste the precious olive-branches he had so much at heart to secure.... I am totally ignorant of the course Sainte-Croix will adopt towards me, but I find myself in perfect readiness to follow the way that may be shown me, even if my expulsion from the Congregation be called for."[61] Closer to home, and aware that he had shortly to go to Le Mans to make his peace with Father Moreau in person and to learn what his future was to be, Sorin was anxious to keep up the spirits of his most devoted collaborators. "Be sure, I shall not forget you in my feeble prayers before God," he promised the sisters' superior at Bertrand. "Had I anything to forgive, I would do so cheerfully. But I have acted somewhat indifferently. . . . *I shall return* [from France], or else I shall be, as much as you, disappointed. It is useless to tell you, my dear Daughter, how much it costs me to leave you all, but I recommend everything to the Blessed Virgin and hope to see you soon, not to part any more."[62]

---

59. Sorin to Purcell, October 1, 1853, AIP.
60. Chappé had been scheduled to travel as Visitor to New Orleans after he left Notre Dame. With the settlement of the dispute, however, he returned instead directly to Le Mans.
61. Sorin to Blanc, October 21, 1853, AIP.
62. Sorin to Mother Ascension, November 9, 1853, AIP. As a member of the nuns' chapter, Mother Ascension had signed the memorandum of February 13.

But the most poignant and yet ironic manifestation of Sorin's chastened mood appeared in another letter to the archbishop of New Orleans. "You tell me, Monseigneur, that poor Father Gouesse has been recalled from the orphanage. Before he departs, I ask you, as a special favor to me and as an act of justice to him, that you regard as null and void all that I have said and written in his disfavor. Certainly he is by no means a totally bad man, and, apart from some vices stemming from his education, he has often pleased me exceedingly by his good qualities."[63] What such an apology, qualified as it was, must have cost Sorin can only be imagined. The wording of it suggests strongly the directive of a confessor, who had insisted that Sorin, if he wanted absolution, was obliged to restore the reputation of a person he had maligned. The expression of regret was in any event consistent with the reflections of that trying time, recorded, as usual, in the third person.

> That the hand of God did not abandon him in his fall and that he was able to rise again, that is what surprises him . . . and fills him with the most lively and the most humble gratitude. God grant that he may never lose sight of the fact that for a religious there is no peace nor safety save in blind obedience, and that after having grieved the Congregation by a scandal heretofore unheard of in her bosom, he should do everything to make up for it by his exemplary submission on every occasion.[64]

Time, the ultimate arbiter of human affairs, would tell.

---

63. Sorin to Blanc, n.d. [October, 1853], AGEN.
64. Sorin, *Chronicles*, 122.

chapter seventeen

Death and Resurrection

ON OCTOBER 10, 1853, A CHASTENED EDWARD SORIN departed Notre Dame du Lac for New York and boarded ship some days later for the voyage to France. By November 17 he was in Le Havre. Here he paused to make a religious retreat, and from here he forewarned Basile Moreau of his imminent appearance in Le Mans, "unless my health or something else might retard my arrival a few days." The submissive mood was still upon him, and during the moments of reflection afforded him by the retreat, he tried to focus his mind on the roots of the recent contention.

> I write in the same style as I started out from Le Mans some twelve years ago, and in the retreat I am making here, . . . I am glad to suffer something for the mission I have left behind. After repassing before God the twelve years of a life so full of responsibility, I do not feel disposed to flatter myself in anything; extremely painful though this last year has been, I cannot but believe it to have been a consolation for you to find me more reasonable than I myself believed I could be. . . . There was merit on my part in exaggerating my wrongs, the better to acknowledge [now] my regret. . . . I am far from wishing to justify, far from even explaining, what took place; it is still a mystery in my own eyes. All I can say is that I would not have wished to offend God in this sad affair. I feared for Bengal and for Notre Dame and was deeply affected by what we were subject to in New Orleans. I believed that Sainte-Croix, better informed, would act otherwise. . . . You know the rest.

And yet he could not but record what had been a noble ultimate objective—"I wished to save the Association in the United States"—and defend, to a degree, the tactics he had employed.

> In the beginning, our declaration of rupture with the Mother House was to be made known to your Reverence alone. I was convinced that in the present circumstances you would agree to everything rather than cause disturbance. In this way I hoped to bring everything to a happy conclusion. Your firmness outwitted me. I bless God for not having permitted me to have advanced farther on so unfortunate a path. I listened too much to the voice of mere nature and not enough to that of faith. My sacrifice comes a year too late. I know this better than anyone.

Though "convinced that he would be sent to Bengal,"[1] Moreau's "devoted son," as he once again inscribed himself, had been reduced to the status of a suppliant: "The only desire I now permit myself to entertain is to return to America and to do there the good I have been unable to do, and to repair here the faults I there committed."[2]

The entreaty did not fall upon deaf ears. In the course of the deliberations carried on at Sainte-Croix during December, it was determined that Sorin would not be transferred to Bengal after all. Precisely why Moreau relented after allowing the matter to have reached such a critical juncture remains unclear. Perhaps he was moved by Sorin's unmistakably genuine contrition; perhaps the various facets of the quarrel had led him to the realization that Sorin was indeed as indispensable to the American mission as he had claimed; or perhaps he concluded that since the Holy Cross mission in Bengal was in place, though still in very precarious condition, it could proceed without upsetting arrangements elsewhere.[3] Renewed tensions between Sainte-Croix and Notre Dame later may well have caused the Founder then to regret his decision of 1853. Sorin at any rate did not go unscathed. He was stripped of his position of provincial for the United States, and the minor chapters of Notre Dame and Bertrand were accordingly dissolved. North America became for the time being a single province, under the jurisdiction of Father Joseph Rézé, headquartered at Montreal. Edward Sorin remained

---

1. Sorin, *Chronicles*, 123.

2. Sorin to Moreau, November 17, 1853, AGEN.

3. Sorin was not alone among Moreau's subordinates in spurning the assignment to Bengal. No less than four other priests also declined. The administrative problem lingered for several years; not till 1859 was a member of Holy Cross consecrated vicar apostolic. For a summary, see Costin, *Priceless Spirit*, 239.

simply local superior in Indiana, or, as he winsomely put it, Rézé's "assistant."[4] These administrative changes were not destined to last long, and even while they were in force they made little practical difference.

On New Year's Eve Sorin left Le Mans for Le Havre. Instead of taking a ship there he went by train the next evening to Paris where he met Father Julien-Pierre Gastineau, whom Moreau had appointed to the mission in New Orleans. Sorin still held the olive branch firmly in hand. "I regret," he wrote Moreau in farewell, "that I cannot return again to Sainte-Croix so that I could one more time acknowledge my fault to each member of the chapter or council and give to each any satisfaction you might judge it prudent to offer." Moreover, "I desired once more to empty my heart into yours and let you see the mingling of regrets and desires, gratitude and devotion, which is rooted there."[5] From Paris Sorin and Gastineau traveled to London, then to Liverpool, where they set sail for the United States on a stormy day in early January. It proved to be a "passage . . . most distressing and most dangerous," lasting twenty-five days. In the little Holy Cross company, along with the two priests were four nuns, one of whom was coming to the convents in Indiana as canonical visitor from the motherhouse,[6] "and another [was] Sister Mary of St. Angela, a young American, . . . who had just made her profession at Sainte-Croix,"[7] a woman destined to play a significant role in the long and storied career of Edward Sorin.

ELIZA MARIA GILLESPIE had been born in 1824, and was thus ten years Sorin's junior.[8] She represented that rarity in early America, a Catholic family of means and social prominence. Her father was John Purcell Gillespie, whose ancestral seat was at Indian Hill, on the west bank of the Monongahela in western Pennsylvania, thirty miles or so south of Pittsburgh and closer than that to fabled Braddock's Road, along which, two generations earlier, that brave but foolish British general had led his army into a bloody trap set by the French and Indians. Eliza's mother was Mary Madeleine Meirs, of Rhenish and English descent, whose family had left Virginia in favor of Lancaster in Fairfield County, Ohio, during the first decade of the nineteenth century. Legal business—he had been certified a lawyer in Philadelphia—brought John Gillespie to Lancaster,

4. Sorin to Rézé, February 20, 1854, AIP.
5. Sorin to Moreau, January 1, 1854, AGEN.
6. See Sorin to Mother Mary of the Seven Dolors, March 7, 1854, AIP.
7. Sorin, *Chronicles*, 123.
8. For much of what follows see Anna McAllister, *Flame in the Wilderness: Life and Letters of Mother Angela Gillespie, C.S.C., 1824–1887* (n.p. [Notre Dame Ind.], 1944), 2–28.

and while in residence there, the young Catholic fell in love with the conventionally Protestant Mary Meirs. They were married in 1821, the wedding presided over by the Dominican friar, Edward Fenwick, later first bishop of Cincinnati. Their first child died in infancy, and, shortly afterward, moved perhaps by this sorrowful event, Mary embraced her husband's religion and practiced it with remarkable fervor for the rest of her life. Two years later, during a gentle February snowfall, her daughter Eliza was born.

The little girl enjoyed for four years unique attention within the Gillespie nursery at Indian Hill. Then, in 1828, Mary Rebecca joined her there, and so also three years later did baby Neal—Cornelius, in the Gillespie family tradition, was a name routinely abbreviated to Neal. Eliza was a precocious child, lively and affectionate, who readily absorbed the rather awesome piety of the household: she recalled from her earliest days lengthy morning prayers and missionary priests celebrating Mass in the commodious Gillespie drawing room. She enjoyed the ordinary pursuits of childhood, and, though her health was never strong, she early on assumed the role of directress of the activities of her siblings and younger cousins. Among the latter was James Gillespie Blaine, who would in due time become one the most powerful political figures in the nation.[9]

The wave of expansion and speculation that marked the booming American economy during the mid-1830s came to sharp halt in 1837. Even before the worst of the depression had made itself felt, the fortunes of the Gillespie family had taken a severe jolt. In the midst of these financial troubles, John Gillespie contracted pneumonia; he died at the end of January 1836. His young widow, with three small children to care for, found herself in relatively straitened circumstances. Nevertheless, that autumn she arranged for the twelve-year-old Eliza to enroll in the convent school operated by Dominican nuns in Somerset, Ohio, near Columbus. Her choice was dictated partly by religious considerations; in this setting, Eliza could be suitably prepared for her first Holy Communion, an episode in her child's life that Mary Gillespie took with the utmost seriousness. But she also took account that Somerset lay only eighteen miles from Lancaster, where the Meirs family resided as well as some relatives of her late husband. By the summer of 1838, when Eliza had completed the very limited curriculum offered by the sisters, Mary decided to leave Indian Hill and to settle herself and her family in the

---

9. Blaine (1830–1893) served as congressman and senator for twenty years and as secretary of state for four. The "Plumed Knight," as he was called, was the Republican candidate for the presidency in 1884. His defeat at the hands of Grover Cleveland was due in part to the alienation of the Catholic vote when one of his overzealous supporters labeled the Democrats as the party of "Rum, Romanism, and Rebellion."

friendly confines of the town where she had been born. Two years later she married a prosperous widower named William Phelan, master of Mount Eagle, the largest property in Fairfield County.

Squire Phelan proved to be an amiable husband and stepfather. And his standing in the community guaranteed that his wife, locally well-connected in any case, would be gladly received in the best homes in Lancaster, like those of the Beechers, the Irwins, and particularly the Ewings. This last named family, headed by the distinguished United States Senator Thomas Ewing and his wife Maria, was in fact related to the Gillespie children on their father's side. Mary Phelan became fast friends with Maria Ewing, whose daughter, Ellen, had been Eliza's schoolmate at Somerset. Catholic piety and charitable good works merged with these women into a kind of provincial aristocracy which crossed confessional lines. Bishop Purcell and Father Stephen Badin were guests of the Ewings and the Phelans, but Senator Ewing practiced no religion, nor did his ward, the young Lieutenant William Tecumseh Sherman, a recent graduate of West Point and later to be his foster-sister Ellen's beau. The elder Ewing, a prominent member of the Whig Party, regularly entertained the likes of Webster, Clay, and William Henry Harrison, the hero of Tippecanoe, who was elected president in 1840.

A few months after her mother's remarriage, Eliza Gillespie, now sixteen, traveled to Washington and joined Ellen Ewing as a student in the Georgetown Academy, a boarding school conducted by the Sisters of the Visitation, that offered probably the best education available in the country to a Catholic girl. Bright and eager to learn, Eliza came away after the two-year course with her mind opened in new ways to art and science and with her religious convictions, if anything, solidified. Back in Lancaster, she shared in various of her mother's good works. She helped her stepfather keep track of his accounts—he was a notoriously inept bookkeeper. She put herself at the service of the parish priest and eventually became the lead teacher in the parochial school. She fussed over Mary Rebecca and Neal, acting the part, as she always did, of assertive big sister. But the years passed without bringing with them a settled direction for the undoubted capacities of her mind and heart. Admittedly the options were limited for one in her position, especially if the opinion of her parish priest was correct: "Eliza should never marry; I do not know a man who is her mental superior."[10] If neither marriage nor the convent held any appeal for her, Eliza could hardly look forward to being more than a spinster moving along the edges of other people's lives. One by one the familiar props fell away. Her Blaine cousins married, Mary Rebecca married Ellen Ewing's brother, and Ellen herself, after a long and contentious courtship,

---

10. Quoted in McAllister, *Flame*, 90.

married the mercurial William Sherman.[11] And then, worst of all, the beloved Neal went away. It happened in 1845. An advertisement for a Catholic boys' school in northern Indiana caught Mrs. Phelan's eye. She had never heard of the place, nor had her pastor, but, at her request, he agreed to make inquiries. The reply came quickly from the institution's president, and within weeks a tearful Neal had been sent off to Cleveland, where Father Sorin met him in person and from there conducted him to the collection of wretched little buildings grandiosly called the University of Notre Dame du Lac. Though no one could have predicted it at the time, this was a fateful moment both for the Gillespie/Phelan family and for the mission of Holy Cross in America.[12]

Neal's first months at Notre Dame were miserable indeed. But once the homesickness passed, and once he grew accustomed to an environment in which English was spoken with a heavy French accent—when it was spoken at all—he came little by little to cherish the place. However rude and even primitive the surroundings may have been, Neal Gillespie found among them the same kind of intellectual stimulation his elder sister had during her stay in Georgetown. He was fortunate in two of his professors especially, François Cointet and Michael Shawe—the latter of whom of course spoke an English even more elegant than that heard on the streets of Lancaster, Ohio. They instilled in him a genuine love of learning, so that, when he graduated in 1849, he decided to stay on, take more courses, and earn his tuition and keep by teaching arithmetic. This decision was in its way an implicit tribute to the progress, despite all kinds of vicissitudes, the college had achieved during his stay there. "Tell me, my dear Ma," he wrote his mother, "what ought I do when I quit studying? I have often been asked when I would finish my studies. . . . I could stay here and study for full eight more years without *finishing* my studies, aye, and study seventeen hours each day. Oh, I'll be sorry when I leave this place!"[13] In the end he did not leave; in September 1851, after pondering his future and finally setting aside other alternatives—a possible career, say, in business or in law—he entered the Holy Cross novitiate at Notre Dame to prepare for the priesthood.

Neal Gillespie's enthusiasm for Notre Dame and Holy Cross was regularly conveyed to his sister through the long and chatty letters he sent her and even more during the happy holidays they spent together at Mount Eagle. Their mornings began, often as not, with a canter in tandem across the adjoining countryside—the Phelan stables were celebrated in the locality and Eliza, now in her mid-

11. John F. Marszalek, *Sherman: A Soldier's Passion for Order* (New York, 1993), 48–51, 79–81.
12. Wack, "Notre Dame Foundation," 133–134, 190–192.
13. Gillespie to Mrs. Phelan, n.d., AUND CEWI, "Ewing Papers."

twenties, was a formidable horsewoman—but their intimate conversations later in the day revealed how their paths in another sense had diverged. Young Neal had found his niche, a noble one indeed and consistent with his gifts and aspirations, while Eliza, his mentor, was left restlessly seeking her own. She continued to resist the notion of the nunnery, though she had for some time been a Dominican tertiary and had quietly performed the devotional practices involved.[14] Neal did not press the matter of a religious vocation; in fact, he rather discouraged it: "If you should ever determine to become a nun," he wrote, "Notre Dame would be a good place to come to, perhaps better than many. But, Lidie dear, would it not be better to stay with dear mother?"[15] This may have appeared an appropriate observation, because just then Mary Phelan's health was showing symptoms of decline. But even concern for her mother could not still Eliza's unease and sense of aimlessness. In the summer of 1851 she agreed to teach for a year in a small school for girls in St. Mary's City, Maryland. Her work there, as a teacher and pastoral helper in the local Jesuit parish, was, predictably, exemplary, and in the course of it she was edging toward a definitive resolution about her future. When she returned to Lancaster in August, 1852, she consulted the pastor, Father Joshua Young, in whose judgment she put great trust, and, at his recommendation, she applied for admission to the newly opened convent of the Sisters of Mercy in Chicago. After so much uncertainty the die was finally cast.

On the face of it Eliza Gillespie's choice of religious congregation was surprising. Familiar with the Dominican and Visitation nuns from her schooldays—orders long established and rich in tradition—she nevertheless determined to join a relatively obscure group organized in Ireland only twenty years before. It remains somewhat mysterious too as to how she became acquainted with their apostolate of service to the poor and sick and especially to afflicted women. Since their first house in the United States had been founded in Pittsburgh in 1843, perhaps she had had some contact with Sisters of Mercy during visits to her Gillespie relatives still residing in the vicinity of Indian Hill. Eliza Gillespie at any rate, now twenty-nine years old, a *mulier fortis* then and ever afterward, knew her own mind. Or at least she thought she did.

On April 2, 1853, as Mary Phelan noted at the time, "Eliza and I started in the stage [from Lancaster] to Columbus, from thence to Notre Dame and Chicago,

---

14. "Tertiary" is the popular term to describe a lay person who associates herself with a religious order by adopting that order's spirit and guidance but without assuming the obligations to take vows and to live in community.

15. Gillespie to Eliza Gillespie, May 10, 1851, AUND, CEWI, "Ewing Papers." "Lidie" or "Lida" was Eliza's nickname within the family.

where my dear child intends to join the Order of Mercy. Oh, I feel very miserable at the idea of separation for life from my dear child."[16] The plan was that mother and daughter should interrupt their train journey at South Bend in order to pay a brief visit to Neal Gillespie. That young man, when he learned of his sister's decision and of her impending arrival at Notre Dame, addressed to her a lengthy appeal not altogether consistent with some of his earlier observations.

> I was truly very much pleased, Lidie dear, that what I had hoped for was in great measure accomplished. I return thanks to our Blessed Mother who has obtained for you, as well as for me, the grace of a religious vocation. . . . You speak of coming this way as you go to Chicago. I am rejoiced at the decision, and I shall pray that you determine to stay here. . . . You must feel yourself, Lidie dear, what an additional happiness it would be to me were you to join the same religious family to which I have attached myself. . . . I know well enough that God sometimes calls a soul to a particular community [like the Sisters of Mercy]. . . . But I do not think this is [true in your] case. . . . I think you should join the Sisters here, [chiefly] because I wish to have my sister in the same family with me. . . . Yet there are more weighty reasons. . . . The occupations of our Sisters would suit you exactly, since they serve God by teaching young ladies and by attending the sick. Moreover, the community is young and needs members. . . . I am afraid that the reason you did not choose at first to join our Sisters is perhaps that my letter to you some years ago, when I was a senseless youngster, may have tended to give you a wrong impression of them. If you have not fully determined to become a Sister of Mercy, do not make any final arrangement, but wait until you have visited me here and have seen our Sisters.[17]

Eliza no doubt carried this letter in her bag as she and her mother, on April 5 or 6, made their way in a hired rig from the railroad station in South Bend toward the Notre Dame compound. Little accustomed as she was to receiving advice from her siblings—since childhood, after all, she had been mistress of the revels—her beloved brother's words could not have been without effect. Then occurred a series of events enshrined and perhaps embellished in the lore of Holy Cross in America. As the women's carriage reached the edge of the campus, it met another going in the opposite direction; holding the reins of the "two beautiful cream-colored horses" was Edward Sorin. The two vehicles stopped abreast of one another,

---

16. Quoted in McAllister, *Flame,* 88.
17. Gillespie to Eliza Gillespie, February 19, 1853, AUND, CEWI, "Ewing Papers."

and conventional verbal courtesies were exchanged. Mary Phelan was known to Sorin from her previous visits to her son, but his real attention fixed upon her younger companion whom he had never met. He knew full well that she was Neal Gillespie's gifted sister, and he already had plans for her. Dismissing the other vehicle and its driver, he invited the ladies to board his own. The team turned around, and at a leisurely pace the buggy proceeded into the grounds. Like a genial tourist-guide, Father Sorin pointed to and identified this building and that, and then, suddenly, he turned to Eliza and said: "You are the one I have been praying for for so long."[18]

The campaign lasted less than a week. Eliza was at first put off, or at any rate confused, by Sorin's abrupt declaration. She had, after all, made a commitment to the Sisters of Mercy and had made it only after a period of reflection that could be counted in years rather than months. She was a mature woman, not a school-girl to be bullied by an overbearing priest. Yet conversation with her eager younger brother only served to intensify her perplexity. Next morning, after Mass, Sorin confronted her again: "Say no more, please, about going to Chicago to be a Sister of Mercy. God has called you here to be a Sister of Holy Cross." Such imperious self-confidence—she would experience it many times more in the future—was hard to gainsay. Mrs. Phelan, though perhaps her maternal sympathies were clear, refused to say more than that the decision had to be Eliza's alone. The train at any rate departed South Bend for Chicago without them, and Eliza consented to go to Bertrand to make a three-day retreat. What she witnessed there, the cheerful dedication of women in the midst of a poverty more than evangelical, appealed mightily to all her idealistic instincts. The superior, Mother Ascension, always a sturdy mainstay to Sorin, did much to alleviate Eliza's doubts, as did, even more, the learned and lovable Father Cointet, who often acted as chaplain to the nuns at Bertrand.[19] At the end of this brief time of prayer and quiet and self-examination, Eliza Gillespie sought out Father Sorin and told him she would indeed follow his counsel, and, after what must have been one of the shortest postulancies in the history of organized religion, she was clothed, on April 17, 1853, in the habit of Holy Cross as Sister St. Angela.[20]

The religious name Eliza chose was that of a Dominican nun of whom, all those years before at Somerset, she had been fond. Sorin meanwhile moved with

---

18. A suspiciously elaborate account is in McAllister, *Flame,* 86–95, from which Costin, *Priceless Spirit,* 73–75, though more restrained, does not differ in substance. Costin bases her account on the unpublished recollections of an aged nun who had been a novice at the time.

19. Eliza Gillespie would in due time write Cointet's biography. See chapter 8, above.

20. See McAllister, *Flame,* 89, 93–94, and Costin, *Priceless Spirit,* 74–75.

his customary dispatch to bring his new recruit into the mainstream of his mission. But he wanted her to serve her novitiate in a setting more sophisticated, and one therefore more befitting for one of Eliza Gillespie's talents and social standing, than that available at Notre Dame. One young sister at Bertrand had been scheduled to go to France at about this time to study the kind of art—drawing, flower design and the like—that would, it was hoped, prove attractive to prospective female pupils in the academy. No nun traveled in those days without a sisterly companion, and so, in his usual arbitrary manner, Sorin simply set aside the originally appointed escort in favor of Sister St. Angela. She went off therefore to the convent of the Good Shepherd Sisters in Caen, in Normandy, not, significantly, to Le Mans. The chronology provides the explanation: this was the late spring of 1853, which marked the very height of the controversy over Notre Dame's proposed secession from Sainte-Croix. By the time she had finished her period of initiation at Caen, that dispute had ended, at least for the time being. So when Father Sorin came to France, at the end of 1853, to effect the reconciliation with Moreau, he summoned Sister St. Angela from Normandy, so that she could make her formal religious profession as a Marianite nun at Sainte-Croix.[21] This she did, and shortly afterward she accompanied him across a storm-tossed sea to her homeland, where she was destined to leave an outstanding testimony of her own.

EDWARD SORIN was fully aware of the prize he had attained for Holy Cross in the enlistment of Eliza Gillespie—"this élite soul," he called her.[22] Before he and she departed Le Mans for home he persuaded Moreau to endorse the appointment of Sister Angela—the "St." soon dropped from her name, as it had in the case of Mother Theodore at Terre Haute—as directress of the academy at Bertrand and its seventy-two pupils.[23] And, though humiliated by recent events as he may have been, Sorin still possessed enough hardihood to warn the Founder that he must not meddle in this assignment: "I forgot to tell you that Mary of St. Angela, because of her family connections, cannot without grave difficulty be removed from the post which you have awarded to her."[24] Nor did his new ally disappoint him. Within weeks of taking up her post, Sister Angela was ready to put in place a plan whereby "we can without any extra expense simply add to the

21. Costin, *Priceless Spirit*, 74–75.
22. Sorin to Moreau, March 8, 1854, AGEN.
23. Sorin to G. Jones, February 9, 1854, AIP.
24. Sorin to Moreau, January 1, 1854, AGEN.

number of pupils [in the Academy] who will pay their board and room and will carry along the others." With Moreau's consent, "the opening of this Catholic school, the first [of its kind] in the United States, can be announced shortly."[25]

The communities at Notre Dame and Bertrand warmly welcomed the return of their superior, reduced in rank as he was. His escape from Bengal was theirs, too. His friend Archbishop Purcell sent jovial congratulations "on your auspicious return and on the *entente cordiale* which now subsists [sic] between the motherhouse and your Institution."[26] During the weeks that followed, however, Sorin continued to mull over almost obsessively the circumstances that had led to his abortive rebellion. The occasion for this further soul-searching was the fulfillment of the congregation's rule that each house keep a running written account of its activities and submit it regularly to the motherhouse.[27] To discharge this obligation in the winter of 1854 meant that Sorin had to recapitulate in writing the recent unhappy altercation.[28] "I do not know what your Reverence will think of these chronicles," he told Moreau in a covering letter. "I have tried to reproduce faithfully the feelings [*sentiments*] that dictated or accompanied each event. But I have not been able to humiliate myself at the cost of the truth." Thus Father Gastineau—who tarried at Notre Dame before reporting to New Orleans— "asked me yesterday if it were not the case, as people at Saint-Croix asserted, that our [proposed] separation was provoked . . . by my fear of going to Bengal."

> I asked him to explain himself, and the good Father simply acknowledged that my refusal of the assignment to Bengal was generally attributed to motives of mine that were completely human. But as a member of the Congregation I owe it to my conscience to redress a very grave error and to recall to your mind, my very Reverend Father, . . . I believed, as did everybody here, that your Reverence wished me to go to Bengal so that in due time I should assume the functions of a Vicar Apostolic. [Gastineau] thinks my self-esteem should have found ample gratification in this prospect, and, as far as he is concerned, Notre Dame appears . . . insignificant and of small preference compared to a miter at Dacca. . . . Happily, though he is more eloquent than all my confreres at Saint-Croix, [Gastineau] cannot succeed in quieting the voice of my conscience. . . . Had I been free and without

---

25. Sorin to Moreau, March 8, 1854, AGEN.

26. Purcell to Sorin, April 3, 1854, AIP.

27. See the explanation in the Preface of Sorin, *Chronicles*, xxiii–xxiv.

28. That is, the account as cited in chapter 16, above, as found in Sorin, *Chronicles*, 108–122.

employment, I still would have refused, as I did. Had your Reverence not spoken of the episcopal dignity, I would have gone to Bengal, but once my refusal on this basis had been established secondary considerations quickly became principal ones in my mind and these prodded me into an obstinate resistance. And, to tell the truth, among these secondary motives that led to our declaration [of independence], it would be wrong to place in the first rank my attachment to Notre Dame.

What then, or who, was the root of the act of sedition? Despite an earlier verbal gesture of forgiveness,[29] Sorin could not dismiss from his mind what he considered the villainy of a particular individual. "There is another cause that sums up in itself alone almost all the miseries we have experienced over the past five or six years, a proper name of two syllables." Gouesse was a proper name of two syllables, and it had been he and his machinations, at both Notre Dame and New Orleans, that "had produced, as I told you before, the true cause of the uproar, although these seemed at the time only the occasion of the events that followed." Certainly "my love for Notre Dame du Lac, great as it was, would not have kept me here one hour in defiance of my conscience; my heart would accuse me of deception [*mensonge*] if I pretended to be indifferent to my immediate surroundings. No one knows better than your Reverence my sentiments on this matter." And then, equating as he had done often before his own status with that of Moreau, he asked rhetorically: "Would you have been able to convince us that you do not have a similar attachment for Saint-Croix?" Surely "I love all those whom Providence has brought together around me, those who have demonstrated over many years their inalterable devotion." But "thanks be to God, I owe nothing to any individual," here or elsewhere. Send me there or keep me here, "whatever pleases you," act with full freedom, and "believe me finally, my very Reverend Father, your very humble and obedient servant."[30]

The contrition or abnegation—perhaps not so comprehensive as the avowal—was nonetheless satisfactory enough to Moreau, who assured his difficult subordinate that, in due time, his former perquisites would be restored. "I am personally very little desirous of any advancement," Sorin replied, "and indeed little alarmed at any humiliation. The only thing I wish for in this world is peace. Each day my soul feels ever more the need for it. The world has seldom fascinated me, but today I am disgusted by the world, even to the point of maintaining my connection

29. See chapter 16, above.
30. Sorin to Moreau, February 24, 1854, AIP.

with it only with pain."[31] But the world, in another sense, was about to buffet him as never before.

HOWEVER BITTER had been the wrangling of the previous fifteen months, the distress of that time was to pale in significance when compared to the year of disaster that lay just ahead for Notre Dame du Lac. When Edward Sorin returned home from France on February 2, 1854, there "awaited him trials such as he had never experienced heretofore." Before the tragedy, however, came a comedy of errors. Julien-Pierre Gastineau, appointed by Le Mans to succeed Francis Gouesse as superior of the mission at New Orleans, had accompanied Sorin to Indiana. There he remained, until the beginning of April, when he departed for the south.[32] After a few days in Louisiana "he disappeared without informing anyone of his intentions or of his place of retreat." Two weeks later Gastineau unaccountably turned up in Rochester, New York, and informed Sorin that he planned to return to Notre Dame. Sorin advised him to report rather to Father Rézé in Montreal, now, since Sorin's demotion, Holy Cross provincial for all North America. Gastineau did so.[33]

This "ridiculous escapade," as Sorin described it, was another chapter in the dreary story of Holy Cross in New Orleans. Indeed, the mission there had become a kind of running sore. Gastineau's inglorious departure meant that Basile Moreau had once more to find a suitable candidate to fill that ill-starred post. Pierre-François Salmon, recently ordained and dispatched from Le Mans to America in 1853, was Louisiana's next victim; he died there within a couple of months of his arrival.[34] With his personnel stretched so thin, the Founder decided he had no choice but to ask Francis Cointet to take up the burden in Louisiana again. That steadfast religious, whose health had been undermined by the eighteen frustrating months he had already spent there,[35] loyally acquiesced. Moreau, however, further instructed him to delay his departure until two brothers on their way from France should arrive at Notre Dame, and should then accompany him to New Orleans. These brothers, and the two nuns traveling with them, endured a terrible, sixty-five day voyage. "When they landed in New York, without money and without resources of any kind, their first act was to telegraph and to write

31. Sorin to Moreau, March 23, 1854, AIP.
32. Sorin to Moreau, April 5, 1854, AIP.
33. Sorin, *Chronicles*, 123–125, and Sorin to Gastineau, May 6, 1854, AIP.
34. Connelly, "Holy Cross in New Orleans," 10–11.
35. Sorin to Rézé, May 6, 1854, AIP. See also chapter 14, above.

[Notre Dame] for the funds necessary to continue their journey. . . . [But] their telegram and letter were both so badly addressed that they were not answered, never having found their way to [their destination]." Eventually, deep into the summer, one of the brothers reached Notre Dame, and money was sent to rescue "his three traveling companions, . . . not one [of whom] could speak a word of English," and "to save them from being sold at auction to pay their personal debts."[36] This curious episode saved Father Cointet from returning to New Orleans, but it did not save his life.

By the time this messy situation was cleared up, other distracting matters had come to the fore, a couple of them gloomy reminders of the past. Father Sorin, always in need of money, had informed the estate of George Woodworth—the "captain" of the ill-fated Callifornia expedition—that he intended to bring civil suit to collect the unpaid debt owed for board, room, and tuition accumulated by the captain's two sons, who had spent four years at Notre Dame.[37] A reply, at once harsh and humiliating, came from a lawyer in Cleveland named F. X. Byerley, son of that Samuel Byerley who had been Notre Dame's earliest patron. The two young men, he claimed, were functionally illiterate: "When they left [Notre Dame], it was a notorious fact, and can if necessary be made to appear [so] in open court, that they had no conception of even the simplest rudiments of an ordinary education."[38] And Captain Woodworth's particular friend in olden days, Samuel Byerley himself, now also living in Cleveland, quarreled with Sorin on an altogether different issue. Why, he asked rhetorically, should Notre Dame have espoused with "the ringing of bells" the politically "dead-bird" cause of the temperance movement?[39] To what specific event Byerley was referring is unclear; Sorin in any case held ambivalent views about imbibing alcohol, sternly forbidding consumption of whiskey by students and faculty alike while winking at beer drinking.[40] Given masculine habit on the Indiana frontier, tobacco, like drink, posed a quandary for administrators at Notre Dame. Father Moreau was consistent in forbidding its use within the congregation—he considered smoking and snuff-

36. Sorin, *Chronicles*, 126. The one traveler who had managed to make his way to Notre Dame was Brother Dominic, a thirty-three-year-old German. He duly reported to the mission in New Orleans and within weeks died there.

37. See chapter 14, above.

38. F. X. Byerley to Sorin, July 3 and October 12, 1854, AIP. Byerley, in a later letter on the same subject (February 3, 1855), referred parenthetically to Sorin's "many and repeated acts of kindness to all our family and to myself."

39. Samuel Byerley to Sorin, June 18, 1855, AIP.

40. John Quinn, "Dry Days: Drink and Temperance at the University of Notre Dame, 1842–1940," 1–8. My thanks to my friend, Dr. Quinn, for showing me this unpublished paper.

taking a violation of the vow of poverty.[41] Sorin tended to agree, and eventually his opinion received formal sanction: "It is decided that in future no man shall be received as a novice who does not promise to cease using tobacco, and that no cigar shall be offered as previous[ly] on extraordinary occasions."[42]

But these more or less permanent concerns seemed of little moment as the dark drama of the summer and autumn of 1854 unfolded. The prelude was grim enough. One night in mid-July, a postulant at Bertrand was suddenly stricken with chest pains, and she died before morning. Twenty-four hours later, a thirteen-year-old orphan was found dead in his bed, having choked, it appeared, on a bit of apple. Shortly afterward two pupils, ailing for some time, also passed away. Then, on August 10, "at eight o'clock in the morning, word was brought to the poor Superior that Brother Alexis, one of the best members of the Society, had drowned in [St. Joseph's] lake during the night." These unrelated fatalities occurred just before the retreat season of mid-summer, and, despite the shock and sorrow they left in their wake, the spiritual renewal these religious exercises were meant to inculcate would provide, Sorin believed, "a well-founded hope that heaven would bless the [mission] for its efforts to please God. . . . Alas, how different are the thoughts of man's heart from the thoughts of God!"[43] The cross first, the glory afterward.

Though for many years Sorin and his colleagues had been troubled by the prevalence of illness at their mission, especially during the summer months,[44] nothing experienced before could have prepared them for the virulence of the epidemic of 1854. The typhus struck first at Bertrand, where five sisters died during late August and early September. With a grisly symmetry the same number of brothers perished at roughly the same time. The first priest to succumb was John Curley, an Irishman ordained only a year before. By early November, when colder weather intervened, death had claimed eighteen members of the communities—fully one-fifth of the mission's complement—and scarcely any of the survivors had escaped the debilitating effects of the dread disease: "At times there was only a single professor [in the college] on his feet while four were incapacitated and out of action." A numbing anguish over the loss of their comrades seized upon those walking skeletons, but no one was grieved over more that François Cointet, who died at the height of the plague, in mid-September.

---

41. See, for example, Moreau, *Circular Letters*, 2: 218, dated August 27, 1861.

42. Minor Chapter Book, minutes, March 29, 1858, AIP.

43. Sorin, *Chronicles*, 127–128.

44. See chapter 12, above.

He was one of those men of solid merit, without the least ostentation, a man of God who saw only God in all things. Each one thought that they appreciated him well during his life, and all now see, after he has disappeared, that the void left by him in descending into the tomb is every day becoming more immense. No one knew him better nor loved him more sincerely than the poor Superior. . . . One need not be astonished to learn . . . that on the night when he was obliged to announce to this other self that he was going to die, to administer to him the last sacraments, and, finally, to receive his last breath, his soul was crushed, his mind bewildered and near to a state of disorganization as sad as death itself.[45]

An appendage to Cointet's death was the further irony that Gouesse, still in New Orleans, reassumed direction of the Holy Cross mission in that city. His triumph, however, if that is what it was, was short-lived; in December he was summoned back to France, and a few months later he was dismissed from the Congrégation de Sainte-Croix.[46]

Bewildered Sorin indeed had to be at thus losing his closest friend and his most stalwart supporter, this "other self," upon whom so much of the work of Holy Cross in America had depended. As the crisis deepened Sorin could offer little solace to his associates. "This year," he told the nuns in Bertrand, "it has pleased Divine Providence to fill up our cups with bitterness."[47] During this grim passage he confided to Mother Theodore in Terre Haute—and perhaps to her alone—how close to despair these afflictions had brought him: "Surely I adore God's purposes even when I do not understand the cause of them or how they relate to each other. Oh, I would not wish for anything in the world to murmur against heaven. God exalts what he has given. I can only bow my head and remain silent. But I fear I have lost all the merit I might have gained from these days of agony."[48]

Yet it was precisely in the midst of such personal sorrow and such bewilderment at the mysterious designs of Providence that Edward Sorin demonstrated his immense capacity for leadership; indeed, this may have been his finest hour. As the death toll mounted, he grasped intuitively how important it was to keep the calamity out of the view of the public and particularly of the boarding students.

45. Sorin, *Chronicles,* 128–131. See also chapter 8, above. The bishop of Vincennes also recognized the loss of one the most effective parochial ministers in his diocese. See Saint-Palais to Sorin, October 12, 1854, AIP.

46. See Connelly, "Holy Cross in New Orleans," 11, and chapters 14 and 16, above.

47. Sorin to Mother Ascension, October 14, 1854, AIP.

48. Sorin to Mother Theodore, October 16, 1854, AGEN.

Edward Sorin in middle and late-middle years

Auguste Lemonnier (1839–1874), Sorin's nephew,
fourth president of Notre Dame

Lemonnier Library, 1890s

Patrick Dillon (1832–1868)

Among early presidents of
Notre Dame,
a favorite and a bête noire.

Patrick Colovin (1842–1887)

Inset: William Corby (1833–1897), war hero and twice president of Notre Dame

Photo courtesy of Indiana Province Archives Center

Thomas Walsh (1853–1893),
after the fire, the shrewd President of the "new" Notre Dame

Mary Gillespie Phelan (1804–1887), patroness extraordinaire of Holy Cross
Photo courtesy of St. Mary's Archives

Cornelius (Neal) Gillespie (1831–1874), Mary Gillespie Phelan's literary son,
Mother Angela's beloved brother

The Belles of St. Mary's, c. 1870

Mother Angela Gillespie (1824–1887),
"The one I have been praying for"
Photo courtesy of St. Mary's Archives

Patrick Condon (1838–1901)
Photo courtesy of
Indiana Province Archives Center

John Toohey (1840–1905)

Sorin's stalwart auxiliaries

Peter Cooney (1822–1905)
Photo courtesy of
Indiana Province Archives Center

Charles Moreau (1823–1899), the nephew
Photo courtesy of C.S.C. Generalate, Rome

The general chapter of 1872, Notre Dame du Lac

Photo courtesy of Indiana Province Archives Center

The Notre Dame Thespians, Exhibition Hall, c. 1878

Alexis Granger (1817–1893), Sorin's gentle and ascetic other self
Photo courtesy of Indiana Province Archives Center

Brother Charles Borromeo
(Patrick Harding, 1838–1922),
architectural prodigy

Pierre Dufal (1822–1898),
bishop of Dacca, second superior
general of Holy Cross, third procurator
general of Holy Cross

Photo courtesy of
Indiana Province Archives Center

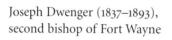

Joseph Dwenger (1837–1893),
second bishop of Fort Wayne

John Henry Luers (1819–1871),
first bishop of Fort Wayne

There were seventy of them enrolled this term, and, "happily, good health reigned among them; only three or four of them were attacked and [were] saved, with one exception." But if word leaked out to their parents that sisters, brothers, and priests had been ravaged by typhus, such news "would have sufficed to empty the college in twenty-four hours," and, short of money as always, the mission would have collapsed. Sorin therefore directed that ordinary routine be maintained at all costs. The situation was almost surreal. Sorin himself carried on his ordinary administrative duties, and dealt as well every day with a massive correspondence, which brought inquiries about the college and petitions to enter the brother- or sisterhood and—needless to say—demands that debts be settled.[49] He further ordered that members of the staff, stricken as almost all of them were at one time or another, nevertheless continue to adhere as closely to normal procedure as possible. True enough, the areas of the compound occupied by the religious had always been out of bounds for the students, who were restricted to the collegiate building and their own recreational grounds; even so, it seems in retrospect almost miraculous that they never realized the extent of the devastation the epidemic had wrought. A determined Sorin added a macabre touch in order to keep the secret: "Half the deaths were unknown to [the students]; the sacraments were administered and burials took place in the evening and in the shadows of the night."[50] Or, as he expressed it to Moreau, "We are reduced to burying our dead secretly. Every day for the past week we have been going in silent procession to the cemetery."[51] Over all this space of time one can almost see the hooded figures and hear the muffled chants, as the sons and daughters of Holy Cross, "in the shadows of the night," laid their loved ones in the cold ground.

A political consideration also encouraged Sorin to adopt a clandestine policy throughout the crisis. Despite his by now wholehearted devotion to all things American, he realized that there was a growing unease among the indigenous population over the scope of European immigration. This feeling helped promote the rise of the bigoted Know-Nothing Party, which, though its overall impact was fleeting, during the mid-1850s gave formal expression to dislike of immigrants in general and of Catholics in particular. As far as northern Indiana was concerned, Notre Dame du Lac was an island of Catholicism set in a Protestant sea, and

49. See, for example, Brother Bonifacius (in Cincinnati) to Sorin, November 15, 1854, relaying a request from the Franciscans in Louisville for teaching brothers, and Harper to Sorin, September 13, 1854, AIP. Harper wrote in behalf of the South Bend Woolen Manufacturing Company and complained harshly that repeated requests for payment had been ignored. This dunning letter was delivered on the eve of François Cointet's death.

50. Sorin, *Chronicles*, 131.

51. Quoted in Moreau, *Circular Letters*, 1: 322. "Poor Father Sorin!" commented Basile Moreau.

staffed—not exclusively, to be sure, but largely—by persons born in France or Ireland. Father Sorin had gone to great lengths to maintain friendly relations with his neighbors of whatever faith, and they out of common decency or, in some cases, out of economic advantage to be gained by the presence locally of a large group of consumers had readily reciprocated. But were the news to leak out that Notre Dame and Bertrand were sinks of disease, where typhus and dysentery and the even more dreaded cholera could flourish, earlier good relations would be of little account.

As the winter came on, and the incidence of illness subsided, Sorin and his colleagues took advantage of the respite to examine, once again, the possible causes of a chronic problem that had now evolved into one of catastrophic proportions. Years before they had hoped the unhealthy environment would right itself once the heaps of soil excavated for construction purposes had been covered over with grass and gardens.[52] This may have been a fanciful notion, but not so fanciful as the view, enshrined in lore passed on by the Potawatomi, that a species of poisonous fish inhabited the lakes. And yet they recognized in this legend a grain of truth, to the extent that the source of the frequent sicknesses seemed clearly related to the compound's water supply. Some people advanced the theory that human waste had somehow infected the wells, but this could not be verified. Sorin himself had long worried that the level of the lakes was too high, so that, after the spring rains, the low-lying land between them became in effect an unsightly swamp that lingered far into the summer. Perhaps, he thought, the noxious fumes that rose from this evil-smelling marsh brought with them the germs that caused frequent sickness. He did not understand at first that the real toxic carriers were the flies and mosquitoes breeding in that slimy ground, but this dearth of scientific sophistication did not gainsay the basic correctness of his judgment. As early as 1847, indeed, he had explored various expedients intended to lower the water level, but to no avail. Even then he strongly suspected, again correctly, that the root of the trouble was a dam blocking the little stream that flowed out of St. Mary's Lake west into the St. Joseph River.[53] Next to the dam stood an unused mill belonging to a man called Rush, who also owned the surrounding farmland. Rush could be moved neither by persuasion nor by threat of a lawsuit to allow egress through the creek during the season of snowmelt and heavy rain.[54] Meanwhile, the lakes routinely overflowed, and the bouts of fever at Notre Dame remained an alarming commonplace. But in the wake of the typhus epidemic the

---

52. Sorin to Moreau, 7, 1847, AGEN. See also chapter 12, above.

53. See Schlereth, *Notre Dame*, 18–19, and especially the map, 17.

54. See Minor Chapter Book, December 13, 1847, and April 3, 1848, AIP.

predicament had assumed a dangerous new dimension, and Sorin determined to approach Mr. Rush once more. The farmer adamantly refused to allow any tinkering with his dam, but, he added, he was prepared to sell the property on which it stood for $9,000, one-third of which had to be paid immediately and in cash. The price and terms were clearly exorbitant under any circumstances, and, even if they had not been, there was not a remote possibility that Notre Dame could raise such a sum.

Then, as the winter of 1855 ended, the angel of death swooped down again. On March 15 a seminarian died of typhus, and two weeks later one of the brothers succumbed to the same disease. Perhaps chastened by this sad news, Farmer Rush approached Father Sorin with an amended proposition: he would sell his property for $8,000 and require only $1,000 as a down payment with the balance to be amortized over four years. Sorin eagerly accepted this offer. The legal papers were duly drawn up, signed, and notarized. But the eccentric Rush suddenly changed his mind again and failed to appear at the meeting at which title and money were to be exchanged. It was, Sorin recalled, Wednesday of Holy Week.

> There are occasions when, by adopting vigorous measures, the enemy is surprised and frightened, and we thus elude his snares. On [Holy] Thursday morning, before Mass, Father Sorin sent five or six of his stoutest men with strict orders to listen to no one and to tear down the dam; they were especially charged to answer anyone who might attempt to stop them that they received no orders from anybody except their master and that the land was his. Never was an order more promptly carried out. Our man [Rush] could not hold out against this bold stroke.... The fall of the dam changed his position vis-à-vis the College. We had a quasi-title to justify us. Public indignation, which was ready to prosecute him for this new piece of trickery, frightened him. One hour afterwards, he went to town and handed over the papers to [our] Brother-commissioner. It is impossible to describe the joy that filled the community when it was learned that the dam was torn down. All returned thanks to Heaven.... Everyone looked upon it as a special blessing and as a promise of health, even if progress did not immediately result.[55]

And the promise was fulfilled: once control over the water-level of the lakes had been secured, never again did the scourge of typhus or any other terrible plague fall upon the Notre Dame compound. The place so fair to behold was

---

55. Sorin, *Chronicles*, 138.

from the spring of 1855 also healthy to dwell in. If Farmer Rush had expected Know-Nothing allies to rally to him—if indeed there were any of this ilk in South Bend—he was disappointed. Edward Sorin, shrewd as well as daring, had employed his "vigorous measures" against a vulnerable target. "We, in common with the whole town," he observed mildly, "had a very unfavorable opinion of [Rush]."

A NEWLY SALUBRIOUS ATMOSPHERE was not the only benefit that came with the purchase of the Rush property. A farm of 185 acres of good land, with a sturdy house and barn, was a welcome acquisition in itself. Possession of it would moreover guarantee Notre Dame a local monopoly over lime- and marl-production, if that endeavor were ever to prosper.[56] But the ever-fertile mind of Edward Sorin was plotting a more ambitious and, as it turned out, a brilliant long-term strategy. The Marianite Sisters were at this moment scattered into three locations. Some still served as domestics at Notre Dame itself. Their major center, however, with their academy, was still in Bertrand, Michigan, but the formerly friendly relationship between Sorin and Bishop Lefèvre of Detroit had soured markedly, partly because, after Hailandière's retirement, the nuns' novitiate had been moved to the Notre Dame campus—in questionable and possibly scandalous proximity to young men, in Lefèvre's view—and partly because the bishop disapproved of Sorin's stance in the quarrel with Basile Moreau.[57] Sorin, therefore, now that a less hostile prelate presided in Vincennes, had already begun to contemplate bringing all the sisters into Indiana and so removing them from Detroit's canonical jurisdiction. With this in mind, three nuns along with some orphans and other dependent children were transferred from Bertrand to Mishawaka, a village a few miles from South Bend. The house established there, in December 1854, was modeled on the brothers' manual labor school.[58]

Mishawaka proved to be a place unfriendly, even hostile, toward the sisters and their work. "It is one of the towns of the North," Sorin observed, "that has best preserved the spirit of bigotry and hatred of everything Catholic."[59] But such small-town intolerance he could brush away with a flick of his hand as his plans for the Rush property matured. "Father Granger, in his walks with his novices, had noticed an admirable site on this piece of ground, on an elevation seventy-

56. See chapter 11, above.

57. Lefèvre to Sorin, February 25, 1854, and Sorin to Lefèvre, April 10, 1854, AIP. See also chapters 9 and 16, above, and Costin, *Priceless Spirit,* 78.

58. See Costin, *Priceless Spirit,* 83–84.

59. Sorin, *Chronicles,* 173.

five feet above the river and at a distance of a mile and a quarter from the college. He had from the very first desired it for the Sisters. Examined by the Superior and by the Sisters themselves, there was found to be such a combination of advantages that it was resolved to establish there . . . the residence of [the Marianites] and their headquarters."[60]

With his mind made up, Sorin moved with his customary dispatch. Less than two weeks after Mr. Rush had reluctantly handed over the title to the farm, the decision to consolidate the sisters' convents had been adopted. All operations and personnel—professed nuns, novices, postulants, boarding students, orphans—were to be removed from Bertrand, Mishawaka, and Notre Dame and were to be consolidated on that "admirable site" above the river. The process, Sorin estimated, would cost about $3,000, but in two years time, he said with characteristic bravura, the resulting economies would more than match that sum. And who could overvalue the spiritual advantages and simple convenience of such a project? Nor would implementation of the plan be allowed to wait until suitable construction could be arranged. By midsummer, under the supervision of that hardy farmer, Brother Lawrence, usable buildings and parts of buildings began to be dragged by ox teams from Bertrand and Mishawaka to the spot above the river. Only then did the sisters realize that a profound change was about to occur in their lives. On August 15, the feast of the Assumption of Our Lady, the whole community gathered at Notre Dame for Mass and dinner, followed by processions around the grounds and, finally, sung Vespers. Afterward, swathed in the golden light of early evening, Father Sorin conducted two of the nuns across the fields to show them the site of their new home. One of them—it would have outraged propriety had she gone with him alone—was, appropriately, Sister Angela, née Eliza Maria Gillespie.[61]

T HE DECISION TO ESTABLISH the sisters at what would in time become St. Mary's College included on Edward Sorin's part a determination to curtail drastically all other expenditures. Three thousand dollars, after all, was a large sum for the chronically insolvent community, and 1855 was a year of high prices and an uncertain economy overall. Yet even extreme frugality would not have saved enough to pay for this project and cover other necessary expenses, including, not least, the installments due the peculiar Farmer Rush. Available, to be sure, was a benefaction that had come out of the blue a year earlier from a priest

---

60. Sorin, *Chronicles*, 139–140.
61. See Costin, *Priceless Spirit*, 86–87.

named Philip Foley, who lived in Toledo and who offered to endow two student-scholarships at Notre Dame. Not coincidentally, the figure he mentioned was exactly $3,000, to be paid by the end of 1855.[62]

But the Providence in which Father Sorin put such unclouded confidence had a far richer prize in store for him. Even before the destruction of Mr. Rush's dam and the subsequent purchase of his property, the Phelans of Lancaster had intimated their intention to endow Holy Cross in America with the bulk of their assets. The moving spirit behind this idea was the fervent Mary Phelan, who, now that two of her children had joined the congregation, persuaded easygoing William that support for its great work would be a fitting testament. A few weeks before the fete of August 15—a few weeks, that is, before Sorin and Sister Angela had taken their evening walk together and inspected the two ramshackle buildings recently moved to St. Mary's from Mishawaka—he learned from Mrs. Phelan that she and her husband had decided to donate the bulk of their property to "the Congregation of Holy Cross established at Notre Dame, Indiana," in exchange for a life-annuity for both of them. The total value of the gift—real estate, bonds, mortgages, and cash—ranged, when certain encumbrances were taken into account, between $70,000 and $80,000—three times the institution's indebtedness. "That this gift must appear Providential, especially under the circumstances," Sorin solemnly attested, "everybody at Notre Dame understood. They saw in it the fulfillment of the words: 'In the evening weeping shall have place, and in the morning gladness.'"[63]

Not even the most cynical observer could mock Edward Sorin's conviction that the Divine itself had intervened at this climactic moment to preserve the work he and his gallant companions had selflessly undertaken. But on the lesser, human level the contribution of the Gillespie/Phelan clan to the survival of Holy Cross and its mission can hardly be overemphasized. Yet that too throbs with implications scarcely explicable to someone unwilling to recognize the maneuvering of an unseen Hand. Mary Phelan had by chance seen an advertisement for an obscure preparatory school for boys in northern Indiana, of which she and her intimates had never heard. Her daughter, Eliza Maria—"the one I have been praying for for so long," Sorin said of her—had come to Notre Dame, fully intending, after a brief visit, to pass on to somewhere else; but she did not. Mary's son Neal Gillespie—who, recently ordained priest, was studying theology in Rome during

---

62. Sorin to Foley, May 6, 1854, and a copy of the contract signed by both men and dated June 5, 1854, AIP.

63. Sorin, *Chronicles*, 142–144. The quotation is from Psalm 30. For details of these transactions see also Wack, "Notre Dame Foundation," 292–296, and the authorities cited there.

the course of these crucial events[64]—was destined to bring honor to his congregation and his university. And, finally, Mary's second husband, William Phelan, very much a successful man of the world, pledged his hard-earned fortune to support a religious endeavor far removed from the commercial preoccupations of a lifetime. It is no affront to the courage and dedication of Edward Sorin and of the brothers and sisters who had joined him in the early 1840s, nor to the vision of Basile Moreau who had commissioned them to venture for Christ in a far-off land—no affront at all to proclaim that without the Gillespies it would have all gone whistling down the wind.

---

64. Sorin to "Reverend Father," July 16, 1854, and Gillespie to Sorin, August 26, 1854, AIP. Gillespie went first to Sainte-Croix. His immediate impression was that, though he might enjoy a month's holiday in France before matriculating in Rome and a rather longer stay after completing his studies, he already looked forward to returning to America.

chapter eighteen

The Quest for Maturity

T HE PHELAN LEGACY DID NOT IN THE END RETURN
as large a sum to Notre Dame du Lac as both parties to the
agreement had originally anticipated. This unpropitious result was due mainly to the unease of the American economy during the mid-
1850s, which reached a climax in 1857 when a full-fledged recession gripped the
whole country. Property values fell, return from bonds was less, and debts were
difficult to recover. Nevertheless, the financial pressures that had weighed so
heavily upon Edward Sorin ever since his arrival in Indiana were to a considerable extent relieved. Not that everyone shared in his jubilation. The centerpiece
of the donation had been Mount Eagle farm, to which Sorin, in the late summer
of 1855, dispatched four brothers to work the land in conjunction with William
Phelan's hired hands.[1] Only weeks later, on September 29, did Sorin inform his
friend, the archbishop of Cincinnati, of what had transpired, with special reference to the farm. Purcell was not amused to learn that one of the wealthiest
Catholic families in Ohio had settled its estate upon an organization outside his
jurisdiction. Recalling how Sorin had sought and received his support during the
recent quarrel with Le Mans, the archbishop expressed his annoyance at being
confronted now with an unwelcome *fait accompli* that seemed to him to smack
of ingratitude. Sorin, he replied with some asperity, had kept him in the dark
about the negotiations with Phelan: "How then could I have any 'desire or advice'
to express concerning [Mount Eagle's] present or prospective condition?"[2] The
next time Sorin visited Cincinnati, Purcell left him to cool his heels for an hour

---

1. William Phelan to Sorin, September 1, 1855, AIP.
2. Purcell to Sorin, October 4, 1855, AIP.

before seeing him, though good feelings between the two were eventually restored.[3] "I will avow to you candidly," the archbishop admitted once he had calmed down, "that I did feel *nettled* and *annoyed* that the splendid property of Mr. Phelan, from whom the Catholics of Lancaster had a certain right to expect assistance for church and educational purposes [had been] deeded away, out of the diocese; and without any stipulation whatever, as far as I had any means of knowing, that it should be used, at least in part, for the benefit of religion in that neighborhood. . . . I did not regret your receiving that splendid present, but I was sorry to see that this diocese was to reap no benefit from it."[4]

Another benefaction from outside its immediate ambit came to Notre Dame at about the same time. This one, a piece of property near Detroit valued at $6,000, was donated outright to Father Sorin by a seminarian then in residence named William Corby, who was destined to perform great deeds for his university and his country.[5] The Phelans, meanwhile, divided their time between Lancaster and a little cottage—it had been the priest's house, moved from Bertrand—located on the grounds of the new St. Mary's Academy, the former Rush farm. Mary thus could now at her pleasure reside in close proximity to her two children; indeed, she outlived both of them. William, however, whose generosity had been to a degree awakened by intimations of mortality, had scant time to adjust to this arrangement; he died in March 1856.[6]

Despite this loss, it seemed, in the late summer of 1855, that Sorin's unwavering optimism about the prospects of the Holy Cross mission in America, an optimism in defiance of every conceivable disaster, had achieved a measure of realization. Those who attended the commencement exercises at Notre Dame that July—presided over by Bishop Young of Erie, Sister Angela's friend and mentor—marveled at the double-spired Church of the Sacred Heart and toured through the new wings added to the collegiate building, which could now accommodate up to 250 boarding students.[7] Nor were these visitors surprised, as later generations would have been, at the variety of instruction on offer. In residence there were boys as young as five or six—the so-called Minims[8]—who were taught their fundamental letters and numbers; the adolescents who made up the juniorate

---

3. See Sorin to Purcell, September 11, 1856, AIP.

4. Purcell to Sorin, February 13, 1856, AIP.

5. Sorin, *Chronicles*, 144, and Hope, *Notre Dame*, 109.

6. Costin, *Priceless Spirit*, 87, and McAllister, *Flame*, 129–132.

7. The addition of the two wings, postponed because of a lack of funds (see chapter 8, above), was completed in 1853. See Schlereth, *Notre Dame*, 26–28.

8. According to the third meaning of the word in a contemporary dictionary (1992), "an insignificantly small portion or thing."

and received the equivalent of a high school education; and finally the members of the collegiate department, who, perhaps less well-served than the others, were expected to unravel the mysteries of the classical languages and the intricacies of accounting. And all these students, whatever their ages, were, as a matter of course, subjected to a religious regimen worthy of a French seminary. Those among the attendees at commencement who had chosen to do so, might also have strolled the mile or so to the splendid site on the other side of the lakes, perched above the St. Joseph River, where the rude buildings transferred only weeks before from Bertrand and Mishawaka gave some pledge of the bright future St. Mary's Academy might in time achieve. Visitors who exchanged greetings with Father Sorin heard him at his most sanguine, suggesting, among other things, that he planned soon to institute a law school and a medical school within the Notre Dame compound. However chimerical such a boast may have been, the enrollment in that autumn term of 128 pupils boded well for the morrow, as did the sixty boarders who matriculated at the nascent St. Mary's.[9]

Sorin could also tick off a roll of dependent houses, most of which, as he said of the one in Cincinnati, gave "full satisfaction."[10] In nearby Hamilton, Ohio, "a pretty little town of six thousand souls," a brothers' school had been opened, as well as another in Louisville, Kentucky, a state where Holy Cross's original experience had been less than happy.[11] These three stations served a mostly German clientele, which provided Father Sorin an opportunity to compare ethnic groups: "In general, what is done among Germans in this country offers more for the future than that among the Irish and the French. The Germans are honest, if not generous. The others do not keep their promises. Among the former there is order and system; among the latter great negligence and little perseverance. There is no doubt but that our German brethren will succeed better than any other nationality in America." A case in point was the new Holy Cross foundation in Toledo, where the brothers had to deal with much Irish drunkenness "and, consequently, much misery and immorality." A fairer prospect presented itself in Milwaukee, also predominantly German. Closer to home viable missions—served by both brothers and sisters and usually by a priest for Mass on Sunday—had been established in the Indiana towns of LaPorte, Michigan City, St. John's, and on the outskirts of South Bend itself.[12] Even after the sisters' manual-labor school had been

9. Sorin, *Chronicles*, 147, and Wack, "Notre Dame Foundation," 297–298.

10. For a short list see Sorin to Moreau, March 5, 1855, AGEN.

11. See chapters 12 and 13, above.

12. Strictly speaking, the area of South Bend, on the north bank of the St. Joseph River, at this date was still called Lowell. See chapter 7, above.

transferred to the new St. Mary's, a few nuns remained behind in Mishawaka to teach about thirty or forty pupils; "they are obliged to admit boys and girls, the congregation not being able to pay the salary of a Brother in addition to that of two or three Sisters. Just now [in 1855] a pretty little frame church is going up on the sisters' property, together with a house for the priest."[13]

Not contributing directly to the mission's explicitly religious activities, but, in Sorin's mind, never unrelated to them, were the initiatives undertaken to assure the institution's local solvency long term. Thanks to the Phelan legacy, some working capital was available and a measure of credit established. Sorin was not slow to take advantage of these relatively favorable circumstances. A small farm adjacent to the Rush property was purchased, and a hundred dairy cows were added to the original herd. Property on the road toward Bertrand, prudently acquired years before when the sisters' convent was located there, had been disposed of, while the area directly south of the Notre Dame compound, still open fields, had been divided into house lots—to be sold for $25 down—with the intention of encouraging Catholic immigrants to settle there.[14] A village of sorts did eventually develop on the site called, appropriately, Sorinsville, until the expansion of South Bend absorbed it.[15] All these transactions required a good deal of legerdemain on Sorin's part: purchase a piece of land one day and borrow against it the next. His skill in this regard seems, in retrospect, emblematic of a pioneer entrepreneur.

THIS NOVEL PROSPERITY for Notre Dame and its connections, due in part to Father Sorin's stubborn devotion and dexterity and to an unexpected cache of good fortune, had another, broader cause. In 1828, when Edouard Sorin was a lad of fourteen keeping under his thumb his playmates in Ahuillé, Charles Carroll of Carrollton, the ninety-one-year-old *doyen* of America's premier Catholic family, turned over the ceremonial first spadeful of earth to begin construction of the epoch-making Baltimore and Ohio Railroad. "I consider this," Carroll said on that occasion, "among the most important acts of my life, second only to my signing of the Declaration of Independence, if even it be second to that." A prescient statement that, because the creation of a railway

---

13. Sorin, *Chronicles*, 161–164, 173–178.

14. Minor Chapter Book, minutes, May 5, 1856, and November 12, 1855, AIP. The project, however, was of long standing. See Minor Chapter Book, minutes, March 5, 1849, AIP.

15. Wack, "Notre Dame Foundation," 307, points out that the streets in this section of the city still bear Notre Dame names: Sorin, St. Vincent (for Brother Vincent), Corby, Angela, and Howard (Timothy, professor in the college, local historian, and judge).

system was to effect another revolution in America, economic, social, and political. But at the start the going was rough. Two years passed before thirteen miles of track were laid, and teams of sweating horses could pull the cars from Baltimore to Endicott Mills, Maryland. In Indiana the first rails went down in 1838, in Madison, on the banks of the Ohio, and it took ten years of toil and frustration before the line reached Indianapolis, eighty-six miles away. Technology and equipment had to be imported from Britain, and Britain also provided a precedent for the fundamental question policymakers, especially in the Midwest, needed to decide: would internal transport better depend upon this novel steam-driven machinery or upon the older system of canals? As the ribbons of steel gradually spread and intersected across the countryside—made possible, ironically, by laborers and matériel often conveyed to work-sites by the canals—the solution became obvious, as it had before in Britain.

At the beginning of 1850 there were still only a hundred miles of track laid in Indiana. Two years later that total had quintupled, and, until it was temporarily slowed by the financial panic of 1857, the expansion continued at a frantic pace. The results were profound and immediate. With a network of railroads established and extending farther along ever more spurs to ever more towns and settlements, linking heretofore lonely outposts to population centers east and west, local markets for commodities were converted into national ones, so that virtually overnight, for instance, the value of an Indiana farmer's wheat doubled to almost a dollar a bushel. Two competing Michigan companies, each anxious to establish a rail-link between Detroit and booming Chicago, pushed construction across northern Indiana, and in October 1851 a locomotive chugged its way into South Bend for the first time.[16] Less than a year later Henry and Clem Studebaker opened their blacksmith shop, and a couple of years after that James Oliver started his foundry, thus laying the foundation for the vast industrial enterprises that would define South Bend economically for the next century.[17] Without the railroads neither farms nor factories could have advanced into the modern capitalist era.

And without them Edward Sorin's grand endeavor might well have withered on the vine. From the beginning—even in the far-off days at Black Oak Ridge—Sorin had acted on the principle that the Holy Cross mission in the United States could survive only if it were based upon a profitable *collège* or, now that he oper-

---

16. Richard S. Simons and Francis H. Parker, *Railroads of Indiana* (Bloomington, Ind., 1997), 5–12.

17. Howard, *St. Joseph County,* 1: 395–401.

ated in a more Americanized mode, upon an educational institution in accord with the norms of his adopted country. Notre Dame had been officially called a "university" since 1844, but that title had been at first hollow—a mockery almost—not only because of inadequate faculty and primitive facilities but, most of all, because of the paucity of students. The critical mass necessary for any successful scholastic enterprise could never have been accrued so long as Notre Dame's base of recruitment was restricted to the hamlets and farmsteads in its immediate environs. The coming of the railroads changed all that. The railroads meant that Notre Dame could be reached by prospective students from places like Chicago, Detroit, and Cleveland, and indeed from all across the Midwest, with relative convenience. It meant too that Holy Cross's outreach to and control of its missions in Cincinnati or Louisville, to say nothing of those closer by, could be immeasurably more effective.

The entrepreneur in Sorin recognized instantly how important this development in the mode of transportation was to the fulfillment of his plans and aspirations. He recorded the "loud burst of joy from all northern Indiana" when the Michigan Central brought its line through Elkhart, South Bend, and Mishawaka. But, he observed delightedly, in addition to the commercial advantages such access would introduce into the whole area, the railroad would guarantee to Holy Cross an agreeable new aptitude

for attending [its] many missions, for the journeys and visits of the Brothers and Sisters assigned to teach, and, finally, for the pupils of the College and the Academy. Moreover, this new railroad would bring European emigration in this direction and would thus facilitate what had been so painfully organized for Catholicism. . . . It would be difficult to set a money value on the benefit of this railroad to an establishment like Notre Dame du Lac, [which] . . . will be, by means of it, within two days of New York, twenty hours from Cincinnati, eight hours from Chicago, and a few hours from even its most distant missions.[18]

"Within two days of New York"—how times had changed since the fateful day in 1841 when Father Sorin and his six companions had boarded the Hudson River boat to begin their toilsome journey westward.

---

18. Sorin, *Chronicles,* 98–99. The importance of the railroads to Notre Dame's development was first pointed out to me by my dear friend and colleague, Professor Thomas J. Stritch, the last of the Notre Dame "dons," who first arrived on the campus in 1930.

HOWEVER ALERT HE WAS to the "money value" inherent in the emergence of the railroads, it was hardly uncharacteristic of Sorin to remark that "Notre Dame du Lac did not, like so many others, offer superfluous thanks" to the officials, public and private, "who had secured a triumph for the rights of the region." After all, "the prayers of the Association had frequently been offered up for the success of this enterprise. . . . In the eyes of the children of Holy Cross [it was] a blessing for which heaven was above all to receive their thanksgiving."[19] This routine melding of the secular and the sacred manifested itself again a little later, and even more colorfully, when the Rush property, gained by quite worldly strong-arm tactics,[20] was formally converted to its new and pious purposes. "This dear house," Sorin announced, in anticipation of blessing its first stone, "shall be called St. Mary of the Immaculate Conception."[21]

The traditional, though often disputed, Catholic persuasion that the Virgin Mary had been from the first preserved from the stain of original sin was given solemn dogmatic endorsement by Pope Pius IX on December 8, 1854. News of this great event reached Notre Dame du Lac just as the new year began, through the pages of the French journal *l'Univers.* Given Edward Sorin's deep devotion to and fervent practice of the cult of Christ's Mother, this formal ratification by the petrine office of what he and most Catholics had always believed was a source of enormous significance to him. "To the ends of the earth," he exulted to Moreau, paraphrasing the psalm, "even to the depths of our forests, their words have resounded. We have heard the voice of the successor of St. Peter, and we have responded to it from the bottom of our hearts. Oh, only God knows with what happiness!" In the campus church the Virgin's altar was decked out with lavish decoration, and at the festive Mass sermons devoted to her dignities were preached in French, German, and English—the last by Sorin himself. Outside joyful pandemonium reigned. As all the bells in the compound, big and small, rang out together, and the college band played with a zest and a volume unprecedented. "We have over a radius of four or five leagues no doubt stirred up a veritable panic. Tomorrow our neighbors will be demanding explanations from us."

Edward Sorin is often portrayed, necessarily, as an entrepreneur and executive caught up in raising money or speculating in real estate or, alas, engaging in unseemly quarrels. It is relatively easy to invoke the shade of the man who strode among the smoldering ruins of his church with new and expanded blueprints al-

19. Sorin, *Chronicles,* 98–99.
20. See chapter 17, above.
21. Sorin, *Chronicles,* 141.

ready in his mind, or the man who tore down Mr. Rush's dam. But integrity demands that the depth of his faith also be reiterated, a characteristic without which he could never—indeed, *would* never—have endured and overcome the lifetime of trials that confronted him. And although through this commitment he embraced the full panoply of Catholic belief and practice, he reserved a special place in his heart for Our Lady, for *Notre Dame.* The definition of the doctrine of the Immaculate Conception was therefore cause for genuine celebration. It is all very well, and of course true, to say that such reverence was typical of nineteenth-century religious, especially French religious. But such a generalization does scant justice to the intensity of Sorin's devotion to the Virgin and no justice at all to the sheer joy he experienced in doing her service. Yet he could not be other than he was even in performing such service; he was a practical man of affairs, not a contemplative.

"It has occurred to me," he told Father Moreau, "that the Holy Virgin would be happy if we worked a little harder in her interests, if we did a little to make her known, at least in our district." Since it would not be possible to reach out to the thousands of souls who ought to hear about her wonders, "I have resolved to publish a small monthly pamphlet (*brochure*) exclusively in honor of Mary. I shall entitle it the Immaculate Conception, because over these next months nothing will be more appropriate. . . . This is a unique way for me to make known and to love Mary; it will be new and full of interest for our House here and likewise for the Congregation generally, an organ to make her better known at such an opportune moment."[22] In a few short years this same enthusiasm would lead to the founding of the *Ave Maria,* a weekly journal which, in Sorin's own judgment, was by no means the least of his achievements.

THE SCRIPTURAL PHRASE, "a sign of contradiction," seemed to apply with full force to Holy Cross in the United States during the mid-1850s. In many ways the mission was prospering as never before. The dreadful problem of chronic disease at its home base had been definitively solved. Its finances were more secure than they had ever been, despite the hard times that prevailed nationally. Its outreach had spread to several key venues in the Midwest. The number of fee-paying students at Notre Dame and St. Mary's, now more accessible thanks to the railroads, increased from year to year. If young men willing to embrace the vocation of Salvatorist priests remained disappointingly hard to find, recruits for the Brothers of St. Joseph and the Marianite Sisters abounded. A

---

22. Sorin to Moreau, January 4, 1855, AGEN.

foundation of nuns in New York, for example, which lasted only a year—and which, as will be seen, proved to be another bone of contention—attracted twenty-five postulants within a few months.[23]

So many favorable auspices inevitably turned Edward Sorin's restless mind once more to the tangled problem of governance. Did not achievements of Holy Cross in America demonstrate the merits of independent action? He even submitted a plan to Le Mans in which he proposed that Sainte-Croix adopt a federal polity in frank imitation of the United States. The existence of the central government in Washington, he explained, does not hamper "local administration in each state. I do not wish to press the comparison too far but only to note that the idea is admirable in itself. For us our Washington is Sainte-Croix, or, if you prefer a churchly comparison, Sainte-Croix is our Rome. Your provinces would be like [individual] states or dioceses, whose important acts would require the sanction of Highest Authority upon which they ultimately depend. But in matters of detail jurisdiction would remain necessarily within the jurisdiction of each locality."[24] The tone of this communication was calm and courteous, but it must nonetheless have raised eyebrows in Le Mans, so recently confronted by Sorin's threat of secession. Indeed, echoes of that crisis were about to be heard again.

"Calm ought now to [have] succeed[ed] the tempest," as Sorin mournfully observed, "if, indeed, peace can ever become the lot of the poor children of Sainte-Croix."[25] Yet not peace but a sword—to invoke another biblical allusion—asserted itself despite all the evidence of well-being. The source of the trouble was, once again, New Orleans—now not just a continuing festering wound for Holy Cross but, it must have appeared, a mark of providential disapproval. After Father Gastineau's flight from the scene and Salmon's death,[26] the post of superior to the mission fell once again into the hands of Sorin's inveterate enemy, Francis Gouesse, who had remained in residence in Louisiana thanks to the benevolence of Archbishop Blanc. At the end of 1854, however, the archbishop acceded to Moreau's directive that Gouesse should be recalled to France.[27] Moreau further ordered that a new superior should be sent directly to New Orleans from Sainte-Croix, while, in the meantime, he accepted the offer of a rather overeager local Sulpician priest named Gilbert Raymond to oversee the mission and its various works. Raymond was "local" only in the sense that he had come as a *soi-disant*

---

23. Sorin, *Chronicles*, 165.

24. Sorin to Moreau, January 17, 1855, AGEN.

25. Sorin, *Chronicles*, 171.

26. See chapter 17, above.

27. Gouesse was dismissed from the Congregation a few months later. See chapter 16, above.

missionary to Louisiana in 1854; a native of Angers and an acquaintance of Basile Moreau, he had become pastor of a parish in the environs of New Orleans, and he had, with startling alacrity, assumed the status of liaison between New Orleans and Le Mans. However welcome such intervention may have been for the moment, the Founder did not intend to keep the mission permanently supervised by an extern. At the beginning of 1855 he assigned the new French superior; at the same time he instructed Sorin to provide a priest from Notre Dame to act as assistant-superior and stated his intention to institute Louisiana as an independent province.[28]

Sorin, with whatever reluctance—"The administration of [Notre Dame] had no desire to reappear in New Orleans, where it had been so grossly insulted and humiliated by [Gouesse]"[29]—nevertheless complied with this order and dispatched Father Michael Rooney to New Orleans. Rooney—a twenty-five-year-old Irish-American, ordained at Notre Dame in 1853—arrived in the late winter[30] and immediately estranged most of the Holy Cross community by his negativity and high-handed manner. Nor was he slow to communicate to Sorin his opinion of the venture of which he was temporarily in charge: "This is a much God-forsaken, Lord-abandoned place, and the sooner you wash your hands of it the better." He soon followed his own advice: in mid-May he departed Louisiana seeking "a more congenial sphere [and] singing 'Te Deum' for my deliverance."[31] That anthem might well have been chanted also, albeit in a different key, by those he left behind. Rooney in any case, once back in Indiana, did not find that a "congenial sphere" either; he seceded from the congregation later in the year.[32]

There were twenty-two Holy Cross religious in New Orleans by now—ten nuns, six brothers, and a total of six postulants—still conducting the orphan asylum, the workshop for indigent girls, and the little foundling home. Rooney's brief passage among them had only exacerbated their divisions and confusions. Respite of a sort, however, was at hand. Isidore Guesdon, the thirty-year-old priest Moreau had appointed superior, arrived in New Orleans about the time Rooney was contemplating leaving. Guesdon proved an able administrator and, more importantly, a conciliatory and soothing presence; during the brief time allotted him he put to rest much of the dissension and ill-feeling that had so long plagued

---

28. Catta, *Moreau*, 2: 46–47.
29. Sorin, *Chronicles*, 159.
30. Sister Mary of the Passion to Sorin, March 25, 1855, AIP.
31. Quoted in Costin, *Priceless Spirit*, 111.
32. See Sorin to Blanc, May 29, 1855, AIP.

the mission. But the dark cloud that hovered over it was not dissipated: on September 18, 1855—the climax, as it were, of the dreadful year of epidemic, both at Notre Dame and New Orleans—Guesdon died of yellow fever.[33]

This was a particularly dreadful time for Basile Moreau too: it seemed as though the burden that weighed down Holy Cross and its Founder could scarcely be borne. The finances of the motherhouse had fallen perilously close to bankruptcy. The exasperatingly drawn-out negotiations with Rome, to secure formal approbation of the congregation, were apparently as far from resolution as ever. Casual defections, like that of Father Rooney, had become well-nigh commonplace. The almost incredible series of disasters that had befallen the mission in New Orleans now was capped by Guesdon's death. And that unhappy news had hardly been taken in when Sainte-Croix learned that three prize missionaries in Bengal had been lost, one to disease and two to shipwreck.[34] Little wonder that during this autumn of 1855 Father Moreau experienced a searing spiritual crisis, something akin to what the mystics call "the dark night of the soul." Whether he was a mystic in the classical sense may well be open to debate—this must in every instance remain always a deeply personal mystery—but certainly at this time he endured that woeful sense of abandonment by the Lord he was striving to serve which is said to be characteristic of one stage of the mystical vocation.

> At that moment I understood something of our Lord's abandonment in his agony, as he went from his Father to his disciples without finding any consolation. I then understood perfectly the suicide of Judas. . . . At night alone with myself I suffered still more from a sleeplessness which was practically continual. Still I found the night short! "O God," I said to myself, "how fast the time passes! Is this the sun that is appearing again? Why cannot this night be eternal?" Finally, convinced more than ever that everything was crumbling around me, I saw myself destined to become a beggar from door to door. I saw myself mocked and stoned, and I said: "My God, I consent, provided that the Congregation be saved and that thou be glorified."[35]

Little wonder too that the compulsively methodical Moreau, never, even at his best, altogether adept at dealing with the vagaries of the human situation, should have shown small aptitude to handle the crises at hand during this moment when he was so peculiarly vulnerable. "I am in a continual state of affliction

33. Brother Ignatius to Sorin, September [18], 1855, AIP.

34. Catta, *Moreau*, 1: 913–915.

35. This was from a memoir written after the fact. See Charles Moreau, *Moreau*, 2: 38–40.

and extreme distress," he told Edward Sorin at the end of September. "May God have pity on us and watch over you in a very special way."[36] As for New Orleans, Sainte-Croix, with the death of Guesdon, had no candidate available to assume the ill-omened position of superior. Responsibility for the mission there, Moreau reluctantly decreed, had to revert to Notre Dame. Yet, even as he admitted this necessity, he insisted that over the long term Louisiana must remain autonomous—indeed, the very day Guesdon died, documents arrived in New Orleans from Le Mans establishing the mission in the Crescent City an independent province.

Edward Sorin, now formally restored to his rank as provincial, responded to this new mandate in an unexpected fashion.[37] Instead of sending a priest to replace Guesdon, he designated two brothers and three nuns, who were, in Sorin's words, "to make the regular visit of that foundation."[38] Not the least charge in his commission was a financial one, the collection of money he claimed New Orleans owed Notre Dame.[39] Included in the group of investigators, and lending it a kind of constitutional validity, was Sister Mary of the Immaculate Conception, who had come with Sorin from France in January 1854 as the formal Visitor to all the Marianite convents in America.[40] Brother Stephen[41] was to perform the analogous function in the name of the Brothers of St. Joseph. But included also was Sister Mary of the Ascension, lately superior at Bertrand, and one of Sorin's most stalwart supporters. From literally the moment of their arrival in New Orleans—early in November 1855—the emissaries were received, as Sorin recorded the event, in a manner that "trampled underfoot even the arrangements of Sainte-Croix and insulted the envoys from [Notre Dame] in the most outrageous manner." The opening salvo, trivial in itself, established the pattern for the weeks that followed. The party from Indiana appeared at eight o'clock in the evening, an hour after the New Orleans residents had dined—an unwarranted intrusion, said they. The deeper issues were soon joined, and wherever the fault may have lain—whether the visitors were arrogant and imperious, or the residents were unduly

---

36. Moreau to Sorin, September 27, 1855, AGEN.

37. Sorin to Blanc, November 1, 1855, AIP, contains the formal announcement of the Visitation to the archbishop of New Orleans.

38. Sorin, *Chronicles,* 150.

39. See Guesdon to Moreau, n.d. [mid-July, 1855], AGEN. Guesdon complained mildly that Sorin demanded payment but failed to provide the necessary documentation—"for good reasons, no doubt."

40. See chapter 17, above.

41. Brother Stephen, né Finton Moore (1811–1869), served in many responsible capacities at St. Mary's and Notre Dame. See Klawitter, ed., *Adapted to the Lake,* 375.

sensitive[42]—the visitation was a conspicuous failure. Sister Ascension, considered Sorin's spy by her New Orleans co-religionists, had by mid-December returned to Notre Dame, "to the great surprise and mortification" of her colleagues in Indiana, once they learned "of the strange proceedings of the Sisters in New Orleans."[43] Brother Stephen lingered for a month or so, long enough to inform Sorin: "It seems Reverend Father Rector [Moreau] approved the conduct of the members here in resisting your authority."[44]

So, as 1855 drew to a close, Notre Dame's hapless relationship with its daughter-house in New Orleans sputtered toward a quietus. The last fiasco was, for all practical purposes, the last straw. "I am more sorry than I can say," Sorin wrote Archbishop Blanc on December 17, "that we have caused your Excellency further embarrassment, though that was far from our intention." Nonetheless, "I cannot repent for having sent the Visitors, even though their reception and their sojourn were so painful. I owed this proof of my obedience to my Superior whose directive (*requete*) was urgent; and I owed as well this final mark of good will and devotion to you."

> I had not intended to say any more, but at this last moment I wish to be frank and straightforward in a matter that seems to me very grave. To sum up, Monseigneur, I owe it to myself to tell you that if we were to have anything further to do with our original establishments in your episcopal city, it could be only with the assurance of being able to do better than what has been done up till now. Our existence at New Orleans *is a continuous scandal;* the very thought of it makes me blush.[45] I had hoped to see all this sad past rectified, but if my views cannot be realized, and if our Visitors cannot be admitted to perform their functions, it is useless to prolong their stay, and I ask you, Monseigneur, to let them depart immediately.[46]

Archbishop Blanc, ambivalent as ever, needed no urging on the point.

One may reasonably doubt Sorin's claim that the Visitors had been assigned at the Founder's behest; Moreau had in fact wanted a priest-superior to be sent

---

42. See the detailed and finely balanced account in Costin, *Priceless Spirit,* 113–127. Much of this material is treated in the same writer's "The Disastrous Visit: 1855," a paper delivered to the Conference on the History of the Congregations of Holy Cross (1990).

43. Sorin, *Chronicles,* 158–161.

44. Stephen to Sorin, January 30, 1856, AIP.

45. All too characteristically Catta, *Moreau,* 2: 56, quotes this sentence without context in order to put Sorin in the worst possible light.

46. Sorin to Blanc, December 17, 1855, AIP.

from Notre Dame, and certainly the religious in New Orleans had expected such a person rather than a squad of inquisitors. However that may be, the petty quarrels brought on by the Visitation provided hardly more than an epilogue to a sad story that had already been written; indeed, the interdependence of Indiana and Louisiana—which Sorin had promoted for seven or eight years—appears, in retrospect, to have been doomed from the start. The finger of blame could have pointed in many directions: at Moreau's chronic indecisiveness, at the disreputable Gouesse's machinations, at Sorin's ambition and the obsessive revulsion he felt toward Gouesse and his "cruel deception," "his *hypocrisy,*" "his sad conduct in our midst [that] presses down my poor spirit."[47] But at work even more decisively than this combination of human frailties were forces no one, even with the best will, could have controlled: immense distances, crushing poverty, and the ravages of disease.

At any rate, Edward Sorin finally had to recognize the southern game was up. Whether he recognized too that the break represented a divide deeper than a merely geographical one is perhaps less likely. Hot and sultry New Orleans was, to be sure, far removed from the lakes and woodlands and snowy winters of northern Indiana. But it was also a real city, an urban milieu with problems and opportunities very different from the preoccupations of semirural Notre Dame. Moreover, Notre Dame based its missionary activity upon the success of its educational institutions; Holy Cross in New Orleans, by contrast, spent its energies on what could be broadly called the social apostolate. And finally New Orleans still manifested in some degree its French heritage, and the blithe shedding of cultural roots and language—the process of Americanization which Father Sorin had so enthusiastically espoused—left some of his erstwhile colleagues in Louisiana uneasy and even resentful. The Sulpician, Father Raymond, still hovering protectively around the New Orleans mission, was perceptive enough to grasp something of this scarcely conscious antagonism. "All the time," he told Moreau in the midst of the disputed Visitation, "the Sisters [here] were thinking that, if you had known the actual state of the house, you would never have [called upon] Father Sorin, especially if you had known the ardent desire of all the Brothers and Sisters to remain dependent on the Motherhouse, particularly considering the innumerable inconveniences for a house in a hot, feverish climate inhabited by people of a special kind of character to be mixed with a house of an entirely different style."[48] To his credit, Raymond kept watch over the beleaguered mission until reinforcement came from Le Mans in 1857, after which the independent Holy Cross

47. Sorin to Moreau, January 25, 1855, AGEN.
48. Quoted in Costin, *Priceless Spirit*, 123–124. The letter was dated November 28, 1855.

province of Louisiana, with its own character and style, settled into a permanent and successful enterprise of worship and service.[49]

B UT THE SPIRIT of New Orleans had one last trauma to inflict upon Holy Cross in America. The thirty-nine-year-old Sister Mary of the Five Wounds had come to Indiana from France in 1844. A woman of considerable ability and spunk, she had served as superior and then as mistress of novices in Bertrand, during the convent's earliest and harshest days. She had gone with the ill-starred mission to St. Mary's, Kentucky, in 1847 and, when after two troubled years that venture collapsed, had proceeded by riverboat directly to New Orleans.[50] There too she held responsible positions within the community and, later, oversaw the labor school for poor orphan girls. Her behavior, however, was erratic enough to irritate the mild Brother Vincent, who thought her "a little busybody or at least too moody." She returned the compliment by complaining that a "Brother Director of an establishment where there are some Sisters should not believe that he has the right to keep the same Sisters in ignorance of what concerns them."[51] Devoted to the mission and to Father Sorin personally as her spiritual guide, Sister Five Wounds remained restless and unsure of her vocation as a nun—perhaps not too surprising within the chronic anarchy that prevailed in New Orleans. She spoke mournfully at any rate of "difficulties" which she "feared too much to try to challenge them. God grant that he may soon deliver me from them."[52]

In 1854 Sister Five Wounds traveled to France on a begging tour in support of her workshop. While there she "somehow or other obtained an obedience from [Basile Moreau] to found a similar house in New York, and she had even collected funds for that purpose."[53] "Somehow or other" seems to have been an appropriate phrase, because it is unclear precisely how a French nun from Louisiana could have convinced the Founder in Le Mans that she had established contact with patrons as far away from her original posting as New York City—particularly since Moreau surely recalled his annoyance when this same nun had come looking for French money some years earlier.[54] The primary agent in the New

---

49. Connelly, "Holy Cross in New Orleans," 12–14.

50. See chapters 13 and 14, above.

51. Vincent to Sorin, September 19, 1849, and Five Wounds to Sorin, n.d. [December, 1849], AIP.

52. Five Wounds to Sorin, August 6, 1849, AIP.

53. Sorin, *Chronicles*, 164.

54. See chapter 11, above.

York affair appears to have been a priest named Benedict Madéore, a Frenchman who, somewhat mysteriously, had been detached from his affiliation with the Fathers of Mercy and who had nominated himself as the new foundation's superior. Madéore had communicated the proposal to Archbishop Hughes and had gained that prelate's assent.[55] In May or June of 1855 Sister Five Wounds went to New York with the intention of getting the new institution underway, and toward the end of that year Madéore assured Moreau that the project would be underwritten by a prominent Catholic businessman and by other similarly well-disposed and prosperous New Yorkers. In the interval, however, the new Holy Cross superior in Louisiana, Father Guesdon, ordered the nun to return to her duties in New Orleans, but after he died, in September, Sister Five Wounds apparently "thought herself at liberty to . . . act for herself" and returned to New York.[56]

There followed twelve months of confusion and misunderstanding which reopened all the old wounds at Notre Dame and Le Mans, if indeed they had ever been closed. Much of the problem arose, as always, because of the awkwardness in communicating over long distances. Much of it too was traceable to the extreme stress Basile Moreau was at this period undergoing, a circumstance that seriously affected his ability to govern. Through most of 1855 the spiritual malaise that darkened almost his every hour was compounded by the deepening financial crisis confronting Sainte-Croix. In this at least the impulsive Sorin could offer some solace: "It is a great consolation to me," he wrote on October 16, "to be able to come to your aid at this moment of distress. If I have to sell the last acre (*apernt*) of land that has come into my hands in this new world, you will have without delay the 15,000 francs ($3,000) you judge necessary."[57] Actually, instead of selling land, he borrowed the money at a high rate of interest, offering land he owned as security. But even in the midst of making this munificent gesture, Sorin was listening to disquieting rumors about rampant maladministration at the motherhouse, about the Founder's inability to delegate or to maintain the loyalty of his subjects; even his personal agony of soul was dismissed by some "in a very flippant way" as "proof of mental aberration."[58] The death of Bishop Bouvier of Le Mans at the end of 1854 should have been a source of encouragement for Moreau, since it removed the single most powerful obstacle to Roman approval of the congregation, thus opening "a new phase" in its development with a

---

55. New York was elevated to metropolitan status in 1850, and Hughes, bishop since 1842, became first archbishop.

56. Sorin, *Chronicles*, 165–166.

57. Sorin to Moreau, October 16, 1855, AGEN.

58. Sorin, *Chronicles*, 169.

promise of "extraordinary blessings."[59] But even this seemingly providential intervention did not itself assure final success in the negotiations.

Basile Moreau, in short, was hardly in a frame of mind to handle circumspectly still another contretemps with his unruly children in the United States. The proposed Marianite mission to New York nevertheless challenged him with one. At first all went surprisingly smoothly. Sister Five Wounds, assuring all her correspondents that financial support had been secured, requested that staff be assigned her from Notre Dame, Canada, and Le Mans, and each of these centers complied; included in the pair sent from Indiana was the often troublesome Sister Mary of Calvary.[60] With seven nuns as a nucleus, a house was set up on Twenty-ninth Street in Manhattan, and it soon attracted a large number of aspiring postulants. When the workshop-orphanage opened its doors, Archbishop Hughes was delighted with the institution's prospects and grandly predicted that within ten years the three branches of Holy Cross could have as many as twenty-five missions in New York state alone. Confirming such euphoria was talk of the Josephite Brothers procuring a farm outside the city and establishing a school for boys there, and even a rumor that an existing archdiocesan parish might be given over to the ministration of Salvatorist priests was bruited about.[61]

One condition, however, Hughes insisted upon and forcefully expressed through his spokesman, Father Madéore: Holy Cross foundations in New York were to be directly subject to the motherhouse in France. On this point the archbishop remained adamant. He was prepared, he said, to deal amiably with a superior appointed by Sainte-Croix, but—recalling perhaps the unfortunate events in Brooklyn in 1847[62]—he wanted nothing to do with Notre Dame du Lac or Edward Sorin. John Hughes was never a man to mince his words, but Sorin chose, with his usual optimism, to mollify their import. After a three-day visit to New York in the late autumn, he claimed "that neither the archbishop nor Father Madéore nor the Sisters themselves knew on whom the establishment depended and that everybody was tired of the uncertainty." He further asserted "that he was authorized to take the house under his direction and to assume the responsibility for it."[63] Nothing could have alienated Hughes more than this, to him, act of ag-

---

59. Sorin to Moreau, February 12, 1855, AGEN. For Bouvier's opposition see chapter 15, above.

60. See Five Wounds to Sorin, September 6, 1855, AIP. As early as 1844 Sorin had complained about Mary of Calvary's "mischief-making spirit and extravagant imagination. Up till now," he wrote then to Moreau, she "has been my cross." See chapter 10, above.

61. See Catta, *Moreau*, 2: 287.

62. See chapter 13, above.

63. Sorin, *Chronicles*, 166.

gression; to keep Notre Dame out of his diocese, he told Madéore, he would, if necessary, bring suit in Rome.[64]

This confrontation between two strong men placed an already distracted Basile Moreau in a quandary. In his all-too-tenuous peace accord with Notre Dame, he had promised that Sorin should exercise jurisdiction as provincial over all houses in North America, except those in Canada and Louisiana. The Founder could hardly renege on that pledge so recently given without stirring up another hornet's nest. So he indulged in a weak verbal subterfuge: "The New York foundation," he told Madéore, "will depend on the motherhouse through the intermediary of Notre Dame du Lac."[65] Such evasion, however, did not satisfy Hughes in the least. Implicitly, but plainly, he threatened that if Sainte-Croix did not create a separate province in New York—with all the appropriate paraphernalia of distinct novitiates, obediences, professions—he would convert the present Marianite foundation into a diocesan institute. Nor was Holy Cross the only target of the archbishop's resolve to exert control on his home turf; the Jesuits and the Sisters of Mercy were feeling similar pressures. "It is no secret," Sorin observed, "that Monseigneur Hughes is no friend of religious orders."[66] Here was manifest again the constitutional problem inherent to the Catholic system of governance, tension between a bishop and congregations striving to remain exempt from his direct supervision; here again was Moreau versus Bouvier, Sorin versus Hailandière.[67]

Just as these difficulties were taking shape, a familiar southern shadow, though darker now than ever, fell once more across the landscape. Sorin had scarcely come home from New York when, during December, his five emissaries began to trickle back from their aborted charge in New Orleans. The rudeness and contempt with which, allegedly, the official Visitors had been treated had driven the provincial who had sent them there to a furious determination that such an outrage should not be endured twice. By mid-month Sorin's stoutest ally among his envoys to the south, Sister Ascension, had returned to Indiana, and he immediately dispatched her as provincial Visitor once again, this time to New York City. Only a few weeks there convinced the Visitor that her sister in religion, Mary of the Five Wounds, "was not a person to properly manage [the foundation]. Each

---

64. See Sorin to Moreau, June 5, 1856, AGEN.

65. The original agreement between New York and Le Mans was amended by the last phrase ("through the intermediary . . ."), added by Moreau himself. See Catta, *Moreau,* 2: 285.

66. Sorin to Moreau, June 11, 1856, AGEN.

67. For a lengthy defense of Sorin's actions in New York, see Sorin to Drouelle, October 8 and October 30, 1856, AGEN. Not only former intimacy but also the *entré* to various high ecclesiastical officials enjoyed by the Holy Cross superior in Rome prompted Sorin to maintain a heavy correspondence with Drouelle.

day there were new projects, new journeys, and nothing stable, but a constant state of endless changes. Then there were quarrels, dissensions, and sullenness altogether unbecoming in a religious house."[68] Sister Five Wounds, in order to plead her case in person, traveled to Notre Dame on two occasions over succeeding months, but she accomplished thereby nothing substantive.[69] The ambiguity that issued from sources of authority could not but have ended in a mishmash of good intentions and bad feelings. Thus the superior of the Marianites in Canada, a woman known in the community as singularly trusted by Father Moreau, insisted that all directives from Notre Dame du Lac be ignored;[70] Moreau himself, on the other hand, conferred upon Sorin the option that "if the house in New York does not function in dependence on Notre Dame, recall the Sisters."[71] In the midst of such contradictory advisories it is small wonder that "the Chapters of [Notre Dame and St. Mary's] were pained beyond measure at the conduct of the motherhouse. . . . It is useless to write . . . of the suspicions that were entertained as to the causes why Sainte-Croix has offered New Orleans and New York to [Notre Dame]. Oh, there are in the lives of religious societies, as well as in those of individuals, moments of trial which are akin to discouragement, not to mention despair."[72]

But this pious sentiment was expressed after the fact. More directly relevant was Father Sorin's unabated fury at what had happened to his Visitors in New Orleans. On December 31 he coldly informed Moreau that the offer of 15,000 francs of aid to the motherhouse, made only two months before, was now withdrawn and that the money must be returned to Notre Dame posthaste. The explanation he gave was that, though he expected shortly to sell Mount Eagle, the Phelan farm, the proceeds from this transaction would be realized only over a period of years, and such delay, combined with pressing local demands for funds, rendered the earlier generous proposal unfeasible.[73] The real reason, however, he revealed only later.

---

68. Sorin, *Chronicles*, 166–167.

69. For the second visit see Sorin to Moreau, August 26, 1856, AGEN.

70. Costin, *Priceless Spirit*, 133. See also Mary O'Sullivan, "The First Fifty Years in New York," a paper read at the Conference on the History of Holy Cross in the U.S.A. (1985), 1–3, and Graziella Lalande, "Mother Mary of the Seven Dolors as a Person and as Moreau's Collaborator," a paper read at the Eighth Annual Conference on the History of the Congregations of Holy Cross (1989), 1–6.

71. Sorin quotes Moreau directly in Sorin to Moreau, October 24, 1856, AGEN. See the accounts of these events, not altogether consistent, in Catta, *Moreau*, 2: 280–294, and Costin, *Priceless Spirit*, 128–135.

72. Sorin, *Chronicles*, 169.

73. Sorin to Moreau, December 31, 1855, AGEN. "As for the fifteen thousand francs," says Catta, *Moreau*, 2: 59, "the mother house found it absolutely impossible to reimburse them at that time."

The genuine occasion and the partial cause of my change-of-mind was the shocking and disgraceful deception worked upon [Sister Ascension] and Brother Stephen in New Orleans. One could see that these unhappy persons, officially commissioned, had depended for everything upon the authority of Sainte-Croix, just as dear Father Guesdon had done, without much skill, and just like his predecessor [Gouesse] had insolently done over the years. One could see, I say, in this last occurrence a reflection of the sentiments our associates at Sainte-Croix really feel toward us at Notre Dame. The whole past was revived. . . . I had hoped that with great prudence one could come in the end to forget the outrages at New Orleans. *Voila,* the whole business has started anew.[74]

Edward Sorin could not subdue his obsession with New Orleans; it swelled like a cancer within his spirit, or, as he expressed it, it had been "the poison of my existence these seven years."[75] "*You owe it to yourself,*" he wrote Moreau with frantic underscoring, "more even than to us, to take advantage of this latest expression of scorn for your directives by condemning unequivocally all the scandals that the Society of Holy Cross has given over these five years at New Orleans, most often perpetrated in your name as a way of disguising a conduct unworthy of our Congregation."[76]

This baneful attitude strongly affected Sorin in the course of his negotiations with New York. It seemed as though he thought poor Sister Five Wounds had carried with her to Manhattan poisonous fumes straight from the Louisiana bayous. "The sentiment I find prevalent here [in New York]," he reported dejectedly, "is not favorable toward our Congregation; they all know by heart here about our history in the South, and they have no confidence in us." When he sought to parley with the archbishop, Hughes "refused to treat with me personally, because he remembered the failure of our Brothers [in Brooklyn] nine years ago and all the miseries of our mission in New Orleans—as if I were responsible for all those loathsome events."[77] Sorin saw the same specter at every hand. As he argued with the recalcitrant Madéore in New York, he heard a suspicious echo from New Orleans, the allegedly seductive voice of the inoffensive Sulpician, Father Raymond, now presiding informally over the Holy Cross mission there. "I have learned

74. Sorin to Moreau, n.d. [August, 1856], AGEN.
75. Sorin to Moreau, August 25, 1856, AGEN.
76. Sorin to Moreau, January 1, 1856, AGEN.
77. Sorin to Moreau, June 5, 1856, AGEN.

from reliable sources here," he reported with some sarcasm, "the whole history of Mr. Raymond. What a pity that such similar men, set aside by their Order or their Bishop, should find admission into the modest ranks of our young family. Well, seeing that this man still cannot make known to Sainte-Croix his, in our eyes, peculiar activities, it might be beneficial to inquire into them at Baltimore and find out why Mr. Raymond did not remain there very long as head of the St. Mary's Seminary nor even as a member of the Society of Saint-Sulpice. *Voici* the model now copied in New York by Father Madéore."[78]

But, gossip aside, the issue raised at New York was the old familiar one. Now, however, there was a new participant in the game, or rather several new participants. "Sister Angela is very sad, my Reverend Father," Sorin told Moreau,

> to see the dishonor of our Society. Sister Emily,[79] a confidante of hers, told me two days ago some things that made me regret very much that you have not taken steps sooner to assure everybody's peace of mind. I do not hesitate to share my fears with you. . . . They include the ruin of our Congregation in the United States. Mr. and Mrs. Phelan are so happy to be here near their daughter, so devoted, and so forth, but if a misfortune occurs, it will be the end. My Father, our future here is bright, but, alas, it is also precarious! We need to take unlimited precautions. An awkwardness, a blunder (*étourderie*) could place us two fingers from destruction. All that I ask today is to be either entirely discharged or else to be furnished with the full powers of a provincial in the United States; to be assisted by your prayers and those of the Motherhouse; to be vigorously and firmly and unbendingly supported, without intervention from Father Rézé [in Canada] or from anyone in Le Mans; and to deal, finally, on all matters with your Reverence alone. . . . Otherwise, my Reverend Father, I can only tremble for the future.[80]

---

78. Sorin to Moreau, June 11, 1856, AGEN. Unlike the Fathers of Mercy, to which Madéore belonged, the Sulpicians do not compose a religious order. Therefore it was in accord with French usage for Sorin to call Raymond "Mister" and Madéore "Father." For Raymond's problems in Baltimore, see Charles G. Herbermann, *The Sulpicians in the United States* (New York, 1916), 238 and 245. Raymond was "a very attractive man [but] not endowed with executive gifts."

79. Sister Emily was the nun who had accompanied Eliza Gillespie to France for her novitiate at Caen and had made profession with her at Le Mans. See Costin, *Priceless Spirit*, 74–76, and chapter 17, above.

80. Sorin to Moreau, January 1, 1856, AGEN. William Phelan died a few months after this letter was written. See above.

In Sorin's mind the Gillespie/Phelan connection remained absolutely crucial, and not only because of the financial advantages that had accompanied it. In the Gillespie children he had found kindred spirits. Young Father Neal, soon to return from his brief studies in Rome, would be, Sorin asserted, "absolutely indispensable here as vice president [of the university]."[81] As for Eliza Maria, now Sister Angela—"the one I have been praying for"—Father Sorin, impressed as much by her background and social standing as by her undoubted competence, turned more and more to her for counsel. After all, he explained to his surely uncomprehending confrères back in France, this was the woman who "during her two years as a student in Washington received from the hands of the President of the United States himself the top scholastic awards from the convent of the Visitation in Georgetown."[82] That this claim was doubtless apocryphal mattered little, since Sorin's regard for Sister Angela's talents rested upon much more solid grounds. Indeed, he worried that if she grew disenchanted with Holy Cross, and her widowed mother with her, the result could be calamitous. "Occasionally Sister Emily shares with me information she thinks important. Yesterday I learned from her that Sister Angela was experiencing serious temptations about her vocation. She was shocked at our scandalous discords, and almost all she had seen about Sainte-Croix, and especially"—the rebuke was, predictably, directed at Father Moreau—"at your conduct with regard to New Orleans. . . . Suppose she retired [from the Congregation] and . . . Madame Phelan, today so happy and so glad to be near her daughter, should consequently repudiate us. What right would we have in the eyes of the world to preserve their benefaction to us? My Father, if you do not take care, thus shall we perish."[83]

Whatever her inner misgivings, however, Sister Angela gave little outward sign that the scandalous debacle in New Orleans would bedevil her as it had Edward Sorin. Indeed, from the beginning of the crisis in New York she assumed a strong and straightforward position. It was due to her insistence, supported by that of her friend Sister Emily, that Sorin had in the first place sent Sister Ascension to New York as Visitor.[84] In April 1856 she went there herself and found the disarray and muddle she probably expected. She was in any case at the same time engaged in negotiating with the bishop of Philadelphia, who appeared much more amenable than his episcopal colleague in New York to support an institute not unlike that which Sister Five Wounds was attempting to set up in Manhattan but

81. Sorin to Moreau, July 20, 1856, AGEN.
82. Sorin to Moreau and his Council in Le Mans, December 10, 1856, AGEN.
83. Sorin to Moreau, n.d. [August, 1856], AGEN.
84. Sorin to Moreau, January 1, 1856, AGEN. See also above.

which would maintain a Notre Dame affiliation. In June, Sorin himself, after a fruitless stopover in New York, went to Philadelphia where he found "the Bishop[85] enchanted at our work, especially among young girls. He wants to have our entire Congregation in his diocese. This will pour oil over the wounds of New York. . . . If the Archbishop [of New York] remains intractable, we shall move our camp to Philadelphia."[86]

One last attempt was made, however, to reach an accommodation with Hughes and Madéore. Under the misconception that the archbishop had softened his position, Sorin, in the late summer, sent Father Richard Shortis to New York in the vain hope that he would be accepted as superior by the diocesan authorities. This was a somewhat chancy appointment, because Shortis, a schoolfellow of Neal Gillespie, had earlier given evidence of a drinking problem;[87] to have put him into such a pressure-packed situation testified to Sorin's restored confidence in the forty-one-year-old Irishman or else simply to the sparseness of priests available within the ever-expanding Holy Cross mission—or probably to both. Shortis's assignment in any event changed nothing: "Scarcely had he arrived in New York when he discovered that the archbishop entertained the same sentiments" as Sorin had encountered in June. Secure in Moreau's directive to "recall the sisters" if matters went awry in New York, Sorin, in August, dispatched four nuns to the "solidly founded" institute in Philadelphia and three others to an orphanage in Washington.[88] "We have nothing to fear from the fall of New York," he assured Basile Moreau.[89]

The final act in the drama was played out by Sister Angela, but not without unpleasantness. In October, formally named Visitor by Father Sorin, she went to New York "to save the mission there if she could see any way to do so. . . . But after a painful interview with the archbishop and a thorough examination of the situation," she telegraphed Sorin that the house was beyond remedy and should be closed. She acted, Sorin said, with an "admirable tact" which should have "shut every malicious mouth." Some of the affected nuns, however, thought that this parvenue Visitor had come with no intention of preserving their house, and in

---

85. John Neumann (1811–1860). Sorin, *Chronicles*, 184, with foresight called him "the holy bishop"; Neumann was canonized in 1977.

86. Sorin to Moreau, June 21, 1856, AGEN.

87. See Shortis to Sorin, August 12, 1854, AIP, in which Shortis admits to a "scandal" he had been responsible for. He promised to abstain from whiskey and brandy, "but, as to wine, beer, cider, or other liquors not called *ardent*, I believe they may be used occasionally without danger to the person or scandal to others."

88. Sorin, *Chronicles*, 185.

89. Sorin to Moreau, October 24, 1856, AGEN.

this judgment, despite Sorin's protestations, they were no doubt correct. Some of them, especially the unstable Mary of Calvary, reacted with violent language and even with a push and a shove. A postulant present told Sorin of the insults Sister Angela had had to endure. "They treated her as Jesus Christ was treated in his passion. God had to help her in a special way."[90] But Eliza Maria Gillespie was not one to be easily intimidated. She briskly closed the house in New York, sent the nuns willing to go to Philadelphia—but not Mary of the Five Wounds, who withdrew from the community[91]—and the postulants back to Notre Dame. Most of the orphan girls were transferred to a new foundation at Susquehana, in northeast Pennsylvania.[92]

EVEN AS IT WAS BEING SHUT DOWN, the house in New York gave Edward Sorin one last distressing moment. Neal Gillespie, on his way home from Italy, disembarked in New York just as his beloved sister was enduring tribulation on Twenty-ninth Street. He was not pleased at what he learned from her. "Father Gillespie," Sorin reported worriedly on October 24, "has left New York and gone to his family [in Ohio], so aggrieved that he has not written here or sent any notification."[93] Two days later word had still not come from the young priest. But Sorin's fears in this instance proved illusory, and soon Gillespie had returned to Notre Dame and assumed the vice-presidency reserved for him. It was well that he did so for, just at this moment, his mother was causing Sorin no little anxiety. Mrs. Phelan had grown despondent since her husband's death, not least because the $3,000 annuity due her was temporarily in arrears. "I am afraid," Sorin lamented, "that she has lost confidence in me. . . . We count too much on the patience of our friends, and we do not know well enough how to keep them."[94]

The Gillespie connection, despite some rocky passages, was, in fact, safe and enduring. Meanwhile, there was much else for Holy Cross in America to rejoice about as 1856 neared its end. The failure in New York, the sour memories of New Orleans, and even the lingering and mutual mistrust between Notre Dame and Sainte-Croix could not obscure the astonishing expansion over which Father Sorin had presided in so short a time. Indeed, the setbacks almost paled in comparison with the measurable progress. "My contention is," he proudly informed Moreau

---

90. Sorin to Moreau, October 24, 1856, AGEN.

91. See Costin, *Priceless Spirit*, 240. Mary of Calvary was given $25 for a ticket to New Orleans.

92. Sorin, *Chronicles*, 183–184, 186.

93. Sorin to Moreau, October 24, 1856, AGEN.

94. Sorin to Moreau and the Council in Le Mans, December 10, 1856, AGEN.

and the council at Le Mans, "that the actual state of the Congregation [in the United States] is prosperous and full of promise for the future."

> We now have eighteen establishments. Holy Cross now counts 238 members: eighteen Salvatorist priests, 80 Josephite brothers, 140 Marianite sisters. The figures show that we are teaching a total of 3000 children, of whom 131 and 66 are boarders respectively at Notre Dame and St. Mary's. As to personnel and foundations, the numbers exceed by more than a third those of 1855. The Congregation is regarded most favorably, and the odds at this moment are ten to one that it will succeed in this country. From all sides we are asked to establish foundations, and if only a little prudence guides the whole administration of the work, there can be no doubt about its development and great utility. The public has confidence in our work, and this is today our guarantee; if this confidence should disappear, the work will almost certainly (*immanquablement*) disappear also.[95]

New York and New Orleans were, to be sure, lost to Sorin's roll call, and Canada remained unattainable. Still, footholds in Washington and Philadelphia, combined with the establishments across the Middle West, afforded plenty of compensation. But potentially "the most important of all the dependencies of the Province of Indiana," Sorin claimed, was that set up by contract with the bishop of Chicago that same year, 1856. "The House of Chicago will probably share in the destinies of the city . . . which . . . [in] the opinion of the public . . . will be one of the first cities of the Union." So came to fruition, at least for the time being, the seeds planted by the invaluable Brother Stephen six years before.[96] The bishop, Anthony O'Regan by name, first proposed to sell to Holy Cross his infant and moribund St. Mary's University for $60,000, payable in twelve annual installments with no interest. In return Sorin agreed to operate day schools in the extant buildings for both girls and boys, assign brothers and sisters to teach in several parishes in the city, and eventually to open an industrial school. A key element in the transaction was O'Regan's commitment that Holy Cross be given the pastorate of a relatively large parish, from which, it was presumed, revenue could be realized to help meet the yearly purchase payment.[97]

The formalities were almost completed when Father Sorin hesitated, perhaps because he was intimidated by the prospect of an annual outflow of $5,000 for this

95. Sorin to Moreau and the Council in Le Mans, December 10, 1856, AGEN.
96. See chapter 15, above.
97. The text of the agreement is printed in Sorin, *Chronicles*, 225–226.

single undertaking. He decided to consult Hugh Ewing, son of Senator Thomas Ewing, brother of Maria Ewing Sherman, and so part of that Lancaster, Ohio, coterie that had included Eilza Gillsespie.[98] Young Ewing, now practicing law in St. Louis, thoroughly examined the terms of the contract and advised Sorin against consummating it, on the grounds that the diocese's legal right to sell was suspect. O'Regan, still anxious to obtain the services of Holy Cross, then offered to lease the same property for fifty years, for payment of a $2,000 annual rent.[99] Sorin in turn pledged "to maintain . . . a select and very respectable school, with full liberty to add thereto any other school for Brothers, Sisters, of trades, a Catholic bookstore, etc." Furthermore Notre Dame du Lac was promised preference when it came to the staffing of diocesan grammar schools, as they eventuated, and a parochial center to act in concert with and in support of the educational institutions.[100] "The first years of this establishment cannot but be onerous to the Congregation," Sorin granted, "but afterwards it is more than probable that these advances will be fully refunded." After some inevitable and, to the bishop, irritating delay,[101] two priests, five brothers, and fifteen sisters were assigned to this endeavor, and, although in the long run the arrangement did not work out,[102] Sorin can surely be forgiven for his euphoria at the prospect, nor can he be faulted for his judgment. "Chicago is the center of the West. . . . Now Illinois seems especially destined, considering its proximity and its Catholic population, to become the granary of Notre Dame. There was therefore no recoiling from any sacrifice, no matter how great, to secure such an advantageous position."[103]

Certainly this remarkable growth and widespread acceptance did not constitute the whole picture for Holy Cross in the United States. Financial danger lurked just around the corner, making "everything here precarious. Although the totality of our indebtedness does not equal that of our possessions (*avoir*), nevertheless, if Heaven permitted this very night that fear should suddenly grip of all our creditors at once, after tomorrow our ruin would be inevitable." Taking account of outstanding loans, mortgages, and regular interest and annuity payments, the mission's debt amounted to $32,000. Sorin was confident that the property at

---

98. See chapter 17, above. Sister Angela was personally involved in the negotiations with the bishop of Chicago (see O'Regan to Sorin, July 26, 1856, AIP), and it is not unlikely that Ewing was consulted at her behest.

99. With an additional 7.5 percent interest, the actual yearly payment totaled $2,150. See Sorin, *Chronicles*, 229.

100. See "Memorandum of Agreement," dated May 28 and amended August 4, 1856, AIP.

101. See O'Regan to Sorin, July 26, 1856, AIP.

102. See chapter 20, below.

103. Sorin, *Chronicles*, 187–189.

Notre Dame and St. Mary's "would be valued today, without exaggeration, at $100,000, but I doubt that if it were sold at auction it would fetch more than a quarter of that sum."[104] Vigilance was still the watchword.

But celebration was appropriate too, after this time of extraordinary progress. On November 12, 1856, a carillon composed of twenty-three chimes, ordered from a foundry in Le Mans, was blessed and fixed in the bell towers flanking the entrance to the campus church. Archbishop Purcell, his fences with Sorin mended, presided at the ceremony, which "was attended by a numerous concourse of priests and visitors" and which "was as solemn as it could be." The original donor had reneged on his offer of funds, and so the community, after four years of negotiation and argument with the manufacturers,[105] had had to absorb the cost of 18,000 francs ($3,600). Sorin tried to evade paying import duties on the bells, but his repeated appeals to the local congressman for special legislation were in vain.[106] If this investment in chimes was an extravagance, it belonged to the same genre as the purchase of the "museum" a decade and more before, and was perfectly characteristic of Edward Sorin at his most flamboyant. "There is no doubt," he said, "but that the effect of this magnificent carillon, the first of its kind in the United States, is a most favorable one for Notre Dame."[107]

---

104. Sorin to Moreau and the Council in Le Mans, December 10, 1856, AGEN.

105. See, for example, Bollée to Sorin, March 4 and December 15, 1854, AIP, demanding payment. In Sorin to Bollée, February 22, 1854, AIP, instructions were given as to how the bells were to be inscribed. The first was to bear the names of Pius IX, Purcell, Saint-Palais, and Moreau; the next nine were to honor the Virgin under various titles ("Mary of the Annunciation," etc.); and each of the final thirteen was to display the name of a saint (including Basil, Edward, and, for France, Denis).

106. Colfax to Sorin, April 9, 1856, and January 7, 1857, AIP. Schuyler Colfax (1824–1885) served in the House of Representatives from 1855 till 1869, the last six years as Speaker. He was vice president during the first Grant administration (1869–1873).

107. Sorin, *Chronicles*, 190.

chapter nineteen

Mixed Blessings

B Y THE BEGINNING OF 1856 BASILE MOREAU'S GRIM passage through doubt and spiritual dryness—what he himself called this "terrible temptation"—had run its course. His trials were far from over, but never again would his soul descend so deep into the slough of near despair. And an answer was shortly to come to the prayer which, his intimates affirmed, had been constantly on his lips during even the darkest days: "My God, I accept everything, provided the congregation be saved and that Thou be glorified."[1] On May 19 a pontifical Brief *ad laudandum*—a formal statement "in praise" of Holy Cross and its works—was signed at Rome; in effect this declaration meant that full recognition of the Congrégation de Sainte-Croix as an exempt religious order within the Church would presently follow. "My dear Sons and daughters in Jesus Christ," the Founder wrote exultantly a few days later, "at last, after five years of waiting, and just after the close of the most painful trial of my life, it is my privilege to satisfy your holy impatience by laying before you the authentic documents which have come from the highest authority on earth. . . . I know you will share my joy and gratitude on reading these documents, whose date will be most memorable in our annals, particularly because it will bring to mind the sweet month of Mary." Details remained to be worked out, and, characteristic of the leisurely Roman *modus operandi*, it was not until eleven months later that the congregation's Rules and Constitutions received official approbation.[2]

---

1. Catta, *Moreau*, 2: 110–111.

2. For a copy of the decree, dated May 13, 1857, and signed by Cardinal Barnabò, Prefect of Propaganda, see Sorin Papers, AIP.

The distinction between these two categories was not always precise, but, in general, "Rules" defined the code of personal conduct appropriate to a religious of Holy Cross, while "Constitutions" set out the principles of the congregation's governance. In this latter sphere, Moreau followed for the most part a pattern adopted by most of the orders founded during the nineteenth century. The supreme governing body was the general chapter, which was to meet every four years or more often if extraordinary circumstances required it. All the local communities were to be represented in the General Chapter, both by ex officio members and by elected delegates. The superior general, chief executive of the congregation, was to be elected by the General Chapter, over the meetings of which he presided. He was to be aided in central administration by a Council of Advisers, attached to the motherhouse, as well as by two assistants, a secretary, and a steward or financial officer. A special post, that of procurator general, was created in order to assure that Holy Cross was properly represented at the curia in Rome, where this priest normally resided. The congregation for administrative purposes was to be subdivided into smaller, geographically limited units—"vicariates" at first and, as numbers increased, "provinces"—and these entities mirrored in their structure the organization of the motherhouse: the ruling body was to be the local chapter with legislative powers for the houses in the relevant region, a vicar or provincial as director, advised by a permanent council—what was called in the early days at Notre Dame the "Minor Chapter"—and aided by a variety of assistants and lesser officers. All in all, though he drafted them in accord with a conventional model, the Rules and Constitutions nevertheless reflected the Founder's neat mind and his obsession with theoretical detail.[3]

Moreau was disappointed, however, in one of his fondest ambitions, the fulfillment of his "general plan" whereby priests, brothers, and nuns would be welded into a single corporate body. Approval had been granted only to "a Community of priests and brothers, the question of the sisters being postponed for special discussion at some future date." The pope had proved immovable on this issue, a decision that sowed seeds of trouble for the future. But for the moment rejoicing was in order: "Thanks be to the God of all consolation for dispelling the anxiety and trials which have so long plunged us in sadness."[4]

---

3. Over the years this fundamental document has inevitably been refined, but the basic spirit and structure remains. The term "Rules," however, was eventually eliminated. See *Constitutions of the Congregation of Holy Cross* (n.p. [Rome], 1951).

4. Moreau, *Circular Letters,* 1: 342, dated May 25, 1856. For the "general plan" and Pius IX's opposition to it, see chapter 15, above.

Whatever pious expressions of grief may have issued from Sainte-Croix, the death of Bishop Bouvier had without doubt facilitated Holy Cross's negotiations with the curia and had opened the way as well to the appointment of a much more amicable successor. Indeed, the passing of that sturdy Gallican permitted Rome without much fuss to divide the vast diocese of Le Mans and to institute a new bishop at Laval (whose jurisdiction, incidentally, included Ahuillé, Edward Sorin's birthplace). Meanwhile a second mission was opened in Italy and a new one in Poland and several more in metropolitan France. A tangible sign of this newfound exuberance could be seen in the erection of a conventual church in Sainte-Croix. It was a neo-Gothic structure, set within the quadrangle of other of the congregation's buildings, its hillside site making it visible from the four corners of Le Mans.[5] After a series of eight daily sermons preached by a notable Dominican friar, on June 17, 1857, the new church was dedicated by the cardinal-archbishop of Bordeaux, in the presence of a glittering company, including, from Rome, Count Marino Torlonia, who had been Sorin's genial host some years before.[6] Amidst a host of fulsome oratory, perhaps Moreau's speech was the most heartfelt, delivered as it was to his persevering confreres: "Dearly beloved brethren, continue to live this holy life. . . . This is your life. Live it, if possible, even with more holy zeal than in the past. . . . Go forth then, humble and noble soldiers, some to lowly schools, others to far-off missions. Go forth!"[7]

In far-off Indiana, to which so many sons and daughters of Holy Cross had gone forth—and to whom had been added so many others who knew nothing of France—the news of the Roman decree of approbation was received with appropriate, if somewhat muted, appreciation. "What made the year [1857] forever memorable in the annals of the Congregation," Father Sorin recorded, "was the . . . the approbation by the Holy See. . . . Thus was raised to the rank of the regular orders of the Church a society which had only a few years of existence and for which such an early encouragement became a pledge of other special favors from heaven." Such lofty endorsement, he believed, should put to rest the agitations of certain "unbelievers" and "discontented spirits," unnamed, who "took occasion to [readdress] the list of their grievances against the society and its venerable Founder." But whoever such malcontents may have been, and however baneful their influence was, Sorin himself maintained that "willy nilly the

---

5. Today the church still stands, fronted by its little piazza, somewhat shabby and forlorn, but still in parochial use. The adjacent buildings have since disestablishment (1905) been converted to other than ecclesiastical purposes. To the church's left, for example, is a military barracks.

6. See chapter 15, above.

7. Catta, *Moreau*, 2: 230–231, 233–239.

work of Sainte-Croix in the United States will bear its own characteristic mark, its family escutcheon, the royal seal of the cross." Indeed, as ready as he was to acknowledge the triumph of Moreau's Roman negotiations, Sorin's immediate source of consolation, as 1857 unfolded, came from favorable statistics closer to home: "The year was remarkable," he said, "by the growth of the College [at Notre Dame]," in which "there were about 200 entries . . . [and] a mean of 140 [students]. . . . St. Mary's Academy kept pace in this movement and, . . . [though] there was a lack of accommodations, . . . yet there were at least ten entries more than in the best years at Bertrand, more regular classes," thanks to Sister Angela, and a total of sixty boarders at the new property, still being developed, on the banks of the St. Joseph River.

Not only was Sorin encouraged by the increased figures for matriculation and residence: "A good number of the students," he observed, "belong to a higher and more comfortable class." Sprung from the gentry himself, he presumably could recognize the difference between the barefoot farm boys from the immediate neighborhood who had predominated at Notre Dame during the 1840s and those of a better social standing, recruited now, thanks to the railroads, from all over the Midwest. This combination of greater numbers and enhanced gentility led him at any rate to alter his administrative style in one significant respect and to usher in the disciplinary ethos that was to characterize Notre Dame for a century. During the early years Sorin—much to the immense irritation of the priggish Brother Gatien—had adamantly refused to impose upon the students a strict code of conduct for fear that to do so would drive them away and thus threaten the institution's very existence.[8] Now, however, confident that the college was on solid footing, he reversed himself and endorsed a severity which, in truth, was much more consistent with his authoritarian temper. One student, for example, who had insulted his teachers, had to endure "a severe lecture, public recantation, and at least one day's meals on his knees in the refectory." Non-Catholics who refused to kneel during prayers offered before and after class were expelled.[9] These grim and sometimes draconian measures became the norm, though Sorin chose to express his revamped policy in rather laconic terms: "More order and greater respect for rules were seen, discipline was more vigorous."[10]

---

8. See chapter 10, above.

9. Council Book of the Faculty, minutes, February 15, 1857, and February 20, 1858, UFMM, AUND. It should be recalled that non-Catholics were excused from any formal or informal instruction in religion but were required "to assist at the religious services with decorum." See *Annual Catalogue of the University of Notre Dame* (1855).

10. Sorin, *Chronicles*, 192.

Yet it seemed that as ever the mission's steps forward were appended by one back, some sobering reminder of how precarious its situation really was. Thus on the eve of this "remarkable" expansion, just weeks after the festive blessing of the new carillon, fire—so often Notre Dame's nemesis—had broken out in the stable, "and in spite of all efforts the building and all that belonged to it were swept away. . . . Two horses were reduced to ashes, with a quantity of corn, oats, salt, meat, harness, [and] farm implements. . . . The loss amounted to fifteen thousand francs. There was no insurance." This "severe scourge" had disheartened Sorin exceedingly, and, with his accustomed hyperbole, he described it as having "brought us to the very verge of total ruin." Not only had "two fine horses [and] 10,000 pounds of meat" been consumed by the flames: "During a whole hour the church and college were in imminent danger. . . . Never had we been yet so near our complete annihilation."[11] Even so, frightening as the conflagration had been— Sorin watched from the bell tower of the church and saw "the air . . . afire with sparks"—it had in the end been contained. "Doubtless the Blessed Virgin did not permit that all [our] labors would be destroyed in one stroke."[12]

The destruction of the stable proved an ill omen of more difficulties to come. Sorin was uneasy once again at the fresh rise in indebtedness—amounting in all to about $7,000, not counting interest payments—thanks to the debacle in New York and the latest initiative in Chicago, then to "the purchase of the carillon and our recent fire and our foundation in Philadelphia," the house organized the previous year by Sister Angela.[13] It might be necessary, he mused, to sell some real estate in order to cover these costs. But retrenchment was also imperative. He directed the sisters' superior in Philadelphia to watch her accounts scrupulously: "Our present embarrassments preclude all serious thought of any unessential expenses for the present year." This did not mean, however, that the nuns were to endure any deprivation beyond what holy poverty required: "I am told your table is too scanty. This will be ruinous; use your discretion but see all [your associates] comfortable." To augment their apostolate in the city, he dispatched two brothers from Notre Dame, Ignatius and John Chrysostom, both, Sorin said, promising young men.[14] "You had better send their meals to the brothers," which, however, did not mean that socializing should be encouraged: "Be severe in forbidding

---

11. Sorin to Sister Mary of the Immaculate Conception (in Philadelphia), January 2, 1857, AGEN.

12. Sorin, *Chronicles,* 190–193, 179.

13. See chapter 18, above.

14. The previous summer Sorin had pledged to send brothers to serve in a parish in Philadelphia. See Sorin to Frenaye, July 24 and August 22, 1856, AIP.

unnecessary intercourse [with the sisters]."[15] All in all, therefore, he spent the eight days of his mid-February visitation to the community in Philadelphia in a mood of cautious optimism. The bishop and clergy of the city, he reported to Moreau, were highly supportive of Holy Cross. "I found an establishment with a bright future. There is a labor-school with 29 [female] boarders and a few day-pupils; ten postulants are in residence; in one school four sisters teach 200 little girls, and in another two brothers teach 200 little boys."[16]

But by the spring Father Sorin had to change his tune. "I have seen financial crises in the United States before, but nothing that resembles what I see today." The panic of 1857 was in full swing. "There is absolutely no money available to us. We are at the mercy of a crowd of creditors; up till now God has inclined them toward patience in our regard, and I would like to perceive in that patience a token of very special protection from on high." This was an awkward moment for the motherhouse, also severely strapped for cash, to request a draft for 1,500 francs as an unspecified reimbursement. Sorin acknowledged the debt, but, he maintained, "it is impossible to borrow any money today. . . . I cannot respond in any manner beyond what in fact we can do."[17] Two months later he protested that not only could he not borrow with property as collateral, he could not even sell real estate, at least not any located east of the Mississippi. "I ask you therefore," he appealed to Moreau, "for permission to authorize me placing on sale a piece of land of about 400 acres in Iowa which perhaps can be sold more easily than the rest, given at this time the flow of westward immigration."[18] How he had come into the ownership of such property Sorin did not bother to reveal.

Whatever the source of this asset, by the summer of 1857 the financial situation across the country had so deteriorated that, among other crises, the richly promising institute in Philadelphia—where the financial disarray "was more severe than in other city of the Union"[19]—stood "in extreme peril." One of the two dwellings originally rented to Holy Cross had to be vacated for lack of funds, and the operations of the sisters consolidated uncomfortably into a single residence. "They obtained from Bishop Neumann permission to take up a collection, which so far has brought in $1,400, and they plan a fair this autumn which might produce between $5,000 and $7,000." Perhaps that prediction was overly sanguine,

15. Sorin to Immaculate Conception, January 26, 1857, AIP. The word "intercourse" in this context should not be misconstrued.

16. Sorin to Moreau, February 16, 1857, AGEN.

17. Sorin to Moreau, May 19, 1857, AGEN. See also Catta, *Moreau*, 2: 299–302, where, as usual, the worst construction is placed upon Sorin's motives and actions.

18. Sorin to Moreau, July 24, 1857, AGEN.

19. Sorin, *Chronicles*, 196.

but the pluck of the sisters, in the midst of this emergency, was remarkable in any case. "They have decided," Sorin reported, "after consultation with the good bishop, to buy a house almost new, . . . an excellent brick structure of three storeys with a good cellar, built on a lot 200 by 250 feet, close to a large and magnificent Protestant cemetery, where they can take the air and go for agreeable walks."[20] What meditations the sisters may have entertained as they strolled among the heretical graves remains unrecorded. They met at any rate the asking price for the property of $16,000, put $2,000 of it down, and, as Sorin expressed it, hoped to find the balance in "the treasury of Providence."[21] The move to quiet, bucolic West Philadelphia ultimately proved over the next decade to have been a success-ful gamble. The sisters, eighteen of them by this time, held their fair in Sep-tember, the increasingly assertive Sister Angela traveling east from Indiana to supervise it.[22]

"I would have preferred," Father Sorin observed, "that the sisters delay their purchase until the receipts from the collection and the fair were in hand. But the good Sisters of St. Joesph"—another French community, active in Philadelphia since 1847—"were also interested in acquiring the property, and had the bishop not expressed a preference for us, the house would have been sold to them."[23] So in this instance of competition among religious Holy Cross had prevailed. Not so, however, in a venue much more important to Sorin than Philadelphia.

The Reverend Father Jesuits have come to Chicago and established them-selves at our very doors. They have already bought a ground-plot for $20,000. They plan to build a church on this site and afterwards a college. Father Daimon [sic],[24] Belgian by birth and, by all reports, one of their more impressive members, has been sent to Chicago after working marvels in St. Louis for eighteen years. I cannot prevent myself from sincerely re-joicing at this contribution to the public weal; but neither can I prevent myself from seeing in the arrival of these good Fathers the grass of our best pasturage cut from under our feet, to the detriment of our house in Chicago

---

20. Sorin to Moreau, July 14, 1857, AGEN.

21. Sorin, *Chronicles*, 196.

22. For full and interesting details, see Mary Campion Kuhn, "Holy Cross in Philadelphia: 1856–1865," a paper read at the Conference on the History of the Congregation of Holy Cross (1982), 2–8.

23. Sorin to Moreau, July 14, 1857, AGEN.

24. Arnold Damen, S.J. (1815–1890), was a prodigious missionary who labored in Missouri and Illinois. See Gilbert J. Garraghan, *The Catholic Church in Chicago, 1673–1871* (Chicago, 1921), 169–175.

and of Notre Dame. If we had foreseen this development, we would scarcely have taken on the project in Chicago; now it is necessary for us to believe that Heaven will provide adequate resources.[25]

But heavenly aid was not forthcoming. From the beginning the arrangements with Bishop O'Regan went awry, because, as far as Sorin was concerned, the bishop refused "to abide by his own promises. . . . The school-houses of the Brothers and Sisters were left in such a miserable state that there was [sic] no means of doing good. The promised collections and fairs had been restricted," just at the moment when funds were so desperately needed. And to cap it off, "the Jesuit Fathers had come to Chicago with the intention of building a church and a college, thus unintentionally destroying one of the principal objectives of the Congregation of Holy Cross when it settled in that city."[26]

D ESPITE PLENTY OF THREATS AND ALARMS, this was a time not without its homely joys. July 17, the feast of St. Alexis, and so "the good Father Granger's festival," was celebrated with a special banquet. Then two days later "came the turn of old Brother Vincent, and we all took a walk out under his beautiful trees; [the moment] will never be forgotten by the good, venerable Patriarch. In three hours everything was prepared, and it was the best celebration ever seen at Notre Dame. Dear good old friend, how much I enjoyed it with him! We held Benediction of the B[lessed] S[acrament] in the dear little rotunda chapel at eight o'clock in the evening. The children and professed [sisters] from St. Mary's were there and sang, and at quarter of nine all went home. There is no place in the whole world where I rejoice more or as much to meet."[27] But the great event of the summer was the arrival at Notre Dame du Lac of the Founder himself.

Basile Moreau had long pledged to visit his congregation's missions in North America. Indeed, he might well have undertaken the journey as long before as 1848, had not the revolution of that year so sharply unsettled matters in Le Mans.[28] After that he was largely preoccupied with the Roman negotiations, all through

25. Sorin to Moreau, May 19, 1857, AGEN.

26. Sorin, *Chronicles*, 196. O'Regan (1809–1866), notoriously cantankerous, was forced into retirement in 1858. See Garraghan, *Catholic Chicago*, 167–179. For Sorin's continuing problems in Chicago, see chapter 20, below.

27. Sorin to Immaculate Conception, July 21, 1857, AIP. Since the reform of the liturgical calendar during the 1960s, the memorial to St. Alexis, formerly observed on July 17, has been eliminated, and that of St. Vincent de Paul transferred from July 19 to September 27.

28. See chapter 13, above.

which he had had to guard his flank locally against the hostile maneuvers of Bishop Bouvier. Nor can it be concluded with certainty, after all the bickering and disagreement, that he did not hesitate at the prospect of facing Edward Sorin on the latter's own ground; Father Moreau's administrative skills were limited, and direct confrontation was not one of them. But now Bouvier was dead, and Rome had approved Holy Cross's constitutions. In the wake of the euphoria engendered by these developments, and perhaps still warmed by the glow of the splendid ceremonial consecration of the mother-church of Sainte-Croix, Moreau turned his eyes and aspirations westward. The steamer *Fulton* departed Le Havre on July 28, 1857.

The voyage across the north Atlantic was difficult, marked by contrary winds and bitter cold. Nevertheless, the passage was swift compared to what had prevailed so recently when vessels were propelled only by sail, and the *Fulton* docked in New York on August 11. After a courtesy call on Archbishop Hughes, Moreau the same day boarded the train for Montreal. He spent two weeks in Quebec province and confessed himself much edified by the spirit of the Holy Cross communities there. He came as formal Visitor, and his self-imposed official charge was to promulgate the newly approved constitutions, which involved presiding over the elections to councils and the canonical installation of superiors for the priests and brothers on the one hand and for the sisters on the other.[29] But, quite in character, he also expended much time and energy in devotional ceremonies of various kinds, and offered spiritual direction to each religious individually. The favorable impression he left was summed up by one of the nuns: "Our Very Reverend Father could tear the house down, and no one would say a word."[30] From a constitutional point of view, the most important directive issued by Moreau in Canada was that, given the qualification insisted upon by Rome, the finances of the male members of Holy Cross had to be kept separate from that of the Marianite Sisters. This directive was accepted without debate.

On the morning of August 26 Basile Moreau stepped off the train at the station in South Bend. His arrival was of course expected, but not on that day and not in that place. Father Sorin was in Chicago preaching a retreat, and Father Granger had been dispatched to Detroit under the impression that he would meet the Founder there and conduct him to Notre Dame du Lac.[31] They failed to

---

29. Catta, *Moreau*, 2: 303–308.

30. See Moreau, *Circular Letters*, 2: 31, dated September 25, 1857, "on the Atlantic Ocean."

31. For the proposed rendezvous in Detroit, see Letourneau to Sorin, August 19, 1857, AIP. Louis Letourneau, having finished his theological studies in Rome, was accompanying Moreau on his journey to America. He was ordained for the Indiana province shortly afterward.

connect, so Moreau had to hire a conveyance to bring him the two miles or so to the campus.

> I got out of the carriage at the post office [he recalled], and my presence astonished the Irish Brother who was busy sorting mail. The news of my arrival soon spread. The large church-bell and the twenty-two others that make up the magnificent [carillon] began to ring out. Just as at Saint-Laurent [in Quebec] there was much running about, and everyone was asking: "Why are they ringing the bells? Why all the excitement?"[32]

Granger returned later in the day, as did Sorin, who, however, came back pale and ill. Nevertheless, he declared himself rejoiced to see Moreau "received with all the demonstrations of the most sincere and most enthusiastic joy."[33]

The Visitation lasted about three weeks. Many of the same organizational procedures that had gone on in Canada were replicated now for the province of the United States. On the day after Moreau's arrival a solemn ritual was held in the church at which Sorin, in accord with the new constitutions, was formally given the additional title of "vicar," while Granger was named master of novices and assistant superior and Patrick Dillon—an Irishman ordained the year before and destined to succeed Sorin as president of the university—was appointed steward or chief financial officer of the community.[34] "To the day," Sorin wrote afterward, "[Moreau] added two-thirds of the night, and when the time came for him to take his departure for France, it was found he had done the work of several months. He had organized everything according to the new Constitutions, formed the chapters and councils of Notre Dame and St. Mary's, presided at the elections of officers in both places, heard everyone in direction, admitted to the novitiate and to profession all who were prepared, and finally arranged the separation in temporals of the Sisters from the other two societies."[35]

This rather abrupt summary did scant justice to the Founder's single incursion into Indiana. To be sure, much time was spent in liturgical and devotional exercises and spiritual exhortation, both corporate and individual. Ceremonies of welcome were elaborate, and heartfelt protestations of loyalty and devotion to

---

32. Moreau, *Circular Letters*, 2: 33.

33. Sorin, *Chronicles*, 193.

34. For a sympathetic summary of Dillon's brief and somewhat checkered career in Holy Cross, see Lyons, *Silver Jubilee*, 75–77.

35. Sorin, *Chronicles*, 194.

Moreau's person were readily proffered. But almost palpable was an undercurrent of perplexity and unease, what Moreau sensed as a "resistance" inspired by the devil himself: "I felt as if some invisible force were working against me. I encountered a mysterious kind of resistance from this bitter enemy of all God's work."[36] Predictably this restraint, whatever its origins, manifested itself on August 27 and 28 when Moreau met formally with the Notre Dame chapter. After he reiterated the basic rules requiring his permission for alienation of significant parcels of land and for building initiatives, he asked to see the account books. Sorin, still suffering from a minor bout of ague, was absent from these meetings, but his colleagues mirrored his point of view and indeed his haphazard bookkeeping style.[37] They presented the Founder with some general estimates of the mission's financial status, but, when he asked for precise figures indicating assets and indebtedness, they told him no such records existed. Long inured to, and critical of, Notre Dame's performance in this regard, perhaps Moreau was not surprised by this admission. In any event he demanded a thorough audit, and young Father Dillon was assigned to provide one. This task, his first as steward, took Dillon nearly two anxious weeks to accomplish.[38]

Meanwhile there occurred a jarring incident which showed that past recriminations had by no means been forgotten. On August 29, a third meeting of the chapter was convened, and Edward Sorin, now recovered, was in attendance. Included on the agenda were items relating to the relatively small sums allegedly owed to Notre Dame du Lac by the missions in New Orleans and Canada. In the course of the discussion, however, Sorin contended that an additional 15,000 francs ($3,000) was owed by the motherhouse itself; he was referring to the money he had advanced to Le Mans in the autumn of 1855, and then, after renewed quarrels over New Orleans, had demanded returned with interest.[39] Moreau expressed surprise, saying that he had considered this allowance at the time—and considered it so still—to have been a generous gift offered at a moment when Sainte-Croix had been in dire straits; surely the motherhouse had exhibited comparable largesse to Notre Dame when need had arisen, and in any case, he added, the congregation was a single family whose members were pledged to assist each

---

36. Moreau, *Circular Letters,* 2: 33–34.

37. Present were Fathers Granger and Gillespie and Brothers Vincent, Amédée, and Antoninus. Brother Lawrence, also ill, was absent. Thirty-three-year-old Amédée (né Jacques Dayres) was French-born, forty-three-year-old Antoninus (né David Barry) Irish-born. See *Matricule générale,* 989 and 1065, AIP.

38. Minor Chapter Book, minutes, August 28, 1857, AIP.

39. See chapter 18, above.

other. But Sorin would have none of it. His claim, he insisted, must be honored, because the money had been raised through mortgages on real estate which, if the loans were not promptly repaid, might well be lost. As the tension in the room mounted, the other members of the chapter uneasily indicated their willingness to have the debt, if that was what it was, considered canceled. But the waspish provincial vicar demurred. Finally a rough compromise was worked out, one that Sorin surely had foreseen: he had lately received his share of his deceased father's estate, amounting to approximately 15,000 francs. This legacy he would place in the treasury of Notre Dame du Lac, with the official notification that the money paid a legitimate debt owed by the motherhouse.[40] The meeting then adjourned, with Sorin stubbornly maintaining he had acted out of principle, and Moreau nursing a bruised spirit and feeling the cold hand of diabolical "resistance."

On September 10 Dillon submitted the results of his research: the Indiana mission's total debt amounted to an alarming $63,000, but its assets—real and movable property and accounts receivable—exceeded this figure by nearly $160,000. The financial statement, in short, revealed a mixed picture, but one which overall was encouraging. So at least it must have appeared to Moreau, however aggravated he might have been since the earlier contretemps; for all practical purposes he waived restrictions on the alienation of real estate, except with respect to the original 524 acres which had come to Holy Cross from Stephen Badin through Bishop Hailandière.[41]

The writ of the Founder's Visitation extended also to St. Mary's. Here, thanks to the Roman decree, the situation was radically different. A community of Salvatorist priests and Josephite brothers had secured papal approval, while the Marianite sisters had been left, so to speak, in limbo. Or, to be precise, from the legal point of view their status remained what it had always been, that of a diocesan institute. To be sure, the pope, in a private audience, had assured Moreau that "you will govern [the nuns] separately; I bless them also, and later on you will present their rules [for the curia's examination]."[42] Nonetheless, technically the local bishop continued to be the ultimate superior, just as the intractable Bouvier had been for so long in Le Mans. Their standing was further complicated for the sisters at St. Mary's because, just at that moment, the forty-two northernmost counties in Indiana were detached from Vincennes and placed under the canonical

---

40. Minor Chapter Book, minutes, August 29, 1857, AIP.

41. Minor Chapter Book, minutes, September 10 and 11, 1857, AIP. Wack, "Notre Dame Foundation," 360–361, prints the detailed statement.

42. Quoted in Moreau, *Circular Letters*, 1: 347, dated May 25, 1856.

jurisdiction of the new diocese of Fort Wayne, and so the bishop to whom they would be accountable remained an entirely unknown quantity.[43]

In the immediate term these legalisms made little practical difference.[44] The division of temporalities, though Moreau, as he was bound to do, imposed it in theory, was in fact postponed until such time as Sorin would judge it expedient.[45] Meanwhile the financial administration would remain centralized, and the exchange of personnel—sister-infirmarians and laundresses at Notre Dame, priest-chaplains and brother-farmers at St. Mary's—would go on as before. Once installed in office, the new bishop chose not to interfere with these arrangements. Yet at another and more important level the separation put a severe strain upon the sisters and their morale. Instead of being co-laborers with the priests and brothers in the Lord's vineyard, they now were required to see themselves as occupying a different and subordinate position. Not that they objected to subordination to the priests of Holy Cross as spiritual directors and overseers; this they accepted without a murmur. But now they had to do so as though they were servants rather than members of the same family, as adjutants rather than full-fledged members of a society gloriously sanctioned by the pope. Though they had worked as hard and had suffered as many trials in behalf of the common cause, the door to full participation had been slammed in their faces. They did not *belong* any more.

The disappointment was keenly felt by most of the nuns, and it affected the welcome they accorded Father Moreau.[46] Not that they felt any thing but warmth and reverence for the venerable Founder's person. His reputation for holiness had preceded him, and his gentleness and ethereal demeanor confirmed all they had heard, as did his slight, diminutive figure bowed by fifty-eight years of rigorous self-discipline, his face gaunt from suffering, his great, dark eyes. They and their charges greeted him with enthusiasm.

[I] saw the entire community of Sisters [he remembered a few weeks later] lined up in procession, with the boarding students in the lead, and after them the orphans carrying their banner and holding flowers in their hands. It

---

43. On September 22, 1857—Moreau had sailed for home only three days before—the formal announcement was issued in Rome creating the diocese of Fort Wayne. The new bishop, John Henry Luers, was consecrated the following January.

44. For much of what follows, see Costin, *Priceless Spirit*, 137–146, and the same writer's "The Voice from the Island: Father Basil Moreau's Visit to St. Mary's, 1857," a paper read at the Conference on the History of the Congregations of Holy Cross (1992).

45. Catta, *Moreau*, 2: 312.

46. For lengthy quotations from the sisters present, see Brosnahan, *King's Highway*, 207–210.

was a touching scene when they all fell on their knees to receive the blessing of the poor pilgrim, and then intoned the *Magnificat,* which was followed by several French hymns. Then it was that tears betrayed my emotion! I marveled at the work of God and blessed his Providence.[47]

Although the sisters' status now was somewhat anomalous—indeed, because of that circumstance—Moreau as Visitor was obliged to supervise the formation of a conventional structure of councils and superiors for them. The most significant result of this otherwise quite ordinary procedure was the metamorphosis of Sister Angela into Mother Angela, as she now assumed the new office of provincial. It was she, moreover, enterprising and indefatigable as ever, who arranged the decorous series of fêtes and ceremonials that marked the Founder's progress during his sojourn. On one such occasion, a reception in the sisters' parlor, Father Sorin asked Sister Elizabeth—an American who spoke no French—to play the piano for the assembled party. Play, he said, my favorite tune, the *Marseillaise,* and play it with spirit. Sister Elizabeth recalled the episode long afterward.

> When [I] was through, the Very Reverend Father [Moreau] came to the piano. Of course [I] stood, but, not understanding a word he said, was surprised at his long speech. [I] listened attentively, and when by the inflection of his voice [I] recognized the termination of a sentence, bowed in assent. . . . I [later] asked Sister [Emily] what Reverend Father [had] said to me. She burst out laughing. "He was so astonished that you played that piece. If you were in France, you would be put in a prison, and he really scolded. . . . He must think you very amiable, for you bowed just in the place you were being so severely admonished and looked so calm."[48]

Sorin's suggestion that the young nun play the stirring anthem of the French Revolution—presuming her memory was accurate[49]—may have been intended merely to tease Basile Moreau, who was a notoriously staunch and lifelong royalist.[50] On the other hand it may have been a more or less playful attempt on

47. Moreau, *Circular Letters,* 2: 33–34.

48. Costin, *Priceless Spirit,* 140.

49. Sister, later Mother, Elizabeth, née Harriet Redman Lilly (d. 1901), toward the end of her life prepared a long manuscript memoir, which Sister Georgia Costin has used skillfully. Harriet Lilly came originally from Lancaster, Ohio, where she had been a close friend of Eliza Gillespie. The two women joined the Marianites at about the same time. A widow, Mother Elizabeth lived to see both her children become religious of Holy Cross—indeed, she outlived them both.

50. See chapter 3, above.

Sorin's part to remind the Founder that Holy Cross in the New World could not succeed if were merely a mirror-image of Holy Cross in the Old. Not only were politics different in the sprawling American democracy; distances were vastly greater, individual initiative was more necessary, entrepreneurship more valued, social classes more fluid, the religious milieu itself more varied and competitive. If this is what Sorin had in mind, it would have struck a sympathetic chord among most of the sisters, though not among all of them. Indeed, a fissure had already opened up within their ranks, and Moreau's visit had inevitably widened it. The fault-line revealed itself primarily, though not exclusively, by way of differing cultural attachments. The French-born women tended to be protective of the language and traditions they had learned in their girlhood and during their training in Le Mans; for them Basile Moreau's ideal of reproducing Sainte-Croix "in the midst of these age-old forests"—to use his own phrase—obviously provided the best means to fulfill their calling. But for the American- and Irish-born, their numbers ever increasing, Sorin's more pragmatic and flexible approach, his readiness to adapt to the everyday realities they encountered, seemed the only sensible way to carry on the apostolate; nor did they think that such a formula compromised their religious vocation. The spirit, they maintained, not the letter, breathed life into any system or set of rules. The division was further exacerbated by the poor quality of some of the nuns sent recently from Le Mans, women who, Sorin bitterly commented, "did not even preserve amongst themselves the appearance of charity" and gave themselves over to "jealousy, indiscretion, [and] levity."[51]

Besides, ready as the sisters were to offer due honor to the revered Founder, it was the magnetic, single-minded, adventuresome Edward Sorin who won their deepest devotion, as he did the brothers and priests at Notre Dame. Moreover Sorin was ever on the scene, each day exhibiting his powerful personality. Moreau, by contrast, except for this one brief sortie, dwelt 3,000 miles away. There was a deep irony at work here. Pope Pius IX had forbidden the amalgamation of the sisters of Holy Cross with the priests and brothers on the benevolent grounds that in similar arrangements in the past the men had tyrannized over the women. The Marianites, therefore, were to go on their independent way. The unintended result over the succeeding years was a rising tide of complaint by American women, who claimed they were being tyrannized by French women. In the end a rupture was inevitable, and with it, testified to by a seemingly trivial semantic alteration, came the foundation of the sisters of *the* Holy Cross.

---

51. Sorin, *Chronicles,* 169.

But that development still lay in the future. Basile Moreau said his *adieus* on September 12, after consultations with representatives from the mission in New Orleans who had traveled to Indiana to report to him. Accompanied by Father Sorin, he paid a formal Visit of a couple of days duration to the new Holy Cross establishment in Chicago, and then repeated the exercise in Philadelphia. The apparent success of these urban missions prompted Sorin in the course of their travels to extract from Moreau a fateful pledge—the sowing of dragon seeds indeed—affecting the greatest urban area of all; the Founder promised that no new foundation would be established in New York City "without the consent of Notre Dame du Lac."[52]

At one o'clock in the morning of September 19 the two men parted at the Philadelphia railroad station. "We embraced each other," Moreau wrote, "with all the effusion of two souls who felt themselves united like Jonathan and David. . . . I had to leave, and what cost me most was separation from this beloved confrere, who had not ceased to shower upon me all the attentions of most thoughtful charity. The extreme fatigue from which he was suffering did not permit him to return with me to New York."[53] That evening Moreau boarded the steamer *Arago*, which lifted anchor a few hours later.

The Founder's acknowledgment of Father Sorin and his "thoughtful charity" was published, it must be remembered, in a communication circulated to every member of the congregation. It was, as so often in Moreau's public statements, meant to edify more than to inform. His inclusion in the same circular letter therefore of references to the "resistance" he sensed at Notre Dame and St. Mary's takes on heightened significance. He came away from Indiana immensely impressed at what Sorin and his colleagues had accomplished, but at the same time his worry that a stubborn spirit of rebellion lurked along the shores of the two lakes and on the banks overlooking the lordly St. Joseph River had been by no means dissipated—this despite the warm welcome accorded him by his American children. During his stay in Indiana, on every issue of substance under discussion, Sorin had got his way, and Moreau—perhaps to his credit in the eternal scheme of things—had clearly demonstrated a lack of that ruthlessness any leader of a great enterprise, religious or secular, must from time to time exhibit. But, spiritually creditable or not, as an administrator Moreau was neither tough enough to make his will prevail nor pliant enough to adjust his predispositions to the re-

---

52. Sorin, *Chronicles*, 270. See chapter 22, below.

53. Moreau, *Circular Letters*, 2: 37. In typical fashion, Catta, *Moreau*, 2: 315, places a sinister construction on Sorin's failure to accompany Moreau to New York.

alties at hand. In one sense the society he had founded remained for him an abstract construct—no surprise, given the temper of his mind. He preferred to lay out theoretical plans and to draw up rules and constitutions covering any possible future contingency precisely in order to avoid the human rough-and-tumble that is the lot of any governor. Such a consequence, however, lay beyond his grasp. He prized the order and regularity and, indeed, the predictability associated with the kind of traditional society in which he had grown up. But when confronted with the vagaries of an unfamiliar culture, like that turbulent American one with which Edward Sorin had so smoothly come to terms, Father Moreau became troubled, confused, and suspicious. Prudence, the ancients had taught, was the virtue proper to rulers, and *prudentia* proved to be the virtue in which the Founder of Holy Cross was most sadly wanting. Not the *prudentia carnis* of expediency that Basile Moreau would have rightly despised; but rather the prudence defined by Aristotle as *recta ratio agibilium,* an habitual readiness, that is, to settle firmly upon a policy calculated to achieve a precise objective and, in implementing it, to take proper account of all relevant circumstances, positive and negative—to accept, in short, the world as it really is.

Reflecting upon that embrace on a platform of a deserted railroad station in the middle of the night, one wonders who, in Moreau's mind, was Jonathan, and who was David.

ACCOMPANYING BASILE MOREAU aboard the *Arago* was the venerable Brother Vincent, who had been appointed an Assistant to the Superior General for a three-year term.[54] He resided in Le Mans for nearly a year, but, like Edward Sorin, his heart abided in America, and by September 1858 he was home again.[55] In the meantime Sorin took up his ordinary duties, without, however, failing to pay flattering homage to the Founder's recent visit. "Very Reverend and dear Father," he wrote, "I like to think that you have at last arrived home in France safe and sound and somewhat rested after your labors. How often, since you left us, have I admired the prodigious strength that Heaven has dowered you with to accomplish your great mission! Compared to your Reverence all of us are but pygmies." But, as ever, Holy Cross in the United States confronted problems that even the visit of the Founder could not dispel.

---

54. Moreau, *Circular Letters*, 2: 15, dated July 3, 1857.
55. Minor Chapter Book, minutes, September 20, 1858, AIP.

In a sense all is well with us up to the present, but the money crisis has during the past week become frightful in the extreme. All the strongest banks, even [those] of New York, have closed down, and we find ourselves enmeshed for 5,000 francs. We do not know how we are going to weather the storm; in a sense we could well say that we too have closed down, since daily we refuse payment, since our treasury is empty. Up to this week no lawsuit has been begun against our House; but the law has just passed in the Court, now in session, which holds one of your drafts for 4,000 francs. I cannot tell you what is to become of us, but I beg you, Very Reverend Father, to pray and to get others to pray for us. Never has the country been so tried. The panic is general, and if Heaven does not work a miracle for us personally, we are done for.[56]

If Sorin rather exaggerated in asserting that "the crisis came so suddenly that no one had time to prepare for it," and that "Notre Dame was less prepared than anyone else in the country," the plight of the institution was grave enough. "[Holy Cross], had, it is true, real estate more than enough to cover its indebtedness without touching on the grounds of the university or the academy [at St. Mary's]; but at that time there was hardly any sale [possible] except at a sacrifice of half the actual value of the property."[57] That indeed was the rub. Notes came due as did contractual commitments, and the usual source of ready cash—sale of the various parcels of land Sorin had acquired—had simply dried up. Furthermore, mortgages on much of that property had to be honored to avoid foreclosure. Among Notre Dame's daughter-houses, those in Chicago and Philadelphia continued to be under the most grievous threat. Even before Father Moreau's Visit, the abrasive Bishop O'Regan of Chicago had written directly to Sorin calling for rental payment in accord with their prior agreement, "for I am in urgent want of money."[58] Nearly a year later the bishop's surrogate, the Jesuit Father Damen, rather more plaintively renewed the demand,[59] but even a year after that, when O'Regan had departed the scene, the administration at Notre Dame had to confess its "embarrassment" at not being able to meet its obligations there.[60]

Buffalo proved to be another trouble spot. In November 1856 four brothers and three sisters had been assigned to conduct an orphan asylum in that city,

---

56. Sorin to Moreau, October 17, 1857, AGEN.

57. Sorin, *Chronicles,* 194.

58. O'Regan to Sorin, January 4, 1857, AIP. For the agreement, see chapter 18, above.

59. Damen to Sorin, December 1, 1857, AIP.

60. Minor Chapter Book, minutes, December 13, 1858, AIP.

"under the patronage of the saintly Bishop Timon."[61] But Sorin's high estimate of John Timon's sanctity did not last. From the beginning negotiations were difficult: Timon maintained that he could not "in justice" accept the level of compensation proposed by Notre Dame, twice what the Sisters of Charity received, he said, "and at least fifty percent more than the Brothers of Christian Schools."[62] Though a compromise was worked out, the drearily familiar quarrel over money persisted, even after the Holy Cross personnel had taken up their duties.[63] Once they had done so, however, the bishop found them lazy and incompetent. "After mature reflection," he told Sorin, "and recommending the affair to God, I have come to the conclusion that you please recall your brothers and sisters. It seems that they cannot realize the object I had at heart, *teaching trades to the boys,* as I explained to you."[64]

Whether the bishop of Buffalo's specific strictures were or were not justified, one generalization seems pertinent. Ever since the misadventures in Kentucky and Brooklyn, more than a decade earlier,[65] Edward Sorin had shown a propensity to commit staff to far-flung missions without a guarantee of sufficient resources and without assurance that the personnel involved were properly trained for the assignment. As time passed and Notre Dame matured, these deficiencies were gradually corrected, and expansion paid solid dividends. But in the beginning boldness appeared to be almost foolhardiness. Curiously, since they differed so radically in temperament, Sorin and Basile Moreau acted much alike in this regard, and both, in the end, could claim success in their distinct spheres. Perhaps they both thought that the old saying—nothing ventured, nothing gained—was a motto taught by the Providence in which they placed their trust. Neither of them, even so, was willing to gamble on a foundation amidst the deserts of the southwest United States; the invitation of Bishop Lamy to send two brothers to Santa Fe was respectfully declined.[66]

No vicissitude could shake Father Sorin's confidence: "In all the great difficulties in which the work of Holy Cross at Notre Dame was involved since it came to the United States, Divine Providence always came to its aid in a manner so evident that it was impossible not to recognize its intervention."[67] He penned

---

61. Sorin, *Chronicles,* 179. See Timon to Sorin, November 30, 1856, AIP: "Your good brothers and sisters have arrived."

62. Timon to Sorin, January 12, 1856, AIP.

63. Timon to Sorin, January 29, 1857, AIP.

64. Timon to Sorin, April 5, 1857, AIP.

65. See chapter 13, above.

66. See Minor Chapter Book, minutes, August 17, 1858, AIP.

67. Sorin, *Chronicles,* 197.

these words as he reflected upon the severe austerity brought on by the depression of 1857–1858. Nothing proved the point to his satisfaction more tellingly than a tale of two creditors. Daniel Maloney was a secular priest who served in Indianapolis and, later, in Lafayette. In the spring of 1856 he loaned Notre Dame $5,500, with a strict schedule for payment of interest and principal, which, unsurprisingly, Sorin failed to meet.[68] Father Maloney, a man apparently of volatile disposition, protested the dilatoriness with growing irritation, until finally, after eighteen months, his wrath boiled over. "[Since you are] unmindful of the code of honor or your sacred character," he fumed at Sorin, "you wish [in effect] to have an exposé of your chicanery and my gullibility. . . . I am much deceived if I do not make your heart sore and heavy before I sheathe, not the sword, but the press."[69] He coupled this threat of causing adverse publicity with notice that he had put the matter into the hands of an attorney. And then, within a week, unaccountably—Providentially?—he calmed down and drew back. "I have determined to wait a while longer for justice to issue from Notre Dame."[70]

Simultaneously Sorin experienced an even more remarkable instance of what he considered the mysterious designs of Providence.

> God holds the hearts of men in his hand and turns them as he pleases. The Congregation had a very striking proof of this in those days of [the financial] panic. One of the neighbors, a rich German Catholic farmer, had at different times . . . obtained notes from [me] amounting to sixty thousand francs [$12,000]. In the month of July [1857], and several times subsequently, he had declared positively that he wanted his money about the beginning of autumn. As he had no mortgage and no security but the honesty of [our] house, the financial crisis naturally made him more uneasy. . . . In the first days of November he came to inquire if his money was ready for him, and he expressed himself rather forcibly on the subject.

Sorin managed to scrape together five thousand francs, promised to deliver twenty thousand more shortly, "and to give him the balance in notes, secured by mortgage."

> What was the answer of the good man? That he did not want to be paid anything at all at the time; that he had no need of his money which he

---

68. Maloney to Sorin, May 15, 1856, AIP.
69. Maloney to Sorin, November 28, 1857, AIP.
70. Maloney to Sorin, December 5, 1857, AIP.

would have to put out at interest elsewhere or to deposit in a bank; that he had no confidence in any bank and that he would prefer to leave his money at Notre Dame rather than anywhere else, until he should need it.

That the farmer, "a naturally suspicious German," should "decline to accept his money when offered him, . . . is not the ordinary way in which men act. But when God directs them for a special purpose, they do, without knowing it, what God wants them to do."[71]

Edward SORIN NEVER WAVERED in his belief that his work was guided by a divine hand. This confidence, however, did not smack of fideism; God, he also believed, helps those who help themselves. Sometimes—and increasingly as the years passed—his activism involved him in great affairs, but he took pains as well to deal carefully with more mundane matters. If attention to detail is a mark of genius, then perhaps it is fair to say that Sorin displayed a measure of that rare attribute. A legitimate distinction is often drawn between a ruler and a leader; Sorin achieved the considerable feat of being both. As leader, the grand and sweeping vision of the destiny of Notre Dame and of Holy Cross in America was ever before his eyes and on his lips. As ruler, except for careless bookkeeping—and even this may have been a calculated effort to maintain his independence of action—he attended to the minutiae of day-to-day governance with abundant vigor.

Sorin's first responsibility in this regard was as priest and religious superior. After the brief period at Black Oak Ridge and the first few years at Sainte Marie des Lacs he never again, once Father Cointet had joined him, acted as a parish pastor, and his romantic notion of ministering exclusively to the Potawatomi had proved a quickly passing fancy.[72] But as provincial and vicar he had to assume the burdens of an ultimate spiritual director for Notre Dame and St. Mary's and, indeed, for houses scattered between Chicago and Philadelphia. This was no easy task, particularly as the community under his charge increased in numbers and diversity. The larger the house the more complex its character, the more likely to witness personality clashes and to harbor misfits, and so the more necessary the superior be sensitive and flexible. Flexibility, however, had its limits for Sorin: though he consistently urged that Holy Cross adapt to the American milieu, he was punctilious in insisting that priests, brothers, and sisters perform their spiritual

71. Sorin, *Chronicles*, 197–198.
72. See chapters 6 and 7, above.

exercises regularly, keep to the rule, and display proper decorum. He routinely censored all the mail received by community-members, and no one was allowed to depart the premises without having his luggage examined.[73] However much he may have disagreed with the Founder on other matters—indeed, however much he may have concealed from Moreau—Sorin always felt himself accountable to the motherhouse in carrying out these strictly spiritual duties.[74]

For the management of affairs at Notre Dame itself Sorin had at hand an instrument in accord with the congregation's constitution. A committee or council of administration—the names varied over the years—of the Minor Chapter met weekly and, if business required it, even more often. Sorin always presided and, though votes were sometimes taken, clearly dominated the meetings; if he were away from home, Father Granger replaced him. The sessions invariably began by formally recording the amount of ready money available; during the stressful last weeks of the panic-year 1857, the cash box contained $297.23 on November 16, $2.00 on December 8, and nothing on December 28. Discussion ranged over a host of topics, from the need to harmonize the Notre Dame and St. Mary's budgets to the feasibility of constructing a school in flourishing Sorinsville. And some of the decisions arrived at were far-reaching. For example, on September 20, 1858, in order to "ameliorate" the performance of the farm, it was determined that at the following spring's planting 150 acres should be given over to wheat, 50 to potatoes, 50 to sugar cane,[75] 10 to beans, 10 to buckwheat, 50 to oats, 100 to clover, 100 to pasturage, and 75 acres were to be left fallow. Other resolutions seem in retrospect trivial, though they demonstrated how meticulously Sorin kept his finger on the local pulse. On September 28, 1857, it was decided by the Chapter that the boarding students in the college would be furnished with butter at breakfast on Wednesday, Friday, and Sunday, and apples and molasses on two other days. "Brother Bernard is to be admonished by Reverend Father Superior for his obstinacy in striking the children" (March 8, 1858). "At meals chairs instead of benches [were to be provided] for the students of classics" (August 30, 1858). "The new privy near the infirmary must be moved in[to] the Boarders' yard near the old ones, and a clean box must be kept for Reverend Father Superior and strangers" (November 9, 1857).[76]

---

73. See, for example, Sorin, *Chronicles,* 265–266.

74. See, among many examples, Sorin to Moreau, August 4, 1858, AGEN.

75. Eighteen months earlier Congressman Colfax secured a pint bag of sugar cane seed from the Department of Agriculture and forwarded it to Sorin. See Colfax to Sorin, January 6, 1857, AIP.

76. See Minor Chapter Book, minutes, 1857–1858, AIP, *passim.* "Strangers" probably meant visitors.

A parallel assemblage was of relatively little moment in the superintendence of affairs at Notre Dame. Regular meetings of the instruction staff had become a tradition by the late 1850s, and though it gathered in plenary session nearly every Sunday afternoon, often as not it adjourned without debating, much less deciding, anything. This dearth of action may have occurred simply because the curriculum in place was working adequately. The number of teachers had, to be sure, doubled in a decade, from seven in 1847 to thirteen in 1857; yet, as a group, they enjoyed relatively little influence and much less than had their predecessors. The reason is not hard to discern. The old Council or Board of Professors, during the 1840s, had been chaired by Edward Sorin himself, who had in those days doubled as a classroom instructor. This newer version—though it employed the prestigious term "Faculty," which implied a certain corporate independence—was presided over by the vice president of the university, the young Neal Gillespie, who, whatever his merits, did not bring to his office any particular clout. Everyone knew where the only meaningful authority at Notre Dame resided. Perhaps this realization explains why at the faculty meeting that opened the academic year of 1857 only eight of the thirteen professors bothered to attend.[77] Not untypical at any rate of the level of discussion that might have been heard was this complaint by Professor Moriarty, who "represented the necessity of having the blackboard fastened to the wall in his classroom, as he suffered some inconvenience from its then existing position."[78]

On those rare occasions when Sorin joined the Sunday afternoon conclave, there was little room for doubt as to who was in charge. "It was decided at a particular meeting of the faculty, invoked on the 30th of September and presided over by the Very Reverend Father Superior, that catechism would be taught for ten minutes in all the classes of the College [between] 2:00 and 3:30 P.M." A few weeks later Sorin attended again, and this time directed the faculty to determine whether a certain student should be "detained" or "expelled."[79] His most striking intervention, however, occurred six months later, when the conduct of a few Protestant students, already referred to,[80] was at issue. At a regularly scheduled faculty meeting, one of the professors descried the refusal of five Protestant students to kneel during the prayers routinely said before and after class, and fretted at "the bad consequences" of this act of defiance, because, he said, "upon the same principle all the Protestant students might refuse to comply extexioirly [sic] with the

---

77. Council Book of the Faculty, minutes, September 1, 1857, UFMM, AUND.
78. Council Book of the Faculty, minutes, March 15, 1857, UFMM, AUND.
79. Council Book of the Faculty, minutes, September 30 and October 11, 1857, UFMM, AUND.
80. See note 9, above.

several religious practices required of all the Protestant students for the sake of order, by the rules of the College." Father Gillespie replied mildly that he "thought it would be more prudent to overlook these delinquencies, as they might think we were trying to compel [non-Catholics] to religious practices." The minutes of the next meeting revealed with brutal candor how decisions were made at Notre Dame du Lac: "The question contested at the last Council, namely, concerning those who refused to kneel during prayer, was not spoken of in the Council, as the question had already been decided by the Very Reverend Superior, who gave them the alternative of obedience to the rules or expulsion from the College. They chose the latter, which took place immediately."[81]

Despot Sorin surely was, but, for the most part, an enlightened one. Or at least enlightened in the sense that without the assertion of his self-confidence and single-mindedness there would have been no faculty to ignore and no students to expel. Without Sorin there would have been no Notre Dame; without him it would have dissolved like a dream, as did so many other institutions, private and public, founded during the same era.[82] This not to say that other individuals—Granger and Cointet and Brother Vincent, Michael Shawe, the Gillespies and, of course, Basile Moreau, to name only the most prominent—did not play crucial roles in this great adventure. Nor should it be forgotten that had the railroads reached northern Indiana a decade later than they did Our Lady's University might well have been only a dim memory. Even simple luck must be taken into account; what if, when the stable burned down, the wind had driven the sparks onto the church and the college? Yet, when all the other factors are acknowledged, the paramount truth remains that Notre Dame survived because Edward Sorin—domineering, charming, supple, courageous, sometimes duplicitous and always devoted to God's cause as he saw it—refused to fail.

---

81. Council Book of the Faculty, minutes, February 14 and 20, 1858, UFMM, AUND.

82. Of the sixty-five Catholic colleges founded between 1841 and 1860, twenty-two survived into the next century. See Gleason, "Indefinite Homogeneity," cited in chapter 13, above.

chapter twenty

Jousting with Bishops

UST BEFORE CHRISTMAS 1857, FATHER SORIN RECEIVED AN invitation to attend the consecration of the recently appointed bishop of the new diocese of Fort Wayne.[1] He accepted readily enough and was in attendance at the numbingly long ceremony, held at the cathedral in Cincinnati on January 10 of the new year. His feelings were mixed, however, because, although he had long been anxious to be delivered from the jurisdiction of Vincennes and had been frustrated that the rumor of a new see in northern Indiana had taken so long to be realized,[2] the man finally selected was a somewhat disappointing surprise. His own preference lay with Julian Benoit, the parish priest in Fort Wayne with whom Sorin had enjoyed cordial relations over the years. Benoit had also been the candidate of Bishop Saint-Palais of Vincennes, but J. B. Purcell's influence in Rome prevailed, and one of his own priests was awarded the office.[3] "A German bishop in a Western state," the archbishop of Cincinnati observed, "where there has been hitherto only a French one, and where the German Catholic population is more numerous than [the] French, is much wanted, or could do more good, I think, than a French one."[4] Sensible as

1. Luers to Sorin, December 19, 1857, AIP.

2. See Sorin to Purcell, April 20, 1857, AIP.

3. Copies of the Roman documents of appointment, 1857–1858, CDWF, AUND, "Diocese of Fort Wayne."

4. See Schroeder, *Diocese of Vincennes,* 138–140. At this date the metropolitan province of Cincinnati included as suffragan sees Cleveland, Detroit, Louisville, Covington (Kentucky), Sault Ste-Marie (Michigan), Vincennes, and, finally, Fort Wayne. As archbishop Purcell had jurisdiction only over the area directly connected to Cincinnati; as metropolitan he enjoyed only some vague appellate powers with regard to the other dioceses. But he was *primus inter pares* and spokesman for the province as far as Rome was concerned. It was most unlikely that any suffragan would have been appointed over his objections. It surely has been noted in these pages how assiduously Sorin cultivated Purcell.

this conclusion may have appeared to some, to others the appointment smacked of ecclesiastical empire-building on the Irish-born Purcell's part—a phenomenon not unknown in Catholic hierarchical circles before and since. In any case, the fifty-year-old French-born Benoit was destined to continue in his parochial post until his death in 1885.[5]

John Henry Luers, eleven years Benoit's junior, was born in Westphalia and came as a boy to the United States in 1833. The family settled on a farm in southern Ohio, and young John eventually moved to a nearby town and went to work as a clerk in a general store. A chance meeting with Bishop Purcell, as he then was, proved to be the determining moment in his life. As the bishop's protégé he enrolled in the local seminary, was ordained in 1846, and promptly assigned as pastor of a struggling new parish in Cincinnati. His success there gained him a diocese of his own before he was forty.[6] Once arrived in Fort Wayne, however, the new bishop was quickly disillusioned. Instead of the 40,000 Catholics he had been told lived in his jurisdiction, he learned that the real number was scarcely half that many. "Fort Wayne is a poor place for a Bishop to accomplish much," he complained to Purcell. Benoit's rickety frame church, Luers's cathedral, yielded hardly more than three or four dollars in the weekly collection basket. So, with more presumption than common sense, the bishop, the oil of episcopal consecration still wet on his hands, began to look round for an alternative site. A relatively prosperous congregation in Lafayette might serve, he thought, but even better as a see-city would be Indianapolis, which, he opined, "ought to be the seat for northern Indiana; it is the capitol of the state and has a fine English congregation, besides good church property." He proposed to offer Vincennes some other town or even several counties in exchange for Indianapolis, until his patron, Purcell, warned him to cease indulging in such foolish pipedreams.[7] It was a bizarre beginning.

Luers "made his first visit to Notre Dame du Lac on the patronal feast of the Brothers, St. Joseph's Day [March 19]. He ordained one man to the priesthood and presided at the religious profession of another. He spent nearly a week in the two houses, and went home, it was said, well pleased and edified."[8] Edward Sorin remained uneasy, however, even though at least one highly placed personage had

5. For a biographical sketch see H. J. Alerding, *Diocese of Fort Wayne, a Book of Historical Reference, 1669–1907* (Fort Wayne, 1907), 60–62.

6. See Alerding, *Diocese of Fort Wayne*, 30–34.

7. See Schroeder, *Diocese of Vincennes*, 139–141, and the authorities cited there.

8. Sorin, *Chronicles*, 200.

tried to reassure him beforehand. "So you have at last a Bishop," wrote Joshua Young, Mother Angela's old friend, now bishop of Erie. "I am sure it is not the one you have expected, [but] he is one you will be pleased with on further acquaintance. Now if somebody you could be better pleased with should get into the see of Chicago," the bishop of Erie added consolingly, "you might be made up [sic] on two sides, to say nothing of the other side of the triangle. Father Benoit might yet do in Chicago." In all such discussions, Young concluded with some prelatial smugness, Sorin should deem himself among the "happiest, because no visions of miters bother you."[9]

Sorin's ambitions did, to be sure, lead in a different direction, but he soon had reason to be less than happy with the intentions of his lately mitered neighbor. "The favorable impressions which the new and worthy bishop of Fort Wayne had carried away with him from Notre Dame were not of long duration." Luers's disenchantment came into the open in May 1858, when he went back to Cincinnati to participate in the second provincial synod convened by Archbishop Purcell.[10] All the suffragans were in attendance, and, as was customary on such occasions, superiors of male religious orders were also invited, though not granted formal franchise. Purcell wrote cordially to Sorin: Come a few days early "and you will find useful occupation."[11] "A thousand thanks for your gracious invitation to the council that assembles next Sunday," Sorin replied. "I extremely regret that I am obliged to decline (*renoncer*) the honor you do me, . . . but engagements over which I have no real control (*disposition*) . . . will not leave me free until the middle of next week, which would be too late to be of any use and would also be scarcely respectful [to the synod]."[12] This rejoinder was entirely disingenuous, as Sorin promptly admitted. "Perhaps it would have been better," he recorded in the third person, "to give the archbishop a statement of affairs just as they stood, but this would have been a complaint; Father Sorin preferred to give as his excuse that he had engagements which prevented him from assisting at the council. Here, as on many other occasions, Father Sorin made a mistake."

How in fact did affairs stand on the eve of the synod, and why was absenting himself from that meeting a mistake for Sorin? Pressing, as always, were money-

9. Young to Sorin, December 20, 1857, AIP.
10. See John H. Lamott, *History of the Archdiocese of Cincinnati* (New York, 1921), 214–216. The first synod was held in 1855.
11. Purcell to Sorin, April 20, 1858, AIP.
12. Sorin to Purcell, April 27, 1858, AIP.

problems, but at this moment, in the slough of the nationwide depression, these had taken a peculiar twist. Rumors were circulating that the titles to Notre Dame property were faulty, which understandably caused no little anxiety among those creditors who held paper secured by mortgages on that property. An inquiry proved that the talk was more than gossip. At Sorin's own initiative, it was discovered that the title to the 524 acres originally given Holy Cross by Bishop Hailandière in 1842 had never been properly registered with the competent state agency. Confusion was compounded by a careless mistake in wording on the deed, which, in effect, "twice confirm[ed] the possession of seventy-five acres of land of little value and [left] Father Sorin without a title to the location on which buildings had stood for fifteen years. The error was palpable," and Sorin appealed to Bishop Saint-Palais, as Hailandière's successor, to correct it. But the bishop of Vincennes unaccountably put the matter off, and then, once his diocese had been divided, assigned to Fort Wayne "a general title to whatever property he [Saint-Palais] possessed in northern Indiana." When Luers paid his visit to Notre Dame in March, he had without objection agreed to provide "a deed to correct the famous error." This document, however, was useless until Saint-Palais formally recorded the transfer, and this he refused to do, he said through an intermediary, until he had returned from the synod of May 1858 in Cincinnati. It was hardly paranoid of Sorin to find this decision an ominous sign of times to come: "The affair now looked mysterious to the administration of Notre Dame."

It looked alarming to the creditors, one of whom chose this awkward moment to bring suit in circuit court then holding its sessions in South Bend—an "immediate consequence," Sorin believed, "of this unfortunate matter of defective titles." In the long term, this action could effect an "increase [of] public distrust" of Notre Dame; in the short term, "Father Sorin was politely informed that if, in the present state of affairs, he left or attempted to leave . . . Indiana he would be arrested at the station."

Complicating Sorin's state of mind was a report he received simultaneously from Fort Wayne, according to which "the sentiments of the young and pious prelate [Luers] were the very contrary of what had been expected, that is to say, that he was now well known as an enemy of all communities in general and that of Notre Dame du Lac in particular." Luers, still in shock at the impoverished status of his infant diocese, had allegedly adopted "this unexpected change," first, because of complaints he had heard at the synod from Saint-Palais, and, second, because of the hostility of "an ex-Jesuit of unsavory reputation, . . . the sworn enemy of Notre Dame," whom Luers had incardinated into his diocese. This second source of trouble Sorin brushed contemptuously aside, but, in retrospect, he concluded that in absenting himself from the council in Cincinnati and so losing an opportunity to rebut the charges of the bishop of Vincennes he "had made a mistake."[13]

To rectify it he decided to compose an apologia and send it to Archbishop Purcell. "Being obliged to submit annually a narrative of our doings to the motherhouse," Sorin wrote on June 9, "I believe it my duty to have you see what I have had to say [in it] relative to recent events, which will perhaps not be without interest to you. I have never forgotten the services your Grace has rendered to our young society from the first day I had the honor to meet you. . . . If you take the trouble to read the enclosed account of these past fifteen years, you will find in it with what we began, and whether it is true that we have labored in vain. Please return to me after you have read it."[14] Purcell did take the trouble, but his reaction was negative. "You have been misinformed," the archbishop wrote sharply, "as to the Right Reverend M. de St. Palais' edifying, or scandalizing, the late Provincial Council of Cincinnati about you or yours. I cannot remember his having once mentioned your name during all its proceedings." This assertion could have been literally true, without precluding the possibility or even the likelihood of private conversations between Saint-Palais and Luers. However that may have been, Purcell was disturbed at the tenor of Sorin's written defense.

> Could you see the letters of Bishop Luers to me, you would find damaging evidence against you, confidential letters written from Fort Wayne. As a sincere friend I tell you [your] memoir betrays a morbid feeling in its authors and conveys, while they may be unconscious of a moral fault, most false impressions. If it is ever disinterred from your Archives and made a page of History—Ecclesiastical, American—it will be regrettable. Better not hear, record, remember, report evil words—or deeds—especially when we are so liable to be deceived by false reports and to exaggerate what may have some foundation in truth.[15]

If the archbishop judged silence in this case to be golden, Edward Sorin did not agree. The "memoir" was incorporated into the Chronicles and so found its way into the archives of Holy Cross: "These pages will remain for our successors, and it would not be just for them to be left in ignorance of the appreciations [sic] of their predecessors in regard to the men and things that concerned them."

---

13. Sorin, *Chronicles*, 200–203.

14. Sorin to Purcell, June 9, 1858, AIP. What Sorin asked Purcell to read is the material in *Chronicles*, 200–214, which is elaborated upon below.

15. Purcell to Sorin, June 17, 1858, AIP.

THE BISHOP OF VINCENNES routinely addressed Sorin as "*Mon cher ami,*" but tension between them stretched back to the days when the Saint-Palais, as pastor at Madison, had rudely dismissed the brothers from Notre Dame assigned to teach in his school.[16] Now, twelve years later, Sorin elected to assume, despite Purcell's denial and disapproval, that at the meeting in Cincinnati the bishop of Vincennes had defamed him and his apostolate. A rejoinder was imperative, because "it was only natural that a bishop should be believed by all his colleagues, especially in matters he ought to know well." The crowning insult was further word from Fort Wayne that Luers, convinced by these falsehoods, "was going to take all his [parochial] missions from [Sorin] and to confine him strictly to the limits of the Notre Dame property, and that without any pity whatsoever."

Sorin put what he perceived to be Saint-Palais's specious accusations under four headings, of which the first was the most serious and arguably the most legitimate: "The only [purpose] for which we had come, and the only important thing, the Brothers and their schools, had been neglected."[17] It could not be denied that the original appeal to Basile Moreau from Saint-Palais's predecessor, Hailandière, had been for brothers to teach within the confines of the diocese of Vincennes. Sorin's presence had been incidental to this purpose, or rather his presence had been, from the bishop's point of view, an accident related to the constitutions of Holy Cross, which required that a priest be superior of every local community.[18] Moreover, Sorin the visionary almost from the moment of his arrival in America strove to expand the brothers' apostolate outside Indiana—to expand it indeed across the country—much to the distress of the bad-tempered and mistrustful Hailandière. Bishop Bazin had formally granted Sorin's principle, but his episcopate had lasted only six months, and Saint-Palais, protective of his turf like most bishops, hankered after the earlier restriction.

Sorin defended his policy over the previous fifteen years by pointing out that now, in 1858, there were 107 Josephite brothers teaching 2,400 children in twelve distinct establishments. ("In these figures we do not include their first foundation in Louisiana, which has just been made into a separate province, and which would considerably increase the above figures.") Such numbers, however, impressive as they were, begged Saint-Palais's question—if in fact he had posed it—because only a handful of the brothers were teaching in the dioceses of Vincennes

16. See Brother Mary Joseph to Sorin, October 26, 1846, in Klawitter, ed., *Adapted to the Lake,* 111–112, and chapter 12, above.

17. Sorin, *Chronicles,* 203.

18. See chapters 3 and 4, above.

and Fort Wayne. Indeed, there were more of them hewing wood and drawing water at Notre Dame and St. Mary's than were actually employed in a classroom. But Sorin was on firmer ground when he asked rhetorically: "Would it not be somewhat more just to acknowledge that . . . the clergy have generally taken but little interest in the matter of vocations, and just as little in the means of making [the brothers] useful after they have been secured?" Too often a pastor would solicit the services of a single brother "and could provide him with no other refectory but his kitchen amongst the servant-girls; and as for the school, . . . a miserable cabin in which it was a mockery to attempt to keep a school."

Another hindrance, in Sorin's view, had to be acknowledged. Americanized as he may have become in many respects, Sorin had not yet shed his earlier suspicion that the United States did not offer the cultural milieu in which vocations to the brotherhood could flourish.[19] "Real vocations are rare," he protested. "When [young men] have entered the novitiate, where they can no longer enjoy the liberty and comforts of the people of the world in this country, they are ever haunted by the thought of the pleasures which they could enjoy and the money which they could so easily earn." A further consideration only exacerbated the problem: "Bishop Hughes [of New York], being consulted on this subject . . . fifteen years ago, did not believe in the possibility of success [for a brothers' institute]. One of the reasons given by him was this: if you have subjects possessed of ability, they will want to become priests. All the difficulties pointed out by the illustrious bishop . . . have been met with in turn, and often all together."[20]

But Bishop Hughes (from 1850 an archbishop), had also underscored another quandary to which Father Sorin chose not to advert: the sheer incompetence of many of the brothers sent out on the teaching mission from Notre Dame.[21] Timon of Buffalo, if called upon, would have seconded such a remonstrance, as would have Blanc of New Orleans, Spalding of Louisville, and Saint-Palais himself. Much more troubling to Sorin were the strictures, uttered a little later, by another illustrious prelate who, like Hughes, was promoted to archiepiscopal rank in 1850. "We have none or hardly any resources to oppose [the anti-Catholic bias in the era of the Know-Nothings]," complained J. B. Purcell. "We have neither male nor female teachers for common schools, or hardly any—surely not in sufficient numbers. Who knows how to teach? I told Reverend Mr. Letourneau that your principal English teacher at St. John's [parish] in this city could not speak five minutes without a grammatical error. [The brothers] cannot speak, they cannot

---

19. See chapter 6, above.

20. Sorin, *Chronicles*, 203–206.

21. See chapter 13, above.

write, they cannot spell the English language correctly." Somewhat illogically he added: "They cannot sing, cannot teach singing."[22] Sorin's only riposte was lame at best: "The business of teaching was never lost sight of. Whenever a candidate presented himself with the intention and the requisite talents for study, he was put to study. . . . A work of this kind was very ticklish. Time was required to lay the foundations before thinking of building the edifice. The work," he said with more confidence perhaps than he felt, "is now founded, and if heaven continues to bless it, it is ready for development."

To the second allegation, that Notre Dame had profited from the parochial missions it had administered, with the implication that such parishes should revert to the secular clergy, Father Sorin reacted with bitter resentment, and for good reason. Indeed, if such charges had in fact been made in the chanceries of Vincennes, Fort Wayne, and Detroit, they were not only unjust but in the poorest possible taste. From 1842 the bishops of these dioceses had been more than content that the men of Holy Cross should minister to the Catholic populace for whom they, the bishops, could not furnish the required personnel. To forget such service now, when the frontier was receding and a more conventional parochial structure had become feasible, and even to accuse those who had provided the service of enriching themselves, would have displayed the shabbiest kind of ingratitude. An angry Sorin at any rate had no difficulty refuting aspersion, whatever its source.

> Let it be permitted us to remark that upon his arrival in South Bend in November, 1842, in the thirteen counties entrusted to him by the bishops of Vincennes and Detroit, Father Sorin found only a handful of poor Catholics, scattered here and there over a tract of more than one hundred miles in diameter and containing scarcely 150 families in all, most of whom had been without spiritual aid for three years and more. . . . Add to this number about as many poor Catholic Indians scattered over the same territory, and you will have an idea of the mission of Notre Dame. Then it excited only pity; no one was envious of it. It was poor in all ways with a poverty to make the heart bleed. There was a flock . . . dispersed, led astray, dissolute, destitute of almost every Catholic sentiment. Fortunately, Father Sorin was yet fresh from his beloved France, rich in zeal and devotedness, and with a boundless confidence in the protection of the Queen of Heaven. His most ardent desires were gratified; he was at last a missioner, as he had so earnestly longed to be.

---

22. Purcell to Sorin, April 22, 1859, AIP.

Clearly Sorin had seen the nasty insinuation as an indictment of himself, but more than personal pique sustained his argument. He paid special tribute to Francis Cointet, his "cherished friend . . . of such happy memory in all this vast district. He worked like an apostle for eleven years in the mission, which he watered with his sweat whilst edifying it by his great virtues and instructing it by his knowledge." Four other priests had come from France, and fourteen more had been ordained at Notre Dame, and all of them—even Francis Gouesse—had labored manfully in the vineyard. "God saw the needs of this mission, and in his own time he provided the men and the means necessary."

> Let it be remembered that this foundation of Notre Dame was carried on without the least local assistance, that the country where the foundation was laid was deeply imbued with prejudices and low bigotry, that the very name "Catholic" was a proverb of reproach, that the very spot given by the bishop of Vincennes for this purpose was nothing but a forest of 524 acres, ten of which were cleared and worn out. . . . Every cent . . . had to come first from the outside; the labors of the members of the [Holy Cross] institute did the rest. Providence blessed their common devotedness beyond all their hopes.

But a vague imputation of fiscal impropriety was best rebutted by firm numbers, and Sorin scoured his records to produce them. For one often blamed for faulty accounting, his search bore results impressive in their precision. "Here is the list," he announced triumphantly, "year by year, from the beginning. It includes absolutely everything that was received as stipends for masses, fees for marriages, for baptisms, in pew rent, collections, offerings, etc." He then appended an annual inventory of missionary activity since 1843. In that year, one priest, Sorin himself, received compensation of $112.08; in 1857 four priests, working in eleven stations in northern Indiana and southern Michigan, collected a total of $569.82. After the arrival of Cointet and Marivault in 1844, there were always at least two priests on the mission; the largest number was six, reached in 1848 and again in 1853. Eighteen forty-eight also registered the highest return of all, $1,034.18, while Sorin's lonely ministry to the likes of the Coquillards and the Potawatomi brought in the lowest. The average therefore amounted to "$143 per year for each priest, that is to say, a sum on which no bishop in the United States would ask his missioners to live. And yet this is all that went into the treasury of Notre Dame, and that was brought in by this long and hard labor of fifteen years."[23]

---

23. Sorin, *Chronicles*, 206–210.

"The third accusation is a double one. The College and the Sisters have taken up too much of our time, it is said." In response Sorin adopted a more sardonic tone: "If by this is meant that besides the institute of the Brothers, for which we had been principally wanted, we also did what was not asked of us, namely, put up a college and established Sisters, we grant it; but we cannot see that in this we were wrong." The accusers contended that the Josephites had been neglected for the sake of the Marianites and the Salvatorists at the university, while the opposite, Sorin maintained, was the truth: "The good Brothers . . . have gained by the establishment of the other two branches, which took an equal interest in them as in their own members, and which have, in fact, procured for them their best vocations." As for the college itself, most American bishops favor institutions of this type, and "we are . . . convinced that it is for us a means of doing good. . . . If there is no reason to boast, neither is there cause to despair of a house which is growing year by year, and which this very year has about 150 boarders and enjoys the confidence of the public." Similarly, the nuns are "doing good in their sphere. We could not regret our sacrifices of time and money unless they had interfered with the success of the Brothers or with anything of more importance. Now this did not occur, and if at this day, after fifteen years of painful labors, there is anything to console us, it is to see that Providence has given us the means to keep the three Societies which had been confided to us under obedience marching side by side."

Finally, the fourth complaint, trivial and mean-spirited, "that Father Sorin had kept the money collected for the [orphan] asylum at Vincennes, needs no other answer than the exhibition of the receipt for this same money, written entirely in the very hand of the good bishop [Saint-Palais], who must have forgotten." The receipt, in the form of a letter of thanks to Brother Lawrence, dated March 28, 1858, was duly exhibited.[24]

Archbishop Purcell may well have disliked this narrative, because he interpreted it as a not-too-veiled assault upon his colleagues of Vincennes and Fort Wayne—bishops, like most persons who share the same profession, tend to stick together—and so he advised against its circulation and even recommended its deletion. But such caution would have been out of character for Edward Sorin, who never suffered insult or animosity gladly. To be sure, he might have waited until the negative rumors and evolved into specific charges, with their sources plainly identified, before he counterattacked; yet often rumors take on a life of their own and do immense damage without ever revealing how they started or who started them. Purcell in any case could not have been displeased at the man-

24. Sorin, *Chronicles*, 210–212.

ner in which Sorin concluded his summary of Holy Cross's early adventures in America.

> In terminating this review of the first fifteen years of Notre Dame du Lac, let it be permitted us to add here that in this country the community has hardly found real and permanent sympathy except from the illustrious Archbishop Purcell. It was doubtless the will of heaven that one part of its trials should consist in this painful disappointment; but the more it felt the lack of this direct encouragement from those from whom it felt that it had the right to expect it, so much the more appreciative did it feel for the kindness and protection of the glorious archbishop, which was a sufficient compensation for all the rest.[25]

A bold conquistador in this new land Edward Sorin surely was. But he was not ready to burn *all* his boats.

The manifesto just reviewed provides evidence, as if any were needed, of the tension that has historically existed within the Catholic community between the organs of territorial and of universal authority. Or, to employ a less exalted idiom, it displays the age-old strain between regulars—members of religious orders, with international pretensions—and seculars—clergy subject to a diocesan bishop. Once the Congrégation de Sainte-Croix had secured Roman approval, it stood free of direct local control, a circumstance that invited discord. But the tension has never been absolute; a more or less amicable balance has been the norm, with the rights of each party spelled out in the canon law. More often than not, Rome played the role of referee rather than autocrat when contentions arose. And the persons involved on both sides, whatever their flaws of character, had all committed themselves to the furtherance of the same gospel. Nevertheless, contentions did arise, and a man of Sorin's impetuous temperament might have been expected to be embroiled in his share of them.

But volatility did not rule out pragmatism, quite to the contrary. In the rough-and-tumble of human relationships, storm could quickly give place to calm, yesterday's enemy could well be tomorrow's ally. Analogously, if Sorin indicted some prelates for failing to offer him and his mission "real and permanent sympathy," at the same time he appreciated the importance of cultivating the good opinion of J. B. Purcell. Once he had defended himself, he was prepared to compromise and to fall in with the archbishop's wishes. "I confess that every day," he wrote to Cincinnati, "this question [of education] seems to become more momentous in

---

25. Sorin, *Chronicles*, 213.

its bearings. Demands for teachers are becoming so numerous and so urgent that it seems to call forth on our part every exertion possible to meet at least some of these great wants." Then, he added blandly, as though unaware of Bishop Luers's designs on the Holy Cross missions: "I have thought of giving up all missionary and pastoral duties and consecrating to one single purpose the exclusive attention of our Congregation in this country, namely, to education."[26] "That is precisely, as it seems to me," Purcell replied with some relief, "what you ought to do: give up the care of the missions and devote yourselves to the care of youth. I believe I betray no secrets when I say that Right Reverend Bishop Luers would wish, does wish, to have the disposal to his own clergy of the missions with which you are now charged." What Sorin had written implied that the Salvatorist priests would in the future teach and also supervise the work of the Josephite brothers, which conformed to the archbishop's own predispositions. "Without priests exclusively charged with the instruction of the male youth, they are gone! This Province is wide awake on the subject, but while they are negotiating, souls are perishing. . . . God speed to your project."[27] Sorin quietly implemented the policy, though he appended a sensible qualification: "The Father Salvatorists were successively recalled from their missions and gave up their pastoral charges to devote themselves with the Brothers to the work of education. Still, they might accept parishes where there was a possibility of establishing schools of the Brothers and Sisters, but only when two Fathers could find employment."[28]

Luers was satisfied, indeed gratified, by this decision. "I am really glad," he told Purcell, "that the Reverend Mr. Sorin has given me up the missions; it is the only way to live in peace with him, and I will have no difficulty in getting them attended."[29] The bishop was happy enough to let Notre Dame see to the spiritual needs of Catholics living in its immediate environs "for some years to come."[30] The road ahead for the superior of Notre Dame and the bishop of Fort Wayne proved smoother than either of them had at first expected.

"THE YEAR 1858 ENDED PEACEABLY," even though the harvest that autumn had been a severe disappointment. "Wheat was not two-thirds

---

26. Sorin to Purcell, April 19, 1859, AIP.

27. Purcell to Sorin, April 22, 1859, AIP.

28. Sorin, *Chronicles*, 224.

29. Luers to Purcell, May 2, 1859, AIP (Sorin Papers).

30. Luers to Sorin, April 30, 1859, AIP. About 150 Catholic families went to Mass on the Notre Dame campus. Another fifty did so at a chapel, also served by Holy Cross, in the area north of the river still at this date called Lowell, and this evolved into what is now St. Joseph's parish, South Bend.

of what it is in an ordinary year, Indian corn still less, and potatoes did worse. Fruits had been a complete failure." But what Mother Nature took away one season she compensated for the next, as has been her wont since time immemorial. In 1859 the farm yielded 2,500 bushels of wheat, "or about half of what would be consumed [by the mission] in a year. This was a great help, because the year just ended had cost more than twenty thousand francs [$4,000] for this article alone." The recovery of the orchards and cornfields was likewise encouraging, and there was hope even for a good return from the sugar cane "or at least molasses." The "floating debt," though "slightly diminished," remained very high. A larger than usual grant from the Propagation of the Faith in Paris, together with an unexpected tuition-payment in the form of an ample mortgage, staved off any immediate financial crisis, affording "at least a beginning of hope that Divine Providence would again save the house." A further good sign was that "the College did not appear to suffer from the hard times, the number of pupils remaining about the same, . . . and the payments being made with about the same regularity."

The fluidity of the outlying foundations continued as before. New schools were opened in Fort Wayne and Toledo, and the one in Columbus was significantly expanded. The establishment in Milwaukee, on the other hand, was "suspended for an indefinite period . . . for want of a suitable place." Brother Dominick, in charge of the German school in Hamilton, Ohio, fell ill and then decided "to make an end of everything in one stroke. Without asking the advice of anyone, he left his post and his vocation." "In order to refresh both body and mind," he informed Sorin, "it is necessary for me to leave the Congregation and dedicate myself to a life of more corporal [sic] exercise."[31] Dominick's defection— "he persisted in his infidelity"—was not an isolated phenomenon. Two other professed brothers were also lost to the community: one "who had been an annoyance to the society for nearly ten years by his spirit of conviviality, levity, and murmuring;" and the other who went mad: "One fine morning [he] declared positively that the Pope had called him to Rome and that he was going . . . [and] that he had no doubt of his future election to the See of St. Peter." Seven brother-novices departed as well, some with permission, some without it. "None of them," Father Sorin recorded sourly, "was regretted as a loss." The slippage extended during these months to three priests who exchanged their commitment to Holy Cross for pastorates in Fort Wayne and Chicago.[32] The prevalent mood within the community gave the superior cause for alarm, though he could not bring

31. Dominick to Sorin, January 10, 1859, AIP.

32. See Kilroy to Sorin, February 23, 1859, AIP. Aloysius Mayer departed in 1858 and Bernard Joseph Voors in 1859. See *Matricule générale*, 692 and 1204, AIP.

himself to describe the malaise precisely: "The demon had asked for power to sift the Congregation. . . . Father Sorin did not hesitate to say . . . that if he saw the demon with his own eyes he would not believe more firmly in his presence and his efforts to destroy the work. . . . Prudence fled from those that should have remedied the evil. . . . Falsehood fell from the lips that had never before been suspected; multiplied and ruinous negligences were of daily occurrence even amongst members of the Chapter."

Some comparable restiveness showed itself among the secular boarding-students. In January 1859 and again in December "there was an uprising, or rather a mutiny, of about forty young men in the College." This unprecedented insubordination might have wrecked "the prospects of the whole scholastic year . . . had not the spirit of religion, which had its weight with the greater number, been brought to bear." Religion indeed had been at least partially the cause of the trouble, since renewed complaints of non-Catholic students appear to have sparked the rebellion.[33] But Sorin admitted that bad food badly prepared, always a hazard to a boarding school, had also played a role in fomenting trouble, as had "an overzealousness" in enforcing discipline. And he hinted at a darker possibility when he linked "certain faults" among the students with "particular friendships." Yet, despite these difficulties, he pronounced the academic year overall a success, and particularly "consoling was the excellent spirit that prevailed in the College at the end of the year."[34]

Not so auspicious, however, were developments ninety miles away.[35] Sorin had reckoned the foundation in Chicago to be crucial to the future of Holy Cross in America. As the railroads converged upon it and the traffic on Lake Michigan expanded, the city promised to emerge shortly as the commercial hub of the entire Middle West. Sorin's sound instinct told him that association with this robust focal point of rapidly growing population and of economic and political power would furnish Notre Dame a golden opportunity to enlarge its apostolate to a significant degree and, not incidentally, to guarantee it as well a rich source of vocations and financial support. With this conviction in mind he had entered into the agreement with Bishop O'Regan and dispatched a large

---

33. See chapter 19, above.

34. Sorin, *Chronicles,* 215–224, 242.

35. Sorin's account of the last phase of Holy Cross's mission in Chicago is a lengthy memorandum prepared for Cardinal Barnabò, Prefect of Propaganda, dated June 6, 1861, AGEN. Incorporated in this document are word-for-word sections of the *Chronicles,* as well as relevant correspondence. The memorandum was never delivered to Barnabò. See below.

number of personnel to serve the University of St. Mary of the Lake and other diocesan institutions.[36]

The timing of the transaction had not been propitious. The depression of the late 1850s had accentuated the difficulties that would have attended such an initiative in any case. As Notre Dame could not for the moment fulfill its rental obligation of more than $2,000 per annum, the diocese fell far short of the promises it made with regard to the upkeep of facilities and collateral funding. Sorin understandably gave emphasis to the latter rather than the former.

> It was soon discovered that the Congregation had bound itself to more than it had reckoned on. Instead of fifty dollars which it was said [by O'Regan] would be sufficient of repairs [at St. Mary's], it was absolutely necessary to contract at once for seven hundred dollars for a single item; moreover the bishop required the Congregation to take the old furniture of the college, which made an additional sum of five hundred dollars.... More than once, by word of mouth and by writing, Father Sorin reminded [the bishop] of his promise to build new school houses, but he always answered that he was obliged to defer this expense, however pressing he himself considered it. Yet such was the deplorable condition of those poor hovels in which the schools of the Brothers and the Sisters were taught that it was out of the question to expect any but the children of destitute families, especially when the free schools of the city were provided with magnificent buildings in which nothing was wanting.[37]

In addition to these embarrassments Sorin had to acknowledge that Basile Moreau, in this instance at least, had judged the American scene better than he had himself. In September 1857, at the end of his sojourn at Notre Dame, the Founder—it may be recalled—had in Sorin's company paid a formal, if brief, Visit to the Holy Cross houses in Chicago. "The only schoolhouse he had time to inspect . . . appeared to him so unfit that he forbade the Brothers who taught there . . . to continue until the building had been thoroughly repaired." Nor had a courtesy call on the bishop lightened the mood: "[O'Regan] was eulogizing Father Sorin, whereupon the Very Reverend Founder remarked that he did not consider Father Sorin deserving of much praise in the contract he had made with his Lordship, and that unless some help were given him, he did not see how the [Holy Cross] establishment could pay the annual rental of $2,150." The bishop

---

36. See chapters 18 and 19, above.
37. Sorin, *Chronicles*, 228.

placidly replied that, since income from the schools was indeed deficient, he would authorize an annual citywide collection which "would bring in, he was sure, a thousand dollars. A circular to this effect was addressed to the pastors, but the collection was made in only one church and brought in sixty-six dollars. . . . It was no more spoken of by either party."[38]

A year later the unfortunate and unpopular O'Regan was gone. His successor was thirty-three-year-old James Duggan, also an Irishman and originally a missioner in St. Louis.[39] Even before he was installed in January 1859, Father Sorin had heard a rumor to the effect that the new bishop did not look favorably upon the Holy Cross foundation at St. Mary's and elsewhere. Accordingly, in April, he addressed an inquiry to Duggan, who replied with brutal candor: "Since I have been here I have always desired to see this property restored to the diocese, and since you have not fulfilled the contract [to pay rent annually], you leave me no alternative but to rescind it. I do not think the gain received by the diocese from the presence of the community compensates for the property it holds. . . . Without further useless discussion of what is unalterably decreed in my mind, I request that you take your measures, because I myself am beginning to take mine."[40]

And so another name was added to the roster of hostile or at least uncooperative bishops: Hailandière, Saint-Palais, Luers, Lefèvre, Spalding, Hughes, Timon, O'Regan, and now Duggan. "It would be useless to tell of the surprise and the pain caused at Notre Dame by this first letter. To dismiss more than thirty members without any other pretext than that of the violation of a contract . . . was something hardly credible." Sorin immediately consulted a lawyer in Chicago, who declared the contract perfectly valid. Duggan, when apprised of this judgment, cheerfully agreed, but he contended, not without justification, that a valid contract, when its terms were not met, could be voided. This unpleasant reality of course was, and remained, the fatal flaw in Sorin's position. Nevertheless he secured an audience with Duggan "and begged the bishop to bear in mind that the Congregation could not thus, either in honor or in justice or according to its Constitutions, abandon the establishment [in Chicago], and concluded that it was obliged to retain it. The question seemed to be settled, and for about two months nothing more was said of it."[41]

He was whistling in the dark. By mid-June it was unmistakable that Duggan had not altered his intentions. Sorin then proposed a compromise, whereby Holy

---

38. "Memorandum," June 6, 1861, 3, AGEN.
39. See Garraghan, *Catholic Chicago*, 180–218.
40. Duggan to Sorin, April 18, 1859, AIP.
41. Sorin, *Chronicles*, 231.

Cross would withdraw from St. Mary's of Chicago if the bishop would concede that "select schools should be established in different parts of the city for [our] Brothers and Sisters." Duggan was noncommittal. Sorin's anxious letters went unanswered, and his visits to Chicago bore no result; indeed, after several "mortifying" interviews, Duggan refused to see him and insisted that any future discussion be carried out in writing. Accordingly, on July 13 Sorin wrote that "having prayed, reflected, and consulted, we respectfully beg to inform you that we have come to the same conclusion as at first, namely, to keep our contract, and whilst we are determined to do our best to correspond to your views, we think ourselves secure in the expectation that you will appreciate our efforts and will grant us your protection." Duggan responded the next day: "In answer to your note in which you inform me of your final resolution, I now write to let you know mine. It is simply this: that you vacate the college and the premises by the first of next August, and that the community, men and women, leave the city by that day. I will take the property such as it is, with its improvements whatever they may be, and will be satisfied not to demand the payment of arrears [in rent] for the past two years."[42]

But Edward Sorin had not carved out of a wilderness an increasingly thriving, if still somewhat rude, organization by accepting at face value every *diktat* from on high. Duggan's peremptory dismissal "astonished" him, he protested. "If I were the only one interested, I would not have waited for a second similar injunction; but I am charged with the interests of other people who trust me to protect them. . . . Your order to vacate the college can be founded only on the fact of the nullity of our lease. Without doubt your lawyers have told you that it was in effect annulled; but ours tell us just the contrary, including even the lawyer that drew it up for Bishop O'Regan. Up to the present therefore I see no legal decision in virtue of which we should give up our possession."[43] This appeal Duggan did not answer, and Sorin's argument continued to be hampered by the hard reality that the eviction notice had resulted from the nonpayment of the rent called for by the contract. A vague invocation of the assurances of O'Regan's lawyer did little to meet that contention, nor did it allay Duggan's implicit threat to put the matter before the civil courts.

The bishop, however, could be challenged by a different legal strategy. Thanks to the recent papal ratification of its constitutions, the Congrégation de Sainte-Croix now enjoyed an enhanced status in church law, which was applicable to the priests and brothers, if not to the sisters. Sorin sensed that here he had an

---

42. Duggan to Sorin, July 14, 1859, AIP.

43. Quoted in "Memorandum," June 6, 1851, 5, AGEN.

advantage. "Last evening," he reported in mid-July, "I had an interview with the dear bishop of Chicago." It was a testy conversation, during which Duggan had blurted out his disbelief that Holy Cross had in fact acquired Roman approbation, though he surely knew better. "I had hoped for a better result, and now I see before us only a choice between retiring in silence or remaining in the middle of an uproar (*éclat*) brought on by a scandalous legal procedure." Father Sorin was "certain our cause would be vindicated in the American courts and probably at Rome." And if this were too sanguine an assessment, he still preferred uproar to retirement. "In truth, even though it is the daily bread of religious communities, and especially that of Sainte-Croix, to suffer injustices, insults, and ingratitude, even from bishops, I still feel an inclination to resist that which seems to me to be clearly unjust and disastrous."[44]

So he addressed a long appeal to Duggan, stating once again various aspects of his oft-repeated rationale: "We were urged by Bishop O'Regan to come to Chicago. I cannot see that we failed through our own fault in anything we had undertaken to do, except in the payment of the rent, which we thought ourselves justified in delaying for a time"; "If an impartial judge would make a comparison between the state in which we found all things three years ago [and now], we should not fear the result"; "We made no profit, but rather find a deficit of more than a thousand dollars . . . because of the hard times and the non-payment of schooling." But now he brandished his new weapon and leveled it above these familiar protestations. "You seem to have no fear of the scandal that would result from legal proceedings in this matter. I assure you that I could not be so insensitive thereto." And the bishop should bear in mind that there existed another and, as far as both parties were concerned, a higher tribunal to take account of: "If up to the present I have refused to our withdrawal from Chicago, it is because I thought it contrary to Canon Law."

To drive home this point, Sorin enclosed in his letter a lengthy extract from a treatise by a prominent French canon lawyer. The quotation showed that Sorin had chosen his ground shrewdly, and without doubt it had its effect, for a while anyway, upon the bishop of Chicago.

A religious house once legitimately established in a diocese, the bishop can no longer suppress this house or deprive a congregation of the right to maintain a house. The Apostolic See, in approving an institute of this sort, confers upon it thereby the right to extend itself into various parts of the world, the only requisite condition remaining to be fulfilled that the con-

---

44. Sorin to Moreau, July 20, 1859, AGEN.

sent of the ordinary[45] be had for any new foundation. When this condition has been fulfilled, that is, once the consent of the ordinary of the place has been obtained, the right of domicile in that diocese has been acquired by a congregation by virtue of papal approval. Thereafter, neither the bishop nor any of his successors can suppress the religious house. If, however, suppression seems urgently necessary, recourse will be had to the Holy See.[46]

This learned commentary brought the young bishop up short: if Sorin was vulnerable because he could not pay the rent required by the contract, Duggan was vulnerable from another angle: if could not prove that O'Regan had not canonically established Holy Cross in the diocese of Chicago, his only recourse was an appeal to the Roman court.

As the bishop pondered this unwelcome prospect, there occurred an unexpected and somewhat mysterious intervention. In the late spring, when the quarrel had first broken out, Sorin had had turned for advice to his one good friend in the hierarchy. Purcell had counseled him to approach Duggan's metropolitan (and, indeed, his patron), the archbishop of St. Louis, and to ask him "to lend his attention to the difficulty and settle it." Father Sorin did write St. Louis, but the archbishop answered with discouraging candor: "I ought not to be [the] person chosen to arbitrate between you. My relations with the Bishop of Chicago are so intimate that, with every desire to do justice, I should always fear lest I might either be, or appear to be, unduly influenced in his favor."[47] Then, one day in late August, when the Chicago crisis was at its peak, "the bells of Notre Dame were suddenly heard" singing out the arrival of the archbishop of Baltimore, "the primate of the United States."[48] This grand dignitary, Francis Patrick Kenrick by name,[49] "had heard of the difficulties of the Congregation with Bishop Duggan

---

45. In canon law the local bishop's normal jurisdiction is defined as "ordinary," and so this word is used as a synonym. In this case, to suppress a religious congregation once established in his diocese, the "ordinary of the place" would need "extraordinary" jurisdiction, to be found only in Rome.

46. "Memorandum," June 6, 1861, 6–7, AGEN. The canonist quoted was Marie-Dominique Bouix.

47. Peter Kenrick to Sorin, June 28, 1859, AIP.

48. Sorin's flattering designation was not accurate. However, during the mid-nineteenth century several petitions were sent to Rome in hopes of securing this honorary title for the archbishop of Baltimore. They were denied. "Rome makes no secret of its dislike for primacies," observed J. B. Purcell. See Thomas W. Spalding, *The Premier See: A History of the Archdiocese of Baltimore, 1789–1989* (Baltimore, 1989), 152.

49. See John P. Marschall, "Francis Patrick Kenrick, 1851–1863: The Baltimore Years" (unpublished doctoral dissertation, The Catholic University of America, 1965).

and, as he himself said, those difficulties made him wish to see the house [at Notre Dame]."

Kenrick "remained for twenty-four hours, showed himself most gracious to everybody, listened to the whole story of Chicago, suggested what was to be done, and all but gave assurance that everything would be arranged."[50] When he left next day for Chicago, he carried with him Sorin's twenty-page memorandum on the dispute to be delivered to James Duggan. Baltimore's parting advice was that Sorin should "claim the return of this memorial if matters were not [satisfactorily] arranged, and send it to St. Louis, to the metropolitan." Some days later, in accord with this recommendation, Patrick Dillon, at that time Sorin's most trusted lieutenant, was charged to go to Chicago, reclaim the memorandum, and proceed with it in hand to St. Louis. But when Father Dillon was admitted to Bishop Duggan's presence, "all was changed. His Lordship now only desired to have an understanding with the Reverend Father Sorin and to retain the Society [in Chicago] that it might continue to do there all the good possible."[51] Duggan's change of mind was remarkable, though, as events were to prove, only temporary. How much it had to do with Kenrick's pressure can only be guessed at. Perhaps Edward Sorin's signal that he was prepared to appeal the dispute to the Roman curia, combined with Baltimore's admonition, was enough to move him. Or maybe the genetic connection between Baltimore and St. Louis played a role; Francis Patrick Kenrick's younger brother, Peter Richard, was the archbishop of St. Louis. It is not inconceivable that a discreet brotherly consultation may have led the latter to advise his protégé in Chicago that the struggle to reassert diocesan control was not, at this moment, a winning proposition.

The reconciliation at any rate was sealed by a cordial meeting between Duggan and Sorin, though "Monseigneur's change to our way of thinking," the latter confessed to a friend, "remains a genuine mystery."[52] The bishop confirmed the arrangement agreed to by his predecessor, and also awarded to the priests of Holy Cross the administration of St. Joseph's, one of the largest and most prosperous parishes in his diocese. Father Sorin for his part renewed his pledge "to keep a respectable day-school," to provide staff for various parochial schools, and, going beyond the original commitment, to introduce genuine collegiate courses at St. Mary of the Lake. On the ticklish matter of the unpaid rent, he remembered

---

50. Yet less than three years later, when Kenrick wrote a letter of recommendation for Sorin to a friend in Ireland, he said: "Although I have never had the pleasure of meeting [Sorin], he is known to me by reputation as a zealous clergyman." Kenrick to Dooley, November 25, 1861, AIP.

51. Sorin, *Chronicles*, 240.

52. Sorin to Drouelle, August 18, 1859, AGEN.

Kenrick of Baltimore's warning that no rapprochement would be possible without at least a partial settlement of that debt. Sorin therefore promised to place $3,000 in Duggan's hands by the May of 1860. "With considerable difficulty, the Congregation managed to pay him that sum by the specified time."[53] And, as a token of goodwill as well as of the importance he attached to Holy Cross's presence in Chicago, he saw to it that some of his most promising young men— including Patrick Dillon and Neal Gillespie—should serve, at least for brief periods, as local superior.[54]

Peace had hardly been established, however, when Sorin received an indication that hostilities might soon resume. "Next Saturday," Father Dillon wrote from Chicago, "the rent will be due, and we should be prepared to meet it unless we wish to be exposed to ejectment [sic]. It is needless for me to say that this installment at least must be paid from Notre Dame. Perhaps we will be able to help the next time."[55] Sure enough, within days an ominous augury came from Duggan's agent. "Having no evidence of anything been [sic] paid," he wrote at the end of September, "I give you a statement of the whole." The rent in arrears totaled $7,525.[56] Yet, despite this reminder, relations appeared to be relatively smooth until the summer of 1860. At the ceremony closing the academic year, "the bishop, who was in town and whom everybody expected, did not make his appearance. If the cause of his return to his earlier coolness was not easy to discover, the object was less enigmatic; the bishop again wanted to resume possession [of St. Mary of the Lake]." As though this rudeness had been a portent, Duggan decided "suddenly to take St. Joseph's church from the Congregation and to transfer it to a secular priest." Only with the income derived from this parish could Holy Cross possibly meet the required rental-payments, and so in losing it "the Congregation was deprived of the principal support which it found there to meet its engagements. This was not merely withholding [the bishop's] protection, but it was ratifying a loss which he well knew would be fatal to the Congregation in Chicago." Meanwhile, the brothers and sisters who taught in parochial schools went unpaid, and the buildings in which they toiled "were left in a shocking state of neglect. The efforts of the most devoted members [of Holy Cross] were thwarted; each superior lost courage when . . . he saw not only the precarious condition of the establishment but the unmistakable proofs of bad will on the part of the ecclesiastical authorities."[57]

---

53. "Memorandum," June 6, 1861, 9, AGEN.
54. Sorin to Moreau, August 22, 1858, AGEN.
55. Dillon to Sorin, September 28, 1859, AIP.
56. McMullen to Sorin, September 29, 1859, AIP.
57. Sorin, *Chronicles*, 257–260.

Sorin was away in Rome[58] when the crisis reached its apex. By the time he returned home at the beginning of May 1861, Fort Sumter had fallen and the nation stood at the brink of civil war. "Everything was changed in the United States; commerce was entirely paralyzed, and in money transactions everybody understood that patience toward a debtor had become a necessity." But Bishop Duggan did not so understand: the rent had not been paid and therefore Holy Cross must evacuate all diocesan property if it did not want to be summoned before a civil magistrate. Icy letters were once more exchanged, acrimonious and fruitless conversations indulged in. Finally, in June, Sorin asked for a definitive episcopal statement in writing, and Duggan quickly complied.

> In answer to your letter I have only to repeat to you what I have often said before: that since the contract between you and Bishop O'Regan has been violated by you in almost every point, I have only to take back the property of the Church which you are occupying. The college has not been properly kept; the schools in the parishes have been neglected; and the rent which you agreed to pay has not been paid. For these reasons and others, I require that you no longer retain the property of the Church; and remitting you the several thousands of dollars now due, I simply demand possession of our own property. If I must resort to legal measures to attain this object, let all the scandal and all the consequences fall back on you. For three years I have borne much for the sake of peace; but I am now resolved not to be any longer trifled with.[59]

In Sorin's "eyes and conscience, this letter did not contain a truthful phrase."[60]

Holy Cross nevertheless had to relinquish its mission in Chicago, a bitter blow for Father Sorin, who had staked so many future hopes on its success. To be sure, only his side of the story was ever fully told,[61] and he was never one to minimize his and his colleagues' accomplishments or to exaggerate the virtues of his opponents. Yet in fact the mission had all kinds of internal troubles, and Bishop Duggan had legitimate reasons for dissatisfaction. The expulsion from St. Joseph's parish, for instance, was less an arbitrary act on the bishop's part than Sorin suggested; it was largely due the unpopularity of the Holy Cross priests assigned

---

58. See chapter 21, below.

59. Duggan to Sorin, June 11, 1861, AIP.

60. Sorin, *Chronicles*, 262.

61. For example, Garraghan, *Catholic Chicago*, 213, states merely that unspecified financial troubles prompted the priests of Holy Cross "to discontinue their educational and parochial labors in Chicago, where their zeal had merited general commendation, and return to Notre Dame."

there. And they were not only unpopular among the parishioners. Charles-Antoine Exel was the last in an unhappy series of pastors of St. Joseph's, about whom the mission's overall superior, Patrick Dillon, could hardly speak rationally.

> It grieves me to the heart [he told Sorin] to write to you as I feel compelled to do. I will not remain here . . . if Father Exel is not called away from here. I cannot, will not, do it. If Father Exel is not withdrawn from here, I will go home to Notre Dame. He treats me very unjustly, in fact, acts like a crazy man. But whether he be crazed or only eccentric, I cannot bear to be treated like a dog, abused (in language) in the hearing of the students, and some who understood [sic].[62]

The canny Brother Stephen, sent by Sorin to Chicago to keep an eye on the confrères,[63] also recognized, if not quite so viscerally, the problem posed by Exel. "I am at a loss," he reported, "to know how or what to do [with] the Trustees of the German church [St. Joseph's]: ask for the key to lock it up?" One bright June day he confronted four angry laymen at the entrance to the church: "[I] ascertained that they want no more to do with your Congregation. They will not have Father Exel.[64] They will lock the church and give the key to the bishop."[65]

Father Dillon, meanwhile, had lost all sense of confidence that the brothers would adhere to his direction. Two of them had already absconded "without letting us know. . . . Father," he wrote Sorin, "I am becoming tired of my obedience [i.e., his assignment in Chicago] *as far as the Brothers are concerned.* I fear they have no confidence in me, and of course [they] do not like me." Moreover, the physical state of the mission had become deplorable. "The house here [at St. Mary of the Lake] is generally in a state of filth that should [make] any member of the community here blush for shame. It is probable that I will have to get the housecleaning done by strangers."[66]

When he gathered together the material about the *l'affaire* Chicago into a memorial for Cardinal Barnabò at Propaganda, Sorin put upon it, understandably, the best possible construction from his own point of view. He sent it to his old friend, Victor Drouelle,[67] who had for some years been the Holy Cross

---

62. Dillon to Sorin, April 18, 1860, AIP.
63. See Stephen to Sorin, April 20, 1859, AIP.
64. Exel, born in Strasbourg in 1826, seceded from Holy Cross in 1863. See *Matricule générale*, 1279, AIP.
65. Stephen to Sorin, June 15, 1860, AIP.
66. Dillon to Sorin, March 1, 1860, AIP.
67. See chapter 14, above.

superior in Rome, with the request that it should be delivered to Barnabò. Drouelle, however, used to curial ways, immediately discerned the weakness in Sorin's case: the nagging problem that the agreed-to rental had not been paid to Bishop O'Regan's successor left Holy Cross in Indiana in an indefensible position, and so Drouelle never submitted the memorandum.[68]

Thus did a promising venture come to a sorry end. And when all is said and done, the conduct of James Duggan through these years was particularly mean and reprehensible. And mysterious too. What, for instance, prompted him to quarrel, reconcile, and then quarrel again, all within less than three years and always on the same issue? What part, if any, did the archbishop of St. Louis play in Duggan's judgment that Rome would support Holy Cross and then that Rome would not? Were the bishop's violent mood-swings precursors to the complete mental collapse he was to suffer later in the decade? In their inventory of intellectual sins, the moral theologians include *delectatio morosa,* which they define as taking pleasure in someone else's distress. Edward Sorin could have been forgiven had he indulged in some small *delectatio* at the thought that Bishop Duggan was to spend the last thirty-three years of his long life—he died in 1899—in an insane asylum.

---

68. See, however, Sorin's apologia in Sorin to Drouelle, June 12, 1861, AGEN.

chapter twenty-one

The Venerable Hand

"ABOUT THE MIDDLE OF THE YEAR," EDWARD SORIN recorded, "the pupils organized a military company, the members of which, thirty-seven in number, adopted a very graceful uniform. This company, even till the very last day, bore itself most honorably and added much to all the celebrations at the end of the year."[1] The year was 1859, and these students, belonging to the senior department of the college, called themselves the Continental Cadets. They wore a uniform of buff and blue, intended to be remindful of the soldiers of the American Revolution. They drilled regularly on the Notre Dame campus, and on the fourth of July, when they marched in close order into South Bend to participate in the civic festivities, their gallant appearance evoked much admiration among the townsfolk. The younger boarders were not to be outdone and organized a little battalion of their own, the Washington Cadets.[2] Sorin saw these martial exercises as conducive to good order and discipline as well as pleasantly decorative. He did not foresee that in less than two years many of his Continental Cadets would march off to battle, and some of them would die. Indeed, when the war between the states broke out, he described it as an event "contrary to the anticipations of all thinking men."[3]

Perhaps this failure of vision was due simply to Father Sorin's keen desire to keep clear of any connection with secular politics—a prudent stance for an immigrant Catholic priest to assume in the wake of the Know-Nothing era. Certainly he did not appear to be gripped by the great social issue of the day. In the

---

1. Sorin, *Chronicles,* 223.
2. *Golden Jubilee,* 93–94.
3. Sorin, *Chronicles,* 276.

southwest corner of Michigan, only a few miles away, lay a series of stations along the underground railroad in active defiance of the Fugitive Slave Act; there is no evidence that runaway blacks sought refuge on the shores of the Notre Dame lakes.[4] Not that Sorin sympathized with bond slavery, but his deepest commitment was, as ever, to the survival and well-being of his mission; not even "Bleeding Kansas," the *Dred Scott* decision, and the fateful election of Lincoln in 1860 could distract him from his single-minded purpose.

These immediate prewar years presented an amalgam of the heartening and the disappointing for that mission. The amount of overall debt "slightly diminished, . . . but it was still very high." Notes came due with dreary regularity; "still, there was at the bottom of each one's soul a conviction that the same providential hand which had so often drawn [Notre Dame] out of its difficulties would not fail." That same hand reached out protectively over the superior himself: "The Brother infirmarian, who had been accustomed . . . to bring [Sorin] a dose of bitters before dinner, made a mistake one morning and presented him with a large dose of the preparation known as Pain-Killer. He would certainly have soon been a corpse if he had taken the dose."[5]

The dependent houses continued to experience mixed fortunes. Enrollment at St. Mary's Academy held steady, and the number of postulants and novices among the sisters continued to expand remarkably. The foundation in Chicago experienced severe crisis, then a preternatural calm, and finally—though the dénouement was still in the future—a crushing reversal.[6] Vocations to the brotherhood were highly encouraging; by the beginning of 1860 the novitiate counted a complement of twenty-one. Yet, during the same period, several more brothers departed, manifesting a tenacious inconstancy which Father Sorin routinely ascribed to demonic influence. While he thankfully acknowledged providential progress in the work of Holy Cross, he discerned simultaneously the machinations of the evil one, of whose morbid presence he possessed almost as palpable an awareness as he did that of the Virgin Mary. Edward Sorin—tough, opinionated, self-willed, often ornery and obstinate—was nonetheless a fierce Christian believer. If the devil was a vivid reality to him—"a raging lion," as the Scripture has it, "seeking someone to devour"—equally real was the antidote with which to confront the enemy of humankind. He was never embarrassed by his own devotional practices, never diffident in recommending them to others, and never ir-

---

4. Hope's assumption (*Notre Dame*, 118) that Sorin was at least tangentially involved in the underground railroad is not persuasive.

5. Sorin, *Chronicles*, 218–220.

6. See chapter 20, above.

resolute in demanding the like from those subject to him. To ward off the diabolical effects of chronic financial uncertainties and negligent auxiliaries and mutinous students, he did not hesitate to invoke the ancient remedies of prayer and fasting. Not untypical of his pattern of spiritual leadership was this circular dispatched a little more than a year before the beginning of the Civil War to all the houses of Holy Cross in the Province of Indiana.

> Once more I have to call upon every member of the community for a new effort and particular prayers to secure again extraordinary help from above.... For this I prescribe an extra Communion weekly, and every day after evening prayer the litany of the Blessed Virgin, with the *Memorare* and the invocation to St. Joseph. Meanwhile the strictest economy should be observed in all our Houses and by every member in a true spirit of religion with a view to please God and to save something for the Congregation in its distress. You may imagine ... how painful it must be for me to hear that in one of our establishments ... scarcely any regard is paid to the Rule on meals and food. I commend that establishment to the prayers of the community.... What blessings can attend the labors of Religious who have made, as St. Paul says, their belly their favorite idol? ... Thank God such members are not numerous in our ranks. There are others whose spirit of regularity, devotedness, and self-sacrifice fills our minds with edification and our hearts with joy and hopes for the future.... Let all try and offer a holy violence to Heaven and trust in the mercies of God. Above, all let a perfect regularity mark the life of everyone in the community.[7]

One consideration presses itself upon the Christian believer as he makes his pilgrim way through the world and ever more urgently so as time passes. Edward Sorin, now in his middle years, began to turn his thoughts toward his own mortality. Perhaps the near escape from the lethal dose of "Pain Killer" had pushed such reflections to the forefront of his mind. "The Blessed Virgin has doubtless watched over that life which may still be useful to her work." And yet, he added soberly, the episode "was an additional proof of the uncertainty of life and of the necessity for a religious as well as for any other Christian to be always prepared." In the autumn of the year, when construction began on a new chapel for the

---

7. Sorin, "Circular Letter," December 19, 1859, AGEN. The *Memorare* (vocative, meaning "remember") is a short prayer dating to the fifteenth century and one especially recommended by Pope Pius IX. It begins, "Remember, most gracious Virgin Mary, that never was it known, that anyone who sought thy protection should go unaided."

brothers' novitiate, he determined to give material expression to his heightened sensitivity. "Here Father Sorin had dug for Brother Vincent, his first companion, and for himself a burial vault where they are both to rest in the expectation of a blessed resurrection. The vault is under the floor in the center of the nave." It was a gesture entirely appropriate for a man who dearly loved those who strove with him for a common cause and who therefore proposed to seek eternal rest in their company. And it was consistent too with the genius of Catholicism, a religion so richly enmeshed in sacred symbols. The modest memorial in the floor of the chapel would be a kind of sacrament, an outward sign of a hidden reality.

But there was more. "In this spot is to be erected a little monument in the shape of a prie-dieu to receive the right hand of the Very Reverend Father Moreau, the founder of Holy Cross. The hand will be suspended as if giving a blessing."[8] The idea had been broached the preceding February, on Moreau's sixty-first birthday and just a week after Sorin's own forty-sixth.

> However strange this letter may appear to you at first sight, it is never-theless one of the most important you have ever received from this Province. Though it has to do with a future which, I hope, is still far off, yet since we are never assured of a tomorrow, we think it our duty to present to you in due time a request which your spirit of faith will immediately understand and which, we hope, your heart will approve without hesitation. If we thought for a moment that you were attached to this life, perhaps we would not dare to hint that one day it must end. But we are well aware that that you see in its approach a relief (*soulagement*), a joy. In fact for you death can only be a gain, for who better than you has fought the good fight, and who can be more assured of the reward the just Judge has promised?

When that day comes, "some keepsake of him so loved will be for everyone a lightening of their sorrow." But "we carry our thoughts still farther," to a commitment outweighing individual consolation. "We wish to give you an unfailing means (*un moyen des plus infaillibles*) of uniting forever the East and the West and of drawing still tighter the bonds which should forever unite the children of the same family, whatever differences in climate there be, whatever the seductions of the time or place." And so, incorporated into the brothers' new chapel, "which is to rise . . . between the old oak tree and the funeral cross which crowns the community cemetery," will be the "final the resting place for the two patri-

---

8. Sorin, *Chronicles*, 219, 243–244.

archs, for Brother Vincent and for me, who was the first to plant the standard of Holy Cross on American soil."

> But in order that the entire Province may find there all the lessons and con-solations which the dead can offer the living, we want a monument to be erected [where] . . . one day the venerable hand which directed their eyes and their steps to the New World, which signed their obediences for the vast forests of America, and which for more than twenty years has never ceased to support, guide, protect, defend, bless, feed, and clothe them. It is this venerable hand they desire to see raised above their mortal remains as a hand that blesses and protects them still. It is to this same hand that they would have their successors come . . . to learn that the very same hand which founded Holy Cross likewise founded Notre Dame du Lac and that it continues to keep the well-beloved daughter united with its dearly-loved mother. . . . O, if we had no fear of going beyond the limits of a letter, how happy we would be to speak of how the sentiments of faith and love will rise under the hand of a Father who will remind them of so many virtues and so many wonders, the sight of whom alone will calm all storms and fears, and be an unfailing source of joy and blessing.[9]

A "strange letter" indeed, but one which affords at least a partial view of the complex psyche of him who wrote it. Enough has been said in these pages already to establish the incessant rivalry between Moreau and Sorin, the lack of sym-pathy, the proneness to mutual misunderstanding, the clash of personalities; and much more will have to be said. Yet through all these bruising contentions and harsh recriminations a part of Edward Sorin's most intimate self maintained a profound reverence for the Founder, which this extraordinary petition reflected. The temptation is strong to discern a schizoid strain in Sorin's attitude, a duality which, although he scarcely recognized its existence, he struggled through vari-ous gestures of reconciliation to dislodge. But it is perilous to indulge in amateur psychoanalysis about persons long dead, and in any case a better explanation lies at hand. The son of the gentleman from Ahuillé and the son of the impoverished wine-peddler from Laigné-en-Belin represented different social classes and hence different styles, assumptions, and spheres of fellowship.[10] In the ordinary course

---

9. Sorin to Moreau, February 12, 1860, AGEN. Moreau's natal day was February 11. For Moreau's courteous but firm refusal of the request, see Catta, *Moreau*, 2: 371–372.

10. Shortly before his death, I asked the venerable Louis Putz, C.S.C.—who had been trained in Le Mans in the 1930s—why, in his opinion, Sorin and Moreau could not get along. "Simple," Father Putz replied. "Sorin was a nobleman, Moreau was a peasant."

of things they would never have met, much less have entered into a symbiotic relationship.

They did meet, however, and bound themselves together in commitment to a common cause, to the propagation of post-revolutionary French Catholicism with all its emotional overtones. In order to achieve the goal, the gallant gentleman, even as he went off to the ends of the earth, solemnly promised to obey the sturdy peasant. The pledge was given in good faith and yet it produced conflict and pain and finally alienation, because, in a culture Moreau knew nothing about, it became impossible for one of Sorin's temperament and antecedents to fulfill. The two men appeared to get on well when they met face-to-face,[11] but such encounters were rare and fleeting, and the enormous distance over which they normally had to communicate served to undermine any sense of comity. Yet Sorin admired Moreau and, in his own way, loved him. To express affection artlessly was an attribute of the religiosity both men practiced. A later generation of Catholics, not much attracted to the veneration of relics, might think Sorin's proposal to embalm the Founder's hand and "to suspend it as if giving a blessing" over his own grave to have bordered on the bizarre. For Edward Sorin, it was a *cri de coeur*.

T HE BLOOD OF A MAN very much alive still quickened that guiding hand, but, after the buffeting of thirty-five years, it had plainly lost some of its resilience. The ambitions of his youth, to do great things for God, Basile Moreau had largely fulfilled. The scars, however, left by so many struggles, were there for all to see. Nor, as he entered the twilight of his life, had the struggles abated—indeed, they had swelled into a seemingly chronic state of crisis, in the face of which he sought refuge more and more in the solitude of his chapel and his study. His own selfless dedication stood as a constant example to the best instincts of those who joined him, and no one could doubt his personal integrity or the profundity of his prayer-life. Inspired by a disinterested zeal he had created virtually out of nothing a religious organization so symmetrical, well-ordered, and serviceable as to rank him with the Loyolas and Ligouris of the Catholic past. Yet, as so often in persons of illustrious achievement, Moreau's very strengths were the occasion of weakness. He had indeed put together a system which, on paper, could answer any question and provide for every contingency. But the structure of his mind and the habits of a lifetime led him to think that the art of governance consisted primarily in the promotion of a conceptually validated

---

11. A fact emphasized to me by my friend and colleague, Thomas E. Blantz, C.S.C.

framework. So it was that nothing brought him more satisfaction than the composition of rules and abstract directives. In 1843, for instance, when the first of his sisters departed for America, Father Moreau promised them "a little book of Constitutions, which would be a safeguard and a guide"; the finished "little book" filled up 400 pages of print.[12]

Real men and women do not live by theory alone. The tragic end of Moreau's brilliant career stemmed not from any lack of labor or noble purpose on his part. Doubtless the opposition toward him that arose within the congregation stemmed partly from unworthy motives of ambition and jealousy among some of those most closely associated with him; one is reminded of the dramatist's description of the aging Henry II: "Round him waiting hungry sons."[13] But contributing also to the misfortune was Moreau's own rigidity, which hindered him when confronting the vagaries of the human condition. In his administration, moreover, he displayed a set of peculiarly contradictory dispositions. On the one hand, he was thoroughly committed to the centralization of authority; complaints about his "tyranny" became common as the years passed. Yet, at the same time, once he had established to his satisfaction the *theoretical* claims of the mother-house to be the fountainhead of all decision-making, he proved remote, lackadaisical even, in implementing them. He seemed content instead to issue constitutional proclamations, pious entreaties, interminable circular letters, reams of paper, in short, admirable as doctrinal exhortation but hardly calculated to amend the unruly. His failure to rein in an independent-minded Edward Sorin has been amply recorded in these pages. Ironically enough, like his counterpart in America, whom he often reproved for overexuberance, Father Moreau routinely persisted in expanding Holy Cross's operations beyond the resources available to him; unlike Sorin, however, he did not keep his hand—that venerable hand—firmly on the tiller, and his ship drifted ever nearer the whirlpool of financial and administrative collapse.

The disastrous Marie-Julien affair, about to burst into the public domain just at the time Sorin dispatched his remarkable petition, was a case in point. For many years Father Moreau had hoped to establish a Holy Cross foundation in Paris, but no favorable opportunity had presented itself. Then, in 1856, came an invitation to participate in the supervision of a Catholic *collège* already functioning in the capital. Moreau chose Sorin's old friend and contemporary, Louis Champeau,[14] to head the small contingent sent promptly from Le Mans. The

---

12. Costin, *Priceless Spirit*, 147.
13. See T. S. Eliot, *Murder in the Cathedral*, Part 1 (the third temptation).
14. See chapter 14, above.

choice was, in theory, an appropriate one: Father Champeau was a senior member of the congregation, had served in several responsible positions, and had earned the reputation of being an excellent teacher and even something of a scholar. Yet he was a moody, querulous man who had seldom shown any talent for administration; only recently the bishop of Orléans had dismissed him from the rectorship of the seminary there for incompetence. With this deficiency in mind, Moreau assigned forty-three-year-old Brother Marie-Julien to accompany Champeau to Paris and to act as his assistant and fiscal officer. This religious had for some years performed similar duties more than adequately at the motherhouse.

But unfortunately, and incredibly, the Founder and his council had neglected to examine the financial terms of the Parisian arrangement, and the euphoria in Le Mans turned into bitter consternation as it gradually became known that Sainte-Croix had assumed responsibility for 75,000 francs ($15,000) of the college's previous indebtedness. Father Champeau, meanwhile, instead of retrenching, initiated an ambitious building program, in which folly he was aided and abetted by his reputedly prudent assistant. Worst of all, Marie-Julien fell in with a set of Parisian swindlers, led by a retired general named de Brossard, who hoodwinked him into issuing fraudulent notes against the credit of Sainte-Croix. Speculation followed upon ever wilder speculation until in 1861, with Champeau in a state of nervous hysteria and Marie-Julien in hiding, Moreau discovered that Paris had sucked up 235,000 francs ($47,000), which almost doubled the motherhouse's total debt to 576,000 francs ($115,200).[15] Or, to be precise, the burden fell upon Moreau personally. Under French law male religious orders enjoyed no more legal existence in 1860 than they had in the far-off days of Canon Dujarié.[16] If such organizations could not own property, neither could they be sued, and so the Founder himself stood liable for the fraudulent paper issued in his name. Early in the 1840s Moreau had apparently foreseen some such unhappy eventuality and had organized a "civil society," a corporation based on the principle that French citizens could pool their resources to pursue whatever purposes they liked. Included in this body were priests, brothers and, later, selected laymen. Unfortunately, however, Moreau neglected to put the "society" to use and to transfer titles of property to it until he himself was about to be removed from his position of leadership.[17]

Almost simultaneously this same legal technicality led to another adverse legal judgment which, if not as directly expensive as the Marie-Julien fiasco,

---

15. Catta, *Moreau*, 2: 395–446.
16. See chapter 3, above.
17. See Catta, *Moreau*, 1: 451–453, and chapter 24, below.

was equally damaging to the reputation of Sainte-Croix and the prestige of its Founder. At the end of 1856 Father Moreau learned that a pious spinster of his acquaintance, recently deceased, had bequeathed him a large sum of money. Her only surviving relative, a niece, challenged the validity of the legacy on the grounds that the testatrix's probated will had been forged, or, if it had not been, that it had been drawn up under the undue influence of the legatee, or, if that too fell short of verification, that the award amounted to an illegal trust. Only the third of these allegations proved decisive. The first of them was absurd, the second unprovable, and no one across the whole *département* of Sarthe lent them any credence. Indeed, Moreau won the suit in the first instance, but, after the case had dragged on for better than four years, he lost twice on appeal, the second time in the supreme civil tribunal in Paris. The judges found for the plaintiff, because, they said, shrouded in the words of the will was a "tacit trust," that is, the old lady really intended to leave her money to the *congrégation* of which Moreau was the head. But since the religious order in question could not own property, real or moveable, neither could it inherit any. Therefore, an intention to deceive had lain at the heart of the spinster's bequest, leaving it null and void. This verdict entailed the loss of the 200,000 francs ($40,000) that the will had awarded to Moreau, as well as a huge expenditure in lawyers' fees. Worse than that, since all three of the plaintiff's charges continued integral to the suit throughout the process, the judicial writ included a formal rejection of Father Moreau's denial that he had contrived at counterfeiting a legal document or had exerted sinister influence over a naïve and ailing woman. Such a conclusion furnished much grist to the mills of an eager anticlerical press.[18]

These two spectacular events were symptomatic of the administrative malaise that was gradually undermining the fabric of Sainte-Croix and the standing of Moreau himself. Other difficulties, manageable perhaps taken individually—the heavy debt, for example, of the Holy Cross house in Rome—assumed a larger dimension in the wake of the machinations of Brother Marie-Julien and the cynical behavior of the French courts. But Moreau himself had to bear much of the blame. Over the three years before the scandal broke, he had pleaded, in vain, for some accounting of the finances of the Parisian house. Champeau and Marie-Julien had ignored him, had in fact accused him of hardness of heart for hesitating to pour ever more money into an establishment which they themselves, out of blindness or presumption, were systematically demolishing. Almost as troubling was the intervention of another influential member of the congregation,

---

18. Catta, *Moreau*, 2: 319–340.

Victor Drouelle, the suave Holy Cross superior in Rome, who lent his support
to the schemers in Paris and, indeed, became himself involved in their dubious
transactions.

Except for anguished appeals on paper, Moreau did little directly to fend off
the approaching calamity. He had complained endlessly that Edward Sorin did
not provide sufficient documentation for his various initiatives, and worried that
the account-books sent from Indiana did not adequately reflect the economic realities of the mission of Holy Cross in America; yet from inattention or gullibility
he allowed the situation in Paris to disintegrate into chaos and scandal. There
might have been an excuse in the first instance: Notre Dame du Lac, after all, was
3,000 miles away and supervision over its condition was accordingly difficult.
Paris, by contrast, was only a couple of hours from Le Mans by train, and so inevitably the question arises as to why Moreau, after three years of frustration, undertook no serious investigation of the circumstances *en scène* and allowed his
increasingly truculent subordinates to pursue their destructive path without hindrance. As for the spinster's legacy, he stubbornly decided to persevere in the suit
despite "the [negative] advice I have received from reliable persons who have made
a study of the law a lifetime occupation [and] the advice of ecclesiastics of well-
known piety." The result of such wrong-headedness was defeat and humiliation.

EDWARD SORIN had nothing to do with the case of the spinster's
legacy and only a peripheral connection with the Parisian scandal. He had scarcely
known Brother Marie-Julien, with whom he had had only minimal relations during the years the latter had served as steward at the motherhouse.[19] But Champeau and Drouelle were Sorin's treasured friends and had been the companions
of his youth. His sympathies naturally lay with them, nor did they hesitate to
enlist his support. "General de Brossard has turned out to be the greatest rascal
(*coquin*) in the world," a wrought-up Champeau complained from Paris at the
height of the crisis. "Brother Marie-Julien has signed notes for fabulous sums of
money. An immense scandal is beginning, and we know too well what will result
from it. We are overwhelmed. You and Father Drouelle are involuntarily involved
in this business. Pray and have others pray. Never has such a storm struck the
Congregation which nevertheless is innocent, since nobody knew what was going
on. . . . The times fail me; I am ill and confounded."[20] Sorin might reasonably have

---

19. See, for example, Marie-Julien to Sorin, n.d. (c. 1855), AIP, a memorandum recording payment of travel expenses for a nun coming from Le Mans to Notre Dame.

20. Champeau to Sorin, February 6, 1861, AGEN.

asked why somebody, Champeau himself in particular, did not know. Instead he replied with fellow feeling: "My God, dear Father, what a catastrophe! What will become of the Congregation if God does not have pity on us? . . . What a blow! *Mon Dieu,* how shall we hold things together?"[21]

Before this exchange took place, however—before the two legal crises in France had reached their climax—another serious dispute was looming, one which did involve Sorin directly. Since the Roman approval of his constitutions for the congregation of priests and brothers, and, conjointly, their separation from the Marianite sisters, Father Moreau had been planning to convene general chapters for both groups. As usual he proceeded in a tortuously slow manner, but finally he scheduled these meetings for Le Mans in the late summer of 1860. Meantime he prepared a revised and expanded set of constitutions for the nuns, the sort of task he liked best. He also named Mother Mary of the Seven Dolors as superior general of the Marianites. Leocadie Gascoin, as she was before she entered religion,[22] was a woman of strong character and genuine piety. Her devotion to Moreau and his ideals was total, as was his confidence in her: in correspondence he often addressed her as "My dear Mother and Daughter." Since 1849 she had governed the community in Canada, and now, aged forty, her mandate was extended to embrace all the sisters in Europe and America. Moreau assumed that the new constitutions and Seven Dolors' appointment would be confirmed by the general chapter, as indeed they were.

But not without a ruinous fight. Father Sorin had always exhibited a wary suspicion toward the Holy Cross mission in Canada; his personal relations with the superior there, Joseph Rézé, had been chilly at best.[23] His objection to Mother Seven Dolors, however, had little to do with her geographical location and nothing at all to do with her admirable character. He took exception rather to her orientation, to her dedication to a religious life for women that he deemed inappropriate for the American apostolate. If Seven Dolors was Moreau's *belle idéale* of the nun—contemplative, docile, given over to domestic pursuits—the energetic, resourceful, and well-educated Mother Angela Gillespie played that role for Sorin. Thus the old disagreement emerged with a new face: what may have been commonplace and praiseworthy in the Old World did not necessarily apply to the New. This is not to say that Sorin encouraged any laxity among his American

---

21. Sorin to Champeau, February 8, 1861, AGEN.

22. See Graziella Lalande, "Mother Mary of the Seven Dolors as a Person and as Moreau's Collaborator," a paper read at the Conference on the History of the Congregations of Holy Cross (1989), 1–4.

23. See chapter 13, above.

sisters in the performance of their pious duties; indeed, his directives sound extremely rigorous to a later, more adaptable generation.

> I wish you . . . to try more generously than ever . . . to show the most perfect regularity in all things pertaining to the Religious Life; namely, rising at 5:00 A.M. and retiring at 9:00 P.M.; meditation, Holy Mass, [the] little office whenever it can be said;[24] silence in all employments through the day, pious reading during meals, particular examen,[25] charity in recreations; visits to the Blessed Sacrament, spiritual reading, [rosary] beads, evening prayer [joined to a consideration of] the subject of [the next morning's] meditation, confession [weekly], the hour of adoration [of the Eucharist]; the monthly retreat, . . . the observance of the vows, the spirit of economy, the love or retirement and humility; . . . avoiding trouble, discord, or dissension and endeavoring to procure at any sacrifice peace, union, and harmony.[26]

Such guidelines hardly suggested any compromise with secular values or practices. Moreau, however, continued to harbor reservations about the continuing "abuses" and "unruly spirits" among the American nuns which he thought had first discerned during his visitation in 1857. But, again manifesting his fatal weakness as an administrator, he refused to face the consequences of his own convictions and simply advised Mother Seven Dolors for the time being not to assert her new authority in Indiana. The coming general chapter, he assured her with all the confidence of a theoretician, would put matters right.[27]

Father Sorin, meanwhile, was, predictably, forging an agenda of his own, in conjunction with supportive spirits like Mother Angela and Mother Ascension. If the Marianites were to be centralized, the focus of their organization ought to be, he argued, in America. If Seven Dolors were to act effectively as superior general, she ought to establish St. Mary's of Notre Dame as her motherhouse and take up

---

24. The Little Office of the Blessed Virgin Mary is an abridged version of the Roman Breviary, the use of which became common in the twelfth century.

25. Particular examen is the pious practice whereby the religious examines her conscience daily, not in some general way, but with regard to a fault—anger, sloth—she regards as most strongly tempting.

26. Sorin to "Dear Daughters," January 14, 1862, AGEN. This admonition was written on the eve of a canonical visitation (see below, chapter 22), but it was not untypical of Sorin's ordinary direction. See, for another example of general exhortation, Sorin to "Dear Daughters," March 10, 1859, AIP. But he was ever ready to deal sensitively also with an individual nun who was "discouraged and unhappy": see Sister St. Martha to Sorin, July 6, 1860, AIP.

27. See Costin, *Priceless Spirit,* 154.

residence there herself. And, in the short term, if there were to be a general chapter in 1860 intended to give validity to the Marianite constitutions that would then be sent on to Rome for definitive approval, that meeting ought to be convened at St. Mary's. Proposals of this sort were anathema to Moreau, but there was ample statistical evidence to bear them out. In 1860, the Indiana province could boast a complement of 180 sisters, while that in France had barely fifty. Of the American nuns only thirty-two, or eighteen percent, spoke French as their first language—the rest, reflecting the patterns of immigration, were overwhelmingly Irish, with a substantial mixture of German- and native-born members. And though among the French minority some women still yearned for the consolations they had enjoyed in their youth at the convent in Le Mans—as the ancient Israelites had longed for the fleshpots of Egypt—there were others, like Mother Ascension, who had adapted with enthusiasm to an American milieu and had no intention of ever returning to France. Little doubt remained that Sorin could count upon the preponderant support of the sisters in his province, as had been the case when they had had to confront the controversial appointment to Bengal some years earlier.[28]

These numerical disparities, however, were less significant in the long run than the philosophical differences with regard to the mission of the nuns that separated Sorin from Moreau. The Marianite sisters in France, and in Canada too, were, with few exceptions, engaged in domestic work, cooking and sewing and cleaning, attuned with equal zeal to the care of the stock and to the care of the sick, and thus lending indispensable support to the Holy Cross houses to which they were assigned. There was nothing ignoble in such activities, quite to the contrary, and Father Sorin, in establishing a distinct convent on the campus at Notre Dame, assumed that the sisters would provide these same services, as in fact they did. But from the beginning, from the moment of the arrival in Indiana of the first nuns from Le Mans in 1843, Sorin had insisted that their primary function would be to act as teachers.[29] This calling would be analogous to that of the brothers for whom Hailandière had originally petitioned Moreau in 1841, concerned as the bishop of Vincennes had been to promote the Catholic education of the boys in his vast diocese. But Sorin, grasping the American mood better than most of his contemporary missionaries, understood that the training of girls and young women demanded commensurate attention. The example of the revered Mother Theodore and the Providence Sisters at Terre Haute was not lost upon him, and so an academy was founded at Bertrand even when the sisters

28. See chapter 15, above.
29. See chapter 9, above.

who conducted it were poorer than church mice, when they had to rinse dirty laundry in the waters of the St. Joseph River, "a process perhaps no harder on the sisters' backs than carrying pails of water up the steps [to the convent] would have been."[30] By 1860, when the future of the Marianites swayed in the balance, Sorin's vision had achieved a remarkable vindication. Besides the academy at St. Mary's that had replaced the original foundation at Bertrand, the sisters operated three other flourishing boarding schools, a manual labor institute, and eight parochial schools, as well as two orphanages. Their presence in Indiana may have been a matter of course, but it had also extended to faraway places like Baltimore, Washington City, Philadelphia, and the suburbs of Chicago.[31]

So Father Sorin's insistence that the headquarters for the Marianites should be most properly established in America, and specifically at St. Mary's, was not without warrant. His campaign to bring this about, however, was not without petulance. His lobbying efforts with Moreau gained no ground, nor did those with Mother Seven Dolors, who visited St. Mary's early in 1860 and received there a mixed reaction. Both she and the Founder took the line that all problems would be solved at the general chapter scheduled to be held at Le Mans later in the year. But holding the meeting on that site was precisely what Sorin wished to avert. He complained, with justification, at the slowness and inadequacy of the translation of the new constitutions—a "massacre in English" he described it[32]—which meant that the overwhelming majority of the sisters in his province would remain ignorant of the crucial document the chapter was supposed to debate and vote upon. Less justifiably he threatened to prevent the delegates chosen in Indiana—not surprisingly Mother Angela and Mother Ascension—from attending the chapter. This maneuver, however, Moreau promptly checkmated, and on June 20 Sorin told Seven Dolors that, though "I have not changed my opinion about the expedience of our two mothers making this journey," nevertheless "I recognize it as my duty to assure you that you must feel free to take from here anyone you choose. I will abstain in future from doing anything to prevent the journey, seeing that the vexation that afflicts me about this matter is part and parcel of another, namely, that my motives have been consistently misconstrued. We have come upon bad times which we never knew before." And then, with a remarkable absence of veracity, he said, "I wish to assume no responsibility what-

---

30. Brosnahan, *King's Highway*, 134.

31. See Costin, *Priceless Spirit*, 20, 149–150.

32. Nor was an acceptable translation available eighteen months later. See Sorin to Moreau, August 17, 1861, AGEN.

ever with regard to the sisters. Please consider as *invalid* anything which appears as opposition to your views."[33]

A week later, however, Father Sorin regretted so sweeping an assertion. "I regret to have to tell you again," he wrote, "that I do not see how our mothers [Angela and Ascension] can possibly attend the general chapter." Then he added a threat intended more for Moreau than for Seven Dolors: "If they do indeed depart from here, one of the consequences will be that, in the present circumstances, I myself will positively not be able to attend [the priests' and brothers' chapter]," which was to convene at the same time as that of the nuns.[34] And a few days after that he elaborated on his position, this time giving vent to his true convictions.

Very reverend Mother, Pardon me if I come so soon again to trouble your repose. . . . The moment we have arrived at is most important. The chapters which are about to convene will no doubt help us search out and discern the designs of Providence. I do not wish to, nor can I, prejudge their results. . . . It is true of course that for three years the material assets of the sisters have been [by Roman decree] separated from ours. But it cannot have escaped your attention that for fifteen years now the two houses [at Notre Dame and St. Mary's] have worked from the same treasury and have shared everything from their inception until the day before yesterday (*d'avant hier*); they cannot be ruthlessly separated without the one or the other suffering loss or, indeed, mutually experiencing a severe ordeal. In the eyes of the public we constitute one and the same Catholic institution, interdependent (*solidaire*) one with the other. I doubt very much that had you taken into consideration anything other than the directive you received [from Moreau] you would have agreed to demand the absence of Mother Ascension [the local superior at St. Mary's] from her house.

Then, with scant regard for Mother Seven Dolors' feelings, he laid out clearly his own recapitulation of the crisis at hand.

The general chapter will examine if the destiny of the congregation in the United States ought to be left to the discretion (*merci*) of a woman who does not appear to be disposed to acknowledge very readily the efforts and sacrifices of every kind the sisters here have endured over all these years. Inspired by the gratitude due their admirable devotion, it has never occurred

33. Sorin to Seven Dolors, June 20, 1860, AGEN.
34. Sorin to Seven Dolors, June 29, 1860, AGEN.

to us to question the advantages of our union. We have been sustained through this time of sacrifice by the aspirations of our venerable Founder, which, for me at least, would have been all sufficient.

But, alas, such was not the case. The choice of Le Mans as site of the general chapter was itself an indication that the American apostolate of Holy Cross would not receive its due, as was the implication that the future source of direction for the sisters would be lodged firmly in France. And he claimed a personal affront as well.

It is useless for me to tell you how bitter I find the dregs of this chalice; but you will force me to drink it to the last drop. Because you press this issue I shall be prevented from enjoying the sight of the motherhouse and seeing again my much beloved confreres and the venerable Founder, which I surely regret. But even more so do I regret the duties I foresaw, numerous and important, which now will have to be put aside because of your order.[35]

Neither this rather sentimental plaint that the departure of Angela and Ascension would keep him from attending the priests' and brothers' chapter in Le Mans, nor the verbal bullying which underlay the whole of Sorin's rationale, made much of an impression on Mother Seven Dolors. Her insistence that the two delegates from Indiana should meet her in New York was complied with, and together they sailed for France. The nuns' general chapter met at Sainte-Croix in mid-August, and Moreau's revised constitutions as well as the appointment of Seven Dolors as superior general of the Marianites were unanimously approved and sent on to Rome for final endorsement. More ominous in the long run was the resolution, also passed without demur, that a sisters' house should be reopened in New York City. Angela and Ascension, even so, voted as they were expected to do, but perhaps their respectful reticence during the *pro forma* debates spoke more eloquently than any insubordination might have done.[36] Mother Angela at any rate, her term as provincial completed, returned home and assumed the less prestigious post of local superior at St. Mary's; but change of titles notwithstanding, no one doubted where the leadership among the American sisters resided.[37]

---

35. Sorin to Seven Dolors, July 3, 1860, AGEN.
36. See Costin, *Priceless Spirit*, 152–153.
37. McAllister, *Flame*, 162.

Edward Sorin, meanwhile, was true to his word: he absented himself from the chapter of the priests and brothers, nor did he, as requested, send a delegate in his place. "Nineteen years have passed," he wrote Moreau on August 5, "since we left Sainte-Croix for America. I would have rejoiced had I been able to celebrate this anniversary with my venerable colleagues at the general chapter under the presidency of you, our venerable Founder." It is worth observing, he continued, that our apostolate in America now encompasses "as many as 300 religious, male and female.... We have a total of thirty-three schools, in which 3,500 children are enrolled. At this moment we have to take care of two colleges. I am not free in the face of our miraculous achievement to absent myself for two or three months, so long as the chief officers at St. Mary's are also away, lest our work should suffer extreme difficulties; we need to devote all our energies to the maintenance of our hard-won standing."[38]

THE GENERAL CHAPTER of the men of Holy Cross, which opened on August 8, 1860, was as stormy as that of the women was deceptively placid. Through twenty sessions over twenty days priests and brothers examined the administrative and financial condition of the congregation. Much of the debate was heated, and much bitter criticism was leveled against the Founder. Leading the assault were Victor Drouelle and Louis Champeau, who chided Moreau for alleged fiscal carelessness, for executive tyranny, and for a marked failure to maintain adequate standards of training in the novitiates. It may have been graceless that such charges should have emanated from two men whose own conduct in these areas was hardly above reproach, especially considering their concurrent involvement in the Marie-Julien affair. But passionate feelings had been stirred up even before the chapter convened through a pamphlet written and distributed by another disaffected priest of the order, which, while dedicated unctuously to "your Reverence," in effect called for Moreau's resignation or, if need be, his removal from office. However hurt the embattled Founder may have been by these signs of rebellion, he remained as ever a fighter. The pamphlet he dismissed as "this audacious scribbling, published and circulated without my permission, whose dedication to me I reject." As for weightier opponents like Drouelle and Champeau—and their absent comrade, Edward Sorin—Moreau took accurate measure as to how far they were prepared to press their dissidence, at least for the time being. He concluded the final session of the chapter, on August 28, with an offer he knew none of his insurgent sons had the audacity to accept.

---

38. Sorin to Moreau, August 5, 1860, AGEN.

I beseech you not to allow me to be any longer an obstacle to peace and union of hearts in the Congregation of Holy Cross or to the development of this institute. Please accept my resignation or, if you prefer, let me place it in the hands of the Vicar of Jesus Christ, either of which you can do by means of an extraordinary session of this General Chapter. I feel the need to live a life of recollection in solitude before going to render my accounts before a different tribunal. . . . Whatever may happen, you can count on my gratitude for your devotion, and you can be assured that instead of harboring discouragement I thank God for having given me in the founding of Holy Cross a taste of contradiction and humiliation.[39]

This proposition, needless to say, was not agreed to by the chapter, out of respect and affection, no doubt, but also out of the realization that whoever replaced the Founder would find himself saddled with the same disabilities, especially the financial ones as dictated by French law.

Edward Sorin had originally planned to attend the general chapter and to combine fulfilling that duty with a European holiday. He had invited Bishop Young of Erie, Mother Anglea's old friend, to accompany him.[40] His own bishop, Luers of Fort Wayne, now as firm a supporter of Sorin and Notre Dame as he had been at first a competitor, was particularly solicitous when he heard of the proposed journey. "I understand you will go to Europe in the coming summer," he wrote, "and rumor has it that you may *possibly not return* but be replaced by someone else. To this I would be obliged to object, that is, *to you not returning,* since the interest of [my] Diocese would suffer from it; for I cannot see who, under existing circumstances, could supply your place."[41] In the event Father Sorin traveled alone, and, having arrived at Sainte-Croix a few days after the chapter adjourned, he presumably basked in "the sight of the motherhouse and of his much beloved confreres and venerable Founder," of which joy he had only weeks before accused Mother Seven Dolors of depriving him. His very presence in the wake of a studied and disdainful refusal to appear at an all-important meeting was meant, of course, to reiterate his displeasure at the proposed organization of the Marianites, and so no doubt it did. Given the tempestuous nature of the chapter, however, it may have been to Sorin's long-term benefit that he had not participated in it. His stay in Le Mans at any rate was brief, though long enough to permit some

39. See Charles Moreau, *Moreau,* 354–360.
40. Young to Sorin, May 22, 1860, AIP. The bishop declined, pleading a full schedule, and then added: "There is, I trust, no danger, of your detention or deflexion [sic] to some other mission."
41. Luers to Sorin, January 10, 1860, AIP.

substantial conversations with the Founder. "Very Reverend Father," Sorin wrote from aboard ship about the middle of September, "I bless God that you were able to listen to me calmly and that you chose to repeat to me your appreciation of the state of our establishments in America in all its gravity." Nevertheless, "each day since I departed has convinced me anew of the importance of the further re-marks I am going to confide to you." Not least among these was a stout defense of a friend who had fallen under Moreau's displeasure.

> If instead of this letter a message should reach you bringing news of this ship being wrecked, I know of only one man who could save our missions in America, and that man is Father Drouelle. And even he might arrive too late. If his presence in Rome has become less necessary since the approba-tion [of the congregation and its constitutions], I do not hesitate to ask you to consider seriously his dispatch to America, where he has shown the talent to make himself loved and to make the motherhouse loved. . . . He is moreover a bosom friend (*ami de coeur*) whose presence would be hailed at Notre Dame and be a special joy to me. He is my elder brother,[42] and I would be very happy to place in his hands the burden which weighs me down, without, however hesitating to help him with all my might and within the limits you would prescribe.

"To place in Drouelle's hands the burden"—Moreau was not the only one to show the resignation-card without seriously intending to play it. Sorin's thoughts indeed were much more preoccupied with the deployment of the sisters as talked about at Sainte-Croix.

> I told you then that their motherhouse would be better placed at St. Mary's than anywhere else. I still believe this to be the case, and I am confident the future will prove me right. Of the three branches, the sisters will be the one most mixed as regards the French and English languages; already more than half of them are English-speaking. A Mother General who speaks only one language cannot be put over them without injustice being done to the gen-eral interests of the Society. Neither Canada nor Louisiana can seriously pretend to be an appropriate locale. Let the balance be struck between Sainte-Croix, administrative center for the male members of the congrega-tion, and St. Mary's for the sisters. At St. Mary's not only is unity guaranteed

---

42. Drouelle was born in 1812 and hence was two years older than Sorin.

but also development in every direction. . . . If the Mother General [Seven Dolors] returns to Canada to take up residence there, she will in effect set aside the obligations of her office in order to act as provincial of the least important of the four sisters' establishments.

Father Sorin had clearly changed neither his mind nor his priorities, but, perhaps aware of the turmoil that had marked the recent chapter, he adopted a conciliatory tone toward the beleaguered Founder: "I believe I have no need to apologize for the candor of this letter. I have intended only to serve the Congregation, and I do not doubt that you will take my observations into consideration."[43] Even so tentative an era of good feeling was not destined to last.

T WO MONTHS LATER Edward Sorin was back at Sainte-Croix. "Would you believe that I have once more and so soon returned to France?" he wrote a friend on November 27. This time he intended to spend several months abroad, though very little of it at Le Mans. His first item of business took him to Antwerp in pursuit of a Belgian priest "who cheated me out of 50,000 francs." He was referring to notes given him several years earlier by Joseph Biemens, on the strength of which he had borrowed the money to buy the cherished chimes for the church at Notre Dame as well as several pieces of property.[44] "I come to settle his notes, which now are dead paper in my hands. God bless him! Now the money borrowed on his notes is coming due." Sorin's efforts to track down Biemens proved fruitless, and he had to turn to Moreau for help: "The Very reverend Father Rector has promised me a loan of 15,000 francs for which I am extremely obliged to him."[45] In exchange for this favor, Moreau requested that Sorin, when he went to Paris to treat with the Propagation of the Faith, inquire into the mysterious and increasingly alarming schemes of Brother Marie-Julien.

Father Sorin, however, was in no hurry to be drawn into that sorry situation. After the profitless venture in Belgium, he spent much of December visiting friends and relatives in the neighborhood of Ahuillé and, as ever, soliciting funds for his mission from individuals and parishes across the *pays de la Loire*. Shortly before Christmas he did go to Paris and brought his requests to the ever muni-

---

43. Sorin to Moreau, September 27, 1860, AGEN.

44. Payment for the chimes dragged on for years. See chapter 18, above. Biemens had been briefly a novice at Notre Dame. See Sorin, *Chronicles*, 189–190, 194.

45. Sorin to Mother Columba, November 27, 1860, AGEN.

ficent offices of the Propagation.[46] While in the capital he lodged with Louis Champeau and heard from him the details of the impending financial crisis. He may also have learned that the distraught Champeau had recently dispatched a denunciation of Basile Moreau's administration to the Roman curia.[47] But Father Sorin, whatever his sympathies for his old friend and his loyalty to his chief, had no intention of involving himself directly in a disaster of other people's making. "I have done what I could with regard to the brother [Marie-Julien]," he informed Moreau laconically. "May God provide the grace to make everything work to the good. Please do not forget my plea in behalf of Father Champeau."[48]

A few days into the new year Edward Sorin set out from Paris for Rome. The eternal city, still in 1861 a political as well as a religious capital, had always been the primary objective of this European journey. He intended to report, in characteristically flattering terms, on the state of his mission in America and its progress since his first visit nine years before.[49] His host, as on the earlier occasion, was the Holy Cross superior in Rome, Victor Drouelle. He passed therefore straight from the confidences of one malcontented friend and confrere to those of a second, and the earnest conversations that occupied the long Roman winter evenings were perhaps the prologue to the formation of the triumvirate destined to revolutionize the Congrégation de Sainte-Croix.

But Edward Sorin, for the moment, was more interested in cultivating the favor of the Roman curia and specifically that of Alessandro Cardinal Barnabò, the Prefect of the Congregation of Propaganda Fide. Barnabò was a hardworking, garrulous, somewhat vulgar Italian, a careerist and bureaucrat to his fingertips, and yet an ecclesiastic not without kindliness and a rough sort of piety.[50] As head of the department charged with the oversight of Catholic missions worldwide, he was the ultimate authority, next to the pope himself, in matters affecting an order like Holy Cross. He had at first strongly encouraged Basile Moreau's endeavors and had been something of a patron to the Founder. The recent financial troubles, however, along with the growing internal discontent—carefully if subtly chronicled for him by Father Drouelle, who had recently passed along to him

---

46. In anticipation of his visit Father Sorin wrote a short report to the Propagation from Antwerp, November 20, 1860, AGEN.

47. Catta, *Moreau*, 2: 397–399.

48. Sorin to Moreau, January 3, 1861, AGEN.

49. See chapter 15, above.

50. Recall Newman's description of Barnabò: "And who is Propaganda? Virtually one sharp man of business, who works day and night, and dispatches his work quick off, to the East and the West; a high dignitary indeed, . . . but after all little more than a clerk, and two or three clerks under him." Quoted in Wilfrid Ward, *The Life of John Henry Cardinal Newman*, 2 vols. (London, 1913), 1: 560.

Champeau's criticisms—had given the cardinal second thoughts. Moreau's heavy spiritual hand, his fussiness and legalistic approach to his subjects, did not wear well with the usually genial Barnabò, and it may well have been he who inspired Pius IX's sad final judgment: "[Moreau had] an admirable head for himself, but [an] abominable [one] in the guidance of others."[51] Barnabò in any case even came to doubt Moreau's carefully crafted constitutional arrangements. "Personally," he observed to Sorin, "I am not in favor of the complete fusion of the priests and brothers. . . . Their spirit ought always to be interpreted in favor of hierarchy, so as to protect the legitimate expectations of the priests and to keep the brothers in due humility."[52] The provincial from America, by contrast, the Prefect found charming and judicious. In the course of a month "I saw his Eminence Cardinal Barnabò eleven times at his home," Sorin almost chortled, "and sometimes for hours at a time."[53]

Aside from acquainting the cardinal with the flourishing state of the Indiana province—the contrast with Le Mans was transparent enough to remain unspoken—Sorin wanted Propaganda's endorsement of two other innovative projects. The first of these was creation of an "Association for the Development of Catholic Schools in the United States." This grandiose title was rather less inclusive than its wording implied; what Father Sorin really intended was to establish an instrument whereby money could be raised in Europe, and particularly in France, to support the educational initiatives undertaken in America by the religious of Holy Cross. "No one in Europe can ignore," he explained in the formal prospectus, "the great hopes for the Catholic Church in the United States.[54] But neither can one ignore the prodigious efforts launched by the Enemy of all good to destroy these hopes at their very source." Godless or heretical education: here, he said, was the manifestation of that demonic enmity. "Everywhere, thanks to government help, sumptuous and free schools are being built." The immigrant families which brought the ideal of religious education to this new land "will soon give place to a generation reared without faith or religion." But a solution lay at hand.

Upon a plot covered only lately by forests stands today a great religious institution called Notre Dame du Lac. It is the provincial house of the Congregation of Holy Cross in the United States. Here are formed its mission-

---

51. Quoted in Sorin, *Chronicles*, 296.
52. Sorin, memorandum, n.d. [1861], AGEN.
53. Sorin to Mother Angela, March 1, 1861, AGEN.
54. Sorin's French here seems oddly archaic or perhaps merely calculated to appeal to a European sense of superiority: "United States" is rendered, not "*Etats-Unis*" but rather "*les provinces unies de l'Amérique septentrionale.*"

aries and teachers. . . . Besides its full novitiates, it is even now educating more than five thousand children. . . . Its Superior has returned to Europe in order to appeal to devoted persons who feel the desire and the courage to dedicate themselves to this sublime and consoling ministry and who are generous enough to assist in the development of this work through their financial help.

The prospectus was duly submitted to Barnabò and by him to the pope, who indicated his cordial assent by attaching to the giving of alms to the Association a spate of indulgences under the usual conditions.[55]

Father Sorin "consecrated the Association to the Holy Family and placed it under the patronage of the Cardinal Prefect of Propaganda." It was to be governed by a president, a vice president, and a committee centered at Holy Cross in Paris. Cells of ten members each were to be organized, and affiliation would cost one franc per year. Father Louis Champeau would act as director and treasurer. Back in Le Mans, however, the proposal, when fully spelled out, met a chilly reception. The matter had been discussed informally, Moreau complained, but no such detailed initiative, indulgences and all, had been sanctioned by the motherhouse and its council. Furthermore, Sorin had had no right to describe himself as provincial of the congregation in the "United States"; was not Louisiana part of the United States? Champeau's involvement alone would have sufficed to arouse in Moreau sharp misgivings; even worse was the appointment of General de Brossard as president of the Association, the same de Brossard who, it was now publicly manifest, had connived at and perhaps had even incited the swindles of Brother Marie-Julien.

By mid-February, Sorin had departed Rome and had arrived at Lyon, where, amid fund-raising activities—there was a branch of the Propagation of the Faith in Lyon—he reacted to Moreau's reproofs, which, he said, he found *"excessively painful."* Moreau, driven to distraction over the Marie-Julien scandal and suspiciously aware of Sorin's recent presence in Paris, had suggested collusion, along with a censure for what had transpired in Rome.

Nothing could surprise me more than to be suspected by my colleagues of having connived with a brother whom I knew only slightly and in whom I had never placed any confidence except to the degree that you had done so.

55. "Prospectus," with confirming documents (copies), January 20, 1861, AGEN. "Under the usual conditions" meant that the work of charity had to be performed by an individual in the state of grace and accompanied by certain prayers or sacramental acts.

Indeed, I told you my fears about [Marie-Julien] even before you shared your reservations with me. I have tried in this matter to warn you, but, since it seemed a case of conscience, charity did not permit me to do so adequately. In any case, am I supposed to have known more about it than you did? . . . I owe [Marie-Julien] nothing, absolutely nothing, and nobody can prove that I am indebted to a single sou. On this score, I am perfectly at peace. [Marie-Julien] never offered to tell me his secrets; all he did was repeat over and over that some day he would *let me know all about what was going on,* but he never did. The news of his sad circumstances has been more a thunderbolt for me more even than for you. For mercy's sake (*de grace*) do not any more ascribe to me any part in an affair with which I had nothing to do.

More immediately relevant were Moreau's qualms about Sorin's Association and the aggressive way in which he lobbied for it in Rome. "The accusation that my educational enterprise did *not* have your authorization is a mystery to me, making me wonder if I understand anything any more. Must I return to Rome to look for your letter, in which you entreat Father Drouelle to help me get on with the project?" This bit of sarcasm was followed by a shrug as far as the naughty general was concerned. "De Brossard was awarded the honorary presidency, because I once heard Father Champeau, who had served on an academic committee with him, describe the general as a worthy personage. Nothing will be easier than exchanging one name for another." And, finally, Sorin challenged Moreau to set aside a proposition already commended by Barnabò and the pope himself: "In order to obtain the approbation of the Holy See it was necessary that the project be presented in detail; it is a viable whole, but it is now in your hands to put into execution or to toss into the fire, whichever you prefer."[56] The Founder, when it came to implementing what he perceived as improper procedure, feared no one's displeasure, no matter how highly placed; the Association was never heard of again.

Father Sorin did not risk his second Roman initiative suffering a similar fate: he simply refrained from telling Moreau anything about it until the negotiation was completed. A persistent problem for institutional Catholicism, especially since the formalization of clerical propriety in the wake of the scandals at the time of the Reformation, has been the discipline and rehabilitation of wayward priests. Religious communities of any size, like Notre Dame du Lac, could be presumed to possess sufficient resources to deal with its own erring members internally.

---

56. Sorin to Moreau, February 13, 1861, AGEN.

Not so individual bishops, especially not those presiding over the impoverished American dioceses of the mid-nineteenth century. They had to look to a monastery or some other large religious establishment to provide a *refugium peccatorum* for their secular clergy. Notre Dame had already for many years rendered this service on an *ad hoc* basis at the request of this or that prelate and now Sorin determined to institutionalize the function by building a special facility for the purpose within the Notre Dame compound.

In most cases the dereliction stemmed from excessive drinking, a frailty that Father Sorin recognized as dangerous within his own house[57] and, indeed, one that had induced him to become a stern advocate of total abstinence.[58] The foundation he had in mind would offer therapy and penance to the offenders, but one may be sure that penance would take precedence. "Humbly prostrate at your feet," wrote Sorin, employing the servile language customary at the time in addressing the pope, "I recommend a work which is certainly the work of your Holiness." "I invoke," he continued, "the memory of an apostle of eighteen centuries ago, who, having denied his Master three times, swore that he knew not this Man. Jesus looked at him, says the sacred text, and Peter went out and wept bitterly." The Prince of the Apostles was given a chance "to amend his triple denial with a threefold protestation of his love. . . . Such is the model and principal patron, very Holy Father, that your Holiness is entreated to accord to these poor disciples [today] who have also wounded the heart of the Divine Master. . . . We trust that this new monument of your consonance with the infinite mercy you represent on earth will be for a long time a source of consolation to your paternal heart."[59] Such convoluted rhetoric was not surprising, given the sensitivity of the subject matter. Barnabò, in his concurring recommendation, spoke cryptically about "the pious intent" to build "a house in the United States in which priests might be free (*vacare*) to perform special exercises whereby they will be able to resuscitate the spirit of their vocation."[60]

---

57. See Shortis to Sorin, June 3, 1860, AIP. Irish-born Richard Shortis was professed in Holy Cross in 1850. His second bout with drunkenness (see chapter 18, above) led Sorin to detach him from the Indiana province and send him to Louisiana.

58. See Samuel Byerley to Sorin, March 24, 1859, AIP. Byerley, Holy Cross's first patron in America (see chapter 5, above), chided Sorin for aligning himself with "the temperance party." He became increasingly eccentric in his later years. See, for example, Byerley to Sorin, July 2 and 25, 1860, AIP. But Sorin, like most Frenchmen, regularly drank wine, though sparingly. See, for example, Sorin to Corby, March 7, 1878: "Your splendid Rhenish wine does me a great service. The first bottle will last until tomorrow and the second the other six days. I find it excellent."

59. Sorin to Pius IX, January 24, 1861, AGEN.

60. Barnabò, "Littera," January 23, 1861, AGEN.

Father Sorin had prepared the ground well. Before submitting the proposal to the Roman officials, he had secured the endorsement of a dozen American bishops, including his own, John Luers, who later in the year presided at the laying of the cornerstone of the new institution. The highlight of this ceremony, Sorin told Barnabò, was "a magnificent sermon" preached by a visiting Jesuit, "which emphasized with remarkable felicity the grandest leader of our century, the immortal Pius IX, and which was impossible for a true Christian to hear without tears."[61] Moreau also, after the fact, however, and without notable enthusiasm, gave his approval—"*Commendamus,*" he scribbled at the bottom of the prospectus presented to him on February 25. That such an institution answered a need quickly became clear: "Six urgent applications have been made since a month," Sorin reported. "We should go on with the Missionary House, and [sic] I do not know how."[62] Some financial assistance was forthcoming, though the support was not unanimous. The two archbishops Kenrick, for instance, declined to participate. Francis of Baltimore pleaded his poverty, and Peter of St. Louis responded to Sorin's appeal with a hint of the sardonic that characterized his long career: "I regret I cannot comply with your request by adding my approbation, which, surely, cannot be necessary after that of the Cardinal Prefect."[63]

Characteristic of Father Sorin was the enthusiasm with which he publicized the new facility. "The location is healthy and fine," he proclaimed, "ten minutes from the University on the shores of St. Joseph Lake, of which it commands a beautiful view. . . . The plan is extensive: 136 feet in length and 75 in width, three stories high, containing 48 private rooms, . . . with every convenience to promote the comfort of the reverend gentlemen for whom the House is intended." And characteristic too was the supple manner in which, as time went on, he shifted his emphasis from providing a penitential hospice for drunkards and other ne'er-do-well clerics to setting up "a home for venerable priests too far advanced in years to discharge any longer the arduous duties of the sacred ministry, or incapacitated by sickness, or simply desirous to retire, for a while, into solitude to renew in their hearts the fervor of their holy vocation." This last phrase suggests that that the original intention was still operative, even though it may have proved to have been less attractive as a fund-raising device than Sorin had anticipated. At any rate, the house whose cornerstone Bishop Luers blessed was to be known as "a home for Missionaries." The cost of the foundation Sorin reckoned at $20,000, some ten percent of which—including a personal donation from Pius IX of 2,000

61. Sorin to Barnabò, September 7, 1861, AGEN. See also Sorin, *Chronicles,* 274–275.
62. Sorin to Purcell, October 6, 1861, AIP.
63. Francis Kenrick to Sorin, November 15, 1861, and Peter Kenrick to Sorin, July 9, 1861, AIP.

francs ($400)—he had collected before he left Europe in April, 1861. For the rest of the needed money, he set out a payment schedule whereby American priests, by a yearly contribution ranging from $10 to $30, depending on their age, could "secure a right for life in the Missionaries' home"—and, *sotto voce,* bishops could likewise place those pastors in need of drying-out or expiation for some other dereliction.[64]

AFTER HE DEPARTED ROME, in early February, Edward Sorin continued his begging tour in France, traveling in a leisurely fashion to Marseilles and Lyon, and then to Vendome, to St. Brieuc on the Breton coast and finally, by mid-March, back to Le Mans.[65] Before he reached there, however, he broached one last piece of unfinished business. "For eighteen years," he wrote Father Moreau, "I have been in charge of the [Marianite] Sisters, and this responsibility has been for me the occasion of many perils, trials, and troubles of every kind." Fervent hopes that the situation would change for the better have been in vain, "and I foresee only an increase in difficulty. I ask therefore to be relieved of all obligation toward this Society."[66] The ultimatum, however, was clearly a negotiating ploy; eight weeks earlier Sorin had remarked that "if you [Moreau] should accede to the bishop of Fort Wayne's request that the nuns' motherhouse be established at St. Mary's, it would reconcile me entirely to taking care of them."[67] Nor had he altered his basic strategy, for even as he asked that the burden of governance be lifted from him, he insisted that, "in order to simplify the administration at St. Mary's, the absolute authority of the Mother Superior [Seven Dolors], be modified, so that she undertake nothing without consultation with the local superior [Mother Angela] or with the assistant General [of Holy Cross]." This last designation referred to Sorin himself, a title that Moreau, desperate to appease his gifted but refractory son, had awarded him, while assuring him at the same time that "your ideas about authority will become mine."[68] Yet again the Founder's administrative mettle had given way when confronted by a stronger personality. Sorin for his part left no doubt as to the practical effects of this surrender: "The government of the Society of the Marianites in our Province

---

64. See Sorin's circular "Letter to the Clergy," November 22, 1861, AGEN. The account in Sorin, *Chronicles,* 274–276, makes no reference to the foundation as a house of priestly penance, which is in marked contrast to the Roman documents, cited above.

65. See Sorin to Villecourt, March 12, 1861, and Sorin to Drouelle, March 11, 1861, AGEN.

66. Sorin to Moreau, February 26, 1861, AGEN.

67. Sorin to Moreau, January 3, 1861, AGEN.

68. See Moreau's notation attached to Sorin to Moreau, February 26, 1861, AGEN.

having been transferred to me exclusively for three years without any foreign reference on their part, their special prayers are required to enable me to justify the appointment."[69]

But Moreau, once Sorin had returned to America, backed away from such a sweeping commitment. "I have found it necessary," he wrote sourly to the Indiana sisters on May 8,

> to charge your Father Superior to use all his authority as my representative, in order to reform these abuses by subduing unruly spirits and compelling all to observe the Rule, thus releasing your Mother General [Seven Dolors] from all responsibility in this matter until further orders from me. Besides, I shall send a Visitor who will make a conscientious report on present conditions in this province, and after conferring with me, he will, with Father Sorin and the Ordinary [Bishop Luers], take the needed measures to bring about peace and order.[70]

What "these abuses" were the Founder did not say, nor did he specify why he thought "peace and order" in Indiana were at risk. It would seem likely that the difference in *esprit* between France and America remained the fundamental issue. The remedy he proposed at any rate—a tripartite division of authority at some future date[71]—was all too symptomatic of an administration gone awry. Indeed, the solution merely led to another crisis. Yet it would have been premature to conclude that a weary Basile Moreau was ready to yield to the tide running against him. The right hand he raised in blessing over Edward Sorin on the eve of the latter's departure from Sainte-Croix—the hand so recently petitioned as a future relic—did not tremble.

---

69. Sorin to "My dear Sons and Daughters" (circular letter), April 14, 1861, AGEN.
70. Quoted in Costin, *Priceless Spirit*, 154.
71. See the astute comments in Costin, *Priceless Spirit*, 154–155.

chapter twenty-two

War and the Nephew

EDWARD SORIN DISEMBARKED IN NEW YORK FROM the steamship *Fulton* just in time to learn of the fall of Fort Sumter and of President Lincoln's call, on April 15, 1861, for 75,000 volunteers. Musing on this grim news some considerable time later, Sorin ruefully recalled "the prediction of Mr. [William] Seward, the Secretary of State, that the rebellion would be put down within three months. His declaration was believed by many if not by all."

At the end of three months, however, peace was as far away as it had been at the beginning, and the terror that haunted the land was the same as that inspired by the first cannon-fire in the harbor of Charleston. We all became conversant with the idea of warfare, and we in the north came to understand that the principal theater of battle between the two belligerents would be in Virginia. Never before had the [American] public had to puzzle out (*examiner*) who would stand upright and who would fall in the face of a tempest like this. If one looks closely, one will appreciate that there are as decisive moments in the life of institutions as in the life of armies. A bold initiative sometimes disconcerts a powerful enemy and brings about a success otherwise unattainable.

Bold initiatives were Father Sorin's stock-in-trade, and it is no surprise if he saw a parallel usefulness for them in the conduct whether of institutions or of armies on campaign. Indeed, his first worry as the Civil War broke out and threatened to drag on was its possible impact upon the audacious policies with which he had built up his own institution. "Panic," he wrote, "has seized upon the banks and the houses of commerce. The war preoccupies everybody. Notre Dame du Lac must look with trepidation to its finances. . . . The floating debt exceeds $60,000, and nearly every creditor, up till now full of confidence in us, will begin to press for repayment. If Providence does not protect us with particular solicitude, this moment could be more critical for us than any we have experienced."[1] The anxiety was perfectly understandable, but in fact Providence turned a kindly eye on Notre Dame. "The hard times this year, which caused half the colleges of the country to close, has thus far had no such effect on this institution. The number of boarders has even exceeded that of [1860], owing to its distance from the theater of war." Certain economies were introduced—for example, priest- and brother-novices replaced some laymen as classroom-instructors—as well as a streamlining of billing procedures. All in all, "the morale of the institute has been the gainer, and that is the main point."[2] Still, although the faculty, staff, and student body of the university were overwhelmingly unionist in their sympathies, there were in residence some boarders from the southern states. A few unpleasant confrontations and brick-throwing incidents occurred, but Sorin and his colleagues, insisting forcefully on maintaining an academic ambiance, clamped down on such outbursts, and by and large an uneasy peace was preserved on campus.[3]

Father Sorin himself remained somewhat remote from the war; his battles during these years were fought, as will be seen, elsewhere from the bloody fields of Shiloh and Antietam. This is not to say that he was indifferent to the outcome of the conflict—he never wavered in his devotion to the Union—nor, as superior of a large religious community, did he fail to encourage his associates to offer spiritual and physical solace to Lincoln's soldiers. The priests of Notre Dame and, even more so, the sisters of St. Mary's, wrote some of the most glorious pages in their histories during the Civil War. Seven Holy Cross priests served as chaplains in the armies of the Union. The most notable among them was the bearded William Corby, later twice president of the university, whose moment of immortality, memorialized in a famous portrait, came on the second day of the battle of Gettysburg when, just before the Confederates attacked the federal positions on Seminary Ridge, he raised his hand in general absolution to the Catholic lads of

---

1. Summary memorandum, Sorin to Moreau, 1861–1863, AGEN.

2. Sorin, *Chronicles*, 277–278.

3. See Hope, *Notre Dame*, 118–120.

the famed Irish brigade, who, with the marching and counter-marching of previous weeks, had had no chance of making their sacramental confession.[4]

The status of chaplains during the Civil War, particularly of Catholics in an overweeningly Protestant culture, was anomalous and ill-defined.[5] And reckless prejudice played, alas, too large a part in estimating their worth, as the first Holy Cross chaplain to volunteer learned to his sorrow. Paul Edward Gillen, born in Ireland in 1810 and a professed member of Holy Cross since 1857, was in New York drumming up financial support for Sorin's "Home for Missionaries"[6] when the war broke out. Though he had passed his fiftieth birthday, he proceeded immediately to Washington, attached himself to the twenty-second regiment, New York volunteers, and, in July 1861, marched with that regiment to Manassas Junction in Virginia. As Corby did more famously later, Gillen, on the pitch black night of July 20, dispensed general absolution to his raw, frightened Catholic recruits, many of whom died the next day in the first battle of Bull Run. Gillen escaped back to Washington, unaware that his priestly standing was about to fall lower even than that of the defeated Union army. His only anxiety at the moment was to secure himself a horse, which, through the intercession of General George McClellan, he managed to do.[7] In October, however, Sorin received notice from the archbishop of Baltimore that Gillen had been discerned guilty of habitual drunkenness, a complaint echoed by the bishop of Philadelphia, who said that the Holy Cross priest had been scandalously observed by a reputable officer "and by the men in his regiment in a state of brutal intoxication." He had moreover been scrounging illicitly for money.[8] "I have just received your honored communication," Sorin replied to Kenrick. "It surprised me as much as it grieved me. This is indeed a severe trial . . . and I shall waste no time in complying with your request . . . to send on immediately . . . another of our fathers to wait upon your grace and to go [to the troops in] Washington. I could scarcely express how much I regret the misfortune."[9]

Such concern, however, proved precipitate; Father Gillen, though he may have hoisted a glass or two, was entirely innocent of the charges leveled against

---

4. See W. Corby, *Memories of Chaplain Life* (Notre Dame, 1894), especially 179–193. Strictly speaking Corby was chaplain to the Eighty-ninth New York, one of the five regiments composing the Irish Brigade. Often, however, he was the only priest available within the brigade.

5. For details, see O'Connell, *John Ireland,* 72–73.

6. See chapter 21, above.

7. Gillen to Sorin, September 14, 1861, AIP.

8. Francis Kenrick to Sorin, October 15, 1861, and Wood to Sorin, October 18, 1861, AIP.

9. Sorin to Francis Kenrick, October 19, 1861, AGEN.

him. By late November Kenrick had ascertained that the accusations of scandalous behavior were totally without foundation and, moreover, the "collections" of money the priest had allegedly solicited from the men of the regiment were for his own support and, ironically, "in aid of the pious project which you [Sorin] have in view," the refuge for erring priests.[10] Paul Gillen, his reputation and priestly faculties restored, went on to serve honorably through most of the Civil War, and his name, along with that of Bourget, Cooney, Corby, Léveque, Carrier, and James Dillon (Patrick's brother), was emblazoned for ever after on the honor roll of Holy Cross and Notre Dame. In 1868, Gillen founded the Catholic parish in Keystone Iowa, where he died in 1882.[11] Prosper-Julien Bourget was not so fortunate; the thirty-year-old Frenchman, who had arrived from France only a year before, died in a military hospital in the spring of 1862.[12]

EARLY IN THE EVENING OF Monday, October 21, 1861, a message came to Notre Dame by courier from Indianapolis. Father Sorin immediately took up a lantern and trudged across the fields to St. Mary's. He asked Mother Angela to assemble the sisters in the parlor. There he read to them a letter from Governor Oliver Morton, describing the acute shortage of medical personnel available to the Union troops concentrated near Cairo, in the far southern tip of Illinois, and asking for volunteers to serve as nurses. A hush was followed by a hubbub of eager voices and then another hush, as Angela announced that she would leave for Cairo the next day. Six others were selected to accompany her, and on Tuesday morning they set out on the five-hundred-mile journey. They arrived in Cairo on the Thursday and were greeted by the local commandant, Brigadier General Ulysses Simpson Grant. He courteously pressed the hand of each of them and bent over that of Mother Angela with a particularly chivalric flourish.[13] So Eliza Maria Gillespie, now thirty-seven-years old, had embarked upon her greatest adventure.

And not just Eliza Gillespie. Upwards of eighty-five Holy Cross sisters tended the wounded and sick during the Civil War, and two of them, both born in Ireland, died of their exertions. In makeshift hospitals in Cairo and nearby Mound City, then to St. Louis and Paducah and Louisville, to Memphis and Washington City, on hospital boats plying the Mississippi, sharing in all the filth and degrada-

---

10. Francis Kenrick to Sorin, November 25, 1861, AGEN. Se also chapter 21, above.
11. See *Matricule générale*, 1125, AIP.
12. Summary memorandum, Sorin to Moreau, 1861–1863, AGEN.
13. McAllister, *Flame*, 170–171.

tion and danger endured by their charges—they forged a record of selfless heroism hard to match.[14] These women, till now tucked away in their obscure convents and schools, became at a critical moment truly angels of the battlefield. Their first extended exposure to the horrors of war came in Mound City in February 1862, when the stretcher-bearers carried into their converted warehouse the maimed and half-frozen casualties from Grant's campaign against Forts Henry and Donelson; even more harrowing were the swarms of wounded, many with their legs or arms torn off, thrust upon them after the awful bloodletting at Shiloh two months later.[15] In the wake of the battle of Antietam, Maryland, the following September, the two nuns in charge of the hospital in Washington admitted in a single day 450 injured men. But the sisters remembered most painfully the survivors they cared for following the massacre at Fort Pillow, Tennessee, in April 1864, when the ferocious Confederate cavalryman, Nathan Bedford Forrest, overwhelmed a garrison composed of white Tennesseeans loyal to the Union—renegades in Forrest's lexicon—and, even worse in his eyes, freed Negroes; with the club and the bayonet the rebels wreaked fearful vengeance on those they did not manage to kill with a bullet. Yet the sisters for their part never discriminated in the tireless solicitude they offered to shattered bodies and tormented minds; the hospital boat *Red Rover,* on which Holy Cross nuns served throughout the war, treated 2,500 wounded soldiers, nearly 400 of whom wore the butternut grey of the Confederacy.[16]

By no means was Eliza Gillespie the only heroine, nor would she for a moment have claimed to have been. Still—perhaps because there was something inherently romantic about her—Mother Angela's feats seemed to attain a more than ordinary level of drama. Her coworker, Sister Francis de Sales, recalled that on a

> February day in 1862, soon after the battle of Fort Donelson, . . . Mother Angela was assisting the Chief Surgeon on the lower floor. He was performing a difficult operation, the exact accuracy of which would determine the life of the soldier. His head and that of Mother Angela were bent over the poor boy. Suddenly from the ceiling a heavy red drop fell upon the white coif of Mother Angela, who . . . did not move. Another, and still

14. Their commitment was to serve "without compensation than our board and lodging, with the consciousness of doing good." See Mother of St. Ligouri to Sorin, November 10, 1861, AIP. Ligouri, at that time provincial superior, had taken a group of nuns to St. Louis and then to Jefferson City, shortly after Angela and her companions had departed for Cairo.

15. See the lengthy quotations in Brosnahan, *King's Highway,* 233–238.

16. Costin, *Priceless Spirit,* 179–194.

another, drop after drop came till a little stream was flowing. At last, the final stitch had been taken, and the two heads . . . rose simultaneously. Not till then did the doctor know that a stream of blood, trickling through the open chinks in the upper floor, had fallen steadily upon the devoted head of Mother Angela, who now stood before the Surgeon with her head and face and shoulders bathed in the blood of some unknown soldier.[17]

EDWARD SORIN PAID DUE HONOR to the men and women of Holy Cross who had provided so much physical and spiritual solace to those hurt by the terrible engine of modern warfare.[18] As a priest he found special satisfaction in the accounts of conversions to the Catholic faith, many of them enacted at a poignant deathbed: during the course of 1862 the sisters "baptized with their own hands more than seven hundred soldiers, after having duly prepared them and made them desirous of belonging to the religion of their good nurses." The three religious who had died—Sisters Fidelis and Elsie and Father Bourget, all immigrants[19]—"were greatly lamented by those for whom they had sacrificed their lives, as well as by their fellow religious at Notre Dame and St. Mary's." But Mother Angela and her companions had scarcely finished scouring the filthy interior of the drab old warehouse in Mound City when Sorin, in accord with the habit of twenty years, was already estimating the value of their ministry in terms of its favorable publicity. "This is a genuine success for the Society," he wrote a friend in France. "In six weeks our . . . sisters have won more favor with public opinion than might have been gained in six years by some other devotional activity."[20] And in retrospect, even as he mourned the loss of his three associates, he could not refrain from assessing the overall advantage this sacrifice might bring to the mission. Never mind that his religious had more than once encountered open bigotry during their tours of duty—most notably in Kentucky, so long a melancholy place for Holy Cross.[21] What would matter in the

17. Costin, *Priceless Spirit,* 180–181.

18. For an expanded treatment of Holy Cross ministries during the conflict, see James T. Connelly, "Holy Cross Communities in the Civil War," a paper presented to the Conference on the History of the Congregations of Holy Cross (1993). For a useful and readable summary, see John F. Marszalek, "Call to Arms," *Notre Dame Magazine* 21 (Fall 1992): 15–19.

19. Zéphyrin-Joseph Léveque, born in Quebec in 1806, who joined Holy Cross just after his fiftieth birthday, had volunteered for chaplain service, but died before he could assume his duties. For an account of his last days, see "Priest of Jersey City" to Sorin, February 13, 1862, AIP.

20. Sorin to Champeau, November 21, 1861, AGEN.

21. See chapters 12 and 13, above.

long run was the recognition that these Catholic nuns and priests were anxious to serve their adopted country, even at the cost of their lives: "[Their] sacrifices were undoubtedly a gain for each of these dear victims; [but] they [also] gave the Congregation of Holy Cross, in the eyes of the public, a consecration that it had not before received and which must surround it with a happy prestige in the midst of the New World."[22]

Sorin himself, after an absence of six months in Europe, returned to Indiana "thank God with a mind rested and enriched with an affection for each member of our family, increased by separation." The war notwithstanding, he set about resuming his ordinary duties of governance, enhanced now by his recent appointment as assistant Superior General. He resolved to adhere to a strict schedule. "The division of my time will be, when at home, as follows: I shall devote Mondays and Tuesdays to the Society of Priests, Wednesdays and Thursdays to that of the Sisters, Fridays and Saturdays to that of the Brothers," making himself thus available to everybody on an equal and predictable basis.[23] How faithfully he complied with this self-imposed regimen cannot be established, but the affection and regard that prompted it were not held in doubt by the members of "our family." One of Father Sorin's great strengths was his ability, even as he was framing in his mind one grandiose project after another, to deal straightforwardly and, if need be, compassionately with the individual man or woman. He was a strict constructionist when it came to the ideals of the congregation; he could be, and often was, stern when dealing with recalcitrant subjects; his very decisiveness led not infrequently to unpleasant confrontations within the community. But nobody who lived or worked with him disputed his motives or questioned his zeal for the well-being of all. His colleagues, men and women, reveled in his flamboyant style of leadership, they took heart, even at the darkest moments, from his unflagging optimism, they appreciated how deep was his piety, different as it may have been from that of the revered Founder. There was an excitement in following such a man, a kind of religious *joie de vivre*. There was also mutual love and respect.

Of course a good share of the time Sorin was not "at home." Not long after settling in at Notre Dame, he was on the road again, to Cincinnati for the sitting of the third synod of that ecclesiastical province. "The decrees of the council are not out yet," he reported, "but one of the bishops told me they will certainly thank the Holy Father for what he has done to found the House [for erring and aged priests]. They seemed to be perfectly pleased with the thing itself. Now the

22. Sorin, *Chronicles*, 279–281.
23. Sorin to "My dear Sons and Daughters" (circular letter), April 14, 1861, AGEN.

certainty of its being the work of God is fully recognized."[24] (This endorsement he underscored later for Cardinal Barnabò: "I have never witnessed in this New World an enterprise which has won such a high degree of universal sympathy. Clergy and people are at one in applauding its utility.")[25] In mid-July a rather more secular purpose took him to Washington, just as that city had fallen into panic at news of the disaster at Bull Run. "I am going to Washington to try to save our post office, if it is not too late. Here is the visible work of the Demon. I cannot express to you the pain I feel at an attack so gratuitous and so unexpected. It could not be, could it, that Heaven wishes now to destroy a work taken on for its glory, and at such expense!"[26] This typically Sorinesque exaggeration does not explain just why the Notre Dame post office was under attack and why, if it were, the deed should have brought about such cataclysmic consequences. The "visible Demon"—always for Sorin lurking nearby—he may in this instance have thought to be incarnated in the person of Schuyler Colfax, the South Bend congressman who now presided as Speaker of the House of Representatives. Colfax had been deeply annoyed a year or two earlier when Sorin had chided him for not supporting a proposal to change the name of the town of South Bend to St. Joseph. The congressman had taken the not unreasonable position that, since the county and the all-important river already bore the name of the Virgin's spouse, further honorary embellishment would be a gilding of the lily.[27] But there was more to the plot than that. Though Sorin liked to refer to Colfax as "a friend,"[28] in fact he entertained ambivalent feelings toward the congressman. Colfax was a notorious leader of the anti-Catholic Know-Nothings, who, as editor of the *St. Joseph Valley Register,* routinely "condemned the efforts of the Papal Church and its dignitaries to stride onward to commanding political power in the Nation."[29] It seems unlikely nevertheless that the powerful Speaker, whatever his concerns for his constituency, would have troubled himself overmuch about a minor postal appointment, especially as he and the rest of the political establishment witnessed that July day the demoralized remnant of McDowell's army streaming back into the capital after their defeat in northern Virginia. And, whether or not due to Sorin's lobbying, the post office at Notre Dame in any event survived and functions to this day.

24. Sorin to Sister Columba, May 5, 1861, AGEN.
25. Sorin to Barnabò, November 8, 1861, AGEN.
26. Sorin to Moreau, July 22, 1861, AGEN.
27. See Colfax to Sorin, April 18, 1860, AIP.
28. See, for example, Sorin, *Chronicles,* 289.
29. See Willard H. Smith, *Schuyler Colfax: The Changing Fortunes of a Political Idol* (Indianapolis, 1952), 53–60.

The most important principle, in Sorin's mind, gained at Le Mans at the conclusion of his European excursion, was the exclusive jurisdiction granted him over the Marianite sisters in the United States, except for those in the distinct province of Louisiana. Once disembarked from the *Fulton* in late April, 1861, he went directly, not back to Indiana, but to Philadelphia, where he invoked his powers as "Plenipotentiary of the very Reverend Father Superior General [Moreau]" to conduct "a regular Visit." He discovered there no religious problem—"there is regularity and a good spirit generally in the House," which included twelve nuns and 130 pupils—though the debt amounted to a troubling $13,000.[30] A similarly formal Visitation was conducted at the flagship convent, St. Mary's, Indiana, from the middle of May through the first days of June. Sorin found it in a flourishing state indeed. Twenty-five professed sisters were in residence, along with forty-two novices and nine postulants. The educational apostolate for young ladies no less than that for impoverished orphans and for female pupils in the industrial school proceeded, the report claimed, with remarkable success. If there existed an outstanding debt of $3,000, this was more than compensated for by outstanding amounts payable to the institution, although "the possibility of collecting a quarter of this sum remains uncertain."[31] St. Mary's, in short, was more than solvent and ready to confront whatever lay ahead. Governor Morton's entreaty would shortly test that appraisal.

FATHER SORIN soon found himself caught up in a different conflict from that to which the governor had beckoned Mother Angela and her companions, though they too were intimately involved in it. Or perhaps it would be more accurate to say that Sorin's war was a tediously familiar one, the continuing struggle between antagonists with opposing definitions of the mission of Holy Cross. And if the contention remained rooted in the differing visions of France and America, the opening salvo this time was sounded in Canada. Sorin had long been wary of the Canadian community centered at Saint-Laurent, near Montreal; his relations with its superior, Joseph Rézé, had been, at best, uneasy, and he was deeply vexed that Mother Seven Dolors had established the generalate of the Marianites there.[32] The occasion for renewed hostilities, however, were the machinations of a lesser individual, which, superficially at least, appeared to bear

---

30. Memorandum, April 23, 1861, AGEN. Sorin relied to some extent upon the cordial support of the bishop of Philadelphia. See Wood to Sorin, July 17, 1860, AIP.

31. Memorandum, June 3, 1861, AGEN.

32. See chapter 21, above.

an eerie resemblance to the disastrous schemes that had so recently brought Holy Cross in Paris to its knees.

In fact, Brother Amédée proved to have been a mere eccentric when compared to Brother Marie-Julien. The two men did share a perceived gift for accountancy, and both had served their respective institutions as financial officers. Yet while Moreau's treasurer bilked the community out of thousands, Sorin's could hardly, at his worst, have managed more than a few hundreds. Amédée, born Jacques-Pierre Dayres in Agen in southwestern France, was twenty-nine years old when he entered the congregation at Notre Dame du Lac in 1853. He assumed his responsible position within the Indiana province four years later.[33] Sorin's later harsh portrait of him—"a man of a fickle, somber, mysterious character, whose ways were secret and erratic, having the zeal of a Pharisee in regard to others, but with a way of his own of understanding poverty and obedience as applied to himself"[34]—cannot disguise his own carelessness in having appointed a clever but disreputable person to an important post within the provincial administration. Edward Sorin, it would seem, like Basile Moreau and even Homer himself, was wont to nod on occasion.

Brother Amédée began a lengthy visit to Sainte-Croix in September 1858. His departure from the motherhouse for America the following March coincided with the entry into the novitiate there of Swiss-born Jules-Charles Petitpierre, who took the name Brother Charles Borromeo. Whatever interchange occurred between these two men, both French-speaking and of the same age—and perhaps none did—their fates soon became entangled together. In mid-July 1860, at any rate, Brother Amédée suddenly and "stealthily" absconded to Canada. "Last night," Sorin recorded,

> after I refused him leave three times over the past several days, he departed for Saint-Laurent anyway. He had an authorization from [Moreau], dated January, 1860. His action was particularly unmanly. He has taken with him whatever he wanted without accounting to anybody, and has not said *adieu* to anybody so far as I know. All the duties with which he was charged are this morning undone, and I have no one to replace him. The statistics, the budget, and everything related to them he has left annoyingly scarcely sketched out, when two days of work done with good will would have sufficed to prepare the material for the General Chapter [scheduled to

---

33. See chapter 19, above.
34. Sorin, *Chronicles*, 265.

meet in Le Mans two weeks hence]. He accuses the whole world, and the whole world accuses him. May God in his Holiness keep him far, far from Notre Dame du Lac![35]

What Father Sorin did not know when he uttered this aspiration was that among the materials Brother Amédée had taken with him to St. Laurent in the dead of the night was a bundle of checks or negotiable notes signed by the provincial himself. "These papers," Sorin bitterly observed later, "had been signed in haste at [Amédée's] request, in order to facilitate routine payment of specific sums for specific objects, in the meanwhile to be kept in his care." Instead, he used them "to betray my confidence."[36]

The plot thickened a few months later when, in early October, Sorin returned from the first of his two 1860 journeys to Europe accompanied by Brother Charles Borromeo, who had tentatively been designated for service in Canada but who, at the last moment, had been assigned by Moreau to Indiana instead. Then, the following April, Sorin, fresh from his voyage aboard the *Fulton*, encountered Amédée in Philadelphia, where he, Sorin—as has been seen—was carrying on a formal Visitation. What the brother was doing in the city of brotherly love remains unclear, but he was in any case full of cordiality and showed "himself to be animated by the best dispositions." Once back in Indiana, however, Sorin discovered that Amédée "was working to bring Brother Charles Borromeo to Canada." Since this change of venue seemed to accord with Borromeo's own predilections, Sorin raised no objection, provided that he be recompensed for the 1,200 francs that the brother's passage to America had cost. Brother Amédée responded by sending enough money to defray Borromeo's expenses from Notre Dame to St. Laurent. Sorin returned the check without comment, "whereat Brother Amédée is displeased!!! [sic] He insolently writes that he has five means to destroy Notre Dame, that he holds the honor of the superior [Sorin] in his hands, and that his superior [Rézé], under whose eyes he is writing, thinks as he does."[37]

Amédée's insolent missive was forwarded to Le Mans, but the response from the motherhouse was "evasive." Meantime, the brother promised that if Sorin would allow Charles Borromeo to depart for Canada and waive his demand for the 1,200 francs of compensation, he, Amédée, would return the materials he had filched from Notre Dame's administrative files. For the sake of peace, Sorin agreed, but the brazen Amédée, implicitly supported by Rézé, reneged on his pledge.

35. Sorin, memorandum, July 17, 1860, AGEN.
36. Sorin to Moreau, August 10, 1861, AGEN.
37. Sorin, *Chronicles*, 268–269.

"The Canadian situation," Sorin complained to Moreau, "is worse even than before I, to settle it, humiliated myself even to the dust (*poussière*) before this brother. I believed his promises; I imagined that he was going to return my papers." Yet, "having done all that he asked," Amédée now declared that "the Canadian house owes us nothing, and he has sent nothing." Father Sorin "on Monday last laid this sad affair" before the members of his provincial chapter: "Surprise was less pronounced among them than simple indignation." There was more at stake, however, than merely the shenanigans of an erratic confrère. Saint-Laurent was bent upon a larger aggression which Sorin would not abide, and he did not hesitate to remind the Founder of the cordial relations he had recently established in the Eternal City. "I make no threat, but I simply declare my intention to bring this matter to the attention of the Roman authorities. I owe it in justice to this Province to explain to his Eminence [Barnabò] and to the Holy Father what condition we have at arrived at here."

> To do this I need only send to Rome a copy of my [official] chronicles composed since my return [from Europe] last May. Canada has always looked upon us with a jealous eye. And nobody here has forgotten the conduct of the Reverend Mother General [Seven Dolors] last year, nor her refusal [to accommodate our sisters]. I know for certain that she has tried to lure away to Canada some of our most capable nuns.

But Brother Amédée, in his insolent correspondence from Canada, had intimated that a threat still more odious to Notre Dame was in the offing.

> The foundation that is being prepared for New York and for some other sites in the United States, as propounded by this brother, stands as an insult to this Province. Such plans moreover are directly contrary to your own commitments! Besides, however, there is at issue just now an unfortunate set of circumstances (*coincidence*), and, if I may make so bold as to offer advice ahead of time, it would be to plead with you to draw back immediately from any foundation or proposed foundation issuing from Saint-Laurent to the United States, and to respect strictly the limits that the [Civil] War will continue to impose [upon us all]. Each Province has its territorial limits. I will say nothing more on this subject; but I have said at least enough this time to acquaint you with my mind fully.[38]

---

38. Sorin to Moreau, August 9, 1861, AGEN.

New York City was about to become, once more, the heart of contention between Notre Dame and the larger Holy Cross apostolate. Sorin's frenzy over the matter, though certainly not a sham, nevertheless did not emerge without a certain measure of calculation. He had known for a year that the nuns' general chapter in Le Mans, sanctioned by Father Moreau, had authorized a Marianite venture in New York; two of Sorin's sturdiest allies, Mothers Angela and Ascension, had been in attendance at that meeting. Earlier failures in that pivotal sector of Holy Cross's mission in America, in which both Sorin and Angela had played a depressing part,[39] now assumed a revived significance. As he had before, Archbishop Hughes insisted that than any such foundation should be subject directly to the motherhouse in Le Mans and not in any way related to the Province of Indiana. In the midst of the flurry of correspondence that followed, Sorin, spontaneously or not, grew ever more agitated. He demanded Brother Amédée's expulsion from the congregation, and when Moreau demurred, offering instead only to "investigate" the charges, Sorin reiterated his intention to submit the matter to Rome. To justify his determination, he quoted for Moreau a letter received from Amédée in early August: "'To put your mind at rest, I will return your notes . . . once you have provided me with a new pair of trousers, a dress-coat (*habit*), and a cloak. . . . This will be a small price to pay for the peace and tranquillity of your soul.' I transcribe these squalid lines," Sorin wrote angrily, "in order to persuade your Reverence to reconsider. . . . If it is possible to live as a religious with religious of this kind, it is more than I know."

But his personal repugnance was mild compared to the apprehension he felt that Amédée and other Canadian upstarts might encroach upon his own ground. "Your Reverence can judge whether I want to effect a union with brothers of this ilk in our (*nos*) States. So I come to ask you to tell me once and for all if I should regard it as certain that the Canadian Province will make no Foundation in the United States, and if any Foundation which is set up from there will become dependent immediately upon the Province of Indiana. This is very grave for us."[40] Too grave indeed not to receive corporate attention. "My chapter here has determined to open an investigation of the encroachments from Canada into this province, rendered doubly odious by the vanity and bragging of this shabby brother." Two questions were at issue, "and they are mixed together:" Amédée's blackmail and the perfidious plan to establish the Marianites once more in New York.

---

39. See chapter 18, above.
40. Sorin to Moreau, August 10, 1861, AGEN.

You will not be surprised that everyone expressed confidence that your Reverence will give prompt justice in both these matters, but the chapter also deemed it a duty to tell you in all simplicity that, if not, it will be impossible not to inform Rome *about everything.* I leave all this to your prudence, very Reverend and dear Father, and I am sorry to see the cup of your griefs thus overflowing. But what can I do? Who has launched this monstrous attack upon us and [thrust] these foundations onto our terrain without even informing us? The spirit of Rome is very clear on this subject. Never will the chapter here consent to see a single foundation of priests and brothers or of sisters set up in the States of the north which does not depend on this Province, without a formal decree from Rome. . . . Why must we have these wars when we all share such a great need for peace.[41]

Signs of conflict, however, continued to accumulate. On August 24 Sorin received a letter from Father Rézé, the Canadian superior, in which he praised the *"extreme delicacy"* Brother Amédée had demonstrated during this fracas. And another from Amédée himself, who jauntily informed Sorin that he and confrères from Saint-Laurent were about to open a facility to serve soldiers in training at Burlington, Vermont. These communications predictably pushed Sorin's fury to an even higher pitch.

They seem to reveal clearly the suppositions of the house at Saint- Laurent. Indeed, in everything the tone of our dear Canadian brethren seems to breathe a limitless confidence in the support and sanction of Sainte-Croix. However that may be, my very Reverend and dear Father [Moreau], I will tell you my thinking once more. My resolve is unshakable, as is that of my chapter. Providence has opened our eyes in the nick of time (*à temps*). If this double affair is not put right immediately, and particularly if the smallest Canadian foundation in the United States is maintained one more day after my first request for removal or your first order to withdraw, without delay in either case, please understand, and do not doubt, that I consider it one of my duties toward the Congregation and Religion to send a memorandum to Rome. It is moderate, but these letters from Canada will be enclosed and all the facts recited.

Why should Moreau, engulfed in so many troubles in France, invite turmoil in the most successful of his missions? The question was more than rhetorical as

41. Sorin to Moreau, August 17, 1861, AGEN.

far as Sorin was concerned. Archbishop Purcell, just back from Rome, related the current unfavorable gossip. "Entirely *entre nous*," he told Sorin, "M. Moreau and your Society in France are in bad odor in Rome. If you know not why, I might tell you *viva voce*."[42] Sorin of course knew why, but he replied discreetly. "Would you be kind enough, most Reverend Father, to tell me what you have heard of our very Reverend Father Moreau and [the] Society in Rome? I long to hear it, even though it must pain me."[43] In fact Purcell had little precise information: "Have you heard of certain law-suits in France, involving wills, money, *and something else*"—this last, though underscored, remained unspecified.[44] And Sorin had Roman testimony of his own with which to badger Moreau.

> I heard with my own ears his Eminence [Barnabò] declare that if the Holy See were to send an Apostolic Visitor [to Sainte-Croix], it would probably be the end of us. . . . Mark well, you have the fate of the Congregation in your hands. . . . If you have encouraged the brother [Amédée] in these encroachments upon our terrain, you alone will be responsible for the crisis. . . . You could cure this disease in a half-hour. If you choose not to, do not blame me for the consequences. You will have forced me to seek elsewhere for a remedy which you had at your fingertips.

Angry, strident, impudent, insulting—any of these adjectives, or all of them, might apply to this tirade. And yet the ambivalence of feeling toward the Founder, so often manifested before, still haunted Father Sorin's inner self. "This is for your Reverence alone: alas! my Reverend and well beloved Father, a *secret horror* tells me we are approaching our end. The will of God at any rate be blessed. You must remember that I am one of your *oldest sons* and that my last morsel of bread will be for you and not for me."[45]

Though nothing came of Brother Amédée's outlandish foray into Vermont, by the beginning of September 1861, Mother Seven Dolors, accompanied by several Canadian sisters, had formally opened a new Marianite house on west Twenty-sixth Street in Manhattan.[46] By the end of the month Sorin could report bitterly that "in the most recent dispatches from Saint-Laurent, along with asking whether we are aware of the *seizure* of *New York* by the *Sisters* of *Canada,* we are

---

42. Purcell to Sorin, October 11, 1861, AIP.

43. Sorin to Purcell, October 15, 1861, AIP.

44. Purcell to Sorin, October 24, 1861, AIP.

45. Sorin to Moreau, August 25, 1861, AGEN.

46. O'Sullivan, "Fifty Years in New York," 3.

assured that we will suffer no harm if we acquiesce [immediately]." In fact, "we are being made sport of, people are laughing at us; and I suppose Sainte-Croix imagines that we too are amused. . . . I assure you, we are not." Moreau had, it is true, tendered him a wilted olive branch. "Your Reverence proposes to recall [Amédée] to France. I accept this offer and have confidence in it. Please take note of this: you will thereby ward off a more terrible blow than would be the loss of such a man for the Congregation."[47] Nevertheless, the unjust aggression in New York had to be countermanded: "Once your Reverence has rendered justice in this regard, we shall take account of it and give more than justice in return."[48] The same day he sent a more explicit ultimatum to one of Moreau's lieutenants: "If the Sisters do not leave New York immediately, . . . my memorandum will go to Rome. Nothing will change my mind about this. . . . Yesterday Brother Amédée informed me that [the Canadians] are going to take possession of a facility in a diocese whose bishop will welcome them. . . . We shall see what Rome has to say about that." Indeed, such an intervention from on high could prove providential: "I see in all this the assent of Heaven to find a way to end our troubles. Only Rome can accomplish it."[49]

Though he hesitated to follow through on this threat, Edward Sorin felt the sting of the "Canadian aggression" into New York more keenly than any event since the abortive appointment to Bengal, and, like that earlier quarrel, it undermined his sense of status within the Congregation of Holy Cross. "Father Sorin," he wrote of himself in the third person, "had returned from Europe [in late April 1861] with increased devotedness to the Motherhouse, but, to his unspeakable regret, the conduct of Sainte-Croix towards him [with regard to the intrigues of Brother Amédée and to the foundation in New York] disenchanted him. . . . He would have been only too happy to prove anew . . . his personal affection for the Very Reverend Father General, whose critical position he understood. . . . Unfortunately the two incidents just spoken of caused bitterness of heart, and when the heart was no longer at Sainte-Croix, it was all the worse for the latter."[50] It seems undeniable that there was manifest in these tortured feelings a measure of paranoia and, perhaps, an overweening ambition. Yet it should be borne in mind that, just as this crisis over New York confronted him, Sorin in the summer of 1861 was passing through the last stages of the collapse of his fondest hopes for the mission

---

47. Brother Amédée did return to France and, in 1866, formally withdrew from the congregation, as did his friend Charles Borromeo the same year. See *Matricule générale*, 989 and 1309, AIP.

48. Sorin to Moreau, September 27, 1861, AGEN.

49. Sorin to Séguin, September 27, 1861, AGEN. Father Armand-Baptiste Séguin held the title of Procurator to the motherhouse. See *Matricule générale*, 730, AIP.

50. Sorin, *Chronicles*, 271–272.

in Chicago and of his duel with the half-mad Bishop Duggan.[51] His defeat in that contest was a heavy affliction. But however depressed or frustrated or alienated he may have felt, he did not lose sight of the larger issue. As always—the point bears repetition—at the heart of the contention with Moreau were the differing perspectives in France and America as to how the Holy Cross vocation should be carried out. "*Voila*," cried Sorin, "I have sacrificed myself in order to establish the Congregation in the New World, and you [Moreau] know the extent of my success. I bless the Heaven that has preserved me, alas, from so many dangers; but in my inmost sentiments, reinforced over the last few months, it seems foolish to proceed any further."[52]

The imbroglio in New York City underscored an administrative muddle which, with some reservations, must be laid at the feet of Basile Moreau. He had sanctioned the closing of the second of the two failed missions there—the first, in Brooklyn, had disappeared with hardly a whimper after a few months in 1848[53]— and he had, moreover, promised that no re-establishment would be permitted without Sorin's consent. "Having been made aware of the circulation of gossip calculated to trouble souls," Sorin quoted him, "touching upon an intention on our part to reopen the House in New York, closed by the Father Superior of Notre Dame with our authorization, we declare these rumors void of foundation and in every case null. Furthermore, no enterprise of this kind will be undertaken in the future without the consent of the Father Superior at Notre Dame."[54] This pledge the Founder now broke, out of weakness, no doubt, not out of malice. For Sorin's real opponent in New York was not Moreau but the archbishop, John Hughes, a man as tough and single-minded as Sorin himself, an ecclesiastical autocrat who had amply earned his nickname, "Dagger John."[55] And, Hughes having flatly refused to have any dealings with Notre Dame, Moreau did not have the stomach to oppose him; if Holy Cross were to secure a foothold in the premier city of the United States, Sorin had to be left out of the equation. This was a conclusion he bitterly resented, though he could not successfully refute it. "You tell me," he said to Moreau, "that I have to understand the archbishop of New York's hostility toward me. But I do not understand it. Yet, even if it does exist, is this hostility the *reason* the sisters are returning to New York, and does it explain the earlier sup-

---

51. See chapter 20, above.
52. Sorin to Moreau, November 20, 1861, AGEN.
53. See chapter 13, above.
54. Quoted in Sorin to Drouelle, November 25, 1861, AGEN.
55. See Richard Shaw, *Dagger John: The Unquiet Life and Times of Archbishop John Hughes* (New York, 1977).

pression of the mission there, a suppression ordered by your Reverence?"[56] In fact, however, such a surrender to pragmatic necessity, which involved breaking his word, did not overly disturb the pious Founder; he continued to judge the nuns in Indiana as undisciplined and worldly, as too much given to an American *esprit.* Their sisters at Saint-Laurent, by contrast, especially when led by his fervent disciple, Mother Seven Dolors, displayed what was to him an appropriate docility and sense of religious decorum—they were, in other words, much like the Marianites under his direct eye in France. Let such admirable women religious bring the genuine *esprit* of Sainte-Croix to the sidewalks of New York.[57]

As THE CONTROVERSY DEEPENED, Basile Moreau gave further evidence of his ability to muddy the jurisdictional waters. Only weeks after he had given Sorin "plenipotentiary" powers over the sisters in Indiana, he issued a decree setting up an authoritative troika: superintendence over the nuns in the Province of Indiana was to be exercised by Sorin, to be sure, but also, on an equal footing, by Bishop Luers and by a Visitor to be sent shortly from France, a functionary "who will make a conscientious report on present conditions in this province and, after conferring with me, . . . will take the needed measures to bring about peace and order."[58] This peculiar arrangement, which on scant evidence presumed a lack of "peace and order" in Indiana, would have been workable only if Sorin, Luers, and the unnamed Visitor were in complete agreement. Yet again Moreau's failure to come to grips with the practical consequences of his theoretical schemes led ultimately to confusion and recrimination. Sorin at first did not react negatively to this three-headed design, largely perhaps because he knew that he had an ally in John Henry Luers, so that whoever the Visitor from France proved to be, or whatever his point of view, an automatic preponderance of two to one appeared assured. Nor could the canonical rights of the bishop of Fort Wayne be deemed in this regard inconsequential: until the Marianite Constitutions had received formal approbation from Rome, the association of sisters remained an institute dependent upon the diocese in which their motherhouse was

56. Sorin to Moreau, January 14, 1862, AGEN.

57. I have resisted more often than not in these pages the inclination to point out the vicious anti-Sorin bias and the consequent tendentious reasoning routinely employed by Etienne and Tony Catta in their *Moreau.* No better example of this obsession of theirs occurs in 2: 472, where an attempt is made to explain away, by impugning Sorin's character, Moreau's moral fault in breaking his solemn word about the reopening of a mission in New York.

58. See Costin, *Priceless Spirit,* 154, and chapter 21, above. Moreau's *diktat* was dated May 8, 1861; Sorin had left Le Mans during the first week of April.

located. So the nuns of the Indiana Province, whether they resided at St. Mary's or in Washington or Philadelphia, or, indeed, were acting as nurses aboard the *Red Rover* in the middle of the Mississippi, were the direct responsibility of Bishop Luers.[59] "Monseigneur Luers is German [by birth]," Sorin warned Moreau, but "in order to avoid the reproach of his [original] nationality, he has become thoroughly American in all his conduct, following the example of his archbishop [Irish-born Purcell of Cincinnati]."

Such a caution was wasted on Moreau. Meanwhile, the vehemence of Father Sorin's objection to the new mission in New York may have helped to stiffen the back of the increasingly embattled Founder. "*My position has become untenable,*" Sorin wrote on November 18. "In view of the reopening of the mission in New York, it seems that there is no administration in Holy Cross . . . except one of guile. . . . Alas, there is no retribution . . . *for solemn written commitments* abrogated." Moreover, "New York is only the occasion of my desire to retire," and then his bitterness overflowed.

> For a long time I have searched in vain in the Congregation and particularly in its government the essence of what should prevail in religious houses. And I have found the contrary. The [Roman] approbation, [the deliberations] of the General Chapter [in Le Mans] have in turn given me hope that a change was in the offing. But today I no longer have hope, and, whatever hope remained until recently, the reopened house in New York has destroyed it entirely. And sooner than confront these new vexations and all these discords, dissensions, and scandals, . . . which redound each day to the dishonor of my first Superior [Moreau] and which *ridicule* my religious simplicity . . . I would have preferred ten times to have been expelled from the Congregation.[60]

As though there were not already enough bad feeling in the air, the ever-constant contention over money further poisoned the atmosphere. Father Moreau, desperate for cash in the wake of the Marie-Julien disaster, now reminded Sorin of the 15,000 francs advanced to him in November 1860,[61] and requested that it be repaid in full and at once. The original agreement called for a repayment schedule

---

59. James T. Connelly, "Bishop Luers and the Autonomy of the Sisters of the Holy Cross," a paper delivered at the Annual Conference on the History of the Congregations of Holy Cross (1987), 7–9.

60. Sorin to Moreau, November 18, 1861, AGEN.

61. See chapter 21, above.

of 5,000 francs per year, dependent "upon the future allocations of the Propagation of the Faith. This loan and this promise of repayment were a proof as well as a result of the reciprocal sentiments of the Motherhouse and her eldest daughter." Sorin, as usual short of funds himself, managed to send to Sainte-Croix 1,000 francs in the late spring of 1861. However, "it was his intention to settle the whole account [in the course of the same year], in order to help the Congregation, whose existence was threatened;" indeed, "Sainte-Croix would have received more than it advanced." But then Brother Amédée intruded, and the nuns from Canada were sent to New York. Though he pleaded for the record the "precarious" financial condition of both Notre Dame and St. Mary's, "in the midst of the horrors of a war which no one would have believed," he left no doubt as to the real reason for default: "The filial love that would have prevailed" had given way to "bitterness of heart."[62] "Your urgency about your 15,000 francs," he told Moreau, "should have reminded you of my cries of distress throughout this year. You could have been very just, you could have said, *omnia reddam*. But you left me to cry out in vain."[63]

"Seventeen times Sainte-Croix insisted upon payment before the time, and just as often Father Sorin was obliged to defer." Characteristic hyperbole, to be sure, but characteristic too was the decision he made, even as the Chicago enterprise was disintegrating and Brother Amédée was issuing his threats, to build a new St. Mary's Academy. And even as a war was raging, and "banks and well-founded houses of commerce were declaring themselves insolvent." Catholic institutions, like "the Dominican College of St. Joseph in Ohio, the one in Bardstown, Kentucky, and even St. Louis University, advanced their graduation schedules and announced that they would not reopen until after the war." At this moment, Sorin displayed yet again his astonishing resilience. "The council at Notre Dame du Lac conceived of the only project that could save the Institution"—hyperbole once more—"that is to say, to astonish the country by the construction of a new St. Mary's Academy." And even the war played directly into his bold hands.

> It proved to be a magnificent edifice,[64] in the building of which a good portion of the local workers and merchants took a deep interest, since commerce and employment had been virtually suspended. The initiative could not have come at a better time for them. Labor costs were kept down by employing brothers from Notre Dame, along with other workers who had

---

62. Sorin, *Chronicles*, 271–273.

63. Sorin to Moreau, November 18, 1861, AGEN. "*Omnia reddam,*" I shall restore everything.

64. It was built to last. On the St. Mary's College campus it is now called Bertrand Hall.

literally nothing to do otherwise and rejoiced in finding jobs even at a reduced wage, only a third of which had to be paid in ready cash. Merchants
sold almost all the matériel under the same conditions. It was therefore not
necessary to consolidate Notre Dame's debt as far as the local financial élites
were concerned. And so St. Mary's was saved. Left to their own credit-
resources, the Sisters could have done nothing but watch the material decay
of their property, already advanced, and would soon find it impossible to
maintain their school in the old House which was already scarcely tenable.[65]

The claim that the nuns, "left to their own credit-resources" would have been
inevitably consigned to failure, was Sorin's more or less explicit assertion that the
separation of temporalities, so much insisted upon by both Rome and Le Mans,
was not an unmixed blessing. The sisters themselves at any rate, except perhaps for
Mother Angela, were not informed about the project until after the first spade-
full of earth had been turned over. And Sainte-Croix was not informed at all until
the building was up, having cost in excess of $20,000 (100,000 francs).[66] When
Moreau's procurator repeatedly raised the matter of the 15,000–franc debt, Sorin's
rejoinder was at once bland and disingenuous. "I can do nothing at this moment," he replied, even as the pilings were being driven into the ground on the
St. Mary's campus and the country was being scoured for funds to support the
Missionary Hostel at Notre Dame. "This is a disappointment, but what can be
done about it (*mais encore*)? You forget too readily the better times, when I sent
by a single courier to Sainte-Croix 15,000 francs to his Reverence [Moreau] and
10,000 to the Mother Superior." That this gesture of generosity has gone unrecorded—most likely because it never happened—does not diminish one's admiration for Sorin's cheek. "Who then has done more than I have up to the
present? So much for your surprise. Moreover, it is very likely that you will never
see a penny of this debt. We are very close here to imitating what happened in
Paris. . . . If God does not save us, we are lost."[67]

As the year neared its close, despite the new construction at St. Mary's and
the generally favorable reaction his prized *refugium* for aberrant and ailing priests
had generated, Sorin's mood grew ever more somber, especially after he learned
that, of all people, Brother Amédée had been formally assigned to act as an aide

65. Summary memorandum, Sorin to Moreau, 1861–1863, AGEN.
66. See Costin, *Priceless Spirit*, 158.
67. Sorin to Séguin, July 16, 1861, AGEN.

to the nuns in New York.[68] "It is not without profound distress that I come to add to the gravity of the circumstances in which I see the Congregation languishing," he wrote Moreau on November 20.

> I am asking permission to return to Rome, and I have so informed his Eminence [Barnabò].[69] Pardon me, very Reverend Father, I fear that you will deny me this request, but given the absolute impossibility I find in gaining recognition of my impressions now for a long time, I believe it my duty to secure an audience [with the cardinal]. I cannot make known my situation through letters, and I am fully confident that as soon as his Eminence understands, he will agree that it is untenable. It is useless to try to tell you what I feel at the thought of withdrawing from Notre Dame du Lac and from the Congregation. For a long time I have resisted the thought, always hoping for a change, but now any hope is gone. Pardon me all the pain I have caused you over these twenty-two years, and particularly for that related to my opposition to your recent foundation in New York. What I have done, I still believe, stems from a sincere devotion to the well-being of the Congregation. . . . I believe I understand the terrain I have moistened with my sweat for so many years. You will regret, my good and very Reverend Father, not having followed the counsel I have repeated consistently. The Congregation is two fingers from ruin, when it should be entering a new era of prosperity. But my devotion will not save it, nor will it be I who gives it the deathblow. You have not wished to understand! I shall retire in order not to witness the last gasp.[70]

Perhaps because he had heard such threats of retirement so many times before, Father Moreau gave them no credence on this occasion. But he did, as Sorin predicted, forbid the proposed journey to Rome. "You have already, my friend, left your province too frequently without my permission. Besides, in addition to the expense involved, a trip to Rome would be both imprudent and contrary to the right of the general council [at Sainte-Croix] to hear your complaints before you go higher."[71] And he did announce that the canonical Visitor, who was to put all things right, would depart for America without delay. The person chosen for this commission was the Founder's nephew.

---

68. See, among several examples, Amédée to Sorin, December 28, 1863, AIP.
69. See Sorin to Barnabò, November 8, 1861, AGEN. The letter dealt with the Priests' Hostel and concluded: "I have a need to see your Eminence and bring another matter to your attention."
70. Sorin to Moreau, November 20, 1861, AGEN.
71. Quoted in Catta, *Moreau*, 2: 478.

CHARLES MOREAU, son of Basile's older brother René, was just short of his fortieth birthday when he embarked on his ill-fated journey to the New World. His uncle had overseen his education, first in arts and sciences in Paris and then in theology at the seminary in Le Mans; the young man had proved to be in both settings an accomplished student. Ordained priest by Bishop Bouvier in 1843, he had immediately applied for entry into Holy Cross. Five years later he succeeded Louis Champeau as prefect of studies in the *collège* at Sainte-Croix. His work in this post was exemplary, and, like Champeau, he combined teaching prowess with scholarly endeavors; the Greek grammar he composed came to be widely used. Not only did the dead languages attract his studious attention; he was fluent in English and German, and he wrote French with commendable style. His rise through the administrative ranks of the congregation was predictably swift. In 1850 he assumed a place on the general council; two years later he was named an assistant general; and in 1860 he became his uncle's chief auxiliary.[72] In appearance Charles was short and slender, and his wide and thin-lipped mouth and pinched eyes gave his face, under a mop of dark hair, a haggard look. He combined a brusque and formal manner with a reputation for impatience; he did not suffer those he considered fools gladly. A posed portrait shows him seated, with, appropriately, his right hand resting on a book on the table next to him, and the left clenched into a fist on his lap. In rigidity of mindset, in devotion to duty and scrupulous regard for the protocols of the religious life, he was a mirror image of Basile Moreau—but without the older man's charm and his intimation of holiness.

There is a parable in the gospel about a landowner who, after dispatching fruitlessly a series of emissaries seeking justice from his violent tenants, decides finally to send his son. "They will respect my son," he mused.[73] Whether Basile Moreau had in mind this passage when he appointed Charles to go to his unruly subjects in America—a spiritual son bound to him intimately by blood as well as by religion—the inspiration went for naught; over the course of a twenty-one month Visitation, "they" did not come to respect Moreau's "son," because that son did not earn their respect or indeed their understanding. This failure, how-

---

72. Catta, *Moreau*, 2: 480–481. One may be pardoned for taking these lines of Catta with more than a grain of salt: "In [Charles's] rapid rise there is not the slightest foundation for any accusation of nepotism. There had been no past indication of any trace of favoritism on the part of the Superior General. Consequently, the only motive for the general council's choice was that Father Charles's exceptional talents could not be ignored."

73. Matthew 21:33–37.

ever, did not stem from any moral or intellectual fault on Charles Moreau's part; it resulted rather from the increasingly heightened tension between Notre Dame and Sainte-Croix, from the conflicting visions of what a mission in America ought to be. Whether or not an increasingly embattled Founder had determined that now was the moment to launch an all-out offensive against his recalcitrant children in Indiana, it would have been difficult, if so, to imagine a more suitable ambassador to achieve such a goal at that particular moment. Father Charles was a man of personal integrity and inner strength who had no reason to deal with the issues at hand except with disinterested motives. But, at the same time, he demonstrated not a scintilla of diplomatic flexibility; he stood as the epitome of a French religiosity that denied the possibility of any cultural deviation from the conventional pietistic principles appropriate to a small town in western France. Stiff and rude, a pedantic stickler with regard to the very principles which were to be the subject of challenge in America, Charles was bound to collide with the charismatic Edward Sorin. Narrow-minded in the extreme, he regarded a question raised as tantamount to a rebellion contemplated. And the fact that he was the Founder's blood relative only served to lend intensity to his every decision and initiative and to his every misstep, so that as his own moral authority ebbed away through one failure after another, that of his uncle was undermined too.

Charles Moreau, after a stormy passage, landed in New York on December 31, 1861. He sent a note to old Brother Vincent announcing his arrival and asking that Father Sorin be so informed. Here was the first small sign of impending trouble. Nonetheless, Sorin, sensitive as he was, took in stride this implied slight, and, since the governance of the sisters was the most pressing issue at hand, he addressed to them a graceful introduction of the Visitor.

> We are informed by the Reverend Father Charles Moreau, the first General Assistant [sic] of the very Reverend Father General, that he has already reached New York on his way to this Province, which he comes to visit in lieu of the General Superior himself. I need not speak here of his eminent qualifications for such an important office; for you all know his reputation as a ripe scholar and as a perfect Religious. He speaks English and German fluently and has the confidence of all the Congregation. I trust he will take time to visit thoroughly. I purpose taking him to all our Establishments and giving every member of the Community the opportunity of seeing him and going to confession to him.[74]

---

74. Sorin to "Dear Daughters," January 14, 1862, AIP.

It is worth observing that however harshly candid Edward Sorin showed himself in speaking to or corresponding with the officials at Sainte-Croix, including Basile Moreau, he was always careful not to share negative sentiments with the generality of his subjects. Nor did he, or so he claimed, ever disparage his superiors in Le Mans to the Roman authorities: in his exchanges with Barnabò, he assured Moreau, "I have never uttered a word or written a line that was not favorable to you and the Congregation."[75] His old friends and comrades, Victor Drouelle and Louis Champeau, were no doubt privy to some of his inmost thoughts and doubts, and, on the local scene, Father Granger, Mother Angela, and perhaps Brother Vincent probably were; but not the rest of the community. At any rate, the crucial message in this communiqué to the nuns, aside from its tone of respect for the Visitor, was this one: "I purpose *taking* him to all our Establishments and *giving* every member of the Community the opportunity of seeing him."

Father Sorin naturally assumed that the Visitor, once rested from his voyage, would as a matter of course proceed directly to provincial headquarters at Notre Dame du Lac, and begin his work there. Then he could be conducted to the dependent houses by Sorin himself, who could hardly be blamed if he intended thereby to maintain some control over the agenda of the Visitation. In fact, Charles Moreau was determined not to be "taken" anywhere by anyone, especially not by Sorin. It would seem that in collusion with his uncle he had planned all along to snub the provincial of Indiana. "I have no idea," Basile Moreau observed blandly, "what order [Charles] will follow in visiting our various houses. . . . [I] shall leave it to him to decide what plan he will follow in his itinerary."[76] The obvious upshot was to let Sorin cool his heels until the august Visitor deigned to favor him with an audience, a reminder that among the higher reaches of administration at Sainte-Croix all subjects were of equal insignificance. Thus the Visitation originated with a slap at the most important individual in the congregation aside from the Founder himself, and ordinary standards of efficiency as well as of simple courtesy were forfeited for the sake of a foolish gesture worthy of a schoolyard bully. It was hardly an auspicious beginning.

Charles carried out his insolent plan by formally visiting first the re-opened Marianite house in New York, which he knew was so resented at Notre Dame. Then he moved on to examine the establishments in Philadelphia, Baltimore, and Washington—all three constituents of the province of Indiana. He decided

---

75. Sorin to Moreau, August 25, 1861, AGEN.
76. Moreau, *Circular Letters,* 2: 239.

next to travel to New Orleans, but, when the military situation made this unfeasible, he turned north to Canada instead. It was mid-March 1862 by then, and a deep chill of disappointment seized upon the residents at Notre Dame and St. Mary's, who awaited the Visitor's arrival with growing disillusionment. Sorin professed himself eager at first to greet Father Charles, but the latter's dilatory tactics soon shriveled away any enthusiasm. "Instead of the favorable results that everybody looked for from this visit, through some mystery not to be explained unless by the wiles of the evil spirit, none of those hopes was realized, and a series of troubles . . . began one after another to arise."[77] Among the troubles unleashed by the Visitation was a decree from Sainte-Croix that reached Notre Dame in early April 1862.

> It is with a view to establishing uniformity [wrote Basile Moreau], which is the mother of union, that . . . I have not hesitated to deprive myself of the assistance of Father Charles, in order that he may resume and complete the Regular Visit of our houses in America. . . . Speak to him with open hearts; share with him your difficulties and troubles; follow whatever advice he gives you. . . . Present to him all the acts of your Councils and Chapters, in order that he may be able to furnish me with a conscientious report and obtain my approval. . . . This approval is essential especially for admission to profession, and until it is obtained all professions will be postponed, as well as the reception of Sacred Orders. . . . As regards the Sisters it will be necessary in every case and without exception, and notwithstanding any concession made in this respect in the Vicariate of Indiana, to obtain previously the written consent of their Mother General [Seven Dolors]. Without this consent of the Mother General, I would never give my approval for perpetual vows, and thus the profession would be null and void.[78]

The sweeping character of this ukase was only one of the aspects of it that troubled Notre Dame. Its timing was peculiar. Dated March 26, 1862, it announced the "resumption" of Father Charles's Visitation, when in fact that procedure had begun the previous December and had continued uninterruptedly since then. The document could have been read as though the Visitor were being armed with additional faculties before venturing into the lion's den of Indiana. At any rate, in mid-June, Charles finally left Saint-Laurent after a three-month sojourn there. He still avoided Notre Dame, however, visiting instead Holy Cross missions in

---

77. Sorin, *Chronicles*, 281.
78. Moreau, *Circular Letters*, 2: 238–239.

Cincinnati, Toledo, Columbus, and Zanesville—all of them founded by Edward Sorin. Sorin's irritation grew apace at "having awaited in vain for Father Charles's arrival and not knowing when he will deign to come to us."[79] On July 7 young Moreau was in Fort Wayne, where Bishop Luers received him and granted him priestly faculties for the duration of his stay in the diocese, and at noon on Saturday, July 11, as though determined finally to bite the bullet, he alighted from his hired rig in front of the imposing collegiate building at Notre Dame. The carillon did not ring out to celebrate his arrival, and only a skeletal staff was on hand to greet him. The campus was half deserted, since the summer commencement exercises had been held only days before. That the Visitor had failed to attend them was one more black mark against him. "The disappointment was greatly felt," said Sorin, "and from that time the desire for his arrival soon changed to indifference," a point he underscored by absenting himself and declining to offer the Visitor a personal welcome.

Informed that Father Sorin was across the fields at St. Mary's, Father Charles made his way there. The two priests remained closeted in the nuns' parlor the rest of the day, in the course of which Sorin told the Visitor that, since Basile Moreau's circular of March 26 was clearly directed at him and clearly broke faith with earlier commitments, he had no choice but to resign as superior of the sisters. Charles replied that he, as Visitor, had no authority to accept a resignation. The next day, July 12, Charles formally received from the provincial, Mother Ligouri, the list of novices recommended for profession; he duly dispatched copies for final approval to his uncle in Le Mans and to Mother Seven Dolors in Montreal. In doing so he was simply conforming to Basile Moreau's directive, which, however, for Sorin was just one more *casus belli,* justifying him in his determination to resign. He drew up a formal document to this effect, and two days later presented it to Charles, who refused to comment upon it. By this time Sorin's disdain for the nephew was so sweeping that he shifted strategy and went directly at the uncle. "Very Reverend Superior General," he wrote,

> in presenting formally my resignation, I regret only that it will reach you so late. But of course I am only telling you what I have told you twice over the past six months without receiving any answer from you. I have therefore assumed that I would be replaced by the Reverend Father Visitor. There will be no time to lose if you wish a replacement should enjoy proper advantage. As for me it is simply a matter of conscience that I should resign from all administration. And if I cannot succeed in doing this without

79. Sorin to Moreau, July 4, 1862, AGEN.

leaving the Congregation of Holy Cross, then I humbly solicit your Reverence to grant me a dispensation from my Vows. . . . I ask nothing more than what I asked ten months ago, although I would never ask anything that did not appear to me important for our Work in America. All I want now is . . . a small corner of a room where I can enjoy peace and leave [contention] to others. If twenty-three years devotion to Holy Cross has not merited me this privilege, I shall seek for it elsewhere. I hope at any rate to succeed, with your blessing.[80]

And so the competition between the Founder and his eldest and ablest collaborator continued along curiously parallel tracks, each man constantly protesting his intention to withdraw from the hurly-burly of administrative responsibility in order to find "peace" in a "small corner of a room," and neither man seriously intending to do so.

Charles Moreau meanwhile proceeded with his Visitation to the nuns at St. Mary's. He preached their retreat and, on July 16, formally called into session their provincial chapter. His attempt to add two French-speaking members to the chapter was thwarted by Sorin, who, his "resignation" notwithstanding, was determined to maintain his standing with the nuns. The provincial's objective in this regard was hampered by the absence of his two most stalwart allies; Mother Angela was engaged in overseeing the sisters' nursing efforts from Mound City to Louisville to Memphis, and she returned to the St. Mary's campus only intermittently; and Mother Ascension had become superior of the house in Philadelphia. The provincial *en scène*, Mother St. Ligouri, a thirty-one-year-old French woman, was of a different stripe altogether. She had come to the mission at Bertrand as a seamstress in 1853, had served later in New Orleans and Philadelphia, and had been elevated to her present position in 1860. Her connection with Edward Sorin was complicated by her strong dislike and disapproval of his confidante, Mother Angela, as well as by the circumstance that, whenever resident in Indiana, she, Ligouri, had Sorin for her spiritual director. This latter relationship manifested on her side an intensity of the sort which indicated, as she put it, that "some women cannot, without great danger and difficulties, be governed by a [male] superior because of the tendency of our sex toward a natural love, so subtly dangerous for men." Yet eleven months before Charles Moreau arrived at St. Mary's she assured Sorin that "my conscience as all else is and ever shall be open to you—as far as you will allow me. No, nothing do I wish to hide from my most

---

80. Sorin to Moreau, July 14, 1862, AGEN.

venerated Father and superior; good and bad and very bad are all the same to his charity."

An element of hysteria or at least of personal anxiety punctuated Mother Ligouri's correspondence with Sorin during 1861 and the first half of 1862, which startled him and led him to recommend strongly that she be replaced as provincial.[81] She sensed his rebuff of her even before another male authority figure suddenly was at hand; her excitable reaction to Sorin's announced "resignation" proved to be the prelude to a shift in her dependence to Charles Moreau. "My mind is made up," Sorin replied to her demand for an explanation for his act. "It is well known now that I had accepted the direction of the Sisters under certain conditions. For a while these conditions were observed, but they having now been laid aside, I consider myself free. Were I to share with you [information] which had just come under my eyes, you would then understand whether we have reason *now* to distrust our Canadian associates. I am as ever the friend of the Sisters. I have absolutely nothing to complain of in this affair, but I am no longer their Superior."[82] In this assertion Ligouri appears to have discerned the dark contrast between the Founder's proper nephew and her once "venerated Father and Superior," whom she chided now for employing resignation as a bargaining chip with the Visitor. Sorin's response was sharp and direct: "I do nothing nor write a line *for effect*. I wish you and all your [colleagues] to understand clearly that the reason why I retire is unwillingness to bring again our administration among persons disposed as I know them to be in Canada. . . . I now beg to close all correspondence on this matter."[83]

The case of Mother Ligouri was an unhappy one, so unhappy indeed that by mid-September 1862 she had departed Indiana for good and gone off to Canada.[84] Having won the allegiance of this troubled if talented woman, however, and one or two of her associates, proved to be for Charles Moreau a pyrrhic victory. Despite respect for his person and his mission, few others of those he visited showed him much sympathy, mostly because he was such an awful scold. He upbraided the sisters at St. Mary's for the unwarranted expenses involved in building the new academy, when in fact, as Sorin expressed it in the third person, "it was to Father Sorin and his council that [Charles] should have addressed himself and not to

81. See the correspondence as quoted and paraphrased in Costin, *Priceless Spirit*, 163–168.

82. Sorin to Ligouri, July 17, 1862, AGEN.

83. Sorin to Ligouri, July 18, 1862, AGEN.

84. It should be noted that Mother Ligouri was not without worth or talent. Thirty years after these unpleasant events she became Superior General of the French Marianites, succeeding Mother Seven Dolors.

the Sisters, who should not have heard one word of his displeasure."[85] The Visitor also pronounced his shock and dismay that novices had been allowed to participate in the nursing ventures taken on at the beginning of the war; he demanded their immediate and humiliating return to the confines of the nunnery. And perhaps most eloquently Father Charles demonstrated the narrow, inflexible, and unenlightened model of religious life he represented on a later visitation to Washington. He came to the little parish hospital operated by Sisters Theodore and Rose at a time when the facility was jammed with wounded men. The Visitor expressed sharp displeasure that the sisters were not regulating their day in accord with the Marianite constitutions—which, it should be recalled, had still to be properly translated into English—and he insisted that, whatever the demands of their ministry to the maimed and the dying, they give precedence to performing at the required time their various exercises: spiritual reading, telling their beads, preparing for their morning meditation, and, in short, offering spiritual guidance to all by their "modesty, silence, and punctual accomplishment of their religious practices."[86]

Father Sorin's first impression of the Visitor displayed merely a light-hearted disdain. "Father Charles arrived about two and half weeks ago," he informed Drouelle.

> He has not yet found an occasion to enjoy anything here, not a thing seems worthy of his commendation. He is very reserved. We waited to hear from him some praise for our pretty lakes and our pretty river which enchant many old ladies etc. But our dear Visitor is as cold as a marble statue. That's not surprising, since he is part of Sainte-Croix in its ice age, and he has just come here after spending four months in frozen Canada. And so he has come here frozen himself, frozen so that he can put at defiance the sunshine of the dog-days (*canicule*) of Indiana.[87]

But during the weeks that followed the relationship deteriorated to the point that the two men scarcely spoke to one another.[88] Then, in September Bishop Luers came to Notre Dame to administer the sacrament of confirmation. Not surprisingly Father Sorin informed him of his resignation as local superior of the sisters.

---

85. Quoted by Costin, *Priceless Spirit*, 158.

86. Costin, *Priceless Spirit*, 190–192.

87. Sorin to Drouelle, July 28, 1862, AGEN.

88. For a detailed summary from Sorin's point of view, see Memorandum, Sorin to Basile Moreau, May 28, 1863, AGEN.

The bishop's reaction was prompt and unambiguous. He summoned Charles Moreau to his presence and told the Visitor that, by virtue of his episcopal authority, he was instructing Sorin to resume his post as the sisters' sole director. He furthermore warned Charles to refrain from interfering in any way himself with the governance of the nuns who belonged to a house, St. Mary's, in his diocese and therefore ultimately responsible to him.[89] A month later, irritated that the Visitor had not appeared ready to abide by this injunction—in effect, to restrict his activities to an investigation of the state of the Holy Cross priests and brothers—the bishop returned to Notre Dame. His vicar general sent Sorin a friendly notice beforehand. "I had heard two or three times the bishop express his dissatisfaction concerning your lack of *égard,* and I thought I would give you a timely warning."[90] But surely it was not Sorin's failure in *égard* or deference that was at issue, as Father Charles readily understood. In another demonstration of diplomatic ineptitude he declined to meet Bishop Luers, and went off instead to visit the hospital in Mound City. An irked Luers for his part, having intervened with regard to "the conduct and doings of the Reverend Visitor and Mother Ligouri" and having thereby challenged the position of Basile Moreau himself, realized that the matter now had to be referred to Rome—a determination by no means unwelcome to Edward Sorin.

"Until Rome has decided," the bishop wrote him early in the new year, "and all things are arranged, you will remain the Director of the Sisters as heretofore, notwithstanding the prohibition of either Superior General Moreau or the Visitor to the contrary." Nor did Luers manifest any particular esteem for the senior Moreau or for his pious principles. "I did not answer the last letter of the Superior General, because I saw no good reason for doing so."

> Unless a permanent [set] of Rules and Constitutions are drawn up by him for the Sisters as will also suit this country, *and I can approve;* and unless he will promise to send no other Visitor from time to time except one who has *practical* experience in such matters, and who will confer with and uphold the local authorities, and change or interfere no more than is really necessary, the sooner the separation from Europe takes place the better, because there can be no peace, as fifteen or twenty years bitter experience has shown. There must be order and obedience on the part of the Sisters without doubt; but it must be a *rationabile obsequium.* As long as it is such,

---

89. Connelly, "Luers and Autonomy," 5.
90. Benoit to Sorin, October 11, 1862, AIP.

depend upon it, I shall uphold the authority of their Superiors, whether in this or any other country. I could not be a true Bishop or save my soul otherwise. But I will not uphold folly or caprice.[91]

This message was music to Father Sorin's ears, as it would have been, it seems safe to say, to those of most of the sisters had they heard it. The writing in any case was clearly on the wall: "The sooner separation from Europe takes place the better." The divorce did not take place immediately nor for some years; but with the support of the sturdy bishop of Fort Wayne the issue was no longer in serious doubt.

---

91. Luers to Sorin, January 8, 1863, AIP.

chapter twenty-three

War and the Virgin

THE CANONICAL VISITATION OF THE ESTABLISHMENTS of Holy Cross in North America, conducted by Father Charles Moreau, lingered into the late summer of 1863. The procedure became, however, increasingly irrelevant, because, due to the intervention of the bishop of Fort Wayne, the matters under investigation and dispute were to be settled by the responsible department of the Roman bureaucracy, Propaganda and its prefect, Cardinal Barnabò. Strictly speaking, young Moreau's mandate to examine the doings of the Congregation of Holy Cross—that is, the priests and brothers whose status as a religious order had been officially approved by the Holy See—continued undiminished, and indeed Edward Sorin voiced strong annoyance that this primary duty had been neglected at Notre Dame and elsewhere. "When the Reverend Father Charles Moreau came to this country, we assumed that the principal object of his mission was to visit the foundations of the Salvatorists and Josephites. . . . We received him (when he was pleased to honor us by his presence) in accord with the canons for such an occasion and . . . offered him the welcome we would have offered the Superior General himself. But scarcely had he begun his Visit here, scarcely had he appeared among us, when he vanished." Sorin's complaint, however, was disingenuous as well as sarcastic; he had made no such assumption. Neither he nor anyone else was under the illusion that the Visitor had been sent from Sainte-Croix to deal with any substantive matter save the status of the Marianite nuns. So Sorin could only feign surprise that Charles "had gone into residence at St. Mary's and had taken in hand a Visitation of the Sisters when he had hardly begun to deal with us [men]. Then, in accord with the decision of his Lordship the bishop of Fort

Wayne, the Visitor was restrained from exercising any powers vis-à-vis the Sisters, and so we expected to see him among us anew. He never came."[1]

At this moment Father Sorin could afford a condescending tone. For many months he had pressed to have his criticisms of the administration in Le Mans brought directly before the Roman curia. He was confident that his own friendly standing with Cardinal Barnabò, so recently reinforced during his 1861 stay in Rome,[2] would give him an advantage in any bureaucratic debate that might eventuate. But now, with Bishop Luers initiating his own suit in the same court with the same general intent—and, even more specifically, calling into question the credentials of Sainte-Croix's formal representative in North America—a favorable verdict seemed guaranteed. Moreover, from his friend Victor Drouelle, still stationed in Rome, Sorin had learned that Basile Moreau's repute among the officials at Propaganda had continued to deteriorate. The scandal associated with the intrigues of Brother Marie-Julien was followed by several other dicey financial affairs, and the drumbeat of complaint against the Founder's person and policies echoed through the curial corridors.[3] Barnabò decided that a formal inquiry was called for. This "Apostolic Visitation," as it was called—its very convocation a severe embarrassment for the Founder—took place in August 1862; it was conducted by the bishops of Le Mans and Angers, acting for this purpose as the pope's delegates. Their conclusions pointed to serious shortcomings in the congregation's performance, though this judgment was assuaged somewhat by the expression of a cautious hope for future amelioration. There was a similarly mixed view of Father Moreau himself.

> [He] is simultaneously Superior-General of the entire congregation, Provincial of France, local superior of the professed house and the college, master of novices for the Brothers and the priests, and professor of theology. . . . Although [he] assured [us] that at the beginning of the next school year he would turn over the direction of the college and the novitiates to serious-minded and capable priests, it would not be out of order for Your Eminence to insist on this important point and to obtain from Reverend Father Moreau a commitment that, after appointing these priests to these offices, he will not hamper their activity by excessive interference. The [Holy Cross] religious . . . point out the ardent, imperious, and oftentimes unduly sharp and changing character of their superior. But all of them add that he is

---

1. Memorandum, Sorin to Moreau, May 28, 1863, AGEN.
2. See chapter 21, above.
3. See, for example, Catta, *Moreau*, 2: 506.

filled with faith and love for the Church, and that, even in his excesses, his zeal is always animated with the purest of intentions.[4]

The picture drawn up for the report to Propaganda does not seem unfair; Basile Moreau regularly gave evidence to a combination of qualities which aroused feelings of resentment and affection, often at the same time and in the same breast. Certainly this was the case with Edward Sorin, whose "deplorable relations"[5] with Le Mans did not nullify his genuine love and admiration for the Founder. Those relations, curiously, did not figure in the examination carried out by the two French bishops, which omission apparently furnished Sorin with a new lyric for an old song. Only weeks after the conclusion of the Visitation at Sainte-Croix, while in America Charles Moreau had been reduced to surly silence, his mission clearly a failure—"I sent a messenger to dear Father Charles," Sorin wrote his uncle blandly, "but, like my previous letters and appeals, he treated that person with scant regard"—he proposed to follow the precedent so fresh in everybody's mind: let the miscarriage of the internal Visitation be put right by instituting a Roman one. "With all possible calm we come in docility to ask you to find good and reasonable, Very Reverend and dear Father, the only means that appears to us capable of bringing about the elements of a durable peace, *voici*, to petition humbly the Holy See to extend to us the blessing of an Episcopal Visit of the kind conducted recently by the bishops of Angers and Le Mans." And as Frenchmen appropriately did the job in France, "please, Very Reverend and dear Father, rest assured that in asking the Holy See to give us for a Visitor a prelate of our own country . . . we in no way intend to annoy the motherhouse but rather to suggest the mechanism to adopt if we are to secure between the motherhouse and ourselves the harmony everybody wants."[6] The person he had in mind for Apostolic Visitor was Archbishop Purcell of Cincinnati, *patrono* to Luers and, he hoped, to himself.

In due time Sorin's aspirations in this regard were realized. First, however, Roman officials had to be satisfied on several outstanding matters affecting the governance of the sisters. Moreau's dilatoriness in formulating a definitive set of rules and constitutions for the Marianites caused much impatience at Propaganda, since without them no final determination as to canonical status could be settled. Even more irritating to Barnabò and his colleagues was a dereliction in which Sorin was judged to be no less culpable than Moreau. The pope himself,

---

4. Catta, *Moreau*, 2: 508–515.

5. Memorandum, Sorin to Moreau, May 28, 1863, AGEN.

6. Sorin to Moreau, September 26, 1862, AGEN.

when he had insisted upon the formal separation between the men and women of Sainte-Croix,[7] had further directed that, as a means of practical implementation, the resources of the two groups be equitably divided. But in the largest province, Indiana, this basic requirement had gone unfulfilled.[8] And, to Barnabò's disgust, when Charles Moreau was named Visitor to America, his uncle neglected to include in his commission this all-important subject. By such an administrative blunder,[9] occasioned no doubt by all his troubles and distractions, Moreau created the impression in Roman circles that he was unconcerned about the separation of temporalities. It also gave the ever-supple Edward Sorin, who was by no means innocent in this regard, to let Barnabò know, through Drouelle, that "the Father Visitor said not a single word to anyone here or at St. Mary's, nor to the Bishop of Fort Wayne, about carrying out the division of temporalities."[10] He quickly seized the advantage thus opened to him, as did his ally, John Henry Luers. For enclosure in correspondence shortly to be sent to Barnabò, the bishop solicited from Sorin "a few lines . . . in French" stating

> first, that the Visitor did not say anything about his coming especially to attend to the division of the Property of the Congregation of Holy Cross from that of the Sisters; second, that that property is divided now (as Mother Angela told Reverend Mr. Benoit [the vicar general] it was); and third, should that in the estimation of the proper Superiors not be deemed a just and proper division, that you will aid the Visitor to the best of your ability to see it justly arranged. I am sure you desire to see the wishes of the Holy Father complied with, and so do I, and we may therefore freely state this to Propaganda.[11]

Father Sorin had indeed, as Mother Angela said, moved to settle the temporalities question that so vexed the Roman authorities. By early November 1862, after pledging a cash payment to St. Mary's totaling $37,000—a figure the sisters found more than acceptable[12]—he was able to render moot the legitimate query as to why the division had not transpired years before. Now that the injunction had been complied with, even so tardily, his position with Luers and Barnabò was strengthened. As for the Indiana sisters themselves, they appeared, most of

7. See chapter 19, above.

8. See Barnabò to Luers, December 13, 1862, quoted in Charles Moreau, *Moreau*, 2: 376.

9. Even Catta, *Moreau*, 2: 491, grants that the omission was "a mistake" on Basile Moreau's part.

10. Sorin to Drouelle, January 21, 1863, AGEN.

11. Luers to Sorin, January 28, 1863, AIP.

12. "Sisters at St. Mary's" to Sorin, November 7, 1862, AIP.

them, quite ready to welcome the reinstatement as superior of the man they considered their founder, solidly supported as he was by the diocesan bishop. The departure of Mother Ligouri had caused scarcely a ripple within the community; it had in fact enhanced the influence of Sorinites like Mother Angela and Mother Ascension, who had returned from Philadelphia.[13] Charles Moreau, as a result of these developments, wandered ever deeper into the wilderness or rather—to discard the metaphor—sought for solace with the community at Saint-Laurent in Canada. An instance of his frustration occurred in early April 1863, when, at his uncle's direction, he summoned a general chapter of the sisters to meet in Philadelphia. The bishop of that city, a courteous and somewhat timid man, had little desire to act as host to a group of bickering nuns. Charles Moreau, he told Sorin, "asked my formal permission to hold the General Chapter in Philadelphia. I did not refuse, but gave him such reasons against it that he has now decided to assemble the members of the Chapter at Saint Laurent."[14] That meeting, predictably dominated by Mother Seven Dolors and other French-born sisters, accomplished little besides passing a resolution thanking Father Charles for his "disinterestedness, conciliation, charity, and devotedness," and another protesting "against all acts originating from a condemnable insubordination." This last was plainly directed at Indiana which went unrepresented at the chapter, because Bishop Luers forbade any of his subjects to attend.[15]

In Le Mans the Founder could hardly have found such a shadowy assembly much comfort, as he watched in dismay his credit in Rome and in America melting away. By February 1863 he had finally submitted the Marianite Constitutions to Propaganda for approbation. In a covering letter, addressed directly to the pope, he argued that the association of devoted women he had instituted was thriving and hence deserved papal favor. To make his case persuasive, however, he had to award special accolades to the most flourishing group of sisters, those in the province of Indiana, which maintained seventeen of the thirty-three Marianite houses worldwide. Yet, even as he boasted about the nurses serving in five military hospitals, Moreau cast dark aspersions over these same women. "After all the enemy of good has done," he wrote to all the female communities, "to develop the cockle of disunion sown by him among your sisters of the Indiana Vicariate, it is important to destroy it to the very roots by opposing to this spirit of discord that of union which can be strengthened only by religious obedience. . . . The union did exist everywhere until certain of your companions in Indiana

13. See chapter 22, above.
14. Wood to Sorin, April 10, 1863, AIP.
15. Costin, *Priceless Spirit*, 198.

chose to ignore the authority of your Mother General and of my own, in the person of the Visitor."[16] It remains a mystery that Basile Moreau, subtle and sensitive as he was in many respects, could not grasp the irony of the stance he had adopted.

Not particularly subtle or sensitive was the bishop of Fort Wayne, though straightforward and earnest. What carried weight with Luers was anything that preserved the sisters' service in his infant diocese, and, since he was willing to play the canonical game to achieve that end, he fell in with Sorin's plan. "The Superior General of the Congregation of the [sic] Holy Cross, Father Moreau," he wrote Purcell of Cincinnati,

> is leaving Father Sorin no peace, and things have come to such a pass that I have deemed it my duty to ask for an *Apostolic Visitor* to investigate the whole affair. I have suggested to Cardinal Barn[abò] that you would be the most proper person for this purpose, since you were nearby and well acquainted with the whole Community. Should he accede to my request, of which I have no doubt, I hope you will do me the kind favor to accept.[17]

Luers was only the latest and by no means the most important figure to come snapping at the Founder's heels. In Rome, Cardinal Barnabò, abetted by the subtle Victor Drouelle, showed growing irritation at the apparent inability of Holy Cross to settle its internal quarrels and to put its financial house in order. Moreau, increasingly isolated, did little to help himself. In March 1863, Sorin asked Mother Angela to forego for a time her duties as nursing administrator and, in the company of his other dear friend, Mother Ascension, to go to Le Mans in hopes of patching up some sort of agreement about the American sisters' status. Moreau not only refused to parley with the two nuns; adamant that their business be taken up with the Visitor-nephew, he even refused to see them.[18] Desperate as he must have been for allies, there is a measure of benighted nobility in the Founder's consistent willingness to adhere to his theoretical principles, alone if need be.

The general chapter of Holy Cross men, scheduled for that summer, promised to be stormy. Sorin, as he had often done before, at first declined to attend on the grounds that his absence would work a hardship on his province. In the end, however, at the urging of Drouelle and Champeau, he agreed to participate in the

---

16. See Costin, *Priceless Spirit*, 195–196.

17. Luers to Purcell, April 3, 1863, AIP (Sorin Papers).

18. Costin, *Priceless Spirit*, 199.

meeting held at Sainte-Croix during the last days of August.[19] Indeed, he arrived some weeks earlier, participated in the community retreat, visited Ahuillé and environs, and ruminated gloomily about the prospects of the chapter. He shared his anxieties with Father Granger, whom he had left in charge back home.

> I cannot *imagine* what we may come to. Rome is visibly out of temper with his Reverence and his nephew. The feeling of all the capitulants is the same, but how will they express it remains yet a secret. The greatest and most serious reproach against the general administration is the *arbitrary* and ever-changing spirit it betrays in most of its measures. Pray that we may even profit if we can, at Notre Dame and St. Mary's, on the difference which happily exists between France and America. As much as possible let us fear despotism.

"I fear you are going to be a little despot too," he added playfully. And, in a wistful and nostalgic aside, he remarked: "There is here an admirable regularity. It is a great edification and consolation to me. But for other reasons, not unknown to you, there is no spirit of comity." And, edified or not, "I have not *modified* one single conviction since I left."[20]

Father Sorin's melancholy prediction proved correct. There was much wrangling during the course of the chapter and very little comity. Sorin brooded bitterly for years at the palpable "resentment" displayed by "the Very Reverend General and his nephew, who sought merely to lower Notre Dame du Lac. It was pitiful to hear them talk of its insolence, etc. According to them and some others, this poor mission of Notre Dame hardly deserved to live, and its suppression or its ruin would not cause a single tear." Plenary sessions of the chapter were interspersed with committee meetings, resolutions were debated and passed, but no minds were changed on the outstanding matters of dispute. One major decision, however, sponsored by Basile Moreau, was agreed to: the congregation was to be reorganized into two large provinces, one embracing France and Italy and the other all the communities in North America. The growing administrative chaos that gripped the congregation's scattered foundations might have seemed to justify such a reform. Yet Sorin from the first suspected it to be a ploy, merely one more "means to be revenged on Notre Dame. The fusion had no other cause. . . . The pretended impartiality of His Reverence was from the beginning to the end

---

19. See Catta, *Moreau*, 2: 556–568.
20. Sorin to Granger, August 16, 1863, AGEN.

of this assembly nothing but a thinly disguised mockery"[21] He probably overstated the reality, but, if not, Moreau's strategy went badly awry, as will be seen.[22] Opposition to the Founder, in any event, had not yet reached the point of no return: he was confirmed in his post as superior-general of the congregation.[23]

At the conclusion of the meeting occurred a contretemps that smacked almost of comic opera. Sorin, hinting that such was Cardinal Barnabò's desire, requested permission to go to Rome and present formally the chapter's decrees to Propaganda for its approval. Moreau, undeceived by this maneuver, refused, and Sorin went with Drouelle and Champeau off to Paris, from where he telegraphed Barnabò: "Before returning to America I want to accompany Drouelle to Rome. The bishop [Luers] approves. The superior refuses. What shall I do?"[24] The weary cardinal-prefect told him to go home, and so, accompanied by an old rival, he boarded ship at Le Havre: "I shall have to cross the ocean with Father Rézé."[25] But before he departed, he fired one more shot across the Founder's bow: "I wish I could tell you I leave content and consoled, but I cannot. On the contrary, my heart is heavy and my spirit unquiet." Moreau had declined even to discuss the governance of the sisters in Indiana, and so had Mother Seven Dolors. "From this I conclude that she thinks as I do for reasons she knows better than anyone. Abraham allowed Lot to leave his side;[26] in the same way (*ainsi que*) there is vast territory for the sisters' endeavors. And if these dear souls cannot stay together in the peace of God, then it would be better it they were given the peace of separation."[27]

"WHEN A MAN IS ONCE AROUSED to what he considers his duty, there is no knowing how far he will go." Thus did Edward Sorin cryptically describe his own reaction to the events that followed upon Charles Moreau's disastrous Visitation. "Instead of the favorable results that everybody looked for from

21. Sorin, *Chronicles*, 296–297.

22. See chapter 24, below.

23. The vote was twenty to three in favor of maintaining Moreau in his post. Catta assumes (*Moreau*, 2: 568) that Sorin, Drouelle, and Champeau were the naysayers. But, since the ballot was secret, there is no evidence to sustain this nevertheless likely conclusion.

24. Sorin to Barnabò, August 27, 1863, "Testo del Dispaccio" (copy), AGEN.

25. Sorin to Sister Columba, August 27, 1863, AGEN. Sorin told Granger (see note 19, above) that Rézé, the Canadian superior, "tells of Father Charles [Moreau] a very different story. He also complained bitterly of his arbitrary measures and ways—and yet he represents himself as perfectly satisfied!"

26. Genesis 13.

27. Sorin to Moreau, August 29, 1863, AGEN.

this Visit, through some mystery not to be explained unless by the wiles of the evil spirit, none of these hopes was realized, and a series of troubles . . . one after the other began to arise." A constitutional crisis was surely approaching. Yet, intimately involved as he was in both the hopes and the troubles that distracted the Congrégation de Sainte-Croix, Sorin could not neglect the large institutions he headed, nor the numerous personnel he supervised, nor even the daily grind which consisted for the most part in making small but necessary decisions. As usual worries over money occupied a good part of his mind, worries intensified by the Civil War that dragged on, inflicting ever more horrors and exerting its dire influence on every aspect of American life. "Confidence, which is the soul of commerce, no longer existed. Whoever happened to be in debt when the war began, could not escape being embarrassed to meet his liabilities. Notre Dame had to suffer from this, especially since provisions and all other articles were going up in price, and paper money was daily less trusted by merchants." This last consideration led to a policy that required each prospective student at Notre Dame to pay $160 in gold for tuition and room and board, and twice that amount in script.[28]

Yet, as Sorin had conjectured from the beginning, the war need not prove to be an entirely ill wind. "The College and the Academy were [during 1862] in a prosperous and most encouraging state. The war had ruined several institutions, . . . [while] thus far the north of Indiana . . . lost nothing by this scourge of the nation, but, on the contrary, had in a way gained by the misfortune of others." The high enrollments continued into the next year: "Our College, thank God, and also St. Mary's Academy are more flourishing [in 1863] than ever. We number here 240 boarders and 160 at St. Mary's."[29] This expanded student body included boys from the southern states, but a firm hand on the academic tiller kept regional contention to a minimum: "It is a testimony which it is consoling to record, that those young men who, at Notre Dame, represented the various shades of the politics of their families and of their States, lived in harmony, even whilst their fathers and brothers were slashing one another some hundreds of miles away."[30] The expansion called for construction of "a recreation hall for the Junior Department" at Notre Dame, to which project the ever-generous Mary Phelan contributed $1,000. The hall could also double as small auditorium and theater, "thus saving the institution an annual expenditure of from eighty to one hundred dollars." In short, thanks to "the protection of its heavenly patroness,

---

28. See Hope, *Notre Dame*, 138.
29. Sorin to Sister Columba, November 11, 1863, AGEN.
30. Sorin, *Chronicles*, 290.

[Notre Dame] maintained its credit and position," leaving "it more solidly established than ever in public confidence."

A different but chronic concern was addressed at about the same time. Because of the war "laborers [had become] so scarce that it was hard to find men to cut wood. . . . After the most serious deliberation [the council at Notre Dame] resolved to introduce steam heating as an escape out of the difficulty." A happy precedent had been set a year before at the new St. Mary's Academy, whose modern heating system "had much to do with the [addition's] great reputation." Now "there was not a day to spare: it was November. . . . By Christmas the College was heated delightfully and economically, as it had not been before. . . . [Steam] was everywhere considered a blessing, saving on an average twenty to twenty-five dollars a day." And the uniform warmth within the building put all those affected, it seems, into a receptive frame of mind: "The administration took this occasion to raise the board by twenty dollars, and no one found fault."[31] So faultless indeed, that the following autumn the number of fee-paying *pensionnaires* reached 320 at Notre Dame, while St. Mary's Academy counted 195.[32]

Sorin had pledged that once the total number of students in residence in the college reached 200 he would entertain the whole scholastic community at a banquet. At the beginning of the academic year, in September 1863, 220 had matriculated and two months later—a certain informality about a requirement to attend all classes during a given semester continued to prevail—when twenty more had done so, the president kept his promise. On an evening in early November the festive dinner was held, followed by a fireworks display. The bishop of Fort Wayne, now Sorin's bosom friend, was the guest of honor for the gala occasion. His presence, however, was due also to another circumstance, one very close to Edward Sorin's heart. On the morning of that day—November 4, 1863—Bishop Luers, in the church on campus, had ordained to the priesthood twenty-four-year-old Auguste Lemonnier. Sorin's eldest sister had married a man named Lemonnier-Dubourg, and, having come into possession of the ancestral Sorin house of La Roche on the outskirts of Ahuillé,[33] they raised their family in those familiar surroundings. Two of their sons, Auguste and Louis, had enrolled in the theological seminary at Le Mans, and both of them, having dropped the second part of their hyphenated name, had come out to America to serve with their uncle in the missions.[34]

---

31. Sorin, *Chronicles*, 281–286.

32. Sorin to Moreau, September 21, 1864, AGEN.

33. See chapter 1, above.

34. Auguste did not use Dubourg in his American setting, but he did when communicating with friends and family in France. See the correspondence in AUND, CPLE, "Lemonnier Collection."

Louis was ordained first, in the winter of 1863,[35] though not without some hesitancy on Bishop Luers's part. "If your nephew has a vocation to your Society," he told Sorin, "he ought to wait until things can be properly arranged, because I am almost certain that Father Moreau would not receive him if ordained as you suggest"—ordained, that is, without explicit clearance from the motherhouse, one of the contentions most central in the wrangles between Notre Dame and Sainte-Croix.[36] The Founder, however, raised no obstacle, perhaps because he knew from the experience with *his* nephew how consoling it was for a celibate to have a near relative associated with him in his life's work. So the bishop set aside his scruples. Father Louis, however, could never quite forsake his French roots and habits, which led to much disagreement with his uncle and, after a year or two, to his return to France.[37] When Auguste's turn to receive holy orders came, he, in contrast to his brother, showed himself to be much more Edward Sorin's disciple, much more amenable to the ideal of adjusting the original genius of Holy Cross to the specific spiritual needs of the New World. "Last week," Sorin told a friend, "my second nephew was ordained a priest here; as you see, even now I have some consolations among my little trials."[38]

One of those trials was the mixed result he was encountering from his nation-wide appeal for support for his priests' hostel. "The work on the house of ecclesiastical retreat"—the variety of titles Father Sorin used to denominate an institution hinted at its purpose to succor the erring as well as the old and ailing—"was continued in proportion to the resources. The Reverend Father [Patrick] Dillon spent some weeks in the city of Pittsburgh, where he collected nearly eleven hundred dollars for the project."[39] But Dillon's success among the good Catholic burghers of western Pennsylvania was no more representative than was Chaplain Gillen's canvas of the union soldiers to whom he ministered.[40] Sorin's hope was that the bishops who endorsed the idea of such a hostel would support it by an annual subscription; but his friendly antagonist of former years, Bishop Martin Spalding of Louisville—soon to be promoted to the premier see in the

35. Auguste Lemonnier-Dubourg to "Cher Papa, cher Edouard, chérie Marie," April 13, 1863, AUND, CPLE, "Lemonnier Collection."

36. Luers to Sorin, January 19, 1863, AIP.

37. See Sorin to Moreau, November 5, 1865, AGEN, recommending that Louis, whose health was "*mauvaise*," might do light duty in a parish where "the air is good. He is very pious, very orderly, but he will do better without us and away from us than in the midst of us."

38. Sorin to Sister Columba, November 11, 1863, AGEN.

39. Sorin, *Chronicles*, 282–283.

40. See chapter 22, above.

United States—told him candidly that such a funding-base was beyond realization.[41] Cardinal Barnabò and his colleagues at Propaganda continued in general support, though it may be reasonably concluded that they were less than *au courant* with the real situation when they simply ordered that "the Provincial Chapter of America shall devise means of erecting and regulating [this] pious undertaking"— a rather characteristic Roman injunction.[42] Sorin himself remained sanguine but down-to-earth: "The Missionary's Home is left for another year, but I trust in God it will go on and meet some day with the glorious end it was destined to."[43]

"THE NEW CONSCRIPTION LAW passed in the Senate yesterday," Father Sorin reported with some alarm early in 1863. "This time (*pour le coup*), unless there is miraculous intervention, the existence of the Community will be seriously under threat."[44] Whatever President Lincoln's original hopes, the progress of the War between the States soon made it clear to him and the other authorities in Washington that victory could not be won on the strength of volunteers alone.[45] At first the government depended upon a set of awkward arrangements with state militias in order to satisfy the ever-growing demand for manpower, and, since Indiana and most other states offered exemptions for clergymen and conscientious objectors, the situation of the men of Holy Cross seemed secure enough. But "this time," in Sorin's phrase, in the legislation passed at the federal level in 1863, no such provision was included. A national lottery was established, and men thus chosen could avoid service only by providing a substitute or by paying a commutation fee in cash. The law was hugely unpopular and sparked riots in many places. At Notre Dame du Lac, "by the beginning of June, the conscription law (*décret*) having been everywhere promulgated, all the Fathers and Brothers between the ages of eighteen and forty-five and of sound mind and body were registered for military service. Lots were to be drawn shortly, and this circumstance caused more than a little alarm across the Province. More than ever the destinies of the Congregation in the United States were exclusively and visibly in the hands of Divine Providence."[46]

---

41. Spalding to Sorin, May 4, 1863, AIP. Spalding was appointed archbishop of Baltimore in 1864.

42. Memorandum (copy), Barnabò, September 30, 1864, AIP.

43. Sorin to Sister Columba, November 11, 1863, AGEN.

44. Sorin to Seguin, February 28, 1863, AGEN.

45. My account follows for the most part an untitled and, so far, unpublished article by Dorothy Pratt. I am grateful to Dr. Pratt for her permission to make use of her research.

46. Summary memorandum, Sorin to Moreau, 1861–1863, AGEN.

No one believed more firmly than Edward Sorin in the workings of Providence, but he did not for that reason eschew the old saw that God helps those who help themselves. He was confident that the generosity with which the small Holy Cross community had answered the army's need for chaplains—seven priests in service and one of them a fatality—would redound to its credit at the War Department. And the heroic response of the nursing sisters spoke to the same end with special eloquence. The implementation of the federal draft law, however, might well have put the Josephite Brothers in jeopardy. Strictly speaking they were not clergymen, and therefore could not claim the same consideration as ministers of the gospel, Catholic or Protestant. Yet they possessed no property of their own and received only a subsistence income, and therefore they had no money to pay the commutation fee of $300. By definition they lived within a closed community, so that finding substitutes was most unlikely. But they were young and healthy, most of them, and the Catholicism they professed was not considered a pacifist denomination. The possibility that the lot should fall upon a goodly number of them was real.

Moreau believed that the prudent course would have been to transfer the brothers under threat to Montreal.[47] Father Sorin, given his bitter feelings toward the Canadian mission, was not likely to accede to that idea. He determined instead to appeal for an exemption to the highest civil authorities, but, taking advantage of current circumstances, he did so in a roundabout way, as though the road to Washington passed, metaphorically, through Lancaster, Ohio, and even through Vicksburg, Mississippi. Those circumstances turned upon the person of Ellen Ewing, who—it may be recalled[48]—was the daughter of the powerful Whig politician, Senator Thomas Ewing. She was also the cousin once or twice removed, schoolmate, and best friend when they were growing up of Eliza Maria Gillespie. And, in 1850, Ellen married a recent graduate of West Point and her father's ward, Lieutenant William Tecumseh Sherman. The ceremony in Washington was a highlight of the social season; among the glittering company in attendance were President Zachary Taylor, Daniel Webster, and Henry Clay.[49] Now, in the summer of 1863, Ellen's enigmatic soldier-husband was a corps commander in U. S. Grant's army which, since the previous Christmas, had been vainly attempting to reduce the great Confederate fortress at Vicksburg. General Sherman had also of course known Eliza Gillespie back in Lancaster, and he had renewed his acquaintance with her when, in her nun's garb, Mother Angela came to Memphis during

---

47. See Sorin to Moreau, March 4, 1864, and Moreau to Barnabò (copy), May 5, 1864, AGEN.

48. See chapter 17, above.

49. Anna McAllister, *Ellen Ewing, Wife of General Sherman* (New York, 1936), 49–63.

the first year of the war to set up a hospital. He admired her and the other sisters for their dedication and for the solace they brought to the wounded, just as he respected his wife's fierce devotion to her religion, though he never felt any attraction to it himself.

Ellen Sherman, meanwhile, who had never lost contact with the prized friend of her youth, drew ever closer to Holy Cross. In 1862, with the prospect of affording them Angela's tutelage, she enrolled her eleven-year-old daughter Minnie at St. Mary's and her eight-year-old son William junior—"Willy"—among the minims at Notre Dame. "They *must* have religious instruction," she wrote her husband in Memphis, "so that they will have strong faith. Sister Angela sent me a kind letter praising you. . . . Your account of the Sisters' visit to headquarters amused us greatly. I am sorry to hear that Sister Angela is likely to be recalled from Memphis. She will probably take charge of the academy at Notre Dame this winter. They have completed a fine new building and have it well supplied with baths and every modern comfort."[50]

Born to privilege, there was an imperious streak in Ellen Ewing Sherman's character, which by no means diminished as her husband's military reputation and responsibilities expanded. Perturbed that two of her brothers, serving in the army besieging Vicksburg, were without the ministrations of a priest, in the spring of 1863 she virtually ordered Edward Sorin to supply them a chaplain. Not unaware of how important the Lancaster connection still was for Notre Dame, he complied and sent to the western theater Father Charles Carrier. A thirty-year-old French native and professed as a member of Holy Cross since 1860,[51] Carrier was an extremely gifted young man, whose good manners no less than his zeal won the esteem of the Ewing brothers and their anxious sister, and that of Generals Sherman and Grant as well.[52] As he pondered this last consideration during the waning days of September, Father Sorin hit upon an idea that might, he hoped, promote the exemption of the Josephite Brothers from the draft. He drew up a formal statement which contended that Holy Cross's contribution to the war effort by way of priest-chaplains and nun-nurses was rendered out of genuine patriotism, "but to bear arms even in a war we deem right and just is very repugnant to our religious and sacred calling." This appeal was directed to President Lincoln, but, instead of forwarding it at once to Washington, he sent it Carrier and instructed him to ask Grant and Sherman to countersign the docu-

---

50. Quoted in McAllister, *Flame*, 205–206.
51. Charles Carrier should not be confused with Joseph Carrier. See *Matricule générale*, 1378 and 807, AIP.
52. See Ellen Sherman to Sorin, March 24, 1863, AIP.

ment. They both did so, and Carrier then took it to Washington, where it won the sanction of the secretary of war and the president.[53]

During these early war years Mrs. Sherman shuttled between her father's house in Lancaster and residences in midwestern and southern cities relatively close to the operations of Grant's army. With two of her six children at school in northern Indiana, she came with increasing frequency to South Bend as well. Thus in mid-June, 1863, she attended prize-day at Notre Dame, and was pleased to witness her dear Willy carry off several awards. These boyish triumphs, however, proved to be prelude to tragedy. The happy little child, now on holiday, accompanied his mother to St. Louis and then to Memphis, where his father took him in hand. Vicksburg had fallen at last, on July 4, and the general could spare some time and attention for his son and heir. Dressed in uniform and dubbed "the little sergeant," Willy during those bright summer days rode proudly next to his father through the campsites to the good-natured cheers of Sherman's hardened veterans. Then, at the end of September, just as Grant ordered Sherman to advance to the aid of a defeated union army besieged in Chattanooga, Willy fell ill of a mysterious "camp fever." He died in Memphis, October 3, aged only nine. The general was devastated, but at least he was distracted from his grief by the preoccupation involved in relieving Chattanooga and then initiating his great Georgia campaign, on the eve of which he told Edward Sorin that he was reconciled "as much as possible" to Willy's death.[54] The burden of sorrow bore more heavily upon his wife who, however, found some consolation in Holy Cross. She was deeply grateful to Father Carrier, who had scarcely left her child's bedside during his illness, and among the many letters of "heart-felt condolence and sympathy" she received none more consoling than those from Father Sorin and Mother Angela. She thanked Sorin specifically for his offer to write "a Catholic sketch of Willy's short life," though with more than ordinary sensitivity she added: "I hope you will be in no great haste." She was convinced that "God alone, *in Heaven alone,* can comfort my heart for the loss, though time [will] shed its balm into the wound." She longed to see again, she said, "the peaceful scenes of Notre Dame," and indeed, as her husband proved that war was hell—leading sixty thousand soldiers on the celebrated march from Atlanta to the sea—Ellen Sherman, enrolling a second daughter at St. Mary's Academy, took up part-time residence in South Bend.

The Josephite Brothers appeared to be safe from conscription as the Civil War entered its fourth year. But when Sorin withdrew several of them from two

---

53. See Pratt, 7–8.
54. Sherman to Sorin, May 3, 1864, AIP.

missions in Philadelphia, on the grounds that they would remain vulnerable to the law away from Notre Dame, loud protests were raised by the bishop and, especially, by one of the pastors thus deprived of staff. He accused Sorin of "breaking a solemn contract" for specious reasons, particularly since he and his fellow pastors had pledged to pay the exemption fee for each serving brother.[55] "The measure adopted, though severe, was necessitated by the war," Sorin replied tersely. "I am satisfied and believed it my duty that, in order to save all our members, I had to recall them temporarily to our House here, even if the decision redounds to my dishonor in Philadelphia."[56] This straightforward assertion, however, probably did not tell the whole story; the prevailing view in Sainte-Croix was that the contemplated North American province might well be headquartered in Philadelphia rather than at Notre Dame, an unwelcome eventuality Sorin thought he could forestall by withdrawing from there all Holy Cross personnel. It appears significant at any rate that Philadelphia was the only place whose missions were so affected.[57]

And, as it turned out, the federal conscription law still posed a danger to the community; or rather through his own conceit Sorin managed to spark a renewal of the threat. He liked to refer to the congressman from South Bend, Schuyler Colfax, as "an old friend," when in fact that lawmaker had been a leader of the Know-Nothings and had remained, even after he enthusiastically joined the new Republican party, sternly and philosophically hostile to Catholicism.[58] Notre Dame nevertheless was the most significant economic and educational institution in his district, and Sorin ranked among his most important constituents; Colfax therefore found it expedient to muffle his distaste and to maintain amicable relations. Sorin, usually a good judge of people and their motivations, foolishly took this behavior, quite predictable in a politician, as indicative of genuine fellowship.

Proof of this misconception came in the wake of the general election of 1864. The dreadful casualties sustained by Grant during his summer campaign in Virginia, and worries that Sherman's strategy in Georgia could well produce a similar result, made the Republican administration and its supporters—of whom Colfax, now Speaker of the House, was perhaps the most prominent—uneasy over their electoral prospects. A month before this momentous poll Sorin was holding forth grandly about his influence with Colfax, citing the case of the Catholic bishop of

---

55. Stanton to Sorin, December 27, 1863, AIP. P. A. Stanton, O.S.A., was pastor of St. Augustine's parish. Bishop Woods wrote an endorsement on the back of Stanton's letter.

56. Sorin to Stanton, March 28, 1864, AGEN.

57. See the editor's comment in Sorin, *Chronicles*, 286.

58. See chapter 22, above.

Natchez, Mississippi, who a year earlier had fallen afoul of the federal authorities.[59] "The very day the telegraph brought this news," wrote Sorin to a friend in France, "Mr. Colfax, Speaker of the House (*président de chambre*) of Representatives, dined here. He is the third man in our government, and his influence in Washington is almost without limit. For twenty-two years we have been, if not exactly intimates, at least very good acquaintances." So Sorin raised the plight of the bishop of Natchez with Colfax, who promised to take the matter up with the Secretary of State "and with Mr. Lincoln." Within days the bishop was released. "I don't like to claim that my protest had such a great effect; many others protested as well. But Colfax's letter to the President was enough to have the proscription revoked."

Sorin did not hesitate even to assume some credit for Colfax's political eminence. "This dear man, Mr. Colfax, owes a good part of his position to our Holy Father Pope Pius IX." In 1848, when the pope had been driven out of Rome,[60] Colfax, editor of the *St. Joseph Valley Register,* had opined in print that if the papacy expired such would be a joyful boon for mankind. The Catholic Irish, as Sorin remembered it, were infuriated at Colfax for his anti-papal rhetoric, and at an election a few months later

> my dear Colfax was defeated and realized he owed his defeat to the Irish.[61] I met him the day after the election and gave him some *good advice* which he has *never forgotten.* Since then there is no journal more circumspect than his when dealing with Rome and Catholics. He is devoted to me, and, for the general well-being, I sometimes avail myself of this good will, all the more readily on offer since he knows that I have at my disposal from sixty to seventy-five votes here [at Notre Dame] each election, either *for* him or *against* him.[62]

Pride goeth before a fall. A month after Sorin penned these condescending lines the Holy Cross men went to the polls and three-quarters of them voted for

---

59. When Federal troops entered Natchez in October 1863, William Henry Elder, bishop there since 1857, was instructed by the commander to offer public prayers for the President of the United States and for the success of Northern arms. Elder refused and was placed under house arrest for several weeks.

60. During the short-lived Roman Republic, 1848–1850, Pius IX had had to take refuge in Gaeta, in the Kingdom of Naples.

61. In fact Colfax ran for office for the first time in 1851, not 1848. He was defeated. See Smith, *Colfax,* 38–41.

62. Sorin to Sister Columba, October 4, 1864, AGEN.

the Democratic candidate for the House, David Turpie, or "Dirty Dave" or "David Turpitude" as Colfax partisans dubbed him.[63] The secret ballot was still a phenomenon of the future, and the Speaker, "who as a matter of course [had] counted on the votes from Notre Dame," was outraged when he learned what had happened. "Now," as Sorin recorded this turn of events—and no doubt tried to explain it to Colfax—"most of the Irish in this country imagine, rightly or wrongly, that the Republican Party is hostile to them." The provincial council, despite this bias, had directed the community members to support the Republican ticket, but the member to whom it had been entrusted to communicate the council's resolution had "foolishly" failed to do so. It was a lame excuse but, to Sorin, preferable to an admission that his recent boast of holding his confrères suffrage at his own "disposal" stemmed from empty hubris. Colfax's wrath at any rate was not appeased, even though he won reelection comfortably. In December, "the exemption [from the draft] which Father Carrier had obtained . . . was revoked, the post office threatened, and all . . . privileges were to be suppressed."

In the crisis at hand, Sorin claimed that he "did his best to direct all minds and hearts to the glorious Patroness of the Lake. . . . Every member [of the community] promised to say one thousand Hail Marys, [and] this time, as so often before, she showed that her arm was not shortened and her maternal heart had not grown cold." Perhaps so, but an earthly patroness proved no less indispensable. When in South Bend, Ellen Sherman had taken rooms, ironically enough, in the house of Schuyler Colfax, who, a childless widower, had little need for his large residence, even when campaigning in the district. The summer and autumn of 1864 was a time of excruciating difficulty for Mrs. Sherman; still mourning the loss of Willy, she bore another son, Charles Celestine, in June of that year—a baby her husband the general was destined never to see—only to watch over his deathbed too, in early December.[64] Nevertheless, burdened with grief as she was, when Father Sorin appealed to her, she immediately sent letters to the president and to the secretary of war. "Heaven permitted that those letters were received in Washington on the very day when the general telegraphed to the government the fall of Savannah."[65] Sherman's announcement—that his army had triumphantly completed its march across Georgia to the sea, and, in effect, had doomed the Confederacy—reached Lincoln's desk on Christmas day. If a petition from the general's lady in behalf of an obscure group of mendicants in northern Indiana arrived at the White House at just about the same time, little wonder the presi-

---

63. Smith, *Colfax*, 197–201.
64. McAllister, *Ellen Ewing*, 284–291.
65. Sorin, *Chronicles*, 288–289.

dent gladly acceded to the request it contained. The exemption from the draft for the Josephite Brothers was restored.[66]

And two years later Edward Sorin demonstrated that he seldom made the same mistake twice. "My dear Sir," Speaker Colfax wrote him after his successful campaign in 1866,

> I cannot let the election pass by without thanking you earnestly for the aid you rendered me therein, and the majority that was thus given me in your township, generally so heavily the other way. I assure you I shall never forget it, and hope always to be worthy of the confidence you and your brethren have expressed.[67]

ON THE VERY DAY President Lincoln received the two Sherman communications, Christmas 1864, Ellen wrote another letter, this one to Edward Sorin: "Accept my subscription of $20 and allow me the honor of being among the first to subscribe to the paper about to be published in honor of the Blessed Virgin."[68] For nearly a decade Sorin had aspired to found a periodical which would encourage Marian devotion.[69] He resolutely intended it to be a devotional magazine, something quite different from the Catholic literary reviews which had occasionally emerged here and there in the United States, only to fade quickly away. In April 1865 the first number of the *Catholic World* appeared, "a monthly Eclectic Magazine of General Literature and Science," destined for a long and honorable publishing life; but in its beginnings it depended almost exclusively on reprints from European journals, while Sorin intended to rely mostly upon original American compositions.[70] A prospectus was accordingly sent to the American bishops and to other influential persons shortly after Mrs. Sherman had advanced her money.

The reaction to the idea was mixed at best. Many of Sorin's friends and acquaintances attempted to dissuade him from a project which, they argued, was

---

66. See Pratt, especially 13–15. Dr. Pratt thus confirms a venerable Notre Dame tradition, as stated in Hope, *Notre Dame,* 133–135, though she is much more sophisticated in analyzing the historiographical problems involved.

67. Colfax to Sorin, October 11, 1866, AIP. At this date elections to the House were held in October.

68. Ellen Sherman to Sorin, December 25, 1864, AIP.

69. See Sorin to Moreau, January 4, 1855, AGEN, and chapter 18, above.

70. See Thomas T. McAvoy, "The *Ave Maria* after 100 Years," *Ave Maria,* 101 (May 1, 1965): 6–9, 21. The *Catholic World's* first editor was the celebrated Paulist, Isaac Hecker.

almost certain to fail. There were not enough American Catholic writers of any stature to sustain such a publication, it was said. As for readership, the Church in the United States was composed of immigrants, many of whom were illiterate and almost all of whom were poor. Homage to the Virgin Mary was indeed incumbent upon all Catholic believers; but in a dominant Protestant culture, was not the kind of journal Father Sorin proposed an incentive for bigots to trot out all the old accusations about Mariolatry? Would it not be more prudent to express Marian piety without such public display and fanfare? The apprehensions of the archbishop of Baltimore were not untypical.

> Though I yield to none in love for the Blessed Virgin, yet I hesitate to approve in advance the idea of a newspaper or journal to propagate devotion to her. This is, to a great extent, a novelty; and unless the subject be *very carefully* and *skillfully* handled, the experiment might possibly do more harm than good to her cause. Hence, while I applaud your zeal, you will not be offended if I ask to see more of the publication before giving to it my sanction.[71]

Besides resistance of this more or less expedient sort, there emerged more pragmatic objections. For example, Sorin miscalculated when he sought the support of Archbishop Purcell, a man whom for years he had taken great pains to cultivate: "Allow me to present you the prospectus of our new little journal with my humble request to favor it with a kind smile; otherwise I fear the Ave Maria would never dare make its appearance again [sic] before you."[72] But Cincinnati was cool to the notion of a publication that might compete for limited resources with his own diocesan newspaper.[73] *Ave Maria* was indeed to be the name of the new journal, and, though Edward Sorin meekly thanked the archbishop for pointing out "errors" in the prospectus,[74] neither Purcell nor any one else could deter him from implementing his plan. "I may be deceived, disappointed, laughed to scorn," he said, "but with all that I will still retain my conviction that the Ave Maria will be the source of most abundant blessings, one of the best things ever done in the Congregation, and ultimately a glorious work for our Blessed Mother."[75]

---

71. Spalding to Sorin, April 10, 1865, AIP.

72. Sorin to Purcell, March 31, 1865, AIP.

73. See Maria Assunta Werner, "The *Ave Maria*," a paper presented at the Conference on the History of the Congregations of Holy Cross (1993), 2–3.

74. Sorin to Purcell, April 9, 1865, AIP.

75. Sorin to Neal Gillespie, March 29, 1865, AUND, CEWI, "Ewing Family Papers."

Father Sorin acted as editor of *Ave Maria* only for the first eighteen months of its long and distinguished history—it appeared weekly without interruption until 1970. Such had always been his intention: "The paper is not to depend on me for anything more than my efforts to spread its circulation and to secure for it the assistance of the ablest pens in the country."[76] One important way to enhance distribution was to gain *entré* to the churches where the Catholic faithful gathered every week. So early on he circulated a plea to pastors, couched in terms to catch their attention and to applaud their own spiritual status. "We have not undertaken this new publication without serious consideration," he wrote. "The object manifested by its title is real and honest; it stands first and foremost in our mind and heart. But there is a second (which is perhaps the best means to secure the first) which we have nearly as much at heart, namely the honor of the priesthood." He concluded by beseeching the priests "to introduce the *Ave Maria* to your faithful people."[77] Nor did Sorin fail to keep his commitment: the first issues of *Ave Maria* contained a continuing narrative on "The Virgin and the Priest."

Whatever doubts others might have entertained, one source of support for the project never wavered. "A novena for the success of your periodical?" wrote Mother Angela on January 21, 1865. "Most certainly we will perform it, my dear Father; or rather we have already commenced it. Ah! Sad should I be if you gave it up because worldly guidance thought it would not be popular." More than offering mere verbal encouragement, she also canvassed her well-fixed relations for funds; the result was a small but significant endowment of $336.[78] The first number of the new journal was duly published the following May 1.

> The AVE MARIA [Father Sorin wrote by way of introduction] is, in the truest and widest sense of the word, a *Family Newspaper,* in which we intend to speak exclusively of our own family affairs. It is published to meet the wants, and interest the heart of every Catholic, from the grey-haired grandsire who tells his beads at eventide, to the prattling child who kisses his medal as falls asleep in his downy cradle, with rosy dreams in which the loved images of his mother on earth and his Mother in Heaven are sweetly blended. . . . Our Country is flooded with "Family Newspapers," and of what are they composed? With the exception of our few good Catholic papers, they are filled with "Sensation Tales and Romances," the best of which are only calculated to give the youthful mind false views of

---

76. Sorin to Purcell, April 9, 1865, AIP.
77. Sorin to "Rev. Sir," April 11, 1865, AIP.
78. McAllister, *Flame,* 230.

life, and the affairs of eternity are either distorted or ignored. . . . This is why the AVE MARIA comes to speak of family affairs. It is entirely for Catholics. Those outside of the Church could not understand it; they would cavil at many things and dispute many points, which their eye cannot see neither can their heart comprehend; and as the AVE MARIA will not dispute with any one, its pages are evidently for Catholics alone. It wishes to speak to hearts that love the Blessed Virgin; and it would be a pain for such hearts to be constantly reading discussions or apologies for their Mother, or vindications of her honor.[79]

These words testify to the reality that the spirit of ecumenism in 1865 was further in the future than the secret ballot. Yet their very forthright insistence that American Catholics, mostly poor and ill-educated, had as much right as their Protestant neighbors to expound upon their faith without "apologies" or "vindications" represented a certain coming of age.

Father Sorin's introduction also testified to something else quite different, namely the facility he had acquired in expressing himself in English; indeed, when judged by the rhetorical standards of his time, he had attained a measure of eloquence. Still, though there is no direct evidence, it is safe to assume that the passage just quoted was proofread before publication by Mother Angela, and not only because the Gillespie clan seemed particularly endowed with the verbal arts. The early issues of the *Ave Maria* were attributed to "The Editorship of the Reverend Edward Sorin and Religious Assistants," but this latter term really referred to the formidable nun. And in fact it was she who really guided the magazine week-to-week during its first eighteen months.[80] As ever Sorin proved the initiator, the organizer not to be gainsaid, without whom the project would never have been launched. Thus it was he who persuaded his friend in Fort Wayne, Father Benoit, to contribute the $250 which made possible the purchase of a printing press.[81] But, absorbed as he was by so many other commitments, he cheerfully left implementing the plan to someone equipped to do so.

Nor could he have chosen better. Fresh from her exertions in the military hospitals, Mother Angela took on this new task with her usual vigor. Besides applying her literary discernment to the short articles, reminiscences, and bits of poetry and fiction contributed to each issue, she oversaw the sisters who were

---

79. *Ave Maria* 1 (May 1, 1865): 1–4.

80. See McAvoy, "The *Ave Maria*," 8–9.

81. Sorin to Purcell, April 9, 1865, AIP. "It will be here in a few days, and then we shall do our work at home."

charged with the typesetting and overall physical layout of the sixteen double-columned pages of rough paper, stitched together by hand.[82] She also solicited essays from prominent Catholics—most notably from the famous convert-journalist Orestes Brownson. The *Ave Maria,* incidentally, demonstrated for its time a noteworthy disposition to publish material about and by women, ascribable no doubt to the influence of the former Eliza Gillespie as well as of the Lady whom the magazine purported to honor.[83] It was Mother Angela, not Sorin, who chided Archbishop Purcell, a friend since her Ohio girlhood, for his negative reaction to the venture: "I am really grieved. . . . One of my earliest and deepest impressions of devotion to our Blessed Mother was made upon my mind by a sermon you gave in Lancaster many years ago. . . . I thought in all simplicity you would be pleased to hear that your spiritual children up north were doing all they could to honor her."[84] Whether due to this call upon nostalgia or simply to the Gillespie magic, the strategy succeeded: a few months later Purcell granted his public approbation to the *Ave Maria,* albeit somewhat grudgingly.[85]

Even as the original prospectus was being circulated, Father Sorin never kept it a secret that Mother Angela would be the actual director of the new magazine "Fortunately," he wrote her brother playfully, "I have here my Angel, whose exclusive occupation will be the Ave Maria."[86] This aspect of the enterprise, however, troubled another high prelate, Spalding of Baltimore. "I doubt whether a woman," he warned Sorin, "even one so accomplished as Mother Angela, will be capable of handling well and judiciously so very delicate a topic, involving so many nice theological distinctions."[87] The "topic" to which the archbishop uneasily referred was the Church's nuanced teaching about the place of the Virgin Mary in the economy of salvation. Once he had perused the early numbers, however, he was for the most part satisfied, though he had discerned a "few exaggerations and inaccuracies."[88] These were not serious or frequent enough to deter him from attaching a fulsome "Introduction" to the bound volume of the first year's issues: "A weekly periodical devoted to the Blessed Virgin, successfully established

82. See John W. Cavanaugh, "Father D. E. Hudson, C.S.C.," *Ave Maria* 59 (February 10, 1934): 168–173.

83. See, for example, the unsigned "Women's Character Elevated by the Blessed Virgin's Divine Maternity," *Ave Maria* 1 (July 22, 1865): 161–162.

84. Quoted in McAllister, *Flame,* 232.

85. See his statement in *Ave Maria* 1 (July 29, 1865): 187.

86. Sorin to Neal Gillespie, March 29, 1865, AUND, CEWI, "Ewing family Papers."

87. Spalding to Sorin, April 10, 1865, AIP.

88. Spalding to Sorin, June 5, 1865, AIP.

in this cold calculating age of Mammonism . . . is truly one of the wonders of this wonderful nineteenth century."

Mrs. Sherman's twenty dollars purchased her a lifetime subscription to the *Ave Maria*. A single copy cost a dime, while a year's subscription was three dollars and two years' five dollars. These prices must have been competitive, because within a year Sorin could boast that the journal had achieved a circulation of six thousand.[89] This good news prompted him to offer two prizes of $200 each to be awarded to the best piece of prose and the best poem composed in honor of Our Lady and then to be published in the *Ave Maria* during 1867. Not uncharacteristically, he decided to divide the prizes and so please four people rather than two. This contrivance did not set well with the only celebrity among the four. Though he acknowledged and accepted the $100, Orestes Brownson grumpily added, "but I expected the whole or none. The division of prizes was not on the programme [sic]."[90]

By then Father Sorin had surrendered his nominal editorship, an abdication which affected not at all the substance or direction of the *Ave Maria*. It was, of course, given the temper of the times, impossible for Mother Angela to assume the title, even though her direction of the creative accomplishment as well as of the tedious physical work had in effect made her editor and publisher. In both capacities she had guided the magazine expertly; the *Ave Maria* from the start had earned glowing reports about the excellence of its prose and about the virtual absence of typographical errors.[91] But there was a solution to the problem of the magazine's directorship perfectly acceptable to Eliza Gillespie: if not she, why not her beloved younger brother? In 1863, Neal Gillespie—fatigued by his assignment as superior in Chicago just as the Holy Cross mission there was disintegrating[92]—had gone to France. After a year of desultory study in Paris, he had reported to the motherhouse at Sainte-Croix, where for two years he held a minor administrative post. Always something of a dilettante, he had achieved nothing in particular there, not even bothering to stake out a clear position in the ongoing struggle between Sorin and Moreau. He thought about writing a history of France for children, or perhaps some other books for juveniles, but he never got

---

89. See John Debitetto, "The *Ave Maria*," Master's dissertation, University of Notre Dame (1941), 5–7. By 1874 circulation had reached 10,000. By 1884 the subscription price for one year had fallen to $2.50 and the lifetime option had been eliminated.

90. Brownson to Sorin, June 21, 1866, AIP. See Orestes Brownson, "Mary, Mother of God," *Ave Maria* 3 (February 9, 1867): 81–85.

91. Cavanaugh, "Hudson," 170.

92. See chapter 20, above.

around to it. The emergence of the *Ave Maria*, however, sparked his imagination and inspired him to hope that here was a project in which his literary abilities might be put to use. Mother Angela encouraged him to write for her magazine, and he readily responded. "But I wish it to be clearly understood," he told her,

> that your partiality for me must not allow you to put into the pages of the Ave Maria any of my contributions that may not be up to the standard— and you should place your mark pretty high—for the Ave Maria should shine not only by the beauty of its piety but [also] by the manner the piety is presented to its numerous and, I hope soon, its numberless readers.[93]

Neal returned from Le Mans in September 1866 and was immediately appointed editor of the *Ave Maria*. Shortly afterward he himself founded *The Scholastic Year* (later renamed *The Scholastic*), a student publication of remarkably high caliber, which opened opportunities to fledgling writers among the students at Notre Dame and St. Mary's. Father Gillespie had found his niche, and he performed in it splendidly till his premature death, at the age of forty-three, in 1874.

The success of the *Ave Maria*—as well as that of the printing company that evolved from it and bears its name to this day—stands as a tribute to Edward Sorin's audacity and to his managerial skills. It attests likewise to his conviction that nearly a quarter century of experience had taught him how to appraise not only the spiritual needs of his fellow American Catholics but also their tastes and intellectual capacities. From the start the magazine complied with its founder's inaugural pledge to assert Catholic doctrine and spirituality without being contentious. The articles moreover were kept short and pithy so that the reader—an immigrant farmer or hod-carrier or, more likely, his harried wife—could appreciate their message without undue strain. To peruse the opening numbers of the *Ave Maria* is to be forcefully reminded of Sorin's deep and continuing dedication to the cult of the Virgin Mary, to *Notre Dame*. The brand of piety revealed in its pages reflects surely the emotional character of that cult as practiced in the mid-nineteenth century, which may not necessarily have recommended itself to later generations. But, it should be borne in mind, the same devotion to the Virgin, expressed in the same robust idiom, was shared by Sorin's Catholic contemporaries, a generation that witnessed the apparitions at La Sallete and Lourdes and the papal definition of the dogma of the Immaculate Conception. Nor were other facets of Catholic teaching and piety neglected; the journal was relentlessly orthodox and compromised not a whit with the premonition that it might prove

---

93. Gillespie to Mother Angela, March 3, 1866, AUND, CEWI, "Ewing family Papers."

culturally offensive.[94] And though some of the Marian apocrypha printed in the magazine ruffled the sensibilities of the likes of Spalding and Purcell—and, closer to home, of Bishop Luers too[95]—the distinction between "the Legends of Mary"[96] and strictly authorized dogma was minutely observed. Indeed, the first potentate to whom Sorin disclosed his intention to publish a popular review was the pope himself: "I wish to inform your Holiness of a journal in English called the AVE MARIA," and Pius IX, after an interval during which curial officials examined the early numbers, sent back a cordial sanction and a blessing.[97] Even before that, however, Father Sorin promised to fulfill "a duty which is no ordinary gratification to our heart, namely, not only to submit in advance, and with perfect obedience, to the judgment of the Church every line the AVE MARIA may ever publish, but [also] to assure our Venerable Prelates who may notice it, that every remark or correction they may see fit to address us will be received with due deference."[98] Deference he would give, but prior restraint he would ignore, as he had so often done in the past.

---

94. See, for example, the pieces on devotion to the Sacred Heart of Jesus and to an explication of the doctrine of purgatory, *Ave Maria* 1 (September 9 and November 4, 1865): 269–270, 392–396.

95. See Luers to Sorin, April 15, 1866, AIP. A few months later, however, the bishop of Fort Wayne sent Sorin a piece he wished to be inserted into the *Ave Maria*. "If the English is not correct," he added, "let Mother Angela rectify it." Luers to Sorin, November 20, 1866, AIP.

96. See, among many examples, *Ave Maria* 1 (June 10, 1865): 71–72.

97. Sorin to "Très Saint Père" (copy), n.d. [probably November 1864], AGEN. For the pope's response, dated September 5, 1866, see Debitetto, "The *Ave Maria*," 4.

98. See note 77, above.

chapter twenty-four

The Changing of the Guard

W HEN THAT REMARKABLE WOMAN, MOTHER
Angela Gillespie, turned over direction of the *Ave Maria*
to her younger brother, she was on the verge of nervous
exhaustion. During the war years she had acted as teacher, supervisor of the nuns
in the Indiana Province, nurse, hospital administrator, envoy to foreign parts,
and, in everything but name, editor-in-chief of a new and precarious publishing
venture. She had moreover prepared textbooks in reading and grammar, the sale
of which, the New York publisher said, "has been very large considering the times.
We have given Mother Angela credit for all up to January [1863]." By the same
date 2,000 copies of the catechism she composed had also been sold.[1] To maintain contact with all her projects she traveled incessantly at a time when public
transport was dirty, crowded, uncertain, and could even be dangerous. She kept
up a copious correspondence. And she accomplished all these tasks while fulfilling her obligations as a nun in an era when religious exercises were required
with a rigor and a punctiliousness later generations would be tempted to label
Manichaean. Little wonder Edward Sorin marveled at what she had brought to
the mission of Holy Cross in America: "Mother Angela *is a person whom Heaven
blesses in everything she touches.*"[2]

But he could see that such strenuous activity had taken its toll on his friend
and co-worker. Shortly after she had passed the reins of the *Ave Maria* to Father

---

1. James Sadlier to Sorin, February 5 and May 4, 1863, AIP. D[enis] & J[ames] Sadlier & Co. was
a Catholic publishing house located in Montreal and New York. Mother Angela also obtained contributions for the *Ave Maria* from the poetess Mary Anne Madden, who was James Sadlier's wife.

2. Sorin to Seguin, February 19, 1863, AGEN.

Neal Gillespie, Sorin ordered her to take a holiday with her peripatetic cousin, Ellen Sherman, then residing in St. Louis. "She looks as usual," Ellen reported, "but Sister Athanasius [Angela's traveling companion] tells me her health has been exceedingly delicate." This brief and restful interval away from her multitude of responsibilities restored Mother Angela somewhat, but in fact her weariness was as much psychic as physical. She said little if anything about her feelings, until a worried Sorin required her, under obedience, to do so. She replied by quoting some lines from the published *Letters* of the English hymnologist, Frederic Faber: "'For some years past, even when not ill, my life has been such a joyless burden that every evening I feel as if the past day were an enemy conquered, or a punishment inflicted and over, but there was no strength left to bear another tomorrow.' Such in all simplicity express[es] my feelings exactly. . . . So much for health, which I would not have mentioned had you not required it."[3]

Surely Angela Gillespie felt for a long time—perhaps throughout her life—the sting of Basile Moreau's rebuff, when, in March of 1863, he declined to see her.[4] And that sorry moment was merely a passing incident in the seemingly interminable strife between Sainte-Croix and Notre Dame, between France and America. The depressing stalemate continued. Father Sorin had sent to Propaganda his long threatened memorandum of complaint, the first of whose ten separate headings of protest was the constitutional plight of the sisters and the sins of Charles Moreau. It requested virtual autonomy for the Indiana province, especially in financial matters, and concluded by asserting that "we no longer have *any confidence* in the Motherhouse or the General Administration."[5] This initiative, however, miscarried. Cardinal Barnabò, aggravated as he may have been at the ineptitude of Sainte-Croix, was nevertheless unready to accede to a policy that might result in the breakup of the order. He was moreover irritated at the strong language employed in the memorandum from Indiana, and he appeared poised to call down a plague on both houses. Sorin therefore found it expedient to try to soothe the prefect's ill temper while not surrendering his essential position. "I infinitely regret the displeasure of your Eminence," he wrote, using the servile rhetoric officers of the Roman curia required and expected. He could not vouch for the attitude of all the signatories of the memorandum, "at this moment

---

3. See McAllister, *Flame*, 241–242. 255. Frederick Faber (1814–1863), a product of the Oxford Movement, became a Catholic in 1845. After his ordination in 1847, he joined the Oratory of St. Philip Neri, recently introduced into England by John Henry Newman. In 1849 Faber founded the London Oratory and served as its head until his death.

4. See chapter 23, above.

5. "Memorandum," Sorin et al. to Barnabò, May 28, 1863, AGEN. The document was signed by twelve priests and eight brothers.

dispersed," he added disingenuously, but as far as he personally was concerned anything objectionable should be considered "null and void." In any case, "all of us would be happy if we were able to acknowledge, some day or other (*quelque jour*), that our complaints deserved to be forgotten. In crises of this kind, it would be necessary to have the intelligence of the angels and the virtues of the saints in order to avoid a wrongful path." As far as Moreau was concerned, "yesterday I wrote his Reverence in a manner most humble and most amiable as possible. And I said to him what we believe in our hearts, we wish to live in peace and with seemly relations with the Motherhouse." Never fear, "we shall preoccupy ourselves with those responsibilities which have lately dismayed us. Your Eminence *knows everything*. We are at peace."[6] As a token of his "humble and amiable" intentions, Sorin duly sent in advance to Le Mans an itemized $90,000 budget for 1865, which showed a deficit of a little more than $1,000 and which Moreau endorsed, signed, and returned.[7]

The rather puzzling pledge to Barnabò, offered in an appropriately obsequious idiom, evidently satisfied the cardinal prefect. A few months later, in May of 1864, the bishop of Fort Wayne arrived in Rome and, after a couple of conversations with Barnabò, dispatched to Sorin a blend of information, some of it titillating, and advice.

> I have been twice with Cardinal Barnabò, whom I am astonished to find so well [informed] on our American affairs—and also on that of our own, that having to do with our Sisters. He spoke kindly and well of you, but not so of the Very Reverend Superior General Moreau, who, I think, has lost all credit with him on account of his fickle-mindedness. . . . He [Barnabò] has also a poor opinion of Father Charles M[oreau] and detests, I may say, Brother Amedeus [Amédée], by reason of his intriguing; [Barnabò] has severely blamed the General for again putting him [Amédée] in authority in New York.

Luers assured Sorin that "your affairs and that of the Sisters will be settled *this year*." From what the bishop could discern, "the Sisters will receive probably much such regard as other similar communities. . . . Father Moreau at any rate will have nothing more to do with them; this the Holy Father has all along required from him [Moreau], but he has not obeyed, and the Pope knows it." So, the bishop told Sorin,

---

6. Sorin to Barnabò, March 6, 1864, AGEN.
7. "Budget for 1865," September 14, 1864, AIP (Sorin papers).

what both you and the Sisters must do *without delay* is to make out in full [a] disquisition that all you want is to live in peace. Be sure not to ask for *too little,* but also state clearly . . . the *reasons* for the necessity of such a request. Do not make any more complaints; it is not necessary, [since] the Cardinal knows them all. . . . It will be better for you and the Sisters to say nothing to him about separation [from Sainte-Croix], but tell him plainly that unless you obtain *at least the main objects* of your demands, you will have to separate in order to save your communities from ruin. . . . [The Sisters] in America have a different object from those in France. . . . They may be entirely separated from Europe or they may not; but in case they are not, they must ask for plain, simple rules and simple liberty of action. . . . *It must now be settled once for all.*[8]

The bishop's prediction that "this year" would see the settlement of outstanding problems proved far too sanguine; Mother Angela and her sisters in Indiana had several years still to live with bickering and uncertainty. Some significant steps, however, were taken. On August 22, the cardinals who constituted the governing board of Propaganda, presided over by Barnabò, met formally to discuss the decrees passed by the general chapter of Holy Cross held at Le Mans the previous year.[9] The policy decisions that emerged from these discussions were gall and wormwood to Basile Moreau. Moreau's proposal to divide the congregation into two large provinces was approved, but, in direct contradiction to his wishes, Propaganda ordered that the headquarters of the French province should be located in Paris, not in Le Mans, and that of North America at Notre Dame du Lac. So, thanks to Barnabò, the Founder's wicked plan to use "fusion" as a means of "placing his nephew in New York as Assistant General in charge of all American foundations" had been foiled—at least that was Father Sorin's assessment of the matter.[10] Their Eminences also swept away a terminological confusion: Sorin had for years considered himself the "provincial" of Indiana, while Moreau had used rather the word "vicar" and "vicariate," which implied his more direct control over his subordinates. Now there was to be no ambiguity. The cardinals of Propaganda, Barnabò formally notified Luers,

have limited the authority of the Superior to those things only which relate in general to the government and the administration of the whole Congre-

8. Luers to Sorin, June 29, 1864, AIP.
9. See chapter 23, above.
10. Sorin, *Chronicles,* 296–297.

gation, to the approbation of the acts which . . . ought to be submitted to him, and to supply [sic] the negligence of officers, as it is his duty. [But] he should not prevent in any manner whatever the others from exercising freely their duties, unless the general good of the whole Order requires the contrary in case of true necessity; in which case, however, he must inform the same officers concerning the determination taken by him on account of the aforesaid necessity. . . . For it is conformable to the desires of my heart that the Religious of the [sic] Holy Cross in America should attend to the formation of the new Province there . . . without experiencing any difficulty from the aforesaid Father Moreau.

Indeed, Luers told Sorin, "The Cardinal thinks it would be a great blessing if the General would resign. I doubt very much whether he [Moreau] will ever get into his good graces again." And so the upshot was that Victor Drouelle became provincial of France (with Louis Champeau as his deputy), and Edward Sorin, unambiguously, provincial of North America, including New Orleans, Canada, and even New York, where the ineffable Brother Amédée, with four other Josephite brothers, was teaching in a parochial school. "Perhaps," Father Moreau commented ruefully, "this decision will surprise the houses in Canada, New Orleans, and New York, which have remained aloof from the troubles of Indiana."[11]

The triumphs of the Luers-Sorin coalition did not end there. Since the August deliberations at Propaganda had dealt only with the general chapter of the priests and brothers of Holy Cross, Barnabò took it upon his own person to give a directive about the sisters.

Turning my consideration also to the Sisters of the Holy Cross, . . . and weighing all the things which have been brought before me concerning their differences, I have resolved that until [Propaganda] shall have given its definitive decision on their Rules and Constitutions they will continue to depend on the House of St. Mary's of the Lake alone and at the same time be under your [Luers's] jurisdiction. For that end, our Most Holy Lord [the pope] approving, I deliver to you, by these my Letters, the necessary faculties. But I wish you to know that the above-mentioned Father Moreau has been informed by me of this delegation made to you.[12]

---

11. Moreau, *Circular Letters*, 2: 336.

12. Barnabò to Luers (translated copy), September 30, 1864, and Luers to Sorin, July 11, 1864, AIP. The last sentence of Barnabò's letter to Luers appears to contradict Catta's assertion (*Moreau*, 2: 661) that Propaganda's "orders had been modified, especially with regard to the chapter in America, without any notification being sent to [Moreau]."

What the cardinal failed to acknowledge in this edict was his and his agency's share of responsibility for the nuns' predicament. If Baslie Moreau had been slow to submit to Propaganda a coherent set of "Rules and Constitutions," Propaganda had been even slower in reviewing what the Founder did propose and rendering a "definitive decision." This characteristic curial insouciance would lead to further confusion later on.

Moreau reacted to the direct intervention of the Holy See into the affairs of his subjects in America with frosty silence, moving Edward Sorin, still torn between affection and antagonism, to try to reestablish even a minimal contact: "I would like it tremendously (*infinement*) if you would have the kindness to write me even a few lines at one time or another. It is painful at my age and in my position to be almost completely set aside. But if such is the will of God, I shall have to resign myself to it."[13] In accord with the faculties given him as apostolic delegate, Bishop Luers summoned two provincial chapters to convene at the Lake during March and April of 1865. The men of Holy Cross, members now of the short-lived Province of North America, met at Notre Dame and promptly, to no one's surprise, elected Father Sorin provincial.[14] "The chapter seemed to have established peace and harmony, and during some months it might have been believed that concord would finally succeed the interminable miseries of the past."[15] When he forwarded a copy of the chapter's proceedings to the Founder, he enclosed what proved to be a final appeal for a personal rapprochement: "Here will begin for all of us, I hope, a new era in our religious life. Deign, very Reverend Father, to assure us of a pardon for anything which has saddened you in the past and return to your first benevolence, which gave us such joy in the midst of our trials of every kind."[16] If Le Mans gave no indication of renewed rapport, a different response came from the mission at New Orleans—so long a thorn in Sorin's side—whose superior signaled his recognition of the revamped circumstances by petitioning for personnel from the provincial of North America: "I hope you will soon send us some Brothers, as we are much in need of them."[17]

The chapter of the sisters gathered at St. Mary's did not go as smoothly. Here Bishop Luers assumed a more assertive role as Barnabò's delegate. He first of all

---

13. Sorin to Moreau, January 10, 1865, AGEN.

14. See the official document, with the seal of the bishop of Fort Wayne, May 11, 1865, establishing the province with Sorin as provincial, AIP (Sorin papers).

15. Sorin, *Chronicles*, 297.

16. Sorin to Moreau, May 12, 1865, AGEN.

17. Shiel to Sorin, August 25, 1865, AIP. Even before this Patrick Shiel (1829–1867) had maintained relatively friendly relations with Sorin. See, for example, Shiel to Sorin, June 18, 1862, AIP, with its implicit criticism of Charles Moreau.

imposed a system of proportional representation, whereby ten of the capitulants were from Indiana while the remaining seven spoke for Canada and New Orleans. Despite this distribution, which in fact gave the non-Indiana sisters a broader franchise than the raw numbers would have indicated, a nun from New Orleans was elected provincial. But when Luers announced that Propaganda desired that the Marianites should emulate the men of Holy Cross and set up a single novitiate for the whole province—which institution would inevitably be located at St. Mary's—the minority balked, citing the distance from New Orleans and the language difference in Canada. The motion nevertheless passed, by the vote, significantly, of ten to seven. The rest of the meeting centered on an examination of the Constitutions submitted by Father Moreau to Propaganda in 1863 (and still gathering dust there in some functionary's desk drawer). The most important amendment requested by the chapter was that each local house, while committed to responding liberally to reasonable assessments from the motherhouse, would routinely retain surplus income for its own projects—a reform long advocated by Mother Angela and, incidentally, by Sorin himself. But, though passed unanimously, the most controversial resolution adopted by the chapter proved to be the proposal that "the members of the Congregation will bear the name Sisters of Holy Cross." For those women, wherever situated, still faithful to Moreau and to Mother Seven Dolors, such a semantic change bore with it momentous symbolism. "Marianite" was a sacred appellation to them, calling to mind more than twenty years of devoted religious service. Indeed, Seven Dolors could remember the day in 1841 when she and three companions had formally received the Marianite habit from Moreau's hands;[18] small wonder she appealed to Propaganda to approve the original Constitutions without amendment. At the same time, the sisters from New Orleans and Montreal entreated the same authority to preserve their separate novitiates.[19]

T HAT THE SISTERS from New Orleans were able to travel north unhindered to participate in the general chapter of March 1865 was a sign that the Civil War had entered its final phase. In April, Lee and Johnston surrendered the pitiful remnants of their once mighty armies, and the same month, on Good Friday, President Lincoln was shot. As dedicated an Americanist as he was, Father Sorin understood that the terrible bloodletting just concluded in the New World could create a bad impression in the Old. "I suppose they look upon us," he

18. See Lalande, "Mother Mary of the Seven Dolors," 2–4, and chapter 3, above.
19. See Costin, *Priceless Spirit,* 200–203.

observed to a French friend, "as a set of Yankees down here, not much to be reck-oned above the four-footed beings that ran through our plains and forests a few years ago, especially since we have shown our primitive, ferocious proclivities in that awful war."[20] But in fact, aside from the crisis over conscription, the war had intruded little into Sorin's preoccupations, and the last winter and spring of the fighting were not exceptional in that regard. The routine chores of gover-nance, both of institutions and personnel, went on relentlessly, as did the inces-sant scramble to raise necessary funds. The ever darkening crisis within Holy Cross at large was never absent from his consciousness, and it committed him to a large correspondence with his allies abroad and especially with the often touchy and always deliberate Roman officials. And, during the early months of 1865, he launched a new magazine and arranged for the first chapters of the Province of North America.

As though this were not activity enough, in late April, while Mother Angela and her sisters were stitching together the first issue of the *Ave Maria*, Provincial Sorin was busily overseeing the accumulation of materials for a major construc-tion project at Notre Dame.[21] The expansion of the four-storied college building put up in 1844, with substantial annexes added in 1853, was necessitated by the steady growth in the number of students. "It will be huge," Auguste Lemonnier reported to his family, "but they like to build like that in the United States. They like big rooms, long, large, and high."[22] The plan called for the structure to stand on the same site as before, next to the twin-spired church, and to incorporate into it much of the old building. The total cost ran to $35,000, a figure which would have been much higher had not the brothers done much of the manual and skilled labor. The Main Building, as it now came to be called, stood a tall six stories, boasting a length of 160 feet and a width of 80, all of brick and with a handsome porch of wood across the front. It continued to function, as had its pred-ecessor, as an all-purpose facility. On the lower floors were refectories, kitchens, offices, and study halls. Classes were held on the third floor, while dormitories occupied the fourth and fifth. Also on the fifth floor was a small chapel. Atop the roof was a dome painted white with a little balcony abutting it, and upon the dome was fixed a statue of the Blessed Virgin, which was blessed with much cer-emonial pomp by Sorin's new friend in the American hierarchy, Archbishop

---

20. Sorin to Sister Columba, March 14, 1866, AGEN.

21. See McAvoy, "The *Ave Maria*," 6–7.

22. Lemonnier to "Cher Papa, chers frères, chérie Marie," March 22, 1865, AUND, CPLE, "Lemonnier Collection."

Spalding of Baltimore.[23] Sorin had always reveled in the melodious tones of ringing bells, and at this celebration, during "a solemn procession of the Blessed Sacrament around St. Joseph's Lake, the . . . beautiful sounds electrified, as it were, for two hours all who attended the grand ceremony."[24] He confessed himself, however, unsatisfied until he would be able to place at Notre Dame "*the first chime in the world,*" able to be played from a keyboard, which would "secure . . . primacy for many years to come." For Sorin, the publicity was no less sweet than the music.[25]

It was no small feat to have begun and finished this considerable engineering and construction job between the time the boarders departed in June 1865 and returned in September. Patrick Dillon, whom Sorin had placed in day-to-day supervision of the project, deserved much of the credit for the speed and efficiency with which it was completed. From the moment the Irish-born, thirty-three-year-old Father Dillon—a stocky man with strikingly Celtic good-looks—had joined Holy Cross at Notre Dame in 1856, he had earned his superior's high regard, first as community steward and then, like Neal Gillespie, as administrator of the lost cause in Chicago,[26] after which Sorin appointed him vice president of the university. In that capacity he proved himself a steadfast and effective lieutenant, uncovering, for example, the secession plans of a group of discontented teaching brothers, which Sorin was then able to nip in the bud.[27] Dillon had won the assignment to direct the conversion of the old collegiate into the sparkling new Main Building primarily because of the success he had enjoyed in performing a similar task during the construction of St. Mary's Academy in 1862. Besides his managerial skills and personal loyalty, he had demonstrated a thoughtful interest in education, and so, when Sorin, as head now of the North American Province, determined it appropriate for him to forego the presidency of the university he had founded twenty-one years earlier, the choice of a successor was hardly in doubt.

The brief tenure of the second president of Notre Dame was notable on several scores. The institution's clientele still included a hodgepodge of aspiring collegians and seminarians, high school pupils, labor-school apprentices, and even small children—the minims—but the senior department had gradually developed a distinct program which could justifiably claim to provide, by the criteria

23. See Hope, *Notre Dame,* 139–140, and Schlereth, *Notre Dame,* 36, and the photographs, 38–39. The blessing and placing of the statue was delayed until the following May 31. See the detailed account of the solemnity in Sorin to Barnabò, June 14, 1866, AGEN.

24. Edward Sorin, "Bells at Notre Dame," (n.p. [Notre Dame, Ind.], n.d. [c. 1880]), 1.

25. Sorin to Corby, n.d. [1868?], AIP.

26. See chapter 20, above.

27. See Dillon to Sorin, June 12, 1865, AIP, and Sorin to Purcell, June 13, 1865, AGEN.

of the times, a genuinely "higher education." Its curriculum, however, despite the assertions in the annual catalogues, had remained largely permeated by the old-fashioned classical and literary ideal. Dillon introduced an important two-year commercial major, which offered standard courses in accounting and mathematics as well as, for some unknown reason, in German. He also organized Notre Dame's first thorough program in the physical sciences; the students who took courses in the higher mathematics, geology, and chemistry were, significantly, freed from the ordinary requirements in Latin and Greek. These innovations were to bear much fruit in the future.[28]

There is no reason to suppose that Edward Sorin judged Dillon's educational initiatives adversely. He had always maintained that Notre Dame students ought to be prepared as much as possible to go into the real world of business. And though he was unsophisticated with regard to scientific inquiry, his insatiable curiosity inclined him to sympathize with the cultivation of any legitimate branch of knowledge. Nevertheless, he and Patrick Dillon did not see eye to eye. One reason was that the president tended to adopt a more relaxed attitude toward student conduct than did his predecessor and religious superior. The day had long passed when Sorin had had to endure Brother Gatien's taunts about his disciplinary laxity.[29] Now behavior of the students was prescribed down to the smallest detail.

> All the students of this Institution are required to attend the exercises of public worship with punctuality and decorum. They shall assist at Mass on Sundays and Wednesdays. Catholic students shall go to confession every month. . . . Students are not permitted to visit private rooms. . . . The time of recreation excepted, silence must be inviolably observed in all places. . . . The use of tobacco is forbidden. Intoxicating liquors are absolutely forbidden. . . . No branch of study, once commenced, may be discontinued without the permission of the Prefect of Studies. No one shall leave the University grounds without the permission of the President or the Vice President. . . . In winter, on Saturday, at 4 o'clock P.M., the students must wash their feet. In summer this regulation is rendered unnecessary by the rule which requires the student[s] to bathe in common twice a week in St. Joseph's Lake.[30]

---

28. See Hope, *Notre Dame*, 141.
29. See chapter 10, above.
30. *Catalogue* (1864–1865), quoted in Hope, *Notre Dame*, 142–143.

Edward Sorin had crossed the sea and enthusiastically embraced the mores of his adopted country, without, however, repudiating the stern code he had learned in a French seminary.

Another source of friction arose when Dillon had deemed it "expedient" to reduce the charge in the cost of residents' board by $50. He had taken this step without consulting Sorin, who, when he learned of it, "expressed his fears to the administration." The result of the measure was "a real deficit of ten thousand dollars. . . . After such an experience, [Sorin] insisted on having the former charges restored, which was done."[31] And done immediately; whoever held whatever title at Notre Dame, the real power rested with him who had virtually created it out of nothing and without whom it would never have survived. The same could be said about St. Mary's, though there the strength of Mother Angela's personality and influence interposed some restraint. In August 1866, the priest-hero of Gettysburg, William Corby, was appointed third president of Notre Dame. Patrick Dillon felt no particular chagrin at his removal from office; for all his talents, he was a restless man for whom a sedentary position soon lost its charm. Nor did he forfeit Sorin's trust and affection.

MEANWHILE, the reputation of Holy Cross in America, no matter who held the presidency of Notre Dame, burgeoned robustly across the country. The war had scarcely ended when Archbishop Peter Kenrick of St. Louis, not always friendly in the past,[32] sent a delegation of distinguished laymen to Indiana to ask Sorin to provide staff for a farm/orphanage in his archdiocese.[33] Similarly, the bishop of Covington, Kentucky, offered a sound brick building and a church, standing on 200 fertile acres, if Holy Cross would set up an "orphan asylum" there.[34] The Dominicans in Wisconsin came forward with a proposal that tempted Sorin enough for him to consult his bishop about it. John Henry Luers, much grown in self-esteem since becoming an apostolic delegate, did not hesitate to proffer advice and more. "Sinsinna Mount [sic] College [would be] a bad bargain for you even when offered *as a gift*," he declared. The place lies too far north, and "if the Dominicans cannot keep it up, who have twice the number of members that you have, how will you succeed?" If, as Sorin had contemplated, he

31. Sorin, *Chronicles*, 302.
32. See chapters 20 and 21, above.
33. Kenrick to Sorin, May 15, 1865, AIP.
34. Carrell to Sorin, November 10, 1865, AIP. On this letter Sorin scribbled a notation: "We could not at present."

had assumed ownership of the site and then sold it off in parcels, he would only annoy the bishop of Milwaukee.

> You should do all you can to put Notre Dame on a good and secure foot-ing; and try as much as possible that that [sic] you can do all with your own force [i.e., religious personnel]. As it now stands, one half at least, if not two thirds, of the teaching, *and that of the higher branches,* is done by laymen or priests not belonging to your community.... In my opinion you should undertake nothing which you cannot fully carry out. Otherwise you will destroy your reputation and credit, which I should be sorry to see.[35]

The counsel was sound, if a bit peremptory in tone, and Sorin abided by it.

Among all these requests for services, the most bizarre, at least in retrospect, issued from the bishop of Charleston, South Carolina, at the beginning of 1866. Patrick Lynch[36] described for Sorin the parlous state of his diocese in the wake of the brutal war which had begun in the harbor of his see city. The group most desperately in need of ministry was the tiny number of Negro Catholics in his charge, who, the bishop maintained, could neither understand their new civil sta-tus nor practice their faith without some special structure designed to cater to their unique spiritual wants. Therefore he had determined to purchase an island seven miles off the Carolina coast and establish there a colony of Catholic blacks, who would form an institution reminiscent of the enclaves set up in the Fran-ciscan missions in California and the famous Jesuit "Reductions" in Paraguay. Would Holy Cross, Bishop Lynch inquired with considerable eloquence, have the "courage" to participate in such a venture?[37] Father Sorin was not a little

---

35. Luers to Sorin, April 20, 1865, AIP. Sinsinawa Mound College, near Madison, closed Septem-ber 5, 1864, but, shortly afterward, the Dominican sisters founded in the area a convent that flourishes to this day. See Mary Paschala O'Conner, *Five Decades: History of the Congregation of the Most Holy Rosary, Sinsinawa, Wisconsin, 1849–1899* (Sinsinawa, Wis., 1954), 106–108.

36. Patrick Neisen Lynch, bishop of Charleston for twenty-five years (1857–1882), earned a repu-tation as a learned and literate prelate who, in the midst of immense difficulties, governed his diocese with spiritual integrity and financial acumen. It seems fair to say that his proposal to Sorin, which sounds grotesque at the beginning of the twenty-first century, should be judged according to the criteria of his own time.

37. Lynch to Sorin, January 6, 1866, AIP. In the late seventeenth century, Jesuit missionaries had established pseudo-states in what are now vast stretches of Paraguay, Brazil, and Uruguay. These in-dependent economic and political entities were intended to protect the natives from the depreda-tions of the European colonists. They implicitly proclaimed at the same time the conviction that the Indians were neither socially nor intellectually prepared to be integrated into a Western society. The so-called "Reductions" collapsed when the Jesuits, in the mid-eighteenth century, were proscribed by the Spanish and Portuguese governments and then suppressed by the papacy.

intrigued by this invitation, and he promptly communicated his interest to Charleston. Then, on second thought, he decided it was the prudent course to advise, not Le Mans, but, in the present state of affairs in the congregation, Rome. "I have informed the worthy Prelate of Charleston," he told Cardinal Barnabò,

> that I would submit his request to your Eminence without delay and that I would be happy to follow any direction in this matter that you might suggest. We can, I believe, take the preliminary steps in setting aside personnel (*avance du sujets*) and perhaps begin a work that would probably be welcomed by all true friends of humanity and even by the Government, which really does not know how, from a policy point of view (*dans ses calculs*), to satisfy the interest of the poor blacks. . . . An example of this sort might be copied elsewhere, and Catholic colonies might be organized and thereby contribute to the salvation of forlorn souls.[38]

Happily for Father Sorin's long-term reputation nothing came of this initiative.

But another project of his, dear to his heart, was wilting on the vine. The home for "missionaries"—a place of retirement for ill and elderly priests and of disciplinary therapy for those who had fallen into disrepute—continued to receive only limited support. The building whose cornerstone had been laid with so much optimism stood unfinished. Bishops nevertheless kept on referring—and in some instances assigning—to Notre Dame troubled clergy for whom space had to be provided somewhere on the campus. Then, late in 1865, came confirmation of the need for such a facility when one of the hierarchical elders himself came to need its ministration. Sorin had first learned of the case earlier in the year; it involved a man he had known casually for some time, James Whalen, bishop of Nashville. "Last spring," he reported to Barnabò,

> one of our fathers, a chaplain in the Union army, passed through Nashville, where he heard about the deplorable scandal being given by this poor bishop, who seems to have lost every vestige of decorum. I believed I would render a service to the Church by inviting him as an old friend to come and stay here. He promised then that he would, but he did not. And now [in November] when we did not expect him, *voici*, he has arrived. We have no vacant room for him; I have given him mine. . . . I must ask your direction as to what lines of conduct I should follow with regard to him. We are in

---

38. Sorin to Barnabò, January 18, 1866, AGEN.

full session here with upwards of four hundred boarding students. Certainly it is not edifying for these young scholars, half of them Catholic and the other half Protestant, to see a bishop with episcopal ring and pectoral cross, still young and healthy but without any visible function. He should not be in a college; but even less so should he be in Nashville.[39]

Irish-born Whalen had joined the Dominicans in Ohio, where he had also become something of a protégé of Archbishop Purcell. A theologian and preacher of some repute, he had served as provincial of his order until he was appointed to Nashville in 1859. Stories about his drunkenness emerged early in his tenure, but even more damaging to his position was the widespread conviction among his Confederate flock that he was sympathetic to the Union.[40] Barnabò acted swiftly and forced Whelan's resignation, but that did not answer Sorin's problem. Bishop Luers proposed a solution, while displaying little sympathy for his deposed colleague. "Treat him as a bishop," he instructed Sorin, "else you will give scandal." Allow him to say Mass and preach, "but not to celebrate in pontifical vestments." He is, after all, a Dominican friar, and therefore he should be trundled back to his priory in Ohio "*as soon as possible.*"[41] So a shepherd melted into the mist, and the Home for Missionaries remained, for the time being, only a partially fulfilled aspiration.

"IT IS A THOUSAND PITIES," Father Sorin said, even as he wrestled with what to do with the unfortunate Bishop Whelan, "a thousand pities that the work on the Home has been interrupted." But he had to acknowledge that to a degree "our unhappy family troubles have lost us more or less the credit and confidence which would have been so useful in order to bring this work to a worthy end."[42] He recalled bitterly, for instance, the scorn Visitor Charles Moreau had cast upon the project. Indeed, however preoccupied he was by the tasks he confronted daily, the quarrels within the Holy Cross "family" figured uppermost in his mind. From Le Mans there issued a scathing denunciation of the chapters held at Notre Dame and St. Mary's under Luers's presidency, declaring their provisions null and void.[43] But not a personal word came from Basile Moreau, and

39. Sorin to Barnabò, November 11, 1865, AGEN.
40. See Thomas Stritch, *The Catholic Church in Tennessee* (Nashville, 1987), 142–145.
41. Luers to Sorin, November 12, 1865, AIP.
42. Sorin to Barnabò, November 11, 1865, AGEN.
43. See Sorin's lengthy rebuttal in Sorin to Barnabò, n.d.[July, 1865], AGEN.

Sorin had to admit that his hopes that the Founder would come himself to Indiana and thus learn first hand "how much the dispositions of the Province were misjudged" were futile.[44] He tried, without much success, to adopt a stoic posture. "I've been awaiting news from Rome or Le Mans," he wrote Father Champeau, "but nothing has come from either place. The situation makes us live from day to day, and we have stopped tormenting ourselves with worry about a future which is entirely invisible to us, which we cannot see even in a confused manner."[45] Then, a few weeks later, the future suddenly burst into clarity.

On November 25, 1865, while preaching a retreat in the village of Grand Lucé, Basile Moreau was handed a letter forwarded from Sainte-Croix, where it had been received the day before. Although couched in terms of an invitation, this communiqué, signed by Cardinal Barnabò, was clearly a command that the Founder present himself in Rome at his earliest convenience, in order to review what Propaganda had determined "to insure the proper administration of the Congregation of Holy Cross." But the tough old man, convinced that his domestic enemies had captured the redoubt on the Tiber, refused to comply. Instead he took up his pen and addressed a letter directly to Pope Pius IX. "It is as one crushed under deepest affliction that I come to prostrate myself at the feet of your Holiness, to beseech you humbly to allow me to tell you that for some time the good faith of the Holy See has been deceived with regard to me." Often before he had dared his colleagues to accept his resignation; now "I place in the hands of your Holiness all the authority I received from you to govern the foundation of Holy Cross." It was an adroit turn of phrase, not surprisingly, since Moreau had always displayed masterful verbal skills. But it was self-defeating in the end, because the rest of the missive was a denunciation of "the intrigue and ambition" of his subjects and a truly breathtaking assertion of self-righteousness. He, who had been sole head of the order he had founded through all the nearly thirty years of its existence, declined to accept any responsibility for the woeful condition into which it had sunk. Any "faults" ascribed to him had been minor and in any event committed "unwittingly." Why should he be summoned to Rome to defend himself? "My conscience reproaches me with the violation of no rule or decree of the Holy See." Therefore, he was arguing implicitly, if the pope accepted the proffered resignation, he would in effect be surrendering to a gang of conspirators. "If there is a question," he concluded, "in the new decisions [of Propaganda] of substituting certain ambitious individuals for the officials regularly elected by the general chapter, I am sure that the congregation will go to pieces." In Moreau's

44. Sorin, *Chronicles*, 287.
45. Sorin to Champeau, November 3, 1865, AGEN.

mind leading the charge of "ambitious individuals" were Edward Sorin, certainly, but even more prominently, since they were *en scène,* Victor Drouelle and Louis Champeau.

Father Moreau wrote also to Barnabò in roughly the same spirit. The cardinal answered sharply that Moreau was to report in person to Rome without delay. Still the Founder refused. Barnabò then instructed the bishop of Le Mans to intervene and to impress upon Moreau the seriousness of the summons. "Rome has felt free," Moreau told the bishop, "to accept all sorts of accusations against my administration and to take action on them, without even giving me the opportunity to reply." Let the sovereign pontiff, he insisted, commit himself by accepting or rejecting the resignation; when apprised of such a decision, he would undertake the difficult winter journey. "He is alleging pretexts," the bishop reported to Propaganda. "His conduct strikes me as inexplicable, and it makes me fear that he may cause many difficulties for his successor." Clearly the bishop had no doubt that the superior general was to be removed from office; indeed, he had heard the pervasive rumor that Moreau, once arrived in Rome, would be required to remain there—*ibi maneat.* Finally, on January 21 an emissary from Barnabò appeared at Sainte-Croix bearing an unambiguous order that Moreau was to set out for Rome *tout de suite,* that no further written communications would be sent or received, and that the congregation stood in danger of dissolution if Propaganda's directive continued to be ignored. Eight days later the Founder departed for the eternal city.[46]

The four months spent there brought Basile Moreau to his personal Golgotha, and, as a man of deep faith, he endured it with courage and dignity. Whatever his shortcomings—whatever his extravagant commitment to the abstract at the cost of misreading the hearts of other men, combined with an imperious temper—he had performed a work of majestic magnitude, a work the fruits of which flourish into the twenty-first century. He never wavered in the principles he had imbibed at the altar and at the prie-dieu in his Spartan room at Sainte-Croix, even when adherence to those principles put him into conflict with others whose principles were held just as honestly. He was not altogether wrong to assert that he had become the victim of the ambition of others; but he was wrong to assume that that ambition was always crass and unworthy, or that persons of goodwill could not differ from him for honorable reasons. There is something sublime in the stubborn integrity of this old man who, in the end, was deserted by everybody, and surely in his loneliness he felt akin to the Jesus whom he had served, the Jesus who faced *his* trial with no one to comfort him. Nevertheless, the comparison

---

46. Catta, *Moreau,* 2: 659–669.

"I send you from Paris a fine Velocipede. The price is 250 francs, unpaid, for the good reason that my treasury is out." (Sorin to Corby, 1868)

The church and Main Building before the fire of 1879

The Main Building, April 1879

The Main Building, September 1879

The Notre Dame faculty, c. 1885

The first Notre Dame varsity football team, 1887

Science Hall, c. 1890

John Zahm (1851–1921),
priest, scientist,
intellectual pacesetter
Photo courtesy of Indiana
Province Archives Center

Schuyler Colfax (1823–1885),
powerful politician, Sorin's
sometimes friend, sometimes adversary

Timothy Howard (1837–1916),
the consummate Notre Dame man

The Minims

Edward Sorin in old age
Photo courtesy of Indiana Province Archives Center

cannot be pressed too far. Basile Moreau was indeed the victim of his disciples' disaffection and of a bureaucracy anxious to maintain its authority; but he was a victim too of his own weaknesses, which ill-equipped him to guide the splendid institution he had erected into the next stage of its development.

During the brief papal audiences granted him the pope displayed no personal displeasure, but Pius IX was by nature a kindly man, and, though not always acute in his judgments, in this instance he had already made up his mind with some shrewdness: Moreau, he said, had "an admirable head for himself, but abominable in the guidance of others."[47] Besides, the pontiff sensibly left the tedious and unpleasant dénouement to the responsible department of the curia. So Father Moreau almost daily wended his weary way from St. Bridget's, the Holy Cross residence, to the vast fortresslike building of dark stone on the Piazza di Spagna that housed Propaganda. As usual the curial mills ground slowly, but grind they did, and little by little he became aware that his cause was hopeless. The accumulated complaints of Sorin, Drouelle, and Champeau, and, probably more importantly, those of the bishops Fort Wayne, Angers, and even Le Mans, could not be ignored. On April 23 Father Moreau met Barnabò for the last time, and the next day he sent the cardinal a formal statement in which he renewed his offer to resign, "the only condition being that I shall be relieved of all financial responsibility. In order to facilitate this resignation, I shall renounce all my rights over the property of the congregation . . . through the organization of a new civil corporation." This was an important concession, given that the tangled confusion of French property-law had long given pause to the malcontents among his subjects, who otherwise would have sought his removal from office years before.[48] And it was a *beau geste* as well, as was his commitment to "accept whatever position is assigned me . . . [by a] new Superior General, whom I shall obey without difficulty, as I shall do also for the local superior under whose authority I shall spend my last days." Nevertheless he admitted no malfeasance in his administration of the order, and ascribed the accusations against him as "calumny." If the pope and Propaganda were to dismiss him, they would have to do so knowing that he acknowledged not a jot or tittle of the charges. Then the quite understandable bitterness bubbled to the surface: "My greatest trial has been to see myself calumniated at Rome and thus exposed to losing the good will of the Holy See to which I have consecrated the whole of my priestly life, teaching what it teaches."

Basile Moreau spent a restless month of May waiting for a definitive judgment. In the meanwhile he was still superior general of the Congrégation de

47. Quoted in Sorin, *Chronicles*, 296.
48. See, for example, chapter 21, above.

Sainte-Croix, and so it was his duty to tend to its business. Specifically he sought an ecclesiastical purchaser for St. Bridget's, which was loaded with debt, only to learn that even this modest endeavor was frowned upon by the mandarins of Propaganda. Barnabò and his colleagues were scheduled to meet to determine Moreau's fate on June 4, 1866. Next day, when no summons had come from the Piazza di Spagna, he shook the Italian dust from his feet and departed for home. Two weeks later the bishop of Le Mans informed him of the decision: Moreau's resignation was accepted and Father Pierre Chappé was appointed vicar general of the congregation until the next general chapter convened to elect a successor. Shortly afterward Father Moreau received a bleak communiqué from Barnabò, ordering him "to refrain from any scheming or interference, either in the general affairs of the congregation or, more particularly, in the elections to be held in the future chapter," and reprimanding him for leaving Rome without permission— a transparent sign that the intention all along had been that the Founder *ibi maneat*. Propaganda obviously had assumed that were the Founder on hand at the elections in Le Mans he would attempt to "interfere."[49] The cup of sadness was nearly full.

But not quite. Father Chappé, long associated with the central administration of Holy Cross, was widely admired within the congregation, more, however, for his benign temperament than for any outstanding talent or qualities of leadership. His peace mission to Edward Sorin in 1853 had been perhaps his most conspicuous achievement.[50] Chappé did what he could to ease the personal awkwardness involved in Moreau's transition from superior general to simple religious. But as soon as arrangements for the general chapter began to be made—it was scheduled for late August—the Founder, quite in character, issued a prickly demand for adherence to what he considered the letter of the law. Propaganda had decreed that the capitulants of 1863 would compose this new and emergency chapter. Moreau maintained that he had been a member of the earlier body and that therefore he should participate in this one too. When that petition was rejected, he then insisted, despite the pleadings of Chappé to the contrary, that he be allowed to draw up and present a formal statement defending his administration. There is an obligation, he told the vicar, "of enlightening the good faith of the members of the chapter, whom efforts are being made to deceive in such a manner . . . as to ruin the foundation of Holy Cross under the pretext of saving it. . . . I do not think that any councilor or member of the chapter can keep silence in conscience, once he is made aware of the scheming and the conspiracy which

49. Catta, *Moreau*, 2: 671–697.
50. See chapter 16, above.

is boldly lying and spreading contempt for the authority regularly constituted for the government of the congregation." Indeed, it would be better "if the congregation were to be stricken with dissolution by the Holy See than to die by inches through a compromise with injustice and ambition." This plea for a chance at vindication was also turned down, in which decision Moreau rightly saw the fine hand of Victor Drouelle, now the provincial of France, whose ascendancy over the timid Chappé had been established early on.[51]

The provincial of North America, meanwhile, kept abreast of these sad and decisive events from afar, but he commented little. In the late winter, while Moreau was enduring his Roman agony, Father Sorin assured a friend who lived Le Mans that "we are now at peace" in the United States, "and I myself too, with not a particle or molecule of hatred or antipathy, no, not even against a single one of your neighbors, whom I hope to meet in heaven. . . . We are getting on pretty nicely and comfortably here," he added lightheartedly. "France troubles us very little. Which is a good thing, because paper is expensive and postage too."[52] His mood was more sober when, accompanied by Patrick Dillon, he arrived at Sainte-Croix at the end of July to attend the chapter. "We hope for better things in the year ahead," he wrote Cardinal Barnabò, whom Sorin now addressed with much more familiarity than before. "Our future in America will be consoling, provided that the Chapter for which we have come from such a great distance provides a *radical* cure for the malady from which our dear family has suffered for so long a time." But his hopes had been dashed too often for him to be sanguine; "each day here increases my apprehensions. The state of our finances is alarming beyond calculation," and it is hard to find here a cheerful face.

> Will the General we came here to elect have the courage to render his position *tenable?* I have my doubts. Either he will have to submit to the old influence, or else make war without end and without profit. My wish is that the day after his election he would go and take up residence in Rome with two assistants. This, in my view, would be the only guarantee (*gage*) of rebirth and peace. The Head of the Congregation thus placed in the bosom of enlightenment (*lumière*), with the help of two arms strong and free, one from the Old World the other from the New, the body can revive and perhaps even acquire a robust constitution. Otherwise I have nothing but anxiety.[53]

---

51. Catta, *Moreau*, 2: 707–712.
52. Sorin to Sister Columba, March 14, 1866, AGEN.
53. Sorin to Barnabò, August 12, 1866, AGEN.

The chapter convened on August 20. Father Drouelle, in his capacity as French provincial, outlined the financial distress under which the houses in his jurisdiction labored. Aside from a plea for direct contributions—Sorin reluctantly promised 35,000 francs ($7,000) at some unspecified future date[54]—the expedient most seriously discussed was the sale of many of the properties Moreau had accumulated in Le Mans. With regard to Sorin's own bailiwick, the chapter decided to recommend to Rome that Indiana, Canada, and Louisiana constitute distinct provinces, to which realignment the provincial of North America offered only token opposition.[55] The only high drama of the meetings occurred when Charles Moreau, in harsh language, resigned his position as assistant general and declared that, were it not out of respect for his uncle, he would have withdrawn from the congregation as well. The crucial business of the chapter, the election of a new superior general, took an unexpected turn. However amicable his relations with Barnabò had become, Edward Sorin could not have been surprised that the cardinal-prefect had vetoed his candidacy, along with that of his partisan allies Drouelle and Champeau. The bishop of Le Mans, who was presiding at the chapter, recommended the inoffensive Chappé, but there was no chance that so ineffectual if amiable a nominee could win approval. Instead the chapter chose a person far removed from the recent quarrels and upheavals, far removed even geographically. Forty-four-year-old Pierre Dufal had gone to Bengal in 1858 and assumed the position Sorin had so stormily refused five years before.[56] In 1861 Dufal, as Rome had promised, had been consecrated to episcopal orders as vicar apostolic of Dacca.[57] His election was in due course confirmed by Propaganda; it remained to be seen how this missionary to the exotic East would react when confronted with the congregation's desperate problems now chronic in Europe and America.

After the chapter adjourned, Father Sorin proceeded to Rome, where he secured the pope's cordial approval for the *Ave Maria*,[58] and took care to nurture his connections with Propaganda. By the beginning of October he was in Baltimore, at the invitation of Archbishop Spalding, to attend as an observer the meeting of the American bishops.[59] He returned home to Notre Dame at the end of that month without his traveling companion, Patrick Dillon, who, by a reso-

---

54. By way of comparison, Rézé of Canada offered 2,000 francs ($400).

55. In the end, Indiana and Canada were accorded provincial status, with Louisiana forming a separate vicariate subject to the motherhouse.

56. See chapter 15, above.

57. Catta, *Moreau*, 2: 712–721.

58. Sorin to Chappé, September 11, 1866, AGEN. See also chapter 23, above.

59. The Second Plenary Council of Baltimore (October 7–21, 1866).

lution of the general chapter, had been assigned to serve a term—as Neal Gillespie had done previously—in the central administration at Sainte-Croix. Sorin, as ever filled with ideas and initiatives, plunged into the familiar round of governance with his accustomed zest. Perhaps most satisfying to him personally was the solution of a problem that had long vexed him: by "a decree of the Provincial Chapter [of 1865 it was decided] to finish the Missionaries' House at the expense of the Congregation [and] to make it [as well] the residence of novices who, finishing their novitiate before the age required for profession, would there continue their studies until they made their perpetual vows." Once completed, a handsome telescope, donated by the Emperor of the French, Napoleon III, was fastened to one of the building's turrets. More important in the long run "was the acquisition this year . . . of 1320 acres, . . . five or six hundred of which are a deposit of turf." St. Joseph's Farm,[60] as this parcel of land came to be known, lay eight miles northeast of Notre Dame and was destined to become an integral part of the institution's economy. At first, however, it was the production of peat that pleased Father Sorin; he estimated that a thousand tons of turf could replace twelve hundred cords of wood, representing a significant saving. "Our neighbors are astonished beyond measure to see that Catholics from beyond the sea have come to discover such a treasure for them. They could not be convinced until they saw the fire that this black earth made in our boilers."[61]

Even as he followed his day-to-day routine, Edward Sorin, like every member of the congregation, waited anxiously for the inauguration of the new superior general. Bishop Dufal's immediate response to the dignity conferred upon him by the general chapter was to decline it. Propaganda, however, confirmed the chapter's choice and ordered him to proceed to forthwith to Europe, though, in accord with its wonted leisurely mode of operation, it did not do so until March 1867. Even then Dufal delayed, and not until July did he reluctantly set out from Bengal. Meanwhile, the situation at Sainte-Croix grew ever more precarious. The hapless Chappé, still technically in charge until the new superior general arrived, found himself caught between two fires. Victor Drouelle was pressing for the transfer of the motherhouse to Paris and for the sale of the real estate in Le Mans as well as of the *Collège de Sainte-Croix* itself. This last was especially outrageous to Basile Moreau, who, increasingly belligerent, resisted any such proposals and, taking advantage of the complexities of the French property law that had so tormented him before, contested the transfer of holdings in his name to the

60. See Schlereth, *Notre Dame*, 149, 195.
61. Sorin, *Chronicles*, 303–305.

newly formed civil society. The Founder also chided Chappé for what he called a breakdown in religious discipline and carefully recorded doleful instances in a memorandum for Dufal. The need for money was becoming desperate, as worried creditors demanded payment and appeals for loans were routinely turned down.[62] Patrick Dillon kept Sorin informed of the rapidly deteriorating situation. "It is *dreadful,*" he wrote on July 25, "that Monsignor Dufal is so long absent. The conduct of the Very Reverend Founder and his followers is most deplorable and cannot continue much longer without bringing ruin on the house here. *He is doing everything in his power to ruin the congregation that he founded.*"[63]

Dillon had scarcely sealed this letter when Father Chappé asked to see him, after which meeting the young Irishman picked up his pen again. The vicar "said that he considered it his duty to inform you of the actual state of things, moral and financial. . . . Notwithstanding all his faith and confidence—and both are boundless—I must say that I never saw him so shaken."

> I need say but little as to the moral state of the house here. You have already had insight enough to form your opinion thereon. The Founder with Father Charles [and a few others] are [sic] in opposition to the new administration. This division is known not only in the Community but [also] among the students and outside. . . . Father Charles has, I'm told, a paper in circulation justifying his public refusal of obedience to the Vicar. The Very Reverend Founder has another, . . . claiming there is no real authority here. . . . His Reverence has also said . . . that he could not understand how *I* could be supported in the house, that I was an *intruder.* . . . His object is to prove the present administration *illegal,* and here is how he does it. It seems there was a letter found in your room after your departure [from the general chapter in September 1866] written to you by the bishop of Le Mans. . . . The letter, they say, proves a *cabal* to change the form of government and various other sundry crimes.

Moreau's object in concentrating his censure on Dillon's status "is but a preparatory step to repudiate *all* the acts of the Chapter and amongst them the election of Monsignor Dufal, if he doesn't think fit to be led and controlled by the Very Reverend Father Moreau. The deplorable delay of his Lordship gives time for this poison to take deep root."

---

62. See Catta, *Moreau,* 2: 726–746.
63. Dillon to Sorin, July 25, 1867 (1), AIP.

Chappé also wanted Sorin to realize just how grave was the motherhouse's financial predicament. The prospect of securing 100,000 francs by selling St. Bridget's in Rome had quieted the creditors briefly. "They have been patient," said Dillon, "hoping that in the division of the proceeds they would at least get a portion of their claims." But Drouelle's promises to them in this regard came to nothing when the sale was thwarted yet again. "You know that *promises* will do for a while, but redeeming one promise by making another soon exhausts all patience." Chappé and Dillon were agreed that rescue could come from only one source.

> The result of the financial failure of Notre Dame de Sainte-Croix would necessarily bring on the suppression of the Congregation in France by the Government and maybe its entire suppression by Rome. *We have not here the resources to save us from ruin.* Of our establishments, Notre Dame du Lac is the only one that can effectually save us. The salvation of the Motherhouse and maybe of the whole Congregation is therefore in your hands. But can even you do it? With your heavy load of debt, can you advance enough to get us out of our difficulty? May it not be in the designs of God to make known to you the valuable discovery of the turf to enable you— *you* who formerly were so blackened and cried down by the late ruling powers—to be the only one in the Congregation to pay off debts contracted by that same (mal)administration. . . . Say then, Very Reverend and dear Father, what you [can] do in our otherwise hopeless case. Could you effect a loan of, say, 50,000 francs?

Dillon understood that Sorin, though indebted himself, had learned, through adversity over a quarter of a century, how to manage debt. Because Notre Dame was a bustling, even a booming enterprise—at least when compared to Sainte-Croix—he could approach the financial markets with some confidence. Whether he put his credit rating to use in response to this appeal remains unclear; he had pledged 35,000 francs during the general chapter, and later he rather tersely remarked "that America subscribed a sum total of 70,000 francs."[64] Dillon at any rate was clearly torn between two allegiances, between two superiors, both of whom he admired. He was not, as Moreau charged, simply Sorin's spy. "[Chappé] says that, if you can, he will guarantee to pay you back. . . . Of him I can say he is an *honest* man and *means* what he says. He will not set a trap for you. . . . It has

64. Sorin, *Chronicles*, 301.

pleased God to bless you with an abundant harvest and a rich treasure [of turf], I hope, in the marsh. Come, be generous and share it with your *impoverished* brethren."[65]

Pierre Dufal finally arrived in Le Mans on September 25, thirteen months after his election. He had previously heard rumors and garbled accounts about the troubles at the motherhouse, but he was nevertheless appalled when he discovered the magnitude of the problem. Rampant factionalism and virtual financial collapse made him long for the dusty streets of Dacca. His attempts to raise a loan ended in failure and humiliation. Badgered by the partisans of Drouelle from one side and by those of Basile Moreau from the other, the bishop soon concluded that the restoration of peace was an achievement beyond him. He stayed at his post for scarcely three months. At the beginning of 1868 he departed for Rome, where he vainly hoped to find help in sorting out the hodgepodge of conflicting claims and mutual denunciations. Neither the pope in an audience that lasted an hour and a half nor Cardinal Barnabò in several lengthy interviews offered him much encouragement, and one wonders why, if they were not ready to support him strongly, they had agreed to—indeed, insisted upon—his appointment to an office for which his missionary experience had plainly not prepared him. "May God have pity on the healthy part of the congregation," Dufal wrote Father Chappé, "in order that, if we are to be sifted, the good grain may be forever separated from the bad. As for myself, my role at Sainte-Croix is finished, and I have only to wait in anxiety and impatience the order of the Holy See to go back where I came from." In early March he formally indicated to Propaganda and to the council in Le Mans his intention to resign.[66]

Father Sorin, who was kept abreast of the general state of things across the sea if not the details, described these months as a time of "expectation" for Holy Cross in America but also as a period of "patience and peace."[67] His ordinary concerns and obligations continued apace. Thus he set up a committee to inquire into ways to save money by revamping the domestic staff at Notre Dame. Thirty lay women were employed in the "kitchen, washhouse, clothes rooms, and drying rooms" at $12 a month for ten months, for a total annual expenditure of $3,600. The committee recommended, as the provincial wanted it to, that these workers be replaced by nuns, each of whom would receive $100 per year.[68] Curiously, for

---

65. Dillon to Sorin, July 25, 1867 (2), AIP.

66. See Catta, *Moreau,* 2: 752–771.

67. Sorin, *Chronicles,* 302.

68. See Brother Lawrence et al. to Sorin, January 19, 1867, AIP. See also chapter 27, below.

all his management skills, a solution to this seemingly small problem plagued Sorin for many years.

While he maintained his usual hectic pace—he persisted, for example, in soliciting subscribers and contributors for the *Ave Maria*[69]—he was heartened by two unrelated developments that assuaged some unhappy memories. The bishop of Louisville, Spalding's successor there, sent an "urgent request" that Holy Cross assume direction of the college in Bardstown, which the Jesuits had closed at the beginning of the Civil War.[70] Long gone were the days of hesitancy and incompetence that had spoiled the original incursion of Notre Dame into Kentucky.[71] Even more gratifying as a symbol was one of the few decisions Bishop Dufal actually made as superior general, this one inspired by Patrick Dillon: Sorin was appointed Visitor to the Holy Cross mission in New Orleans, whose superior had recently died.[72] He returned to the scene of so much past heartache and strife not, to be sure, as a conquering hero, but nonetheless with a sober feeling of vindication. His Visit coincided with one of that city's frequent epidemics of yellow fever and, to his credit, he immediately organized a drive to raise funds to relieve "our poor fellow beings" in Louisiana.[73]

But the news from abroad inevitably intruded and pushed all other preoccupations aside. When he learned of Dufal's resignation, Sorin contacted the bishop of Le Mans. Charles-Jean Fillion, nephew of an old friend and patron of Basile Moreau, had worn the miter in his native city since 1862. His attitude toward the Founder of Holy Cross had evolved from ambivalence to hostility, or at least to the conviction that, if there were to be peace in his diocese, radical change was needed at Sainte-Croix. Sorin had known him casually since their student days. "Monseigneur," he wrote,

> yesterday I heard very disturbing news. Still, I cannot convince myself that the situation of the Congregation of Holy Cross is so desperate that it will have to be abandoned. I cannot easily reconcile myself to such ruin when so many prayers have been said and so much confidence placed in God and

---

69. See Eliza Starr to Sorin, January 21, 1867, and Mary Huntington to Sorin, March 7, 1867, AIP. Eliza Starr was a poet.

70. Lavialle to Sorin, January 29, 1867, AIP.

71. See chapters 12 and 13, above.

72. See the "Obedience," signed by Dufal, September 27, 1867, AIP.

73. Sorin to Purcell, October 16, 1867, and Purcell to Sorin, October 19, 1867, AIP. The archbishop of Cincinnati told Sorin that special collections in several of his parishes had already netted $600.

in the Blessed Virgin and St. Joseph. I come then to ask you, Monseigneur, as our good friend and as one most knowledgeable about our affairs and about the sentiments in Rome,[74] what you judge it best for us to do. I am emboldened to do so by our old friendship of nearly forty years and still more by concern for the well-being of so many souls in France and in America. Tell me frankly what you think, without fear or evasion (*détour*). *Your response will guide my actions.*"[75]

This sentiment directed to such a personage was politic, but one may legitimately doubt that Edward Sorin, that self-sufficient man, would be guided at this moment of crisis by something other than his own convictions. At any rate, events in France and Rome over which he had no direct control were unfolding rapidly and relentlessly. Propaganda instructed Dufal to convene an extraordinary general chapter to be held in Rome during the early summer. The bishop, much influenced by the increasingly erratic Victor Drouelle, accordingly summoned Father Moreau and ten priests and ten brothers, representing the various Holy Cross missions, to assemble at St. Bridget's; it was Dufal's final official act. The term "extraordinary general chapter" was significant, because the list of capitulants drawn up by Dufal and Drouelle did not include some of those who, *ex officio,* would normally have been called to participate. Basile and Charles Moreau predictably seized upon this procedural point to question the canonical validity of the whole enterprise, Charles in a sharply worded protest which Cardinal Barnabò found offensive. Indeed, the prefect, and the pope as well, sent out distinct signals that, unless the congregation could put its house in order for good and all, suppression was inevitable.

The chapter opened on July 14 without the presence of the Founder. As had happened two years before, he refused to comply with the command to come to Rome, and this time he persisted, even when an angry Barnabò threatened him with censure, possibly even excommunication. Once again it is difficult not to admire the lonely courage of this aged warrior, now in his seventieth year, who would not bend to what he perceived to be a plot to destroy his life's work. He rightly assumed that an assembly whose agenda would be largely set by Drouelle, his bitterest enemy, would file a harsh indictment against his administration. Nor was he mistaken to surmise that once he left his base in Le Mans and went to

---

74. Since the Visitation of Sainte-Croix ordered by Propaganda in 1862, Fillion had continued in the capacity of apostolic delegate.

75. Sorin to Fillion, March 19, 1868, AGEN.

Rome he might well be forced to remain there, out of the way in some convent garden—*ibi maneat* once more. So, with head held high, he addressed his Eminence, the cardinal-prefect:

> If there were no other question for me than to continue the role of victim which has been imposed upon me by duping the good faith of Propaganda and his Holiness, I would continue in this path with pleasure, limiting myself to private prayer for those who are persecuting me. But there is a question here of the honor of the Holy See, to which I have devoted my entire life, and of the temporal interests of which I must render an account to my congregation. Now these interests have been gravely compromised by scheming and ambition, and everything gives me grounds for fear that the chapter in session at Rome may aggravate the situation still more.

And to Bishop Fillion: "In a spirit of most respectful submission, I shall accept the canonical penalties with which I am threatened, and shall offer them to God as an act of reparation to His justice for the faults of my life."[76]

By mid-June Sorin had arrived in Rome, where the prayers of his subjects back in Indiana followed him. "Thank you, thank you, very beloved little children," he wrote the novices at St. Mary's. "I trust I will soon have the happiness to meet you again at your Eden-like St. Mary's. . . . I speak sometimes of my dear Novices, but pray oftener for them."[77] As the members of the extraordinary chapter gathered at St. Bridget's, most of the conversation turned upon the behavior of Basile Moreau: "They all consider our poor Founder as a man out of his senses or without a conscience. . . . [He] is now in plain rebellion against the Holy See." A report from Le Mans stated that Moreau, in a sermon preached before "a considerable audience," declared that he had indeed been "threatened with ecclesiastical censures, but that the day he would be excommunicated would be the most glorious in his life. . . . It would appear that the two Moreaus have become perfectly incomprehensible."[78]

The chapter adjourned on July 20, and two days later the capitulants were granted a farewell audience by a somber Pius IX, who expressed "hesitancy" over future prospects because of past "threatening" and "scandalous" behavior. Nevertheless, "*Deus est caritas*," the pope said to them, "God is love. It is my hope that

---

76. Catta, *Moreau* 2: 808, 818.
77. Sorin to "Very dear little Novices," June 13, 1868, AIP.
78. Sorin to Granger, July 10, 1868, AGEN.

your congregation will become a congregation worthy of its name, that it will carry everywhere the marks of peace and charity, and that henceforth it will live in harmony." The priests and brothers of Holy Cross, after receiving the papal blessing, filed solemnly out of the audience chamber. The last to leave was the new superior general, elected by the extraordinary chapter with virtual unanimity, Edward Frederick Sorin.[79]

79. Catta, *Moreau*, 2: 808–832.

chapter twenty-five

At the Helm

EDWARD SORIN WAS NOT UNAWARE BEFOREHAND that he would likely emerge from the extraordinary chapter of July 1868 as the third superior general of the Congregation of Holy Cross. He hinted as much to his friend and confrère Alexis Granger ten days prior to his election: "I cannot say when I shall leave [Rome] for Notre Dame. . . . I may be with you on the 15th [of August, the feast of the Assumption of the Virgin], but I may not. Serious events may shape my course differently from what has gone on previously." Whatever the theoretical advantages of impartiality, the strategy of placing at the head of the order a man uninvolved in its dissensions had badly miscarried. Indeed, the last state of affairs was worse than the first, and Bishop Dufal was soon on his way back to Bengal. In the oppressive heat of the Roman high summer, the sheer inevitability of Sorin's elevation had become unmistakable. Although he claimed, in accord with the protocol required of clerics, that he begged his colleagues not to impose such a burden upon him, one may be excused for doubting that he anticipated tackling this new challenge with anything but relish.[1]

He alone among his senior colleagues had demonstrated the skills required in managing a complex enterprise; a record of accomplishment was before the eyes of the electors and of the watchful Cardinal Barnabò. They recognized that Sorin's decisiveness, his capacity for work, and his attention to detail had brought him through many a crisis. He had proved himself tough and resilient. If he had experienced severe financial difficulties in establishing, maintaining, and

---

1. Sorin to Granger, July 22, 1868, in Edward Sorin, *Circular Letters*, 2 vols. (Notre Dame, Ind., 1885), 1:5.

expanding his mission, he had by craft and stamina, and sometimes by bluff, succeeded in surmounting them. Nor was his protracted feud with Basile Moreau any longer a hindrance to promotion, now that the Founder's stock at the Vatican had fallen so low. Sorin, by contrast, had prudently cultivated the Roman authorities at a time when they felt sorely threatened: the aggressive absorption of the last remnant of the Papal States into the new Kingdom of Italy was only two years away. And his Marian piety was deemed no less genuine than his devotion to the embattled Holy See. His earlier combat with the likes of Hailandière and Duggan had given way to a close alliance with his own bishop and a cordial relationship with the powerful archbishops of Cincinnati and Baltimore. He was fluent in both the languages spoken by the members of the congregation and by their associates, the sisters. He possessed magnetic charm in abundance. If he had forged his reputation in the forests of the New World, he still displayed the polish of a *gentilhomme* appreciated by the Old. But perhaps what recommended Edward Sorin most was his unwearying and infectious optimism. "We are all perfectly united in views and sentiments here [in Rome]," he assured Father Granger. "The Congregation will pass through the present crisis and will come out of it, in my firm belief, purified and strengthened, even if it must be somewhat reduced through the loss of defective members."[2]

Father Sorin was in his fifty-fifth year when he assumed his new responsibilities. His health overall was sound, though he had inevitably added some flesh since the day he had boarded the *Iowa* in Le Havre and embarked for the great adventure in America. The jawline had softened somewhat, but the clean-shaven face—the famous long white beard was grown later—with its firm wide mouth and its bright eyes behind the spectacles still radiated self-confident energy. His hair had turned all grey now, and it receded a little from his forehead; he wore it, as before, full and with sweeping sideburns that covered his ears. If the passage of time had altered his physical appearance, it had also smoothed away some of the impetuousness of his youth—he would not again indulge in reckless pursuits like the expedition to the California goldfields or permit a quarrel to drag out needlessly as he had over the mission in New Orleans. This is not to suggest that the man in his late middle age had altered his goals or ideals or that his personality had undergone radical change. He remained as ever an activist, a risk-taker, often pragmatic and sometimes volatile, usually sensitive to the feelings of others but, if he saw the need, ruthless in pursuing his objectives, eloquent, dictatorial, and captivating. But fundamental to all else was the conviction that Providence had singled him out to perform mighty deeds. "I see clearly," declared young Fa-

2. Sorin to Granger, July 10, 1868, AGEN.

ther Sorin on the eve of his departure for America, "that our Lord loves me in a very special manner."[3] He bore that certainty with him to his dying day.

Up to 1868 Edward Sorin's life in its maturity had been played out in a drama of two acts: the creation of a great institution in the middle of a wilderness, and a tragic quarrel with his spiritual father. The curtain had fallen on those scenes, and the stage had been cleared for a third and final act, which promised to have a dramatic rhythm of its own.

A WEEK OR SO before he was elected superior general Father Sorin offered Mass in a Roman parish church. Over the altar hung the portrait of "a Madonna of a heavenly beauty, whose eyes a few years ago were seen to move for more than a month. All unworthy as I am, I am certain that I saw myself, more than a dozen times, the same eyes, *not moving* but *moved*, completely different at one time from where they were a moment before and a moment afterward. Oh, how I prayed at that altar for all my precious friends beyond the waters!"[4] To presume the benevolent gaze of the Virgin on himself and all his works was at the heart of Sorin's piety, strikingly vindicated, he must have thought, by the chapter's decision of July 20.

His "precious friends beyond the waters" were never far from his thoughts and prayers, and not only out of reverent affection. For upon those nearly 400 priests, brothers, and sisters, serving in a plethora of ministries scattered across the eastern half of the North American continent, rested any expectation that the Congrégation de Sainte-Croix could survive and experience a renewal. Little could be counted on from a few stray Josephite brothers still teaching in Algeria or from Dufal's mission in Bengal, which could barely sustain itself. And the congregation's plight on the European shores of the Atlantic was dismal in the extreme. Two of the three houses in Italy had been closed, and the third, St. Bridget's in Rome, loaded with debt, limped along only because all efforts to sell it had failed. But the situation in France, the congregation's center and heartland, was even more discouraging. Several Holy Cross foundations had simply shut their doors, including the colleges at Flers and Saint-Brieuc in Brittany. The collegiate facility in Paris, the occasion of so much financial distress, was abandoned in favor of a new site in the suburb of Neuilly-sur Seine; this institution had been set up by Victor Drouelle and Louis Champeau—in defiance of Basile Moreau's direct order—as a corporation legally distinct from Sainte-Croix, itself a gesture

---

3. Sorin to Hailandière, n.d. [summer, 1841], AGEN.
4. Sorin to Granger, July 10, 1868, AGEN.

in despair. The most distressing, and most poignant, scene, however, was that revealed in Le Mans itself. The college had ceased to operate, and hopes that the Jesuits or even the bishop might purchase it to keep it Catholic hands proved illusory. The indebtedness of the motherhouse, which had swelled by 75,000 francs ($15,000) since the election of Bishop Dufal in 1866, required complete "liquidation," in Drouelle's infelicitous word. To satisfy the looming creditors the house itself had to be sold along with whatever could not be easily stored: furniture and chattels of any kind, the adjacent farm buildings and the cattle, even the furnishings of the conventual church, unless the diocese could be persuaded to lease it for parochial use.[5] In human terms such draconian measures meant the expulsion of the religious who had long lived and prayed on this cherished spot, some of them for three decades. Besides the relatively healthy priests and brothers thus to be expelled—several of whom sought dispensations from their vows: on August 16 Père Charles Moreau reverted to Abbé Charles Moreau—the roster of evacuees included twenty aged and infirm Marianite nuns who had occupied one wing of the complex.[6]

In the immediate wake of his election the new superior general avoided viewing the worst of this wreckage. On July 23 he boarded a train for the thirty-hour journey to Marseilles, and from there, accompanied by Drouelle and Champeau, he went on to Paris. On his way to catch the packet for the United States at Brest he paused in Le Mans only long enough for ceremonial calls on the bishop, the prefect, and the mayor. In the interval he oversaw the publication and distribution of a *Circular* which, in effect, recapitulated the harsh critique of Basile Moreau's administration that had dominated much of the discussion at the chapter. Moreau predictably replied in a public letter of his own, mimeographed and sent round to all the houses of the order. "If," he wrote, "as we find in the circular of our general chapter, . . . I were not afraid of becoming for you a source of scandal, I would maintain absolute silence on the treatment accorded me in the aforesaid letter." There followed the by now hackneyed complaints of calumny against his person and of misrepresentation of his financial dealings.[7] Father Moreau was without doubt a man of honor and principle who endured much suffering not of his own making; yet his posthumous stature might well have stood even higher had he been able to emulate the resolution of Princess Cordelia: "Love, and be silent."[8]

---

5. Establishment of a parish involved legal and financial negotiations with the commune of Sainte-Croix. They were prolonged. See Sorin to Bardeau, March 14, 1869, AGEN.
6. Catta, *Moreau*, 2: 885–893.
7. Catta, *Moreau*, 2: 836–846.
8. *King Lear*, act 1, scene 1.

With so much trouble afflicting Holy Cross in France, Sorin's hasty departure—he landed in New York on August 11—perturbed even his closest allies. "We are like a family without a head," complained Father Champeau, who assumed that the superior general would ultimately take up permanent residence in the new motherhouse planned for Paris, where he, Champeau, could exert his influence. This assumption indicates how little even the closest of Sorin's French allies grasped his discernment of the proper future course for Holy Cross. The congregation had succeeded in America—in which the superior general now, setting aside past disputes, generously included Canada[9]—and had languished almost everywhere else. Its enterprise everywhere therefore needed an injection of the bold and energetic American spirit. Even so, Sorin understood the European propensity to view the affairs in the New World as somehow mysterious and even outlandish. When he heard rumbles that Barnabò was perplexed by his hurried exit to Indiana, he hastened to reassure the cardinal-prefect, aware that that eminent prelate was never indifferent to financial concerns. Fulfillment of the terms of certain contracts and fiscal commitments, he wrote in September, "made my presence absolutely necessary at Notre Dame du Lac." He did not elaborate beyond insisting that "we have here great interests to safeguard. I do not see what real utility there would have been for me to be in France these two months." Moreover, his location did not prevent him from addressing the continuing internal squabbles: "From here I have been able to rebut the circulars which the Very Reverend Founder has unhappily addressed from Le Mans to our Establishments and to various bishops."[10] As for Champeau's lament, let him, Sorin advised with some sharpness, busy himself usefully with matters within his ken. The extraordinary general chapter had attached great importance to the kind of texts employed in the schools conducted by Holy Cross: "Dear Father Champeau, whom Providence has so richly endowed for the accomplishment of a task of this sort, ought to occupy himself with it immediately."[11]

Despite all his determination and unflagging optimism, however, Father Sorin, on his return to America, had to accept the loss of his most trusted adjutant. "My difficulties," he explained to Barnabò,

> have been much increased by the secession of Father [Patrick] Dillon. He learned that his widowed mother, his grandmother, and several younger siblings were confronted with a debt of 13,000 francs, which was more than

9. See Sorin to Rézé, August 30, 1868, AGEN.
10. Sorin to Barnabò, September 27, 1868, AGEN.
11. Sorin to Drouelle, August 10, 1868, AGEN.

equal to all that they possessed. Seeing these loved ones without resources and without any other source of support save himself, he has believed himself strongly obliged to solicit a dispensation from the vows of poverty and obedience. His brother [James], also a professed member of our order and dying of lung disease, has insisted upon joining him. However much I regret it, I have had, in the light of public opinions here, to accede to their petition.[12]

Patrick Dillon's withdrawal from Holy Cross was duly registered in June 1868. He was offered and accepted a pastorate in Chicago. In that ministry he was joined by his younger brother James, who, despite his chronic bad health, had served honorably as a chaplain during the Civil War. Patrick died there the following November, as did James a year later.[13] Both were buried in the community cemetery at Notre Dame. "Poor dear Fathers Dillon!" Sorin told Mrs. Phelan, "how I miss them. Thus we pass and disappear when least expected."[14]

Patrick Dillon had entered upon his fatal illness when Father Sorin, on the last day of October, departed Notre Dame for France.[15] Once he had arrived at the motherhouse on November 11, the tension was almost palpable, though Sorin acknowledged that the Founder had greeted him "kindly." Even so, a confrontation was not long in coming, as Sorin explained to the procurator general in Rome, Nicolas Bardeau—the Holy Cross priest assigned to act as agent with the curia, the post Drouelle had held in earlier years. Bardeau was to reassure the officials at Propaganda that "I have committed myself (*j'ai épousé*) to the future of the Congregation of Sainte-Croix and that I am determined to make their concerns *mine* until the my last breath. The *actual situation* is certainly critical, but I do not despair. Now that it has been *purged*, . . . [the congregation's] convalescence will perhaps take time; but it is more viable than it was six months ago." Sorin had taken pains to visit "the principal personages of Le Mans" and to "examine the overall condition of things." Even so,

the great obstacle is as ever the same, the poor dear Father Founder. I adore, without really understanding them, the designs of Heaven with regard to this dear man and the foundation of Sainte-Croix; but I could not conceive

---

12. Sorin to Barnabò, September 27, 1868, AGEN.

13. See *Matricule générale*, 1014, 1090, AIP. James Dillon never formally withdrew from the congregation.

14. Sorin to Mary Phelan, February 9, 1869, AUND, CEWI, "Ewing Family Papers."

15. Sorin to Sister Columba, October 11, 1868, AGEN.

of a person more adamantly opposed to the congregation's rebirth. Three times he has insisted, and I have refused, supported by Monseigneur Fillon, that he should keep in his possession a Roman Missal given *him* by the pope, despite the declaration *to the contrary* by the bishop. Last evening we had a long discussion about a *point* that he desires absolutely to use to his own advantage, namely, that professed religious in our Congregation have the right to dispose of their property without the permission or the consent of the Superior, an assertion I denied.

Besides the missal, Moreau claimed possession of other liturgical accouterments, including a chalice valued at 1,000 francs, and, overall, a collection of ritual equipage totaling six times that amount.[16]

In fact Moreau's contention was correct. In the Constitutions and Rules which he had drawn up—and which, needless to say, Sorin had subscribed to—the vow of poverty taken by the members of the congregation did not oblige them to relinquish ownership of property that might come to them by gift or inheritance. Sorin, for one, had considered himself free to spend any way he liked the money he received from his deceased father's estate.[17] But the position Moreau now took went far beyond concern over a stray missal or chalice. To what degree, he demanded rhetorically, were the properties of Notre Dame de Sainte-Croix, now so deeply indebted as to be in danger of seizure by its creditors, at the disposal of the new administration—at the disposal in his view, that is, of calumniators and traitors like Sorin, Drouelle, Champeau, and Chappé? It will be recalled that in French law a religious congregation of men had no standing and therefore could not own or alienate property. To circumvent this prohibition Father Moreau had adopted a common practice by forming a "civil society" to act as legal guarantor of the financial dealings of Holy Cross. As initiator and chairman of this body, the Founder's signature was routinely affixed to all transactions. A series of disasters—most spectacularly, but by no means uniquely, the Marie-Julien affair of 1860—had brought down upon the society, and therefore the congregation, immense debts as well as widespread discredit on Moreau personally. By 1866 the overall situation within the order had so deteriorated that the Roman authorities had forced Moreau's resignation as superior general.

At that time, in a gesture of conciliation, Moreau had offered to dissolve the civil society and so expedite the formation of a new one, so long as he was ab-

---

16. Sorin to Bardeau, November 14, 1868, AGEN.
17. See chapter 19, above.

solved from any individual liability.[18] His successor, Bishop Dufal, accordingly headed a similar association until succeeded himself by Edward Sorin. Father Moreau, however, soon came to regret his concession. His grounds were partly principled, partly highly personal. As he watched with dismay the hasty sale of the motherhouse's furniture and livestock and books, he wondered with reason whether the congregation's creditors, including several members of his own family, would have any chance of receiving a fair settlement, particularly those who did not hold mortgages. The law prescribed that, in cases of an institution's virtual bankruptcy, those whose claims were temporally prior had to be satisfied before others who had become creditors later on. If the "liquidation" did not produce funds equal to the total indebtedness, many in this latter category would receive nothing; nor was there a legal remedy available to them. Various persons, moreover, had loaned money to Holy Cross because of their affection or esteem for Father Moreau, and he felt, again rightly, a special obligation to see that their interests were protected. Finally, he professed himself appalled at the inflating of the motherhouse's debt during the short two years since his resignation; officially the figure stood at 75,000 francs, but Moreau alleged the sum was nearly twice that much. No one in any case could blame him for that deficit.

But the Founder's posture on these and related issues was darkened by what he conceived to be the injustices done to him personally. During the week the superior general was in residence, Moreau treated him with frosty courtesy and never hinted at his future strategy. Deep within him, however, the hurt and anger toward the man who had once been his protégé and now was his enemy, continued to fester, as he revisited in his mind the catalogue of ill treatment. The superior general, meanwhile, in consultation with his general council, gave vent to his habitual optimism by proposing that Sainte-Croix's fiscal troubles in France might be solved by mounting a regional appeal for money or even a national lottery. Nothing came of these schemes in the end—the intermingling of church-state relations during the Second Empire led to too many bureaucratic complications—but Sorin still harbored hopes for them when he left Le Mans for Paris on November 19. The evening before, "feeling it my duty," he explained his plan to Moreau. "He appeared pleased and told me . . . he would pray for its success."[19] In the report he sent to Propaganda a few days later Father Sorin mentioned the liquidation process only in passing and emphasized instead "that, true enough, at this moment our dear Congregation resembles a sick man who has been bled almost to the last drop in order to save his life. It appears weak, but in the eyes of

18. See chapter 24, above.
19. Sorin to Barnabò, November 30, 1868, AGEN.

the wise it has simply been purged of all that impaired its system. Henceforth it will be healthy, as it now enters upon a path of natural vigor which it has probably never enjoyed before. With a little patience one will soon see, I hope, that it has recovered the luster of its youth."[20]

The superior general was in for a rude awakening. The day after Basile Moreau pledged his prayers, his lawyers introduced into the civil court in Le Mans a petition that the association legally responsible for the financial transactions of Sainte-Croix be dissolved and that the claims of creditors upon that corporation be settled by an independent arbitrator. If this suit were approved, the new administration's right through the civil society to dispose of the motherhouse and related properties in Le Mans as it saw fit would be disallowed. Sorin's stern reaction was a measure of his shock and outrage. "Very Reverend Father," he wrote from Neuilly-sur-Seine, Louis Champeau's headquarters in the Parisian suburbs,

> I have heard with as much pain as surprise that you have had recourse to the civil courts in hopes of dissolving the Civil Society of Sainte-Croix whose mandate, according to our original statutes, rests as arbitrator with the bishop [of Le Mans]. I cannot understand how you, my Reverend Father, a professed Religious, can act in this way, without having consulted the Superior of the Congregation, in defiance of the condemnation written in your own hand in Constitution 8, article 54.[21] Since the right of the approval of such of such measures is reserved to the Superior General, I therefore order you, in the name of our Lord Jesus Christ and in virtue of your vow of obedience, to cease this pursuit and to annul immediately everything you have done in this legal matter.[22]

A copy of this communication was sent to Cardinal Barnabò and to the bishop of Le Mans, and it was inserted into the local newspapers.

The Founder's affidavit was not intended to avoid bankruptcy; quite to the contrary, by formally admitting to overwhelming debt and paucity of resources, the petition guaranteed that liquidation would occur. What Moreau did hope to accomplish was to slow down the process. The civil society, controlled by his enemies, wanted to hurry to the auction block. If a more leisurely method were adopted, perhaps something could be saved from the wreckage. He firmly believed that a sale of the encumbered properties over time would bring a better

20. Sorin to Barnabò, November 21, 1868, AGEN.

21. "The Superior-General directs and administers the congregation; he represents it and acts in its name before all jurisdictions. . . . No lawsuit may be undertaken without his permission."

22. Sorin to Moreau, November 22, 1868, AGEN.

return and thus benefit all the creditors. This was a perfectly legitimate aspiration, however improbable of fulfillment, as was a similarly forlorn hope that in the end the college might reopen under different auspices, even under the direction of his nephew Charles. And—it need hardly be said—Father Moreau sought no pecuniary advantage for himself. But his intention also—less laudable, if no less understandable—was to thwart his enemies, the chief of whom now had the presumption to call him to his duty. When chided for his disobedience by Bishop Fillion and, later, by Cardinal Barnabò, he responded with bitter reminders of the past.

> You close your [written remonstrance], my Lord [he wrote Fillion], *by asking me what I would have thought when I was superior, if one of my religious would have disregarded my authority.* Alas, my Lord, I have had only too many occasions to show my stand on similar incidents. Father Sorin, who is fighting me today so arbitrarily, comported himself in a very disobedient manner when I, as his superior, commanded him to do certain things which were just. I have not forgotten his constant refusal to reimburse me for a loan of fourteen thousand francs;[23] nor the letter in which his assistant, Father Granger, notified me of the separation of Notre Dame from the motherhouse, which it is today his mission to destroy; nor the reception accorded the two Visitors I sent, Fathers Chappé and Charles; nor his memorandum to Propaganda against me; nor his protestations to Rome . . . after the chapter of 1863; nor his stubborn persistence in the construction of a retreat house for suspended and sickly priests; nor his refusal to have an understanding with me in keeping with the will of the Pope, to bring about the separation of the temporal interests of the Sisters from those of our own religious; nor especially the schism which he occasioned and which he is still fomenting with these same Sisters [in America], who have completely disregarded . . . the constitutions approved by the Holy See.[24]

To his superior general Father Moreau sent no response.

The suit was not withdrawn, much to Sorin's disgust. "The real object of the uncle and nephew," he assured Granger, "is to ruin, directly and shamefully to ruin the Congregation, in order to verify their prophecies that it could never live

---

23. Actually the sum was fifteen thousand francs. See chapter 21, above. Moreau's resentment was as understandable as Sorin's conduct was reprehensible, but, drowning as Sainte-Croix was in a sea of red ink, it is doubtful that $3,000 would have made any long-term difference.

24. Moreau to Fillion, December 13, 1868, quoted in Catta, *Moreau,* 2: 911–912.

without them, and next to rebuild it upon its ruins in complete independence from Rome. If it were in their power to destroy it in a day, its destiny would be sealed at once."[25] That Sorin was prepared to believe that Moreau intended to break with the papacy attests to how harsh the contest had become and how deep the estrangement. Nothing at any rate could move the Founder, not even an offer from the members of the civil society to dissolve voluntarily and to appoint liquidators agreeable to Moreau. By that time, mid-February 1869, the legal process was nearing its conclusion, and Sorin decided to make one last appeal. "What more can you obtain from the courts in Le Mans [than this]?" he asked. "Let me conjure with you one more time, my Very Reverend Father, to desist from a procedure which your best friends reprove you for and which appeared so foreign (*éloigné*) to your own thinking only months ago. You know that everything I have done in your Reverence's regard has been to avoid scandal." And speaking of scandal: "You have taken no account of it. You have continued to say Mass! I have never ceased to pray for you, and I have gotten your best friends to pray for you, that you desist from this action. It has all been useless, *a useless evil*."[26] There was no reply.

Evil or not, Moreau's initiative did prove useless. The court's judgment[27] was indeed favorable to his petition, providing for, among other things, a year's hiatus before the properties had to be sold, but by March 9, when it was handed down, it had become a dead letter. Sorin and his allies had resorted to a legal maneuver of their own. After the Founder rejected their compromise, they had secured, in effect, a prior injunction, by having a mortgagee serve a writ of attachment on all the property. The result was a series of auctions which began on April 21 and which netted just under 400,000 francs.[28] As Father Moreau had predicted, some creditors salvaged only twenty percent of what was owed them. Whether they would have done better under his court-sanctioned strategy, however, remains problematic. In any event, the overall debt of the French houses still totaled nearly 300,000 francs, the resolution of which was to preoccupy the superior general for years to come.

Once the judicial matter had been settled, Edward Sorin left Le Mans for Rome, where he stayed for several weeks. His presence was then required, because Propaganda was reviewing the acts of the general chapter of 1868, which,

25. Sorin to Granger, December 2, 1868, AGEN.
26. Sorin to Moreau, February 27, 1869, AGEN.
27. See "*Jugement*," March 9, 1869 (copy), AGEN.
28. See Catta, *Moreau*, 2: 962.

with trifling adjustments, were approved.[29] While there, however, he also lobbied hard to persuade the Roman officials to order Moreau's removal to a religious house elsewhere in France. If the Founder were allowed to reside in Le Mans, he argued, he might well become the focal point of resistance to the new administration. "I have never witnessed in my life any similar opposition," Sorin protested. "I bear toward Father Moreau personally only profound pity, without any resentment or animosity. I ask God each day to forgive him. But I cannot pretend that he has not undermined, indeed ruined the community." [30] This effort did not succeed, perhaps because of an intuition Sorin had had earlier: "Well he, the good Cardinal . . . must be horribly tired of us by now."[31] Barnabò and his colleagues at any rate, whether out of compassion or weariness, declined to force the old man into exile. And so, on April 28, Basile Moreau departed the vast institution he had created, and, with the help of his nephew, moved some articles of clothing, a few books, and the armchair in which for years he had slept, to a small house nearby occupied by two of his spinster sisters, now aged like himself. The Marianite convent was not far away, and the nuns there begged "the favor . . . to allow us to bring you your meals. . . . We wish and desire to do the same thing for Miss Victoire and Miss Josephine." It was poignantly fitting that the Founder should have been the last to leave Notre Dame de Sainte-Croix.[32]

FATHER SORIN was in Paris at the moment this sad scene was played out.[33] Among the statutes sanctioned by Propaganda was the transfer of Holy Cross's general administration to the French capital, for which he sought the formal permission of the archbishop there: "I dare to hope that your Excellency will welcome a measure which we look forward to as promising happy results for the development of our work and for the good of the Church."[34] After a brief stop in Le Mans, Sorin boarded the *St. Laurent* at Brest for the voyage home. He had much to ponder. During the first ten months of his generalship he had not only endured the final crisis with Basile Moreau and witnessed in person the plight of the congregation in France. He had also discovered how many and

---

29. See Sorin to Granger, April 13, 1869, AGEN.

30. See Sorin to Barnabò, February 27, March 10, and April 2, 1869, AGEN. The quotation is from the letter of March 10.

31. Sorin to Bardeau, January 14, 1869, AGEN.

32. Catta, *Moreau*, 2: 948–950.

33. See Sorin to Corby, April 28, 1869, AGEN.

34. Sorin to Darboy, May 5, 1869, AGEN. Georges Darboy (1813–1871), archbishop of Paris since 1863, was shot to death by the Parisian Communards. See below.

multifarious were the obligations he had assumed. Much of the work he had to do was tedious, and much of it trivial.

Yet a good part of Sorin's genius was his willingness to deal with detail. Hence from France he dispatched back to Father Corby at Notre Dame du Lac "a big Frenchman worth his weight in gold and double that. . . . He is a regular baker, and an admirable one. Give him good flour and you will have bread worth eating. His name is Brother Simon: splendid health, excellent temper, and [a] good Religious." Nor did he refrain from interjecting himself into the affairs of the university of which he was no longer president: Brother Paul, whom he also assigned to Indiana, "is a first rate teacher of penmanship . . . and besides something of a musician." "Musicians are difficult to procure for a place like [Notre Dame]," and if Brother Paul did not do, there was always Brother Leopold, "very amiable with students, a model gentleman, and worthy of all confidence," who "would be the leader of the band." The general did not only commission fresh personnel to Corby, who was now the president and, under the new regime, local superior as well: "I send you a fine Velocipede which may serve as a model. Such is the furor of the people about this new invention I almost had to wait two months for getting one. The price is 250 francs, unpaid, for the good reason that my treasury is out." Disappointed in securing the Bordelais wine Corby wanted, Sorin considered his "promise [in this respect] . . . now redeemed in four boxes of cigars at one cent apiece. The first is always charming, but the second has no flavor." Nor did he forget the imperatives of contemporary piety: in consigning to Corby's solicitude a "trunk full of Relics," he insisted that care be taken in their distribution. "They have cost a large amount of money and immense expense in time for sixteen long years of exertion in Rome and here [Le Mans] for two years more."[35]

Not that Sorin neglected more urgent matters. He maintained the structure of governance he had inherited from Moreau—legislative chapters general and local, standing councils at each level, and an executive system ranging from himself at the top down to the lowliest household steward[36]—though he compressed its size and characteristically kept a firmer hand upon its operations. More pragmatic in policymaking and implementation than the Founder had been, if no less prone to arbitrariness, Father Sorin took pains to avoid the temper tantrums that had compromised so much of Moreau's administration. What would be called today interpersonal skills Sorin possessed in a far greater degree than did the often remote, formal Moreau. This does not mean that either man suffered fools gladly; but the younger of them did know, perhaps instinctively, how to soften

---

35. Sorin to Corby, November 28 and December 18, 1868, and February 18, 1869, AIP.
36. See chapter 19, above.

even a sharp reprimand with a gesture of warmth.[37] Perhaps also Sorin's robust physical health promoted the contrast between administrations, particularly when one assesses the ascetic Founder's latter years. Sorin's modus operandi in any case committed him to a long and vigorous daily schedule, as well as to the combination of an immense correspondence and incessant travel. He appeared to take it all in stride, until age caught up with him.

In putting together his team of high officials within the congregation Father Sorin, not unexpectedly, employed a sort of spoils system and rewarded priests whom he regarded as friends and allies. Victor Drouelle carried on as provincial in France, though that may have been a dubious favor; Alexis Granger was named provincial in Indiana; Nicolas Bardeau, a trusted if not an intimate lieutenant, was given the sensitive post of procurator general in Rome; and Pierre Chappé became one of the two assistant generals. The appointment of the second assistant general, however, showed that Sorin was capable of a certain Machiavellian shrewdness. Joseph Rézé, the longtime Holy Cross superior in Canada, was a man whom Sorin disliked and distrusted. To him a letter of special import was written from Le Mans in early February 1869.

Very Reverend dear Father, At a General Council held this morning, you were named assistant General to replace the late Reverend Patrick Dillon. This is a proof well deserved, be sure, of the confidence we place in your virtue, your ability, and your devotedness. The vote of this Council was unanimous in calling you to this office, and no one feels more happiness than I over your nomination. We are perfectly aware of the difficulty in replacing you at Saint-Laurent; we shall await your arrival here to proceed to the selection of your successor with [your] perfect knowledge in order to make a suitable choice.

It does not seem presumptuous to assume that Sorin's "happiness" had really to do with dislodging a seasoned opponent from the North American continent and immersing him in the chaotic French environment, where Champeau and Drouelle could be left to neutralize his potential for mischief. Sorin at any rate could not resist tweaking whatever *amour de soi* Rézé might have found endorsed by

---

37. For example, he quarreled with Timothy E. Howard, a lay member of the faculty at Notre Dame (see below), but when Howard and his wife lost a child, Sorin, then in Paris, wrote his condolences: "I do not know what to beg of you to convey to your excellent Mr. Howard for the loss he has sustained in his little family—my condolences and my congratulations: they have now an Angel Guardian to gaze from above upon every step of theirs on earth, and they have faith enough, both of them, to realize the Providential dispensation." Sorin to Corby, February 10, 1869, AIP.

this advancement: "Let no one in your Province, however, get excited over your promotion. Nowhere are we necessary to God." And then he added with a shameful lack of sincerity: "Notre Dame du Lac is better off since I left."[38]

Paramount of course to the anxieties of the new superior general was the question of the congregation's finances. In analyzing this crucial matter, there emerges the substantial irony that he who had been so often criticized in the past for careless bookkeeping exhibited in his present capacity the zeal of a certified accountant. "I am in receipt of your incomplete Statistics," he wrote Granger. "I much regret the delay which this must unavoidably occasion in my official report demanded nearly three weeks ago by his Eminence [Barnabò]." The stern admonishment of his oldest friend continued:

> I therefore beg of your Reverence, once for all, to make it clearly understood by all your Houses that an incomplete Statistic is no Statistic at all. I am bound to wait until [the accounts of] all the Establishments of the Province come in, or to report to Rome by name the Superiors who refuse to comply with one of the most important rules of the Congregation. I wait. If any House has been dispensed by me [as previous provincial] from the obligation of paying the Provincial House for Vestiary [sic], Stationery, and so forth (of which I have not the slightest remembrance), let it be now stopped forever.

And speaking of stationery, the general instructed the provincial to cease affixing excess postage to communications sent abroad: "Please procure light paper and light envelopes, and thus you can enclose three or four letters under a fifteen cent stamp without danger or injustice to your treasury."[39] Not even Peter Cooney, who enjoyed a justified reputation as a Civil War hero, was immune from accountant Sorin's probing inquiries. "What is Father Cooney doing?" he asked Corby, now that Cooney was a pastor in South Bend and so subject to the local superior at Notre Dame as immediate superior. "Has he no time to give me an answer to my question? I am very anxious to receive his Statistics."[40]

A tardy report from a little parish in South Bend was of course a minor irritant compared to the parlous financial condition of the French houses the superior general had to confront. He had contemplated for a while the possibility of floating a huge loan—up to a million francs ($200,000)—with Notre Dame du

38. Sorin to Rézé, February 7, 1869, AGEN.
39. Sorin to Granger, February 25, 1869, AIP.
40. Sorin to Corby, February 10, 1869, AIP.

Lac and St. Mary's as collateral.[41] He declined, however, to risk seeking the money in American capital markets, and the banking circles in the west of France were cool to the notion of investing their assets in mortgages held on property thousands of miles away. So, in the end, the idea foundered on this incompatibility, in accord perhaps with the biblical aphorism: Where a person's treasure is, there will his heart be also.[42] Whatever new responsibilities Edward Sorin had to take on as superior general, and however his style of governance had to accommodate to those responsibilities, his heart remained as firmly committed as before. "I may live in France as long as obedience and duty will require," he wrote from Paris on the last day of 1868, "but to consider myself happy, . . . no, never." Not that people had been unkind, and indeed to have revisited his boyhood home and "the few relatives time has spared me" had brought him "pleasure for a moment. But neither persons nor places here can distract my mind from the spots where . . . my best sentiments are centered." He knew where his real treasure lay.

> Notre Dame and St. Mary's, with their varied and delightful dependencies and associations, will forever stand paramount in my mind. . . . No people appear as happy as are the dear inmates of Notre Dame and St. Mary's. I find nowhere in France a little world of students as . . . at Notre Dame. Could I say less of St. Mary's? I may be blinded by affection, as parents are generally suspected to be, but thus far I am not conscious of it. The more I reason with myself for fear of being too partial in my appreciations of persons and places and things, the more clearly I see . . . that my preferences are well-grounded, and that my own very dear little family in the New World is the best entitled to my predilection and devotion. . . . Divine Providence has blessed us not only with local and temporal advantages . . . but also with spiritual and religious privileges. . . . It has blessed us with a spirit of devotedness and energy which will remain, I trust, as the characteristic feature of all the children of Holy Cross in America.[43]

AMONG THOSE CHILDREN one group was fast approaching a definitive solution to a long-standing crisis, though not without much distress. Early in 1867 Rome finally approved the Constitutions of the Marianite Sisters sub-

---

41. See Sorin to Raguideau, January 18, 1869, AGEN. M. Raguideau had been for many years Sainte-Croix's legal consultant.

42. Matthew 6:21.

43. Sorin, *Circular Letters*, 1: 7.

mitted by Basile Moreau four years earlier. The Founder, so recently removed from the headship of the men of Holy Cross, was confirmed as the sisters' superior—something of a consolation prize in the midst of his troubles. With typical bureaucratic hauteur, Propaganda also waved away all the interim arrangements put in place since Father Charles Moreau's hapless Visitation to America in 1862,[44] and ordered that a general chapter be held in New York under the presidency of Archbishop John McCloskey,[45] at which the Constitutions were to be formally promulgated and a new mother general elected. This meeting, dominated by French-speaking delegates, was duly held in June 1867. The doughty Mother Angela Gillespie, though she understood French too, was nevertheless a minority of one. When she presented to the chapter a petition signed by 132 sisters, which requested, in effect, that the Indiana Province be granted autonomy for a ten-year experimental period, McCloskey ruled the motion out of order. The chapter's majority then reacted by passing a resolution stating that "should, God forbid, our very dear Sisters of the Indiana Province persist in their refusal to [accept the Constitutions in their entirety], we wish them to be no longer considered as belonging to the Congregation of the Marianites of Holy Cross."[46] Whether the vote represented a challenge or a gesture of surrender to the inevitable, it appeared that a solution of sorts was within sight—and particularly so since Mother Angela had taken the precaution to entrust a copy of her petition to Bishop Luers, who forwarded it along with his own plea for separation to Propaganda. "They *must have* what they ask for," he said flatly.[47]

As usual the Roman tribunal proceeded slowly. In the interval, Edward Sorin, temporarily in residence at Sainte-Croix as superior general, found the nuns there bitterly estranged from him. One of them indeed tried to cite him in civil court for an alleged debt to her of 2,000 francs. "They want to make a scandal and destroy me and all I have in hand here and in America," he told Mother Angela. "To put an end to their mischievous designs among the Sisters . . . in our Province, let the Council adopt the following measure, to be submitted to and sanctioned by the Apostolic Delegate [Luers]: that every message coming from the Marianites of Le Mans be at once enclosed in a clean envelope and sent back as a letter, *unpaid*, to Mother General. They want money and not a little of it, and disturbance." But a more personal word needed saying too. As her friend and spiritual

---

44. See chapters 22–24, above.

45. Archbishop John Hughes, Sorin's opponent, died in 1864.

46. Costin, *Priceless Spirit*, 204–206.

47. Luers to Purcell, June 8, 1867, AIP (Sorin papers). Purcell was then in Rome, and Luers prefaced the remark in the text: "Please say a good word to Cardinal Barnabò in favor of the Sisters of the Holy Cross here."

director, he realized that Angela, for all her courage and talent, was still passing through her own dark night of the soul, but he also appreciated her worth and her unique importance: "As for you, my dear child, be ever and everywhere a circuit of union, a conciliating adviser, full of wisdom and moderation, as also of confidence in God's Providence; do not fret overmuch."[48]

The spirit of conciliation he recommended, however, had to do with "the great commotion" that uncertainty had bred within the community at St. Mary's, not with the Marianite general administration.[49] Assuaging the feelings of the nuns he encountered in Le Mans did not figure very prominently in his official communiqué to Propaganda, a document he dispatched in support of the bishop of Fort Wayne's earlier appeal for dissolution. "As for the Sisters in America," he wrote Barnabò,

> it is necessary to observe that the conduct, especially in recent months, of Reverend Father Moreau has so pained and scandalized them that it will take a generation before they could contemplate the possibility of a continuing union with Le Mans. They realize that the whole central administration of the Marianites is so permeated with sentiments of hatred and vengeance of the Reverend Father and of Monsieur [sic] Charles Moreau, his nephew. They will therefore not consent to any connection or rapprochement with the Sisters of France, at least not *today*. In order better to grasp this repugnance which the madness of the Reverend Fathers Moreau has rendered for the moment *invincible*, one must understand the American temperament. It naturally dislikes trouble and vexation of the kind Father Moreau scatters around himself perpetually; with him there is no repose. But in America, where everything in religion has to be created anew, we need peace. Otherwise attentions are diverted and good will (*bonheur*) flies over the Community's walls. With [Moreau] the nuns have witnessed nothing but frivolous changes, abandonment of foundations, battles with bishops and espionage against priests, and have experienced dissensions at home and reproaches abroad. Once relieved of this yoke, they will live in harmony, succeed brilliantly, enjoy the esteem of the hierarchy, the clergy, and the public, and see open before them a magnificent future.

If Sorin in this indictment conveniently forgot his own frequent "battles with bishops," he spoke now with the assurance that with the maturity experi-

---

48. Sorin to Mother Angela, December 2, 1868, and January 10, 1869, AGEN.
49. See Sorin to Granger, December 9, 1868, AGEN.

ence had given him he had managed to mend most of his episcopal fences and, more importantly, that the sisters in Indiana, almost to a woman, supported him. But in case the cardinal-prefect were to judge this proposed secession too radical, the superior general offered, if not conciliation now, the inducement of a possible reconciliation at some later date. "The personal animosities will disappear with the present generation, and then, with the calming of passions, one may see a more advantageous occasion for *a reunion;* but if there is to be a chance for *an ultimate reunion,* it seems today more opportune that there be . . . complete independence between the *French* and the *English* communities." Mother Angela, seconded by Bishop Luers, had requested a ten-year trial during which Indiana would go its own way, as would Le Mans with Canada and New Orleans in tow. "In ten years time," Sorin concluded, "let Propaganda judge which of the two has more vitality and which had better fulfilled its mission."[50] He had little doubt as to how that judgment would fall, at the present or in the future. As he expressed it in terms he would not have used with Barnabò: "Father Moreau would prefer to devastate [the nuns' ministry in] America by re-establishing the government of his four cooks, his washerwomen, menders, and seamstresses. God forbid!"[51]

During the spring of 1869, the pope gave formal approval to the reappointment of Mother Seven Dolors as general of the Marianite Sisters, with Father Moreau as titular superior. Ten weeks later the petition for autonomy presented by the bishop of Fort Wayne was also ruled upon favorably. Father Sorin was promptly named superior by Luers, who, still apostolic delegate, continued as the ultimate authority over the nuns of Indiana. Sorin busied himself putting together a set of constitutions for his sisters. In July the provincial chapter met at St. Mary's. "[The] Constitutions for the use of the Sisters belonging to this Province," read the chapter's minutes, "[have been] already examined by the [local] Council, but it now remained [that they] be examined and voted by the Chapter. Therefore it was necessary to know if the members preferred to be reunited with France or to form a Community by themselves by the adoption of said Constitutions. The secret votes being taken, the separation was unanimously agreed upon."[52] So, after years of tumult and shouting, the Congregation of the Sisters of *the* Holy Cross became a reality on a quiet summer afternoon.

A few messy details still required clarification. Several sisters resident for some years in the Canadian province petitioned for reentry into Indiana. Sorin

---

50. "Quelques observations sur la question des Soeurs," Sorin to Barnabò, n.d. [January 1869] AGEN.

51. Sorin to Bardeau, December 17, 1868, AGEN.

52. Quoted in Costin, *Priceless Spirit,* 207.

promised that if their "return" were endorsed by Rome, "they will be received cordially." Also unresolved was the claim by the "washerwomen" of Le Mans that money was owed them by their former colleagues at St. Mary's. The amount was not large, especially when compared to the overall debt Sorin had to contend with, but he refused to pay it until Propaganda eventually insisted. "We will honor [this debt]" in due time, he observed. Nevertheless, "[Propaganda's decision] does not give them the right to be paid immediately. It is a debt in equity, religious rather than legal."[53] Meanwhile, "the Decree of Separation has earned [Barnabò] eternal gratitude. Perfect peace reigns in our Province. [The nuns'] joy is inexpressible. They now operate eighteen establishments. They enjoy an excellent reputation among their pupils. They owe . . . their most encouraging future to the blessing of Heaven and of the Holy See."[54]

IT WAS NOT UNUSUAL in the Catholic rhetoric of the mid-nineteenth century to rank the munificence of the Holy See only slightly less than that of heaven. This protocol reflected the real clerical world, and Edward Sorin, ever a realist—even if a somewhat emotional one—accepted it without a second thought. During his tenure as superior general of Holy Cross he traveled to the eternal city no less than twenty times, and a large percentage of his correspondence was directed either to his agent in Rome or to the prefect of Propaganda himself—Barnabò till his death in 1874 and Cardinals Siméoni and Franchi afterward. Sorin understood perfectly well that the curia was a bureaucracy much like any other and had to be dealt with as such. But his employment of *Realpolitik* in his relations with Roman officials did not diminish his veneration for the person of the pope, which, if anything, was intensified by the political maelstrom which was about to envelop the pontiff.

By the time the sisters in chapter cast their unanimous vote for separation, July 1869, Father Sorin had been back in Indiana for about six weeks. He had stopped at Montreal first and had succeeded, he believed, in "raising the spirits" of the personnel in that mission—an implicit rebuke to the now departed Rézé. Once at home, various administrative items, most of them routine, required his attention. One of them, however, was a matter of future consequence: "Happily, I have been able to prevent the construction of the new railroad line across

53. Sorin to Battista, December 7, 1871, and Sorin to Siméoni, January 8, 1870, AGEN. Ferdinando Battista or Prebrobattista was Bardeau's successor as Holy Cross procurator general in Rome (see chapter 26, below). Archbishop Siméoni was secretary and later prefect of Propaganda.

54. Sorin to Barnabò, September 16 and 17, 1869, AGEN.

this property, and so Notre Dame du Lac will preserve its principal charm, its solitude."[55]

The charm at this time was shared by about 600 people altogether, with another couple of hundred across the lakes at St. Mary's. At Notre Dame, the number of boarding students fluctuated somewhat, especially during the Civil War, but steadied out to between three and four hundred afterward. In addition were the fifty apprentices attached to the Manual Labor School, and twenty-five or so boys of grammar school age—the minims—now under the charge of the sisters. The student body represented many states of the union, though by far the largest contingents hailed from Illinois and Indiana. The only pupil who verged on celebrity came from New Mexico Territory. A grateful Father Sorin had promised William T. Sherman that any boy the general recommended would be educated at Notre Dame *gratis,* and Sherman designated the son of his friend, famed mountain-man Kit Carson; unhappily, the younger Carson could not meet even the rather loose standards then required and soon drifted away.[56] For collegians without benefit of such largesse the cost of attendance varied with the state of the national economy; for President Corby, however, the fiscal situation varied little: "Money is very scarce, *east* and *west.*"[57] In 1870, as reported in the student magazine, board and tuition stood at $150, added to which, inevitably, were a collection of special fees: $5 for matriculation, $10 for special language instruction (including Gaelic), $12.50 for training in instrumental music, $10 for use of a piano and $2 for a violin, $5 for use of "Philosophical and Chemical Apparatus," and $10 for a diploma. If a student wished to stay on campus during the summer holiday, the charge was $35. "*Payments to be made invariably in advance.*"[58] It need hardly be said that admission was entirely open.

The university was gradually coming of age. The number of instructors, religious and lay, had risen to the mid-thirties. As Patrick Dillon had introduced programs in commerce and science, so President Corby gave emphasis to the study of languages and to musical performance.[59] A law school was inaugurated in the fall term of 1869, with an ambitious curriculum engaging the three students

---

55. Sorin to Barnabò, September 16, 1869, AGEN.

56. See Stanley P. Hirshon, *White Tecumseh: A Biography of William T. Sherman* (New York, 1997), 337.

57. Corby to Sorin, January 11, 1869, AIP.

58. *The Notre Dame Scholastic, Devoted to the Interests of the Students,* 4 (November 24, 1870): 7. The early *Scholastic* bore a motto on its masthead of which Sorin would have approved or, indeed, he may have inspired it: "Labor Omnia Vincit."

59. The whole issue of the *Scholastic,* 3 (October 30, 1869), was devoted to music on campus.

and two professors: "Ethics; Constitutional and International Law; Common Law in all its divisions; the Law of Contracts; Criminal Law; the Law of Evidence, Pleading, and Practice."[60] In conjunction with the observance of the institution's silver jubilee the same year, an alumni association was formed and promptly chose Corby as its director. Indeed, the priests kept a firm control over all Notre Dame organizations, including those of the students, which proliferated at the end of the 1860s. Thus Auguste Lemonnier, university vice president (and Sorin's nephew), directed the St. Edward's Literary Association. Other societies included the St. Cecilia Philomathean Association, which sponsored debates. On October 8 and 15, 1870, the question before the house was, "Resolved, That the Indians possess a right to the soil;" this issue "was pretty ably and forcibly [sic] discussed," and the affirmative side prevailed.[61] The Philharmonic Society vied with the Orchestra and choir for the allegiance of those musically inclined. The Thespian Society also flourished, producing in the fall of 1869 an original play written by Professor Arthur Stace and entitled "The Enchanted Hostelry." At the same time the St. Aloysius Philodemic Association, with its library of 300 books of "history, poetry, and general literature," attracted a considerable membership.[62] The recording secretary of this group, incidentally, was a youth destined to achieve great prominence at Notre Dame and in the scholarly world at large. In 1867 John Augustine Zahm, an Ohio native whose aunt was a nun at St. Mary's, had indicated a serious interest in joining the Holy Cross community. Sorin replied to the teenager's inquiry in a manner fully characteristic: "As you seem so anxious to come and try yourself here, I am willing to accept your offer, namely, on your paying $50 to keep you for five months in the College. You may come any time your parents will deem it expedient."[63]

Young Zahm and his contemporaries did not spend all their spare time and energy debating "forcibly" or attending structured meetings. Boat races were held regularly on St. Joseph's Lake. In the spring "base-ball" [sic] games predominated among various athletic pursuits. In one contest the Star of the East club defeated Juanita 38 to 24, scoring eight runs in the second, third, and seventh innings; the winners were awarded a barrel of apples, donated by one of the brothers.[64] The students participated too in those highly formal occasions, religious

60. *Scholastic*, 4 (January 22, 1870): 5.

61. *Scholastic*, 4 (October 22, 1870): 7.

62. *Scholastic*, 3 (October 2, 1869): 11.

63. Sorin to Zahm, November 14, 1867, AUND, CAZA, "Albert Zahm Collection." See also the excellent study, Ralph E. Weber, *Notre Dame's John Zahm, American Catholic Apologist and Educator* (Notre Dame, Ind., 1961).

64. *Scholastic*, 4 (March 25, 1871): 7.

and civic, so much favored in the middle of the nineteenth century. October 13, the feast of St. Edward—Sorin's name-day—was always marked by a convocation with long and flowery speeches, stout avowals of patriotism and manly piety, and the rendering of music by Rossini or some other fashionable composer—and with a better than usual meal. Commencement exercises, or the "distribution of prizes" as Sorin insisted on calling them, were events conspicuous for pomp and circumstance at St. Mary's no less than at Notre Dame. In June of 1871, an "interesting exhibition" was on view during graduation ceremonies at what the editors of the *Scholastic* called "St. Mary's Female Academy." A "Crown of Honor was bestowed by last year's winner, Eleanor Ewing, on her good friend Hattie Neil of St. Louis. We saw the personification of virtuous beauty crowning her twin sister." Several short plays were then performed by the students followed by a tableau depicting "Isabella [of Castile] surrounded by Faith, Hope, and Charity, crowned by the Angel of the New World; [it] was in good taste and much admired." The commencement orator, a politician from Iowa without a gift for metaphor, "congratulated the sisters and students for the richest intellectual repasts he had ever witnessed."[65]

Over all these and related activities Edward Sorin presided with paternal satisfaction. Little wonder he insisted that the genius of Holy Cross had flowered in the New World as it withered away in the Old. When his duties as superior general summoned him back to France in late October 1869, the comparison was effectively brought home to him. Seeing him off was a convocation featuring laudatory addresses from representatives of the three academic departments—senior (collegiate), junior, and the minims—followed by a musical *soirée,* and his return the following March precipitated a similar celebration.[66] Indeed, in the midst of his own establishments he enjoyed an esteem that bordered on veneration. As one enthusiastic student writer put it in a sketch of the history of Notre Dame: "Father Sorin still lives, thank God, and long may he live! His deeds already accomplished and those hereafter to be done need another to recount them. The feeble pen which traces these lines were [sic] not worthy to reveal in full the life of Father Sorin."[67]

The external prosperity of Notre Dame—its new and refurbished buildings, its swelling numbers, its student societies with pretentious names like "Philodemic" and "Philomathean"—in which its founder took justifiable pride, did not, however, tell the whole story. The internal weaknesses of the institution had

---

65. *Scholastic,* 4 (June 28, 1871): 2–4.

66. *Scholastic,* 3 (October 30, 1869): 31.

67. *Scholastic,* 4 (January 8, 1870): 65–66. (The first three volumes of the *Scholastic* employed continuous pagination.)

been laid out for Father Sorin the same year that John Zahm had applied for admission to Holy Cross. Timothy Edward Howard had been a student at Notre Dame during the late 1850s. He had enlisted in the Union army at the beginning of the Civil War and had been severely wounded at the battle of Shiloh. Physically unable to continue his military service, he had returned to Notre Dame as an instructor, in which capacity he discerned much that he judged amiss. This young alumnus—destined for a distinguished career as professor, historian,[68] South Bend city councilman, and state senator, and toward the end of his life chief justice of the Indiana supreme court—did not hold back. "Very Reverend Father Provincial (as Sorin was in 1867)," he wrote,

> Notre Dame is *apparently* prosperous, that is, so far as the physical or *material* is concerned—fine buildings, great numbers of students, and so forth. I will go further and say that as a *school* it is prosperous. But it claims to be a *college*, even a university, and the public tacitly acknowledges the claim. Now from books, reviews, and the like, I know about what a first class College is in America, France, England, Germany and Italy. From personal experience I know that the University of Michigan is pronounced lately, on high authority, to be one of the first of the literary institutions of America.

Howard had been born in Ann Arbor and had served in a Michigan regiment during the war.

> I ought also to know Notre Dame very well, and I am sorry to say that, as a college, it is not successful. . . . Study is superficial; there is scarcely an attempt made to follow the course as laid down in the catalogue. Students study about what branches they please, and those knowing Latin and mental philosophy have been graduated with very little attention to their knowledge of Greek of the natural sciences.[69]

The fault lay primarily, however, not with the students but in the manner in which the faculty had been organized.

---

68. See his *History of St. Joseph County*, 2 vols. (Chicago, 1907), often cited in these pages.

69. Howard in later life published a collection of poetry, in which he romanticized "The Student." "Alone he toiled from vespers' fading light / Until midnight boomed upon his startled ear. / But reason slowly waking soon the cloud / Passed o'er him and he breathed once more aloud. / And then beneath the trembling taper's light / He sought the hazy figures of the night; / And, as he glanced along the hard-wrought scroll, / He felt the life leap proudly in his soul." Timothy Edward Howard, *Musings and Memories* (Chicago, 1905), 62.

My agreement says I am "to teach such classes as are assigned to me"; accordingly I am trying to teach *five* different sciences: Astronomy, Rhetoric, Geometry and Trigonometry, Latin, and Conic Sections. Now I venture to say that no one, no matter how great his talent or how learned he may be, can do full justice to sciences requiring such opposite qualities of mind. Nor can any college ever become remarkable for its scholarship which demands such unnatural and overstrained exertions on the part of its teachers.

Attrition among the matriculated student body was, for Howard, both a sign and an effect of what was radically wrong with Notre Dame: "We do not keep our students, consequently have no graduates who can take their place beside those of other colleges. Next year we shall have very few of our present students." Howard had tried to make this same case when Patrick Dillon was president, "but he was then building this house [the main building], and I suppose did not have time to give due consideration to the subject, though he said that he knew everything I said was true." And anyway Howard understood that no combination of Corbys or Dillons held the reins of genuine power. "Perhaps, Very Reverend Father, I have said too much, but I say it only to you, and I think it better to do that than to run down the institution behind your back."

> I should like to feel that Notre Dame were equal to her reputation. There is a magnificent prospect for this to become a great Catholic university, but we are losing ground every day, . . . in spite of our wonderful *material* progress. . . . We need now not so much to improve the external as the internal, to classify students and professors, to arrange and *follow* a course of study for each department. It is a standing rebuke that we have not better scholarship. . . . Good scholars are more necessary to a College than elegant buildings, and Notre Dame has spared no pains on the latter.[70]

Father Sorin, so accustomed to the adulation of those around him, did not much appreciate the candor of Timothy Howard's lengthy manifesto, and at the end of the spring semester of 1867 the young man's contract was not renewed. The termination, however, was not due merely to personal pique. For Sorin the "elegant buildings" that Howard disdained held an almost sacramental significance, the outward expression of all the blood and sweat and tears that had been expended in constructing them. The "elegant buildings" carved out of the wilderness, and the museum and the telescope and the printing press, these "material"

---

70. Howard to Sorin, January 22, 1867, AIP.

objects had won the public acknowledgment Howard referred to and so had made possible all the accomplishments of Holy Cross in America. It must be borne in mind moreover that Sorin's formal education had been restricted to French seminaries thirty years before. He was never really an academic or an intellectual, in the rarefied sense in which those terms are normally employed. Nor did he ever entirely comprehend the essential difference between a boarding school and a university.[71] He was a missionary, and a spectacularly masterful one, who had realized from the beginning, at Black Oak Ridge, that the foundation of a flourishing *collège* was the key to the success of the broader mission, not only as a source of financial support, but also as congruent with the aspirations of his fellow American Catholics.

Yet he did not toss aside Timothy Howard's long letter; he filed it and pondered over it. Perhaps he recalled from more than two decades earlier the peripatetic Michael Shawe, whose garrulousness had annoyed him but to whom he had entrusted the arrangement of Notre Dame's first intelligible curriculum, simply because Shawe knew more about such matters than anyone else available.[72] As Sorin was realist enough to understand that his Roman superiors had to be accommodated and flattered, so upon reflection, however absolutist his instincts, he knew he had to draw from his subjects the best that was in them, to take advantage of skills he did not possess himself. In 1869 he welcomed Howard back to Notre Dame and appointed him professor in the new law school. Howard for his part, though his principles and youthful ardor were undimmed, had undergone a change of heart, having reflected himself during the two-year interval and so having grasped something of the burden Sorin had to carry. "I cannot find words to express gratitude for your kindness," he wrote. "I shall endeavor by attention to my studies and to the classes you will be good enough to give me to show how thankful I am for your kindness."[73] Notre Dame was the clear winner, as the quest for maturity continued.

---

71. See the comments in Hope, *Notre Dame,* 167.
72. See chapter 12, above.
73. Howard to Sorin, November 10, 1868, AIP. See also Hope, *Notre Dame,* 306–307.

chapter twenty-six

On the Apostolic Trail

E DWARD SORIN, AS HE CROSSED THE ATLANTIC
from New York to Brest in November of 1869, was contemplating the kind of structural and personnel changes within the
Congrégation de Sainte-Croix he could introduce to shape it according to his own
expectations. Traveling with him was Father Ferdinando Battista, lately a theology
instructor at Notre Dame, and now slated to replace Nicolas Bardeau as Holy
Cross's Roman agent. Bardeau had died suddenly the previous September—"a
serious loss," said Sorin, "oh! I regret his loss immensely."[1] The decree of Propaganda confirming the decisions reached at the extraordinary general chapter the
year before had ordered that the motherhouse of the order be transferred from
bankrupt Le Mans to Paris. But Battista's appointment was only one small signal
of the fact that the central administration would be from now located wherever
the superior general happened to reside, and this was most often in Indiana. "I
believe I save and serve bigger interests here than I could have done at Le Mans,"
as he put it to a friend.[2] This did not sit well with his erstwhile allies, Victor
Drouelle and Louis Champeau, who, after all the intrigue they had engaged in
previous years, expected the prize of a loud voice in the order's affairs. They were
in for disappointment.

---

1. Sorin to Sister Columba, September 25, 1869, AGEN. See also the *Scholastic,* 3 (October 30,
1869): 31. Battista could not be named procurator general, as the students at Notre Dame thought,
since that office was in the gift of the general chapter. Sorin therefore asked Barnabò to allow "our
dear Father Ferdinando" to perform the functions of procurator general "without assuming the title."
See Sorin to Barnabò, November 13, 1869, AGEN.

2. Sorin to Sister Columba, September 25, 1869, AGEN.

Sorin went to Paris first and then to Le Mans and then back to Paris, where on December 10 he convened a meeting of the general council, composed of his assistant superiors, Chappé and Rézé, and the other officers of the central administration, priests, and brothers. The crucial item on Sorin's agenda reflected his determination to liquidate the remainder of the debt still crushing the French houses. He took some justifiable satisfaction in announcing that he had shortly before solved at least one of the order's financial embarrassments: "I am happy to have been able [from American sources] to send a payment of 70,000 francs to Father Chappé and so prevent the sale of our magnificent church in Le Mans to shopkeepers who might well have profaned it."[3] But, he told the members of the council, this was only a first faltering step in a process bound to try the patience and the endurance of the whole congregation. He therefore proposed a radical approach to the problem, "a grave measure which the general council unanimously endorsed and which seems required by actual circumstances."

> After having examined the paucity of subjects, especially among our priests [he explained to Cardinal Barnabò], the Council inquired whether the Superior General, aided by his Councilors, could not, at least for the time being, administer directly the Province of France, without harming the government of the Congregation at large. It was said in the discussion that professed members of the said Province would be favorably inclined to this proposal, in the implementation of which they envision an economy in personnel and expense. Moreover, the Congregation would enjoy another advantage, that the indispensable reforms would be more readily welcomed and more surely executed.

"I myself believe this is the proper course to follow," he added disingenuously, as though the idea had not been his in the first place. "For the present, the Congregation has more to gain than to lose from it. It is not a permanent alteration but only a *momentary suspension* of the provincial administration in France for the reasons already described."[4] The strategy adopted served its purpose, mostly because Sorin gave first priority to settling the outstanding French debt and never flagged in imposing ruthless economies on his French brethren and in seeking donors wherever he could find them. By the time normal administration was restored, the debt had been paid off in full.[5]

---

3. Sorin to Barnabò, September 16, 1869, AGEN.
4. Sorin to Barnabò, January 18, 1870, AGEN.
5. Even the invariably and relentlessly biased Catta acknowledged this achievement. See Catta, *Moreau*, 2: 1018.

Many persons, religious and lay, aided in this effort. One of the first was the indefatigable Mother Angela Gillespie, who during the early months of 1870 collected $4,000 from her friends and dispatched the money off to Sorin in Paris.[6] Louis Champeau demonstrated his personal generosity by signing over without condition funds that had come to him in an inheritance.[7] He received a return on his investment, so to speak, by being named at the December 10 meeting to replace Father Chappé as first assistant general. Even so, Sorin qualified this promotion with the significant proviso that it involved "no change in his actual functions"—that is, Champeau, despite his new title, would simply continue as superior in Paris. The inoffensive Chappé became the French province's master of novices, of whom there were lamentably few. Alexis Granger, a similarly ineffective administrator, "having asked to be relieved from the responsibilities of his charge," gave over his post as provincial in the United States to William Corby. "Release me from every superiority," Granger had pleaded, in view of "my little aptitude for government."[8] Corby in turn was succeeded as president of Notre Dame by August Lemonnier, Sorin's gifted nephew. Clearly this administrative reorganization and shuffle in leadership was calculated to reinforce Father Sorin's authority. And odd man out was Victor Drouelle, now that the superior general was to govern the French province directly. Sorin explained smoothly that Drouelle had to be kept in reserve; if Propaganda declined to accept Father Battista as Holy Cross agent in Rome, then he would resume his former post there as procurator general. In fact Sorin did not intend to allow the ever-restless Drouelle to indulge in the kind of bureaucratic maneuver employed against Moreau, and so the bitter estrangement between the two old friends and allies began.[9]

By the beginning of the new year of 1870, when these changes were promulgated, Sorin had made his way to Rome, an almost ritualistic practice now and for the rest of his career. He was scarcely settled at St. Bridget's—still unsold—when a courier delivered to him a communication just received at Propaganda from Le Mans. It appeared that Basile Moreau, now living outside community, was suffering from a scruple that doing so might contravene his vow of poverty. Not that the Founder had abandoned his austere and Spartan style of life in the mean little house he shared with his aged sisters on the rue de la Presche;[10] but

6. See Sorin to Battista, February 19, 1870, AGEN.

7. Champeau's contribution eventually amounted to the very large sum of 80,000 francs. See Sorin to Battista, August 29, 1971, AGEN.

8. Granger to Sorin, March 1, 1870, AIP.

9. Sorin to "Reverend Fathers and dear Brothers in Christ," January 25, 1870, AGEN.

10. See chapter 25, above.

at more than three score years and ten he could not easily cease to be a man who honored the letter of the law almost as much as the spirit. He therefore inquired of Archbishop Siméoni, the secretary of Propaganda, whether he should seek a dispensation, and Siméoni forwarded his question to St. Bridget's. Sorin immediately penned a terse reply. "Very Reverend Father," he wrote, "I have heard from Propaganda that you have requested it to issue you a strange dispensation, and I am charged to ask you to tell me what exactly you are asking for, so that I can then support it to the degree that it depends upon me."[11] But Moreau did not deign to bargain with his rebellious son. Instead he addressed Siméoni again, and this time through the sarcasm all the hurt and bitter remembrances shone through.

> I have had the honor to ask you, Monseigneur, to communicate to me the decrees of the *strange* Chapter of St. Bridget's [of 1868], . . . and I have waited in vain for fifteen months. Further, I have asked for your authorization to apply to my confessor for permission I could need with regard to the fulfillment of my vow of poverty, if indeed it still exists. If to obtain a response I must resort to the good will (*obligeance*) of the Very Reverend Father Sorin, I shall withdraw my request and shall adhere to my vows in accord with the doctrine of St. Thomas [Aquinas] and St. [Alphonsus] Liguori. As to the *strangeness* of my question, it ought not surprise our new Superior General if he remembers what is recorded in our registers, that in 1853 he applied to the Bishop of Vincennes in order to obtain, and did obtain in effect, his independence from the general administration of our congregation for a period of five years, and this unknown to me or even to the members of his own community.[12]

Basile Moreau maintained to his dying day that he forgave those he judged to have injured him; if so, he did not forget either. In this sad instance at any rate Sorin appeared to have read more into the Founder's inquiry than had been intended. "Eminence," he wrote Barnabò, "After having reflected, prayed, and consulted about the request of the Very Reverend Father Moreau for a partial dispensation from his vows, we believe that supporting this request would fulfill a duty toward him and toward the Congregation, in the sense that he seems to in-

---

11. Sorin to Moreau, January 3, 1870, AGEN.

12. Moreau to Siméoni, January 9, 1870, AGEN. For Sorin's "unauthorized" request for a dispensation, see chapter 16, above.

dicate at the end of his letter, that is to say, a total dispensation from all connection with and all duties toward the Congregation."[13]

WHEN FATHER SORIN ARRIVED IN ROME, the First Council of the Vatican was already in session.[14] As general of a male religious order, he might have secured some minor consultative function within the conciliar structure had he so desired, but he was too much taken up with the current parlous state of that order to concern himself with the issues that absorbed the fathers of the council. Besides, those issues, important as they were, held scant interest for him; the relation of faith and reason or the problem of the oriental churches' relations with the West weighed little with the missionary from Indiana who was trying to pay off a huge debt in France. As for the overriding question under debate, Edward Sorin's simple faith had long before assented to the pope's infallibility, and he needed no sophisticated deliberations to shore up that conclusion. As always, when he arrived in Rome, he presented the pope with a small offering and a declaration of loyalty. "What I give your Holiness is a mite," he said on this occasion, "but it is an alms proffered by souls richer in faith and love toward the infallible Vicar of Jesus Christ than all the goods in the world."[15]

Several bishops in attendance at the council, including Pierre Dufal back from Bengal, stayed at St. Bridget's, but Sorin, aside from the normal courtesies, for the most part had little to do with them. An exception was Bishop Fillion of Le Mans, who was housed nearby, and with him, still a key player in the affairs of Holy Cross, Sorin did consult on several occasions.[16] He also sought an audience with one of the dominant figures in the council, the English Archbishop Manning.[17] At the urging of Neal Gillespie who, as editor of the *Ave Maria,* was anxious to extend the sale of his magazine into the United Kingdom, Father Sorin arranged a brief and apparently successful meeting with the former Anglican archdeacon: "The Most Reverend Archbishop Manning could hardly refuse his approbation, and I know it will go very far towards increasing the circulation of

---

13. Sorin to Barnabò, January 15, 1870, AGEN. It is extremely doubtful that Moreau requested complete severance from Holy Cross, as Sorin interpreted "the end of his [original] letter" to Propaganda. But that letter is not extant. See Catta, *Moreau,* 2: 969–970.

14. The council met from December 8, 1869 until it adjourned *sine die* on July 19, 1870.

15. Sorin to Pius IX, n.d. [January, 1870], AGEN.

16. Sorin to Sister Columba, January 18, 1870, AGEN.

17. Henry Edward Manning (1808–1892) became a Catholic in 1851. In 1865 he was appointed archbishop of Westminster and in 1875 a cardinal.

the Ave."[18] One other episcopal contact made in Rome, confirming negotiations initiated a few months before, brought about in time far-reaching results. Claude-Marie Dubuis, a French-born missionary now bishop of Galveston—his diocese then included most of the state of Texas[19]—was eager to obtain personnel to staff his *collège*, which had had to close at the beginning of the Civil War. The institution could revive and prosper, Dubuis's chancellor had maintained, under the aegis of "the society that has done so well at Notre Dame."[20] Sorin had regretfully replied that he lacked the resources to undertake the project. During their conversation in the eternal city—while the world watched the swirling disputation over infallibility—the bishop raised his modest proposal again and in person, and Sorin listened now with more sympathy.[21]

Indeed, back in Paris at the beginning of February, Father Sorin's thoughts were, as ever, concentrated primarily on matters American—if not specifically upon Texas, then certainly upon the center and fountainhead of his mission. "I am always anxious to hear from Notre Dame," he wrote impatiently to William Corby. "A week without a letter is all I can bear. I hope everything goes on as usual. . . . How much I would prefer to take the sea at Brest rather than remain here. Thus we go, not where we wish but where God directs." Nor did he, when far away, refrain from micro-management. Be sure, he instructed Corby, that bills accrued by the sisters at St. Mary's for such services as doctors' visits and shoe-repair be paid by Notre Dame. He keenly missed, he said, "the honorable members of the Faculty and . . . your excellent students."[22] At the Parisian headquarters—or more precisely at the suburb of Neuilly-sur-Seine, where Holy Cross had relocated its *collège*—he attended the heap of business that had accumulated since his departure for Rome. Most of it was of small importance, though taken together it defined the sort of preoccupation that would be his throughout his tenure as superior general. Complex negotiation with a pious French noblewoman about a property transfer—which in the end came to nothing—occupied much of his attention.[23] So did the irritating persistence of the financial claims against the Indiana Province brought by the Marianite Sisters in Le Mans.[24] Meanwhile, as he

18. Sorin to Battista, February 19, 1870, AGEN.

19. The diocese of Galveston was established in 1847. In 1870 it included all of the state of Texas except El Paso County in the far west, which remained under the jurisdiction of the Vicariate of Santa Fé, New Mexico Territory.

20. Chambodut to Sorin, August 26, 1869, AIP.

21. See William Dunn, *St. Edward's University: A Centennial History* (Austin, 1986), 2–5.

22. Sorin to Corby, October 5 and December 22, 1869, AIP.

23. See Sorin to La Baronesse de Béville, February 6, 10, 21, and 22, 1870, AGEN.

24. See Sorin to Siméoni, January 8, 1870, AGEN. See chapter 25, above.

waited for word whether or not Propaganda wanted him to return to Rome, alarming reports came from America about sickness and death at Notre Dame and St. Mary's. Characteristically he exaggerated their import—"the last news from Notre Dame is even worse"; "panic has erupted there and for three days every message has urged me to return without delay in order to calm spirits and restore confidence"[25]—and so, at the end of February 1870, he took ship for home.

His stay there, however, did not last long. He did indeed find severe illness within the community—three of the brothers died in succession shortly after Sorin's return[26]—though it remains a mystery why he estimated that the "panic" involved cost $20,000 which he could otherwise have allotted to the French debt.[27] His most important function during this brief interval in Indiana was a formal Visitation of St. Mary's. The inspection, begun on May 4, left the superior more than satisfied. "After seeing as [spiritual] director every member of the community," he reported, "and examining for more than two months the state of the Institution, comparing [its condition] year-to-year since 1865, we feel safe to say that the present standing of the House is, owing to God's blessing and the devotedness of the Sisters, in general far more satisfactory than at any previous epoch of its existence." Some establishments he had not had time to visit in person, and to these he sent Mother Angela as his delegate: "We are happy to state that the same spirit of devotedness has been blessed everywhere in like manner." Therefore, "we recommend . . . as few changes as possible, if any at all." Nevertheless, amidst the usual reassertion of the nuns' duty to practice economy and regularity in their pious practices, he issued two directives which revealed the fine hand of Angela Gillespie: "The manual labor of the Novitiate shall be reduced, . . . even if outside help has to be procured, in favor of studies"; and "No Sister should be employed in teaching class or music more than six hours per day. Any disregard of this injunction will be visited by a loss of health or of piety. And what will be gained [by excess hours in the classroom] will be purchased much higher than it is worth."[28]

By July 20 Father Sorin was on the road again to New York, and ten days later, aboard the *Lafayette* on his way to France, he composed what amounted to a short treatise on the nature of leadership. Addressed to William Corby—his most trusted lieutenant now that Patrick Dillon was gone—it deserves to be quoted at length.

---

25. Sorin to Battista, n.d. [February 1870], and Sorin to Raguideau, February 11, 1870, AGEN.
26. Sorin, *Circular Letters*, 20–21.
27. Sorin to Barnabò, May 22, 1870, AGEN.
28. "Act of Visit to St. Mary's of the Immaculate Conception," July 7, 1870, AGEN.

Since I left you I have been more preoccupied with you and Notre Dame than the rest of the world. So much now rests on you personally for the furthering of the destinies of the Congregation that you become daily more and more the center of my constant thoughts. Now is your time, I may say, to make your mark as a Religious, a man of God and of the world, a true lover of his Society through difficulties of all sorts from men and things. For this you must not only be esteemed and loved, but feared. Let all know that you love your Congregation more than any of its members. Devotedness, energy, firmness, and no change will aid you materially. Some may and will murmur; but what is that to compare with the result of a vigorous administration? It is not enough to allow every officer to fulfill the duties of his charge. You must see that they do it and support them in the same. You will do well to guard against any postponements. When a resolution has been reached, no time should be lost in its execution. You have around you a class of slow movers who would never have taken Richmond by assault. . . . It would be a waste of time to [await] one of your chapters to promulgate your platform. Proclaim publicly what you expect from all your Religious. Your sphere is entirely changed [and] your responsibilities with it. *I will sustain you.* One of the glories of our present Pope is to have known so well how to say, *Non possumus,* I cannot. I am sure many will tax and seriously tempt your good nature; but I trust they will soon learn you are a man of principle [and] not disposed to sacrifice better judgment to any one's interested desires. Mark it well, it was chiefly on your sound judgment I based my choice of you for the position you now occupy [provincial of Holy Cross in the United States]. You must *rule* and not be ruled. Furthermore, you must do it energetically. Your presence should be felt everywhere and at all times. Otherwise such a large House would inevitably, unavoidably linger [sic], get loose, and go down. Never let your orders pass unheeded. . . . In all things do affirm your authority, not by words but by deeds, not for ostentation but from sheer duty.

"It is not enough to allow every officer to fulfill the duties of his charge. You must see that they do it and support them in the same." It is hardly presumptuous to discern in these lines the distinction Sorin drew between Basile Moreau's failed administrative method and his own more successful one. Had the Founder pounced upon Brother Marie-Julien and his shady associates, and had he, at the same time, "supported" his officer in charge of Notre Dame du Lac, the blow that struck at the heart of Holy Cross might have been warded off. As for sharing these convictions with Corby: "See what a letter I have written you. It is from love and duty too, [and] you will receive [it] as such. I will never write you from any other motive. I esteem you, I love you *propter quod locutus sum* (because of what I have said)."[29]

EDWARD SORIN spent scarcely a month abroad on this trip in the summer of 1870. Aside from the interlude during the retreat for the French houses held at Précigné "without any trouble"—the same Précigné where he had been a minor seminarian forty years before[30]—his only undertaking away from Champeau's *collège* in Neuilly-sur-Seine involved him in a brief trip to Belgium. It was an odd business, calling to Sorin's mind the distant and storied past and intensifying within him the fiercest proprietary instincts. Relatives of Father Louis DeSeille—the heroic Belgian priest who had died at Sainte-Marie-des-Lacs in 1837[31]—had entered a claim to a piece of property allegedly given to their uncle by an Indian chief and now absorbed into the mission of Notre Dame du Lac. Sorin discovered enough documentary evidence to sustain "this old allegation" that he decided, in prudence, to offer a cash settlement of 12,000 francs ($2,400) in order to avoid litigation.[32] This arrangement was agreeable to one of the nephews, but not to his brother and sister, who threatened to refer the matter to a civil tribunal and, for good measure, to Rome. Father Sorin reacted with wrath and scorn. "These *crafty* people," he complained, "more *ambitious* than honest [intend] to denounce me to the Pope; I am called a thief for the first time in my life." As a result he withdrew his offer, and dared the DeSeille family to sue him over "a piece of land that neither Father DeSeille nor the Indian chief had probably ever seen." Such greed was a sad commentary on the career of Louis DeSeille, "who was a holy priest, who came [to Sainte-Marie] to work as a missionary among the Savages, who died *there* a saint, [and] who would never have dreamed of accumulating property for the benefit of his family in Belgium." Let his relations do their worst. "If, contrary to my anticipation, Rome should lend an ear to these *impious* assertions, I will then appeal that the case be sent to our Venerable Metropolitan [Purcell of Cincinnati], . . . who knew and commissioned Father DeSeille."[33]

---

29. Sorin to Corby, July 30, 1870, AIP.
30. Sorin to Battista, August 31, 1870, AGEN. See also chapter 1, above.
31. See chapter 7, above.
32. Sorin to DeSeille, October 11, 1870, AGEN.
33. Sorin to Battista, March 1, 1871, AGEN.

This strong stand sufficed to ward off a potential threat to the physical integrity of Notre Dame du Lac, and Sorin turned to grapple with the harsh realities of the present rather than with the ghosts of the past. Two weeks before his arrival there, on July 19, 1870, France had declared war on Prussia. Napoleon III in person had promptly led his armies, brimming with confidence, toward the German frontier. But the emperor was not the soldier his uncle had been, and by August 6 the French had been badly defeated in two separate battles. As the month proceeded, the situation grew ever more grave. Father Sorin judged the conflict, not inaccurately, to be portentous for the Church as well as for the land of his birth. "At this moment, at six o'clock in the evening," he wrote on August 29, "the destiny of France is being decided on the banks of the Meuse and the Moselle. Great God, what tides of blood are going to flow before this business is finished. We must pray more. It is Luther arising anew and for the last time against Christ! Do not doubt it; Religion has more to do with what is happening than one might think."[34] And two days later: "Everything here is in agitation. Half of Neuilly has fled into Paris. There is emptiness all around us. There are rumors of terrible battles along the Meuse, but for five days we have had no news of the armies."[35] The great fortress of Sedan lay along the Meuse, and there, on September 2, Napoleon III surrendered to the Prussians. The Second Empire ceased to exist.

Sorin may have erred in contending that the shade of Luther inspired the German soldiers—many of them were Catholic Bavarians—but he was correct in predicting that the Franco-Prussian War would have ecclesiastical no less than political consequences. Only a remnant of the thousand-year-old Papal States—virtually just the city of Rome itself—remained under the civil jurisdiction of the pope, and only the presence of a French garrison there prevented the forces of the *Risorgimento* from completing the process of unifying Italy with Rome as its capital. But when war broke out at home, the Emperor of the French began to withdraw his troops—the Vatican Council, its agenda far from completed, hastily adjourned—and by August 19 all of them were gone. A month and a day later, after a token bombardment and token resistance, the Piedmontese triumphantly marched through the Porta Pia and, as King Victor Emmanuel took up residence in the Quirinal, Pius IX withdrew behind the Leonine walls and declared himself a prisoner in the Vatican. At almost the same moment, the German armies, advancing relentlessly from the east, laid siege to Paris.

---

34. Sorin to Sister Columba, August 29, 1870, AGEN.
35. Sorin to Battista, August 31, 1870, AGEN.

By that time Edward Sorin had prudently departed for America, but he brought his misgivings home with him. What troubled him most was the lack of news. "Is the Pope going to remain in Rome?" he asked his agent there anxiously. "Is he so little respected and yet not molested? Are the cardinals free to exercise their offices? Have the Jesuits left the city? What is the true sentiment of the Roman populace? Are they, as we have heard here, in favor of Victor Emmanuel? Is it thought there that the old [papal] order will continue, or is the King going to take full possession? If the latter, what standing does this leave for the Sovereign Pontiff?"[36] Fretting helplessly at home, Father Sorin took the only steps available to him. "No sooner was it positively known here last month that our Holy Father has been robbed of his Capital, . . . that I deemed it my duty to lay at his feet the profound sympathies of the Congregation . . . together with the assurance of the fervent supplications we would offer to Heaven in his behalf, until it would please God to restore to him that which had been so unjustly and sacrilegiously torn from his blessed hands." He ordered Provincial Corby to "assemble the Faculty of this University and . . . with the Honorable Professors [to initiate] immediate measures to organize an indignation meeting of all the Students, to express the sentiments of the Institution and to pass appropriate resolutions. The Proceedings [are] to be published in the Ave Maria or The Scholastic."[37]

Meanwhile, the Prussians girded Paris and its suburbs with an iron ring of cannon and entrenchments. The artillery duels between the invaders and the stout defenders in the Parisian forts tore through the earth and lit up the skies over the course of the last months of 1870. Leaving behind only a skeleton staff, Louis Champeau withdrew into Brittany and Victor Drouelle to a haven near Laval. Paris, its people starved into submission, fell to the Prussians on January 28, 1871. Champeau then returned to his charge in Neuilly, just in time to discover that the worst was yet to come. In March the workers of Paris, organized by anarchists and communists, declared the independence of their Commune in defiance of the central government, located since the Prussian invasion in Bordeaux. The leadership of the rebellion, mostly radical and fanatically anti-clerical, promised war to the knife against the bourgeoisie and the Church. As the Germans stolidly watched—their army drawn up outside the city perimeter—Frenchman battled Frenchman in a bloody frenzy. Once more artillery was called into play, now in an internecine struggle, and the upper floors of the Holy Cross college in Neuilly were destroyed by communard shells. For a while the forces of the Commune prevailed, and Father Champeau and five of the brothers were arrested and

36. Sorin to Battista, October 20, 1870, AGEN.
37. Sorin to Corby, November 23, 1870, AIP.

incarcerated. Luckily for them they did not share the fate of other communard hostages, like Archbishop Darboy, who along with four other priests was executed on May 24.[38] Champeau was for some unexplained reason released and, in the company of one of the brothers, managed in disguise to escape from Paris.[39] The other Holy Cross brothers were freed at the end of May 1871, when government forces, in an orgy of blood and vengeance, finally put down the rebellion. The Louvre and Notre Dame stood unscathed after the street-to-street fighting, but the Tuileries palace and the Hotel de Ville lay in ruins.[40]

Even before the calamities associated with the Paris Commune, Edward Sorin, in far-off Indiana, wondered whether his congregation, already afflicted in its European homeland by mundane financial distress, could endure for long such institutional assaults. "Poor France is to be pitied; the hand of God is visible upon her! We stood in need of this terrible lesson in order to correct ourselves (*revenir à nous*). But we have not yet learned our lesson, and we force that hand to chastise us further, to redouble its blows."[41] "France is lost, she is finished. *Mon Dieu,* what an ending, what a shocking chastisement!"[42] "The signs of the times are alarming," he cautioned Father Battista. "I foresee in Rome and in Paris a religious persecution that cannot be avoided except by a miracle. I believe therefore it is my duty to instruct you not to expose your life uselessly. You should, after consultation with [Cardinal Barnabò], take measures to come here immediately. . . . I have extended the same invitation to all our religious in France, and I think it a special dispensation of Providence that we have been here for thirty years and so have prepared a home for all of our own." Indeed, the prospect lifted him to almost rhapsodic heights.

> What today would be the future of our Congregation if it had only the French foundations? Here is where its real future lies. Just last week a bishop asked, indeed begged, that I bring our Religious from France without delay; he would take a hundred of them himself and immediately put them to good use. You know that we have all the different climates: cold in Canada, heat in New Orleans, moderate in Indiana, delightful (*délicieux*) in Texas and Tennessee, where the springtime is perpetual. Likewise for lan-

38. See Adrien Dansette, *Histoire religieuse de la France contemporaine* (Paris, 1965), 334–339. Altogether the communards executed twenty-four priests.

39. See Sorin, *Circular Letters*, 1: 29–30.

40. See Denis Brogan, *The Development of Modern France, 1870–1939* (London, 1953), 55–74.

41. Sorin to Brother Auguste, January 15, 1871, AGEN.

42. Sorin to Brother Gregoire, January 30, 1871, AGEN.

guages: English here and in Louisiana, French in Canada and Texas. . . . I do not wish to force anyone to leave France but to give complete liberty to each individual.[43]

As events unfolded in France during succeeding months, Sorin's eagerness to provide an American solution to the congregation's crisis only strengthened. And it intensified even more when the news came that heavy fighting had broken out around Le Mans, which fell to the Prussians the same day as did Paris, January 28, 1871. The city and its environs suffered severe damage, especially in the wake of the German evacuation in early March. "May God have pity on our poor France!" cried Father Moreau. The empty religious house at Sainte-Croix was converted into a military hospital, where the Marianite Sisters served devotedly.[44] Father Sorin for his part saw this added wave of devastation as further evidence of the reasonableness of his plan and, moreover, a last chance to effect some kind of reconciliation with the Founder. Accordingly, when he learned of the Prussian depredations in Le Mans, he wrote Moreau and invited him to take refuge in Indiana. There was no reply, and so, in mid-June, he wrote again.

I have just come from offering for you the holy sacrifice of the Mass, and, after having spoken to the good God, I dare to present to you yourself the prayers (*voeux*) that I continue to say for you in my heart. Oh, if you were only here to receive the homages of a whole family which would be so happy to receive today the blessing of its venerable Founder. Some months ago I addressed to you my humble and sincere request in the name of your whole American family, but I received no response. . . . I have now confided the matter to St. Basil, and I am going to hope against hope. . . . If you pardon and forget the past, then you can envisage the future with a Father's heart and can return to America where you would be received, doubt it not, with a joy that will compensate you for past pains. Your Reverence ought no longer stay in France with its limitless sorrows. The horizon brightens, however, somewhere else. Consent, Very Reverend Father, to depart that lugubrious scene, where your age and your waning powers no longer permit you to work successfully for God's glory. Allow us here to assume your care in your last years and to show you each hour the sentiments of veneration with which we want to enfold you either here [at Notre Dame] or in

43. Sorin to Battista, December 12, 1870, AGEN.
44. See Catta, *Moreau*, 2: 983–985.

Canada or elsewhere. If you welcome this heartfelt overture, I will immediately make the necessary arrangements, and you can believe in advance
the inexpressible joy with which you would fill the soul of your old devoted
child in Jesus, Mary, and Joseph.

He could not resist a postscript. "Is it not marvelous that Providence has prepared
in America a refuge for the Congregation? When the storm threatens today to
bring everything in France to grief, the Congregation need not perish for that reason. The resources will not be lacking to it in the New World."[45] Yet, even if these
last lines seem a little self-serving, Sorin's invitation was all in all a handsome
gesture, a genuine olive branch which proves—if further proof be needed—that,
whatever his faults, hardness of heart was not one of them. Sorin asked Mother
Angela to write the Founder in the same spirit, and she did so with her usual
grace. But the old man was immovable. "I did not feel that I could reply," he explained, "because they were not retracting anything, and because they doubtless
wanted to use me as a shield to protect themselves against the charge of being responsible for the break."[46]

THE HOLY CROSS MEN in France, depleted in number, low in
morale, and buffeted from within and without, nevertheless did not rush to seek
refuge in Edward Sorin's brave New World, any more than the Founder did. The
superior general, however, acted as though he expected battalions of reinforcements to cross the sea at any moment. He launched simultaneously, and precipitously, a series of initiatives which stretched to the breaking point the resources
he had at hand. The results were as mixed as they were predictable. Already months
before the outbreak of the Franco-Prussian war, Sorin, in Rome, announced air-
ily "that we have accepted a gift of 3000 acres in the State of Tennessee, on the
condition of establishing a school on the tract." Similarly generous benefactions
were springing up in other parts of the old Confederacy. "A few weeks since, I accepted another [gift] of 4500 acres, with a college already built and furnished, in
Texas." Moreover, "last week our venerable friend, the Right Reverend Bishop
Martin,[47] made me promise a few Brothers to take charge of his own College in

---

45. Sorin to Moreau, June 14, 1871, AGEN. In the pre-Vatican II liturgical calendar, June 14 was
the feast of Moreau's patron, St. Basil.

46. Quoted in Catta, *Moreau*, 2: 981.

47. Auguste Martin, an early patron of Holy Cross as pastor in Logansport and Hailandière's
harassed vicar general, was now bishop of Nachitoches, Louisiana (the diocesan seat was transferred
to Alexandria in 1910). See chapters 5, 10, and 11, above.

Nachitoches [Louisiana], to which is also attached a considerable parcel of land." In the margin of this communiqué he scribbled an addendum: "Finally, within a few weeks, I expect to bring to a happy conclusion another transaction still more important." Also, "on my way to Paris next week, I expect to find in Marseilles a report from our Reverend Father Gillen and upon [reception of] it to close a transaction placing Notre Dame . . . in possession of 8,668 acres in the northern part of the State of New York."[48]

Most of these claims proved to be sheer bluster. The marginal notation was, significantly, later crossed out. Nothing came of the alleged invitations from Tennessee and Louisiana. As for upstate New York, Paul Gillen had his hands full putting together a successful Holy Cross mission in far-away Iowa.[49] Sorin did indeed send a couple of emissaries to investigate a site near Malone, New York, a few miles from the Canadian border, but their reports were negative: "The soil is very poor. The land is valueless, except [for] what timber is on it."[50] Texas, however, did in fact offer a viable mission-field for Holy Cross, which, after much struggle and disappointment, brought forth abundant and lasting fruit.

Upon his return to the United States in the late summer of 1870, Father Sorin followed up upon the conversations he had had with Bishop Dubuis of Galveston earlier that year in Rome.[51] He dispatched one of his ablest adjutants, German-born Brother Boniface Muhler, to scout out the situation in south Texas. Boniface was welcomed enthusiastically by the local chancery, and once shown the facility called St. Mary's College—founded in 1854 under the auspices of the French Christian Brothers, who departed when the war broke out—Sorin's emissary shared in the enthusiasm. Almost immediately he began conducting classes for twenty-four pupils and basked in the approval of the populace of Galveston, Catholic and non-Catholic alike. So promising was this initial response that Boniface deemed it advisable to apply for added personnel from the Holy Cross center relatively nearby in New Orleans. Support from there was not forthcoming, but four brothers were dispatched to Texas from Notre Dame. By the end of the year enrollment had risen to eighty-four. "I candidly invite you," a euphoric Brother Boniface declared to his superior general, "to thank God with me for having called us to this field of usefulness. This seems really our country, where we can do *much* good."[52]

48. Sorin to "Reverend Fathers and dear Brothers in Christ," December 10, 1870, AGEN.

49. See chapter 22, above.

50. Vagnier to Sorin, September 1 and 10, 1869, and Brother Francis de Sales to Sorin, August 5, 1870, AIP. Thomas Vagnier (1839–1926) joined Holy Cross from his parents' farm near Fort Wayne. See *Matricule générale,* 1202, AIP.

51. See note 20, above.

52. Boniface to Sorin, November 27, 1870, AIP.

Early the following spring Father Sorin, together with Mother Angela Gillespie and, for decorum's sake, a nun-companion, traveled down the Mississippi first to New Orleans and from there, by ship along the shores of the Gulf of Mexico, to the island city. They were "very much pleased with Galveston, her bishop, and everything connected with her. Brother Boniface . . . does well." Indeed, Bishop Dubuis maintained that he could make use of any number of religious Holy Cross could supply. Specifically, he indicated possible establishments at the old Franciscan mission in San Antonio, in Houston, Brownsville, and in the fabled Rio Grande town of Laredo.[53] He warmly invited a Notre Dame priest to conduct an eight-day retreat in his cathedral, and Sorin promised to send the eloquent Father Peter Cooney for this purpose. "*Without any doubt* they will pay liberally; the college will gain much by his going and the Congregation even more. What a beautiful country we have seen in Texas!" he added exultantly. "What a beautiful spot Galveston is! We all felt better there than ever before. Brother Philip [who had arrived in October] has gained twenty-eight pounds, and not one among [the community has] had a chill or a headache."[54]

The foundation in Galveston, however, despite all the initial optimism, conformed to the lesson of the gospel-parable, that seed sown in shallow and stony ground may sprout quickly only to wither in the bright sunshine. Within a year's time the enthusiasm for Holy Cross in south Texas had diminished enough to cause Brother Boniface no little anxiety. Two of the teaching brothers had departed, and their replacements had shown little aptitude for the classroom. The priest *en scène,* a pious man and "obedient as a child, . . . can render us no service, except that he says mass for us."

> The College is not in so flourishing a condition as I would wish to see it. Nothing had been done during vacation to encourage and secure boys; this may be one cause. On my return to Galveston [from a summer holiday at Notre Dame] I was pained to learn that several of our most promising boys had entered other schools.[55]

As the enrollment continued to decrease, Bishop Dubius began to manifest some impatience. Then, in the summer of 1873 Brother Boniface was shifted to another assignment, and the departure of this indispensable man hastened the mission's decline. The trouble was rooted in a simple paucity of capable personnel. Edward

---

53. Boniface to Sorin, December 17, 1870, AIP.
54. Sorin to Corby, March 29, 1871, AIP.
55. Boniface to Sorin, October 29 and November 18, 1872, AIP.

Sorin's proclivity—as it had been Basile Moreau's—to overextend his resources once again led to his undoing. Attempts were made to set up foundations in Brownsville and Nacodoches, but these survived for barely a year. Nothing more was heard of San Antonio, Houston, or Laredo. Still, the Holy Cross presence in Galveston lingered for a few more years, till 1877, and this circumstance proved crucial in the end, because it occasioned the singular success the congregation would enjoy in Austin.[56]

In the meantime another disappointment occurred simultaneously in far western Missouri. The pious widow of a well-fixed farmer offered the bishop of St. Joseph a grant of property, provided a cemetery were located there as well as a funerary chapel in which she and her late husband would be buried. The bishop in turn sought to interest a religious order in establishing a school or perhaps a seminary on the 160 acres of committed fertile farm and timber land. Early in 1872 a contingent of Alexian Brothers went into residence there, but after six months they decamped. The bishop then turned to Edward Sorin, who apparently did not see a warning in the Alexians' swift departure: a brother was promptly sent to the scene from Notre Dame.[57] Brother Adolphus, an industrious if somewhat choleric individual, discerned at first considerable promise for the project, though the physical and logistical difficulties loomed large. "I have now only to say," he reported, "that improvements necessary to render the place attractive should be commenced with as little delay as possible."[58] But from the beginning Sorin, for whatever reason, appeared strangely offhand about the venture if not indifferent to it. There was no money and, worse, there was no plan of development. After some months a priest and another brother were sent to Missouri from Notre Dame, without, however, bringing with them any cash or any idea of how to proceed. The widow, moreover, turned out to be as querulous and grasping as she was pious; she complained constantly at the perceived inaction of the struggling little community, and when asked for a loan so that some progress could be made, she insisted upon charging ten percent interest. Through these various difficulties the superior general remained impassive, nor would he, despite oft-repeated pleas, consent to come and visit the site in person. Instead he contented himself with chiding Adolphus for indecisiveness and indicated his intention— and thus implicitly giving a clue to his real priorities—of reassigning the brother

56. William Dunn, "The Early Years of Holy Cross in Texas, 1870–1900," a paper delivered to the Conference on the History of the Congregations of Holy Cross (1982), 5–9. For Austin, see chapter 28, below.

57. See "Description of Property Donated to the Church by Mrs. Amanda Corby," October 11, 1872 (copy), AGEN.

58. Adolphus to Sorin, October 20, 1872, AIP.

to canvass for subscriptions to the *Ave Maria*. In less than two years the Holy Cross initiative in Missouri came to a dismal end.[59]

Such inertia was hardly characteristic of Father Sorin; perhaps it stemmed from a preoccupation with, and brighter hopes for, other enterprises undertaken at the same time, in Texas and, even more so, in Cincinnati. He had gone to great lengths to secure a Holy Cross presence in the Queen City and to maintain cordial relations with the archbishop, John Baptist Purcell. Ever since 1852, when the Josephite Brothers took charge of an orphanage there, Notre Dame had provided personnel to staff several parochial schools to serve an ever-expanding Catholic population. Aside from satisfying the obligations of their religious calling—not of course a trivial consideration—these efforts were aimed at producing, eventually, a regular source of revenue and at promoting vocations. By 1870 the foundations in Cincinnati were normally breaking even or a little better, though the expectation of gaining a significant number of recruits for the congregation did not materialize. The next year Sorin steered through a meeting of Corby's provincial council a resolution to open a college in Cincinnati. As usual with Sorin a college—*un collège*—meant, in effect, a secondary school on the French model. Still, however modest its goals, to staff even an institution of this kind required a commitment of personnel not easily come by within the Indiana Province. The number of available brothers, to be sure, was high and growing—112 professed in 1872—but some of these were designated for manual work of various kinds, while most of the rest were qualified only to teach elementary pupils—a status as fixed in 1871 as it had been in 1841. Once again Father Sorin was testing his optimism and nerve—and his trust in Our Lady—against statistical reality.

Accordingly, St. Joseph's College was founded on October 2, 1871. It operated in cramped temporary quarters—the twelve boarding students lodged in one room, fifteen feet by fifteen[60]—until a building could be hastily erected on West Eighth Street in downtown Cincinnati, on several contiguous lots donated, as had been the case in Missouri, by a pious lady. One priest, several brothers, and a sprinkling of laymen taught a three-year "commercial" course, featuring classes in orthography, letter-writing, bookkeeping, and commercial law. By the following spring an official county audit estimated the monetary value of the institution at slightly less than $52,000. St. Joseph's survived for fifty years, though it never prospered. Indeed, it was a constant drain upon the resources of the Indi-

---

59. For a detailed treatment, see Franklin Cullen, "Cordwood and Calumny: Holy Cross in Missouri, 1872–1874," a paper delivered to the Conference on the History of the Congregations of Holy Cross (1991).

60. Brother Arsene to Sorin, December 18, 1872, AIP.

ana Province. From 1874 till Sorin's death in 1893, the largest graduating class totaled thirteen, and in only two other years did the number reach double digits.
The pious lady in this instance did not cause any difficulty, but hesitant and insecure leadership certainly did. The first president, Brother Arsene,[61] after a year
in office, looted the college's modest treasury and ran off with a woman to Baltimore. Over the next three years five different Holy Cross men attempted to
provide proper direction; even the redoubtable Brother Boniface Muhler of Galveston fame lasted in the presidency for only a single term.[62] It seemed as though
St. Joseph's, aside from scandal, never recovered from the deep national recession
of 1873, which was compounded for Catholic Cincinnati by the collapse of the
archdiocese's finances at the end of the 1870s.[63]

Even as the college building was rising on Eighth Street in Cincinnati, Father
Sorin was finalizing an agreement to launch still another new foundation. In December 1871, a contract was signed between Holy Cross and the diocese of Milwaukee. It called for the congregation to open a school for boys on a parcel of
fifty-one acres on the edge of Watertown, Wisconsin, a bustling little city of eight
thousand, forty miles northwest of Milwaukee. It further specified, at Sorin's insistence, that Holy Cross also assume responsibility for the nearby parish ministering to English-speaking Catholics (there was also a German-national parish
in the town).[64] The superior general took care—as he had not in Missouri or
Texas—to employ the services of a professional appraiser before he made any
commitment: "On the whole I think the terms and circumstances are very favorable for your purposes, and I believe you will meet with every encouragement
from the people of Watertown and surrounding country."[65] The total cost of the
land was set at $12,000, one-third of which was to be paid to the diocese immedi-
ately and the rest incrementally at five percent interest.[66] Sorin signaled the hopes
he entertained for this establishment by sending there forthwith three priests,
three brothers, and two nuns. Not only were plans for construction of a collegiate

---

61. Né John Luther. See *Matricule générale,* 1744, AIP.

62. See Joseph Kehoe, "St. Joseph's College, Cincinnati, Ohio," a paper delivered to the Conference on the History of the Congregations of Holy Cross (1989), especially 2–6, 12.

63. In 1878 the forty-year-old archdiocesan bank, operated by Father Edward Purcell, the archbishop's brother, closed down when the bulk of its loans were revealed to be uncollectable. Many
years were to pass before the liabilities were paid off.

64. See Charles J. Wallman, *Built on Irish Faith: 150 Years at St. Bernard's* (Watertown, Wis.,
1994), 91–107.

65. McIntosh to Sorin, July 8, 1871, AIP. C. E. McIntosh was a partner in a real estate agency in
Appleton, Wisconsin.

66. Sorin to Henni, October 31, 1871, AIP.

facility put on the drawing board, but also others for a new parish church. Most significantly, Sorin demonstrated the high value he placed on the Wisconsin mission by directing his trusted aide, the handsome and now clean-shaven William Corby, shortly to be relieved of his duties as provincial, to assume overall charge there. The commitment of so many relatively skilled religious was a far cry from the neglect accorded to Missouri and the indecision that marked the initiative in Cincinnati. And the investment paid dividends to the degree that, despite some internal bickering—"There is a great want of politeness or rather charity of intercourse of the members toward each other," one of the brothers complained, "some [being] happy only when annoying or backbiting their neighbor"[67]—the "University of Our Lady of the Sacred Heart" seemed during its early years comparatively flourishing, so much so that another brother assigned there told Sorin that it might "throw . . . Notre Dame in the shade."[68]

The superior general also considered expansion much farther afield. As early as 1869 the possibility had arisen of opening a foundation in Newfoundland. He instructed one of his brightest young priests, the Civil War veteran Peter Cooney, then a pastor in South Bend, to work up a preliminary report on prospects in the Canadian maritime. The result of Cooney's research, carried out with books and maps, was negative: "The idea of establishing a University there, I think, is a 'Castle in the air' under present circumstances."[69] Edward Sorin accepted this verdict without demur, and indeed he was uncharacteristically tentative in his dealings with the Canadian Province; perhaps the memories of clashes with the earlier administrations of Joesph Rézé and Mother Seven Dolors gave him pause. For the most part in any case he left matters there to the local superiors, of whom Camille Lefebrve, later famed as the "Apostle to the Acadians" was particularly memorable. Born in Quebec in 1831, Lefebrve had served in a variety of Holy Cross educational and pastoral ministries, but his reputation in Catholic Canada rested largely upon his work in New Brunswick, among the Acadians, the descendants of those original French settlers, celebrated in song and story,[70] whom the British had deported at the beginning of the French and Indian War (1763). A generation later a contingent of them had been allowed to return and settled

67. Brother Gabriel to Sorin, January 10, 1872, AIP.

68. See Franklin Cullen, "Sacred Heart College, Watertown, Wisconsin, 1872–1912," a paper delivered to the Conference on the History of the Congregations of Holy Cross (1989), 1–5.

69. Cooney to Sorin, September 24, 1869, AIP.

70. *Evangeline: A Tale of Acadie,* Henry Wadsworth Longfellow's most popular poem-narrative, was published in 1847.

in small communities along the border with Nova Scotia.[71] Here, with Basile Moreau's mandate in hand, Lefebrve labored tirelessly and successfully to put together a sturdy institutional structure. When elected provincial in January 1871—Hillarion-Charles Villandre had resigned due to ill health and had returned to France, where he died the next year[72]—Lefebrve was reluctant to leave his wind-swept missions and made his disinclination public. Father Sorin, however, insisted: "I trust that you have had time to reflect and so to convince yourself," he wrote sharply, "that in declining . . . what religious obedience requires of you you have assumed a measure of responsibility you would be better advised to avoid."[73] Lefebrve, unwilling as he may have been, took up his new duties in Montreal, and a few months later Sorin did his best to encourage him: "I repeat my advice with regard to your own activities in Canada. . . . Fear less and confide more in Providence. Perhaps in case of need (*au besoin*) I may be better able some years from now to assist you than I am today. Take up the work at Montreal like a man and give to it all the energy and all the devotion you are capable of."[74] That assurance of future support, however, ended as an irrelevance; Lefebrve, who always exhibited the maximum of energy and devotion, served nevertheless only a single term as Canadian provincial, and then returned to his beloved flock in New Brunswick, where his apostolic enterprise earned him widespread esteem.[75]

Finally, among all the initiatives taken on during this time frame, one occurred close to home. "Last Summer," Sorin told the bishop of Milwaukee in October 1871, "I accepted in our own diocese here two new foundations, . . . and one of the two is the house built for the Bishop himself in Fort Wayne, in which our Brothers are now teaching [in] a select school. . . . We are not speculators, neither do we seek for money. But it is my duty to see to a solid basis of operation whenever a new Establishment is offered. For the sake of Religion, I want to make no foundation but what may prove a success."[76] Such protestations, had he heard them, might have surprised the lonely Brother Adolphus languishing in far-off western Missouri. The transaction in Fort Wayne in any case led to a scuffle with

---

71. See Léandre Fréchet, "Holy Cross in Acadia," a paper delivered to the Conference on the History of the Congregations of Holy Cross (1994), 1–5.

72. Sorin to Champeau, September 21, 1871, AGEN.

73. Letter of March 31, 1871, quoted in Pascal Poirier, *Le Père Lefebrve et l'Acadie* (Montreal, 1898), 198.

74. Sorin to Lefebrve, July 23, 1871, AGEN.

75. Poirier, *Lefebrve*, 211–226. In 1890, the aged Sorin asked Lefebrve to serve again as Canadian provincial; he refused. He died in 1895. See *Matricule générale*, 1223, AIP.

76. Sorin to Henni, October 30, 1871, AIP.

John Henry Luers, who had begun his episcopate suspicious of the aggressive Sorin only to become his sturdy ally during the jurisdictional contest over the status of the American sisters.[77] In the spring of 1871, however, the bishop of Fort Wayne appeared ready to revert to his original attitude. The trouble arose out of an arrangement whereby Sorin agreed to pay $5,500 in exchange for a deed to "the ground extending from the new fence put up between [Luers's] and the Brothers' house running up through the garden to the street," and here a teaching facility would be established. The bishop for his part required that Holy Cross maintain on this property adjacent to his cathedral "a good common school (Parochial)" and charge no more than seventy-five cents a month for one child from a family, fifty cents each for the next two, and twenty-five cents for a fourth, "sons of poor widows [to be admitted] free."[78]

All this seemed straightforward enough, until the bishop insisted that the contract include a provision whereby the property would be returned to the diocese if for whatever reason Sorin or his successors closed the school or if his congregation were itself dissolved—the latter a not impossible future contingency given the crises through which Holy Cross was just then passing. This codicil Sorin simply ignored and, much to Luers's annoyance, he refused without explanation to amend the contract. For some weeks the pact looked as though it would founder. "If you think the Bishop may take advantage of you," wrote an irritated Luers, "cannot the same be done by your Congregation? . . . I think you did not sufficiently reflect on the matter, for I cannot bring myself to think that you have an intention to overreach me."[79] Still Sorin maintained a stubborn silence, and Luers showed once again that a lack of candor was not among his shortcomings.

> I cannot for the life of me see what objection there can be to the deed. What is it? And what else do you want? It is hard to do business with you; this mode of acting has turned more than one of your best friends against you, who warn against you as being tricky, and in reality you give yourself the appearance. This does you much harm.[80]

By mid-June Father Sorin had relented, and this small argument was settled amicably, although the contract was not formalized till the following year.[81] A certain

---

77. See chapters 20 and 22, above.

78. Luers to Sorin, April 16, and Sorin to Luers, April 17, 1871, AIP.

79. Luers to Sorin, May 6 and May 7, 1871, AIP.

80. Luers to Sorin, June 12, 1871, AIP.

81. See Dwenger to Sorin, May 21, 1872, AIP. Joseph Dwenger was Luers's successor. See chapter 27, below.

poignancy attaches to these otherwise pedestrian events. On June 29, 1871, John Henry Luers, aged fifty-one, died suddenly and quite unexpectedly of a stroke. "I know neither of us wish it," he had written Sorin in the midst of their recent quarrel. "But twenty years from now we both will be in eternity, and hence we must on both sides do now what is fair and right."[82]

THE APOSTLE PAUL was fiercely protective of the converts he made in the course of his missionary journeys around the Greco-Roman world. "I am jealous over you with godly jealousy," he wrote the Corinthians, and I am weighed down by "a daily preoccupation, my anxiety for all the churches." Hardly any facet of the spiritual or moral fabric within these newborn communities escaped his minute attention—nor, for that matter, did more earthbound concerns: "Drink no longer water," he advised Timothy, "but use a little wine for thy stomach's sake." Something of this Pauline single-mindedness manifested itself in Edward Sorin's administration as superior general. Though he always had at Notre Dame du Lac a secure home base of the kind lacking to Paul, and though, likewise "in journeyings often," he eluded the "perils in the sea" and perils from "robbers" and "the heathen" and from "mine own countrymen" that almost overwhelmed the apostle, Sorin nonetheless expended an enormous amount of time and energy keeping track of Holy Cross's far-flung interests, in person or by correspondence. Indeed, his written exchanges with his agent in Rome, Ferdinando Battista, ran into the hundreds.

The incessant travel to France and Italy also revealed the depth of this holy obsession, as did, even more so, the tireless management of Holy Cross's American heartland. Sorin could not resist intervening in matters that sometimes appeared trivial to his associates. During much of 1871, for instance, he was negotiating with a Belgian musicologist—"I have a beautiful baritone voice"—to fill a faculty position in the university; the young man agreed to come to Notre Dame if he were permitted to give private lessons in addition to his other duties.[83] That same summer, Sorin commissioned one of the lay professors to write an "heroic poem" about Christopher Columbus,[84] while he pondered the advisability of buying a

---

82. Luers to Sorin, May 6, 1871, AIP.

83. Regniers to Sorin, March 8 and April 19, 1871, and January 22, 1872, AIP. Jules Regniers received a salary of 2,000 francs per annum, and Sorin soon revoked the permission to take private students.

84. Stace to Sorin, September 30, 1871, AIP. Arthur Stace requested more than the $80 Sorin had offered "if the poem should prove successful."

steam-driven fire engine.[85] At all times and seasons the superior general's appetite for information was insatiable, and he grew impatient when it was not forthcoming or when it reached him tardily or in an incomplete form. More than one colleague felt the lash of his tongue or his pen for reports he deemed unsatisfactory. For example, in the course of a couple of weeks he chided Peter Cooney, then a pastor in South Bend, for a failure to render a proper account of a fundraising project, and John Toohey for neglecting to send to Notre Dame a detailed enough summary of the state of the mission in New Orleans. Consistent with their differing personalities, Cooney replied sharply and Toohey smoothly and apologetically.[86]

Despite such reprimands, these two priests were very much part of Sorin's inner circle. If St. Paul had his missionary-helpers, Sorin by the early 1870s had gathered round him a cadre of reliable disciples, most of them a generation younger than himself and all of them as mobile as Timothy and Titus had been. The exception in age was Peter Cooney, who had entered the congregation in his mid-thirties and who was fifty in 1872. William Corby that year celebrated his thirty-ninth birthday, while Toohey was thirty-two. Canadian-born Patrick Condon who, like Toohey, had entered the congregation first as a brother,[87] was thirty-four. These men formed the core of Sorin's administration, and to them he entrusted the most sensitive and significant assignments. The confidence their superior placed in them required them to function in diverse capacities and places, a principle honored even after he died. Thus Corby, after his wartime heroics, served as American provincial twice and as president of Notre Dame twice. But he was also twice put in charge of the mission in Wisconsin, for which Father Sorin entertained great hopes. Cooney was director there for two terms as well, as was Condon, while Toohey, after holding a responsible post in New Orleans, spent one spell in Watertown—during which he translated Sorin's *Chronicles* into English—and died in Austin, Texas, another of the superior general's most favored foundations.

Father Sorin for the most part gave these intimates their head, though he never left any doubt as to where the ultimate authority lay. Nor did they hesitate to express their views to him freely. Corby in this regard was the perfect subordinate: loyal and conscientious, with his grave manner and commanding presence, he could be counted upon to fulfill any charge given him precisely and without pretension that the policy was his own. Patrick Condon, if he did not cut the same impressive figure as did Corby, was equally trustworthy, however difficult

---

85. "Silsby Mfg. Co." (Chicago) to Sorin, June 7, 1871, AIP.
86. Toohey to Sorin, August 24, and Cooney to Sorin, September 8, 1869, AIP.

the assignment. When the affairs of the new college in Cincinnati went awry, it was Condon whom Sorin dispatched to try to set matters right. That he did not succeed there, despite his strong support for Brother Boniface—who "did all for the better (he is indeed a good man)"[88]—was not due to any lack of practical skill or dedication. Toohey, by contrast, was the sole intellectual in Sorin's entourage. He possessed literary talents reminiscent, at least in his correspondence, of Timothy Howard. And like Howard, he did not refrain from bearding Sorin on one of the superior general's most conspicuous blind spots. During a time when he was in residence at Notre Dame, Toohey boldly reiterated Howard's negative indictment of the institution and its clerical faculty, and urged Sorin to move to correct this glaring need: "Let the priests see that they are expected to take charge of the higher branches, as well in theology as in mathematics, classics, and the natural sciences. Will they not be compelled as it were to study, in order to fit themselves for such classes?"[89] Finally, the feistiest member of Sorin's inner circle was no doubt Peter Cooney, who never failed to speak his mind, even at the risk of annoying the superior general. A preacher just short of brilliance, the Irish-born Cooney, who, like Corby, had forged an admirable record as a chaplain during the Civil War, was called upon for many an oratorical performance from Wisconsin to Texas. But Sorin also used him as a troubleshooter. When the renegade Brother Arsene fled from Cincinnati to Baltimore, it was Cooney who was sent to find out what had happened to him. The report was characteristically candid: Arsene, who had absconded from Ohio with a thousand dollars in cash, had alleged to local worthies that he was about to open a school in the Maryland city. In fact, wrote the blunt Peter Cooney, he has done nothing of the sort; "He has gone back to his vomit. He is living with that girl again."[90]

Father Sorin still had at his side a good angel, the saintly Alexis Granger, and the aged Brother Vincent too, by now an institutional icon; but neither of them aspired to responsibility beyond that required of them by their religious vows. Neal Gillespie and Auguste Lemonnier were special cases, and not only because they both died young: Gillespie because of his connection to Mother Angela and to the all-important Ewing-Phelan coterie in Lancaster, Ohio, and Lemonnier because he was Sorin's nephew. Although Gillespie never quite shook off the reputation of a dilettante, Sorin demonstrated good judgment by giving him the

---

87. See *Matricule générale*, 1076.

88. Condon to Sorin, September 17, 1873, AIP.

89. Toohey to Sorin, July 4, 1872, AIP. For Howard's strictures see chapter 25, above.

90. Cooney to Sorin, November 25, 1873, AIP. In accord with the recommendation of the archbishop of Baltimore, Sorin petitioned Rome to dispense Brother Arsene from his vows. See Sorin to Battista, December 12, 1873, AGEN.

editorship of the *Ave Maria,* a job he could and did do creditably. As for Lemonnier, his brief tenure as fourth president of Notre Dame had put to rest any misgivings that his preferment rested solely upon nepotism. But he died in 1874, aged thirty-five, his last words reportedly, "Be good to the students."[91] Neal Gillespie followed him to a grave in the community cemetery a few months afterward.

The Pauline analogy admits of further elaboration. Edward Sorin, like the apostle, exhibited a richly varied temperament: assertive, authoritarian, combative, and yet capable of deep emotion and swings of mood. Both men were eloquent, even lyrical at times, at any rate in the written word. And both were driven by a spiritual ideal. In Sorin's case, however, this unworldly goal was often obscured, because so much of his public life was necessarily spent in activities like putting up buildings or raising money—or fending off creditors. Yet in the midst of all these preoccupations he remained a priest and a religious who believed that his destiny would ultimately be decided not in terms of brick and mortar, or of schools founded and young men and women educated, but to the degree that he lived in accord with his vows and in a style consistent with the genius of Holy Cross as formulated by Basile Moreau. One among the many painful ironies of his prolonged quarrel with the Founder was the fact that Sorin never deviated materially from that genius in his person nor in his administration as superior general. In 1871 he promulgated a new set of rules, "almost," as he said to Corby, "the first time we have [had] English Rules." The novelty, however, lay in the language, not in the spirit.

> Please read and explain the new Rules daily at spiritual reading and meditation. The great object . . . is to draw the attention of the Community to them; to inculcate them in all minds; to bring all to their exact observance; to square by them everyone and every thing; to have them so well known, so well kept, that they may be the Rule of the House. I have read them over again, and I feel convinced they are practical, sound, methodical. If well observed, they will keep up Notre Dame and the Congregation. If received indifferently and acted upon carelessly, I must say I do not know what awaits us.[92]

Father Moreau could hardly have stated the principle more clearly.

But man does not live by abstractions alone, and Sorin took seriously his responsibilities as a director of individual souls, particularly of his fellow members

---

91. Quoted in Hope, *Notre Dame,* 170.
92. Sorin to Corby, August 8, 1871, AGEN.

of Holy Cross. Many of the brothers, sisters, and priests subject to him also turned to him for ghostly counsel. The struggle for spiritual maturity was usually composed of small daily encounters with one's self, seldom dramatic and always essentially private. A typical confidence came from a brother stationed in Fort Wayne, who had, at Sorin's urging, made a retreat and felt better for it. Even so, "I do not perform my religious exercises with my former fervor and consequently do not experience the same pleasure as formerly." The cause of this aridity was too much obligatory involvement in "temporalities," a circumstance with which his mentor could no doubt sympathize.[93] Another brother wrote of his internal "dissatisfaction" due, he concluded, to a sense that his talents were not being properly utilized. "But on the other hand I can tell you that the remembrance of the grievous sins of my past life has hitherto been a powerful check against going to [sic] far in this kind of dissatisfaction. I know I have deserved something worse. . . . I [beg] your blessing and your kind interference [sic] in my behalf."[94] Occasionally the problem stemmed from the ordinary human tensions inevitable within a group of people living in close proximity. "We have a member who is no honor but a dishonor to the house," complained a brother from Galveston. The miscreant carps and criticizes and even "refuses to go to Mass."[95]

Such misbehavior was not so common as in earlier days, and the turnover among Sorin's religious was not so pronounced. Sometimes, however, a personal crisis had to be confronted. Father Richard Shortis, whose weakness for alcohol had troubled the community on earlier occasions, had fallen victim to drink once again. "I was laboring under a very severe cold," he wrote plaintively from Saint-Laurent in Montreal, "and on Christmas night I took some punch (whisky and water) and it affected me. I thought it would do me good, but I was too weak to bear it. Only three of four members [of the community] saw me. I feel most grateful for your charity towards me. I certainly have deserved the severest treatment for my relapses. But now at least I trust, through the mercy of God and the intercession of the Blessed Virgin, I will profit by this warning."[96] And sometimes the superior general was presented with an ultimatum. "I demand definitively of you," a brother addressed the superior general from Cincinnati, "to be unbound and entirely dispensed from my vows of obedience and poverty, finally from all to which the Congregation of Holy Cross could hold any claim whatever over

93. John Chrysostom to Sorin, January 20, 1872, AIP.
94. Leo to Sorin, January 8, 1872, AIP.
95. Maurice to Sorin, July 13, 1872, AIP.
96. Shortis to Sorin, January 15, 1872, AIP. For Shortis's earlier difficulties in this regard, see chapter 18, above.

me." He hoped that Sorin would respond to this appeal as "a benign father, because the eternal salvation of my poor soul requires it."[97] A rather more plaintive entreaty issued a little later from a young priest assigned to a pastorate in South Bend. "I am sorry indeed," he confided to Sorin, "that I am so sick in mind, so troubled, so worthless." He had embraced a religious vocation with euphoria, but now, though faithful to his obligations, he had fallen into deep depression. "As for the knowledge necessary for a priest I have, no doubt, some; but even where [sic] I know, I cannot apply the principles of Theology, because I am too timid, wavering, undecided, and excited." He pleaded for an audience "as soon as your will and time permit."[98] Father Sorin took on these and many more such heartfelt perplexities with the spirit of St. Paul: "When any man has had scruples, I have had scruples with him; when any man is made to fall, I am tortured." Nevertheless, he must have rejoiced when he received a note from the apparently unflappable Brother Thomas: "Very Reverend Father General, My troubles, spiritual and corporal, are so commonplace as not to require special consideration."[99]

But in the end Pauline vigor and conviction prevailed whenever Edward Sorin was called upon to exert spiritual influence. "What do I hear, and what can I believe of what I hear?" he wrote to a prominent Catholic layman.

> Your own Reverend Pastor was telling me at dinner yesterday that you yourself had ceased even to make your Easter duty!!! The reason he gave was that you loved money more than your Church! That in having money you were no longer guided by a Catholic conscience, but by a desire to accumulate wealth as fast as possible, disregarding all the prescriptions of the Church on this delicate subject. All this was so new to me that I could scarcely believe it; and even now I rather think there is some misapprehension of the case. But, my dear friend, the doubt itself is too much for me to bear. You are the Director of a pious, excellent, and lovely family, ready to do your will at any time. So much greater is your responsibility. It is from you they have to learn what is right and to guard against what is wrong. . . . Take this letter to your learned and excellent Bishop; explain your course in

---

97. Amédée Joseph to Sorin, October 14, 1872, AIP. Brother Amédée Joseph, né Peter Weyers, changed his mind and remained in the congregation: see *Matricule générale*, 955, AIP. (He should not be confused with the Brother Amédée who caused Sorin so much trouble years earlier; see chapter 22, above.)

98. Lauth to Sorin, October 12, 1873, AIP. Father Jacob Lauth, ordained in 1870, eventually left Holy Cross and joined the Benedictines. See *Matricule générale*, 1731.1.

99. Thomas to Sorin, January 12, 1872, AIP.

pecuniary transactions to him in full and abide by his decision, and your conscience will be in peace; death will lose it horrors; God will bless you in time and forever; your dear children will love your edifying memory; they will pray for you with confidence. And you will rejoice the heart of one of your best friends, E. Sorin.[100]

The unknown recipient of an admonition of this sort might well have imagined himself back in the Corinth of the first century.

---

100. Sorin to "My dear Sir," May 25, 1871, AIP.

chapter twenty-seven

Retreat from Asia and a Death at Le Mans

"IN A FEW HOURS WE SHALL LAND AT BREST, PRECISELY thirty years, day for day and hour for hour, since we left the French coasts in 1841. The voyage could scarcely have been more pleasant, and yet I have never been so long unwell at sea. I do not know how I will fare on land, but if my health should not improve I would make a very brief stay in France."[1] Edward Sorin was a man always sensitive to meaningful anniversaries. He also had long enjoyed sturdy health, else he could not have survived the harsh conditions under which he had labored across those three decades. But he was in his fifty-eighth year now, and he could hardly expect to enjoy the same level of stamina that had been his that Sunday morning long ago when he came off the Wabash and strode along the muddy streets of Vincennes toward Bishop Hailandière's cathedral.[2] Yet, even if age had taken its inevitable toll, the waters upon which Sorin sailed were, in a metaphorical sense, much calmer now. The three great challenges of his life had been met: Notre Dame du Lac was firmly and permanently established; the duel with Basile Moreau was settled, however painfully; and the Congregation of Holy Cross had survived the crisis of the 1860s which had threatened its very existence—"the financial affairs that the Reverend Father Moreau left us as a sad heritage."[3] This is not to say that Father Sorin was

---

1. Sorin to Corby, August 8, 1871, AGEN.
2. See chapter 5, above.
3. Sorin to Barnabò, August 17, 1871, AGEN.

594

now ready to rest on his oars; he realized that plenty of rough rapids might very well loom ahead. But whatever formidable tasks and challenges lay in the future, he knew that the danger of imminent disaster had passed away. As a deeply optimistic and self-assured man who had nevertheless habitually assumed the worst, he viewed this relatively tranquil situation with some skepticism. In fact, however, the patriarchal era of his career had begun. It would prove less dramatic than what had transpired before, more tedious, more taken up with humdrum administrative cares. It would not, however, effect any perceptible change in the forceful, swashbuckling, and yet sensitive personality of him who, as a young priest about to venture into an unknown wilderness, could confidently assert, "I see clearly that our Lord loves me in a very special manner."[4]

The seasickness was forgotten once the *St. Laurent* reached port. Even so, on this occasion Father Sorin did not linger long in the land of his birth. Indeed, the pattern of coming years can be discerned in this summer sojourn of 1871. Frequent trips to Europe, none of them of extended duration, kept the superior general *au courant* with the affairs of the congregation overseas and nurtured his relations with the Roman authorities. As was his wont, he presided over the annual religious retreat of the French priests and brothers, at the conclusion of which nine novices made their profession.[5] The exercise was held at the house at Neuilly-sur-Seine, which had been so badly damaged during the uprising of the Paris Commune and upon which, to Sorin's satisfaction, Louis Champeau had promptly undertaken substantial repairs.[6] The customary side-trip to Rome was omitted, perhaps because Father Sorin hesitated to bring bad news to Propaganda in person. The problem was the Holy Cross mission in Bengal.

> Despite our lively desire [he wrote Cardinal Barnabò from Paris] to replace the missionaries taken away from Monseingeur Dufal by death and illness, we are forced to acknowledge that it is impossible for us to fill these vacancies and even more so to add personnel, in consequence of the situation created in our Congregation by the secession (*scission*) of the Reverend Father Moreau and by the political developments in France, about which your Eminence is fully aware. This is why we humbly request that you accept

---

4. Sorin to Hailandière, n.d. [summer, 1841], AGEN.

5. Sorin to Battista, August 20, 1871, AGEN.

6. See *Sainte-Croix* (n.p. [Paris], 1960), 71. This book is a collection of essays and reminiscences of Notre Dame de Neuilly—as the institution came to be called—which the Congregation of Holy Cross conducted until the legislation of 1903 banning religious orders in France necessitated its transfer to the secular clergy.

our excuses and we confidently leave to your high and paternal benevolence whatever decision you will judge useful to adopt for the greater glory
of God.[7]

This sycophantic language notwithstanding, Sorin had already determined to withdraw Holy Cross from Bengal, the irony of which decision could be fully appreciated by Basile Moreau alone.[8]

Back at Notre Dame by the end of September, Father Sorin put in motion an
initiative he hoped would be more palatable to Propaganda and conducive as well
to the long-term benefit of the congregation. His plan turned upon an advantageous utilization of the encumbered Holy Cross house in Rome, St. Bridget's.
This property, located in a fashionable section of the city and just across the
square from the magnificent Palazzo Farnese, had taken its name from Bridget of
Sweden, the fourteenth-century visionary who had settled and died there. It had
come into the congregation's possession in 1855. Father Victor Drouelle, then the
order's procurator general and Roman superior, had refurbished the building,
provided space in it for theology students enrolled in the Roman universities,
and made it his own headquarters. The flourishing condition of St. Bridget's, however, did not last, and it seemed likely to suffer the same dismal fate as the other
foundations of Sainte-Croix in Italy. But the failure of all attempts to sell it during the recent financial crisis had left it available as the site for the extraordinary
chapter of 1868 which had elected Edward Sorin superior general.[9]

The same chapter had decreed that the motherhouse, in the wake of the collapse of Le Mans, should be transferred to the Parisian establishment at Neuilly.
Sorin, convinced that "France is lost, France is finished,"[10] never much liked this
decision, and indeed he treated it as a dead letter. Whether or not theoretically
presumptuous, he simply acted as though the central administration accompanied him wherever he went.[11] Nonetheless, he perceived that another formality
might have its symbolic and political advantages. As early as June 1871, he opined
that "events will shortly lead us to establish the Motherhouse in Rome. If there is
peace, or at least a peace which leaves the Holy Father master in his [limited] do-

7. Sorin to Barnabò, August 17, 1871, AGEN.

8. See chapter 15, above.

9. See chapter 24, above. Fréchet, "Holy Cross in Italy," 7–8, gives voice to a prevailing and current (1989) bias by describing the chapter of 1868 as "notorious."

10. Sorin to Brother Gregory (Le Mans), January 30, 1871, AGEN.

11. See Sorin to Champeau, December 7, and Sorin to Battista, December 31, 1871, AGEN, as examples of correspondence on stationery labeled "Maison Mère" but postmarked Notre Dame du Lac.

main, we shall come soon and locate ourselves at St. Bridget's."[12] The "peace" to which he referred was of course a hoped for respite from the upheavals of the year before that had resulted in the fall of papal Rome and its absorption into the new Kingdom of Italy. Those events had rendered the disposal of St. Bridget's all the more problematic, and, worse, had made it not impossible that the triumphant anti-clerical regime might confiscate the property, as it had so many religious holdings. And anyway the "Piedmontese aggression," as he and most other Catholics called it, evoked the pugnacious side of Edward Sorin's temperament. Profoundly devoted as he had always been to the papal office and to the person of Pius IX, he ordered now that the for-sale sign should come off the gates of St. Bridget's and that it should be regarded instead as the formal flagship of the Congregation of Holy Cross. "Tell the cardinal," he instructed Father Battista,

> that I am positively determined to go myself to Rome and to fix our Motherhouse there. If he approves, [King] Victor Emmanuel will not frighten me (*ne me fait aucune peur*). Besides, I could have no nobler ambition than to share the perils and the destiny of the Pope. I would be happy a thousand times over to pour out my blood and mingle it with his. I have no confidence in Paris. If Heaven does not miraculously save France, she will be lost beyond recall. And until she has been thoroughly regenerated, I would return there only with the greatest repugnance.[13]

The impulsive romanticism of this resolution stands as testimony to a persisting aspect of Sorin's character, and a most charming one. It is remindful of many earlier bursts of enthusiasm, most notably perhaps the proposal to Moreau of thirty years before that he be allowed to relinquish the office of superior of the Holy Cross mission in order that he might devote himself exclusively to an apostolate among the native Americans of northern Indiana.[14] This intention was soon forgotten in the midst of so many other initiatives, and the notion of bearding Victor Emmanuel in person did not last either. Nonetheless, Sorin had already decided it was prudent to take steps to protect St. Bridget's from the ravenous designs of the Italians. "The House called St. Bridget's, [on the] Piazza Farnese, belongs to me since more than three years," he wrote the American consul in Rome in curiously awkward syntax.

---

12. Sorin to Battista, June 12, 1871, AGEN.
13. Sorin to Battista, November 2, 1871, AGEN.
14. See chapter 7, above.

Being a citizen of the United States since twenty-five years, I am determined to use, as such, every means in my power to secure that property
against all attempts on the part of the Italian Government to take possession of it or in any way to dispossess me out of my rights on it. To you
therefore I now apply, officially begging of your kindness, to see to my request and protect my personal property in Rome, known as St. Bridget's,
and save it from injury. . . . If Honorable Colfax, my neighbor and friend
since thirty years, is now at home, I will send you by next mail from his
own hand in my behalf and for the same.[15]

The consul and his immediate superior, the American minister, were not eager to
challenge the host government before the fact. Let Sorin wait, they directed, until
some hostile move toward confiscation had actually been made, and in the meantime let him furnish to the appropriate department of the Italian bureaucracy
documentary evidence of the fact of his *personal* claim of the property.[16] After
several anxious months it became clear that St. Bridget's was safe from appropri-
ation; it remained in Holy Cross hands until 1892. The very property arrangements that had undone Basile Moreau—vesting community ownership in the
person of the superior—had during this minor crisis served Edward Sorin well.

Still, he had to puzzle out what to do with the house on the Piazza Farnese.
All attempts over the years to sell it had failed; the notion of fixing the congregation's motherhouse there had been only a moment's zealous gesture; and not even
the rapacious oppressors of the pope wanted it. But Father Sorin was never loath
to formulate extraordinary projects, and the grander the better. In this instance it
might even be permissible to employ that ordinarily fallacious and condescending epithet—he was a man ahead of his times. In the proposal he submitted to
the prefect of Propaganda at any rate were displayed his ingenuity, his sound entrepreneurial instincts, and his quite breathtaking imaginative range.

Every year, he explained to Cardinal Barnabò, 50,000 Americans travel to
Europe, "and a good half of them go to Rome." And what do they discover there?
"From the public hotels where they reside, each day they are conducted among
the sacred monuments and holy remains by Protestant tourist guides, who hide
from them all the beauties of Catholicism and who, far from making their stay an

15. Sorin to U. S. consul, September 29, 1971, AGEN. The ungraceful wording, not typical of
Sorin at this late date, may have been a translation prepared by Father Battista. The appeal at any rate
had been sent to Battista who in turn was commissioned to bring it to the consul. Schuyler Colfax
was at this time vice president of the United States, but he was shortly to become embroiled in the
scandals associated with the Grant administration.

occasion to remove their prejudices, send them back to their homes more callous (*endurcis*), more dangerous than before they came to Rome." The American is good hearted, "and he seeks the truth. As soon as the truth is made plain to him, he welcomes it and attaches himself to it. Should it not then constantly sadden us to see these thousands of travelers departing our shores, most often men and women of talent, influence and fortune, and realize that the greater proportion of them will become more estranged from Catholicism than if they had never visited the very center of Light?" St. Bridget in her time cared deeply for the spiritual welfare of her countrymen who came to pray at the tombs of the apostles. "I, as one who knows America, am moved to see so many abandoned, erring souls, often so noble, so pure even, and so well-disposed. I would like to do something for them based on my thirty-two years of labor for their salvation." Let St. Bridget's fourteenth century be reprised in the nineteenth. "Please God, let whoever enters the gates of Rome find there an angelic hand to direct their paths and undeceive their eyes!"

> We have in America some Sisters very well educated, many of them converts, manifesting a remarkable zeal and talent for leading Protestants to the true Faith, as testified to by the 1500 soldiers they baptized during our Civil War. In spite of my well-known admiration for cloistered orders, I am happy to see that in his wisdom our venerable Pontiff-King has brought into his city a certain number of non-cloistered Religious, whom it would be difficult to do without these days. Here is the mission that I would like to see for our American Sisters of the Holy Cross in Rome: in an expanded and refurbished St. Bridget's the inauguration of an American School of Fine Arts for the training of young American artists in painting, sculpture, vocal and instrumental music, with a certain number of apartments set aside for American women of the higher class who desire or prefer accommodation with a religious Society to a public hotel during their stay in Rome, . . . and so experience the real and immediate influence of the Sisters.

"I do not doubt for an instant," he added characteristically, "the success of this project if it is encouraged and blessed by Him whose blessing assures success. . . .

---

16. See Sorin's notarized statement of ownership, April 24, 1872, AGEN, in which he claims the support of "my old friend Louis [sic] Cass Junior" and "my neighbor and intimate friend, S. Colfax." For a summary of the negotiations, see Battista and Quigley to Marsh, June 25, and Marsh to Quigley, June 26, 1872, AIP. George Marsh was the American minister to Italy. Peter Quigley was a diocesan priest from Ohio, resident in Rome, who acted as adviser to Battista. He should not be confused with James E. Quigley, later bishop of Buffalo and archbishop of Chicago.

Under the direction of the American Sisters of the Holy Cross St. Bridget's will rebound before long (*sous peu*) and will become the rendezvous of the female élite of the United States. A series of conversions will be the result."[17]

THE VISIONARY is seldom appreciated in his own generation, which may explain why Edward Sorin's quixotic plans for St. Bridget's were never realized. Or maybe it was because what he called the trifling amount of money needed for its refurbishment—50,000 francs ($10,000)—did not appear trifling to the mandarins of Propaganda. Or, more likely still, the embattled Roman authorities, cabined up now within the narrow confines of the Vatican and with the forces of a hostile regime all round, had more on their minds than the cultivation of budding artists or of the American "female élite" who might travel to the Eternal City. In any case, even as Father Sorin was lauding his "very well educated Sisters" to the cardinal, their high tone was causing him vexation on another front. The solution he contrived was more than usually precipitous, and it brought him into confrontation with the formidable Mother Angela Gillespie.

For some years Sorin had been fretting over the expense involved in providing domestic services at Notre Dame. From their first arrival in America in 1844, the sisters had assumed responsibility for such work. Indeed, they had maintained a convent on the campus, along with their facility at Bertrand, Michigan, a few miles away. Then, with the consolidation of their province in 1855, these household chores were seen to by personnel sent daily across the lakes from St. Mary's.[18] But as the university and its related activities expanded, especially after the Civil War, and as, simultaneously, St. Mary's and its dependent houses increasingly concentrated on educational projects, the need for cooks and laundresses increased while the prospect of acquiring them from among the Holy Cross nuns contracted. By 1867 thirty lay women from South Bend and environs were employed at Notre Dame, and, though paid at the pitiable wage of $12 a month, they represented what was, to Father Sorin, an unacceptable expenditure. He had accordingly commissioned a panel to examine the situation; it had concluded that money could be saved by mustering more nuns and compensating them less. This recommendation—of the sort that heightened Sorin's contempt for committees—obviously solved nothing. Or rather it merely confirmed the status quo ante, a

17. Sorin to Barnabò, n.d. [summer, 1872], AGEN.
18. See chapters 8, 9, and 17, above.

mixed staff, that is, roughly half of which was composed of sisters and half of women hired from the town.[19]

Meanwhile the budgetary pressure intensified along with Edward Sorin's impatience. In the late winter of 1872 he decided to take action, and, though predictably he did not consult a committee, he did confide in his longtime patron, Archbishop Purcell. "Some ten or eleven years ago," he wrote,

> all the work reserved to females was done here by some fifty sisters. The increase in the number of inmates made the task above their strength. At first a few strong women were taken in to help, then a dozen, later on two dozen and more.... The result is ... the unavoidable introduction of twenty-five women without rule or pledge of any kind, moving and leaving as they please, and giving no guarantee beyond those generally found among persons of their class. Besides a permanent necessity, [this situation] is a permanent expense in cash annually of $3,000. Now what is paid for the sisters' clothing, $40 a year, and what is required as a substitution of labor for them at St. Mary's make another amount of $3,000. This tax on the Institution of $6,000 per annum, with the little satisfaction purchased by it, can be tolerated no longer.

The redress he proposed was "to form here something like a Third Order[20] to supply our own wants with a religious element, and by it I feel confident to save $5,000 annually at least." Aside from his prudent practice of keeping his ecclesiastical metropolitan abreast of his doings, Sorin contacted Purcell also because the archbishop of Cincinnati had recently founded a diocesan order of nuns. "I wish to give *à nos nouvelles Tertiaires* the cap and collar of your Sisters of Charity. Would you be kind enough, when you visit some of their houses, to say to the Superioress that I would be much obliged for the loan of a sample of both, and, if you permit, for a copy of their rules."[21]

Sorin assured Purcell that this "new step" was one with which "all parties interested fully agree and by which all will be benefited." This assertion was not

---

19. See chapter 24, above.

20. The term "Third Order" admits of many nuances. What Sorin apparently had in mind was a "Third Order Regular" whose members swore the traditional religious vows, in distinction to a "Third Order Secular," which was composed of lay people who took no vows but who pledged to live in accord with the ideals of a particular religious congregation, like the Franciscans. They were commonly called "tertiaries."

21. Sorin to Purcell, February 10, 1872, AGEN.

true. Several days elapsed between the dispatch of the communiqué to Cincinnati and Sorin's presentation of the plan to the council at St. Mary's. "The administration of Notre Dame is tired and sick of such a state of things. . . . St. Mary's, being daily the eye-witness of the evil and not offering a remedy to it, has been deemed unable to do it. Hence the thought of adopting some other means to help Notre Dame and the Congregation out of difficulty."[22] The sisters reacted to this complaint with consternation; it seemed that the man whom they revered as founder, director, and friend intended to set up a society to rival them and thereby to separate himself from them. Moreover, their other protector, John Henry Luers, had died only months before, and who could predict what stance a new bishop of Fort Wayne might take? Sorin, however, was not to be forestalled. A week later he sent a flyer to a select list of parish priests, soliciting recruits for his "third order."

> Twenty-seven years ago [he wrote], when the first Sisters of Holy Cross arrived at Notre Dame, Indiana, their object was simply to take charge of the various departments of manual labor usually entrusted to their sex. For a long time they rendered a very valuable assistance to the infant Institution in the infirmary, the kitchen, the vestry, the clothes- and wash-rooms, and so forth. Soon, however, the want of Religious female teachers in the West was so forcibly represented and so sadly felt that it was deemed a necessity to modify at first and gradually to change almost entirely the end [i.e., objective] of their Congregation and [to] direct its chief aim towards education. . . . But while we thank God for the success of our Sisters as teachers, we must confess that their original object has by degrees, as anticipated, been lost sight of.

This statement also played rather fast and loose with the truth, or—to put a kinder construction upon it—it suggested a serious lapse of memory. Even before the first contingent of sisters had arrived in Indiana, even while Father Sorin was still at Black Oak Ridge, he had pleaded with Basile Moreau to send nuns to the American mission to act as *teachers*. Nor had he changed his emphasis once settled at Sainte-Marie-des-Lacs.[23] Such a perception was a credit to his foresight. Now, however, confronted by a different set of necessities, he chose to blur the earlier intuition.

---

22. Sorin, "Memorandum," n.d. [February 1872], AGEN.

23. See Sorin to Moreau, October 21, 1841, and December 5, 1842, AGEN. See also the discussion in chapter 8, above.

Hence the opening here at Notre Dame of a separate novitiate to carry out the first and elementary idea of twenty-seven years ago, exclusive of all other and higher aspirations, although partaking of the same religious advantages of a Community life, under the same vows of obedience, chastity, and poverty. Our object is to form a regular training [for] good, pious, and unpretentious subjects to a religious, meritorious and useful life of labor in accord with an EASY RULE, yet sufficient to secure obedience, peace, and union and harmony, and to lead each member to perfection.

To assuage the dismay his plan provoked at St. Mary's, Father Sorin did little more than simply indulge in wordplay: "The Coadjutor Sisters of the Holy Cross are now the branch we wish to revive and develop . . . with only a slight difference in dress . . . and best suited to [their own] condition, earlier habits, or natural inclinations."[24]

Sorin was gratified by Purcell's positive response to his proposition, though the archbishop cautioned him not to denigrate the Holy Cross sisterhood in place.[25] The response to the advertisement to the pastors was similarly encouraging. Would a young woman who "can speak only German and a little broken English" be welcome in "your new congregation of Sisters?" asked a priest from Zanesville, Ohio. From New York City came another endorsement, this one for "Bridget Dunn, a good girl" who might well fit the requirements Sorin had described.[26] Meanwhile, the sisters at St. Mary's, under the leadership of Eliza Maria Gillespie, did not think themselves able to challenge Father Sorin's version of the history of their apostolate. Nevertheless, through of the spring of 1872, they deliberated at length about how to meet what they feared was a threat to their integrity. By June they had reached a determination, the first expression of which issued from the pen of Sorin's "most obedient and devoted child, Mother Angela."

It is needless to say the effect [the proposal of a third order] produced. For the fact [is] that after having dedicated themselves to aid the domestic arrangements at the college [at Notre Dame] ever since their arrival in America, the Sisters are now told by the Fathers of Holy Cross that their services are needed in future only until the Fathers form a new religious order for their colleges, establishments, hospitals, and industrial schools. [They tell us] that at the present time "the material at their disposal is

---

24. Sorin to "Reverend dear Father" (copy), February 20, 1872, AGEN.
25. Purcell to Sorin, February 13, 1872, AIP.
26. Epprick to Sorin, February 16, and McGovern to Sorin, October 25, 1872, AIP.

abundant, the experience and skill together are at hand" to form this new Order. May not the question arise in any mind why, with such means in abundance, . . . did the Fathers not propose to give this material they find so easy to procure to St. Mary's to form for them?

It was a reasonable question. And, since the sisters' Rules and Constitutions were just then undergoing Sorin's revision, "why not make in the Rules that are now being made such provisions as would secure to Notre Dame the proper services?" Mother Angela was especially irritated at Sorin's use of expressions like "abundant material" and "experience and skill."

> While I most emphatically protest in the name of the Sisters that they do *not wish this* I at the same time want it understood that we do not seek to give our services where they are not needed *or solicited.* . . . When you first mentioned this subject to me, I did as I have ever done and with God's grace I shall ever do, sought to cooperate by all means in my power to carry out your wishes. . . . [But] for me it seemed as a *first essay* that would be modified in time in order to bring it to the proper Religious basis, and, at the same time, keep in full vigor the two fundamental principles: first, *to give the domestic help needed for Notre Dame,* and second, *to give that help through the body of Sisters who have been doing it to the present.* If they have not done all that was needed, could not the *same pen* that is forming new Rules for a new Society have proposed to embody such rules in those now being written for the Sisters of the Holy Cross?

The underscorings and occasionally awkward phraseology testify to Mother Angela's deep disturbance, as did her closing demand: "In making a record of this great change in the spirit and work of the Sisters of the Holy Cross, may I beg that it may be fully expressed in the records at Notre Dame as not made at St. Mary's."[27]

Cool heads—and, no doubt, mutual affection and respect—in the end prevailed. The sisters' council put forward a compromise proposition, which strongly denied Sorin's allegation of calculated neglect—"That *we,* the Sisters, have 'virtually abandoned' our *first* work we are scarcely prepared to admit"—and brushed aside his verbal legerdemain of "Coadjutor Sisters"—a gesture "so *frail,* a mere *nominal affair* that sooner or later would end in two distinct communities." At

---

27. Mother Angela to Sorin, June 6, 1872, AIP.

the same time they acknowledged "our lively remembrance of what we have received from Notre Dame in years past and [from] you particularly, Very Reverend Father." To solve the imbroglio, therefore, "we propose to send to Notre Dame, immediately after their first year of novitiate, a sufficient number of suitable subjects for the wants of said place." There the second year of novitiate would "be passed under the careful training of a prudent Superior," who, however, would be a professed member of the St. Mary's community. Once the probationary period was over, the admission of these candidates to final vows would be determined by the sisters' council, though the profession-ceremony might take place at Notre Dame. "In doing this"—and here was an implicit rebuke to the men of Holy Cross—"we shall have to hire domestics for some of our houses here and elsewhere. . . . But in turn we shall expect our Reverend Fathers to take the same interest in securing subjects for our Novitiate as they would have to use to form *a new order of Sisters*."[28]

Sorin accepted this plan, and indeed it may have been the outcome he desired all along. The new arrangement at any rate went into effect after the sisters' retreat in August, when under the charge of his old friend and ally, Mother Ascension, "the subjects received [at St. Mary's] for Manual Labor" moved to Notre Dame to complete their probation. By November Sorin could report "that the Sisters' House here is a complete success; there is perfect satisfaction and harmony among them. They give us perfect peace besides saving four or five thousand dollars." He had set "several of the most intelligent" to learn to operate the *Ave Maria*'s press, so that in a few months, "instead of employing four Protestant printers as we do now to praise our Blessed Mother at $5,000 a year, the Sisters will save that much and do themselves the labor of religion and love, without fuss or trouble."[29] His appraisal was doubtless overly sanguine; if the tensions on both sides of the lakes were much reduced for the time being, the precise status and dubious canonical legitimacy of the divided novitiate continued to nettle relations between the two communities until 1890 when the bishop of Fort Wayne, Joseph Dwenger, at the direction of the Vatican, closed down the Notre Dame branch of the novitiate. By then Mother Angela was dead, and Father Sorin had entered upon his final days.[30]

---

28. Mother Angela et al. to Sorin, June 14, 1872, AIP.

29. Sorin to Corby, December 15, 1872, AGEN.

30. See Costin, *Priceless Spirit*, 211–213, 229–230, and Arthur J. Hope, "Sisters of the Holy Cross at Notre Dame" (n.p. [Notre Dame, Ind.], n.d. [1958]), 17–18.

EDWARD SORIN was away in Texas visiting the new Holy Cross foundation there on April 14, 1872, when Dwenger, the child of German immigrants, was consecrated second bishop of Fort Wayne in a ceremony held in the cathedral in Cincinnati.[31] The portly prelate, a member of the Congregation of the Most Precious Blood, had been, like John Henry Luers before him, a protégé of Archbishop Purcell. It was Purcell who sent word of the appointment to Notre Dame. "Your partiality toward the Bishop-elect," Sorin replied, "goes a great way to prove that he will be the right man in the right place. You console me not a little when you assure me that 'he will cherish our institutions.' Thank you for this timely and delicate remark."[32] During the trying first days of his episcopate—he suffered from depression and insomnia—Dwenger did indeed strike up a cordial relationship with Holy Cross. He took to addressing Sorin, twenty-three years his senior, as "my very dear Friend," whom he solicited for prayers and counsel.[33] The bishop, however, survived these early trials and, by temperament a coarse and assertive man, clashed more than once with his "very dear Friend" over the next two decades.

Father Sorin, even as he tried to solace the sleepless young prelate, and to put in motion the compromise with the sisters, was mostly preoccupied with the convening of the first general chapter of the men of Holy Cross since 1868. The site of this meeting was to be Notre Dame du Lac. The romantic notion of eventually establishing the motherhouse, and himself, in Rome still attracted him, at least at one level of his consciousness. "I have the greatest desire," he told Ferdinando Battista, "to see all the business of the Congregation properly regulated, and afterwards to fix myself with you in Rome." Indeed, "I would have preferred to hold [the chapter] in Rome," but the political situation renders that "impossible at the present moment." As for Paris or anywhere else in France, he dismissed the idea out of hand, not only because of his pessimistic view of the fortunes of the congregation there but also, more pragmatically, because "the French capitulants will be able to sail to America *gratis* and not the Americans the other way round," which meant a saving of several thousand francs. He expected the European participants to depart Le Havre on July 18, 1872.[34]

---

31. Dwenger to Sorin, March 26, 1872, AIP (Dwenger's invitation).

32. Sorin to Purcell, February 29, 1872, AIP.

33. See, for example, Dwenger to Sorin, May 15 and July 7, 1872, AIP. For Dwenger, see Alerding, *Fort Wayne*, 38–45.

34. Sorin to Battista, April 17 and April 26, 1872, AGEN. Why the travelers from France "*auront le passage gratuit*" is unclear.

It is legitimate to wonder whether Sorin ever really intended to give up the home base of his own creation, Notre Dame du Lac, for a house on the Piazza Farnese, where he would have been only one among the scores of religious superiors competing for the Vatican's attention. The wisdom of hindsight suggests the negative, since in fact he never did. But that conclusion would underestimate the volatility of the man's temperament, as well as the indignant reaction most Catholics of his generation felt toward what they perceived as a base injustice done to the beloved Pius IX. Indeed, one of his later complaints against Dwenger was what he called the bishop's disloyalty in promoting "Gallicanism in all its ugliness (*laideur*) four years after the Promulgation [at Vatican I of papal infallibility]."[35] Even Newman's famously nuanced defense of infallibility in the *Letter to the Duke of Norfolk* offended Sorin, the ultra Ultramontane: "The pamphlet of Dr. Newman in response to Gladstone," he declared, "is the unhappy product of a beautiful spirit but also of a heart visibly embittered (*ulcéré*) against the popes."[36]

Even so, Sorin, upon reflection, always tempered his romantic inclinations with a strong dose of realism. Rome was at the moment inauspicious and Paris, though still technically the site of the order's motherhouse, was unthinkable. The general chapter of the Congregation of Holy Cross accordingly opened on August 5 within the familiar confines of northern Indiana. It proved to be by no means so revolutionary as the gathering of four years earlier. The ex officio and elected members spent three weeks pondering and discussing the superior general's prior mandate: "The General Chapter is approaching. . . . Every Religious shall be seriously examined and weighed before [this] assembly, that the Capitulants may form a correct estimate of the real worth of each member and employ him to the best possible advantage. Hence a new motive for this community at large [is] to behave religiously, that we may know how far and how much we may trust and depend on each member."[37] And indeed most of the chapter's twelve formal rulings dealt with the tightening of discipline within the congregation at large and within the individual houses. "The Chapter," read the second canon, "having devoted a great part of the session to a revision of the Common Rules and the principal Particular Rules, . . . decrees . . . that all the Religious of the [sic]

---

35. Sorin to Battista, February 20, 1875, AGEN.

36. Sorin to Battista, February 5, 1875, AGEN. Sorin had wasted no time in getting hold of a copy of Newman's *Letter* which had been published in England only a month earlier.

37. Sorin, "Memorandum," n.d. [February 1872], AGEN.

Holy Cross . . . shall be urgently pressed to return to a stricter observance of even the smallest points of the Rules." This injunction included "the necessity of strict economy," a requirement underscored by "the happy liquidation of the debt of [Le] Mans, [which] was obtained only at the cost of sacrifices . . . upon all our Houses."[38] Finally, the chapter passed a resolution about the substance of which Sorin had already forewarned Cardinal Barnabò: "The Sacred Congregation of the Propaganda shall be asked to relieve the Congregation of the [sic] Holy Cross from the Apostolic Vicariate of Eastern Bengal, to which we cannot furnish subjects in sufficient number, sickness and death not ceasing to decimate the missionaries." Despite this unfortunate reversal, the statistics reviewed by the chapter were impressive enough. Holy Cross included in its ranks, all told, 75 priests, 245 brothers, and 187 aspirants at various stages of their training. They conducted 79 educational enterprises with nearly 10,000 pupils, and administered nineteen parishes as well.

The chapter also revised the list of the congregation's officers. Louis Champeau was confirmed as first assistant general, while Ferdinando Battista was formally named procurator general and Roman agent, a post he had in fact functioned in since the end of 1869. France reassumed its status as an independent province, with Joseph Rézé as its head, while affairs in Canada were to be presided over, however reluctantly, by the charismatic apostle to the Acadians, Camille Lefebrve. Alexis Granger, with similar reluctance, resumed the office of provincial for the United States, now that William Corby had been dispatched to oversee the new foundation in Watertown, Wisconsin.[39]

Notably missing from this roster was the name of Victor Drouelle, himself a capitulant. The former procurator general and French provincial—and the most active agent in the putsch against Basile Moreau—had expected at the very least to be restored to his position in France. Sorin instead offered to appoint him to command in Montreal, where, relatively near Notre Dame, the superior general could keep a close eye on the notorious intriguer. Such an arrangement would have been heartily endorsed by Lefebrve. But Drouelle haughtily declined. "I was entitled to protest," he declared, "for, though I have spent the best years of my priestly life in foreign countries, yet I never contracted any obligation to leave France." At sixty years of age, he protested, he could hardly be expected to take up a post where the climate would play havoc with his health.[40] He returned to

---

38. "Liquidation" at this date was not the exactly correct term. A small portion of the debt remained. Sorin to Barnabò, August 27, 1872, sets the figure at 78,000 francs ($17,000).

39. For these figures and the decrees of the chapter, see Sorin, *Circular Letters*, 1: 46–49.

40. See Catta, *Moreau*, 2: 1014–1015.

France, restless as ever and without the responsible post he believed his seniority and experience entitled him. Months of brooding led him ultimately to draw up a document in defense of his past actions; a copy of this he sent to Sorin along with a bitter enclosure. "Permit me to say only to you and what I do not say in my statement: it seems to me highly indelicate that you kept a calculated silence about the causes of [past controversy] and that you exposed to all possible unfavorable comment the life of one of the Ancients of the Congregation." Edward Sorin remained adamant. "If this communication represents a fait accompli," he scribbled at the bottom of Drouelle's letter, "I regret it and disapprove of it. . . . If it is merely a consultative document, I repudiate it as a direct insult to the Chapter, from which a man can appeal to Rome but not to his fellow Religious, who can then only lose the more readily the respect they otherwise owe him."[41] And so one of the "Ancients" of Sainte-Croix, the talented, urbane, yet radically unstable Victor Drouelle, passed into a limbo of his own. Two years later death found him there.

Despite such an unpleasant and probably, given the personalities involved, unavoidable confrontation, the superior general, as he reviewed the work of the chapter of 1872 for Propaganda, felt justified in claiming "that the overall condition of our Congregation is much more satisfactory than one could have hoped for, after the different crises we have experienced in recent years. These events have resulted in purifying our religious and in strengthening those who have remained faithful. Thanks be to the God of mercy who consoles his own after having tested them." Sorin—it almost goes without saying—assured Cardinal Barnabò that the showcase of this recovery was located "in America, in the United States and Canada, where the material condition of our Missions is steadily improving and where the religious spirit is maintained in a most consoling manner." But things were looking up even in

the Province of France, which has been the most unsettled, because of numerous defections occasioned by the resignation of the first Superior General, because of the necessary closing of important foundations, including the college and motherhouse at Le Mans, and because of the fears that the enormous debt could never be paid. Now, however, I can say that this province has seen peace restored among the religious and its enormous debt almost paid off . . . and manageable. . . . We have the satisfaction of informing your Eminence that the fifty-six French houses are generally

---

41. Drouelle to Sorin, with addendum, n.d. [late August 1873], AGEN.

on the way to prosperity, despite the political troubles the country has recently endured, and that the regular discipline in them has not suffered too much.[42]

As for Bengal, "we wish it were in our power to give your Eminence better news, . . . but the losses suffered by our missionaries are irreparable at present," and the general chapter had therefore seconded Sorin's earlier request to withdraw. Indeed, over recent years, seven Holy Cross men had died in Dacca and its environs and six others had been invalided home. Bishop Dufal, with only five colleagues, could not hope to minister to the vast territory entrusted to him. Rome moved at its usual deliberate pace, and not until 1876 did a small group of Benedictines arrive to take up the work of the Catholic mission in Bengal.[43] Sorin, meanwhile, explained the chapter's decision to Dufal and offered what sympathetic assurances he could.

As for you, Monseigneur, and your pious and worthy associates of the Congregation, you have won by your long and admirable devotion the imperishable right to the recognition and the love of the whole Family of Sainte-Croix. We shall honor you always, whether in Europe or the New World, and we shall be only too happy to contribute by all the means in our power to restoring your precious health, so nearly consumed in the service of God's glory beneath the burning sun of Bengal. You will have for yourself, Monseigneur, as will all your dear missionaries, full and entire liberty in choosing your residence.[44]

Whatever inner thoughts Father Sorin may have had as he thus closed down the mission to which he had refused to go twenty years before, the dénouement of this great spiritual drama had not yet come. In 1888 he sent the men of Holy Cross back to Dacca, and the men of Holy Cross are there still.

ONCE THE GENERAL CHAPTER was adjourned, Edward Sorin indicated his intention "to return within a few weeks to Paris, which continues as the central headquarters of our Congregation, in order to try actively to

---

42. Sorin to Barnabò, August 27, 1872, AGEN.
43. See Edmund N. Goedert, "Holy Cross Priests in the Diocese of Dacca, 1853–1981" (Notre Dame, Ind., 1983), 7–9.
44. Sorin to Dufal, August 27, 1872, AGEN.

remedy some of the sufferings as well as to inspire the courage of our religious who suffered so grievously during the recent war."[45] In fact he did not go to Europe till the following spring. Perhaps the growing tension with Victor Drouelle gave him pause, or maybe the very reality, so distasteful to him, that prudence required him to keep the motherhouse nominally in Paris, at least for the time being, made residence at Notre Dame du Lac seem all the more appealing. There was in any case much to occupy him at home. He needed to oversee the establishment of the new sisters' novitiate and, as he did so, to mend fences with Mother Angela and St. Mary's. The new and so far flourishing foundations in Wisconsin and Texas demanded careful attention. He worried that reinstating the beloved but vacillating Alexis Granger as provincial of the United States might weaken the overall administration. "What think you," he asked William Corby, off in Watertown, "about making our Father Toohey Assistant Provincial? He is regular and attentive to every duty, and is fast gaining universal esteem. Not a thing against him."[46] Nor was further expansion ever far from his mind; several hundred acres of land were secured on the outskirts of Chicago, a city which Sorin had always considered of pivotal importance to the future of Holy Cross and from which it had been ignominiously expelled twelve years before.[47] And some nuisances never appeared to go away. The Marianite Sisters in Le Mans, egged on by Charles Moreau and by their outpost in New Orleans,[48] persevered in their allegation that Notre Dame owed them upward of $20,000, a claim Sorin just as persistently rejected.[49]

The ex officio commitment to combine the functions of spiritual director and religious superior continued apace. A brother stationed in Texas, for example, demanded a transfer to New Orleans, "where I may spend some time in complete repose. . . . It is true I would be anxious to render Brother Boniface [in Galveston]

---

45. Sorin to Barnabò, August 27, 1872, AGEN.

46. Sorin to Corby, December 15, 1872, AIP. Toohey's appointment was confirmed on January 5, 1873. See Sorin, *Circular Letters*, 54.

47. See chapter 20, above.

48. It should not be forgotten that out of the various constitutional crises of the late 1860s Edward Sorin had emerged as superior general of all Holy Cross priests and brothers, wherever they were located, including New Orleans and Canada. But he was superior (and theoretically subject to the bishop of Fort Wayne) of the Sisters of *the* Holy Cross only, that is, of those nuns who had originally formed the Indiana Province. The sisters in New Orleans and in Canada maintained their connection with the Marianite motherhouse in Le Mans.

49. See, for example, Sorin to Perché, June 23, 1872, and March 23, 1873, AGEN. Archbishop Napoleon Perché of New Orleans, Blanc's successor, was a native of Le Mans and an acquaintance in his youth of both Moreau and Sorin.

all the service in my power. But I find it too painful and distressing to continue this same train of occupation . . . [when] I find that constant teaching only aggravates the inflammation of my throat."[50] But Father Sorin's priestly ministry reached a wider clientele than simply his fellow religious. One instance at this time was of particular interest, since it turned upon an issue which was to cause much difficulty for the American hierarchy during the last decades of the nineteenth century. Sorin was called to the deathbed of a local luminary who had indicated a desire to be baptized.

> I knew he was a Freemason. I had known him a long time, and he was an old friend. I hoped to find him disposed to repudiate Masonry. But when I posed the question to him directly, he refused. I tried for ten minutes to guide (*amener*) him to the desired declaration, but it was all useless. During this time the two principal Freemasons of South Bend were in the next room, and they heard our conversation. Finally I departed without baptizing him. He lived another two days, and in the interval he was baptized by a Protestant minister. I have to believe that his good faith will save him.[51]

Here was an aspiration worthy of the man who uttered it.

A few days before Christmas Father Sorin had reason to be pleased with another of his inner circle. "Our Father [Peter] Cooney," he reported, "closed here this morning a very fine retreat with 245 communions. He certainly spared no pains, and the students seemed to appreciate his devotedness and ability. He gave us a very good sermon at high Mass on the priesthood. He succeeded equally well a week before at St. Mary's"[52] But the day after Christmas disaster struck, in the form all too familiar to the missionaries of Holy Cross. "I am just returning from the smoking ruins of our church in Lowell," Sorin informed William Corby. "While our dear Father [William] Demers was here with me yesterday afternoon on a charitable errand, the church was discovered in fire [sic], and in spite of all efforts in less than two hours it was leveled to the ground. . . . A brave convert

---

50. Brother Agathon to Sorin, November 21, 1872, AGEN.

51. Sorin to Battista, January 14, 1873, AGEN. The fiercely anti-clerical and indeed anti-Christian bias of European Masonry was only mildly replicated in the United States. This distinction was never recognized by the Vatican, with the result that the relationship between American Catholics and so-called "Secret Societies" was awkward and ambivalent. See, for example, O'Connell, *Ireland*, 229–231, 404–406.

52. Sorin to Corby, December 15, 1872, AIP.

rushed in and saved the Blessed Sacrament."[53] Corby's reply included, besides conventional expressions of condolence, a hauntingly prophetic note:

> [The rescue of the Eucharist] is a reason to thank God (or rather an occasion) for having saved Notre Dame from the many perils to which it has been exposed. For several years nothing cost me more anxiety than the dangers of fire at Notre Dame, where so much could be destroyed in a few hours and where *so many* lives would inevitably be lost.

Seven years later that foreboding, at least for a frightful moment, would appear to have been fulfilled.[54]

I T WAS CORBY TOO who tried to console Edward Sorin a little later in the wake of another sorrowful event. "Poor Brother Lawrence," he wrote from Watertown,

> nothing that I have heard for years gives me so much pain. A good devoted man, one who never spared himself in the service of the community and one whom I always respected and esteemed. I have had prayers offered for him both by the Brothers and Sisters and Masses by the priests. If he still lives, pleas [sic] tell him so.[55]

Brother Lawrence, né Jean Menage, never learned of these supplications in his behalf. After a three-month illness, he died April 4, 1873, aged fifty-six. "In his death," Sorin declared to all the members of Holy Cross,

> we sustain a serious loss which none can realize better than myself, however much his memory may be held in gratitude and love among those who knew him best, or whom he assisted most by advice or example, or in pecuniary transactions. It was myself who brought him to the community thirty-three years ago; and although I have seen, more than many other men of my age, Religious of undoubted fidelity, of great zeal and devotedness, I

---

53. Sorin to Corby, December 27, 1872, AIP. Demers was the pastor of the parish, now St. Joseph's of South Bend. See also Dwenger to "the Catholics of St. Joseph Congregation, Lowell," December 31, 1872, AIP, in which the bishop urged parishioners to rebuild under Sorin's direction.

54. Corby to Sorin, December 30, 1872, AIP. For the great fire of 1879, see chapter 29, below.

55. Corby to Sorin, April 4, 1873, AIP.

can remember none whom I would place above our dear departed. . . . If any one is to be named as having contributed more than others by earnest and persevering efforts of mind and body to the development and prosperity of Notre Dame, if I did not do it here, the public voice would declare it, and name Brother Lawrence. . . . As to myself personally, I lose a friend who never refused me any sacrifice.[56]

The tribute was surely just. The sturdy farmer from Sarthe had taken on any task asked of him, even the ill-starred expedition to the California goldfields.[57] And so now only two were left of Sorin's original six companions, Brothers Vincent and Francis Xavier.

But some ten weeks before Brother Lawrence's death there occurred an even more momentous passing, one that could not but have aroused in Edward Sorin's heart a rush of memories, some bitter, some sweet. He announced it in another circular letter dated January 31, 1873.

I learn, though not officially but by the public papers, . . . that our venerable Founder died in Le Mans a few days ago. I deem it my duty not to wait for the particulars of this sad event . . . but to immediately recommend to your fervent prayers one to whom we are all indebted for our Religious existence as an Order in the Church. I need not adduce here any further claim on his part to our special suffrages. . . . Whatever may have been within the last few years our regret and pain at the course he seemed to pursue, the tomb has now closed upon the past and leaves us but the memory of our sacred obligations to a Founder whose last years, in God's inscrutable Providence, will be presented to our meditations, purified in the crucible of affliction, and possibly richer in merits than any epoch of joy and human prosperity. For "whom the Lord loveth, He chastizeth, and He scourgeth every son He receiveth."

A schedule of daily "public suffrages" began immediately with a solemn Mass at Notre Dame and continued in all the provinces of the congregation until the end of July, in order "to gratify, as much as possible, the pious wishes of all."[58]

Basile Moreau had fallen ill on New Year's day. His condition steadily worsened, and shortly after noon on Monday, January 20, he died, just weeks before

---

56. Sorin, *Circular Letters,* 1: 56–58.
57. See chapter 14, above.
58. Sorin, *Circular Letters,* 1: 55. The scriptural quotation is from Hebrews, 12:6.

his seventy-fourth birthday. In attendance was his ever-faithful nephew Charles along with Mother Seven Dolors and several other Marianite sisters. The funeral took place the following Thursday. The local Jesuits, who now staffed Notre Dame de Sainte-Croix, offered the church Moreau had built as venue for the obsequies, but their overture was declined. Instead the requiem Mass was sung in the tiny Marianite chapel, only a stone's throw away. The secular clergy of Le Mans presided. Victor Drouelle and Louis Champeau traveled down from Paris and were assigned seats among the lay-mourners. At the graveside there was an awkward moment when Drouelle approached Father Charles Moreau and extended his hand. The nephew took it. Champeau did not fare so well; next day, when he sought to offer condolences first to Charles and then to Mother Seven Dolors, he was turned away in both instances.

Basile Moreau's voice was not stilled in death. He left a kind of written testament which, when read 130 years later, testifies subtly to both his moral strengths and weaknesses.

> With all my heart I pardon those who have harmed me in the exercise of my ministry by their calumnies. . . . I beg God to pardon those of our religious who have unknowingly paralyzed the development of the Congregation of Holy Cross, by having recourse to means which are both out of harmony with the spirit of our constitutions and rules and opposed to religious obedience, simplicity, truth, and abnegation. If they could read in the depths of my heart, they would see there no bitterness, but only indulgence and love for all the members of our family. My conscience tells me that I would gladly suffer much more.[59]

Understandably the aura of sanctity has clung to the Founder of Holy Cross. Still, there is really only One who can read the depths of the human heart, even the heart of a great but flawed religious leader. Edward Sorin's final word seems, after all, to say all that could have been said: "May he rest in peace, and soon help us on the narrow path to heaven."

---

59. Catta, *Moreau*, 2: 996–1005.

chapter twenty-eight

Piety and Progress

"WE WENT YESTERDAY, FATHER CHAPPÉ AND I, to see Bollée," Edward Sorin wrote from Le Mans at the end of 1868. "We had a long conversation with him and his two sons. They are very much taken with the idea of putting up at Notre Dame the finest chime in the world." Outside, in the bell-caster's yard, lay "two magnificent bourdons, just finished, . . . but in no way superior to yours." The recipient of this news was Alexis Granger, back in Indiana. Sorin, always fascinated by bells, was in the process of negotiating for the purchase of a monster bell of 16,000 pounds, and, always the entrepreneur, he had reckoned on a way to pay for it. The carillon he so prized, though it no longer worked properly, could be marketed by way of a lottery, and the unsightly shed in which it had been housed these fourteen years could be disposed of.[1]

> Your lottery [he continued his letter to Granger] should be authorized at once, and your tickets, at fifty cents, should total the round number of 20,000, no less. When people come to consider what they can get for fifty cents, twenty-three bells of the first foundry in Europe, a large cylinder, a splendid clock (and everything should be carefully described), whoever has fifty cents to spare will take a chance. If properly carried out, your undertaking will be a complete success. Not only [at] Notre Dame and St. Mary's, but [at] all your schools, and every one you meet, will get chances; in Canada, New Orleans, New Brunswick the same. Monsieur Bollée him-

---

1. See chapters 18 and 21, above.

self said that at fifty cents he would take some. But mark it, you have not a day to lose. . . . You may secure for Notre Dame a wonder which will not be surpassed for ages perhaps.[2]

St. Anthony's Bell, as it came to be called, eventually did toll the hours, did signal daily the Angelus and in season the great liturgical feasts, did send out its sonorous tones across the lakes and fields of Notre Dame du Lac. But before it could do so a place had to be provided to hang it. The fragile towers of the campus church, which could not support the carillon, would not meet the need. That circumstance did not matter; Father Sorin had determined to provide a grand new setting for St. Anthony and many other artistic wonders as well.

The twin-spired Church of the Sacred Heart had stood on the Notre Dame campus, hard by the main building, since 1848, when it replaced its rude log predecessor. It had served the Holy Cross community and the student body, and also as a place of worship for the Catholics in South Bend and the surrounding countryside. In the early years Edward Sorin had acted as ministering priest to these fifty or sixty families, though, with the passage of time, that designation became more and more nominal as his obligations increased and other priests assigned to the mission were available to assume various parochial duties. After 1858, when by the bishop of Fort Wayne's decree Notre Dame was changed canonically from a mission-station to a full-fledged parish, Alexis Granger took up the formal office of pastor of Sacred Heart, thus adding still another charge to an impressive list: twice provincial, vice president and prefect of religion in the college, master of novices on several occasions, and, more generally, Father Sorin's gentler alter ego.[3]

A decade of remarkable growth later Sorin and Granger agreed that an expanded sacred space was required. True enough, the edifice had been refurbished and modestly expanded over the years, and the opening of two new parishes in South Bend proper, St. Joseph's and St. Patrick's—the town in 1870, having annexed Lowell, boasted a population exceeding 7,000—had reduced the strictly pastoral functions attached to the campus church. But simultaneously the numbers of religious and students *en scène* had multiplied, especially after the Civil War, with every prospect of continuing growth in the future. Moreover, the sisters at St. Mary's did not possess a facility ample enough to meet all their liturgical and devotional needs. And perhaps determinative was Sorin's conviction

---

2. Sorin to Granger, December 13, 1868, AGEN.
3. See White, *Sacred Heart Parish*, 35, 38–40.

that the time had come for a genuinely monumental expression of the Catholic faith to be erected in mid-America.

Such a statement in brick and mortar, in paintings and sculpture and colored glass would necessarily reflect the conditions of its time and place and the predilections of the man who brought it into actuality. However much Edward Sorin accommodated himself to the American milieu, however much his experience had led him to despair of the condition of the so-called eldest daughter of the Church—"France is lost, France is finished!"—the religion he preached and practiced was, in its cultural details, what he had imbibed at Ahuillé and Le Mans, at Précigné and Parcé-sur-Sarthe. His formative years spent in these places had been a time of intense Catholic revival, a revival whose fervor had spilled over into missionary endeavors like his own.[4] In its flush of enthusiasm French Catholicism had rediscovered values furnished by earlier models, the medieval ages of faith before the Protestant Reformation and the dynamic resurgence of the old religion after it. Father Sorin participated zestfully in all the customs and practices the revival brought to the fore. He collected relics with boundless enthusiasm; in the course of his junkets to Europe he sent home to Indiana trunkloads of them with punctilious directives about their distribution. Sometimes he despaired of satisfying all the supplicants for these sacred objects: "Father Benoit has thirty-nine reliquaries," he complained on one occasion, "and the Bishop claims his share. None at all for me and Mrs. Phelan."[5] He was always on the lookout for opportunities to obtain indulgences. He learned, for example, in reading an article in a Belgian devotional magazine, that the Crosier Fathers had secured Roman permission to attach a partial indulgence to the recitation of a rosary blessed by them, "500 days per bead. I would be infinitely obliged if you would procure this faculty for me as well as for the ordained Superiors of our Houses."[6] As for the nineteenth-century restoration of pilgrimage, Father Sorin was an eager participant, particularly when such pious visitations were related to the cult of the Virgin Mary. He was intensely interested in La Sallette, traveled several times to Lourdes—and set up at Notre Dame a modest shrine in honor of Bernadette Soubirous's visions there[7]—and at least once to the magnificent cathedral of Notre Dame de Chartres.

---

4. See chapters 1 and 4, above.

5. Sorin to Battista, September 4, 1874, AGEN.

6. Sorin to Battista, December 18, 1872, AGEN. The Crosier Fathers or, more formally, the Canons Regular of the Order of the Holy Cross, were founded in Belgium early in the thirteenth century.

7. Not to be confused with the celebrated Lourdes grotto established in 1896 and still a center of devotion on campus. See Hope, *Notre Dame,* 264.

I did not leave the church until it was time to go back to the depot and start for Paris, at 8:00 P.M. I was so glad to be able to say Mass and to pray among such fervent lovers of our Blessed Mother. It must have been a rich day for many a soul, and for poor France in general. I cannot exactly say that I came all the way from Indiana for the pilgrimage to Chartres, and yet in one sense I did, for ever since I read the [statement] announcing it, I determined to be there, cost what it would. . . . A lady from Dreux seated behind me in the church seemed to be boasting a little of having come eight leagues to Chartres. I turned and said in a whisper: "I came 1,800 leagues."[8]

Such patterns of behavior might at first blush seem hard to harmonize with the brash, xenophobic culture of the United States during the last third of the nineteenth century. Yet the stress they put upon personal improvement struck a chord with the American temperament, practically if not philosophically. There ran through French Catholicism—and indeed through the Catholic *Weltanschaung* generally—a deep vein of moralistic individualism not unrelated to the Cartesian definition of the autonomous self, and this disposition melded readily enough with the mores of Sorin's adopted country. "If I . . . seek among these characteristics [of Americans] the principal one, which includes almost all the rest," observed the prescient Tocqueville in 1840,

I discover that . . . each American appeals only to the individual effort of his own understanding. America is . . . one of the countries where the precepts of Descartes are least studied and are best applied. Nor is this surprising. The Americans do not read the works of Descartes, because their social condition deters them from speculative studies; but they follow his maxims, because this same social condition naturally disposes their minds to adopt them.[9]

Conjecture about a compatibility between French Catholic religiosity and the American individualistic ethos cannot be pressed too far. For, as Tocqueville

---

8. Sorin to Sister Columba, May 28, 1873, AGEN. In 1846 two children reported an apparition of the Virgin Mary near the southeastern French village of La Salette. Twelve years later a similar event occurred near Lourdes in southwestern France. Both places, and especially the latter, became sites of massive popular devotion.

9. Alexis de Tocqueville, *Democracy in America,* 2 vols. (New York, 1984 ed.), 2: 3–4. I owe this reference to the very helpful conversations with my friend and colleague, Professor Mary Katherine Tillman.

also argued, Americans' fierce reliance on the unattended self befitting to a pioneer status disposed them to deny "what they cannot comprehend; which leaves them but little faith for whatever is extraordinary and an almost insurmountable distaste for whatever is supernatural"—an insurmountable obstacle, one might suppose, to the vocation of a Christian missioner from across the sea. To proclaim the extraordinary and the supernatural was the stock-in-trade, so to speak, of a man like Edward Sorin. But the varieties of emphasis that Catholicism has manifested at different epochs furnish perhaps a clue to understanding what proved to be a successful amalgamation of the French and the American. This is not to say that the Catholics of one generation thought they differed in *substance* from those believers who went before them or who were to come after them. Indeed, Cardinal Newman, Sorin's contemporary, published a treatise the year after Notre Dame received its charter as a university demonstrating that the creed and practice of the Roman Church in the nineteenth century, whatever the differences in detail, were consistent with what had flourished in the Christian community from the beginning.[10] Preachment of the gospel and administration of the sacraments remained, as they had always done, at the center of the Catholic experience, the warp and woof a seamless garment.

Nevertheless, one era of that experience has not necessarily accentuated the same elements of a rich deposit of values as another. Whether out of the implicit Cartesianism that permeated the theology they had studied, or out of what Tocqueville called the "social condition" in which they found themselves—more likely out of both—the priests of the Holy Cross mission centered at Notre Dame du Lac promoted an apostolate which emphasized personal piety and extra liturgical devotion, often encapsulated in sodalities and confraternities, like the "Guardian Angels of the Sanctuary" and the "Sacerdotal Prayer Union," both instituted by Sorin.[11] Sophisticated Catholics a hundred years later would characterize this ministry as too clerical in its orientation, too anxious to cultivate private devotions, too prone to emotional excess, too gullible when presented with accounts of the miraculous, too little concerned with the amelioration of society. They would decry the lack of a sense of integral worship, the failure to grasp the holistic significance of the cycle of feast and fast. The more extreme among them would discern in it a ghetto-mentality and dismiss the whole enterprise as a species of "triumphalism." The critics would, in sum, reproach Sorin and his contemporaries for cultivating an overly individualistic spirituality.

---

10. John Henry Newman (1801–1890), *An Essay on the Development of Christian Doctrine* (London, 1845).

11. See Sorin to Benoit, July 22, 1874, AGEN, and Hope, *Notre Dame*, 174.

Such strictures, quite obviously, reflect simply the passage of time more than anything else, an elaboration of Newman's brilliant theory of development. Although they are not without their merit, they also reveal the condescension the present all too commonly bestows upon the past. Change is an inescapable constituent of the living organism the Church purports to be. "In a higher world it is otherwise," Newman wrote famously and confidently; "but here below to live is to change, and to be perfect is to have changed often."[12] The same principle was expressed rather more laconically in an ancient slogan: *Ecclesia* semper *reformanda est,* the Church *always* needs to be reformed. And reform for Catholics has ever meant organic growth, not destruction of the old and creation of the new. Indeed the old, absorbed but never invalidated, constantly reasserts itself, and the sophisticates at the beginning of the twenty-first century may well wonder why *their* immediate ancestors had so little esteemed private prayer, moral exhortation, warm devotion to the Virgin and the saints, proper reverence for the Eucharistic Real Presence, the consolations of the sacrament of penance, the committed and consecrated life of the vows, and the salutary practice of preceding feast with fast.

Father Sorin at any rate saw his vocation in starkly direct terms. "I was born, it seems to me," he once confided to a close friend, "with a peculiar sense of the simplicity with which a Religious should be, as it were, permeated. Any departure from it is a torment." But the Providence upon whom he so often called had reserved for him an additional obligation.

Alas, whatever care we may take . . . to edify others, there will be, when we are gone, more eagerness to quote what in our conduct seemed to favor nature than what appeared done to overcome and conquer it. God alone knows how much I love the souls He has entrusted to me. I am more than ever resolved to live for them and their future happiness. From the same motive of faith, I believe I feel much more tenderly for whose who, like myself, have to carry the burden of authority. I pity them, and they become doubly dear to me in proportion as their responsibility is extended. Let us all aid each other to become true Religious, much more actively, directly, and efficiently, than to secure . . . a flying comfort, for which we may feel very sorry at the last hour.[13]

---

12. Newman, *Development,* 40.
13. Sorin to Mother Ascension, December 16, 1876, AGEN.

BY 1869 THE PLANS for the new church were firmly taking shape. The first step taken was a change in name. The old worship center had been dedicated to the Sacred Heart. The devotion to the heart of Jesus, with its biblical and patristic roots, had achieved wide popularity in France during the seventeenth century. Its votaries honored Christ's human heart as the depository of a love directed both to heaven and to earth. The popular notion of the heart as the seat of emotional affection had long been celebrated in song and story and in the devotional realm as well—"Our hearts will not rest," cried St. Augustine, "till they rest in thee." St. Francis de Sales (d. 1622) had described transcendent prayer as *cor ad cor loquitur,* heart speaks to heart, a conversation with the divine in which mere words have no role to play. But the cultus achieved its definitive standing with the apparitions experienced by a Visitation nun from Burgundy named Margaret Mary Alacoque (d. 1690), to whom Jesus revealed "the heart which has loved human beings so much," the "heart of flesh" which honors the "heart of God."[14] Margaret Mary was an unpretentious woman who made no special claims to holiness. Under the guidance of her Jesuit confessor, however, she disclosed to the public at large the mystical messages accorded her, with the result that there emerged eventually a vast literature focused on the Sacred Heart, as well as a set of pious practices—most notably her recommendation that a Catholic receive Holy Communion on the first Friday of nine consecutive months. A succession of popes sanctioned the devotion to the Sacred Heart by instituting a liturgical feast—celebrated in June, the month Sister Margaret Mary had had her first visions—and ultimately by her beatification in 1864 and her canonization in 1920.

Edward Sorin and Alexis Granger had grown up imbued with devotion to the Sacred Heart of Jesus, so peculiarly French, and it is therefore no surprise that the first real church built at Notre Dame du Lac in 1848 should have borne that title. But they also had been caught up in the immense revival of Marian piety— so often referred to in these pages—that also characterized the France of their formative years. So in 1869, when Granger at Sorin's instance announced the new endeavor, he proclaimed that the building proposed would be dedicated, in a

---

14. Quoted in Thomas F. O'Meara, O.P., *The Basilica of the Sacred Heart at Notre Dame* (n.p. [Notre Dame, Ind.], n.d. [1992], 13–14. This short work is a moving and informative theological reflection on the decorative aspects of the minor basilica (an honorific title conferred upon the church by Pope John Paul II in 1992). It should be noted that Father O'Meara's "guide" was composed just after the building was restored in its iconography to the scheme instituted under Edward Sorin, 1869–1892.

neat and happy junction, to "Our Lady of the Sacred Heart of Jesus." An advertisement inserted into several pious publications over Granger's name explained
that "gratitude to our Blessed Mother for the many blessings obtained through
her powerful intercession . . . has urged us to begin at once the execution of a
project we have entertained for some years past, . . . to build a church at Notre
Dame, not merely an edifice suitable in size to the want of both students and
community, but a church worthy in some manner of the glorious patroness of
the place." As for financing the enterprise, Father Granger, ever a diffident and reluctant fund-raiser, also instituted "the celebration of a DAILY MASS [from] the
21st of June 1869, [which] *will be continued for fifty years* for all those who shall
contribute $50 to the erection of the church." Despite the pastor's signature, this
proposal had a definitely Sorinesque ring to it, especially in its embellishments:
"Any offering less than $50 will entitle the giver to the fruits of the daily Mass *pro
rata* of the amount contributed. . . . Persons who could not easily give $50 at once
can pay in installments."[15]

There was a complication, however, in initiating the project just then and in
choosing its new name. Mother Angela and the sisters at St. Mary's had intended
to affix the title of Our Lady of the Sacred Heart to the church they were planning
to construct on their campus. Angela indeed had by 1869 raised several thousand
dollars for that end. But Sorin, as usual, got his way. Once she learned of his intentions, she assured him that she would "cheerfully withdraw our petition and
will work for the Church at Notre Dame if you think it best. . . . I *now* feel
satisfied that . . . a great monument to our Blessed Mother . . . should be at Notre
Dame in preference to St. Mary's." The money she had collected was duly turned
over to Granger and so served to augment the amount gathered from the contributors who hoped to share in the in the daily Mass for fifty years or in its
"fruits . . . *pro rata*." Mother Angela for her part had to wait till 1886, the year before her death, for the completion of a community church at St. Mary's, dedicated to Our Lady of Loretto.[16]

Granger's announcement of 1869 stated that the construction of the new
church would begin "at once." In fact the cornerstone was not laid until the spring
of 1871, and the building did not achieve its final form until 1892, the year before Sorin and Granger died (thus providing an odd analogy to Mother Angela's

---

15. Quoted in Thomas J. Schlereth, *A Spire of Faith: The University of Notre Dame's Sacred Heart
Church* (Notre Dame, Ind., 1991), 20. This excellent examination of the historical, architectural, and
iconographical aspects of the church, with its splendid illustrations and charts, is a model of its
genre.

16. See Schlereth, *Spire of Faith,* 17.

experience on her campus). The reason for this gradual process was due largely, though not exclusively, to budgetary concerns. Another factor was a certain hesitancy about style, size, and ornamentation. Father Sorin's original ambition, characteristically grandiose, was to adopt as a model the Gesù in Rome, the mother church of the Society of Jesus. Built during the latter half of the sixteenth century, this great baroque monument to the soaring aspirations of post-Tridentine Catholicism, with its vast interior topped by a dome decorated with magnificent frescoes, represented precisely the kind of triumphalism the founder of Notre Dame wanted to effect.[17] An architect was accordingly hired, but his design—a three-naved domed cruciform large enough to seat 2,000—would have involved an expense beyond what even Sorin could contemplate, rumored to have been as much as $100,000.[18] Instead he and Granger agreed to devise a more modest and, for their time, a more conventional structure, a single-spired neo-gothic edifice of brick and fieldstone which was eventually enlarged by transepts, six small aspidal chapels (1879) and a Lady Chapel (1888) thrusting out behind the sanctuary. A steeple rising to 209 feet (1892) put the final touch to the exterior of the Church of Our Lady of the Sacred Heart of Jesus. Working with Sorin and Granger, or rather the real if self-taught architect who worked with their cordial support and encouragement, was Brother Charles Borromeo. Born Patrick Harding in Ireland in 1838, a carpenter's son, he had joined the Holy Cross community at the age of twenty-four. If the church was largely the creation of his prolific intelligence, so were a host of other campus buildings, many of them still in service more than a century later, put up before his death in 1911.[19]

The interior decoration of the church was a similarly gradual proceeding, presided over by two foreign artists, one French and the other Italian.[20] The stained-glass windows were the product of a native of Le Mans called Eugène Hucher. His studio had evolved from an enterprise initiated by Basile Moreau and Sainte-Croix, which in the 1850s had passed into the control of a convent of Carmelite nuns. The sisters in turn had given the business over to a group of laymen, among whom Hucher was the master craftsman; ultimately he became the

---

17. See Georgina Masson, *The Companion Guide to Rome* (London, 1980), 107–108, and Wylie Sypher, *Four Stages of Renaissance Style* (New York, 1955), 247.

18. Auguste Lemonnier-Dubourg to "Cher Papa et al.," January 17, 1870, AUND, CPLE, "Lemonnier Collection."

19. Schlereth, *Spire of Faith*, 16–21, and *Matricule générale*, 1609, AIP. Harding should not be confused with an earlier and, to Sorin, a troublesome Brother Charles Borromeo. See Sorin, *Chronicles*, 266–269, and chapter 22, above.

20. The interior decoration continued well into the 1880s. See, for example, Gregori to Sorin, October 11, 1883, and Hucher to Sorin, February 21 and April 3, 1883, AIP.

owner of the Carmel Glassworks as well. Sorin knew and appreciated his reputation and, during his frequent visits to Le Mans, kept in constant touch with him as the windows of the church were painstakingly fashioned. Hucher never traveled to Indiana and hence never saw the end result of his brilliant handiwork.[21] Luigi Gregori, by contrast, who painted the church's dazzling murals, spent a major portion of his creative life at Notre Dame. Sorin met him in Rome where for some years he had held the position of artist-in-residence in the papal court. In 1874, aged fifty-five, the dapper Italian began his work in the still unfinished church under the terms of a three-year contract. He remained a fixture on campus for seventeen years and applied his skill to many other projects, including the famous if sometimes controversial paintings depicting the career of Christopher Columbus that still today grace the entrance and foyer of the Main Building.[22]

Once the ground-belfry housing the carillon had been removed, construction of Our Lady of the Sacred Heart had commenced at a point some distance in front of (or south of) the old twin-spired church, which continued for the time being as the site of the community's usual liturgical and devotional functions. By the summer of 1875, with its nave, sanctuary, and transepts finished, the new edifice was ready for regular service and the former one for demolition. On the morning of August 15, the feast of the Assumption of the Virgin, Edward Sorin solemnly blessed the building, still starkly innocent of decoration on the inside, and shortly afterward his old friend and collaborator, Alexis Granger, sang the first high Mass there, bolstered by a choir and a new organ that had cost $6,000.[23] The two priests had journeyed far from the French countryside of their youth, but the church that would from then on serve as the spiritual center of their endeavors might well have stood proudly on a hilltop in Sarthe or Mayenne.

FATHER SORIN took pains to attribute the long process of construction and ornamentation of the new church to Granger—"your bell," he had

---

21. See an "Address" by Stéphane Arrondeau of Le Mans, delivered in the Basilica of the Sacred Heart, Notre Dame, August 11, 1998, based upon his doctoral dissertation (Université du Maine, 1997), *La Fabrique de vitraux du Carmel du Mans (1853–1903): chronique d'une grande aventure.* I owe this reference and the text of Dr. Arroneau's address to the kindness of my colleague, Professor Charles Parnell.

22. See Schlereth, *Spire of Faith,* 31–33. The series of Columbus murals were done for the present Main Building, that is, for the one built after the disastrous fire of 1879. See chapter 29, below.

23. See Hope, *Notre Dame,* 216–218. White, *Sacred Heart Parish,* 48, says Granger blessed the church, in contrast to Schlereth, *Spire of Faith,* 19, who says Sorin did. Sorin's correspondence testifies to his presence at Notre Dame on that date.

written the pastor from Le Mans at the beginning of the project, and years later, from Rome, "I find here the beautiful chalice presented by His Holiness to your new Church of Our Lady of the Sacred Heart. . . . I saw the other day the model of your statue; they all agree here that you have a splendid monument."[24] But Sorin himself was the driving force behind this enterprise and indeed most other initiatives undertaken by the community at Notre Dame du Lac and by the congregation at large. It was he who had petitioned Pius IX for the chalice and had persuaded the pontiff to use it at his own Mass before having it sent to Indiana.[25] The "colossal statue" of Christ was also secured in Rome through Sorin's efforts, although it proved artistically less satisfactory than another gift, "the magnificent portrait of His Holiness which Signor Gregori has just finished and which will probably be judged the most perfect and most lifelike in existence. It is so natural and depicts the Holy Father as I have had the happiness to observe him on his afternoon promenade."[26]

Meanwhile life at Notre Dame du Lac continued apace. The number of students held more or less steady throughout the 1870s, though there was some slippage in the wake of the national recession of 1873. Under Mother Angela's tutelage, St. Mary's Academy began to edge into its collegiate future by instituting a program whereby graduates might stay on for a year or two and take courses they had missed previously.[27] At Notre Dame Edward Sorin's own indifference to serious scholarship still set the intellectual style and mood; despite the pleas of Timothy Howard and Father Toohey, the faculty, priest and layman alike, remained for the most part lackluster. An exception that proved the rule was Augustin Louage, a peripatetic priest who joined Holy Cross in 1872, at the age of forty-three. Sorin appointed him master of novices the following year, and he went on to fashion a distinguished career within the congregation. He published several philosophy manuals in English, the first of which Sorin recommended enthusiastically: "I believe this work is excellent. It answers perfectly an immense need in this country, where up to now we have had, even in Catholic colleges, only on this subject Protestant compositions."[28]

---

24. Sorin to Granger, January 19, 1876, AGEN.

25. Sorin to Battista, August 11, 1875, and Sorin to Sister Columba, October 31, 1875, AGEN.

26. Sorin to Franchi, June 9, 1875, AGEN. Alessandro Cardinal Franchi was the new prefect of Propaganda, in succession to Cardinal Barnabò, who died in 1874.

27. Costin, *Priceless Spirit*, 213.

28. Sorin to Battista, September 24, 1873, AGEN. Louage served as master of novices at Notre Dame, 1873–1880, and provincial of Canada, 1880–1887. He was appointed bishop of Dacca in 1890 (after Holy Cross had reassumed direction of the Bengal mission) and died there in 1894. See *Matricule générale*, 1871, AIP.

Even more exceptional, and more enduring in its affect upon the development of Notre Dame, was the emergence of the brothers Zahm, John and Albert.[29] Young Father John Zahm, ordained in 1875, began his famous series of scientific lectures and fieldtrips the next year, and by the time he died in 1921 he had attained an international reputation as a genuine polymath. Throughout his distinguished career he never ceased to echo Toohey and Howard, specifically lobbying the congregation's authorities to enrich the training offered to the men of Holy Cross by sending them to good graduate schools. Sorin scarcely understood this intent of raising Notre Dame to the level of a real university, but he was sincerely fond of Zahm and never interfered with the younger man's studies and ambitions—an accommodation not always adopted by his successors. Albert Zahm matriculated at Notre Dame in 1879. After graduation he stayed on for ten years as professor of mathematics. Though like his brother he possessed a wide-ranging intellect, his deepest interest lay in the field of aeronautics, and his researches, both before and after the Wright brothers, gained him worldwide fame. The intellectual seeds sown by these luminaries bore fruit in due time, but in the interval Notre Dame abided by Sorin's ideal of providing a cadre of devotedly Catholic laymen equipped to take their place in the world. Commencement statistics tell one aspect of the story: at the exercises in June 1875, a typical year, of fifty-six degrees conferred, forty-three were products of the commercial department.[30]

Besides the tenets rooted in his own limited educational background, Father Sorin may have harbored suspicions of clever men because of the unpleasantness he experienced at the hands of the university's fifth president. Patrick Colovin, born in English-speaking Canada in 1842, joined Holy Cross at Saint-Laurent and was ordained in 1867. His abundant intellectual ability brought him a series of responsible positions, but the course he followed as a religious was troubled from the beginning. Perhaps he was thrust into those positions at too tender an age; if so, Sorin had to assume a measure of blame. Colovin was only twenty-eight when Sorin insisted he be appointed superior in Montreal despite the objections raised by the provincial council. "[I] blame the narrow spirit of your councilors," he scolded the retiring superior, "who see only local interests when the very existence of the entire Congregation is in play. My heart is with you, but my judgment disapproves of the narrow views that have been adopted." A gifted candidate must not be casually thrust aside: "Father Colovin . . . is not easy to

29. See Weber, *John Zahm*, 11–15, 20, 147–149.

30. Hope, *Notre Dame*, 171, 181–182, 207–212.

guide. He is more a philosopher than a Religious. But perfection is not of this world. We have to deal with men, not with angels."[31]

But Colovin quickly proved to be as unruly a subject as he was an unwelcome local superior. He quarreled with Sorin's directive that prayers be offered in all the houses of the congregation for the repose of two recently deceased members. "Do you think, dear Father," Sorin asked him, "that you have acted in a sufficiently religious and edifying manner in refusing this injunction and accompanying the refusal with arguments as though you were the *supreme judge?*" Colovin had objected to a grammatical error he had discerned in Sorin's circular. "You act as though you had come upon a heresy, an incontestable crime! . . . You are so confident in the superiority of your judgment that it seems useless to you to give your poor superior the benefit of the doubt." The issue for Sorin was vowed obedience, not some rubrical detail. "Dear Father, true zeal for the efficacy of religion is efficacious in proportion to the degree that it is humble. You assure me in advance of your submission to whatever I decide, and then in the same breath (*souffle*) you *demand to see . . . the sanction of Rome.* Which of these two do you want me to take as an expression of your true sentiments?"[32]

But worse was to come. A few months after he had composed this admonition, in the late summer of 1871, Father Sorin hurried off to Montreal to deal with a genuine crisis in the Canadian province.

> I am very sorry to learn here such an unpleasant account of poor Father Colovin [he informed William Corby]. A regular and scandalous drunkard; a proud and merciless censor and natural enemy of anyone above him in office; a lazy, irregular, and piousless [sic] sort of Religious, whose spirit here is recalled as subversive of all authority. They predict he will surely prove equally dangerous anywhere else. What to do with such a one is no small difficulty. Here he is lost for life; he cannot come back to Canada. I pity him but do not know what to do with him. There is a report that he is doing mischief . . . as chaplain of the local convent. He should be kept at home."[33]

"Home" for Colovin, after his escapades at Saint-Laurent, was Notre Dame du Lac. Here too his conduct left much to be desired and earned Sorin's reprimands. These Colovin appeared to accept with appropriate docility. "Just allow me the

---

31. Sorin to Villandre, June 15, 1870, AGEN.
32. Sorin to Colovin, February 24, 1871, AGEN.
33. Sorin to Corby, September 17, 1871, AIP.

pleasure of saying to you," he wrote plaintively on one occasion, "that on yester-day I admired alike your delicacy and your manhood, and both greatly."[34] What-ever the superior general thought of such protestations, he decided the gifted if flawed young priest deserved another chance. Colovin was accordingly assigned to the mission in Watertown, Wisconsin, where he was awarded the title of "theo-logian and professor of arts and mathematics" and where the superior, Corby, could keep an eye on him.[35] Father Colovin met this test successfully, at least to the extent of dazzling Corby personally—a circumstance that would have un-happy repercussions later.[36] And Sorin too was apparently impressed. When in the spring of 1874 Sorin's projected trip to Watertown had been thwarted, he in-formed Corby by mail: "Among many things of which I wanted to speak to you . . . was [to] let me know confidentially if Father Colovin could not be re-moved [from Wisconsin]; I have something else for him in view."[37]

What exactly the "something else" was remains unclear, though it is possible that Sorin intended Colovin to act as aide to the president, Auguste Lemonnier, the state of whose health was causing widespread alarm. His "is a hopeless case," Sorin said of the beloved nephew at the end of August 1874.[38] And when Father Lemonnier died six weeks later, Colovin was named to succeed him. The choice seems curious in retrospect, given Colovin's uneven record and especially his weakness for drink. Perhaps Sorin, even as he mourned the loss of his nephew, was anxious to demonstrate that he played no favorites. More likely the promo-tion of Colovin, certainly in many respects an able man, resulted from the thin-ness of competent personnel available to an ever-expanding Holy Cross. Corby and Toohey could not be everywhere. The experiment at any rate was not a suc-cess. Colovin proved efficient enough, and his dignified demeanor as well as his oratorical ability gave his public persona a seemly gravitas. But he lacked Patrick Dillon's verve and Lemonnier's warmth. Most detrimental of all, he lacked the superior general's confidence. Nor was he lucky: Colovin's tenure coincided with the falloff in enrollment caused by the poor national economy during the mid-1870s, a serious problem for Notre Dame's always precarious finances. When the fall term began in 1877, Colovin exchanged positions with William Corby, who assumed the presidency of the university for the second time.

---

34. Colovin to Sorin, August 23, 1871, AIP.
35. Cullen, "Sacred Heart, Watertown," 5.
36. See chapter 29, below.
37. Sorin to Corby, May 4, 1874, AIP.
38. Sorin to Corby, August 29, 1874, AIP.

Colovin's brief second stay in Wisconsin was marred by controversy. Rumor had it that he had begun drinking again, and his overall reckless behavior, along with his persistent expressions of contempt for Sorin and Notre Dame, led six members of the Watertown college's staff to petition for his removal.[39] Sorin, convinced that Colovin had entered into a conspiratorial plot with Charles Moreau, determined to go further than that and expel him from the congregation. "Both of them are capable of it," Sorin commented bitterly. "Their success will simply ruin the Congregation, [and] they both know it."[40] But Colovin was not ready to depart quietly. "This charge," he responded, 'habitual contempt for authority,' I deny. I challenge the proof of it, and until such time as it is established I disregard the 'decision' in so far as it concerns my membership in this community. Out of every right of which I am now deprived I consider as an aggravation of an unprovoked and uncalled for outrage."[41] Nor was he without friends within the congregation. Nine priests, among them Condon and John Zahm, drew up a strongly worded protest against the "arbitrary" and "unfair" treatment accorded their "abstemious" colleague, Father Colovin, and Sorin found it prudent to rescind the order.[42] But Colovin's position in Watertown had been rendered untenable, and he was sent off to Dakota Territory, the deprivations of which he endured for less than a year. "I am here in a position," he wrote Granger, the provincial, "which no authority . . . has the right to place me. I came here as a concession to hate, and to avoid the continuation of the blackguard outrages of which for years I have been the object. But I shall remain no longer than is compatible with honor. . . . You can do just as you see fit in the case." In due time the authorities did see fit to expel Patrick Colovin from the congregation.[43] He retired first to his native Ontario, and from there he launched a last, bitter, scarcely comprehensible broadside at Edward Sorin. "Reverend Sir," he wrote, "you will please send me a simple and formal certificate to the effect that I have never been a member of the Congregation of Holy Cross, or of the Holy Cross, or whatever may be, or may have

---

39. "Address" to Sorin, n.d. [1879], AIP.

40. Sorin to Battista, January 17, 1879, AGEN. Colovin was allegedly colluding with Moreau in promoting the nuisance suit, filed in Rome, with which the Marianite Sisters in Le Mans continued to harass Sorin and Notre Dame. See Sorin to Franchi, April 21, 1878, AGEN: "Monseigneur Fillion [bishop of Le Mans] said to me: 'You owe the Sisters nothing.'" Sorin also nurtured darker suspicions, for which see chapter 29, below.

41. Colovin to Sorin, June 17, 1879, AIP.

42. "Address" to Sorin, n.d. [1879], AIP.

43. Colovin to Granger, June 7, 1881, AIP, and Sorin to Battista, July 5, 1881, AGEN. See also Hope, *Notre Dame*, 170–171, 178–179, *Matricule générale*, 1642, AIP, and chapter 29, below.

been, the name of the institution of which you are superior." He based this demand on the allegation that he had "never crossed the door of a novitiate, never [seen] a master of novices in the congregation until long after my profession. . . . As this is a matter of business, you will please attend to it with ordinary businesslike promptitude."[44]

THE MISSION UNDERTAKEN by Holy Cross in southwest Dakota was occasioned by the discovery of gold in the Black Hills in 1875. Almost overnight towns famous later in legend like Deadwood and Lead sprouted up, populated mostly by ordinary seekers of fortune but also by similarly legendary figures like Calamity Jane, Wild Bill Hickock, and Sam Bass. A secular priest from Nebraska arrived in the area in 1877, but he did not last long among those he called "the very worst Catholics in the world," who spent their money in saloons and "houses of infamy" and wanted a priest only on their deathbeds. The following January his successor, pleading the need for succor in the face of the frequent accidents in the mines as well as the incidence of typhus, diphtheria, and other diseases, appealed to Mother Angela to send sisters to act as nurses. With Sorin's endorsement, she agreed, and in mid-summer five nuns undertook the fatiguing journey from Indiana to Deadwood and began their healing ministry in a rented house on the outskirts of the town. Soon afterward reinforcements arrived from St. Mary's, and a companion hospital was set up in Lead. Sorin indicated his own sense of the import of this new venture by dispatching there the estimable Father John Toohey, the first of seven Holy Cross priests to assume parochial duties there.

The obstacles, however, proved overwhelming. The boom-and-bust culture created by the goldfields and the rough and transient character of the populace resisted the establishment of permanent institutions. Less than three years after their arrival the sisters closed their forlorn little hospitals and withdrew. Toohey was recalled to Notre Dame at about the same time, and the last of his successors had departed by 1885. Two years before that the nuns returned to Deadwood, as teachers now rather than nurses, and opened an academy in their former hospital building. St. Edward's—the name was significant—struggled through a host

---

44. Colovin to Sorin, February 2, 1882, AIP. Father Colovin was apparently maintaining that since he had not undergone a canonically approved novitiate (the fact of the matter is not clear), no later commitments to Holy Cross were valid. He died in 1887 in Wisconsin, where he had been engaged in pastoral ministry.

of adversities till 1897 when the school finally closed. Altogether thirty Sisters of the Holy Cross had rendered their unselfish service to the Dakota frontier over a seventeen-year period.[45]

Northeastern Wisconsin was a more settled and decorous region than was western Dakota during the roaring '70s and '80s, but here too, after a bright and hopeful beginning,[46] the Holy Cross mission soon encountered serious difficulties. As ever, they stemmed from inadequate funds and a shallow pool of competent personnel. In accord with his usual practice, Father Sorin had insisted that the college in Watertown should be linked to a parish, thus assuring mutual financial support. So William Corby acted both as pastor of St. Bernard's parish and president of the University of Our Lady of the Sacred Heart. But as early as 1875 a formal visitation by the provincial, Alexis Granger, revealed much tension within the community, while a little later Sorin himself found the parochial school totally inadequate.[47] Patrick Condon, who was at the time the parochial assistant to Corby, registered his conviction that the jurisdictional union was not working and that parish and college should be separated. He warned moreover that unless a more capable faculty could be assembled and a strenuous effort mounted to recruit students over a wider geographic area, "it would be better to break up the whole thing and have your subjects employed somewhere else, as nothing short of a complete reform will keep this house alive another year."[48] Sorin followed the advice vis-à-vis the administrative separation, and the next year appointed Condon himself president of the college. But there appeared no swift revival of the institution's earlier promise, and by the beginning of 1878 Sorin, depressed by the widespread hard times, had about given up hope: "Watertown College . . . should be closed as soon as convenient; it is an expense and a sacrifice of a large personnel, who could certainly be utilized somewhere."[49] Condon, on the other hand, had grown less pessimistic, and, since the superior general always trusted his judgment, Sacred Heart was granted a renewed if shaky lease on life. The institution never really flourished as Father Sorin had hoped,

---

45. See Franklin Cullen, "Holy Cross in the Black Hills. The Dakota Apostolate, 1878–1897," a paper delivered to the Conference on the History of the Congregations of Holy Cross (1987). Of Brother Franklin's many admirable monographs, this one, in its thoroughness and use of sources, is particularly outstanding.

46. See chapter 26, above.

47. Sorin to "My dear Child," September 20, 1876, AIP. The unnamed recipient of this letter was a nun whom Sorin intended to send to Watertown to take charge of the school.

48. Condon to Granger, June 14, 1875, AIP.

49. Sorin, "Memorandum for the Administration," January 2, 1878, AGEN.

but, except for an interval between 1886 and 1888, it continued to function under Holy Cross auspices as a college for lay students till 1912.[50]

Most of Father Sorin's expansive initiatives during the 1870s experienced similar uncertainties. "New Orleans will remain a dead letter in our hands. I would strongly recommend to dispose of St. Isidore's Farm," the piece of land, now halved in value due to the recession, which had originally been slotted as support for a projected college in Louisiana. "Cincinnati must be kept in the best possible condition," though St. Joseph's College there continued to be an unprofitable drain on the province's resources.[51] But the aged John Baptist Purcell had been a steady friend and patron, and now that he faced a disastrous bankruptcy due to the carelessness of his brother—"he is a good priest, but the very opposite of a man of business"[52]—desertion of the archbishop by Holy Cross was unthinkable. And the mission at Galveston too, after a bright beginning, was teetering on the verge of dissolution.

Nevertheless, the Holy Cross presence in Galveston and the apparent encouragement of its bishop, resulted in Father Sorin's most successful foundation outside Indiana. As early as 1872 Bishop Dubuis contacted Notre Dame to the effect that he had been promised a tract of land near the Texas capital city of Austin upon which the donor was anxious to see the foundation of a Catholic college for boys. Mary Doyle, a widow, was willing to turn over to the diocese her farm of 398 acres for this purpose, so long as she could enjoy its income during her lifetime. Dubuis could not staff such a project on his own, and, since he was so pleased with the progress Brother Boniface Muller had so far made in his see-city,[53] he inquired whether Holy Cross might be in a position to assume the charge. Once apprised of this opportunity Sorin hastened to Austin and held a very satisfactory conference with Mrs. Doyle, during which she indicated her agreement to award the property to Holy Cross if the bishop assented. Moreover, in a characteristic three-day whirlwind of activity, Sorin acquired an adjacent 123 acres from a certain Colonel Willis Robards, fifty of them as a gift and the rest at $50 an acre. He also took care to cultivate cordial relations with the local pastor, a secular priest named Nicholas Feltin. "Our good bishop," Feltin informed Sorin shortly after the latter had returned to Indiana, "writes to me that he feels very happy to know

50. Cullen, "Sacred Heart College," 6–10, 17–19, 24. In 1886 the college was closed to public matriculation and used exclusively as a training school for aspirants to the brotherhood. This experiment lasted two years and was resumed in 1912.

51. Sorin, "Memorandum for the Administration," January 2, 1878, AGEN.

52. Sorin to Battista, March 12, 1879, AGEN. The reference was to Father Edward Purcell. See chapter 26, note 63, above.

53. See chapter 26, above.

that we endeavor to act in good harmony with regard to the affairs of the congregation in Austin."[54] Once back home, Sorin, always trustful of the Lancaster, Ohio, connection, consulted a scion of the Ewing family. "Your prospects in Texas I think are splendid," opined Thomas Ewing, Junior, now practicing law in Cleveland. "I would say that I would consider Austin or San Antonio a far better point for an Institution than New Orleans or Galveston, owing to sanitary reasons."[55]

The "harmony" with Pastor Feltin, however, underwent some rough moments over succeeding months and years. Sorin, as he had done in Watertown, insisted that Holy Cross be awarded the local parish as a hedge against future financial trouble. Feltin raised no objection to this proviso at first, until it struck him that, once he had left Autsin, he might not be recompensed for money of his own he had spent on property and construction over the years. As late as 1875 he complained about the difficulty in securing "a suitable place in which to exercise the holy ministry in the Diocese."[56] In the end affairs in this regard were worked out amicably, when Sorin purchased the parochial school Feltin had built at his own expense—though for a lesser price than the former pastor had requested.[57]

Another advantage Father Sorin perceived in the arrangement in Austin was that, besides the parish, Holy Cross could also count on the farm as a source of income. But here too things did not go altogether smoothly. Mrs. Doyle, in frail health, was anxious that Holy Cross take some discernible steps toward making the school of her dreams a reality. Her impatience was not altogether reasonable, since the income from the farm continued to be hers and since negotiations about the parish were still not complete. Nonetheless, she was irritated at what she considered Sorin's unwarranted silence. "I hope, Reverend Father," she appealed to him, "you have not abandon [sic] the idea of erecting the College in our midst, as it is certainly wish [sic] for. I beg, Reverend Father, you will be kind enough to write me a few lines and let me know your full intentions."[58] Whatever reassurances Sorin gave her made little difference to her personally: a few months after penning her plaintive letter, in February, 1873, she died.[59] And predeceasing her by a few months was Colonel Robards, who left behind a pregnant widow and two small children. His executor trusted that under such unhappy circum-

---

54. Feltin to Sorin, June 11, 1872, AIP. Similarly friendly communications were sent May 2, May 4, December 14, and December 17, 1872, AIP.

55. Ewing to Sorin, April 27, 1872, AIP.

56. Feltin to Sorin, January 19, 1875, AIP.

57. Feltin to Sorin, April 6, 1875, AIP.

58. Mary Doyle to Sorin, November 17, 1872, AIP.

59. Dunn, "Holy Cross in Texas," 8–11.

stances Father Sorin might soon pay at least a portion of the indebtedness which amounted to $4,189.[60]

Negotiations were wound up with a formal agreement signed by Bishop Dubuis and Father Sorin early in 1874. The able and energetic Father Daniel Spillard,[61] aged thirty-five, was promptly sent from Notre Dame to serve as pastor of the parish and superior, and, on April 23, Mother Angela herself conducted another sister to Austin to begin classes for the local Catholic children. Two brothers followed at the end of the summer. This Holy Cross nucleus, however, moved slowly, partly because of the unpredictable moods of the bishop, who seemed to blow hot and cold toward the mission. And despite Spillard's desire to open a college without delay—some of Mrs. Doyle's relatives were rumored to be contemplating a suit for recovery of her property on the grounds that the commitment to Catholic education had gone unfulfilled—financial reality imposed even greater caution. "Our wheat has been harvested, thrashed, and yielded only six bushels to the acre," Spillard reported in 1876. "This is not very encouraging to our industrious Brothers. We had a pretty good corn crop, but not much cotton and at a low price."[62] His outlandish idea of floating a loan of $10,000 drew from Sorin an amused rebuke: "My dear Reverend little Father, I wonder how a little man of your size can talk big words as you do—$10,000 as I would have done for $100 thirty years ago. What security, pray, will you give for such a loan?"[63] Gradual progress in this instance proved fruitful and enduring. When the first classes were taught on the farm in 1878, Spillard referred to this humble entity—it counted a total of six pupils—as St. Aloysius Preparatory School. He later called it the University of Holy Cross, but ultimately, even as the institution enjoyed modest growth till, in the fall term of 1885, sixty-one students matriculated, it bore Sorin saint's name: successively as academy, college, and university, it prospered, as it does to this day, under the ghostly patronage of Edward the Confessor.[64]

The overall success of St. Edward's of Austin may appear in stark contrast to the failure over the long term of others of Father Sorin's foundations elsewhere in Texas, as well as in Missouri, Louisiana, Dakota, Cincinnati, and, much earlier, in Kentucky and New York. Even the mission in which he put his greatest hopes, Watertown, Wisconsin, disappointed him. But such a conclusion would widely miss the mark. The presence of the priests, brothers, and sisters of Holy Cross in

60. Blackburn to Sorin, December 18, 1872, AIP.
61. For Irish-born Spillard (1839–1926), see *Matricule générale*, 1734, AIP.
62. Spillard to Sorin, July 25 and October 12, 1876, AIP.
63. Sorin to Spillard, July 13, 1875, AIP.
64. Dunn, "Holy Cross in Texas," 13–16.

these widely varied apostolates, even over a short span of time, was an immense contribution to the development of the Catholic community in the United States during the nineteenth century. The "Immigrant Church," to employ the conventional phrase, with all its ethnic and cultural variety, with its restless movement from place to place, with its insecurity as it attempted to assimilate into an often hostile Protestant ascendancy, desperately needed, if the faith were to survive, the assurance that dedicated religious could offer. It can never be overemphasized that Sorin and his colleagues, men and women, were missionaries before they were educators or nurses or administrators. Some of them, to be sure, fell short of the ideal; but for every Patrick Colovin or Brother Amédée, a John Toohey or Peter Cooney or Brother Boniface Muller or Mother Ascension stepped to the fore. In a situation that was constantly fluid, to hold the fort, so to speak, until other religious societies were ready to assume the gospel's burden in a certain region—thus the Benedictines opened a hospital in the Deadwood school building the Holy Cross nuns vacated in 1897—was itself an important function. Yet can it be maintained that the earlier work of Mother Angela's sisters over nearly twenty years among the gunmen and prostitutes of the wild Dakota Territory did not yield fruit of its own? Edward Sorin never had enough money or enough personnel to accomplish fully all that his soaring spiritual ambitions strove for. Even so, he understood, intuitively or otherwise, that to put down roots in American society, to build and to sow and ultimately to harvest, was the task that Providence had set for him. This establishment or that might not endure; but he never doubted, within the framework of his highly moralistic, individualist, and Marian piety, that the accounting at the final tally would reflect his own and his colleagues' unambiguous commitment. "Yesterday," he wrote from Paris at the beginning of 1878, even as the mission in Watertown seemed doomed, "I had a settlement with the Blessed Virgin, and this morning I presented a new contract for the future. I think she is pleased with either [sic]; at least I am delighted with both. I never felt more confident [that] she will take proper care of all I left behind. Please see to her interests in every possible manner. May she find every soul in our Family worthy of her love and protection!"[65]

WHEN IT CAME to governance of the Holy Cross houses in Europe, holding ground, rather than American-style expansion, was Edward Sorin's objective. By and large, he attained it, though it was no easy task. To be sure, the

---

65. Sorin to Corby, January 2, 1878, AGEN.

situation in France had stabilized since the disasters of the late 1860s. Most of the indebtedness had been liquidated, and the numbers of vocations had increased modestly. The *collège* at Neuilly-sur-Seine, under Louis Champeau's direction, was a going concern. The political situation, however, continued to cause anxiety. The Third Republic had emerged out of the ruins of the Second Empire, and in its early years the new regime was dominated by Léon Gambetta and his allies. And Gambetta, the only politician to have achieved heroic status during the calamitous Franco-Prussian war, was the party leader who coined the electoral slogan, "Clericalism, that is the enemy!"[66] A repetition of assault by club and pistol in the mode of the Parisian Communards of 1871 may not have been in the offing. Still, churchmen had reason to fear the hostility of a government controlled by elements committed not to the Commune's violence but to its ideological antipathy toward Catholicism. Father Sorin sensed the danger early on, even before the spate of anti-clerical legislation began to issue from the parliament. "I am watching very carefully (*de près*) events in France," he observed on Christmas Eve, 1874, "and each day magnifies my fears for our dear country. Unless there is a miracle, France is marching to her ruin."[67]

However dedicated he was to the missions in America, the superior general did not neglect the houses overseas. He became a constant transatlantic traveler: by 1874 he reckoned he had "crossed the ocean twenty-seven times,"[68] and there was no discernible abatement in the years that followed. Indeed, Sorin grew rather fond of the passage, now reduced thanks to steam-driven machinery to ten days duration. He usually found the ship's officers and crew accommodating, though sometimes, as on a voyage early in 1878, he encountered a tedious fellow passenger. Six of us, he reported, occupied "the first cabin," and one monopolized the conversation.

> He is a young Minister, a Graduate of Yale College in theology, medicine, law, etc., etc. [He] talks much [and] of course pompously, for he ignores nothing, has traveled immensely, speaks all the languages of Europe, without mentioning most of the dead ones, in every one of which he is proficient. He has been accustomed to preach three times every Sunday [and] was very anxious to do so yesterday. But he had to be satisfied with only one and [as a result] could not sleep at all last night. . . . In two words I never yet met such a vain, ridiculous puppy with such an amount of learning as he

66. See Brogan, *Modern France*, 127–152.
67. Sorin to Champeau, December 24, 1874, AGEN.
68. Sorin to Battista, March 31, 1874, AGEN.

boasts of. He is particularly interesting in the care he takes of his health. . . . Before we reach Liverpool I promise to show him off in his true light [as] a despicable and selfish personification of vanity.[69]

The sea had been "a little rough" during that crossing, which may have explained why the minister was so anxious about his health. But it had been a great deal rougher two years earlier when the *Amérique,* seven days out of New York and bound for Le Havre, sustained irreparable damage to her propeller shaft. The result was the hoisting of makeshift sails and two weeks of wandering over stormy seas. Help finally arrived, and Father Sorin and the other passengers were transferred to another vessel, which brought them safely into Queenstown on December 18, 1875. The consternation and alarm at Notre Dame had been hardly less than that aboard the *Amérique* herself.[70]

Sorin spent the bulk of his time on these European junkets in France at Champeau's foundation in the Parisian suburbs, still technically Holy Cross's motherhouse, and his headquarters. But he traveled widely within the country as well, formally visiting the congregation's scattered houses, presiding over retreats and professions, and examining the order's physical facilities and account books no less than its spiritual condition. Most of these executive duties, always carried out conscientiously, were nonetheless by their nature routine rather than momentous. Personnel problems, however, did now and then arise, and it would have been out of character had he not reacted to them bluntly. When a group of brothers complained to the bishop of Laval about their master of novices, Father Sorin, ever on the watch for episcopal interference, rushed to the defense. "Our dear Religious have all responded [to the complaints]," he assured the bishop, "and I can only bless heaven for their excellent dispositions. It has been fully demonstrated that the accusations . . . are gross exaggerations if not absolutely malicious inventions. The evidence proves the bad faith of those who sent the Memorandum to your Grace."[71] And when the rivalry between Louis Champeau in Paris and Joseph Rézé, the French provincial, reached a critical juncture, Sorin intervened with his usual gusto. The province in its budgetary obligations, he scolded Rézé, must always accede to the directives of the central administration of which Champeau, as first assistant general, was a charter member. "This, dear good Father," he wrote, "is a grave and capital error, and it requires a prompt and radical remedy. The evil is done not to Father Champeau but to all of us. I see

69. Sorin to Corby, January 7, 1878, AGEN.
70. See *Golden Jubilee,* 131–132, and Hope, *Notre Dame,* 173–174.
71. Sorin to Le Hardi du Marais, February 11, 1878, AGEN.

only one remedy for it, that you acknowledge freely your error and your regrets." When Rézé responded lamely that he had withheld certain monies at the insistence of the provincial council, Sorin sent back a single withering line: "From now on do not listen to your council."[72]

There were lighter moments. "I am just after assisting at the gymnastic exercises of our boys," he reported to Indiana from Neuilly. "I regret they were not continued at Notre Dame, reducing from them all danger and to what is surely safe and harmless. Here there is no danger possible, and boys and parents absolutely want them. Would it be possible to reinstate gymnastics in order to promote the students' health?"[73] And official duties did not occupy all his attention. During these two or three month sojourns there were also more personal excursions to the neighborhood of Ahuillé, where several of his siblings still resided and where the family of his deceased nephew, Auguste Lemonnier, still occupied the ancestral seat at La Roche.[74] He went with some frequency also to Le Mans, a place that aroused mixed emotions in him, in order to consult with Monsieur Hucher about the windows for the new church at Notre Dame, but also to call upon his old schoolmate, Bishop Fillion, and especially upon his close friend and constant correspondent Sister Columba, who lived in the Visitation convent there. On one such occasion, when she was suffering from a minor illness, Sorin had been unable to visit her and in excuse he fell back on playful self-censure: "Who is going to begin the education of a sixty-five-year-old barbarian? But what reveals the barbarian in his true light . . . is the fact that you have been sick. Oh, the villain! Do not fear to place him in the pillory; he knows very well that he deserves it." The problem was that "he had only fifty minutes between trains," and so "he had to depart . . . desolate that he could not return later and see his old friend of the Visitation and through her offer his respectful homages to her pious household."[75]

Father Sorin usually included a stay in Rome on his European itinerary. Here too the uncertain political atmosphere was troubling, specifically as it affected the status of St. Bridget's. By the mid-1870s he heard the anti-clerical drums beating loud again, and he feared that the threat of confiscation had resurfaced. "If there is really a danger," he instructed his Roman agent, "that new laws are to be passed that will again threaten the House, it would be best . . . to seek to sell it at a reasonable price rather than to risk losing everything through some sudden

---

72. Sorin to Rézé, June 25 and July 5, 1878, AGEN.
73. Sorin to Corby, May 8, 1878, AIP.
74. See Lemarié, *De la Mayenne*, 5–6.
75. Sorin to Sister Columba, June 11, 1878, AGEN.

change (*revirement quelconque*)."[76] Actually after some menacing noises the Italian government once more showed no interest in St. Bridget's, and a buyer for it could not be found at any price. So, faced with status quo ante, Sorin racked his brain, as he had done so often,[77] to find some use for the place. One proposal was "to open there for our Congregation a center of Higher Ecclesiastical Studies and to assign to it a half-dozen of our better American subjects, already ordained, in order to prepare for Degrees [from the Roman universities]."[78] This, however, was an idea whose time had not yet come.

For so devoted an Ultramontane as Edward Sorin, time spent in the aura of *Romanità* was never a burden, despite the hostile political climate and the seemingly permanent uncertainty with regard to St. Bridget's. Even the notoriously dilatory procedures of the papal curia evoked from this habitually impatient man hardly more than a grimace. "I have been here nearly three weeks and not idle," he wrote Granger in the late winter of 1876,

> and yet I could not get to this day [approval] of the acts of our last General Chapter [in 1872]. Every day I send to the Propaganda our good Procurator [Father Battista]. Yesterday the Secretary said to him smilingly, "We are working for you." [Battista] went again this morning. I feel confident he will return at noon with another fine declaration and no Documents. But they are all so polite and so good that you cannot quarrel with them. The fact is they are overwhelmed. After all, a year in America is a day in Rome, they say. One thing is certain: they are very thankful we cause them so little trouble.[79]

More than a month later the hoped-for sanction of the chapter's *Acta*—a formality but a necessary one—had still not been granted. "I am here yet, and to be candid I no longer know when I can leave Rome." Consolations nonetheless abounded.

> As you know I fully intended to return to France fully two weeks ago. But the unexpected kindness of his Eminence the Cardinal Prefect of Propaganda [Franchi] to accept our invitation to dine here on St. Joseph's Day [March 19] detained me in the Eternal City, much to my satisfaction. In the

76. Sorin to Battista, July 13, 1875, AGEN.
77. See, for example, chapter 27, above.
78. Sorin to Franchi, April 13, 1878, AGEN.
79. Sorin to Granger, February 1, 1876, AIP.

interim I went to [the shrines at] Foligno, Assisi and the Portiuncula, and Loreto,[80] which meant a six-days journey actually full of unspeakable enjoyments. I returned in time to see to our festival at St. Bridget's. The dinner passed off, I may say, admirably. At the end of it I made, of course, a little speech, to which his Eminence replied in a manner that pleased everyone present, although too flattering for us. . . . A general clapping around the table made it plain that he had pleased everyone.[81]

As he had once proposed to convert St. Bridget's into a guest house for upper-class female tourists,[82] Edward Sorin, both as ecclesiastical statesman and pious pilgrim, now hit upon a plan to introduce a larger American constituency to the magic of *Romanità*. "The first Pilgrimage to Rome from America" would confirm his ardent devotion to the person of Pius IX and to the papal office as well as his affection for his adopted country. The assemblage, he informed Father Battista, will be relatively small, but "thousands *indubitably* will follow in its wake." It will land in France and proceed first to Lourdes and from there to the Eternal City, where it will be crucial that it be afforded a cordial welcome. Its modest numbers will

> *make it easy for individual attention to be lavished on all of them.* They will return content, enchanted, and will fashion public opinion in the United States over the next decade, a very important thing. . . . Far be it from me to offer counsel to Rome. But I have lived for thirty-three years in the States, and I know the attitude of Americans toward Rome probably better than anyone else. Personally I ask and desire no *personal* favor . . . . This will be rather a natural and honorable occasion for His Holiness to testify to his interest in the New World.

Bishop Dwenger of Fort Wayne will act as titular head of the party, as befitted his rank, but "in fact it is I who will by right be the pilot of this pilgrimage. Nobody has crossed the ocean twenty-seven times as I have done, and nobody knows Rome and Lourdes better than I. . . . Perhaps I suffer from illusion, but it seems

---

80. The tomb of a thirteenth-century mystic, Blessed Angela of Foligno, was a favorite site for pilgrims. The Portiuncula was the church of Santa Maria degli Angeli, which served as the center of St. Francis of Assisi's apostolate. Sorin had erected a replica of it on the Notre Dame campus. At Loreto, a village near Ancona, was located the "Holy House," according to legend the girlhood home of the Virgin Mary, which had been carried by angels to Loreto in the late-thirteenth century.

81. Sorin to Granger, March 21, 1876, AIP.

82. See chapter 27, above.

clear that Divine Providence has disposed these matters so as . . . to allow me to render to the Holy Father a signal service."[83] The pilgrims duly departed New York for Brest on May 16, 1874, and reached Rome via Lourdes about June 10. They remained there two weeks and enjoyed, besides the spiritual and cultural benefits, "the good Orvieto [wine] and good cooking" that Sorin had instructed Battista to furnish.[84]

Aspirations were high that the experience might have been repeated with a different and larger clientele in 1875, a Roman jubilee year rich in indulgences, and a promotional brochure was published with that intent. But it was not to be, mostly because of the lack of an episcopal patron. Purcell of Cincinnati had declined the invitation, and "Monseigneur Dwenger has caused a good deal of unpleasantness. Indeed, we are surprised he has not caused even more. He displays such rudeness and such violence of manner and language that he disgusts every cultivated person. Add to this his Gallican principles, and you will understand that if the choice of an Episcopal Guide were left to the Pilgrims themselves, the Bishop of Fort Wayne would probably be left at home." Father Sorin took some consolation that Purcell had apparently become disenchanted with his sometime protégé. "'Our brother of Fort Wayne,'" Cincinnati confided to Notre Dame, "'tends to imagine he knows more than anyone else, and that with one hand he can lift more than anyone else.'"[85]

JOSEPH DWENGER'S BAD MANNERS and alleged anti-papal prejudices did not constitute Sorin's full case against the bishop of Fort Wayne, or Purcell's either, for that matter. The governance of the Sisters of the Holy Cross became a controverted issue yet again. During Bishop Luers's lifetime the office of apostolic visitor—a sort of remote Roman guardian for the sisters—had been filled by Archbishop Purcell. Luers, bishop of the diocese in which the sisters' motherhouse was located, had exercised overall jurisdiction, though he had done so through Father Sorin as immediate superior and indeed founder. This arrangement suited Sorin and most of the American nuns, especially since Luers was their ally in the struggle with Basile Moreau and the Marianites of Le Mans, and since he left the day-to-day administration to Sorin and to the likes of Mother Angela and Mother Ascension.[86] Dwenger claimed, not unreasonably, the

83. Sorin to Battista, March 31, 1874, AGEN.
84. Sorin to Battista, March 27 and June 25, 1874, AGEN.
85. Sorin to Battista, February 20, 1875, AGEN.
86. See chapter 25, above.

same formal authority as his predecessor, but he also asserted a right to be apostolic visitor, and Propaganda had acquiesced. The first news of this development came in a rueful note from Purcell to Mother Angela: "I am not really surprised, considering his frequent outbursts of sensitivity, that Bishop Dwenger would try to succeed me in the office I have imperfectly held (but never sought) for a couple of years. If he succeeds, I am sure it will only add to your prosperity, but it will not lessen my interest in your welfare." This faint praise for his suffragan the archbishop followed with a rather more explicit sentiment: "Thank God, your flourishing institution is beyond the reach of a vexed influence."[87]

With this communication in hand, Sorin instructed Battista "to learn at Propaganda what conclusion they have reached with Bishop Dwenger, with regard to his demand to visit the Sisters. I know that the Archbishop of Cincinnati would feel offended."[88] The title "Visitor" itself did not matter; what mattered was the bishop's intention to implement it to an unprecedented extent. "The Sisters are very much upset," Sorin reported. "They consider [Dwenger] a MEDDLER [sic]. I shall hold fast to the Constitutions, which of course he does not understand."[89] But it was precisely because the constitutions had not yet been formally presented to Propaganda that gave Dwenger his opening. To counter him Sorin appealed directly to the prefect.

Monseigneur Purcell has been our friend for thirty years. The Sisters have absolute confidence in him. Soon I shall have need for his influence as well as his friendship when I put in his hands the Constitutions of the Sisters for approval in Rome. Last November [1873] I asked him to continue his good offices in the Sisters' behalf for another three-year term. To the great joy of all of us, he consented. . . . The venerable archbishop has always been so good for us, we humbly beg your Eminence to assure us the continuation of his protection . . . and sage counsels, until he has completed his work and has had the consolation of having obtained the apostolic sanction of the Constitutions.[90]

This tactic did not succeed, and much to Sorin's irritation Propaganda granted Dwenger's request, though the bishop of Fort Wayne denied, with some

87. Purcell to Mother Angela, June 17, 1874 (copy), AGEN.
88. Sorin to Battista, June 29, 1874, AGEN.
89. Sorin to Battista, February 1, 1875, AGEN.
90. Sorin to Franchi, July 12, 1874, AGEN.

sophistry, that the word "request" was proper. "Very Reverend and dear Friend," he addressed Sorin at the beginning of 1875,

> I received a decree and letter from Cardinal Franchi abrogating the powers of the Archbishop of Cincinnati as *visitator apostolicus* and placing the Sisters of the Holy Cross within the ordinary provisions of Canon Law. In the decree there is, however, a slight inaccuracy, namely, "that it was granted at my request." I did not request a change and stated this distinctly. I merely stated the state of affairs and left the whole matter to the judgment of Rome. Of course it will be my aim to do all I can for the welfare of the Sisters.[91]

But Sorin did not believe the coarse and aggressive Dwenger had much to offer "the welfare of the sisters," even as they expanded their ministry to Salt Lake City and San Francisco.[92] And, respectful as he was of the curia's authority, since he also understood the workings of a bureaucracy, his lobbying on this subject continued energetically.

> Please ask Cardinal Franchi [he instructed Battista] if the Bishop of Fort Wayne can set aside the Constitutions which I gave [the nuns] five years ago and which have been approved by his Predecessor [Barnabò] and by Archbishop Purcell as Apostolic Delegate. These Constitutions have been often commended (*louées*), and they have perfectly satisfied all needs. My intention all along has been to present them, through Monseigneur Purcell who scrutinized them ahead of time, for the approbation of the Holy See, after a trial of six years duration. The Archbishop of Cincinnati has written to me that the Bishop of Fort Wayne demands to be consulted about the taking of vows, etc., because he considers himself the nuns' Superior.[93]

So had John Henry Luers. But he had left decisions about which aspirants should be admitted to the novitiate or to final profession to Sorin, who had left them, sensibly enough, to the sisters themselves. Dwenger the "meddler" purposed another regime altogether, and as a consequence Edward Sorin, pragma-

91. Dwenger to Sorin, January 15, 1875, AIP.

92. See Alemany to Sorin, April 6, 1875, AIP. Joseph. S. Alemany, as archbishop of San Francisco, had jurisdiction over Utah Territory until 1886, when Salt Lake was erected into an independent vicariate. In June 1875, the Sisters of the Holy Cross opened a school in Salt Lake City. Utah was admitted to the Union as the forty-fifth state in 1896.

93. Sorin to Battista, February 1, 1875, AGEN.

tist as well as pious pilgrim, blithely changed his tune. During the struggle with the Moreaus, it was acceptable doctrine that Luers was superior to all the nuns attached to St. Mary's, wherever they served. It was acceptable no more.

> I regret [Sorin wrote Battista] that [Propaganda] has given such authority over our Sisters to the Bishop of Fort Wayne, whose hotheaded (*emporté*) and imperious character all the world dreads. I know that the good Sisters are seriously alarmed. Please point out to Monseigneur Siméoni that today St. Mary's has foundations in Baltimore (2), Washington (3), Alexandria, Virginia, Illinois (3), Milwaukee, and Lancaster, Pennsylvania. St. Mary's is therefore a *Maison générale,* which cannot be directed absolutely by the ordinary of the place, because other bishops would naturally be fearful that their interests would be sacrificed to his. . . . Of course [Dwenger] enjoys episcopal rights over the houses in his Diocese, as does any other bishop. What I cannot understand is that the bishop of Fort Wayne should have jurisdiction over our Sisters serving, say, the archbishop of Baltimore. . . . God alone knows what it has cost me over these thirty years to establish the Sisters of the Holy Cross in this New World. He has blessed my efforts. They form at this moment well governed and very useful Congregation of 500 members. . . . I hope with all my heart that nothing happens to ruin their beautiful future prospects.[94]

In the end the sisters' "beautiful prospects" were not ruined, and they went on to ever-greater heights. The constitutions received interim Roman approval in 1875,[95] and Bishop Dwenger, though he did indeed meddle in the sisters' business now and then, presided peacefully enough at their general chapter the following year.[96] Purcell had gotten it about right: the institution created by Edward Sorin and Angela Gillespie was "beyond the reach of a vexed influence." Or as Sorin put the legal matter more specifically, professions and dispensations "belong to the General Council [of the sisters] whose votes are usually taken; but for either, the radical power is vested in the Superior [Sorin himself]."[97]

Joseph Dwenger was only the latest among the bishops with whom Father Sorin had had serious difficulties. Indeed, aside from Luers, Purcell, and Martin

---

94. Sorin to Battista, December 6, 1874, AGEN.

95. Sorin to Purcell, January 26, 1875, AIP. See also chapter 30, below.

96. See McAllister, *Flame,* 317. For instances of Dwenger's "meddling," albeit of a largely inconsequential character, see Dwenger to Sorin, August 19 and September 13, 1876, May 12, 1877, and September 12, 1878, AIP.

97. Sorin, "Memorandum," October 17, 1876, AIP.

Spalding—and he had quarreled with each of them at one time or another—his experiences with the members of the American hierarchy had not been particularly congenial. Nor was his estimate of their talent or effectiveness particularly high. Little wonder then that he strongly favored the establishment of a permanent Roman representative in the United States. The prospect of the appointment of such an apostolic delegate had been debated for many years, and most of the bishops had consistently opposed it.[98] Sorin's sturdy Ultramontanism combined with his personal disenchantment with the prelates he had dealt with led him predictably to adopt the opposite view.

> The importance of a Representative of the Holy See in the United States is much greater than is ordinarily thought. . . . The bishops in general do not recognize it, but the clergy desires it, and the common good requires it. Each bishop is all-powerful in his diocese; the archbishops are scarcely recognized in practice and content themselves with ceremonial precedence. But has not this almost limitless freedom of sixty or so bishops, most of whom are poor theologians and none of whom know canon law, become *a danger?* Rome is *far away;* some matters are never reported there or known, and this encourages them to do as they please. If on the contrary each bishop knew that any of his acts could fall next day under the eyes of a Representative of Propaganda, what salutary discretion (*retenue*) would follow immediately, what changes for the better. . . . Another danger is the lack of harmony among prelates denied an accessible center of directing authority. The National Councils announce, it is true, programs calling for unity of action, . . . but they remain visibly without effect. . . . The year 1876 ought not to end without final settlement of this grave question. If a Roman dignitary, well known, prudent, amiable, capable should come to us after the November elections, with the title of archbishop and legate of the pope, within six months a great deal will be accomplished. Rome will have in the New World a security *that she has lost elsewhere.* I have lived thirty-five years in the United States; I believe I understand them.[99]

Eighteen seventy-six came and went. The Apostolic Delegation was finally set up in 1893, a few months before Sorin died.

---

98. See John Tracy Ellis, *The Life of James Cardinal Gibbons, Archbishop of Baltimore, 1834–1921,* 2 vols. (Milwaukee, 1952), 1: 595–652.

99. Sorin, "Memorandum," n.d. [before November, 1876] (copy), AGEN. The occasion for preparing this document is not clear. The original is located in the files of Propaganda.

ONE BISHOP of whom Father Sorin was fond was his confrère and predecessor as superior general of Holy Cross, Pierre Dufal. Propaganda's delay in replacing the missionaries in Bengal meant that Dufal did not leave Calcutta till the end of 1876.[100] He retired first to Rome in hopes of mending his shattered health. He soon grew restless, however, and, while in Rome early in 1878, Sorin took advantage of his connections in Texas and at the curia to secure for the grizzled missionary a useful and honorable position: "We had this noon a most cordial audience at the Propaganda. Cardinal Franchi told us he intended giving Galveston to Monseigneur Dufal, either as Coadjutor or Titular. What a blessing!"[101] Alas, this ecclesiastical marriage proved not to have been arranged in heaven. Dufal's appointment as the increasingly erratic Dubuis's coadjutor soured within months. In December the new coadjutor issued a printed statement to the clergy of Galveston in which he protested "the acts of administration in temporal affairs, which the titular Bishop is transacting alone, as usual, and about which as Coadjutor Bishop I have not been consulted. From this day I withdraw from such irregular and uncanonical administration."[102] This unhappy news reached Notre Dame via a letter from Father Spillard in Austin. "The circular is a declaration of war," Sorin replied sadly. "[It] cannot be ended but by the withdrawal of Bishop Dubuis. I expected the same, but not so early."[103]

Had he not been confined to his room for the past two weeks, Father Sorin added, he "would have gone south" himself to support "the good Bishop Dufal." In fact, the "bad cold" that incapacitated him then was only the latest, and probably the lightest, ailment Sorin had suffered from off and on since the mid-1870s. And not only he: as age crept up on them, many of the major players in his life were similarly afflicted. The patriarch, Brother Vincent, now past eighty, grew more frail by the day. Alexis Granger endured a series of illnesses which alarmed all those—and they were many—who revered him. Mother Angela, though she was ten years younger than Sorin, did not escape the common lot either. Among those worried about her at the beginning of 1877 were Bishop Dwenger and, perhaps more intensely, Ellen Ewing Sherman, who fretted over "dear Mother Angela's illness" and pledged her heartfelt prayers for "my dear cousin Eliza."[104] Angela in turn was keenly anxious as to the well-being of the father of them all.

---

100. See Sorin to Battista, November 22, 1876.

101. Sorin to Granger, February 25, 1878, AIP.

102. Dufal, "Printed Circular," December 17, 1878 (copy), AIP.

103. Sorin to Spillard, December 25, 1878, AIP. Dufal's formal resignation from Galveston was accepted by Rome in 1880. Dubuis resigned the following year and returned to France.

104. Dwenger to Sorin, March 5, 1877, and Ellen Sherman to Sorin, January 18, 1877, AIP.

Once, when no news had come for some weeks from Sorin, who had gone to Europe, she wrote him in no little distress: "This silence makes the days seem longer!! Well, I'll try to make them rich in merits by cheerful and patient resignation—and then I'll sing a grand *Te Deum* when I do get a letter. For I never for a moment believe that you, dear Father, are going to continue this long silence." She insisted that she felt much better than before. But "do please let me know, when you do write, just how *you* are. Ever, my Beloved Father, your devoted Child."[105]

Edward Sorin's physical problems had apparently begun in 1875. In the autumn of that year a brother stationed in Austin extended him congratulations on his "convalescence from a long and painful disease, borne, I am sure, with perfect patience and resignation."[106] One may legitimately wonder whether Sorin, who had for most of his life enjoyed robust health, did indeed endure his period of recuperation "with perfect patience." He was well enough at any rate to travel to Rome early the next year, but while there he learned that his two dearest comrades at Notre Dame, Granger and Brother Vincent, were both ill again: "I now feel very homesick, since I know of the relapse of our dear Father Granger. . . . Oh, you little dream of my home attachments, especially since I came near to part [by my own illness] with all I love forever. And whom do I not love there?"[107] And his own recovery was short-lived. Later in 1876 he was sick enough to retire for a few weeks to take the healing waters at a health spa near Waukesha, Wisconsin. "I cannot say when I will return to Europe," he told Dufal. "My ailment, they say, is serious. Just now I cannot write long letters without overly wearying myself."[108] The ailment, whatever it was, sapped his strength and energy, which for so busy a man was a cruel cross. A week's treatment in the mineral springs at Waukesha gave him some relief: "I feel much better, I may even say *well*," he informed Corby in nearby Watertown. But, he added gloomily, "I hope you will never lose your health and strength; it is a terrible trial."[109] A year later he was still suffering from chronic fatigue. "At the moment I do not know what my health will demand of me. I am no better than I was eighteen months ago. I begin to feel the weight of my sixty-four years soon to be finished, at an age when each day adds worries, some too grave and heavy not to leave a mark on my weak shoulders."[110]

---

105. Mother Angela to Sorin, March 7, 1878, AIP.

106. Brother Killian to Sorin, October 13, 1875, AIP.

107. Sorin to?, March 3, 1876, AIP.

108. Sorin to Dufal, December 7, 1876, AGEN.

109. Sorin to Corby, December 10, 1876, AIP.

110. Sorin to Dufal, November 3, 1877, AGEN.

But despite these intimations of mortality the hectic pace of Sorin's life never really abated. And a specific worry, a venerable one and an especially poignant one in the light of what occurred at Notre Dame a few weeks after he expressed it yet again on March 20, 1879, did indeed leave its mark.

I am glad to find you [President Corby], as I am myself, terribly afraid of fire. When we read daily of disastrous fires, the very idea that one of our 600 personnel is enough to bring 599 others such a calamity makes the President in charge fearfully responsible. [The recent conflagrations nationwide] . . . imperiously force me to help you in adopting every reasonable measure to prevent such an awful disaster. Let it be borne in mind that fully two-thirds of losses by fire are due to negligence. How can we remain in peace unless our 600 inmates are all equally awake to the danger? Providence has given us all the securities that can be wished for; but there is no guarantee against carelessness as an Institution. A public, habitual dread is our only safety. I would advise you to assemble the Priests and Brothers together this afternoon and speak to them on this subject, and to commission your two Stewards to visit every House on the Premises and report to yourself.[111]

---

111. Sorin to Corby, March 20, 1879, AIP.

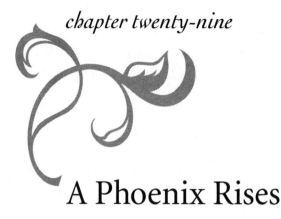

chapter twenty-nine

A Phoenix Rises

THE MINIMS WERE THE FIRST TO SEE SMOKE CURLING up from the roof of the Main Building. April 23, 1879, fell on a Wednesday, a free day from school for the little boys, who were playing in their recreation yard nearby. It was eleven o'clock in the morning. Three hours later the six-story building, which housed classrooms, refectories, dormitories, the college library, offices, and professors' rooms, Edward Sorin's prized museum—that "splendid collection" of "stuffed birds and beasts from around the globe"[1]—stood a grotesque burnt-out shell filled with smoldering piles of rubble. All around it lay a profusion of tattered books and papers, broken bits of furniture, even a mattress or two, that desperate students and professors had thrown out the windows as the conflagration spread. Four other structures to the northeast of the Main—the infirmary, the small music hall, the minims' gymnasium, and the hostel for elderly men (which had evolved out of Sorin's original plan for a refuge for penitent and ailing priests)[2]—had also gone up in flames. Almost miraculously, there were no fatalities and only a few minor injuries.

No one could say with certainty, then or since, what caused the fire. One rumor had it that some students, in defiance of the rules, were smoking in a fifth-floor dormitory. Another conjecture was that a live ember blown from the steam plant's chimney had ignited refuse on the Main Building's roof. But the most likely explanation appears to be that workmen applying new coal-tar to the roof—they had finished their job about a half hour before the children first saw

---

1. See chapter 11, above.
2. See chapter 21, above.

the smoke—had left behind enough combustible material for a stray spark or, just possibly, the heat of the sun to ignite it.

> There were large tanks on the upper floor [President Corby explained laconically], and from these water pipes ran all over the building. The building was deluged with water, but it seems that it did no good. You see, the fire first burned away the supports of the large figure of the Virgin Mary which crowned the dome and weighed about a ton. That fell and made way in the roof for the fire to spread.[3]

Aside from the malfunctioning water tanks, the fire-fighting capacity at Notre Dame amounted to hardly more than a bucket brigade, which, despite heroic and exhausting effort, proved totally inadequate for the purpose. When word reached South Bend, the volunteer firemen were fetched from their shops and forges, harnessed horses to their steam-driven fire engine—which had last been used two years earlier—and hastened toward the campus. They were too late; had they arrived a little sooner perhaps the music hall or the hostel might have been saved, but all hopes for the Main Building had vanished within sixty minutes.

William Corby moved with dispatch. At three o'clock in the afternoon he assembled the whole Notre Dame community in the new church which, thanks to the gentle wind luckily having blown away from it, was undamaged. All classes, the president announced, would be adjourned and all degrees and certificates awarded without further examination. Telegrams would be sent to students' parents informing them of the situation and reassuring them about their sons' safety. Most important of all, he said in a tone remindful of the war hero he was, rebuilding would commence on the morrow, and the institution in all its branches would reconvene, as scheduled, on the first Tuesday in September. Here was a bold prediction, to be sure, but one which, when it was successfully fulfilled, would mark the beginning of a new epoch for Notre Dame and for Holy Cross in America.[4]

Corby made his pledge without prompting from Edward Sorin, although he was probably confident that the superior general would have done the same.

---

3. *South Bend Daily Tribune*, April 23, 1879.

4. I have followed here Hope, *Notre Dame*, 183–191, and Thomas J. Schlereth, *A Dome of Learning: The University of Notre Dame's Main Building* (n.p. [Notre Dame, Ind.], n.d. [1991]), 7–11. Though they differ in a few minor points, these accounts are in substantial agreement. Father Hope's is based almost exclusively on relevant pieces in the *Scholastic*. Among the fourteen buildings on campus untouched by the fire was the print shop where the *Scholastic* and the *Ave Maria* were produced.

Sorin at any rate was not present to witness the disaster. He had gone to Montreal, on his way to New York and still another trans-Atlantic voyage. Father Corby went to some lengths to be sure that the distressing information reach Saint-Laurent not by a stray telegram or news bulletin but by a personal envoy. For this task he commissioned the university librarian, Professor James Edwards, who that evening boarded the train for Canada. Sorin returned with him to Notre Dame on Sunday, April 27. As he somberly viewed the wreckage, he may have recalled the uneasiness about the dangers of fire he had expressed to Father Corby only a few weeks before. Timothy Howard, now a professor in the law school, was beside him.

> He walked around the ruins and those who followed were confounded by his attitude. Instead of bending he stiffened. He signaled all of them to go into the church with him. I was then present when Father Sorin, after looking over the destruction of his life's work, stood at the altar steps and spoke to the community what I have always felt to be the most sublime words I have ever listened to. There was absolute faith, confidence, resolution in his very look and pose. "If it were ALL gone I should not give up" were his words in closing. The effect was electric. It was the crowning moment of his life. A sad company had gone into the church that day. They were all simple Christian heroes as they came out. There was never more a shadow of a doubt as to the future of Notre Dame.[5]

Nor did Sorin doubt that the catastrophe would in the end bind ever closer all the men of Holy Cross, wherever they were. "When I learned of the disaster, I was in Montreal," he wrote the members of the general council in Paris, responding to their "touching letter" of condolence. "I returned here two days later, and I surveyed the debris and the ruins without tears. But when I read your letter this morning, I wept for the first time since the tragedy of April 23. Please accept my humble thanks . . . for sentiments so worthily and so nobly expressed. . . . I had thought that I already loved you with all my heart, . . . but I was wrong; at this moment I realize I love you now as I have never loved you before." Keep up your spirits, he added, "and in the autumn, I hope, I shall come and tell you with my own voice what I think of you and what this moment really means for the Congregation of Holy Cross."[6] And to the community at large, he urged that the ca-

---

5. Howard to Hudson, n.d., quoted by Schlereth, *Dome,* 10, and Hope, *Notre Dame,* 186, with slight differences. Father Daniel Hudson was the editor of the *Ave Maria.*

6. Sorin to "Religieux de Sainte-Croix de Neuilly," May 26, 1879, AGEN.

tastrophe be an occasion of grace: "Immense as it is, our loss may soon be called a real blessing, if it brings every Religious of Holy Cross to resolve earnestly to be, now and forever, a model of regularity and devotedness, of obedience and humility, a cheerful lover of actual poverty—one, in a word, of whom the Community may well be proud."[7]

Crisis had always brought out the best in Father Sorin. It did so again, even though he had now begun to suffer the uncertain health inevitable for a man in his sixty-sixth year. And so it was hardly a surprise that he should have endorsed Corby's resolution to rebuild immediately. Clearing away the rubble began at once, with everybody participating, and an observer for the *Scholastic*, writing with typical adolescent verve, noted that "everyone agrees that Very Reverend Father General can wheel off a load of bricks with great grace and dignity. We do not wish to discourage the efforts of a conscientious worker, but still, regard for historical accuracy compels us to state that Father Granger would scarcely command a large salary among the horny-handed sons of toil."[8] Just as quickly Sorin mounted a nationwide competition to find a suitable architect for the rebuilding project. He and Corby stayed in close consultation with Brother Charles Borromeo Harding, who had demonstrated his own credentials as a builder during the construction of Our Lady of the Sacred Heart,[9] and on May 14 they announced their choice, thirty-six-year-old Willoughby J. Edbrooke of Chicago, an Episcopalian, who already enjoyed an enviable professional reputation and who was destined to become one of the leading lights among American architects.[10]

Meanwhile, amid the tension of the moment, Sorin and Corby, though they agreed about ends, did not necessarily see eye to eye about means. On May 13 they had engaged in a sharp exchange, and later in the day Sorin, who had taken up residence at St. Mary's, sent Corby an uncharacteristic if somewhat tentative apology for "our little altercation this afternoon" about plans to provide a new infirmary.

As I do not wish to increase your many troubles unnecessarily, nor to force my views in any shape or manner, I beg your pardon for anything I may have said or done to try your patience, however good my intentions may have seemed to me. Henceforth you may rest assured of my non-interference.

---

7. Sorin, *Circular Letters*, 1: 129.

8. Quoted in Hope, *Notre Dame*, 187.

9. See chapter 28, above.

10. See Schlereth, *Dome*, 12–18. Professor Schlereth places his discussion very helpfully within the larger context of the history of American collegiate architecture.

Do what you see fit . . . without the least regard to what I said. . . . I shrink from any personal responsibility too much to assume any spontaneously. My interferences hitherto were more apparent than real. My great fear was, and is yet, that you will lose immensely by ending too late.

Specifically, what he had proposed in order to avoid "ending too late" was to "have saved money and time . . . by keeping the [laborers] on the grounds to eat and sleep." However, "in future I shall content myself in praying for your full success, in which no one will rejoice more heartily than your devoted, E. Sorin."[11]

But his basic apprehension would not go away, nor, for that matter, would the imperious habits of a lifetime be satisfied by prayer alone. As he told Corby the next day, "The final adoption of a plan for the rebuilding of Notre Dame, being in its results the most important act ever accomplished by the Congregation here or anywhere, it is our duty to [consider] . . . the magnitude of the undertaking, the brief time allowed for it, and the scarcity of materials, if not of hands, required for its accomplishment [by the] given date. We all agree we must be through in ninety days or lose God knows how much. This loss, however," he added gloomily, "is more probable than finishing in due time." Three days later his fears on the same subject had not lessened. "I confess I feel very uneasy. . . . Two and a half million bricks are to be laid; at 2,000 a day for each, it will take fifty masons to lay 2,500,000 in a month, . . . which is certainly not one-half of the whole job. I see nothing else feasible but to give out the entire building to three reliable head men, each bringing in his own crew. . . . I would telegraph Mr. Edbrooke to get a proposal for . . . three reliable men."[12]

Father Sorin's anxiety on this score was understandable enough, but three and a half months of furious activity put it to rest. By July 1 he was able to tell his "dear and good Sister Columba" that "we are halfway through our work of restoration, a gigantic task, but it is the work of the Holy Virgin and St. Joseph; it is they, not I, who will complete it. We are now at the third story, and in two weeks our sixty masons will fulfill their quota,"[13] which ultimately reached 4,300,000 bricks—most of them the dusty yellow variety produced from Notre Dame's own marl-deposits and kilns.[14] The other technical specialists followed in due course. In all more than 300 workmen wrestled with the tons of stone and

---

11. Sorin to Corby, May 13, 1879, AIP.

12. Sorin to Corby, May 14 and 17, 1879, AIP.

13. Sorin to Sister Columba, July 1, 1879, AGEN.

14. The coming of age, as it were, of a natural resource Sorin had long hoped to exploit. See chapter 11, above.

wood carried, most of it, by rail to South Bend—the Michigan Central Railroad cut its freight charges in half[15]—and then brought to the site from the town by an endless stream of wagons. The construction bosses, with Brother Charles Borromeo overseeing them, did not have to worry about the norms imposed by later labor practices; on the long hot summer days the worker's right to relief after an eight-hour shift was as unheard of as a mandated forty-hour week.[16] Indeed, the young scholars who edited the *Scholastic* even begrudged the laborers a holiday on the fourth of July: "Were it not for this delay, the third story of the building would already have been complete." On the last day of August, Sorin reported exultantly,

> after all the work, the effort, the worry, the disappointments (*déceptions*), false starts, sleepless nights, the new Notre Dame this morning served its first meal to thirty pupils in the east refectory, [a week] before the opening of school. The building now boasts two refectories, two study-halls, and four dormitories, all of them grander and . . . more stately [than before]. . . . The central entrance, with its magnificent Rotunda, will be finished next week. . . . This autumn . . . we shall begin planning construction of a community residence, a recreation and music hall, a gymnasium, a [new] print shop, and a refectory for the Sisters.[17]

The remarkable feat of reconstruction did not of itself solve the financial disaster involved, "a disaster without precedent and capable by itself of ruining any Congregation. But with God's help, Notre Dame will revive," he assured his Roman agent. "I have confidence in the Blessed Virgin. We shall be reborn. . . . I have waited, and I must continue to wait a week or more, before presenting the new plan which I want you to submit to His Holiness and to solicit from him an Apostolic Blessing, of which we have so great a need."[18] Since the total loss stood at $200,000 and the insurance covered hardly twenty percent of that figure, a good deal more than a papal blessing was required. "Would you like to know how much we are spending every day?" Sorin asked Sister Columba. "Between a thousand and fifteen hundred dollars." But nothing could dampen his faith-driven optimism. "St. Joseph is our treasurer," he said, "and up to now no one has suffered, and everyone has been paid on time. But, if you please, you must whisper

---

15. Schlereth, *Dome,* 13.
16. See Hope, *Notre Dame,* 190.
17. Sorin to Battista, August 31, 1879, AGEN.
18. Sorin to Battista, n.d. [late April] and May 9, 1879, AGEN.

in the Saint's ear lest he forget that the largest expenses always come at the end of a project."[19] The various Notre Dame constituencies did indeed spring into action, and for the most part their endeavors bore positive fruit. Alumni were scattered across much of the east and Midwest, and many of them responded generously to the appeals of their alma mater.[20] This was particularly the case in Chicago and its environs, where a large concentration of graduates had settled and where, so many years before, Father Sorin had prophesied that Holy Cross in the United States would ground its future prosperity.[21] "We have endured an immense loss," he acknowledged, but "the widespread efforts to create a new Notre Dame superior to the first are truly astonishing. Even the Protestant Newspapers have made it a *national* endeavor. From all sides pious souls are coming to our aid."[22] Indeed, "our catastrophe, so sudden and so unexpected and so terrible, has been seen as a loss to the whole country, and the American people have marvelously helped us to reverse it."[23] And not only Americans: Irish-born Sisters Valeria and Briggita canvassed the cottages and parishes of their impoverished homeland and brought back 1,380 pounds sterling ($6,900).[24]

Nor did South Bend fail to respond. Sorin circulated in the town a printed appeal on the same day he surveyed the ruins. "Our first resource is the insurance money, $45,000. All I can command myself, from personal resources, is one thousand dollars, which I cheerfully offer as the first donation on the list now open among my old and devoted parishioners of Notre Dame—a feeble tribute indeed, but God knows it is all I, or the Community, can find available."[25] Alexis Coquillard—whose very surname evoked the pioneer days of forty years before and who himself had been one of the original students in the college—promptly contributed $500, and at a public rally urged his fellow townsmen to follow suit. He pointed forcefully to Notre Dame's importance to the local economy, a fact to which, he argued, "every merchant, mechanic, clothinghouse, boot-and-shore store, dry goods store, grocery, lumberman, and miller can testify."[26] Most touching perhaps was the reaction of the girls at St. Mary's Academy who pledged their

---

19. Sorin to Sister Columba, July 1, 1879, AGEN.

20. For a sampling of the flood of sympathetic and supportive mail, see the *Scholastic*, 12 (May 10, 1879): 541–543.

21. See chapter 20, above.

22. Sorin to Battista, July 4, 1879, AGEN.

23. Sorin to Sister Columba, November 24, 1879, AGEN.

24. "Notebook," 1879–1880, with detailed lists of contributions and contributors, as well as a statement of the nuns' expenses, AIP (Sorin papers).

25. Sorin, "Appeal," Second Sunday after Easter [April 27], 1879 (copy), AUND, PNDP, 10–AD-2.

26. Quoted in Hope, *Notre Dame*, 187.

pocket money to bolster the reconstruction effort; more pragmatic was Mother Angela's command—not request—that each sister of the Holy Cross furnish a donation of $20 for the same objective.[27]

One deep and abiding disappointment for Sorin was the failure of many who owed legitimate debts to Notre Dame to settle their accounts even when entreated to do so after the fire. He ordered Corby to acquire "all he can get from old debts from Students,"[28] and he himself sent "a personal appeal to nearly 200 families indebted to Notre Dame . . . I made said appeal as strong and moving as I could, for I knew it covered an amount of $75,000. . . . I received twenty-two dollars ($22)! Ah, this is the lesson I *then learned*. We expected to make friends by patiently waiting, as we had by reducing terms and sometimes foregoing all payments. *We failed;* and what is worse yet we made of those pretended friends, under obligations, *ungrateful beings*—the worst class of people." Given as Sorin was to hyperbole, one may question the strict accuracy of the figures he cited, but the lesson he learned from this misadventure was unequivocal. "I must add here, as a result of my forty years' experience, that, instead of favoring the method apparently forced on Catholic schools in this country, of filling up our halls at any price, on any terms, and even gratuitously. *I condemn it for our Houses,* of which it is a ruin and, as a rule, of no profit to anyone."[29]

The fall term opened on schedule in September as President Corby had promised. The number of students in attendance fell sharply to 324, which included all ages and all classes, but under the circumstances this was surely anticipated. Father Sorin at any rate was not disheartened. "There are 250 [collegiate] boarders here now," he reported in early October. "In three or four weeks there will be 300. It is a magnificent success." True enough, "the edifice is not entirely finished. One hundred fifty laborers will be working into November and costing $3,000 a week." But the end result will be "one of the first religious and literary houses in America."[30] The students were no doubt proud to be associated with so distinguished a building; they may have appreciated even more the new gas lighting and the indoor plumbing.[31]

The ornamentation of the Main Building, including Luigi Gregori's interior murals,[32] took several years to complete. For Edward Sorin, however, the adornment that mattered most, the golden dome and the statue of the Virgin Mary

27. Costin, *Priceless Spirit,* 215.
28. Sorin to Granger, October 29, 1879, AIP.
29. Sorin, *Circular Letters,* 1: 153–154.
30. Sorin to Battista, October 8, 1879, AGEN.
31. See Hope, *Notre Dame,* 190–192.
32. See chapter 28, above.

atop it, was in place by 1882. A dome and a statue had of course been featured on the old building—indeed, as Corby had said, the fall of the 2,000 pound statue onto the roof had sealed the college's fiery fate—but Sorin was determined that their successors would be grander, more striking, and more beautiful, just as the new Notre Dame was to be superior to the old. Even as the bricklayers were still doing their work, he and Willoughby Edbrooke discussed how the massive dome should be constructed and decorated.[33] The architect suggested as inspiration the capitol in Washington, a point of view perfectly agreeable to the patriotic priest, who, nevertheless, had a second beau ideal in mind. He sent a sketch of the new building to Battista to show to Cardinal Franchi: "You will recognize the Dome of St. Peter. I want to be Roman above all else."[34] As for the model of the statue, Sorin felt no need to consult the distinguished Episcopalian architect. Standing on an obelisk on the edge of the Piazza di Spagna, just outside the doors of the vast black-stone palace of Propaganda, was (and is) a statue of the Virgin under the title of the Immaculate Conception. Sorin had hoped at first to secure a facsimile of that sculpture—"it would have satisfied my great ambition and have been my greatest joy"—but the price in Rome, "double what is asked for here," was prohibitive.[35] So he commissioned an artist resident in Chicago named Giovanni Meli, who fashioned the sixteen-feet high, 4,400 pound icon in a matter of months. It stood on the roof of the Main Building's front porch until the dome was finished. There was one last consideration. His confrères urged the superior general to be satisfied to have this imposing pinnacle embellished with gold paint. But Sorin was having none of it. It must be gilded with gold leaf, he insisted, and so it was, and so it has been ever since, as it thrusts skyward 197 feet above the flat Indiana landscape, as enduring a symbol as any in Mid-America.[36]

At THE END OF OCTOBER 1879 Edward Sorin departed for France, where plans were to be laid for the general chapter scheduled for the following spring. This was the journey that had been postponed in the spring because of the great fire. The stress that that crisis had imposed appeared to have endowed him with renewed vigor; the illnesses and consequent fatigue that had troubled him off and on in recent years receded, at least for the time being. Even as he packed his bags his mind was bubbling over with plans for further expan-

33. See Edbrooke to Sorin, October 21 and 22, 1880, AIP.
34. Sorin to Battista, July 4, 1879, AGEN.
35. Sorin to Battista, October 18, 1879, AGEN.
36. See Schlereth, *Dome*, 24–25.

sion, especially to improve the facilities serving Notre Dame's religious faculty and staff. The physical conditions under which the sisters labor, he told Provincial Granger, have become "a shame and danger"—the clothesroom, the washroom, and even the *Ave Maria* printing office—and funds must forthwith be dedicated to correcting these anomalies. Furthermore, "it should be clearly understood in this Province that the Home of our [senior priests and brothers] is not the College, nor any other house, but the Professed House." The present small building has not functioned "in a manner or of a capacity adequate to the needs of a growing family, as ours here. The need of such a House has long been felt by our best Religious; but by the side of a large College it was considered from year to year secondary to the wants of the Students." The moment had come to end this "regretted and protracted delay in providing a suitable general community center."

> I would pity those who would show themselves loath to avail themselves of it. But to insure the advantages intended, I must leave no choice to anyone in this matter. All who are not required to eat or sleep with the Students must take their meals, attend the exercises, and sleep at the Professed House, and also take there their daily recreations and spend their Sundays and festival days. I have no doubt that our worthy Religious will be rejoiced and even delighted with this new arrangement. . . . [We shall] fit up for this purpose the old residence of the Professed which . . . will originate a new era of regularity, of discipline, and religious enjoyments and comforts hitherto ignored.[37]

If anything, the superior general's supervising hand was firmer than ever. On shipboard, only a day or two outbound from New York, he showed how preoccupied he was with "regularity" and "discipline." Chagrined by comments he had apparently heard on his journey east, Father Sorin once again issued a stern directive to the diffident provincial.

> We do not always learn at home all we should know for the government of those committed to our care. We do not travel far from the community before we hear what Bishops and Priests remark about our Religious. I must confess that I have been exceedingly pained of late by various censures

---

37. Sorin to Granger, October 25, 1879, AIP. The result of this expansion was the building directly behind the Basilica of the Sacred Heart, now called the Presbytery. Corby Hall, completed in 1895, was built as a larger Professed House, and, though it has been used for a variety of purposes over the years, serves in that capacity today. See Hope, *Notre Dame,* 263–264.

from such high and respectable sources concerning the strange manner our Fathers *travel, dress, and behave.* . . . To bring our members to [standards] . . . common to all Religious orders, I beg of your Reverence, under pain of very probably severe condemnation from the approaching General Chapter to cure at once the deplorable evil alluded to by an energetic measure fully justified by the gravity of the matter and made necessary by the levity our Rule has been trifled with; namely, to declare *suspended ipso facto* every Religious of Holy Cross in your Province who shall have left his House without proper permission, or remained out longer than permitted, or without strict fidelity to the *rule for dressing on journeys.*[38]

Once arrived in Paris, however, Sorin confronted a problem far more grave than that displayed by the careless sartorial habits of his American confrères. By 1879, out of nearly a decade of brutal political struggle, the anticlerical parties, inspired if not always led by Léon Gambetta, had secured control of all the Republic's tools of power. Along this broad leftist spectrum the politicians feuded among themselves over various issues, and no premier could hope to hold the confidence of the Chamber of Deputies for long. Between 1879 and 1883 four distinct ministries held office. But throughout this period one man kept the same post regardless of who headed the cabinet. Jules Ferry remained minister of education, and his principal policy was bluntly to drive the religious orders out of all French schools. In the legislation he introduced in the Chamber in March 1879 the key provision was the so-called article seven, which in effect banned all but a few congregations from teaching in even private institutions. Ferry's bill passed the Chamber on July 9, even as Edward Sorin was fretfully observing the progress of the masons laying brick for the new Main Building. By the time he arrived in France, in November, the measure had moved on to debate in the Senate, which, in January 1880, threw out article seven. The Chamber promptly retaliated by issuing on March 29 two unreviewable edicts which came to be known simply as *les Décrets:* first, an order for the immediate and complete dissolution in France of the order hated most by the anticlericals, the Jesuits; and, second, a mandate that all other teaching congregations seek governmental "authorization," without which perhaps 10,000 priests and brothers and upwards of 100,000 nuns would be excluded from the schools they presently administered or taught in.[39]

The bad old days Basile Moreau had endured in Le Mans had come again, only now with an even colder and more determined enemy at the gate. Father

---

38. Sorin to Granger, October 30, 1879, AIP.
39. The complicated story is well told in Dansette, *Histoire religieuse,* 413–430.

Sorin, if no more prone to interfere in strictly political affairs than had been his former mentor and superior, could hardly have been expected in 1880 to assume a different stance in the face of an attack similar to that of 1840. His language, however, tended to be a bit more acerbic than Moreau's. "The condition of France today," he informed Granger, "is precisely as the *Univers* describes it, if not worse.[40] After two months of uncertainty, waiting for the fall of Waddington, he has now been replaced by Freycinet, who is even more mischievous. Article seven will surely be approved. Who then," he added sarcastically, "will recount all these beautiful tales about our greed and riches?"[41] As he waited with "the greatest anxiety" for news about the fate of article seven in the Senate, he expressed his judgment of the minister of education: "Every sensible man expresses the most perfect contempt for that Ferry, a third-rate lawyer who cannot even write a correct page in French."[42] Article seven indeed failed to win the approval of the relatively more conservative Senate, but consolation, such as it was, proved short-lived: "The *Décrets* promulgated [by the Chamber] day before yesterday," he lamented on April 1, "show me most clearly that now we have no prospect of success here in France. It would be folly on my part to sacrifice our great interests across the sea which my absence from there puts in jeopardy in every respect."[43]

A profound difference thus existed between how Moreau coped with a hostile state in the 1840s and how Sorin viewed the analogous situation forty years later. Moreau had never doubted for a moment that the foundations of Holy Cross in France provided enough ballast so that the congregation could extend its ministrations to Algeria, Italy, Poland, and even Bengal, to say nothing of the American New World. In 1880, however, Holy Cross in France, at least as Sorin viewed it, was suffering from an institutional malady which looked to him to be terminal.

The French Province is so reduced that there is but a single voice uttering the same cry from every tongue over and over: *we are dying*. Each year the number of foundations diminishes. The Novitiate enjoys the confidence

40. *L'univers* was the right-wing Catholic daily, edited by the pugnacious Louis Veuillot, which exerted immense influence, especially among the country clergy in France. Sorin had been a faithful reader of it since his youth.
41. Sorin to Granger, n.d. [early January 1880], AGEN. The date is presumed from the fact that article seven did not in fact pass the Senate. Guillaume Waddington, who did not favor article seven, had at about this time given way as premier to Charles de Freycinet, who did. See Dansette, *Histoire religieuse*, 416.
42. Sorin to Corby, January 25, 1880, AIP.
43. Sorin to Battista, April 1, 1880, AGEN.

of no one; many of those who come out from it, far from being acquisitions, are an embarrassment or a disgrace. It ought to be the hope of the Province; on the contrary, it is only a serious expense and beyond our resources. . . . The Province itself is not properly administered when the Provincial has the reputation of permitting everything and allowing each member to follow his own fancy. . . . The Province of France has entered its death-pangs. Perhaps it can recover, but not by ordinary means. . . . When in 1868 I was elected and forced to accept [the generalship], I did not know how profoundly the divisions, the quarrels, the frivolousness (*démonstrations journalières*) had so vitiated all the elements of community life in this French Province.

The ineffectual provincial was Joseph Rézé, a confrère with whom Sorin had often been at odds but to whom, out of hope or desperation, he had given several responsible posts.[44] In fact Rézé's inaction was merely one prominent feature in an altogether disintegrating situation. "If the Congregation existed only in France, I would despair of it." But there was a realistic alternative. Holy Cross in America, even if some of its members dressed too casually and occasionally stayed out too late, was flourishing.

Happily, more than two-thirds of our Religious Family are in the New World, with a most encouraging future. There my activity, if Rome approves, will easily build upon the blessings Heaven has already granted. There all the opportunities for success are found united. The spirit of our Religious . . . has not been corrupted as is the case here. One sees there harmony, obedience, regularity, confidence. There prosperity, public esteem, general contentment, unanimous devotion bring only encouragement. . . . Heaven has blessed me in America. To allow such blessing . . . to be put in jeopardy would be on my part an inexcusable infidelity, an aberration bordering on scandal.

This argument, which Father Sorin drew up for his Roman agent, was intended to promote a specific policy objective, one for which the agreement of Propaganda would be needed. Holy Cross, to survive, must be closely wedded to Notre Dame du Lac. Or, as he expressed it negatively, in the form of a veiled threat: "If the Motherhouse must compulsorily (*forcement*) be maintained in France, I shall

---

44. See chapters 13, 15, and 27, above.

be absolutely obliged to abdicate my office."[45] This was the frame of mind which he took with him to Paris and with which he approached the meeting of the general chapter.

From the beginning of his administration Sorin's strategy had aimed to shift the focus of Holy Cross's apostolate away from its faltering French base to its thriving houses in North America. Tactically, however, he had first to overcome the centuries-old presupposition in Paris and in Rome that the Faith was Europe and Europe was the Faith.[46] Should the "Eldest Daughter of the Church" yield primacy to a bumptious new country, peopled by millions of heretics, not to speak of cowboys and red Indians, a country moreover to which French men and women had brought the true gospel in the first place? Perish the thought. The prejudice was surely understandable, but, in the light of the renewed assault against the Gallican Church launched by the likes of Gambetta and Ferry, it had lost much of its credit. And with the passage of the laic laws of 1879–80, Edward Sorin judged the moment ripe to expose it as an anachronism.

And not only he. The new pope, Leo XIII,[47] had introduced a different temper into the Roman curia. A dryly intellectual man, who prided himself on his diplomatic skills, he never won the same measure of love and devotion Father Sorin and indeed the masses of Catholic faithful around the world had tendered his hearty and much-maligned predecessor.[48] But for all his personal warmth, for all his courage and patience in suffering, Pius IX had often exercised his high office with scant regard for the distinction between ends and means. Leo, by contrast, while not repudiating any of Pius's general policies, assumed a much more pragmatic style and demonstrated a willingness to embrace whatever gains short-term flexibility might offer. When the Chamber of Deputies issued the infamous *Décrets* of March 29, 1880, he insisted that the French bishops respond to this act of aggression with cautious restraint. And to a confidant he said, "The Jesuits are finished in France. Try to save the other orders."[49]

Such was the papal mind-set when Father Ferdinando Battista, in accord with Sorin's instructions,[50] sought and was granted an audience in early April.

---

45. Sorin to Battista, n.d. [February 1880], AGEN.

46. A point of view whose classic expression in English is Hilaire Belloc, *Europe and the Faith* (London, 1920).

47. Gioacchino Pecci (1810–1903), elected after Pius IX's death in 1878.

48. Sorin was in France when Pius IX died (February 7, 1878). He received assurances from home that Notre Dame had entered into properly prayerful mourning for the deceased pontiff and that the news of Leo XIII's election "was well received here." Corby to Sorin, March 2, 1878, AIP.

49. See Dansette, *Histoire religieuse*, 414–418.

50. Sorin to Battista, March 29, 1880, AGEN.

The Holy Father questioned me closely and with obvious interest as to what we were going to treat in our General Chapter. I answered His Holiness that among the matters we had to decide was whether or not to transfer the Motherhouse from Paris to Notre Dame du Lac in America. Scarcely had I uttered the words "transfer the Motherhouse" when His Holiness said to me with much emotion: "Yes, my child, you have good reason to do this. In France there is nothing very reassuring in the current state of things." He pursued this subject for a little time, and then he dismissed me with his Blessing for all our Religious and for our Chapter in particular.[51]

So Sorin could count upon papal endorsement of his intentions even before the chapter met. And his own bishop, whose opinion, though not determinative, would have been carefully noted within the corridors of Propaganda, adopted essentially the same line. "Father Sorin," Dwenger declared with his habitual terseness, "should have permission to reside in America or be relieved of the generalship. [Holy Cross's] interests in America are too great," and in the same blunt spirit he stressed the point with Sorin himself.[52] But the superior general, a leader—sometimes a manipulator—of his fellow religious for nearly forty years, recognized the value of proper constitutional ratification as well. "The General Chapter will be short," he confided to Alexis Granger. "There are only a few issues to deal with besides the enforcement of the Rule." And of course the transfer of the motherhouse.

I have not the slightest doubt that it ought to be at Notre Dame and not here. But in order that it should be acceded to here and in Rome, the transfer must be seen as self-imposed and agreeable to all and not as something emanating from us. The work of Providence will be recognized to the degree that the hand of man is not allowed to be seen interfering. If the Motherhouse departs from Paris, we shall receive it gracefully, but we shall not lift it on the point of our sword. One always buys too dearly when one pays for what the passage of time will give free. It will be much better to inter the synagogue with honor.[53]

---

51. Battista to Sorin, April? 1880 (fragment), AGEN.

52. Quoted in Granger to Sorin, March 5, 1880, AGEN. See also Dwenger to Sorin, May 25, 1880, AIP.

53. Sorin to Granger, February 7, 1880, AGEN.

Sorin had little doubt that he could muster the necessary votes—"Do not forget that the Province of France represents scarcely 200 members, while there are 265 in Indiana and another 140 in Canada"[54]—but before they could be counted a decision had to be made by the general council as to the site of the chapter. The superior general, needless to say, preferred Notre Dame, without being prepared, however, to raise serious objections to Paris. The matter in the end was settled by an event which for Sorin had personal as well as professional ramifications. When he arrived at Neuilly in November he found that "the dear Superior is not well."[55] During succeeding weeks Louis Champeau's condition worsened drastically. "Every day he grows weaker. . . . He has received the last sacraments. His death will be a great loss for us. Without a miracle I do not see him getting back on his feet. We shall pray till the last hour for his recovery."[56] The prayers appeared at first to have been answered, and Father Champeau, now sixty-three, though still very sick, appeared to be slowly regaining his strength. By early February Sorin could report that he was "happily much on the mend."[57] Indeed, Champeau felt well enough to announce that he could assist at the general chapter if were held in his own house at Neuilly-sur-Seine.[58]

This development determined for all practical purposes the locale of the chapter. Father Sorin might have dismissed Joseph Rézé and other reactionary members of the French province, but he could not so easily set aside the feelings of Louis-Dominique Champeau. He was not only the friend of Sorin's youth and his constant ally in the old disputes with Moreau, but also the donor whose munificence had contributed significantly to Holy Cross's deliverance from the debts the former administration had accumulated.[59] Champeau had besides made a success of the *collège* at Neuilly despite crises thrust upon him first by the Commune and afterward by a succession of anticlerical governments, and, finally, he held the office of first assistant general. So the capitulants were summoned to assemble in Paris on April 18. Father Sorin admitted to some uneasiness, mostly because another of his intimate friends was in poor health. "Of course," he assured Alexis Granger, "I dreaded a little, when sanctioning the chapter *here*, the

54. Sorin to Battista, April 1, 1880, AGEN.
55. Sorin to Battista, November 10, 1879, AGEN.
56. Sorin to Battista, December 13, 1879, AGEN.
57. Sorin to Sister Columba, February 6, 1880, AGEN.
58. Sorin to Battista, February 19, 1880, AGEN.
59. See chapter 26, above.

necessity of an ocean voyage for you. But I could not help it."[60] Ten days later Champeau suffered an unexpected relapse and died.[61]

The sudden passing of "one of [the Congregation's] best and most worthy members"[62] caused some momentary confusion and consternation as the date for the opening of the chapter approached. In the end, however, the meeting began on schedule. Father Granger survived the voyage handily. Indeed, as Sorin reported back to Indiana, "he says it was he who nursed the others; he was not sick a moment and looks well." Once the sessions start, "lively times will follow for a week. Our American soldiers seem to me ready and able to carry their points or die a noble death on the spot. For my part, I anticipate no trouble; we are all Christians."[63] He was especially heartened by the declaration sent ahead to Paris by the Canadian capitulants, who pledged "to carry by storm (*emporter d'assaut*) the Translation of the Motherhouse to Notre Dame. They want nobody to labor under any doubt or illusion. And so the majority is assured, sixteen out of twenty-one votes."[64]

By May 1 the superior general and his fellow capitulants from North America, their victory won, were aboard ship on the way home.[65] Although, as has been suggested in these pages, the central administration of Holy Cross had been de facto located at Notre Dame du Lac since Sorin's election as general in 1868, the de jure endorsement was more than a mere formality. "God alone knows how I longed for the same," Father Sorin exclaimed. Not that the event should have given rise to any gloating. "In the transfer of the Motherhouse to Notre Dame," he admonished the community there, "none of us will fail to recognize a

---

60. Sorin to Granger, February 18, 1880, AIP. Granger, though he had hoped "circumstances" might have spared him the journey, "one I had never wanted to make again," was ever the good soldier and pledged his appearance. See Granger to Sorin, March 9, 1880, AIP.

61. Sorin to Siméoni, March 14, 1880, AGEN. Giovanni Siméoni, with the rank of archbishop, had served as secretary of Propaganda under Cardinal Barnabò, the prefect. When Barnabò died in 1874, he was succeeded by Alessandro Cardinal Franchi, and Siméoni, himself raised to the cardinalate, was sent to Spain as nuncio. Upon the election of Leo XIII he was named prefect of Propaganda, replacing Franchi. Archbishop Domenico Jacobini then became secretary, the same post Siméoni had held under Barnabò.

62. See Sorin's lengthy tribute, *Circular Letters*, 1: 135–136. Champeau was a benefactor of Holy Cross in death as in life. He left the congregation 50,000 francs. See Sorin to Battista, August 23, 1881, AGEN.

63. Sorin to Corby, April 12, 1880, AIP.

64. Sorin to Battista, April 1, 1880, AGEN.

65. For the list of the twenty-eight decrees of the general chapter of 1880, See Sorin, *Circular Letters*, 1:292–294. Number 19 reflected one of the superior general's current annoyances: "The dress of the Religious of the same Province must be perfectly alike—summer and winter, especially on journeys." See note 36, above.

signal favor from the Holy Father; not a favor, however, to flatter our vanity, but one evidently calculated to impress on our hearts a true and religious gratitude, calling forth our best efforts to acquire that perfection of which we, before all others, must henceforth give the example to the rest of the Congregation." For his own part this achievement seemed to occasion somber reflections rather than any complacency.

> At my age I can but feel that I have only a short time to enjoy your company, and to edify myself with the cheering examples of your virtues. I return [from Paris], not so much to live, as to end my days among those I love best on earth. For, to tell the truth, in proportion as I always feared to be made too much of in life, I dread the idea of being too soon forgotten after death. Indeed, the daily growing preoccupation of my mind is not to be forgotten, but remembered and prayed for when I can no longer help myself or others; and I find an unspeakable consolation in the assurance that, once gone from the spot I have loved so long and so tenderly, many a devoted heart will breathe a fervent prayer over my cold remains, when prayer alone can relieve a poor suffering soul. Sweet as your welcoming congratulations are to my heart on my return in [sic] your midst, I enjoy them especially because they reveal to me a friendship I would vainly seek elsewhere; strong enough to outlive the unavoidable adieus which should be the ruling thought of declining years everywhere, but particularly among Religious.[66]

No doubt his own recent infirmities prompted these sentiments. But perhaps the death of Louis Champeau also contributed to them, as well as the news that Father Pierre Chappé had entered his last illness—he died later in the summer. Champeau, Chappé, Victor Drouelle, with whom Sorin had been at least partially reconciled before he died:[67] the three musketeers of Sainte-Croix, so to speak, all gone now. Only D'Artagnan was left.

ONCE AT HOME AGAIN, however, Edward Sorin found much to cheer him. Work on the Main Building continued apace, so that not long afterward he was able to give a rhapsodic description of the overall aspect of the new Notre Dame.

---

66. Sorin, *Circular Letters,* 1: 136–137, dated May 15, 1880.
67. See Sorin, *Circular Letters,* 1: 80, dated April 5, 1875.

The University building is now finished with its beautiful Dome on the center and its golden statue . . . 200 feet above the ground. That it is a grand sight, we hear it repeated by every visitor, even from the first opening of Notre Dame Avenue a mile and a quarter from the College. But the beauty of the scenery increases as you come nearer to the building and when you enter the main hall, twenty feet wide, recently enriched with that luxurious smooth and colored pavement, covering a space of 3000 square feet on either side of which our Roman Artist, Luigi Gregori, has so admirably traced the life of Columbus. When you stand in the middle of the rotunda and look on the East and on the West, [you] see two vast study rooms of equal size, 100 feet by 80; there you may readily form an idea of the superior arrangements of the new Notre Dame. The same exactly is repeated below for the two dining rooms and three times above for the dormitories. There is ample room for 500 boarders. And despite the hard times we are passing through, there is scarcely a doubt the number will be here soon.[68]

This prediction was only slowly realized. In 1881, only 351 students were in attendance, a figure, however, somewhat larger than that of the year before.[69]

On the whole Father Sorin's health remained sound, though his teeth began to cause him some grief. The illnesses of the late 1870s had pared away some of the flesh gained during his middle years—indeed, he seemed to have recaptured the leanness of his youth. But the most striking change in his physical appearance was the full white beard he now cultivated, which fell richly to his mid-chest and which contrasted exquisitely with the caped black soutane he habitually wore as an example to his brethren who were tempted to garb themselves carelessly. As he stood before the burgeoning campus, with its farms and orchards and lakes, with its fifteen buildings, with the squads of craftsmen and priests and students of all ages over whom he presided, he displayed the mien of an Old Testament patriarch, of an Abraham conducting his herds and retainers toward a promised land of milk and honey, or, better, of a Joseph in Egypt, who oversaw all the riches and monuments of the pharaoh. Edward Sorin's writ, moreover, extended far beyond the confines of northern Indiana. Age had not diminished a whit his direct concern for the missionary activity, down to its smallest detail, that Holy Cross had taken on from Montreal to New Orleans, from Salt Lake City to Washington. His enormous correspondence bears witness to this continuing involvement.

---

68. Sorin, "Memorandum," n.d. [early 1882], AGEN.
69. Hope, *Notre Dame*, 197.

During 1880, for example, he received many hundreds of formal communications from a wide variety of correspondents, each unique—from a lonely nun seeking spiritual solace to the president of the Edison Electric Company in New York explaining that a crown of bright bulbs around the head of the Virgin's statue atop the golden dome was not yet feasible—and each eliciting a prompt and sometimes lengthy reply.[70]

The difference between these and earlier years was that Sorin adopted a rather more relaxed mode. Thus, if he kept a particularly sharp eye on St. Edward's in Austin, Texas—the most successful Holy Cross mission outside Indiana now that the once promising venture in Wisconsin was languishing—he did so with a minimum of negative criticism. He appreciated the merits of Father Daniel Spillard, the superior there, but he could not resist an old man's playful admonition when the occasion presented itself.

> You begin to understand business and business men [he wrote Spillard in 1881]. One third reduction is already something, but one half would be better. I do not want to miss the opportunity to secure that parcel of land; but I want you to secure it for $1,500 instead of $2,000. I leave it to you to arrange your movements accordingly. Perhaps by showing a complete indifference you will accomplish more than by too great a visible anxiety. Say that you can make better use of your little cash in Austin than in buying useless land. In any event tell me immediately the result.[71]

Closer to home Father Sorin enjoyed to the fullest the role that advanced age had afforded him. He relished entertaining the worthies of South Bend society, the Studebakers, the Olivers, and the rest, at sumptuous dinner parties, what he called "Parisian Entertainments,"[72] served in the senior refectory of the new Main Building, at which both his French charm and the French cuisine he offered served to impress favorably these new American oligarchs, heretics though they were. Nor did he forget them and other local notables—or allow them to forget him and Notre Dame—during the Christmas holidays. Thus the president of the Oliver Chilled Plow Company jovially expressed his gratitude "to Santa Claus via Notre Dame" for a gift of a large cake shaped like a pyramid and a bottle of

---

70. Compare the relevant correspondence for 1880 in AIP with that in AGEN. The same exercise is instructive for any other calendar year as well.

71. Sorin to Spillard, November 4, 1881, AIP. See also chapter 28, above.

72. Colfax to Sorin, November 2, 1883, AIP, accepting an invitation to one such fête.

chartreuse.[73] The thank-you note of the chief executive of the Studebaker Wagon and Carriage Company was more fulsome.

> You will please accept my thanks for your usual Christmas remembrance. . . . May you live many more years to enjoy the society of dear friends and receive the blessings from the thousands whom you have been the means of making men of principle, intellect, and Christian witness. After thy work is done, may God so direct that the leader who may take your place may be possessed with the same *noble intellect,* same broad and far-seeing views, same liberal Christian spirit as his <u>Predecessor.</u>[74]

Timothy Howard, now Clerk of the St. Joseph County Court, was also a recipient of holiday largesse, though in his case the gesture had a family ring to it. He promised that he and his wife would dip the cake in the *"liqueur fameuse,"* and then added nostalgically: "I look upon myself as a child of Notre Dame and trust that my character has been, at least to some degree, formed by your noble example."[75] Father Sorin was shrewd enough moreover to realize that in a mass democracy cordial relations with the press were a necessity for an enterprise like Notre Dame, and so he routinely sent the chartreuse and cake to the staffs of both South Bend dailies, with a couple of bottles of claret (vintage '75) thrown in for good measure.[76] But, to his credit, he also remembered during the holidays the mighty who had fallen. Caught up in the scandals of the Grant administration, Schuyler Colfax's political career had withered away; he spent most of his time now lecturing across the Midwest to half-empty halls. To him went a bottle of wine to mark the new year of 1881.

> As we are all Teetotalers, we will have to preserve the wine for sickness. And its presentation reminds me of the delicious bottle you kindly sent me when I returned from Washington in 1871, so feeble and almost at death's door. I can remember yet how every spoonful of it quickened the sluggish blood in my veins. . . . I think back often to our third of a century of unbroken friendship with a gratification that I can but feebly express. I trust it will so remain till the end.[77]

73. James Oliver to Sorin, December 27, 1881, AIP.
74. James Studebaker to Sorin, December 28, 1882, AIP.
75. Howard to Sorin, December 25, 1881, AIP.
76. Hope, *Notre Dame,* 199.
77. Colfax to Sorin, January 2, 1881, AIP. Colfax died in 1885.

The once powerful Speaker of the House had apparently forgotten his vindictive attitude toward Notre Dame in the last year of the Civil War; Sorin at any rate had forgiven it.[78]

No doubt it was his relationship with the minims, his "little princes" as he called them, that demonstrated best the fatherly and benevolent posture Sorin increasingly assumed. A celibate without grandsons of his own, these grammar school pupils furnished him a unique source of consolation. When he visited them he always came armed with gifts of sweets or fruit. He promised them that once their number had reached fifty, he would treat them to the kind of Parisian banquet he had reserved heretofore for prestigious people like the Studebakers. By the spring of 1881, their enrollment fell two short of that total. One day, when he and his guest Bishop Dwenger looked in on their classroom, Sorin suggested that the youngsters designate his grace an honorary double minim, so that the required number might be attained. Given the bishop of Fort Wayne's formidable girth, this proposal might have been tendered with a bit of a twinkle in the eye. Dwenger at any rate genially agreed, and the minims got their banquet.[79]

And shortly afterward they got their own building as well, its blueprints drawn up by Sorin himself with the collaboration of the ever-creative Brother Charles Borromeo Harding. The physical dimensions of St. Edward's House, just to the northeast of the reconstructed Main, were modest, but the boys, since they were princes, exultantly dubbed their hall "the Palace."[80] Here from 1882 they resided and did their studies—reading, history, grammar, mathematics and, for Catholics, catechism and biblical lore—taught mostly by the sisters, while the brothers supervised discipline and organized recreation.[81] At the same time, construction was begun to replace the clapboard music hall that had been consumed by the fire of April 23. Washington Hall, as the new edifice was called, envisioned a much expanded role for the performing arts at Notre Dame; it was inaugurated with a performance of Sophocles's *Oedipus Rex.* Two years later, just as Luigi Gregori was finishing the Columbus murals in the foyer of the Main Building, Father Sorin rejoiced to see the completion of its west and east wings, giving it the massive configuration it has had ever since. The same year, 1884, a new two-story

---

78. See chapter 23, above.

79. Hope, *Notre Dame,* 194–201.

80. See Granger to Sorin, March 28, 1882, and "The Sorin Princes" to Sorin, September 22, 1883, AIP.

81. Till the program was terminated in 1927, about 6,000 boys passed through the minims' school in St. Edward's. Many of them continued their education at Notre Dame. See Schlereth, *Notre Dame,* 88–90.

brick science hall, a project long cherished and nurtured by Father John Zahm, provided the university for the first time with a separate facility devoted exclusively to research and teaching in the natural sciences, photography, and mechanical engineering.[82] Such a burst of physical expansion in the immediate wake of so dire a calamity surely recalled the proverbial phoenix rising from its own ashes.

But even in the midst of so many signs of providential favor—or perhaps because of them—Edward Sorin was not ready to relax his vigilance altogether. "A new scholastic year is opening," he addressed his religious confrères in September 1881, and "who does not wish it to prove a success? For my own part I feel, like you all, fully confident of such a result, provided each of us does his duty." What must be avoided above all is "scandal of any sort on the premises, either from students or professors or Religious." Discipline needed to be reinforced "everywhere and always, . . . mildly but effectually. Among the abuses lately signalized as most saddening and to be avoided I must name drinking, visiting the town [in search of] of light plays, [disturbances] in private rooms after nine P.M., private mails, smoking everywhere, Professors and even Religious not under effectual control."

> What must be chiefly improved may be contained in a few comprehensive words; namely, a greater respect, not only in expressions but in deeds, for religion and religious duties; a more universal attention to secure [for] our own members and students a complete knowledge and love of our holy Faith; a greater attention to manners among all; spiritual reading every day; everywhere a thorough explanation of the regulations and an enforcing of the same; courteous and prompt obedience to all in authority. . . . To secure all the above the President of the University shall act as Superior to all Religious attached to the college and shall preside over all their religious exercises in the chapel of the University, and be responsible for their regularity and conduct at large. He alone will give permissions to leave the premises.[83]

The president upon whom this stern obligation was imposed was not William Corby. From a combination of motives, Sorin was in the process of removing him from office just at the time he wrote the admonition just quoted. The prob-

---

82. See Weber, *Zahm*, 18, 29. After the fire of April 23 Sorin appointed the resourceful Zahm campus firechief. Zahm's original science hall, much and frequently refurbished, is now the La Fortune Student Center.

83. Sorin "Memorandum," September 2, 1881, AGEN.

lem between the two men may have first arisen because of their disagreement over the details involved in the construction of the new Main Building. Or it may have been that Sorin resented the credit widely accorded Corby for the spectacular success of that project[84]—if so it was hardly worthy of the superior general, though not entirely out of character for him. Certainly, however, an additional and perhaps determining factor was Sorin's suspicion that Corby, his most loyal and able subordinate, had fallen under the malevolent influence of Patrick Colovin. The brilliant if unstable Colovin had been Corby's esteemed colleague in the mission in Wisconsin during the mid-1870s. Then, after his lackluster presidency at Notre Dame, Colovin had endured a brief and troubled tenure in Watertown, after which he had gone to the bleak mission in the Black Hills, and there his connection with Holy Cross had been terminated.[85] Or, as Sorin put it, "The General Council [of the congregation] has expelled the infamous Colovin for the third time. What an indignity! It is said that he will appeal to Rome, and so," he told his Roman agent, "I leave him to you."[86] Colovin did not in fact appeal his case to Propaganda and settled instead, for the few years left to him, into a respectable position as a parish priest in Wisconsin. But for Sorin the apprehension, the obsession even, that the location of the central administration of Holy Cross at Notre Dame might somehow be aborted took precedence over all other considerations.

> Here the general administration, where our best Religious so ardently desire the canonical establishment to be located for the well-being of our Work of Holy Cross, appeared threatened by Colovin and his clique. Of course Colovin himself has been expelled from the Congregation, and his principal disciples, Father Corby and the others, have had to lower their sights, and calm has been restored. Father Corby, the very personification of vanity (*la vanité même*), has had to assume charge of St. Bernard's parish in Watertown, Wisconsin, where, in 1873, he built a grandiose church, but in doing so he accrued a debt of 100,000 francs, which Colovin, his adviser and successor, managed only to augment. Father Corby never consulted me about this expense (he habitually consults only sycophants). He has asserted instead that nobody but he could liquidate this debt by himself and indeed that no other Father of Holy Cross could do so. His departure from

---

84. See Hope, *Notre Dame*, 195.
85. See chapter 28, above.
86. Sorin to Battista, July 5, 1881, AGEN.

here bothers nobody; indeed, it has prompted universal relief. . . . His replacement, Father Walsh, . . . has received plaudits from all our world.[87]

One may well doubt that Detroit-born William Corby was scheming to restore the motherhouse to Paris. Nonetheless, he may not have been altogether surprised at his removal from the presidency, because he had long known that Sorin suspected him of having moved into Colovin's orbit. "I was somewhat surprised," he had written Sorin a year earlier, "to think you are of [the] opinion that I favor Father Colovin. When in Watertown I told him openly what he *should* do. When I returned [to Notre Dame] I told you the result but tried to act in the case with all the charity I could. Besides, I had as [a] motive *prudence*. His case is a desperate one, and all I feared was, and is, that he might do desperate things. I did not consider myself a *judge* in the case."[88]

But even though it was due largely to Sorin's personal pique and, in this instance, his weakness for conspiracy theories, Corby's exile to Wisconsin proved in the long run highly beneficial for the development of Notre Dame. Thomas Walsh, only twenty-eight when he assumed the presidency,[89] was cut from far different cloth. Born in Canada, as Patrick Colovin had been, he entered Holy Cross at Saint-Laurent in 1872. The rather chubby young man, pious, studious, and clearly very intelligent, soon caught the superior general's eye, and after a year's novitiate he was sent to Paris to read theology. In 1876 Sorin recalled him, not to Canada but to Notre Dame, where he began his teaching career while completing his theological preparation for the priesthood. This was the final year of Colovin's troubled presidency, but Walsh, showing a prudence beyond his years, took care not to entangle himself in the quarrel between his fellow Canadian and the superior general. Instead, he concentrated on his teaching and, after ordination, on his duties as director of studies, a post to which President Corby appointed him. In this latter capacity he demonstrated remarkable skill, especially in reorganizing the whole curricular structure of the college after the fire. He was, again like Colovin, a genuine intellectual, but unlike that tempestuous man Father Walsh was affable and accommodating. During his twelve-year tenure—the balance, that is, of Edward Sorin's life and indeed of his own—he presided

87. Sorin to Battista, September 8, 1881, AGEN.

88. Corby to Sorin, June 28, 1880, AIP.

89. Bishop Dwenger, never slow to express an opinion, urged Sorin to keep Corby on as president. Walsh, he said, despite all his "estimable qualities," was too young. Dwenger to Sorin, May 25, 1881, AIP.

over not only the physical expansion of the institution but also over its unprecedented advance in sophistication and maturity as an enterprise in higher education.[90]

Thomas Walsh's premature death (July 17, 1893) did not obscure the emergence of a new generation of Holy Cross men to stand where the likes of Corby, Toohey, and Condon had stood before—though, in a poignant sign of continuity, it was Patrick Condon who had ministered to Walsh on his deathbed.[91] John Zahm was coming into his own as a scholar and controversialist. Andrew Morrissey had come to Notre Dame from Ireland as a lad of twelve, and twenty years later he succeeded Walsh as president. Daniel Hudson now edited the *Ave Maria,* as he was destined to do with distinction for more than four decades. Father Sorin viewed this natural evolution benignly, and now, consistent with the patriarchal manner, he was more content than heretofore to allow subordinates freer rein. Nor did he neglect to cultivate young talent among his confrères overseas. "If our Father Français presents himself to board at St. Bridget's for three or four years for theological studies, pray," he instructed Battista, "receive him very kindly. I will settle with you for all expenses he may cause you."[92] Gilbert Français, after his Roman seasoning, became the accomplished president of the *collège* at Neuilly-sur-Seine and then Sorin's successor as superior general of the Congregation of Holy Cross.[93]

FATHER SORIN traveled to Europe twice in 1882. A brief springtime stay in Rome was followed, in the autumn, by a similarly short sojourn in Paris. The Roman visit left him troubled and exasperated. No one, he believed, had demonstrated more heartfelt loyalty to the Holy See than he—not least by the steady if modest financial support he had extended over the years.[94] And as the Italian government had continued to harass the "Prisoner of the Vatican," Sorin had even offered him a place of refuge.

> With all the uncertainties (*éventualités*) which menace Rome and which could in a short time force his Holiness himself to flee, God alone knows

---

90. See Hope, *Notre Dame,* 202–208, and *Golden Jubilee,* 177–180.

91. Hope, *Notre Dame,* 251.

92. Sorin to Battista, April 8, 1881, AGEN.

93. See *Matricule générale,* 1766, AIP.

94. Such support was often in the form of Mass stipends. See, among many examples, Sorin to Battista, February 21, 1882, AGEN, in which Sorin enclosed a check for 15,000 francs to provide for the same number of Masses.

where, let it be known that Notre Dame belongs to the Pope. Here, at the center of Catholicism in the New World, he would be fully secure. The 650 people who live here today would be for him a guard of honor, of devotion, and of filial love, worthy of all confidence.[95]

Sorin probably knew that this proposal was a flight of fancy, but the genuine fealty that inspired it seemed to have won a scant reward when next he parleyed with the officials at Propaganda. "Your Eminence will permit me, I hope," he wrote the prefect from shipboard on his way home, "to share the impressions I take away with me from my recent visit to the Eternal City."

Perhaps, even probably, my apprehensions are not well-founded, but it seems that your Eminence no longer views me the same as before. The silence for two years with reference to the acts of the General Chapter held at Paris in 1880 is incomprehensible to me, as is the failure of Propaganda to suppress once and for all the wicked and ridiculous charges raised against us by the Marianites of Le Mans. These things make me fear a change in your Eminence's attitude toward us. This is especially the case since I am not aware that I have done anything to lose your esteem. Nobody in America is more submissive and devoted to you. Above all, I live for the Holy See, whose causes I have espoused all my life. If I am wrong, Eminence, it would be easy for you with a single word to restore the peace and joy in my heart. For forty-one years I have served the Church in America, for the salvation of souls and in the interests of my Congregation. God has blessed me far beyond my merits and in the midst of extraordinary difficulties. This last, which is not the least, I dare to hope, your Eminence, can shortly become a new source of consolation and devotion.[96]

In retrospect this sense of vexation appears fully justified, especially with regard to the nuisance suit the sisters in Le Mans continued to press at Propaganda.[97] "I scarcely doubt that this indignant piece of information sent to Rome originated with ex-Father Charles Moreau or his community of Marianites at Mans. Since ten years I see no abatement in their brutal fury against me personally."[98] His

95. Sorin to Battista, September 27, 1881, AGEN. During the revolutions of 1848 Pius IX had had to flee Rome and take up residence in the Kingdom of Naples.
96. Sorin to Siméoni, May 18, 1882, AGEN.
97. See chapter 25, above.
98. Sorin to Dwenger, January 11, 1879, AIP.

conclusion was basically correct; the bitterness of Basile Moreau's nephew had, if anything, increased with the passing years. Even so, Sorin knew full well the leisurely modus operandi of the Roman curia, to say nothing of its penchant for maneuvering among its far-flung dependencies by a policy of selective and calculated reticence. Nevertheless his patience with the papal bureaucracy's ways wore thin during his latter years, perhaps because he realized his own time was running out.

Father Sorin found the Roman spring of 1882 disagreeable on another score. Ferdinando Battista had acted as procurator general of Holy Cross since 1870, though he had had to wait briefly before that prestigious title was conferred upon him.[99] Through that decade, resident at St. Bridget's and in regular contact with Propaganda, he had become something of confidant for Sorin. Recently, however, some strain between the two had manifested itself. Sorin was increasingly annoyed at his Roman agent's long silences and his carelessness in maintaining or forwarding important documents.[100] He had been especially vexed when Battista neglected to present to the pope a full report on the reconstruction of Notre Dame's Main Building and then to secure the pope's public "word of sympathy and encouragement." Battista had aggravated his fault by equivocal excuse. "Why this deception?" Sorin demanded. "Bear well in mind that all the world here . . . judges your activities, blames you for the least negligence, and shows the liveliest joy and recognition for all you do for the benefit of the Congregation. It is a painful and inexpressible surprise that you have not sent the Papal Blessing upon the great work of reconstruction, which has won the admiration of all the United States."[101]

But a more serious matter surfaced just before Sorin departed for Rome and his disappointing interviews with Cardinal Siméoni. A routine canonical visitation to St. Bridget's had revealed at best careless bookkeeping and at worst some misappropriation of funds. The trouble arose out of a pension which Sorin, at the direction of Propaganda, had pledged for the support of Pierre Dufal, who, after his unfortunate experience as coadjutor in Galveston,[102] had retired once more to Rome. The money, 3,000 francs—the first installment of an annual total of 24,000—had been dispatched through Battista, but Bishop Dufal claimed never to have received it. When Sorin heard this complaint, he immediately summoned Battista to Indiana to explain himself. The procurator general refused to come.

---

99. See chapter 26, above.
100. See, for example, Sorin to Battista, April 5 and April 18, 1881, AGEN.
101. Sorin to Battista, October 8, 1879, AGEN.
102. See chapter 28, above.

So when Sorin himself arrived in Rome a few months later he confronted Battista with the intention, as he assured Siméoni, "of naming, if need be, a Successor worthy of confidence as soon as possible."[103] The procurator, however, was by now an old Roman hand, and he had friends in high places: no less a personage than the cardinal-vicar interceded in his behalf, and Father Sorin left for home with the situation unresolved.[104] In the late summer he instructed Battista again, this time by cable, "*to come here instantly,*" and again without result. Finally, as 1882 neared its close, he had sorted out the imbroglio to his satisfaction. "I would certainly have removed our poor Procurator, Ferdinando Battista, last May," he assured Siméoni,

> except for the intervention of his Eminence, the Cardinal Vicar, to whom you referred me, and who put all the blame for *these unjust accusations* [against Battista], as he styled them, upon Monseigneur Dufal. . . . The fact is, 3,000 francs were sent to St. Bridget's to be remitted to Bishop Dufal, as was his due according to the directive you had given me. The unfaithful Procurator appropriated the money thus sent from here to fulfill this obligation, which has given in your eyes *the appearance of oversight or of bad will.* Happily, this is only an appearance. I have been faithful to my duty and to my promises.[105]

And so Ferdinando Battista passed out of Father Sorin's life and indeed out of the Congregation of Holy Cross.[106] Irony prevailed in the choice of a successor. "I learn with satisfaction," Sorin wrote Pierre Dufal at the beginning of 1883, "that you are willing to serve our Congregation as Procurator and representative to the Holy See. The General Council, expressing to you its respectful appreciation, can assure you that our religious family will applaud your dedication in this regard, and will be proud to be represented by a Bishop."[107] Perhaps he hoped that the curial authorities might show a little more gratitude and a little less hauteur.

L'affaire Battista was still hanging fire when Father Sorin made his quick journey to France at the end of September. The political situation vis-à-vis the religious orders was still very tense—as it would continue to be into the foreseeable future—but so far the congregation had survived and the *collège* at Neuilly-

---

103. Sorin to Siméoni, February 23, 1882, AGEN.

104. The cardinal-vicar is the officer of the curia who administers the diocese of Rome in the pope's name.

105. Sorin to Siméoni, December 7, 1882, AGEN.

106. See *Matricule générale*, 956, AIP.

107. Sorin to Dufal, January 1, 1883, AGEN.

sur-Seine functioned as before. "Without being directly hostile," the superior general observed sagely, "the officials of the French Republic are by no means our friends."[108] But even if no immediate crisis had to be contended with, the relentless decline of the Province of France, in statistical terms at least, proceeded just as Sorin had predicted. Since 1872 eleven foundations had been closed down, and succeeding years witnessed the demise of eight more. In 1872 207 Holy Cross priests and brothers were at work in France; at the end of 1883 the number would be reduced to 149.[109] Besides confronting these depressing figures and the ever-present danger of dissolution, the stay in Paris was painful for the superior general for another reason: "I have just come from a dentist who has pulled all my upper teeth, and tomorrow morning he is going to pay the same deference to my lower. He tells me I will have to wait fifteen days before I can be fitted with dentures."[110]

Back home, besides the uncomfortable struggle to accustom himself to false teeth, Edward Sorin occasionally suffered bouts of physical disability. In the autumn of 1883, for example, he had a nasty fall, but he recovered rapidly.[111] Despite such passing travails, for the most part he presided happily over the expansion at Notre Dame du Lac and to its growing reputation as a significant religious and intellectual center. As though to underscore this new prestige, he and Father Walsh inaugurated earlier that same year the annual conferral of the Laetare Medal, awarded by the university to a distinguished American Catholic lay person. The first recipient was the historian John Gilmary Shea; the first woman to be so honored, in 1885, was the poetess Eliza Allen Starr, a close friend of Mother Angela and a frequent contributor to the *Ave Maria*.[112] Meanwhile, Father Sorin, himself more than ever benevolent, basked in a veneration that often verged into flattery. For every Colovin and Battista he could count scores upon scores of loyal and devoted disciples. His name-day (October 13) regularly occasioned celebrations in his honor on the Notre Dame campus, featuring plays, musicales, patriotic speechifying, and festive dinners. His birthday (February 6) each year brought floods of adulatory messages from almost all the Holy Cross men and women in

---

108. Sorin to Siméoni, December 7, 1882, AGEN.

109. See Lecointe, "Statistical Review of the *Province de France*," December 1, 1883, AIP. Hippolyte Lecointe (1824–1888) succeeded Joseph Rézé as provincial. See *Matricule générale*, 741, AIP.

110. Sorin to Dufal, September 26, 1882, AGEN.

111. Mary Phelan to Sorin, October 11, 1883, AIP.

112. See the list in *Golden Jubilee*, 193–194. The award was (and is) announced on the fourth Sunday of Lent each year. The first word in the Latin liturgy proper to that day is *Laetare*, Rejoice. By medieval custom the pope, on that Sunday, blessed a rose-shaped ornament and awarded it to some distinguished person, usually a Catholic aristocrat.

America, none more tender than that of Angela Gillespie. The days of early February 1883 were "bitterly long and cold," she wrote from St. Mary's.

> Just think—we have not seen you since the second. Do you wonder why our days are so long? And yet with such weather I'd rather have seen longer days than see you run the risk of venturing out. . . . Although deprived of seeing you on this your *birthday,* yet I do not forget you on this precious festival—reminding me all the more vividly as it does of what I owe you. The debt commenced more than a quarter of a century ago!! All I can give, that is, the gratitude of *time* and *eternity* could never repay it.[113]

So the days came and went, and the years, and though for so pugnacious a man there were still battles to be fought, they were fewer now, and he often indulged in nostalgia, as old men are wont to do. "My dear young Princes," he addressed the minims one snowy day shortly before his seventieth birthday,

> were I a poet I would draw some inspiration from this beautiful snow just now storming from all sides over the Dome and playing all sorts of antics around its crowning monument, our Blessed Mother's golden statue. . . . How delightfully this first snow reminds me of our first departure from France! It was on the feast of Our Lady of the Snows, August 5, 1841. . . . I never believed in chance, but on this occasion I understood at once and realized that the Blessed Virgin herself, for whom we were actually and joyfully sacrificing all—little as it was—had accepted the modest homage of our honest hearts and had herself chosen this beautiful feast for the day of our adoption among her own missionaries, and wished to assure us from the start that she would be our Star of the Sea, and our Guide and Protectress through the snows of the Northwest of the New World. To me it was a revelation. I accepted it in full confidence, and now, after an experience of forty-two years, I confess, with an unspeakable sense of gratitude, that our fondest hopes have been, from day to day, realized beyond all expression.[114]

On occasion, to be sure, Sorin's mood grew more somber. At about the same time, or perhaps a little later, he put down on a sheet of paper a directive to be observed when the sands in the hourglass had finally run out.

---

113. Mother Angela to Sorin, February 6, 1883, AIP.
114. Sorin, *Circular Letters,* 1: 241–242.

When I die, the Community shall not be disturbed by any extra preparations or invitations to strangers for my obsequies. On the contrary, I wish the Community to remain completely at peace, exclusively occupied with the needs of my poor soul. I want nothing more than what is prescribed by the Rule: a simple wood coffin, with the simplest purple vestment. No strangers of any sort are to be disturbed by any telegraphic announcement; no invitation whatever to attend [should be sent]; none present but my own dear children of Holy Cross around my body; no delay to wait for friends at a distance. While laid in state, I want no strangers to look at me and prevent my own dear children from praying undisturbed around my mortal remains. Indeed, I want no visit but from my own family, for which alone I have lived, and whose affections I so much prized since my entrance into the Congregation.[115]

---

115. Sorin, "Memorandum," n.d. [1884], AGEN.

chapter thirty

"The Autumn Is Come for You"

IT SHOULD NOT BE THOUGHT THAT CONTEMPLATION of a plain wooden coffin and himself laid out in it, garbed in a simple purple chasuble, preoccupied Edward Sorin during his last years. Morbidity was no more part of his nature than pessimism or self-doubt. His stamina, to be sure, began to wane, and the heedless activity of earlier times had to be moderated. He could no longer cross the ocean, as he had so often done, with the same energy and verve as before. "The life of man here below is truly an ordeal, a suffering," he declared from Paris in the spring of 1885. "We arrived here yesterday evening at five o'clock; seldom have I been so exhausted, and never so tried."[1] The false teeth fitted for him by the Parisian dentist caused him continual discomfort, and he found it necessary more than once to take the soothing waters of a health spa, as he had done in Wisconsin a decade earlier.[2] Yet he complained rarely, and indeed he worried as much about the chronic infirmities of similarly aging colleagues like Alexis Granger and Pierre Dufal as he did about his own. He displayed a willingness to be patient with the bishop, now his agent in Rome, as he never had to the unfortunate Ferdinando Battista. "I seriously fear your silence is the result of sickness," he wrote Dufal, and then, after adding laconically, "I am not well myself," he passed quickly to the settlement

1. Sorin to Dufal, April 4, 1885, AGEN.
2. Sorin to Dufal, October 2, 1887, AGEN.

of a bill for seventeen francs ($3.40) charged by a photographer who had taken some pictures at St. Bridget's.[3] Man's lot here below might be an "ordeal," but that was no reason to be careless about the smallest expenditure.

If Sorin's travels became more restricted and of shorter duration, they by no means ceased. He went to Europe several more times, and late in 1887, fresh from a personal audience with Pope Leo XIII, he journeyed from Rome to the Holy Land.[4]

> Within a few months [he addressed the men and women of Holy Cross from Bethlehem] I shall have reached, God willing, my 75th year—a long life indeed—one of trials and consolations of no common character. Indeed, I often wonder how I could stand some of them and live. God's holy will has been my comfort, and on the whole my sufferings did not equal my joys. But this unexpected one of a visit to the Holy Land, so long desired, surpasses all others. . . . Since my arrival in Bethlehem I have not been idle. Again and again I have visited the precious grotto which has for me a charm perfectly inexpressible, increasing each time I return to it. . . . The Holy Family sanctified it. Over and over again, floods of penitential and loving tears have washed it for centuries. Among the numberless consolations I enjoy here there is one I must mention. It is written that *all* the words the Blessed Mother heard from the shepherds she preserved in her heart. Why should she not do the same with us? She doubtless heard all my petitions for myself and our beloved family, numerous as they were, so earnest and so often repeated.[5]

But Sorin would not have been Sorin had he not, once returned from the land where Jesus had been born and lived and died, given to his experience a practical application. "I want to publish in English," he told the prefect of Propaganda, "a new way of the cross for the members of our Religious family of Holy Cross. . . . I ask humbly that his Holiness may deign to accord to our . . . Priests, Brothers, and Sisters the precious and ineffable privilege of setting up in all their foundations, with the usual indulgences, this royal way of the cross, which will be from now on

---

3. Sorin to Dufal, April 6, 1885, AGEN.

4. See Andrea Supori, to the Franciscan guardians of the Holy Places, November 12, 1888, Sorin Papers, AIP. Supori, secretary of the Franciscan general in Rome, provided Sorin with this letter of introduction.

5. Sorin, *Circular Letters*, 2: 52–53.

the sacred seal (*cachet*) of our Congregation, of our characteristic devotion, and an abundant source of blessings for its members and for their students."[6]

It was widely noticed within the communities at Notre Dame and St. Mary's that in these his last years Father Sorin's communications to his co-religious took on a decidedly inspirational and even a pietistic tone.[7] If so, such a development was hardly surprising, and in any case a fair analysis would reveal that a decided thread of pious consistency ran through the *Circular Letters* dispatched since his elevation to superior general in 1868.[8] Nor was he, for all his devotion to the Virgin, prepared to wander into a tangled field of questionable orthodoxy.

> A preacher who enjoys a certain reputation has been here for some days, and when talking to the students at St. Mary's about the doctrine of the Immaculate Conception, had the audacity to say *that it was a necessity* and that *God would not have been God if He had not made Mary immaculate at her conception.* I was present at this sermon, and I said to the preacher afterward that he had gone too far. Two days later he repeated the same assertion at Notre Dame. His statement caused an uproar (*bruit*), and he defended it nonetheless. I believe it my duty [he instructed Bishop Dufal in Rome] to inquire, at the highest authoritative level, whether such a view on this matter can be finally sustained.[9]

Clearly it could not.

Increasing age also curtailed Father Sorin's travels within his American bailiwick, though, again, without restricting them altogether. In 1884 he attended the landmark Third Plenary Council of Baltimore, as an observer, however, rather than a participant. He undertook a more strenuous journey the same year, to Utah Territory, where the Sisters of the Holy Cross had established themselves nearly a decade earlier.[10] He was less impressed by the spectacular physical beauty of Great Salt Lake than by admiration for the sisters' accomplishments there and by distaste for the locally predominant religion. "We have seven nuns and four houses there. . . . They could not have succeeded better. . . . I returned enchanted

---

6. Sorin to Siméoni, March 1, 1888, AGEN. Otherwise, Sorin added, "our students would have to go to the parish church, often a considerable distance away, in order to make the way of the cross, a devotion heretofore unknown to them, and yet so rich and vital for the eyes of faith!"

7. See the comment of Costin, *Priceless Spirit*, 230.

8. See, for example, Sorin, *Circular Letters,* 1: 79–83 (February 6, 1875), and 1: 164–167 (January 13, 1882).

9. Sorin to Dufal, May 15, 1885, AGEN.

10. Costin, *Priceless Spirit,* 219.

at all the good they have done among these 'new Saints of modern times,' as they call themselves." Indeed, he claimed some credit for initiating government intervention vis-à-vis the Mormons' most notorious custom.

> I cannot forget that it was *right here* (*ici même*) at Notre Dame that the governmental pursuit of this abominable Sect began. If the Mormons ever realized the initiative Providence had allowed me to take, they would not pardon me readily. [Schuyler] Colfax dined here one day [in 1871] and sat on my right. He had just returned from Salt Lake, where he had had a long interview with Brigham Young, at the conclusion of which he had received [Young's] blessing *on his knees*. The account of this Mormon blessing bestowed on the Vice President of the United States infuriated me. A discussion followed, and Colfax soon blushed with shame. Two months later, after his return to Washington, there began the famous *censure* of the Mormons, which has gradually brought about the *effective* determination to prosecute and imprison any Mormon convicted of the crime of polygamy.[11]

THIS BIT OF SELF-CONGRATULATORY HISTORY was incidental to Edward Sorin's real purpose in pointing out to his Roman agent the achievement of the nuns' mission at Salt Lake. "If Rome appreciated it," he said, "it would serve as an important motive to hasten the approval of their order." Such a seemingly bland remark disguised the fact that he had begun his last campaign, the last struggle in a lifetime of struggle. It turned upon the constitutional status of the Sisters of the Holy Cross, and it involved a complex contest among strong personalities driven by crosspurposes. The seeds of the problem had been sown three decades earlier by the well-intentioned Pope Pius IX, when he rejected Basile Moreau's "general plan" of a threefold religious family and insisted that the Marianite Sisters be kept canonically distinct from the congregation of priests and brothers. Then, in 1869, after much acrimony, the Indiana Province had declared itself independent from the Marianites in Le Mans, a disposition approved by Propaganda for a probationary period of ten years. But 1879 came and went without any further clarification of the American nuns' standing.[12] This

---

11. Sorin to Dufal, October 30, 1885, AGEN. Brigham Young died in 1875. Not till 1890 did the Church of Latter-Day Saints advise its adherents to conform to the civil law with regard to polygamy.

12. In Costin's words (*Priceless Spirit,* 229): "The approbation of 1869 had been for ten years. The year of 1879 had slipped by with no request for renewal, leaving the Sisters in a canonical limbo, a fact to which no one seems to have adverted at the time."

meant that technically they remained under the jurisdiction of the bishops in whose dioceses they served. Propaganda, however—not without prodding from Notre Dame—had named Sorin's friend, Archbishop Purcell of Cincinnati apostolic visitor, and he in turn had benignly designated Father Sorin, already superior general of the Congregation of Holy Cross, superior as well of the Sisters of the Holy Cross. Bishop Luers of Fort Wayne had endorsed this arrangement, but his successor, Joseph Dwenger, had maneuvered Purcell out of his office as visitor and had claimed an ultimate authority over all the sisters wherever they were stationed, on the grounds that their motherhouse, St. Mary's, lay in his diocese.

Sorin, who disliked Dwenger intensely for other reasons, had parried this thrust successfully, partly because of the bishop's high regard for Sorin's staunch ally, Mother Angela, partly because of Propaganda's habitual dilatoriness, and partly because other American bishops were not ready to acknowledge their colleague of Fort Wayne's claim. Notable among these latter was Richard Gilmour, the Scottish-born bishop of Cleveland, who was an old friend of Angela Gillespie and, through her, had established cordial relations with Sorin. Indeed, he was anxious that Holy Cross open a men's college in his diocese: "I feel pretty sure it would be a success from the start." Gilmour moreover had little time for German surnames like Dwenger. "The Jesuits of this diocese," he confided to Sorin, "are Germans and not suited for Cleveland. . . . Now I do not care to get these strongly marked Germans, and hence would prefer an order like yours, American."[13]

In 1882, however, at the sisters' chapter, Angela stepped down as provincial and was replaced by the more problematic—from Sorin's point of view—Mother Augusta, née Amanda Anderson, who had joined the community thirty years earlier and had served since then in several highly responsible capacities—it had been she who had founded the mission in Salt Lake City. A series of undefined illnesses, marked by fever and headache—perhaps migraine—had afflicted Angela Gillespie since the late 1870s, although such physical hindrances had hardly slowed her frenetic pace. Sorin had always counted upon her as his surrogate in overseeing the sisters' foundations, which stretched now from coast to coast. And whatever title she bore—from 1882 directress of studies at St. Mary's and then mistress of novices—Mother Angela continued to exert strong influence within the congregation. Utah, Texas, California, Maryland, Ohio: wherever the sisters had gone, Angela Gillespie was sure to appear at one time or another, giving witness to the ancient administrative formula, *suaviter in modo, fortiter in re.*

---

13. Gilmour to Sorin, August 1 and 4, 1883, AIP. Gilmour (1824–1891), a convert to Catholicism in his youth, eventually had to turn to the Jesuits, who opened St. Ignatius College (later John Carroll University) in 1886.

This cultivated and devoted woman for whose original adherence to Holy Cross, Father Sorin, according to his own testimony, had long prayed, had given so fully of herself that her absence from his life and his mission was quite unthinkable. Nor was he, born to the gentry himself, indifferent to her social and political connections. He learned with gratification that while in New York in the summer of 1884 she called upon her cousin and childhood chum, James Gillespie Blaine, the nominee of the Republican Party that year for the presidency of the United States.[14]

At home, when Mother Angela and the sisters proposed founding a medical facility in South Bend, Sorin readily fell in with their plans, and in a little house on a piece of property he had purchased years before St. Joseph's Hospital, in 1882, began its long and honorable mission to the sick.[15] Her efforts on the St. Mary's campus centered on providing a suitable church for the community, a project she had generously set aside in order to promote the building of Our Lady of the Sacred Heart at Notre Dame. She did not share the resentment of others, including her own mother, Holy Cross's great benefactress, Mrs. Phelan, at what was widely perceived to be Sorin's failure to respond with appropriate enthusiasm.[16] Yet even Angela's steadfast loyalty had been strained when Sorin had proposed the establishment of a separate group of nuns to succor the domestic needs of the male community at Notre Dame. A compromise of sorts on the matter had been reached—a separate novitiate at Notre Dame nominally subject to St. Mary's—but a meeting of minds had not. This lingering disaffection played a role in the disputes which dominated the 1880s. But even more so did Mother Angela's gradually failing powers.

The immediate threat, however, as Father Sorin saw it, was the aggressiveness of those local ecclesiastical authorities always anxious to dominate religious orders.

> Never have religious communities had greater need of protection from the Holy See than now, without the fetters (*entraves*) of individual bishops, who really know nothing about them and who will condemn them as often as the priests of their dioceses ask them to. God alone knows the sacrifices of every kind that have been imposed upon me over the course of forty-four years, because of my *resolve to grant everything* to the Bishops. I have as a result had peace with them, but at the price of thousands of dollars! The bishops here [in the United Sates] have need of religious as nowhere

14. Costin, *Priceless Spirit*, 222.
15. Howard, *St. Joseph County*, 1: 431.
16. Mary Phelan to Sorin, October 11, 1883, AIP. Her rebuke was implicit but clear.

else in the world. But to aid them, protect them, assist them? The history of the New World is no different from that of the Old, a reprise of the opposition between the secular clergy and the religious. Our only hope is in the protection of the Holy See, removing from us as much as possible an arbitrary judgment committed to an opposed position (*à l'encontre*). The independence that would be allotted us by a Rule approved by the Holy See would sustain our courage and would help us much more than the local Authorities who are so various and so often opposed one to another.[17]

What Father Sorin wanted from the Roman authorities was a formal confirmation of his own position, or, expressed more broadly, continuance, through him and his successors, of the integral relationship between the sisters on the one hand and the priests and brothers on the other. In his heart he had never endorsed the canonical separation, as he had demonstrated years before by his stubborn delay in dividing the temporalities. In other words, he had been as dedicated to his own version of Moreau's "general plan" as the Founder had been to his. Given Pius IX's determinative edict in 1857, official union was out of the question. But by the secession of the Indiana nuns from Le Mans, and the consequent benevolent disposition of Archbishop Purcell and Bishop Luers, a coalition—for lack of a better word—had been effected in the person of the superior general of the Congregation of Holy Cross, who was at the same time the superior of the Sisters of the Holy Cross, Edward Sorin himself. Characteristically he brushed aside any alternative. "All [the sisters]," he observed as the matter was making its leisurely way through the council rooms of Propaganda, "they all feel and confess they owe all these blessings of God to the Priests of Holy Cross. The very thought of a [decision] severing them at no distant time from the paternal care and government under which Heaven has so abundantly blessed them, fills their souls with fear and trembling. It is far better, they unanimously say, to remain as they are."[18] The unanimity in the end proved illusory, though no doubt there was substantial support for this position among the sisters, particularly so long as Mother Angela was alive.

In March, 1885, Father Sorin paid a brief visit to Rome, where he was assured that the status of the sisters was being duly considered and that a decision would be forthcoming shortly. A few months later Bishop Dwenger was in the Eternal City, and the first reports of his activities there were unsettling at Notre Dame. "There are men," Sorin commented bitterly, "from whom it is difficult to obtain

17. Sorin to Dufal, October 6, 1885, AGEN.
18. Sorin to Dufal, October 8, 1888, AGEN.

any sign of gratitude. For twelve years I have given [Dwenger] twelve or thirteen sisters *gratis* for his asylums, and three or four brothers also. But it is useless to reason with him. He must have his own way. . . . He promised his recommendation without any reserve. . . . I see that the poor Sisters feel and dreadfully apprehend . . . a painful mortification. The bishop of Vincennes first, then, with the creation of the new diocese, he of Fort Wayne: neither ever spent a dollar in support of the sisters. I bless Heaven which has given us the means to help the good bishop; but to make him the judge of what we ought to do . . . is to close the eyes to the light and to common sense."[19] Meanwhile the months passed and Propaganda's pledge of a swift determination went unfulfilled. Then, early in 1886, Dufal heard Roman rumors that led him to recommend a withdrawal of the petition for approval: "Would it not be better," he asked, "to leave things as they are, with direction of the sisters by their founder and in practice themselves, rather than risk dependence on the bishops?"[20] Sorin was strongly tempted, though he was heartened somewhat by Dwenger's surly mood after the bishop had returned from Rome, obviously similarly unsatisfied, and by the reassurances of the friendly Gilmour of Cleveland, who had been visiting the Vatican at the same time.[21] Still, his mood was bleak: "All I can say is that Rome should do us an immense favor and save us from serious evils by keeping the promise made to me last March. It makes us all feel very badly."[22]

O‌THER MATTERS of course had to be attended to by the superior general. For the most part, however, his faith in young Thomas Walsh proved justified, and he found few occasions to interfere in the day-to-day administration of Notre Dame.[23] Walsh, often advised by the suave and learned editor of the *Ave Maria*, Father Daniel Hudson, recruited new and able lay faculty, most notably perhaps, at the end of the 1880s, the poet and novelist—and later United States Minister to Denmark—Maurice Francis Egan. Another layman, of longer standing on the faculty, James Edwards, began the laborious tasks of reconstituting the college library—10,000 volumes had been destroyed in the fire of 1879—and of assembling an archive of American Catholic history; Walsh broke precedent in behalf of these endeavors and saw to it that a support-line was from

---

19. Sorin to Dufal, May 3 and October 6, 1885, AGEN.
20. Dufal to Sorin, February 10, 1886, AGEN.
21. Gilmour to Sorin, February 23, 1885, AIP.
22. Sorin to Dufal, October 5, 1885, AGEN.
23. For what follows, see Hope, *Notre Dame*, 212–215, 222–226, 227–231.

then on entered into the annual budget, the first sum a princely $500. The president, besides overseeing the construction of new buildings and the completion of others—including the Main and the church—also performed the remarkable feat of introducing electrification to the whole campus as early as 1885. In these endeavors Father Sorin took a more direct interest, especially in the pious uses to which electricity could be put. "After vespers" on the feast of the Assumption, he reported,

> a mile-long procession wended its way round St. Joseph's Lake to the sound of the great bell that can be heard forty-two miles away, and displayed a beauty and magnificence unique in the New World. A demonstration of love and respect for the holy Virgin like this would not be tolerated in [anti-clerical] Rome. Here at Notre Dame it was a feast for the whole country. At eight o'clock the electrical illumination of the statue atop the Dome dazzled the eyes of the whole company.[24]

In another connection altogether, Sorin also approved of Walsh's strict disciplinary policy, particularly with regard to that perennial collegiate problem, student drinking. Expulsion for drunkenness was the norm, and notices, signed by Walsh, appeared routinely in the local newspapers threatening prosecution of anyone who sold liquor to Notre Dame students. Sorin was not a teetotaler like the young president, but neither did he imbibe spirits, and he had consistently recognized that strong drink could turn ordinarily docile youths into unruly louts. Father Walsh was an unambiguous prohibitionist, and as such he stood on the cutting edge, so to speak, of the American Catholic ethos of his time, as defined by such prominent bishops as Gibbons of Baltimore, Ireland of St. Paul, and Keane of Richmond. (One reason Gilmour of Cleveland disliked Germans was his conviction that they drank too much beer.) These "progressive" prelates were the very leaders Sorin was most anxious to be identified with, and their stance on the whisky trade, given the ravages it had effected among the masses of Catholic immigrants,[25] was by no means unreasonable. The superior general therefore applauded, though he did not participate, in the assembly at Notre Dame in August, 1886, of the sixteenth annual convention of the Catholic Total Abstinence Union of America, which attracted 700 delegates from fifteen states.

Father Sorin did not participate, and not only because he did not stand in the front rank of total abstainers. That same month and in the same place he had to

---

24. Sorin to Dufal, August 16, 1885, AGEN.
25. See, for example, O'Connell, *Ireland*, 105–114.

preside over the meeting of the general chapter of the Congregation of Holy Cross. And, as though to demonstrate that in this valley of tears nothing comes easily, all sorts of difficulties had to be overcome before that event could occur. The first of them issued from France. Though the Holy Cross province there had shown nothing but drastic statistical decline over a decade and a half, the hubris among its members had not kept pace. The provincial chapter meeting at Nuilly-sur-Seine had passed two resolutions: that the chapter of 1886 itself be held in France and that the motherhouse be promptly restored to Paris. Sorin must have been reminded of the cynical French saying: *Plus ça change, plus c'est le même chose.*[26] "As for the first demand," he responded, "the general council here has unanimously rejected it as absurdly expensive." As for the second, "more serious, it is for a general chapter, not a provincial one, to treat of such an issue and resolve it. It would have been more honest first of all that if our French confrères had already secured the consent of Rome for the return of the Superior General to France"—Sorin's perpetual fear was that Propaganda, mistrustful of a motherhouse located in the wilds of America, would require a return to a conventional European site—"they will have to find a new Superior General."

> But even in such an eventuality, his place would be here and not in Paris, seeing that the Congregation has a future in the New World that it could never have, without a miracle, in the Old. More than two-thirds of its religious are here, and here without persecution or hindrance (*entrave*), instead encouraged daily by its palpable success and a providential future and the richest hopes. The Province of France has not closed down a single foundation, nor lost a single member, because of its distance from the congregation's central administration. On the contrary, for these past five years France has been a burden for the central administration, perhaps even a danger. Here it has been able to inspire what is done. Here the Superior General has been ever active and indeed has realized each day the importance of his presence at the very center of the action. He knows his co-workers and is known by them consistent with the spirit of the country; in Paris he would be no better than a provincial.[27]

And, as his mood darkened with the coming of another anniversary to remind him of his age and his increasing frailty, he wondered whether even the

---

26. "The more things change, the more they remain the same."
27. Sorin to Dufal, October 1, 1885, AGEN.

office of provincial might be too much. "This morning is the forty-third anniversary of my first Mass at Notre Dame," he wrote on November 30, 1885. "How many tremendous events have transpired since that memorable day! Each year adds new signs (*présages*) of the glorious future the Holy Virgin is preparing for us here, not only for the well-being of the Congregation but for the Church in this New World." But what place was there to be in this "glorious future" for a man too old to contribute meaningfully to it?

> Myself, I am not so much proud of what has been accomplished as confused. My fear, which grows each day, is that soon, because of my age, I shall become an obstacle to the development of this great work. So my resolution is fixed, *irrevocable:* to abdicate, to resign as soon as possible every office, every charge, every responsibility. . . . In two months I shall begin my seventy-third year. I need repose in order to prepare for the last judgment. Great God, what a moment![28]

But though the wheels turned more slowly than before, repose did not fit the man, even now in the eighth decade of his life. The fires had not yet burned out, and the final judgment would come when it came. Meantime there was still work to be done, still presumptuous French brethren to be chastened, still a sluggish Roman curia to contend with.

The general chapter, required by the constitutions to assemble every six years, was the immediate order of business. Despite French objections, the capitulants, elected and appointed, twenty-one in all, were summoned to gather at Notre Dame in May 1886. But then, for all Father Sorin's enthusiastic attachment to the American scene, local upheavals gave him pause. By mid-March a series of railroad strikes had sparked widespread labor unrest. "The general peace," he explained to his Roman agent, "has been sharply troubled by the constantly spreading revolts of laboring men. No one can predict what the result will be. Commerce is paralyzed. St. Louis is in a state of stagnation, and South Bend, right beneath our windows, is the same. Hundreds of thousands of workers have at the uttering of a password (*mot d'ordre*) left their shops and pose a danger to their neighbors." Under these circumstances Sorin doubted the expedience of the "principal members" of the congregation to absent themselves from their establishments. "I would prefer, if Rome approves, to put off the chapter for a year or two . . . and wait for better times."

---

28. Sorin to Dufal, November 30, 1885, AGEN.

The term "password" for Sorin had a sinister Masonic connotation, and indeed the Knights of Labor organization, which fomented the strikes, was a secret society, though not Masonic. The situation in any case did not improve. He sent Dufal several issues of the *Chicago Tribune*, "the most important newspaper in the West," to document "what troubles menace the peace of the country and of the whole world. . . . To hold the chapter in May would be an imprudence. . . . Not one of our chiefs could leave his post without danger, even for three weeks."[29] This judgment appeared to have been confirmed by the events in Chicago in early May. In Sorin's words:

> The social state has become exceedingly serious. Witness the bomb set off in Chicago last Tuesday, killing or wounding fifty policemen, the guardians of the peace who were simply doing their duty. We all hope that this execrable act of Anarchists, Socialists, Communists, Nihilists, and their ilk will serve to reestablish order by creating a universal and well justified abhorrence for them, and that they will either be exiled or fill up our prisons. Society has never seen any like situation. One hardly knows what to do or what to expect.[30]

After the shock of Haymarket, the labor disturbances moderated enough for Father Sorin to reschedule the chapter to meet at Notre Dame in October and then to bring it forward to August, just as the great temperance rally was concluding. Bishop Dufal opened the proceedings on the feast of the Assumption by officiating at a pontifical Mass and bestowing on the capitulants a papal blessing. They met for nine consecutive days, three hours each morning and three more in the afternoon.

> With the exception of a single question [Sorin reported], the most perfect harmony reigned during all the discussions, from the beginning to the close of the sessions. That question was whether to restore the Motherhouse to France. The French capitulants, along with a few Canadians whom they gained to their cause, had approached the matter entirely prejudiced (*parti pris*) and determined before any discussion to achieve their objective, even though that would have had the effect of assuring the resignation of the Superior General, who clearly stood in their way. But two-thirds of the

29. Sorin to Dufal, March 16, 17, and 26, 1886, AGEN.

30. Sorin to Dufal, May 11, 1886, AGEN. The Haymarket riot occurred on May 4. The bomb killed eleven people, including seven policemen. Four perpetrators were later hanged.

assembly pointed out what the disastrous effects for the family of Holy Cross as a whole would be, and the idea was rejected.[31]

The superior general assured Cardinal Siméoni that the chapter of 1886 "was probably one of the most important" in the congregation's history. It is difficult see why. The vote on the removal of the central administration to Paris was a foregone conclusion, and the eighteen capitular decrees appear, at least in retrospect, rather humdrum. One of them however, did address directly a problem which Sorin had long believed undermined the morale of the brothers and of the community as a whole: "Henceforth whoever enters the Congregation as a postulant Brother renounces by [that] fact all right to become a priest in our Congregation."[32] Among the personnel changes to emerge out of the chapter was the appointment of a new provincial for Indiana; all apparently was forgiven if not forgotten, and William Corby was recalled from his exile in Wisconsin. A harder confrère for Sorin to forgive was the perpetual malcontent, Joseph Rézé, who, having failed as provincial in France, now wanted to lead the Canadian province as he had done in former years. "Happily for Canada, no one there wants to see him back as Provincial. France refuses him likewise. Although he is going back there only as assistant [provincial] and hence very unhappy, he will have his vengeance on America! It is a sad case."[33] As for the superior general himself and his "continuation in office," he not surprisingly succumbed to "some moderate pressure" and agreed to stay on.[34]

IN LATE NOVEMBER came another anniversary, "the forty-fourth of our arrival in the middle of a forest. Today it is all cleared land, and 1,100 people live here and praise God and his Holy Mother." And there was astoundingly good news: "Finally, finally our dear Sisters are going to have their constitutions approved. What a blessing! When," he asked his Roman agent, "will you send the official dispatch?"[35] Bishop Dufal continued to hear happy rumors to this effect out of Propaganda and sent them posthaste to Notre Dame. "Your excellent communication has given us great pleasure. God grant that it soon be

---

31. Sorin to Siméoni, September 22, 1886, AGEN.
32. Number 8, which reiterates a similar decree of the chapter of 1880. See Sorin, *Circular Letters,* 2: 23–25.
33. Sorin to Dufal, October 28, 1886, AGEN. See Sorin, "Decree," November 13, 1887, AGEN, appointing Rézé provincial of Canada, "with all the powers attached thereto."
34. Sorin to Dufal, August 24, 1886, AGEN.
35. Sorin to Dufal, November 23, 1886, AGEN.

followed by a telegram saying, 'Constitutions approved without significant alteration.' . . . I am impatient to depart for Rome myself, but I cannot do so before
reception of the said telegram."[36] But the new year of 1887 began without any
formal confirmation, and Sorin, in his frustration, remembered what Joseph
Dwenger had said to him twelve months before: "Do you think Bishop Dufal has
the energy to carry out such a negotiation?"[37] Nor was Sorin unaware that the
bishop of Fort Wayne might have intended to relate the alleged lack of energy to
stories about Dufal's heavy drinking, stories Sorin himself did not believe. Still,
the messenger for whatever reason seemed incapable of delivering the essential
message. Another birthday came round, and it was a sad observance.

> Here I am, since yesterday morning, marching into my seventy-fourth year.
> Will I finish it in this world? I seriously doubt it. Every new year opens my
> eyes to the most somber colors, very menacing for the Church. European
> freemasonry terrifies me. The heresy of Dr. McGlynn spreads in a way to
> make me fearful. Oh! How regrettable that Rome has not sent *its Nuncio*
> these twelve or fifteen years! What an unspeakable loss for the Church in
> this country! Today I waited for your telegram. Nothing has come. I am
> sick of it all and expect nothing more than what sustained St. Paul, to be
> dissolved in the Lord.[38]

But worse was shortly to come, much worse.

Mother Angela Gillespie took to her bed shortly after New Year's, 1887. As
before, she suffered from no discernible disease, but she was suffused with a
numbing weariness that penetrated ever deeper into the center of her being as
the short, cold days of winter passed by. Her sisters in religion attended her faithfully, and Father Richard Shortis, who had been a schoolmate of her brother
Neal, now dead thirteen years, saw to her devotional and sacramental needs. Father Sorin was a frequent visitor, and he, though concerned like the others, was
assured by the doctors that there was no immediate danger. On February 21 she
observed her sixty-third birthday. Shortly after a visit from Sorin on the morning
of Friday, March 4, she heard the bell tolling the funeral procession of a young

---

36. Sorin to Dufal, December 13, 1886, AGEN.
37. Dwenger to Sorin, November 27, 1885, AIP.
38. Sorin to Dufal, February 7, 1887, AGEN. Edward McGlynn (1837–1900) was a priest of the
archdiocese of New York, whose activism in social and economic issues led to his suspension by his
archbishop in 1886 and excommunication by Rome in 1887. He was reinstated in 1892. His personal
demeanor and extreme rhetoric contributed to his difficulties. Pace Sorin, McGlynn's views were not
heretical.

nun who had been a special favorite of hers. She rose from her bed and stood at the window in a kind of farewell salute to her friend and sister. There she collapsed, and at eleven o'clock she died. A few days later, at the funeral, another friend, an old one this time, Bishop Gilmour of Cleveland, spoke over her remains: "How many there are among us here today whom she has molded, attracted, inspired, with high and religious ambition; whom she has led in the paths of life. . . . It is difficult for those who have not known her to realize the extent of her labors. Not everyone can comprehend the depth of Mother Angela's devotion to the cause of God. Many have seen it, but few understood it. . . . For many a long day this community will feel the gap made by Mother Angela's loss."[39]

And not only the community of sisters of which she had been in fact the Foundress. "The terrible shock that was felt all around centered in my poor heart with such a comprehensive effect that I feared I would never recover from it. No death ever affected me as the death of dear Mother Angela."[40] Edward Sorin was one who had seen and understood this woman's devotion not only "to the cause of God" but to himself, to his work, to his ideals—even when his sometimes peremptory manner and autocratic habits bruised her sensibilities. He was devastated by her passing.

> Since my arrival in the New World forty-six years ago, I never remember suffering as I suffer now, at the immense loss that has fallen upon us with unexpected and irreparable death of Mother Angela. She was interred this morning at St. Mary's by Monseigneur of Cleveland, who preached admirably about her rare merits and great successes to a large congregation who came from all parts to pay testimony to the illustrious and humble deceased. The press all over the country has raised a single voice to praise the thirty-seven years she spent here, during which she raised so richly thirty-nine foundations devoted to the religious instruction of the young and to the care of orphans and the sick. This universal impression, coming from all sides, was unexpected and surprised even me, and it opened my eyes to the immensity of the ordeal that weighs me down. I have no tranquillity. I have no idea what will come next.

But he did have an idea about what had precipitated Mother Angela's death, and, in the midst of bitter sadness, he wanted it known in Rome.

---

39. McAllister, *Flame*, 335–337.

40. Sorin to "My Beloved Daughters in Jesus Christ," April 2, 1887, in Sorin, *Circular Letters*, 2: 119.

What overwhelms me most about this sudden death is a secret I can tell to no one. But to tell it to you, Monseigneur [Dufal], is a duty. Here it is. What contributed to shorten the days of this precious and admirable Religious was surely the delay in the approbation of the Constitutions. No one strove harder than she to accomplish it. No one felt more than she the terrible shock at this deception which ended by allowing her no hope. For her it was a mystery. . . . *Voila* the secret that presses down upon my heart, far beyond what I could possibly express.

No evidence survives to suggest that this extravagant indictment possesses any validity.[41] It seems rather to have welled up out of Sorin's present obsession. Indeed, if he were looking for a scapegoat of so abstract a kind, he might have discovered one closer to home. "The magnificent chapel or Rotunda of St. Mary's"—the church of Loretto—"is finished now. She took so lively an interest in it, but now she will never see its dedication."[42] Perhaps she would have, had Edward Sorin been less tardy in pressing her cause, though in the end he did supply funds for the basic structure.[43] No such speculation should question that his grief was profound or that his sense of irreparable loss was in the least contrived.

But his campaign went on, and shortly after Mother Angela's demise it took a tactical turn which appeared to favor Father Sorin's objective. Since 1876, when Holy Cross withdrew from East Bengal, the Benedictines had served the Catholic missions centered in Dacca. Now they too determined to depart that harsh land and unforgiving climate, and Propaganda requested that Holy Cross take up the burden once more. The superior general's response was swift: "It is impossible to take any measure ad hoc before the approbation of the sisters' Constitutions, in the sense in which they have been presented in Rome. It is equally impossible to decide about this before the holding of a General Chapter, which will be convoked the moment we receive the happy dispatch, which will take two months or so." And then, indulging in irony if not a trace of sarcasm, he added: "I am infinitely grateful to Propaganda for having proposed us for this mission. We can take charge of it; but the approbation has to come first."[44] Nor had he changed his mind a month later, and he expressed it even more bluntly. Propaganda had given gratifyingly "prompt and complete" endorsement to the decrees of the chapter of

41. See the sage comment of Costin, *Priceless Spirit*, 228.
42. Sorin to Dufal, March 6, 1887, AGEN.
43. See chapter 28, above. Brosnahan, *King's Highway*, 306, says the building cost $54,000.
44. Sorin to Dufal, May 1, 1887, AGEN.

1886, for which he sent warm thanks. "Unhappily, however, the joys of this world are seldom complete." He had expected a similarly favorable decision with regard to the sisters by the end of May, and now it was June. "It is evident that this approbation has to precede the acceptance of the new mission in East Bengal. If the Superior General of the Priests and Brothers is not recognized as such for the Sisters, acceptance is impossible."[45]

There the matter stood when Father Sorin went to Paris and, despite not having received the desired telegram, to Rome in the autumn, and then on his pilgrimage to Palestine. But a new complication emerged with renewed stories that Pierre Dufal was drinking again. Though he still defended the embattled bishop, Sorin, after some reflection, decided that he had to confront him.

> Now to the painful point [he wrote early in 1888]. Although I do not believe there is a particle of truth in it, there has been a shameful report spread in Neuilly that our Procurator General is a regular drunk, that he is known as such in the City, and that as a natural consequence not only St. Bridget's but the whole Congregation has lost all the confidence of Propaganda and of the Roman officials in the whole curia. What a disastrous rumor! I leave you to show the impudence and malignity of the groundless charge. I pray that you soon vindicate your character and ours.[46]

A bad reputation would imperil not only the lobbying efforts at Propaganda on behalf of the sisters' constitutions but also the plans Father Sorin had worked out for St. Bridget's. St. Bridget's, that Roman albatross hung round the neck of Holy Cross for so long—and of course the procurator general's own residence and headquarters—"shall be retained," in accord with the decrees of the general chapter of 1886, "and made a house of studies," to which "each Province shall pay annually 2,000 francs or 400 dollars, whether two subjects be sent there or not, and the traveling expenses of the subjects sent."[47] This decree was at least partially in response to Bishop Dwenger's harsh criticism of the Indiana province's careless procedures in training aspirants to the priesthood; too often, he charged, seminarians were taken away from their studies and spiritual formation and assigned to teach at Notre Dame or Watertown or Austin.[48] Sorin recognized the justice of this reproach and acted swiftly. "Our little seminary," he announced,

45. Sorin to Dufal, June 2, 1887, AGEN.
46. Sorin to Dufal, February 9, 1888, AGEN.
47. Sorin, *Circular Letters*, 2: 44.
48. Dwenger to Sorin, May 29, 1886, AIP.

"will open here with fifteen talented and pious and promising youths. [It will be] the chief feeder of St. Birdget's Superior School. May God direct and bless our modest plans!"[49] And shortly after the chapter adjourned, he told Cardinal Siméoni, "We are ready immediately to send at least two ecclesiastical students to St. Bridget's from Notre Dame, and we hear that Canada is equally ready."[50]

So vindication of the procurator general's "character" was doubly necessary. Bishop Dufal, a man accustomed to controversy, was nevertheless shaken by the allegations against him and appealed for direct intervention from the mother-house. Sorin declined.

> Your request that I write to Propaganda on the subject of the charges, in order to learn positively whether they are believed there, or whether your removal from office is desired there, goes quite beyond my intentions. I believed it my duty to make known to you what I had heard—without be-lieving it for an instant—in order to put you in a position to deal justly and appropriately with these perverse tongues. What more can I do? . . . I regret having caused you pain, but I am confident it will result in a benefit I have hoped for: the stoppage of an anti-religious insolence (*audace*).[51]

Whether or not Dufal was able unaided to rebut the painful rumors—he re-tired to Neuilly-sur-Seine in the spring of 1889[52]—his personal discomfiture did not diminish Father Sorin's determination to gain his point with regard to the Sis-ters of the Holy Cross. "In response to your last communication," he told Siméoni in mid-April,

> I cannot alter my humble and honest declarations [made recently]. If the actual state of our expectation becomes finally a fixed reality, by the ap-probation of the constitutions of our Sisters, *we shall examine immediately what to do about* [about Bengal], in order to meet the desires of Propa-ganda. Till then I cannot take on another commitment, but rather must de-cline, albeit reluctantly, any responsibility for a task *quite beyond our powers in the present situation.*[53]

---

49. Sorin to Dufal, September 2, 1885, AGEN.

50. Sorin to Siméoni, September 22, 1886, AGEN.

51. Sorin to Dufal, March 15, 1888, AGEN.

52. He was succeeded as procurator general by Father Peter Franciscus, for whom see *Matricule générale,* 2039, AIP.

53. Sorin to Siméoni, April 11, 1888, AGEN.

If the salutation of this letter reflected the writer's conventional and genuine reverence for Roman authority—"May your Eminence deign to accept the homage of profound respect of your humble and devoted servant"—the substance of it showed there was fight in the old man still. And even if this last battle could not be won, he fought it with the same vigor he had borne with him to the wilderness forty-seven years before. The time had come to recognize a truly astounding achievement.

"MY JUBILEE IS FIXED for the fifteenth of August," along with "the consecration of our church and the blessing of all the buildings and premises of Notre Dame. . . . Would it not be proper to have this new marvel of beauty consecrated with the title of Minor Basilica? In point of fact there is nothing like it in the United States."[54] The observance of the fiftieth anniversary of Father Sorin's ordination actually took place in two stages.[55] The first, on May 26 and 27, 1888, was restricted to the immediate Notre Dame and St. Mary's family of religious, faculty, and students. Indeed, eighteen lay professors authorized deductions from their salaries of from five to fifteen dollars to help pay for the local festivities.[56] On the Saturday afternoon "an appropriate entertainment" was held in Washington Hall, "consisting of music, poems and addresses, prepared expressly for the occasion." There had been many such exhibitions in past years, but Sorin, after the singing and the laudatory speeches were done, indicated the special weight he gave to this event by breaking precedent and ascending the stage himself to offer formal thanks.

> In the light of divine faith a Golden Sacerdotal Jubilee . . . of the ordination of a priest to the sacred office of minister of the Most High, to which nothing on earth can compare in real elevation, is assuredly worthy of due commemoration, not alone on the part of one who was raised to such an unparalleled dignity but likewise among those of his friends who can properly appreciate the signal blessing. . . . Were it only to remind him of the eighteen thousand holy masses offered for the living and the dead since

54. Sorin to Dufal, February 9, 1888, AGEN. The church was designated a minor basilica in 1992. See O'Meara, *Sacred Heart*, 45.

55. What follows is based on *Golden Jubilee*, 207–236, and Hope, *Notre Dame*, 235–239. The latter narrative is based on contemporary accounts in the *Scholastic*, while the title of the former refers not to the observance of Sorin's anniversary but to that of the founding of the university. See the enormous collection of material related to the jubilee in AUND, COSR, "Sorin Papers."

56. See the list, dated April 30, 1888, in the Sorin Papers, AIP. The grand total deducted was $185.

the day he was first allowed to stand before the altar of the living God, what an inspiring cause of unbounded joy and gratitude to heaven this fact alone would reveal to faithful souls! . . . But what intensifies still more my gratitude . . . is the selection by God himself of the rich field where I was to labor; oh, how often it has filled my soul with joy! It is not for me to state here the unspeakable consolations which awaited me in this new world . . . and above all on this glorious domain of the Queen of Heaven. . . . Allow me to declare . . . honestly that I claim but a very small fraction of the merits you assign me but justly return it all to the Blessed Virgin herself, and to the devotedness of my modest and faithful co-laborers in the field already promising such an abundant harvest for the advance of science and the salvation of immortal souls.[57]

A festive supper followed, and afterward a band concert, punctuated by the boom-boom of the student-cadets' cannon. Then, just as dusk was falling, a carriage drawn by a team of coal-black horses, the gift of students past and present, was driven up to the porch of the Main Building, where the jubilarian and his colleagues had been listening to the martial music. Sorin, Corby, John Zahm, and the indefatigable librarian, James Edwards, promptly climbed aboard the barouche and rode off into the darkness. As the cheers died away, "out of every window of the massive pile [of the Main]—from spacious study halls, lecture, class, and private rooms, from roomy libraries in the halls—there beamed the noonday brilliancy of the Edison light," while multicolored skyrockets burst above.[58]

The next morning, Sunday, May 27—the exact jubilee day—Father Sorin celebrated a solemn high Mass, at which Father Corby, the restored provincial, preached what was in effect a eulogy. The liturgy concluded, the ministers and congregation filed out of the church's main entrance and across fifty feet or so of lawn, where the celebrant blessed the cornerstone of the building that would soon be called Sorin Hall. This project, designed by architect Willoughby Edbrooke to serve exclusively as a residence composed of private rooms for senior students outside the Main, represented a new departure for Notre Dame, one which critics frowned upon as encouraging unwarranted permissiveness.[59] Yet, in Edward Sorin's willingness to discount such reservations and to accept this proposal urged by Zahm and Thomas Walsh in the name of modern collegiate practice, it represented as well his lifelong ability to accommodate to changing times

---

57. *Golden Jubilee,* 208–210.
58. Hope, *Notre Dame,* 235–236.
59. See Schlereth, *Notre Dame,* 114–116.

and, in this instance, to endorse the initiatives of a gifted younger generation. Later in the day, at a public banquet held in one of the refectories in the Main Building, toasts and flowery speeches paid tribute to the jubilarian, most notable among them perhaps, because of his famous surname, that of Henry Brownson, class of '88, son of the illustrious Orestes (whose remains had been interred at Notre Dame in 1886, ten years after his death). In the afternoon the celebration concluded with a boat race on St. Joseph's Lake and a review of the smartly marching cadets of the junior and senior departments.

That Edward Sorin's sacerdotal jubilee was more than just an occasion for familial rejoicing was amply demonstrated the following August. What had been accomplished at Notre Dame under his stewardship seemed to a wider public emblematic of the growth and maturing of the American Catholic Church as a whole, and there were those in high places anxious to give expression to this fact. To honor the founder of Notre Dame was in effect to proclaim the enduring and legitimate status of the Church, after much struggle, had attained within American society. In accord, therefore, with the late nineteenth century's predilection for gaudy celebrations, featuring bands and banquets, fireworks and fiery oratory, plans were formulated at the beginning of 1888 to solemnize Father Sorin's golden anniversary as a national as well as a personal triumph. Over the ten weeks between late May and mid-August final preparations, choreographed by Corby, Thomas Walsh, and Sorin himself, readied the campus for the great day. Typical of the festive embellishments was

> St. Edward's Hall, the home of the minims and the pride of Father Sorin, who as he grows older seems to love children more and more. [It] was replete with decorations, outside and in. The front wall was about covered with red, white, and blue bunting. Among the mottoes the most conspicuous was "Golden Jubilee," made of golden roses on a white ground. Others were "Salve Pater," "Te Deum Laudamus," "Ave Maria," and the figures "1814," "1838," "1842," and "1888." "Golden Jubliee" and "50" in conch shells were conspicuous against the greensward of St. Edward's Park, in front of the hall. Inside . . . a curtain drawn from the window at the head of the stairway reveal[s] a life-size full-length portrait in stained glass of the founder of Notre Dame. At the bottom in stained glass [are] three landscapes representing the log cabin, the old Notre Dame [Main Building], and the new Notre Dame.[60]

---

60. *South Bend Daily Tribune*, August 15, 1888.

By Assumption eve, Tuesday, August 14, all was ready to welcome a glittering company of Catholic celebrities.

Chief among them was the archbishop of Baltimore. The presence of the diminutive James Cardinal Gibbons, primate in all but name of the Church in the United States, guaranteed the publicity for the event that all the participants desired. He was the first cardinal ever to visit Indiana, and when he arrived at the Lake Shore Depot, shortly after 7:00 P.M., he was greeted by "an immense throng, . . . including among the assembled multitude no less than three bands of music. There were also there the Ancient Order of Hibernians, St. Joseph Society, St. John the Baptist Society, and [the] Catholic Knights of America, all in full regalia." Father Corby, as head of the welcoming committee, escorted Gibbons to the barouche presented to Sorin at the earlier celebration.

> A line of march was then formed, the South Bend Military Band leading. . . . On each side of the carriage . . . marched the Hibernians as a guard of honor. . . . The procession attracted much attention, everyone endeavoring to catch a glimpse of the most prominent Catholic in America. . . . The most elaborate attempt at a reception was in the Fourth Ward where flags, Chinese lanterns, bunting, and other decorations were observable on every side, while fire works, bells ringing, illuminations of stores and private residences all added to the general effect. An immense throng of people had gathered in the East Side's business center and also about St. Joseph's church, from the spire of which waved the papal flag, surrounded by the stars and stripes. At the church little girls dressed in white approached the carriage . . . and literally covered it with choice flowers. . . . The big bell at Notre Dame pealed forth its heartiest welcome as the procession neared the University, while the smaller bells jingled merrily. The procession entered the University campus under an immense canopy of evergreens, and following the carriageway made a circle of the grounds. [It] finally halted in front of the grand stairway of the Main Building.[61]

There Father Sorin and President Walsh, surrounded by a dozen prelates who had arrived earlier, greeted a weary prince of the Church, who, with smiles, handshakes, and embraces, was conducted without further fanfare inside the building.

But the tone for the celebration had been set. Very early the next morning, the feast of the Assumption of the Virgin, Bishop Dwenger presided over the consecration of Our Lady of the Sacred Heart, now virtually complete: the crypt had

61. *South Bend Daily Times,* August 15, 1888.

been opened in 1885 and the Lady Chapel, crowned by the Bernini-style baroque altar so prized by Sorin,[62] late in 1887. Since the ceremony mandated by the ritual of the day was numbingly long and, save for liturgical sophisticates, scarcely comprehensible, it was closed to the public.[63] A little after nine, the three-hour solemn marathon finally concluded. Father Sorin celebrated a low Mass for his religious family. "The church was then thrown open for pontifical Mass, Haydn's Imperial Mass being used for the occasion. His Eminence, Cardinal Gibbons, was celebrant. . . . The great church was packed to its utmost capacity at this service, and the congregation were given a rare intellectual treat in an address by Archbishop Ireland of St. Paul, who paid one of the highest tributes to Notre Dame's founder."[64]

The choice of John Ireland, recently elevated to the rank of archbishop, as preacher of the day was itself significant. Born the year of Sorin's ordination, Ireland enjoyed a national reputation for eloquence. But more than that, he also represented a point of view within the hierarchy by no means shared by all his episcopal colleagues. If the open and often bitter contentions involved in the so-called Americanist Controversy[65] were still some years off, the parties had already begun to form, and Ireland was clearly the leader of the "Americanists," of those prelates, that is, who discerned in the coupling of Catholicism and the American experience a marriage contracted in heaven. "I love too deeply the Catholic Church and the American republic," Ireland said famously in 1884, "not to be ever ready to labor that the relations of the one with the other be not misunderstood." The Church "welcomes with delight the signs of the times that indicate a glorious future for her beneath the starry banner. But it is true also [that] . . . the more America acknowledges [Catholic] teachings the more durable will her civil institutions be made."[66] Some of Ireland's closest allies also participated in the festivities of August 15, notably Richard Gilmour of Cleveland, John Keane of Richmond, the recently appointed rector of the new Catholic University of America, and, if less outspokenly, Cardinal Gibbons himself. Theirs was an ideological position wholeheartedly endorsed by Edward Sorin.

Ireland's rhetoric was very much that of his own day, when pulpit oratory was expected to furnish a measure of learned entertainment as well as admoni-

---

62. See Sorin to Dufal, February 2, 1888, AGEN. The altar, purchased in Rome, cost 4,300 francs.

63. White, *Sacred Heart Parish*, 55–57. White, citing the *Scholastic*, observes that from this time the title of the church alternated for some years between "Our Lady of the Sacred Heart" and simply "Sacred Heart," the designation that finally prevailed.

64. *South Bend Daily Times*, August 16, 1888.

65. See Thomas T. McAvoy, *The Great Crisis in American Catholic History* (Chicago, 1957).

66. John Ireland, *The Church and Modern Society*, 2 vols. (New York, 1903), 1: 28–29.

tion and instruction. The archbishop of St. Paul was a master of the genre, and if his discourses seem in retrospect overly florid, they cannot be reproached for lack of substance or candor. On this day he began by citing Matthew's gospel: "He that had received the five talents coming, brought other five talents, saying: Lord, thou didst deliver to me five talents; behold I have gained other five over and above."

> Venerable priest, whom to honor the princes of your people, your brethren, your spiritual children to the third and fourth generation are assembled, celebrating with you a solemn anniversary, be it mine to salute you on this auspicious day, and in words which, we are confident, the Master is sweetly whispering to your soul, say to you: "Well done, good and faithful servant." Your days have been full. No talent was left by you unused. The autumn is come for you, and the rich fruits of your life perfume the land.

The preacher then predictably narrated an outline of Father Sorin's career, which, he said, so manifestly illustrated how well the jubilarian had employed the talents given him. But there was a special favor in store for the young French priest.

> Fifty years ago the Republic of the West was but emerging from her age of infancy, though her features plainly bore the lineaments of greatness and majesty. . . . With soil most fertile under foot, a benign sky above, the air made genial and health-giving by the breezes of truest liberty, hither, surely, would come millions from transatlantic shores, who, joining hands with the sturdy and pushing American colonists of earlier emigration, would build up a nation unparalleled in the story of ancient ages. Providence was preparing to [sic] the Church a glorious opportunity for work. . . . The newness of their conditions of life, the energy needed to subdue nature, their freedom from beaten paths and narrow groovings, impart to our populations freshness, vigor, buoyancy, predisposing them to hearken to the message of truth, and to be, when made her disciples, the most daring and loyal soldiers of the Church. In America the Church is free as the bird is free in the air to spread out its pinions and fly whithersoever it wills; free to put forth all her powers and tempt the realization of her most ambitious projects for the welfare, natural and supernatural, of men. She fears neither the sword of an avowed foe nor the gilded throne to which a seeming protector would seek to fasten her for her more facile enslavement. Bound to no enervating conservatism, no old-time traditions repressing her movements, she can encounter with the liberty of action which insures success the multitudinous problems, social and philosophic, which have sprung

up from the complications of modern times. Westward, it has been said, the star of empire moves. Westward, methinks, moves too the apocalyptic candle stick. The future arena for the Church's grandest battles and most glorious triumphs, verily, I believe in my heart, is America. Let her soldiers but do their duty, and all will be well. Towards America the young levite of fifty years ago . . . turned longing eyes. . . . Fifty years of ceaseless, brave work in God's kingdom. . . . You never tired, though the burden was heavy. You never faltered, though trials crowded upon you and the shadow of defeat often darkened the sky above you. We might in some measure tell what you have accomplished. What you have endured to bring your labors to completion we could not tell. God knows all, and he will repay.

And so the orotund phrases rolled on, a rough tide of sound out of Ireland's notoriously gravely voice, for forty-five minutes or so. There were some stirring moments, as when the preacher, himself a chaplain during the Civil War, turned toward two greying men sitting in the sanctuary: "Fathers Corby and Cooney are with us this morning to tell the need there was of priests among our soldiers, and of the great things done for religion by themselves and their fellow-chaplains." And then to the jubilarian: "There were other priests and other sisters in the war; those of the Holy Cross made up the greater part of the roster. None excelled them in daring and religious fervor. No other order, no diocese, made . . . sacrifices as did that of the Holy Cross. Father Sorin, you saved the honor of the Church." But perhaps most moving for Edward Sorin—and saddening, both because of recent bereavement and current controversy—was Ireland's evocation of the sisters and "the wondrous prosperity of St. Mary's and its numerous offshoots."

He has been the friend, the guide, the counselor of the community. Their rules and constitutions are the fruit of his wise thought and careful observation of the needs of this country. From him comes their special fitness for work in America; and to this fitness must they in great part attribute their marked success in their schools and their institutions of charity. It is for us all a cause of deep regret that she was not spared to celebrate this Golden Jubilee who for many years presided with rare intelligence and ability over the destinies of St. Mary's, ever ready to lend willing cooperation to Father Sorin's plans for the raising up of her community to the high standard of excellence now belonging to it. I speak of the venerated Mother Angela, one of the worthiest daughters of the Church in this nineteenth century.

The archbishop returned over and over to his basic theme, right to the end of his oration. Edward Sorin's "high-mindedness . . . is his sincere and thorough Americanism. From the moment he landed on our shores he ceased to be a foreigner. At once he was an American, heart and soul. . . . He understood and appreciated our liberal institutions. There was in his heart no lingering fondness for old regimes or worn-out legitimism. . . . Fifty years hence—what will the Church in America be? . . . Let us live and work as Father Sorin has lived and worked, and all will be well."[67]

By half past twelve the last strains of the Haydn Mass, performed by hired musicians from Chicago, had faded away. The festive banquet for a thousand guests followed immediately, with something of the look of a Quaker Meeting: 700 men were served in the two refectories in the Main Building, while 300 women sat down to a loaded board in the nearby infirmary. The menu was printed in Sorin's native language, from a soup of *tomates aux croutons* to *saumon braisé à la taratre* and *poulets à la marengo* to *fromage américain* and *crème glacée à la vanille*. The customary postprandial toasts, however, definitely lacked a Gallic flavor. The Americanist prelates, like President Walsh, were to a man strong prohibitionists, John Ireland almost fanatically so. The strongest beverage available at the feast therefore was coffee, and the toasts were drunk with water. What the jubilarian, known to adhere to the biblical dictum and to take a little wine for the stomach's sake—as well as his South Bend friends seated around the flower-, flag- and bunting-bedecked room, to whom he routinely sent bottles of good claret with which to celebrate Christmas and New Year's—what they may have thought of such abstemiousness has not been recorded. The watery toasts at any rate followed the conventional pattern, one to the pope, another to the United States, another, given the presence of so many bishops, to the American hierarchy. Then, Bishop Gilmour rose to respond to "The Founder of Notre Dame." "Father Sorin," he said, "in the name of this most reverend and distinguished audience I congratulate you today upon this eventful celebration. We today can all feel a profound joy that you have so stood at the altar and so ministered to the people that we can say that there is no blemish on your name. It is therefore with the profoundest joy that I say to you, *ad multos annos!*" Sorin, the bishop of Cleveland continued, "had impressed his influence upon so many thousands of people and places." And, he added with no little shrewdness: "Greatness is shown by readiness in the selection of men and places, and Father Sorin has been especially apt in selection and combination." But the Scot, Gilmour, would not have

---

67. *Golden Jubilee*, 218–236.

been worthy of his Irish brother of St. Paul, would not have shown himself the fervent Americanist he truly was, had he not concluded: "We have thrown off the shackles which Europe would weigh us down with. Europe shall never again dominate over the religious, educational, or political beliefs of the people of the United States. The new form of the Church favors a separation of Church and state." The applause, so the local press reported, lasted a full five minutes, but one might wonder whether the remains of Pope Pius IX, so beloved by Edward Sorin, might have stirred uneasily in his tomb in the bowels of the Basilica of San Lorenzo fuori le Mura.[68]

In the afternoon, from the portico of the Main Building and in the presence of some several thousand spectators, there were more speeches and more felicitations for Father Sorin. The one genuine intellectual among that generation of American bishops, John Lancaster Spalding of Peoria, spoke eloquently and at length about the need for quality higher education for American Catholics and paid appropriate compliments to Notre Dame—though one was never sure whether this suave and often ironical prelate meant exactly what he seemed to say. The ever diffident Cardinal Gibbons also spoke glowingly of Notre Dame, but briefly and, as was his wont, with no hint of ambiguity. Supper proved to be an Americanist love-fest, when the cardinal conferred upon John Ireland his pallium—the circular band of white wool symbolizing metropolitan rank—just received from the Vatican, and John Keane delivered a longish speech praising the new archbishop as well as the old jubilarian. Then the company went outside to witness still another fireworks display, a fitting finale to what had been a more than satisfactory celebration.[69]

It WOULD NOT BE EXCESSIVE TO SAY that after the grand festivities of the spring and summer of 1888, the years remaining to Father Sorin amounted to a lengthy anti-climax. The spirit continued strong as ever, but the flesh weakened relentlessly. The capacity to deal each day with a dozen crises, great and small, was no more. Even the brief remarks he had spoken at the celebration in May turned out to be, as his colleagues recalled, "his last extended public utterance."[70] The hand that had guided the Holy Cross mission in America for forty-seven years and the whole congregation for twenty was now sometimes

68. *South Bend Daily Tribune,* August 16, 1888.
69. *South Bend Daily Times,* August 16, 1888.
70. *Golden Jubilee,* 208.

too unsteady even to write a legible letter.[71] Indeed, the immense official correspondence that had preoccupied him so much for so long dwindled, if not to nothing, then to a bare fraction of its previous bulk. The circular letters became shorter and were published at longer intervals. And they tended to be largely spiritual meditations, often on the subject of death.

> As I advance in years I cannot help foreseeing the day fast approaching when we shall have to part with each other. Many of us may never meet again here below. But as I fully realize what I would wish to recommend above all at my last hour to the dearly beloved children of Holy Cross, I now beg to express it in acknowledgment of your filial and touching expressions of devoted affection, namely, that you, each and all, in any part of the world, may remain united in charity and in an ever-increasing love of the Blessed Virgin; that, in order to honor and widen or further extend her maternal and powerful protection, you may for her sake and delight, observe your holy Rule strictly, manly, religiously, fervently, and heroically forever.[72]

Even before the observance of the golden jubilee Sorin had surrendered one redoubt in his battle to maintain control over the sisters. Holy Cross, he agreed, would undertake a mission in East Asia. "I leave it to you," he instructed Bishop Dufal, "to work out the details of this new endeavor with his Eminence: the precise locality, whether in Bengal or elsewhere; the required number of missionaries; the timing of their departure; their travel expenses, and so forth." But if one line of resistance had been breached he still manned the defenses behind another: "What a tragedy that our Sisters—so capable, so devoted—cannot take part in this foundation!!!"[73] In September the bishop of Fort Wayne offered a sliver of hope. While Propaganda continued to insist on a strict separation "as to property, organization, and so forth," said Dwenger, "I am perfectly convinced that Rome does not intend to disturb your position; yet they will not make your successor . . . *ex officio* the canonical superior of the Sisters for all future."[74] But, as things turned out, neither would Rome force the nuns, led by Mother Augusta, to maintain the connection with their present canonical superior.

---

71. See, for example, Sorin to Siméoni, May 31, 1889, AGEN, for which Alexis Granger acted as amanuensis.

72. Sorin, *Circular Letters*, 2: 76 (October 1, 1889).

73. Sorin to Dufal, May 21, 1888, AGEN.

74. Dwenger to Sorin, September 14, 1888, AIP.

By this time Sorin had appointed five priests to Bengal, three from Notre Dame and two from Canada. "I will advance them $1,000 and give them permission to draw on me for further expenses, since his Eminence says he cannot do so. Unhappily, I am short of money as usual." To lead the mission he chose Michael Fallize, lately pastor of St. Joseph's parish in South Bend. "He is the most capable of the five. He is from Luxembourg and his brother was named a bishop last year in Norway."[75] The subject of Bengal led Sorin to recall Pierre Dufal's sterling service there in earlier years. "I regret more and more that your health will not permit you to conduct them to their mission and put everything in order there, as no one could do nearly so completely as you." Apparently he felt satisfied that his faith in the bishop's good personal behavior had been vindicated.

As the missionary contingent made its way to Paris and then Rome, a weary Father Sorin—"I am not quite recovered yet from the fatigues of last month"—renewed his plea, to which "I have nothing to add except that the Sisters ought to have the privilege of choosing their own Superior General, after my death and forever. But I still hope . . . they will be left for the present in the state in which Heaven has blessed them *every day,* and more and more. . . . We hardly know where to find space for all the boarders who arrive daily at St. Mary's by the half-dozen." And the sisters flourish elsewhere as well: "Nineteen academies, twenty-eight parochial schools, three orphan asylums, five hospitals, fifty-five establishments in all, and they never have been so prosperous. In some cities, like Austin and Salt Lake, the civil authorities have gone out of their way to pay tribute to the admirable Sisters of the Holy Cross. God grant that each year they become more and more worthy of such praise, and that nothing arises to unsettle this confidence and this progress, so promising for the future."[76]

Now and then he showed that the spark of initiative still smoldered. "I am in serious negotiation," he revealed in March, 1889, "to acquire the famous abbey of Claire Fontaine, located on the border between Belgium and the Grand Duchy of Luxembourg. The price of $30,000, though very modest, is beyond our present resources. But for the needs of Bengal, this would be a nursery of vocations! Also it would be a precious place of refuge (*asile*) for our dear French brethren more and more menaced by exile. May God bless this major endeavor in all its details!" But not even enthusiasm for a new and exciting project could still his now years-long apprehension about the matter closest to his heart. "Nothing comes from

75. Sorin to Dufal, September 6, 1888, AGEN. No Holy Cross brothers were sent to Bengal until some years after Sorin's death. See Goedert, "Holy Cross in Dacca," 55. Fallize remained in the Bengal mission for twenty-one years. See *Matricule générale,* 2098, AIP.

76. Sorin to Dufal, October 2 and 16, 1888, AGEN.

the Eternal City," he concluded this note to Dufal. "Not even a word about the question of the Sisters."[77]

Time was running out. On March 26, 1889, Bishop Dwenger informed Sorin that he had received from Rome formal approbation of the sisters' constitutions, which decision would bring finally to closure the administrative connection between the men and women of Holy Cross. This ruling, the bishop said, would be confirmed at the general chapter to be held in July, when a new superior general would be elected from among the ranks of the sisters themselves.[78] Father Sorin pondered this news for some weeks and then registered what proved to be his last appeal to the authorities at Propaganda. He no longer claimed unanimous support among the nuns but pointed rather to "the fears, the dread even, that grows among the better spirits, even as their chapter approaches along with the promulgation of the new constitutions."

> I am not surprised at their reaction. [They are apprehensive] about an administration probably new and unaware of the real state of affairs, which perhaps would enjoy the confidence of no more than half the community. . . . Here is the most efficacious and natural remedy. Let Rome *put me in charge,* under whatever title, of establishing and putting into practice the new constitutions and hold me responsible for the results of this important initiative, with full powers to enforce the rules for the total well-being of the congregation, spiritual and temporal. . . . Nothing important will be undertaken without having been submitted to me. The overall confidence of the Community in its administration . . . will be enhanced and good management will prevail at all levels. Some years of this exercise of positive authority will suffice to establish desirable order and assure the Congregation an encouraging future instead of exposing it to ruin.[79]

"Exposing it to ruin" if he were removed from authority: here in this futile entreaty may have been one more illustration of Sorin's chronic penchant for hyperbole. Yet it had been his supreme self-confidence—sustained, he believed, by the favor of the Virgin Mary—that had seen him and the religious he governed

---

77. Sorin to Dufal, March 7, 1889, AGEN. The idea to establish a Holy Cross foundation in Luxembourg had originated with Michael Fallize, a native of the Grand Duchy. See Fallize to Sorin, September 23, 1887, AIP.

78. See Dwenger to Sorin, March 26, 1889, AIP.

79. Sorin to Siméoni, May 31, 1889, AGEN.

through every conceivable crisis for nearly half a century. His successful administration of the sisters "so visibly blessed by Heaven for more than forty years" could not be lightly set aside. He had established them in the New World, had been their counselor and friend and indeed their inspiration. Prefacing the rules he had given them in 1871, he had asked each of them to bring a special sensibility to the fulfillment of her vocation.

> And what is this precious disposition? Is it the consciousness of having brought to the Community a fortune, an accomplished education, a rare talent? . . . None of these; it is something far more precious, while it is within the reach of all. *It is the spirit of faith.* . . . The spirit of faith sustains her in the hour of fatigue, of trial, of affliction, of sickness. For in the light of faith the tribulations of this life bear no comparison, in her estimation, with the degree of glory awaiting her in eternity.[80]

The sisters' chapter that assembled at St. Mary's in July 1889, presided over by Joseph Dwenger, did not in any sense repudiate the founder's inspiration nor display any diminution of reverence for him. But it did, in accord with Propaganda's decree, formally sever the last administrative link between the Congregation of Holy Cross and the Sisters of the Holy Cross. Pius IX's injunction of thirty years before had at last been fully consummated. Mother Augusta, the provincial, was elected superior general, though only on the third ballot—which may have suggested some residue of support among the capitulants for Father Sorin's position. Sorin, Corby, and Granger at any rate duly resigned from the St. Mary's board of trustees.[81] The following year the controverted sisters' novitiate on the Notre Dame campus was closed down and transferred to St. Mary's. A contract was drawn up whereby the nuns continued to provide domestic services at Notre Dame in return for a flat monetary compensation.[82]

Father Sorin resisted this arrangement almost to his dying breath. He had in fact entered into his last illness when he proposed to the newly appointed apostolic delegate to the United States, Archbishop Francesco Satolli, "a complete separation of the House of Sisters at Notre Dame from the House of St. Mary's and the establishment of a new community at Notre Dame. . . . It is impossible for St. Mary's to supply the help required at Notre Dame. For this we require new vocations . . . [among] those who will come wishing to enjoy the advantages of a

---

80. Quoted in Costin, *Priceless Spirit*, 218–219.
81. Sorin to Dwenger, August 12, 1889, AIP.
82. Costin, *Priceless Spirit*, 229–230.

religious life and at the same time ready . . . to engage in manual labor." Nothing came of this initiative, which, however, included an ironic twist.

> Greater force is given to our request in the present instance, by the fact that the Administration at St. Mary's has refused and still refuses to send Sisters to the Missions of Eastern Bengal. The Sisters who now labor there were sent from the house at Notre Dame.[83] With the proposed new Community established, we have every means to hope that year after year bands of devoted Sisters may be sent to aid in spreading the light of the Gospel through those missions so dear to the heart of the Sovereign Pontiff.[84]

Father Sorin's aspirations with regard to the sisters were not fulfilled, but instead of the "ruin" he had predicted their apostolate continued to flourish, as it does to this day. Old and ailing as he had become, to have established the definitive independence of the women's congregation was doubtless the best course to have adopted. Even in the final throes of the debate he had assured Siméoni that "I leave it to your Eminence in your wisdom to judge the matter."[85] Or, as he put it to Bishop Dwenger after the battle had been lost: "I never thought for a moment of transgressing any Decree of the Holy Father."[86] His own will had been thwarted by the jurisdiction for which he held the deepest reverence, and he accepted the verdict. Edward Sorin probably never heard the adage that has long circulated in clerical circles more cynical than any frequented by him: Always stand by the Holy See, and the Holy See *may* stand by you.

FATHER SORIN WENT ABROAD in 1890 and again in May 1891, when he was accompanied by John Zahm. These journeys, however, had little to do with the kind of business that had preoccupied him in years gone by. "The very thought of parting again with you, even for a short time" he addressed his confrères at Notre Dame on the eve of the second departure, "would of itself

---

83. Ten nuns departed Notre Dame September 5, 1889, and arrived in Calcutta on November 10. Once the novitiate at Notre Dame had been suppressed (1890), however, Mother Augusta recalled them to St. Mary's. See Raymond J. Clancy, *The Congregation of Holy Cross in East Bengal, 1853–1953*, 2 vols. (Washington, D.C., 1953), 1: 92–94. Holy Cross Sisters returned in 1927. See Goedert, "Holy Cross in Dacca," 58–59.

84. Sorin to Satolli, June 10, 1893, AGEN, in John Zahm's hand. Sorin had for many years urged the appointment of a papal delegate: see chapter 28, above.

85. Sorin to Siméoni, May 31, 1889, AGEN.

86. Sorin to Dwenger, August 12, 1889, AIP.

grieve me were it not for the confidence that a sea-voyage will restore my en-
feebled health, and give me the consolation of affording some comfort to our
dear religious in France, so severely tried by the cruel adversaries of our faith."
The recent French general election had indeed lent popular ratification to the
anti-clerical legislation of the previous decade.[87] Whether or not the frail and
aged superior general was able to console his French brethren, the trip did nothing to restore his health. Yet he remained serene. "You may rest assured that this
temporary absence from your midst will only strengthen our old friendship, as it
always did. Indeed, my late failure in health has rendered every loving and loved
member of our dear family more precious to me than ever before."[88]

Early in 1892 he suffered the first in series of internal hemorrhages which
indicated the deterioration of kidney function known as Bright's disease. From
then on he was treated by a specialist from Chicago, who recommended first recuperation at a seaside resort. Father Sorin returned home from there in time to
preside at the general chapter which convened on August 15 and which, understandably, did little more than confirm the status quo. Afterwards he was again
bedridden, though he rallied in time to participate in another anniversary observance, this one, on November 26, marking the arrival of the little band of missionaries at Sainte-Marie-des-Lacs fifty years before. Much on Sorin's mind were
those who had then accompanied him, only one of whom, Francis Xavier, was
left; Brother Vincent, the venerable patriarch, had died July 23, 1890, aged ninety-
three.[89]

> The season in which we came—a long and severe winter of five months
> and of constant snow—multiplied not a little our trials. Sometimes we
> found our beds in the morning covered with snow. What a fine preparation
> for our meditation. "Blessed are the poor, for they shall see God," not only
> in heaven but even here upon earth. "They shall live in him, move in him,
> and have in him their very being." Our little community was never so edi-
> fying. Our dear Brothers, of whom only one remains, had to suffer, God
> alone knows in how many ways, being obliged to take their night's rest on
> the bare floor; and yet not a word of complaint. God's holy will was their
> comfort and the unfailing source of consolation and joy.[90]

---

87. See Dansette, *Histoire religieuse,* 446–448.

88. Sorin, *Circular Letters,* 2: 90.

89. Kilian Beirne, *From Sea to Shining Sea: The Holy Cross Brothers in the United States* (Valatie,
N.Y., 1966), 27. Francis Xavier, who had first been called Brother Marie, died in 1896. See *Matricule
générale,* 420, AIP.

90. Sorin, *Circular Letters,* 2: 95.

In late February 1893, Father Sorin composed his last circular letter, a lenten admonition to renew "within our souls the spirit of prayer and mortification" and so to help us "remember that we are a teaching family and that one of our chief duties is to devote ourselves to those entrusted to our care to secure their eternal salvation."[91] In June, when Archbishop Satolli, the apostolic delegate, paid a formal visit to Notre Dame, Sorin managed to receive him ceremonially and to present him with that last petition about the status of the sisters. A month later came the news of Thomas Walsh's sudden death, and two weeks after that, on July 26, Alexis Granger died, aged seventy-six. When told that his oldest friend was gone, Edward Sorin burst into tears. "Mon cher Alexis!" he cried. "Who next?" There was not much doubt as to the answer.

By the time classes resumed at Notre Dame in September Sorin had taken to his bed for good. Father Andrew Morrissey, Walsh's replacement as president, visited him daily and assured him that all was proceeding satisfactorily. "'Tis well," was all the dying man could reply. On October 13, the feast of St. Edward, he was much too ill to do more to observe his name's day—for so many years an occasion of celebration on the campus—than to wave weakly from the porch of the presbytery at the delegation of faculty and students who had come to salute him. On October 28 the deathwatch began. Two days later he was anointed and given the Eucharistic Viaticum. On the following morning the minims of St. Edward's Hall, the "little princes," were told their old friend and patron was dying. They asked if they could see him just once more; instead the sisters in charge took them to the chapel. Meanwhile, in the presbytery nearby, Edward Sorin opened his eyes and saw kneeling around his bed his beloved religious co-workers in the vineyard of the Lord. The sight seemed to satisfy him, for he closed his eyes again and, with no sign of struggle, he died. It was 9:45 in the morning, Tuesday, October 31, 1893.[92] "The tidings of his demise spread quickly," reported the local press, "and were everywhere received with expressions of the deepest sorrow. . . . The great fire in 1879, the magnificent rebuilding of the university, the golden jubilee of Notre Dame's founder and first president succeed one another in the lapse of time. Then comes death. What better monument could be reared to Very Reverend Father Sorin than the splendid university that overlooks the beautiful lakes on whose banks his active life had been so nobly spent? There can be none."[93]

---

91. Sorin, *Circular Letters*, 2: 96–97.

92. Hope, *Notre Dame*, 254–257.

93. *South Bend Daily Times*, October 31, 1893.

Contrary to his explicit directive,[94] Father Sorin was buried with much pomp and circumstance. A pontifical funeral Mass, a sermon preached by an archbishop, dirge-playing bands and muffled drums leading the cortege to the community cemetery beyond the lakes, mourners young and old from far and wide following the coffin. It could not have been otherwise. Many laudatory words were spoken to mark his passing, poems and ballads written. But perhaps John Ireland had said it best a few years before, on the day of the golden jubilee.

> The gospel of human effort in the work of God needs to be preached to the world today. Were it understood and carried out, we should soon tell of marvelous victories. Father Sorin planned and worked, and worked hard. He was watchful and enterprising in seeking out opportunities for doing good and promoting the interests under his charge. He deserves success, and he has received it. . . . Do all you can, and then your prayer for divine blessing will be heard. The divine is needed, and the priest or the Christian who will succeed must love God and seek his aid. I will mention but one fact—a striking one in Father Sorin's life, with regard to the supernatural element. It is his tender devotion to the Mother of God. He loved her with child-like simplicity and ardor; all his projects were brought by him to her altar to be blessed by her before he sought to put them into execution. His efforts were unceasing to obtain that others love her and commend themselves to her intercession. Need we wonder at the success of his labors with this powerful protectress praying for him![95]

It was November when Edward Frederick Sorin was laid to rest, as it had been November when youth and ardor had first brought him there. "Everything was frozen over. Yet it all seemed so beautiful. The lake especially, with its broad carpet of dazzling white snow, quite naturally reminded us of the spotless beauty of the august Lady whose name it bears." Soon the snow would fall again and offer gentle shelter to his grave.

---

94. See chapter 29, above.
95. Quoted in *Golden Jubilee*, 232–233.

Epilogue

"AT AHUILLÉ, HIS BIRTHPLACE, FATHER SORIN HAS been forgotten. From now on, thanks to the plaque we shall unveil in a few minutes, he will be present among us."[1] Monsieur Lemarié, mayor of the commune, was standing in the nave of the parish church on this Saturday evening, September 16, 1978. "For myself," he continued, "and in the name of the municipal council largely represented here tonight, I want to express profound thanks and gratitude to the American ecclesiastical authorities who have determined to celebrate the memory of this missionary, our native son, whose accomplishments now, thanks to their initiative, will be hereafter appreciated by the parishioners of Ahuillé." Then Father Theodore Martin Hesburgh, Edward Sorin's fifteenth successor as president of Notre Dame, still vested as he had been for the Mass just concluded, pulled aside the curtain in front of the space next to the old baptismal font—in which baby Edouard Frédéric had passed through the rite of Christian initiation 164 years before—and revealed the commemorative plaque. "By this act," Hesburgh said, "we make amends to a man unjustly forgotten."[2]

The Mass had been an impressive affair, concelebrated by upwards of twenty priests, among them the rector of the Université Catholique de l'Oeust, at Angers. Prominent in the congregation were Monsieur and Mademoiselle Dubourg-Lemonnier who, with their father, aged ninety-two, still lived in the manor house at La Roche, the Sorin family seat; due to age and infirmity the elder Monsieur

---

1. See Prologue, above.
2. *Le Courrier de la Mayenne,* September 22, 1978.

Dubourg-Lemonnier—who could still remember his great uncle's last visits to Ahuillé—did not attend the ceremony. Other dignitaries came from Laval and from Paris, including the local member of the Chamber of Deputies. The lively music, sung in French, English, and Latin, was provided by the fifty Notre Dame students enrolled for the year at the university in Angers. After the liturgy and the unveiling ceremony, a reception was held in a hall nearby, during which, as one reporter noted, "cordial contacts were easily established. The American delegation's simplicity and perfect knowledge of our language contributed not a little to lending the occasion the air of a family celebration." At the reception Mayor Lemarié presented Father Hesburgh with an aerial photograph of Ahuillé and environs, and announced that the road out of the village passing by La Roche, formerly the Rue de Bretagne, would now be called the Rue du Père Sorin.[3]

"We make amends to a man unjustly forgotten." Not forgotten, surely, on the banks of the St. Joseph River in northwest Indiana, nor in Texas nor in Utah nor in Dakota nor in Oregon, not forgotten, surely, in all those places, east and west, in Washington and New Orleans and Wisconsin, and among all those apostolates in which the men and women of Holy Cross had brought to bear their salutary influence, their teaching, their nursing, not forgotten, surely, in Montreal and Acadia, not forgotten even in France and Italy where, during Sorin's generalship, forces not merely anticlerical but anti-Christian reached their most strident and most savage extremes since 1792, not forgotten, to this day, among the impoverished Muslims of Bangladesh. One among those who knew him best—had known him indeed since boyhood and had experienced both his confidence and his censure—perhaps gave the truest, as it certainly was the most heartfelt, critique of his mentor's career.

> The venerable Father Sorin, so long our Superior-General—the great captain who led the army of Holy Cross to final triumph—is gone; he is dead. No! he is not dead; his spirit still lives. He so impressed his spirit on the Congregation that it will ever live in the hearts of all devoted members. He was a great man; a man of noble sentiments, of brilliant mind. He had a large heart, full of affection, full of piety, full of love of his patroness, the Blessed Mother of God, whom he loved with the tenderness of a child. So great, indeed, was his affection for her that he seemed to live for Mary, to

---

3. *Le Courrier de Maine-et-Loire*, September 19, 1978, and *Le Courrier de l'Ouest* (*Angers*), September 18, 1978. Press reports and other materials related to the ceremony—including the text of Father Hesburgh's remarks, in French and English—are to be found in UNDA, CZCG, "Sorin Birthplace Commemoration, 1978."

work for Mary. To her he told all his troubles. In her he confided with a confidence truly born of the liveliest faith. If success attended his labors, Mary received the credit of it all.... When I write on this subject, I do not know how to stop; but if Notre Dame holds a prominent place today, if the Congregation has prospered, it is due to this devotion [to] and confidence in Mary, and the lesson should not be forgotten by us who survive Father General! Now, he whose life was an inspiration to us all, whose *enthusiasm* gave new impetus to every work and fired every soul, is gone. Oh! How may we express our grief? Words fail us. The loss is irreparable.[4]

In that word "enthusiasm" Father Corby caught something of the magic which Edward Sorin brought to the multitude of challenges that the mission he embraced as a young priest imposed upon him and which characterized him all his life. This was not an attribute always understood by his confrères in France, not understood, specifically, by that other giant of Holy Cross, Basile Moreau. And here one treads upon delicate ground indeed. During the early years of the twentieth century a predictable and perfectly understandable revisionist school within the congregation looked back upon the sufferings of the Founder and wondered aloud whether Moreau's afflictions had been due not to his own failings, personal and professional, but simply to the malevolence of his subordinates, most notably among them Edward Sorin. If this indeed had been the case, then testimony to the undoubted holiness of Moreau's life must necessarily involve an indictment of those who conspired against him—again, most notably Edward Sorin.

Such a point of view is by no means unusual in human affairs, but it is almost always wrong-headed. It is also almost always too simplistic an explanation of human relationships. To praise someone's virtues should not automatically commit one to denigrate those of someone else, however intimate the two might be. St. Paul "withstood Peter to his face" when he thought Peter was wrong; he did not thereby challenge St. Peter's unique mission. Moreau and Sorin were both men of heroic stature, but, being men, they were not without flaws and weaknesses. And perhaps it was that very "enthusiasm" of which Corby spoke that stood as a barrier between them. Moreau the consummate theoretician of the Old World, Sorin the peerless pragmatist of the New; and so the twain did not meet, and probably could never have met. Even so, if the historical record proves

---

4. William Corby, Circular Letter (as Provincial of Indiana), November 2, 1893, quoted in Sorin, *Circular Letters*, 2: 131–132.

anything, it proves that Holy Cross—and all that Holy Cross has meant across four continents—needed them both. It would be monumentally unjust to forget either of them.

And among the beneficiaries of the two of them were those fifty Notre Dame students who performed the music at the plaque-unveiling ceremony in Ahuillé parish church in September 1978. In the sentiments expressed in one anthem they sang there could have been no disharmony, neither then nor before nor after: *Salve Regina, vita, dulcedo, et spes nostra*—Hail Holy Queen, our life, our sweetness and our hope.

Index

Throughout the index the abbreviation of ES is used for Edward Sorin. The names used in the index are the English/Americanized versions.